The First World War and British Military History

The First World War
and
British Military History

Edited by
Brian Bond

CLARENDON PRESS · OXFORD

This book has been printed digitally and produced in a standard specification in order to ensure its continuing availability

OXFORD
UNIVERSITY PRESS

Great Clarendon Street, Oxford OX2 6DP

Oxford University Press is a department of the University of Oxford.
It furthers the University's objective of excellence in research, scholarship, and education by publishing worldwide in

Oxford   New York

Auckland Bangkok Buenos Aires Cape Town Chennai
Dar es Salaam Delhi Hong Kong Istanbul Karachi Kolkata
Kuala Lumpur Madrid Melbourne Mexico City Mumbai Nairobi
São Paulo Shanghai Singapore Taipei Tokyo Toronto

with an associated company in Berlin

Oxford is a registered trade mark of Oxford University Press
in the UK and in certain other countries

Published in the United States
by Oxford University Press Inc., New York

© The Several Contributors 1991

The moral rights of the author have been asserted
Database right Oxford University Press (maker)

Reprinted 2002

All rights reserved. No part of this publication may be reproduced, stored in a retrieval system, or transmitted, in any form or by any means, without the prior permission in writing of Oxford University Press, or as expressly permitted by law, or under terms agreed with the appropriate reprographics rights organization. Enquiries concerning reproduction outside the scope of the above should be sent to the Rights Department, Oxford University Press, at the address above

You must not circulate this book in any other binding or cover
and you must impose this same condition on any acquirer

ISBN 0-19-822299-8

CONTENTS

Chronology of Publications on the Military History of the First World War   vii

Unpublished Sources   xi

Notes on Contributors   xiii

Editor's Introduction   1

I. *Establishing the Historical Foundations*   13

    1. Early Historical Responses to the Great War: Fortescue, Conan Doyle, and Buchan   15
       KEITH GRIEVES

    2. 'The Real War': Liddell Hart, Cruttwell, and Falls   41
       HEW STRACHAN

    3. Sir James Edmonds and the Official History: France and Belgium   69
       DAVID FRENCH

II. *The Battle of the Memoirs*   87

    4. Frocks and Brasshats   89
       IAN BECKETT

    5. Sir John French and Lord Kitchener   113
       RICHARD HOLMES

    6. The Reputation of Sir Douglas Haig   141
       KEITH SIMPSON

III. Indirect Approaches 163

7. Gallipoli 165
   EDWARD SPIERS

8. Allenby and the Palestine Campaign 189
   JONATHAN NEWELL

9. T. E. Lawrence and his Biographers 227
   BRIAN HOLDEN REID

IV. The Great War Rediscovered 261

10. 'Bunking' and Debunking: The Controversies of the 1960s 263
    ALEX DANCHEV

11. Everyman at War: Recent Interpretations of the Front Line Experience 289
    PETER SIMKINS

Index 315

CHRONOLOGY OF PUBLICATIONS ON THE MILITARY HISTORY OF THE FIRST WORLD WAR

1918 Spenser Wilkinson, *Government and the War*.
1919 J. H. Boraston, *Sir Douglas Haig's Despatches, December 1915-April 1919*.
Field Marshal Viscount French of Ypres, *1914*.
1920 C. à C. Repington, *The First World War* (2 vols.).
Sir Ian Hamilton, *Gallipoli Diary* (2 vols.).
Sir George Arthur, *The Life of Lord Kitchener* (3 vols.).
Sir Charles Callwell, *Experiences of a Dug-Out, 1914-1918*.
1921 Reginald Viscount Esher, *The Tragedy of Lord Kitchener*.
1922 G. A. B. Dewar and J. H. Boraston, *Sir Douglas Haig's Command, December 19 1915 to November 11 1918* (2 vols.).
Brigadier Sir James Edmonds (ed.), *Official History of the Great War: Military Operations, France and Belgium, 1914*, i. (henceforth referred to as 'Edmonds, *Official History*').
1923 Winston S. Churchill, *The World Crisis*, i. *1911-1914*; ii. *1915*.
1925 Edmonds, *Official History: 1914*, ii.
Sir Horace Smith-Dorrien, *Memories of Forty-eight Years' Service*.
1926 Sir William Robertson, *Soldiers and Statesmen*, 2 vols.
Sir Frederick Maurice, *Governments and War*.
1927 Sir Charles Callwell, *Field Marshal Sir Henry Wilson: His Life and Diaries*, 2 vols.
Edmonds, *Official History: 1915*, i.
Robert Graves, *Lawrence and the Arabs*.
Winston S. Churchill, *The World Crisis, 1916-1918* (completed by *The Aftermath* (1929), and *The Eastern Front* (1931)).
1928 Sir Frederick Maurice, *The Life of General Lord Rawlinson of Trent*.
B. H. Liddell Hart, *Reputations*.
Sir George Arthur, *Lord Haig*.
Edmonds, *Official History: 1915*, ii.
Lord Beaverbrook, *Politicians and the War, 1914-1916*, i. (ii. (1932))
E. Ashmead-Bartlett, *The Uncensored Dardanelles*.
1929 B. H. Liddell Hart, *The Decisive Wars of History*.
John Charteris, *Field Marshal Earl Haig*.
Robert Graves, *Good-bye to All That* (reissued 1957).

viii *Chronology of Publications*

      Charles Edmonds, *A Subaltern's War*.
      C. F. Aspinall-Oglander, *Official History of the Great War, Military Operations: Gallipoli* (ii. (1932)).
1930 B. H. Liddell Hart, *The Real War 1914-1918*.
      Cyril Falls, *War Books*.
1931 B. H. Liddell Hart, *Foch: the Man of Orleans* (2 vols.).
      John Charteris, *At G.H.Q.*
      Edmonds, *Official History: 1916*, i.
      Sir Hubert Gough, *The Fifth Army*.
1932 B. H. Liddell Hart, *The British Way in Warfare*
      Edmonds, *Official History: 1916*, ii.
1933 B. H. Liddell Hart, *The Ghost of Napoleon*.
      D. Lloyd George, *War Memoirs*, i. and ii.
1934 B. H. Liddell Hart, *A History of the World War 1914-1918*.
      —— *T. E. Lawrence in Arabia and After*.
      C. R. M. F. Cruttwell, *A History of the Great War*.
      D. Lloyd George, *War Memoirs*, iii. and iv.
1935 A. Duff Cooper, *Haig*, i. (ii. (1936)).
      Edmonds, *Official History: 1918*, i.
      Sir Charles Harington, *Plumer of Messines*.
1936 B. H. Liddell Hart, *The War in Outline 1914-1918*.
      John North, *Gallipoli: The Fading Vision*.
      D. Lloyd George, *War Memoirs*, v. and vi.
      C. R. M. F. Cruttwell, *The Role of British Strategy in the Great War*.
      E. G. French, *French Replies to Haig*.
1937 Guy Chapman (ed.), *Vain Glory*.
      Edmonds, *Official History: 1918*, ii.
1938 B. H. Liddell Hart, *Through the Fog of War*.
1939 Edmonds, *Official History: 1918*, iii.
      E. L. Spears, *Prelude to Victory*.
1940 G. C. Wynne, *If Germany Attacks*.
      Sir Archibald P. Wavell, *Allenby: A Study in Greatness*.
      Edmonds, *Official History: 1917*, i.
1941 Lord Birdwood, *Khaki and Gown: An Autobiography*.
1947 Edmonds, *Official History: 1918*, iv.
1948 Edmonds, *Official History: 1917*, ii.
1951 Edmonds, *A Short History of the First World War*.
1952 Robert Blake (ed.), *The Private Papers of Douglas Haig 1914-1919*.
1953 Major-General Sir John Davidson, *Haig: Master of the Field*.
1954 Sir Hubert Gough, *Soldiering On*.
1956 Alan Moorehead, *Gallipoli*.
      Lord Beaverbrook, *Men and Power, 1917-18*.
1958 Leon Wolff, *In Flanders Fields: The 1917 Campaign*.
      Sir Philip Magnus, *Kitchener: Portrait of an Imperialist*.

Chronology of Publications

1960 Cyril Falls, *The First World War*.
John Terraine, *Mons: The Retreat to Victory*.
1961 Alan Clark, *The Donkeys*.
Lord Hankey, *The Supreme Command 1914-1918* (2 vols.).
1962 Barrie Pitt, *1918: The Last Act*.
1963 A. J. P. Taylor, *The First World War: An Illustrated History*.
John Terraine, *Douglas Haig: The Educated Soldier*. *Oh! What a Lovely War* (Play: Wyndham's Theatre).
Victor Bonham-Carter, *Soldier True: The Life of Field-Marshal Sir William Robertson*.
Correlli Barnett, *The Swordbearers*.
1964 *The Great War* (BBC Television).
A. H. Farrar-Hockley, *The Somme*.
1965 B. H. Liddell Hart, *Memoirs*, 2 vols.
Robert Rhodes James, *Gallipoli*.
P. Guinn, *British Strategy and Politics, 1914-1918*.
A. Marwick, *The Deluge: British Society and the First World War*.
1967 Sir Llewellyn Woodward, *Great Britain and the War of 1914-1918*.
1968 G. A. Panichas (ed.), *Promise of Greatness: The War of 1914-1918*.
1969 (-71) *Purnell's History of the First World War*.
Oh! What a Lovely War (Richard Attenborough's film version of the 1963 play).
Richard Aldington, *Lawrence of Arabia: A Biographical Inquiry*.
1970 S. W. Roskill, *Hankey: Man of Secrets*, i.
1971 Martin Middlebrook, *The First Day on the Somme*.
1973 James Marshall-Cornwall, *Haig as Military Commander*.
1975 Paul Fussell, *The Great War and Modern Memory*.
A. H. Farrar-Hockley, *Goughie: The Life of General Sir Hubert Gough*.
1976 E. K. G. Sixsmith, *Douglas Haig*.
Norman Dixon, *On the Psychology of Military Incompetence*.
1977 John Terraine, *The Road to Passchendaele*.
G. H. Cassar, *Kitchener: Architect of Victory*.
1978 John Terraine, *To Win a War: 1918, The Year of Victory*.
Denis Winter, *Death's Men*.
Lyn MacDonald, *They Called it Passchendaele*.
1980 John Terraine, *The Smoke and the Fire*.
1981 Richard Holmes, *The Little Field-Marshal: Sir John French*.
1982 Shelford Bidwell and Dominick Graham, *Fire Power: British Army Weapons and Theories of War 1904-1945*.
John Terraine, *White Heat: The New Warfare 1914-1918*.
1983 David R. Woodward, *Lloyd George and the Generals*.
Robin Prior, *Churchill's 'World Crisis' as History*.
1985 Ian F. W. Beckett and Keith Simpson (eds.), *A Nation in Arms: A Social Study of the British Army in the First World War*.

J. Grigg, *Lloyd George: From Peace to War, 1912-1916*.
J. M. Winter, *The Great War and the British People*.
1986 Trevor Wilson, *The Myriad Faces of War*.
David French, *British Strategy and War Aims 1914-1916*.
1987 T. H. E. Travers, *The Killing Ground: The British Army, the Western Front and the Emergence of Modern Warfare, 1900-1918*.
1988 Peter Simkins, *Kitchener's Army*.
Gerard De Groot, *Douglas Haig 1861-1928*.
1989 Jeremy Wilson, *Lawrence of Arabia: The Authorised Biography*.
J. M. Bourne, *Britain and the Great War, 1914-1918*.
1991 Denis Winter, *Haig's Command: A Reassessment*.

UNPUBLISHED SOURCES

British Library
Edinburgh University Library
House of Lords Record Office

Imperial War Museum

Leeds University Library
Liddell Hart Centre for Military Archives,
   King's College, London

Liverpool Record Office

National Army Museum

National Library of Scotland

Public Record Office

St Antony's College, Oxford

Macmillan papers
Nelson and Son papers
Lloyd George MSS
Beaverbrook papers
Murray papers
Boraston papers
Fitzgerald papers
Liddle collection
Allenby papers
   (including Wavell's notes
   and correspondence for
   his biography)
Edmonds papers
Liddell Hart papers
Maurice papers
Robertson papers
Swinton papers
Spears papers
55th (W. Lancashire)
   Division papers
Fortescue notebooks
Roberts papers
Buchan papers
Haig papers
War Office papers (WO 32)
Cabinet papers (CAB 45)
Deedes papers

NOTES ON CONTRIBUTORS

Professor Brian Bond is Professor of Military History at King's College, London and President of the British Commission for Military History. His books include: *British Military Policy between the Two World Wars* (1980), *War and Society in Europe 1870-1970* (1984), and *Britain, France and Belgium 1939-1940* (1990).

Dr Keith Grieves is a Lecturer in History at Kingston Polytechnic. His books include: *The Politics of Manpower, 1914-1918* (1988) and *Sir Eric Geddes: Business and Government in War and Peace* (1989).

Dr Hew Strachan is a Fellow of Corpus Christi College, Cambridge. His books include: *Wellington's Legacy: The Reform of the British Army 1830-54* (1984), *European Armies and the Conduct of War* (1983), and *From Waterloo to Balaclava: Tactics, Technology and the British Army 1815-54* (1985).

Dr David French is a Lecturer in History at University College London. His books include: *British Economic and Strategic Planning 1905-1915* (1982) and *British Strategy and War Aims 1914-1916* (1986).

Dr Ian Beckett is a Senior Lecturer in War Studies at RMA Sandhurst and Secretary of the Army Records Society. His books include: *Johnnie Gough VC* (1989) and (as editor) *The Army and the Curragh Incident 1914* (1986).

Dr Richard Holmes is a former Senior Lecturer in War Studies at RMA Sandhurst and Commander of a TA battalion. His books include: *The Little Field Marshal: Sir John French* (1981) and *Firing Line* (1985).

Keith Simpson is a former Senior Lecturer in War Studies at RMA Sandhurst. From 1988 to 1990 he was Special Advisor to the Secretary of State for Defence. He is now co-director (with Richard Holmes) of the Cranfield Security Studies Institute. Among other publications he has edited: *The War the Infantry Knew* (1987) and (with Ian Beckett) *A Nation in Arms: A Social Study of the British Army in the First World War* (1985).

Dr Edward Spiers is Reader in Strategic Studies, University of Leeds. His books include: *The Army and Society 1815-1914* (1980), *Haldane: An Army Reformer* (1980), and *Chemical Warfare* (1986).

Jonathan Newell is a Lecturer in History at the University of Malawi. He has recently been awarded his Ph.D in the Department of War Studies, King's College, London.

Dr Brian Holden Reid is a Lecturer in War Studies at King's College, London and Resident Historian at the Staff College, Camberley. His books include: *J. F. C. Fuller: Military Thinker* (1987) and *American Studies: Essays in Honour of Marcus Cunliffe* (1989).

Dr Alex Danchev is a Lecturer in International Relations at the University of Keele. His books include: *Very Special Relationship: Field Marshal Sir John Dill and the Anglo-American Alliance 1941-44* (1986) and (as editor), *Establishing the Anglo-American Alliance* (1990).

Peter Simkins is Historian at the Imperial War Museum. His books include: *Kitchener's Army* (1988) which was awarded the Templer Medal by the Society for Army Historical Research.

Editor's Introduction
BRIAN BOND

The First World War, with its terrible attritional character and acutely disappointing consequences, has thrown a long shadow over subsequent decades. For the reading and reflective British public it has been simultaneously fascinating and repellent; much further away than the Second World War yet harder to come to terms with as history; a no man's land in the historical landscape. In recent years, however, there have been encouraging signs that a new generation of historians, with wider scholarly interests and without the emotional hang-ups or anguish of their elders and mentors, have overcome these inhibitions sufficiently to place the 'Great War' in a proper perspective. Thus, seventy-two years after the war ended it seems appropriate to attempt an objective historiographical survey without the need for what one contributor has termed ' "bunking" and debunking'.

Since the fiftieth anniversaries of the 1960s evoked a great resurgence of interest in the First World War public demand continues to be virtually insatiable. As Peter Simkins notes:

Evidence of the hold which the war continues to exert on scholars and the general public alike may be seen in the growing numbers visiting the battlefields of Flanders and Gallipoli each year; in the founding of specialist organizations such as the Western Front Association . . . and in the frequent appearance of new feature films and television dramas and documentaries with a First World War setting.

The idea for this book was inspired by the need for a historical counterpart to Paul Fussell's deservedly celebrated literary study *The Great War and Modern Memory* (Oxford, 1975). Many of Fussell's ideas are useful to historians but his approach is emphatically not historical nor is he entirely reliable as a guide.[1] It would be a pity if his highly original work was annexed to the currently influential movement which places excessive emphasis on a very few supposedly representative 'anti-war' poets

---

[1] Paul Fussell's underlying preoccupations with the essential meaninglessness of war have become clearer with the publication of his much more personal account of the Second World War entitled *Wartime* (Oxford, 1988).

and disenchanted memoirists.[2] Indeed, Fussell himself has brilliantly exposed the drawbacks in treating a semi-fictional memoir such as Robert Graves's *Good-bye to All That* as though it were both objective and representative. Moreover, without wishing to detract from the cultural significance of the extremely varied war poetry inspired by the First World War,[3] it is obvious that literature cannot provide a substitute for the *history* of the war which embraces policy, strategy, and tactics as well as the dramatic personal experiences of war on the home and military fronts. All the essays published here testify to the wide range and intense controversies aroused by *historical* interpretations of the war from the earliest wartime narratives, described by Keith Grieves, to the latest depictions of 'Everyman at War' recorded by Peter Simkins.

A second, though more indirect inspiration behind the inception of this venture, was John Kenyon's pioneering study of the historiographical development of British constitutional history and the historical profession in *The History Men* (London, 1983). While disclaiming any comparison with the great range and depth of Kenyon's work, the editor may perhaps modestly describe his team of contributors and their subjects as the *Military History Men*.

The term 'team' is more accurate here than in many collaborative works since the eleven contributors have formed the nucleus of a group which has met once a term during the past three years to discuss the original draft papers of the essays published here and other topics relating to the historiography of the First World War. There has consequently been ample scope for constructive criticism and the exchange of ideas; a process which is acknowledged in the footnotes. Whatever its defects and omissions, this volume should display more coherence than is usual in collected conference papers. Inevitably there is a certain amount of overlap, particularly in the treatment of Sir Douglas Haig, but in the editor's judgement the differing approaches of Richard Holmes, Keith Simpson, and Alex Danchev make for stimulating comparisons rather than mere repetition. It will also be apparent that although the contributors share a common approach to the central theme each is an established scholar with his own special field of expertise. Remarkably few really significant differences of opinion have occurred during the

[2] For the great variety and lack of a clear progression from patriotic euphoria to bitter disenchantment in First World War (and post-war) poetry and fiction see the contributions of Dominic Hibberd and Hugh Cecil respectively in Michel Roucoux (ed.), *English Literature of the Great War Revisited* (Picardie, 1988).

[3] D. Hibberd and J. Onions (eds.), *Poetry of the Great War: An Anthology* (London, 1986).

preparation of this volume, but where these are present—for example over the achievement of John Terraine or the value of the recorded evidence of veterans—there has been no editorial intervention to secure uniformity.

A few words of explanation may also be necessary regarding our decision to concentrate almost entirely on the Western Front with the exception of essays on Gallipoli and Palestine (Allenby and T. E. Lawrence). Quite simply, the most heated and enduring controversies have been provoked by these theatres of the war and the leading (or, in the case of Lawrence, most interesting) participants in them. It is these topics which have provoked—and continue to do so—the bulk of historical writing about the British role in the War. Considerations of coherence and constraints of space have reluctantly caused us to exclude other controversial topics such as the Battle of Jutland, the submarine crisis of 1917, and the Mesopotamian campaign. We have also omitted important aspects which have been covered in other books, such as the role of films, art, posters, and propaganda. In other words we regard this as a trail-blazing exercise and shall be delighted to see other historical thickets opened up.

In the first section, 'Establishing the Historical Foundations', three of our contributors examine the problems encountered, the preoccupations and limitations of the authors, and the controversies they provoked in dealing with the war at different levels: amateur, semi-professional, and official.

Keith Grieves explores the problems encountered by three amateur historians who tried to write general histories before an official model was available; when documentary sources were scarce and bureaucratic obstruction pronounced; and when patriotic Victorian convictions proved a severe handicap to a realistic depiction of the war. Hew Strachan takes the process further chronologically by comparing and contrasting the works of three extremely able and influential historians: Liddell Hart, Cruttwell, and Falls. He brings out the importance of their differing pre-war and wartime experiences in explaining their initial approach to writing war history, and then traces their contrasting development: Liddell Hart becoming increasingly critical of the whole Western Front campaign with Cruttwell surprisingly deferential on this point; while Falls modestly prepared a balanced and unjustly neglected masterpiece.

David French's essay demonstrates the crucial roles of Sir James Edmonds, chief editor and principal compiler of the Official History for more than forty years in imposing his own idiosyncratic views on how the war should be presented to the public, and in guiding, assisting, or obstructing those soldiers and statesmen who wished to write memoirs or histories.

In Part II, 'The Battle of the Memoirs', three contributors have focused on the seemingly unending and often bitter controversies over the reputation of Kitchener, Lloyd George, and the senior Western Front commanders including French, Smith-Dorrien, Hubert Gough, and, above all, Haig. Ian Beckett throws new light on the publishing and financial aspects of these 'battles'; Richard Holmes shows that the French-Kitchener controversy was still burning fiercely in the 1980s.

In Part III, 'Indirect Approaches', the inclusion of Gallipoli requires no special justification since it was from its inception in 1915 and remains to this day the most controversial of all the Allied campaigns; from one (Churchillian) viewpoint the only imaginative strategic enterprise of the whole war, and from others (Fuller or Robertson), an evasion of the only war-winning strategy which demanded total concentration on the Western Front. Gallipoli remains perennially controversial for other reasons including the tantalizingly close possibilities of success—in March, April, and August—and the emotive Anzac involvement. Edward Spiers reviews the historiography of the campaign with special focus on the reputation of Sir Ian Hamilton, while Peter Simkins also discusses the seminal influence of C. E. W. Bean and later historians in celebrating the heroic performance of Anzac troops.

One of the many facets of the T. E. Lawrence legend is that, in sharp contrast to Haig's attritional generalship in the mud of Flanders, he embodied the idea of the relatively clean, mobile, limited, and decisive war in the desert. As Brian Holden Reid shows, this romantic interpretation was given a powerful boost first by Lowell Thomas's picture show and later by Liddell Hart's biography which used Lawrence's exploits as a stick with which to belabour Haig and all that he (Liddell Hart) had come to detest about the Western Front. Reid also brings out the significance of Jeremy Wilson's recent authorized biography which excels in clarifying what Lawrence actually did in the Palestine campaign. As Reid notes, so far from historical investigation diminishing Lawrence's reputation (as Aldington and other critics hoped it would), Wilson's painstaking research has enhanced it by showing why he was held in such high regard by Allenby and others. By contrast, Allenby lacks a really good modern biography and his great achievement tends to be eclipsed by Lawrence's overwhelming popular appeal. Allenby has at least one public house and a famous bridge named after him, but is

Editor's Introduction

unlikely to be the hero of a film or a National Portrait Gallery Exhibition. Jonathan Newell's contribution is therefore a necessary counterpart and corrective to the saga of T. E. Lawrence.

The final section, 'The Great War Rediscovered' consists of two wide-ranging and complementary explorations of how our present notions of the First World War have been influenced by new historical approaches and by the theatre, films, and television since the saturation coverage of the years 1914 to 1918 during the fiftieth anniversaries in the 1960s.

Alex Danchev brilliantly evokes the historical rediscovery of the First World War for a new generation in the 1960s whose chief products in the form of books, a blockbuster television series, and a radical play later transformed into a film have fashioned our attitudes to the war to a much greater extent that has been generally appreciated. Peter Simkins brings the story right up to date by his wide-ranging survey of the intense contemporary interest in the battle experiences of ordinary soldiers. As he remarks, the tape recorder was introduced, by Martin Middlebrook and other pioneers in the collection of oral evidence, in the nick of time because even the most durable veterans of 1914-18 must of necessity soon fade away.

As several of our contributions, particularly Ian Beckett's, demonstrate, the stream of historical publications—general histories, unit histories, personal accounts—continued throughout the 1920s and into the 1930s. Some publishers then began to suspect that saturation point was being reached and there was a falling off in the mid-1930s before the approach of another war temporarily eclipsed the earlier conflict. The 1940s and early 1950s were understandably a very quiet period for First World War histories; as late as 1960 Cyril Falls unluckily missed the tide in publishing his excellent but unsensational study. Soon afterwards, to change the metaphor, the flood gates opened and have not noticeably closed much since in terms of the number of books published annually, not to mention all the other war-related activities discussed by Peter Simkins. This volume as a whole therefore assists historical stock-taking by revealing how much pre-1939 work is still in print and, from a wider perspective, how scholarly views on particular issues have changed and new fields of study have been developed.

An important point, discussed by several contributors, is that the bulk of official documents relating to the war did not become publicly accessible until the 1960s. Consequently, as Ian Beckett points out, Churchill, Lloyd George, and Beaverbrook, who shamelessly exploited their privileged access to state papers (and indeed built up large personal archives of documents which should have been surrendered on leaving office), enjoyed enormous advantages in publishing their own seemingly authoritative versions in the 1920s and 1930s. They derived further benefits, in terms of informed comments, by widely circulating their drafts in proof or typescript among former colleagues and senior civil servants. In this way Edmonds, as the chief official historian, and Hankey as Secretary both of the Cabinet and the Committee of Imperial Defence, exerted enormous indirect influence. Edmonds, for example, with his ambivalent attitude to Haig, fed Liddell Hart with a great deal of classified information and gossip sometimes in conflict with what he published in the official history. Hankey suffered an unjust and ironic fate in that, having helped Churchill and other politicians to publish their own well-documented accounts of the First World War before 1939, he was forbidden by Churchill to publish his own memoirs until long after 1945, by which time they had lost much of their bite and originality. Beckett's essay also brings out the point that so long as the official documents remained closed there was a natural tendency for certain useful and eminently quotable sources, such as Sir Henry Wilson's edited diaries or Churchill's *World Crisis*, to be endlessly cited by other authors.

Liddell Hart deserves special mention in this connection because of the dominant influence he came to exert on First World War historiography through his own prodigious output in the 1920s and 1930s, and his involvement as presiding deity over a large sector of First World War publications. Although his work was not scholarly by modern standards, Liddell Hart listed an impressive range of published sources and enjoyed significant 'inside' contacts with Edmonds and others. Since, as Hew Strachan persuasively demonstrates, Liddell Hart was mainly concerned to inculcate broad strategic views in a polemic style the absence of official sources was not a fatal handicap. His eulogistic study of T. E. Lawrence and his continuing partisan approach to works about his hero, right through to his consultancy over the film *Lawrence of Arabia*, did much to foster the view that the 'real war' (or the correct one) had been fought in Palestine rather than France. His association with Lloyd George and his help with the latter's memoirs was mutually reinforcing in both men's antipathy to Haig. Liddell Hart was always a staunch supporter of Gallipoli as the 'indirect approach' which ought to have succeeded as a far more attractive alternative to Western Front attrition. In the 1960s Liddell Hart vetted the drafts of Alan Clark's and A. J. P. Taylor's irreverent histories which depicted the Western Front generals as donkeys and the war itself as meaningless; he admired Leon Wolff's emotive diatribe against the Passchendaele campaign; and denounced

Terraine for his presumption in daring to defend Haig. Lastly, he served as historical consultant for *The Great War* television series and for the play *Oh! What a Lovely War*. Danchev quotes the revealing remark of Raymond Fletcher, who played an important part in writing the script of the play, that his three-hour harangue to the Theatre Workshop group on the play's message was 'one part me, one part Liddell Hart, the rest Lenin!'

Several of the essays included in this volume provide evidence to demonstrate that First World War histories, and particularly memoirs of leading actors in the drama, reached a large readership and were a profitable undertaking. Thus, John Buchan's *Nelson's History of the War* series was a bestseller during the conflict priced at one shilling and threepence, whereas Fortescue's volumes were hopelessly overpriced at four guineas each. These were at the extreme ends of the price range, the average being about £1. 5*s*. 0*d*. for a single volume and two guineas for a two-volume set. Sir Hubert Gough's memoir *The Fifth Army* sold over 3,000 copies in the first year after publication; Haldane's *Autobiography* sold over 5,000, and Grey's *Twenty-Five Years* nearly 12,000. Soon after publication in 1927 Robert Graves's biography of T. E. Lawrence was selling more than 10,000 copies per week. Churchill's and Lloyd George's war memoirs also enjoyed very high sales: the first volume of the former's *World Crisis* was reprinted twice within a month of publication in April 1923 to attain a print run of 11,380 copies in Britain alone, while Lloyd George's six volumes had sold 54,237 copies in Britain by February 1937. All the major memoirs were also serialized prior to publication in the national press and, as Ian Beckett reminds us, in addition to popular cheap editions, the circulating libraries such as Boots would bring popular war books to a wider readership without the need to purchase what were still relatively expensive luxury items in relation to weekly wages. As for the top earnings, Beckett calculates that Churchill received £27,000 in advance of British and American royalties before a single copy had been sold, and that Lloyd George made about £65,000 from his memoirs.

However, what clearly stimulated publication by most participants (or their supporters and detractors) more than the prospect of financial gain was the issue of personal reputation. Liddell Hart, usually a sensitive judge of the popular mood, encapsulated this interest in his book entitled *Reputations* (1928). Individual reputations were of course intimately connected with particular episodes in the war so that, for example, accounts of the retreat from Mons resurrected the French–Smith-Dorrien clash; and the battle of Loos that of French and Haig; Ian Hamilton and Churchill's reputations were inseparable from Gallipoli, and Hubert Gough's from the catastrophe of March 1918. Just as happened after the Second World War, some publishers began to feel by the mid-1930s that their readers had had enough of this genre, but were often obliged to think again when an anniversary or the belated appearance of a volume of the Official History (the 1917 'Passchendaele' volume for example did not appear until 1948) set the sparks flying again.

Alex Danchev and Peter Simkins both make illuminating points about the remarkable revival of popular interest in the First World War in the 1960s. This phenomenon was mainly prompted by the fiftieth anniversaries falling between 1964 and 1968, but was profoundly influenced by the *mores* of that decade which might be characterized as anti-imperialist, anti-heroic, hostile towards traditional authority and profoundly sceptical of the efficacy of force in general and war in particular to solve political problems. In the 1960s the First World War was not only rediscovered but also refashioned: some of what purport to be the best-known recruiting posters, for example, were probably more numerous and popular in the 1960s than they had been in 1914.[4] There was a revulsion against the 'gung-ho' treatment of war or what Raymond Fletcher described as 'writing at the salute'.[5] Others, such as Robert Kee, revolted against the pious attitude to the First World War exacted at Remembrance Days during their youth in the 1920s and 1930s. Also the First World War came to suffer by comparison with the Second in terms of moral purpose and beneficial outcome. The result was a predominance of ultra-critical historical accounts of the First World War by Alan Clark, A. J. P. Taylor, and others which stressed the incompetence of the high command and the excessive cost, if not outright futility, of the national war effort. Danchev suggests that even the attempt by John Terraine to give the script of the enormously popular television series on *The Great War* a positive message was defeated by the overwhelming power of the negative visual impact of the Western Front battlescapes. In fact John Terraine waged an almost single-handed struggle against the prevailing critical consensus as to the unwisdom of the attritional battles on the Western Front, the quality of Haig's generalship, and the reasons for (and import-

[4] I owe this suggestion to an unpublished paper by Dr Nicholas Hiley.
[5] The most impressive sections of Paul Fussell's *Wartime* comprise a bitter attack on the lies and propaganda disseminated by the US government to its soldiers in the Second World War. Fussell challenges the necessity for such deception even in total war. Robert Graves's *Good-bye to All That* is in part fuelled by rage against similar propaganda in the First World War.

ance of) the Allied victory in 1918. Danchev quotes at length the amusing but patronizing reviews which Terraine received from John Keegan and Robert Kee but, despite his limitations (discussed here by Keith Simpson and others), Terraine's dogged reiteration of his main ideas in numerous books and articles has been historiographically very significant. As Danchev concedes, 'with time, the extraordinary intensity of his commitment became the touchstone, not only of his own work, but of the interpretation he had come to represent'.

In the editor's opinion, despite the saturation coverage of the First World War in the 1960s, little was produced of lasting scholarly value because there was so little attempt to place the war in historical perspective; books such as *The Donkeys* and films such as *Oh! What a Lovely War* tell us as much about the spirit of the 1960s as about the period supposedly portrayed. As Michael Howard acutely observed, the film of *Oh! What a Lovely War*, though ostensibly anti-war, was more emphatically anti-authority, specifically upper-class authority. It was, in a word, anti-officer. This is, to put it mildly, a partial and disputable view of the First World War. Elsewhere, in Peter Simkins's essay, John Keegan (no admirer of the First World War generals) is quoted to the effect that leadership at company and platoon level was perhaps 'of higher quality and greater military significance in the First World War, at least in the British army, than before or since'. It seems appropriate that Danchev should conclude his scintillating review of the First World War as refurbished in the 1960s with references to the music hall and the theatre: the dramatic tragedy of 1914-18 had been reduced to a mere entertainment —a War Game, and a game which Britain lost.[6]

It is, however, not necessary to end on a sour or pessimistic note because in more recent years there have been developments to encourage genuine students of the First World War. First, academic historians have at last begun to exploit the full range of available sources not only to reappraise traditional controversies about policy, strategy, tactics, and personalities, but also to portray war in its full social, cultural, political, and intellectual contexts with a sophistication seldom previously displayed and in marked contrast to the more narrowly military interpretations pursued by even the ablest earlier historians such as Falls and Cruttwell.

[6] In a recent BBC Radio 4 discussion on the baneful influence of the public schools a speaker confidently asserted 'And that is why we lost the First World War'—revisionism with a vengeance but a reasonable deduction from the film version of *Oh! What a Lovely War*.

The publications of contemporary historians such as Trevor Wilson, Tim Travers, David French, and Peter Simkins[7] (not to mention the excellent work being produced in other countries such as France), display a refreshing detachment from the emotional hang-ups and petty vendettas which have characterised so much of the historiography discussed in this volume. At the same time this new wave of scholarship has revealed serious gaps as well as the need for a reassessment of well-worn subjects. Most of the campaigns, for example, deserve to be re-examined in the light of new evidence while some, such as Macedonia, Palestine, Mesopotamia, and Italy have scarcely been explored by modern scholars. Trevor Wilson and Robin Prior are preparing a critical study of Sir Henry Rawlinson which should provide a model in the genre and, as Keith Simpson remarks, despite a score of attempts there is still no really satisfactory biography of Haig.

Secondly, as Peter Simkins stresses, the comparatively recent awakening of interest in what happens in battle and in the recorded recollections of 'Everyman at War', admirably pioneered by the Imperial War Museum as well as by individuals such as Martin Middlebrook and Peter Liddle, has made the First World War accessible to thousands of students who would not normally be attracted by the scholarly works described here. One salutary outcome of this popular interest is the publication of numerous volumes on particular units (notably the 'Pals Battalions' on the first day of the Somme) or particular episodes in battle (Mametz, High Wood, Pozières, Beaumont Hamel for 1916 alone). To Peter Simkins's careful discussion of the value and limitations of veterans' recorded impressions as historical evidence one need only add that such recollections are most valuable when they relate closely to the soldiers' own experience and least so when they refer to wider issues of policy and the conduct of operations.

John Grigg has recently reminded us that Britain entered the First World War only after an agonized Cabinet debate of the moral as well as the strategic issues, and the resultant long attritional struggle was sustained by a greater spirit of idealism than is now recalled (and greater too, Grigg argues less persuasively, than in the Second World War).[8]

---

[7] T. H. E. Travers, *The Killing Ground: The British Army, the Western Front and the Emergence of Modern Warfare, 1900-1918* (London, 1987); Trevor Wilson, *The Myriad Faces of War* (Oxford, 1986); David French, *British Strategy and War Aims 1914-1916* (London, 1986); Peter Simkins, *Kitchener's Army* (Manchester, 1988).

[8] John Grigg, 'Nobility and War: The Unselfish Commitment?', *Encounter* (Mar. 1990).

Most participants, from Prime Minister and commander-in-chief to the ordinary rankers and factory workers, had a clearer conviction that the war was worth while for Britain and that it was necessary to stick it out until victory was won than can easily be imagined now, or indeed was so easy to comprehend by, say, 1933 when the results in both domestic affairs and international relations were so disappointing and so disproportionate to the casualties.

The Hon. Alan Clark, currently Minister of State for Defence, still maintains that 'We should never have fought the First World War *on land* at all. It was the naval blockade that delivered victory. The sacrifice of a whole generation in Flanders was little more than a placebo to the mulish vanity of the General Staff.'[9]

The historiography examined here conveys only fleeting notions of this 'disenchantment' in, for example, the contrast between Liddell Hart's euphoric view of British generalship and staff work in 1916 and his increasingly critical stance in the 1920s. What certainly did cause a great deal of disillusionment about the high ideals of the nation's leaders was the publication of indiscreet memoirs such as Repington's; the inflammatory diaries of Sir Henry Wilson; and Lloyd George's vendetta against the reputations of Haig and Robertson after their deaths.

From our present perspective it is possible to show more sympathy and understanding for the predicament of military and political leaders confronted by a technological revolution in warfare than did, say, Fuller or Liddell Hart in the inter-war years. This is not to say that costly errors of judgement and lack of imagination should be condoned, and historical detachment should certainly not be equated with a bland sympathy for everyone in authority. Rawlinson's reputation is unlikely to be enhanced by Wilson and Prior's study, and our group has, for example, little to say in mitigation for some of the other senior commanders on the Somme.

If pressed to declare their own verdicts, differences of opinion might be detected among the contributors on certain issues such as the wisdom of the Gallipoli undertaking or of Haig's single-minded concentration on the Western Front. We are, however, united in our determination to carry the discussion of First World War historiography beyond popular stereotypes of 'The Donkeys' or 'The Butcher and the Cur'.[10] Such historiographical studies are essential for an understanding of how

---

[9] From a letter published in the *Sunday Telegraph* (8 July 1990).
[10] This tradition is alive and well. See John Laffin, *British Butchers and Bunglers of World War One* (London, 1988).

current views of the war—its conduct, character, and consequences have been shaped. The time is surely approaching, if it has not already arrived, when the First World War can be studied simply as history without polemic intent or apologies. It has taken a long historical march to reach this vantage-point.

I
Establishing the Historical Foundations

1
Early Historical Responses to the Great War: Fortescue, Conan Doyle, and Buchan*

KEITH GRIEVES

During the First World War and immediately after, the relationship between British military historians and the state was frequently uneasy. For the state the need for historical writings which bolstered opinion in support of the nation's war effort was a higher priority than the publication of judicious scholarly works. Official requirements and variable access to source material led to books of diverse quality which sought only to highlight the progress and virtues of the Allied cause. However, such notable writers as John Fortescue, Sir Arthur Conan Doyle, and John Buchan wrote accounts of great individuality in which personal interpretations of the war effort emerged, despite their unwillingness to produce history which the military authorities would find unsatisfactory. They wrote in the context of self-censorship and a buoyant market for patriotic writings, but none of these authors described their historical works as, pre-eminently, propagandist. They all expected their accounts to have a permanent value, not simply because they were supportive of the war effort, but because they could not envisage the emergence of books which challenged the British conduct of the war. They employed historical methods and what they wrote reflected closely the needs of a society at war and its aftermath, prior to the onset of an era disenchanted with the means and achievement of victory. Their accounts reassured participants and onlookers, and were honestly written as history, with the initiative in these major projects taken by the author and not by the state.

* I am grateful to Professor Brian Bond for his interest and support during my work on this area of study and appreciative of the discussion of an earlier draft at the First World War seminar at King's College, London. I should also like to thank Dr David French for his helpful comments on the essay. For permission to quote copyright material, I am grateful to the Trustees of the Liddell Hart Centre for Military Archives, King's College, London, Lord Tweedsmuir, and Edinburgh University Library.

Fortescue, Conan Doyle, and Buchan struggled to cope with the onset of total war and this essay will examine their historical responses. Fortescue was *the* historian of the British Army who attempted to make sense of the idea of official history, but in 1919 he returned to his study of Wellington's army. He acknowledged (and accommodated) the impact of the 1914-18 war on his history writing and the outcome was a curious amalgam of conclusions on two Great Wars. Conan Doyle aspired to official history but wrote without official endorsement and had a more limited appreciation of the task of the military historian. He produced a substantial amount of information, gathered in private correspondence, but was unable to depict the scale of war. Buchan was more successful. His access to source material and leading actors was unrestricted and he coped more effectively with the practical constraints on contemporary history writing. His publications enjoyed wide readership but even in revised form Buchan found, like Conan Doyle and Fortescue, that his view of war was too celebratory and romanticized to be entirely accepted in the long term.

I

The Hon. J. W. (later Sir John) Fortescue, fifth son of the third Earl Fortescue, was unable to pursue a military career, either for reasons of poor eyesight or due to the financial cost to the family of maintaining his three brothers in the army.[1] During the 1890s he conceived the idea of a multi-volume history of the British Army[2] and was only able to sustain this project after 1905 through royal patronage, as Librarian of Windsor Castle. At the outbreak of war he was studying the campaigns of 1813-15, for volume ix, and during 1915 he continued work on *A History of the British Army*. He held the firm conviction that without access to writings on previous expeditionary forces the New Armies would suffer a debilitating absence of *élan* and lack continuity of purpose.

He took delight in receiving letters from officers who were reading *A History of the British Army* at the front. General Sir Horace Smith-Dorrien told him that it was 'the great stand-by of the Army at the front'.[3] In September 1917 Fortescue informed his publishers, Macmillan, 'From letters which I receive from the front I believe that the

[1] *The Times* (23 Oct. 1933).
[2] J. W. Fortescue, *A History of the British Army*, 13 vols. (London, 1899-1930). This project started in 1896 with the original intention of four vols. ending the history at 1870.
[3] Fortescue to Macmillan, 6 Oct. 1917, Macmillan papers, BL Add. MS 55064.

officers—& some of the men would be thankful to have—say one copy per unit—to read in the winter.'[4] He conveyed the expectation of seasonal lulls in the campaign and confinement to secure winter quarters —conditions recognized by Wellington rather than Haig. Fortescue was increasingly vexed by the delayed appearance of an abridged volume of *A History of the British Army*. It was published in 1918 as *British Campaigns in Flanders 1690-1794* for officers to 'study the experiences of their forerunners in the Low Countries in a book which is fairly portable and fairly inexpensive' at eight shillings and sixpence.[5]

Apart from drawing attention to the past experiences of British forces in Flanders, Fortescue sought opportunities to emphasize the virtues and utility of tradition. His pamphlet *The Foot Guards* comprised short articles on the Guards regiments which first appeared in *The Times* in November 1914. He paid homage to the continuity of links between regiments and families. In the long casualty lists of the Coldstream Guards in the first two months of war he noted familiar names from the Scottish border and the West Country. Its 'hereditary prowess' was emphasized,[6] and Fortescue delighted in the existence of Colonel Monck, 264 years after his forebear founded the regiment. Fortescue asserted the continuing significance of birth and honour which was also a strong theme in *A History of the British Army*. Of the Peninsular army he noted, 'No one who knows anything of the subject will dispute the advantage which the habit of command inherited through many generations and acquired in childhood, may confer upon a man.'[7]

The Foot Guards was a distinctive contribution to the recruiting effort at a time when the aristocracy was paying heavily for the privilege of command. He expressed disgust that Britain was unprepared for war, like previous conflicts, and as a direct result the Grenadier Guards was 'pitted for generation after generation against tremendous odds and sacrificed in order to gain time for a sluggish nation to prepare for defence'.[8] An indignant conservatism shone through, particularly in his irritation that the lessons of past wars remained unexplored by policy-makers. By 1917 Fortescue's pamphlet was not selling well but he could not comprehend the diminishing relevance of his views in the emerging

[4] Fortescue to Macmillan, 8 Sept. 1917, ibid.
[5] Fortescue, *British Campaigns in Flanders 1690-1794, Being Extracts from 'A History of the British Army'* (London, 1918), preface.
[6] Id., *The Foot Guards* (London, 1915), 22. See also Lady Fortescue, *'There's Rosemary, There's Rue'* (London, 1939), 196.
[7] Fortescue, *A History of the British Army*, x. (1920), 205.
[8] Id., *The Foot Guards*, 30. See also Lady Fortescue, 'There's Rosemary', 187.

conditions of total war. None of his writings was used for overseas propaganda.[9]

In February 1916 Fortescue was approached for the third time to write an interim history of the war, based on official sources, for the general public.[10] He would have preferred the passage of 100 years and the death of the war's chief actors, but the War Office thought differently and Fortescue 'very reluctantly' accepted the task.[11] In effect he was mobilized to wield the pen, rather than the sword. Lord Kitchener, Secretary of State for War, intended that official material would be supplied to the historian, who would write without impediment. After Kitchener's death this scheme was replaced by the circulation of chapters to appropriate leading actors. Fortescue's work was increasingly subject to close supervision and during 1917 he attempted to resign from this salaried position. His interpretation was diluted and constrained by the 'anxiety of officials that blunders in the Field should not be referred to'.[12] Official material was sifted for him, but sometimes remained inaccessible in France and a profusion of private information was sent to him by proud and anguished parents concerning isolated incidents which were only verified with difficulty. He enjoyed the visits of officers from the front, but feared the impact of 'incorrigible grumblers, men with a grievance, seekers after notoriety' on his work.[13]

During the years 1916-19 Fortescue wrote 1,800 pages about operations on the Western Front up to May 1915. He twice rewrote his account of the Battle of Le Cateau following the return of prisoners in November 1917 and the 'belated discovery' of relevant documents in January 1919.[14] Three months later his involvement in the Official History was at an end and Lady Fortescue noted, 'One of my happiest memories will always be the morning of my Man's liberation.'[15] On his departure Fortescue outlined his long-standing complaints to Brigadier-

[9] None of Fortescue's writings was listed in the *Schedule of Wellington House Literature*, Imperial War Museum, 79/492.

[10] Fortescue, *Author and Curator* (London, 1933), 249; Lady Fortescue, 'There's Rosemary', 194; Fortescue, *A History of the British Army*, ix. (1920), p. v; *Army Quarterly*, 5/2 (Jan. 1923), 276.

[11] Fortescue to Edmonds, 8 Apr. 1919, Edmonds papers, II/2/95a.

[12] Lady Fortescue, 'There's Rosemary', 195.

[13] Fortescue, *Author and Curator*, 251.   [14] Ibid. 253.

[15] Lady Fortescue, 'There's Rosemary', 212. The immediate cause of Fortescue's departure from the Official History project was his critical reviews of Sir John French's *1914* which provided evidence of his 'partiality'. Fortescue to Maj.-Gen. F. Maurice, 1 Nov. 1919, Maurice papers, 3/5/101. Fortescue was always unhappy that the Historical Section, Committee of Imperial Defence demanded the production of positivistic 'ultimate history'.

General James Edmonds whose appointment as head of the military branch of the Historical Section, Committee of Imperial Defence occurred too late to rectify his position. Fortescue wrote,

> You know your mind, & have decided what you want. It is because no one knew his own mind or could report to me what was wanted, that I have been worried to death about the whole business, & have started upon the wrong track. I was told that a popular history was required of me, & now, at the eleventh hour I learn that it is something very different.[16]

Thereafter, Fortescue mischievously speculated on the probable date of publication of volume i of the official history of military operations, without appreciating the scale of revision of the early drafts. Initially, he had envied Sir Julian Corbett's clearly defined position as historian and archivist at the Admiralty, but the delayed publication of the first naval volume confirmed his pleasure in being free of bureaucratic control.[17] On 3 January 1921 Fortescue suggested to his publisher,

> I think that we ought to have a sweep for the publication of the official history, comprising fifty tickets dated 1921-1971. If you draw 1950, I'll buy it off you for 5% more than you gave for it & lodge it with my executors for my wife's benefit.[18]

Fortescue's contribution to contemporary history writing was undermined by the failure to clarify his official role and his own intention to return to work on the Great War of 1793-1814 at the earliest opportunity. However, he could not undo the experience of living through total war, sensitive as he was to the impact of long intense periods of conflict on combatant nations. In his preface to volume ix of *A History of the British Army* Fortescue wrote,

> I do not say that the time spent over the war with Germany was wholly unprofitable for me, for I could assure myself of at least two things, that all the old mistakes of former wars were repeated in high quarters between 1914 and 1918, and that the prowess of the British soldier was worthily maintained.[19]

---

[16] Fortescue to Edmonds, 8 Apr. 1919, Edmonds papers, II/2/95a; J. E. Edmonds, *History of the Great War*, i. *Military Operations: France and Belgium, 1914* (London, 1922), p. ix. See also D. French, ' "Official but not History"? Sir James Edmonds and the Official History of the Great War', *Journal of the Royal United Services Institute for Defence Studies* (Mar. 1986), 58.

[17] Sir J. Corbett, *History of the Great War: Naval Operations*, i. (London, 1920). See Fortescue to Macmillan, 7 July 1919, Macmillan papers, BL Add. MS 55065.

[18] Fortescue to Macmillan, 3 Jan. 1921, Macmillan papers, BL Add. MS 55065.

[19] Fortescue, *A History of the British Army*, ix. p. vi.

Establishing the Historical Foundations

Fortescue's examination of the years 1813-15 cannot be explained without reference to the British war effort 1914-18 because his conclusions highlighted the similarities in civil-military relations in both wars. Volumes ix and x were two-thirds complete at the outbreak of war, but the remaining portion of his manuscript was written during the raising of the New Armies.[20] This section included his review of the manpower problem of April 1815 and the concluding chapter on the significance of the years 1803-14. In May 1919, having left untouched this work for three years, Fortescue remarked, 'It is a joy to get back to the old history again.'[21]

For the author the study of the army was vindicated by the achievements of the British Expeditionary Force in 1914-15. In volumes ix and x he fulminated against political interference and ministerial ineptitude on a greater scale than in the volumes written before the war.[22] With the exception of Lord Liverpool, whom he admired, the blunders in organizing the nation's resources for war in the years 1803-14 were 'one and all sad proof of the unteachable ignorance of our Governors'.[23] While the Italian peninsula lay unexplored by British troops, expeditionary forces were 'inexcusably' dispatched to the West Indies, Egypt, and Sweden, and the recruiting machinery progressively broke down.[24] Fortescue found that the army was well organized but insufficient drafts were available. The delays in its reconstitution during May 1815 were emphasized in support of his contention that the troops fought splendidly and were led by gallant and efficient sons of the gentry who triumphed over poor national organization as well as the enemy. Fortescue wrote that 'the whole of this episode brings into glaring relief the evils of our own party system and the defects of our organization, even after nearly a quarter of a century of war, for National Defence'.[25] This was written in 1915 in the context of the political debate on compulsory military service which Fortescue regarded as an essential element of national preparedness for war and therefore two years too late.

Like many compulsionists, Fortescue was affronted by the search for political consensus on this issue rather than the acceptance of expert opinion from GHQ or from historians with insights into past wars. His

---

[20] Fortescue to Macmillan, 22 Sept. 1914, Macmillan papers, BL Add. MS 55064.
[21] Fortescue to Macmillan, 20 May 1919, ibid. The notebooks containing Fortescue's drafts of *A History of the British Army* are undated, and the surviving material for vol. ix is incomplete. Fortescue notebooks, National Army Museum, 6807-356.
[22] Cf. Fortescue, *A History of the British Army*, viii. (1917, but an entirely complete MS in 1914). [23] Ibid. x. 182. [24] Ibid. 185, 219.
[25] Ibid. 236.

comments on conscription were more pertinent to the age in which he wrote than the campaigns of 1803-15. Consequently, in volumes ix and x expressions of discontent were made with the belated organization of Britain's war effort against Germany. However, Fortescue often forgot human agency and despite his admiration for 'regimental spirit',[26] looked for an exact and, increasingly untenable, science of war. He also preferred military history to be the study of 'a community apart, sojourning in a strange land'.[27] He had little time for the problems of maritime supply routes, let alone the economic implications of munitions production and military recruitment.[28] None the less, he continued to expect that his volumes on the British Army would be read because they delivered lessons on the pursuit of military objectives from past experience of large-scale campaigns.[29]

However, for Fortescue as a student of Napoleonic warfare, changes in the structure of British society after 1918 and the impact of war made history less of an agreeable companion. He observed the collapse of the gentry's purchasing power and the demise of country-house libraries.[30] Moreover, he frowned upon the growing affluence of paper-makers and printers in comparison with historians.[31] His writings became practically a 'patriotic offering'[32] funded by his wife's dress-making and house decoration business.[33] As a result of the war his history writing became a painful labour, and at four pounds four shillings per volume it was not as central to the task of elucidating the lessons of the war as he hoped it would be. Fortescue responded patriotically to the demand for an Official Historian, but encountered all the problems of fettered contemporary history writing. He returned to the years 1813-15 with relief and found that this project gave him an excellent opportunity to express his views on the two Great wars.

II

Fortescue concluded that many years should elapse before a serious history of the war was written, but other notable attempts were made to

---

[26] *The Times* (23 Oct. 1933).   [27] Fortescue, *Author and Curator*, 249.
[28] *Army Quarterly*, 1/2 (Jan. 1921), 417.
[29] Lady Fortescue, 'There's Rosemary', 187.
[30] Fortescue, *Author and Curator*, 263.
[31] Id., *A History of the British Army*, ix. p. vi.
[32] Fortescue to Macmillan, 6 Feb. 1921, Macmillan papers, BL Add. MS 55065.
[33] Fortescue to Macmillan, 13 Mar. 1920, ibid.; Fortescue, *Author and Curator*, 260; Lady Fortescue, 'There's Rosemary', 217.

write early histories. One of the most ambitious works started during the war was the six-volume account by Sir Arthur Conan Doyle entitled *The British Campaign in France and Flanders* which appeared in the years 1916-20. Conan Doyle expected to gain access to official sources, largely due to his propagandist role in the Boer War and in 1914-15. Indeed, most of Conan Doyle's writings on war fulfilled official objectives and in 1915 he was intent on becoming *the* chronicler of the British forces in France.

Early in the Boer War Conan Doyle, aged forty, attempted to enlist in the Middlesex Yeomanry, and in February 1900 he sailed for South Africa as a senior physician attached to a friend's privately funded hospital unit. He observed the capture of Brandfort and enjoyed several minor adventures on reconnaisance. After being interviewed by Lord Roberts at Pretoria, he secured permission to obtain accounts from serving officers and began to write a history of the war.[34] However, he derived more pleasure from his 'incursion into diplomacy' in writing the pamphlet *The War in South Africa: Its Cause and Conduct*. He relished the opportunity to combat adverse home and European reaction to the concentration camps, by highlighting the fair play of the Imperial forces in conditions of irregular warfare.[35] One million copies were printed after an appeal in *The Times* for private subscriptions to fund production. It was freely distributed in France and Germany and in 1902 he was knighted.

At the outbreak of the Great War Conan Doyle was a private in the Crowborough Company, 6th Royal Sussex Volunteer Regiment. He immediately proposed that local guard and garrison duties should be undertaken by a formally constituted National Reserve, or 'Landsturm' of civilians over military age.[36] In Sussex he demanded increased enlistment and noted the apparent dichotomy in the recruiting figures between the splendid performance of the villages and the moderate outcome in the coast towns. Young men in urban areas should enlist or 'feel a cold draught wherever he turns'.[37] In the battle against 'shirkers' Conan Doyle played a major literary role. Two articles from *The Daily Chronicle*

[34] H. Pearson, *Conan Doyle: His Life and Art* (London, 1943), 128-30; C. Higham, *The Adventures of Conan Doyle* (London, 1976), 158-63. I am grateful to Dr Ian Beckett, RMA, Sandhurst for information on Conan Doyle's military writings during the Boer War.
[35] A. Conan Doyle, *The War in South Africa: Its Cause and Conduct* (London, 1902); Pearson, *Conan Doyle*, 131. [36] *The Times* (8 Aug. 1914).
[37] *Eastbourne Gazette* (14 Oct. 1914), quoted in J. M. Gibson and R. L. Green (ed.), *The Unknown Conan Doyle: Letters to the Press* (London, 1986), 210-11.

were published as short pamphlets and the *Schedule of Wellington House Literature*, collated by the War Propaganda Bureau, listed his celebrated recruiting statement *To Arms* which noted 'that it is every Briton's duty to see that England is victorious'.[38] As late as 1917 he happily contended that 'brave slaves led by clever fiends can and will be beaten by freemen led by gentlemen'.[39]

From the moment Conan Doyle attended the meeting of eminent authors at Wellington House on 2 September 1914 his pen was vigorously used in support of the war effort. He suspended his production of novels with the exception of one wartime appearance by Sherlock Holmes. At the meeting the *litterateurs* concluded that the duty and destiny of England was 'to uphold the rule of common justice between civilized peoples, to defend the rights of small nations, and to maintain the free and law-abiding ideals of Western Europe'.[40] As his major contribution to the national task, Conan Doyle wrote a military history of British operations on the Western Front. Ultimately, through controversy and delay, *The British Campaign in France and Flanders* was less significant than Conan Doyle had envisaged and gave him little sense of satisfaction. The deaths of his son and brother at the front and the difficulty of establishing his account as history caused despondency. In 1924 he wrote,

my war history, which reflects all the passion and pain of those hard days, has never come into its own. I would reckon it the greatest and most undeserved literary disappointment of my life if I did not know that the end is not yet and that it may mirror those great times to those who are to come.[41]

Conan Doyle sought to celebrate the British war effort yet from the outset, ironically, his relationship with the War Office was problematic. Early in 1915, while in charge of prisoners of war at Lewes Gaol, he obtained Asquith's approval to start work on the book. Conan Doyle assumed that Sir John French's initial enthusiasm gave him 'official sanction' to obtain material from divisional and army commanders. In practice any arrangement which fell short of the role of Official Historian

---

[38] Conan Doyle, *To Arms* (London, 1914); *Schedule of Wellington House Literature*, Imperial War Museum, 79/492, entry No. 24; P. Buitenhuis, *The Great War of Words: Literature as Propaganda 1914-18 and After* (London, 1989), 23-4.

[39] Gibson and Green, *The Unknown Conan Doyle*, 249-50.

[40] *The Times* (18 Sept. 1914); D. G. Wright, 'The Great War: Government Propaganda and English "Men of Letters" 1914-16', *Literature and History*, 7 (1978), 72.

[41] Conan Doyle, *Memories and Adventures* (London, 1924), 368-9; Pearson, *Conan Doyle*, 170.

was regarded with scepticism in the British forces in France. In April 1915 Conan Doyle wrote to Colonel Edmonds, who had been GSO1 4 Division in 1914, for information on the Battle of Le Cateau. Edmonds was suspicious of 'a "try on" to get information that is War Office property'.[42] Conan Doyle was told to apply for the divisional war diary at the War Office, which decided at the end of April that no information could be divulged.

In reality Conan Doyle enjoyed no greater access to official material than other civilian writers. In one exasperated response he told Edmonds, 'I should have thought that when the C in C gave me leave to ask such questions and named you, as the officer I was to apply to, that it was absolute official sanction.'[43] During May 1915 the military censor ruled that the volume's early appearance was 'undesirable' and the publication of the first volume was delayed until 1916. To acquire information Conan Doyle engaged in an extensive correspondence with senior officers, little of which has survived, and sought discussion with junior officers on leave. French noted Conan Doyle's dependence on private information and the War Office's reluctance to approve and facilitate his research for the first volume. Consequently French withdrew his sponsorship of Conan Doyle and refused permission for the account of 1914-15 to be dedicated to him. Conan Doyle subsequently disparaged French's facile descriptions of modern warfare[44] and the book was dedicated to Field Marshal Sir William Robertson.

In April 1917 Conan Doyle's account of the Somme offensive in volume iii was vigorously blue-pencilled. This official attitude compounded the constant problem of adjudicating the relative significance of divisional roles in major operations. Without official material Conan Doyle was utterly dependent on leading participants. He told Major-General Jeudwine of the 55 Division, 'how impossible it is for me to hold the balance even between the wish of divisions when my information is partial'.[45] From Jeudwine he wanted papers, diaries, and divisional reports on the Guillemont operations with the request, 'I would ask you however to keep the matter between ourselves, for if you refer it for advice or permission, to any high authority then it becomes official,

---

[42] Minute, Edmonds to Col. Hon. W. Lambton, 21 Apr. 1915, Edmonds papers, II/2/58.   [43] Conan Doyle to Edmonds, 4 May 1915, ibid. II/2/61.
[44] Conan Doyle, *Memories and Adventures*, 372-3; Pearson, *Conan Doyle*, 169.
[45] Conan Doyle to Maj.-Gen. H. Jeudwine, 30 Mar. [1917], 356 FIF/43, 55th (W. Lancashire) Division papers, Liverpool Record Office. See Jeudwine's reply of 11 Apr. 1917, ibid.

filters back to the War Office and there is the chance of some annoyance.'[46] Conan Doyle's conspiratorial tone undermined his seemingly patriotic and self-imposed altruistic task of 'rescuing facts' from oblivion. Jeudwine delayed contact by suggesting that they met when he was next in London. He later noted, 'I sent him nothing nor did I meet him—not liking round the corner ways.'[47]

For an author who regarded British military policy as almost entirely successful, the failure to secure information from all sectors of the front was a severe setback for which his lionized role of 1900-2 had ill prepared him. Lloyd George sympathized and suggested to Conan Doyle that 'it was probably better done from direct human documents than from filed papers'.[48] In the aftermath of his visit to France and Italy in 1916, Conan Doyle's writing gained impetus but was channelled in the direction of a further propaganda pamphlet. In *A Visit to Three Fronts* he drew attention to the 'two very great men whom Britain has produced —the private soldier and the regimental officer'. He also noted 'the enormous imperturbable confidence of the Army'.[49] As literary propaganda work to bolster opinion which needed to believe that the liberal rhetoric of 'decency' and 'honour' had continuing meaning in 1916-17 this pamphlet was a significant contribution. However, Conan Doyle's observations and sentiment were less happily accommodated in his volumes of military history.

The British Campaign in France and Flanders served the purpose of sustaining civilian morale by depicting the clash of arms as the advance of good over evil and civilization over barbarism. Despite this clear objective, Conan Doyle expected his volumes to have a continuing validity because he assumed that the war would always be depicted from his perspective. His book mythologized the British soldier but failed to signify the nature of his achievements in a tortuously complex narrative. His central themes are illuminated in volume v which focused on the months January to July 1918. It embodied the 'future was dark and dangerous, but there were also solid grounds for hope'[50] school of history writing, in which British forces were constantly questing for 'equilibrium'.[51]

[46] Conan Doyle to Jeudwine, 30 Mar. [1917], ibid.
[47] Note, initialled by Jeudwine and dated 17 Apr., on Conan Doyle to Jeudwine, undated, ibid. [48] Conan Doyle, *Memories and Adventures*, 424.
[49] Ibid. 382; Conan Doyle, *A Visit to Three Fronts* (London, 1916); Higham, *The Adventures of Conan Doyle*, 251-3.
[50] Conan Doyle, *The British Campaign in France and Flanders*, 6 vols. (London, 1916-20), v. 61. [51] e.g. ibid. 5, 66, 75.

26   Establishing the Historical Foundations

Conan Doyle described a series of troop movements, usually resembling well-ordered field-days, in which the measurement of military success was based on the scale of casualties, explained in obtuse and unilluminating terms. He wrote,

> It is said that during the retreat from Moscow an officer having asked who were the occupants of a certain sledge, was answered: 'The Royal Regiment of Dutch Guards'. It is in a somewhat similar sense that all mentions of battalions, brigades and divisions must be taken at this stage of the battle.[52]

Some scenes were effectively described, but Conan Doyle ignored staff-work, supplies, morale, artillery, and aerial warfare. He examined the progress of individual brigades and divisions in action, using a heavily compartmentalized structure, which failed to emphasize the interrelationship of adjacent formations.

Few descriptions of battles commenced with an overview of the disposition of forces or nature of the terrain and the maps did not help the reader through the complicated maze of paragraph outlines of the activities of individual units. Consequently, linking statements took the form of 'We left the Thirty-fourth Division upon the evening of March 21 still holding its reserve lines',[53] or 'if the story be now continued it leaves too wide a gap for the reader to cross when he has to return to the history of the Fifth Army upon the 21st March'.[54] Conan Doyle frequently and apologetically mentioned the mechanics of his narrative to the reader, who was left to piece the descriptions of each section together and could be forgiven for thinking that GHQ had a purely ornamental role. In volume v Haig merited eight brief references and no insight was granted into decision-making above divisional level. Units moved without apparent reason and German plans remained unclear. Despite the early appearance of memoirs of senior German army commanders after the war, Conan Doyle concluded that his own work was sufficiently cogent and would not have to be revised.

His military history was very narrowly focused on the front line and its major selling-point was that 'for the first time the detailed battlelines of these great encounters have been set out'.[55] In this respect Conan Doyle was remarkably successful, for no reviewer suggested that a brigade or battalion was out of place. After the war he took pleasure in meeting ex-servicemen and ascertaining their regiment, whereupon 'he informed the astounded recipient not only of his former brigade and division but the principal actions in which he took part!'[56]

[52] Ibid. 65.   [53] Ibid. 23.   [54] Ibid. 76.   [55] Ibid. iv. preface.
[56] Adrian Conan Doyle, *The True Conan Doyle* (London, 1946), 18.

In his search for certainties and axiomatic articles of faith *The British Campaign in France and Flanders* revealed the author's vulnerability in the face of vociferous leading participants. Conan Doyle spent many hours with General Sir Hubert Gough after the German attack in March 1918. He concluded, 'there was absolutely nothing upon the military side which could have been bettered, nor has any suggestion ever been made of anything which was left undone'.[57] Conan Doyle was convinced that Gough was unjustly condemned and he sought to challenge that injustice in his remarkably partial account of the retreat, in which good order was everywhere maintained.[58]

His penchant for superlatives was based on thin evidence and revealed an author committed to the propagation of basic statements about British destiny and the inevitability of German defeat. They were predicated on simple cause and effect relationships and avoided the complex interlocking factors of large-scale war. Without evaluating the availability and deployment of manpower, Conan Doyle assumed that 350,000 men sent to France in April 1918 were previously withheld from Haig by the government, when in fact they were mostly unfit, under age, or undertaking other essential tasks.[59] For Conan Doyle, Haig and Gough were faultless and the government guilty of negligence. Twelve years later Conan Doyle remained reluctant to criticize any aspect of the British military war effort. He was concerned that Edmonds's account of the battle of Loos, which referred to the panic of some British units, was 'too vivid'[60] and 'could be softened',[61] particularly for American consumption.

Conan Doyle's inclination to avoid trenchant comment on military organization and performance gave his writing a fantastical quality not far removed from his patriotic verse. He drew attention to 'the yeoman of the Shires, and the infantry of London [which] won once more the ground which Richard the Lion Heart with his knights and bowmen had contested in the long ago'.[62] The same indomitable spirit is present in the poem 'Victrix', which was used for recitation, and whose first stanza asked,

[57] Conan Doyle, *The British Campaign in France and Flanders*, v. 200.
[58] See H. Gough's foreword in Adrian Conan Doyle, *The True Conan Doyle*; *Spectator* (20 Sept. 1919).
[59] Conan Doyle, *The British Campaign in France and Flanders*, v. 202.
[60] Conan Doyle to Edmonds, 6 Dec. 1929, Edmonds papers, II/2/204.
[61] Conan Doyle to Edmonds, 4 Dec. 1929, ibid. II/2/203.
[62] Conan Doyle, *The British Campaign in France and Flanders*, v. 1.

> How was it then with England?
> Her faith was true to her plighted word,
> Her strong hand closed on her blunted sword,
> Her heart rose high to the foeman's hate
> She walked with God on the hills of Fate—
> And all was well with England.[63]

In practice Conan Doyle found it difficult to disentangle his overtly propagandist mode of writing from the more permanent historiographical place he wished to secure for *The British Campaigns in France and Flanders*, which at seven shillings and sixpence per volume was somewhat improbably designed for the poorest soldier, as well as for future generations.[64]

To Conan Doyle's enduring annoyance each volume was severely criticized on publication in the *Times Literary Supplement*. By the appearance of volume v the anonymous reviewer was known to be John Fortescue. The unhappy spectacle arose of an account which was originally approved by the War Office being unflatteringly reviewed by the Official Historian. The prose was too elegant and the style too extravagant and Fortescue concluded of volumes iii and iv, 'He has been much at the front, he has worked hard, and he has felt much; but it is not his *metier* to write military history.'[65] The review emphasized the lack of time in which to assimilate information, lack of source material, absence of an overview, and the failure to relate tactical outcome to preparations at front line and command levels. In highlighting these points Fortescue drew attention to the problems inherent in passionate, unofficial, contemporary history writing, of which Conan Doyle's work was simply a prime example. For him the British army at war was one of the 'most wonderful of military epics'.[66] While Fortescue's reviews reflected a historian in retreat from the study of modern battles, particularly in his statement that only men with front-line experience could describe the conditions endured in France, they were not 'the pettiest details of animadversion' Conan Doyle suggested them to be.[67]

[63] 'Victrix', in Conan Doyle, *The Guards Came Through and other Poems* (London, 1919), 13-15. See also the poem 'Haig is Moving, August 1918' (pp. 20-1).
[64] Adrian Conan Doyle, *The True Conan Doyle*, 24.
[65] Fortescue's review of vols. iii and iv in the *Times Literary Supplement* (11 Mar. 1920). See also ibid. (27 Mar. 1919) (vols. i and ii). For Conan Doyle's response see his *The British Campaign in France and Flanders*, v. preface. See also his letter in the *Times Literary Supplement* (26 July 1917).
[66] Conan Doyle, *The British Campaign in France and Flanders*, v. p. v, dated 1 May 1919.
[67] Ibid. p. vi.

The *Spectator* suggested that the volumes would retain a value for reference purposes,[68] but no mention of his work is to be found in B. H. Liddell Hart's *A History of the World War 1914-1918* or in C. R. M. F. Cruttwell's *A History of the Great War 1914-1918*. Conan Doyle worked tirelessly and without financial profit. Ultimately, his major writing commitment over five years was superseded rather than used as a foundation stone in the historiography of the war. From 1922 onwards this process was hastened by the publication of the Official History of the Great War. Fortescue predicted that *The British Campaign in France and Flanders* would 'share the fate of Entick's "History of the Seven Years War"; and if the reader has never heard of Entick we shall say no more'.[69] Despite Conan Doyle's remonstrations against Fortescue's contraventions of literary etiquette, his charges were valid. With the passage of time military history should not accommodate texts of incessant optimism and stereotypical images, but in the aftermath of war Conan Doyle's work had a relevance to the society for which it was written.

III

At the outbreak of war John Buchan was medically unfit and unable to contribute to the war effort in any other way than to write about it. To occupy his mind and keep the printers and binders of Thomas Nelson and Sons, which he joined in 1906 as literary adviser, in employment, with the cessation of normal literary activity, he began writing *Nelson's History of the War* in instalments of 50,000 words. The firm, of which he became a director in 1915, published 24 volumes from February 1915 to July 1919. The volumes appeared regularly, regardless of Buchan's various appointments which tended to leave him less time to write but also gave him the advantage over Conan Doyle of easy access to public figures and official information. Buchan later recorded in his autobiography that he knew too much and 'was often perplexed as to what I could print'.[70] However, his capacity for self-censorship never gave the Foreign Office or the War Office grounds for concern.

Buchan was a war correspondent for *The Times* at GHQ during the months May to September 1915, and in June 1916 he joined the Intelligence staff at GHQ. He wrote summaries of military operations but was forced to return to Britain in October 1916 after a duodenal attack. As

[68] *Spectator* (6 Mar. 1920). [69] *Times Literary Supplement* (11 Mar. 1920).
[70] J. Buchan, *Memory Hold-The-Door* (London, 1940), 167.

an experienced soldier-publicist Colonel Buchan was appointed Director of Information at sub-ministerial level in February 1917, having previously managed aspects of news control at the War Propaganda Bureau at Wellington House.[71] During the summer months of 1917 Buchan's directorate was the subject of internecine conflict in Whitehall and his work on *Nelson's History of the War* became more difficult to sustain.[72] After February 1918 the development of administrative procedures to regulate information flow was conducted in more autonomous conditions, when Lord Beaverbrook was appointed Minister of Information with Buchan as Director of Intelligence. Howard Spring later wrote, 'It is a mystery to me how he got through the days as he did. He was doing his work as an Intelligence officer; he was writing his history of the war; and he was somehow fitting in novels as well.'[73] As Lord Rosebery asked in February 1917, 'How will you combine all your activities, you multifamous man?'[74] It might be added that during the war he was also almost 'continuously unwell'.[75]

None the less, in *Nelson's History of the War* he wrote an account which was seriously discussed, because, as *The Times* noted, 'it represents the faith which inspired the civil population during five years of war, and it did much to create, or, at all events, to maintain, that abiding confidence'.[76] In the volumes he constantly expressed confidence in the outcome of the war and his disinclination to adopt a degree of detachment was regarded as a virtue by his readership. His publisher was confident in its unrivalled position in the market and during 1916 raised the price of each volume, by threepence, to one shilling and threepence. It enjoyed by far the largest circulation of any war publication.[77] Buchan wrote the

[71] R. H. Lutz, 'Studies of World War Propaganda, 1914-33', *Journal of Modern History*, 5 (1933), 496-516; I. Nicholson, 'An Aspect of Official War Propaganda', *Cornhill Magazine*, 70/419 (May 1931), 593-606; P. M. Taylor, 'The Foreign Office and British Propaganda during the First World War', *Historical Journal*, 23/4 (1980), 875-98; M. Sanders and P. M. Taylor, *British Propaganda during the First World War 1914-18* (London, 1982), 63-76; T. Wilson, *The Myriad Faces of War* (Cambridge, 1988), 733-4.
[72] See Buchan's letters to his mother, 11 June 1917 and 7 July 1917, Buchan papers, Acc. 6975, no. 14(1).
[73] H. Spring, quoted in Lady Tweedsmuir, *John Buchan by his Wife and Friends* (London, 1947), 80.
[74] Lord Rosebery to Buchan, 10 Feb. 1917, Buchan papers, Acc. 6975, no. 13.
[75] Buchan, *Memory Hold-The-Door*, 164.
[76] Undated review, National Library of Scotland, MF MSS 317 (microfilm of MS at Queen's University, Ontario).
[77] G. M. Brown to Buchan, 1 Mar. 1916, Buchan-Nelson correspondence in Nelson and Sons papers, Edinburgh University Library, B/6/57. In 1919 each volume cost two shillings and sixpence. See also note by Buchan attached to letter to Lord Beaverbrook, 13 May 1922, Buchan papers, Acc. 7006.

volumes as a public duty and accommodated all official interests, yet he maintained a perspective which was essentially his own. His expression of values and opinions in war was not dissimilar to his peacetime writings. As a result of the accessibility of official information, Buchan never needed to pursue Rider Haggard's suggestion in 1915 that he should apply to become the official historian.[78] Instead, he drew confidence from the many compliments he received throughout the war. Lord Haldane noted as early as June 1915, 'You have written in a fashion which has brought the splendid fighting quality of our troops vividly before the public mind. That is a real service to the nation.'[79] John Galsworthy had 'much admiration for your indefatigable energy and efforts'.[80]

An indication of the official endorsement enjoyed by Buchan, unlike Conan Doyle, was the remarkable decision to allow the publication of *Nelson's History of the War* to continue after he was appointed to Haig's Intelligence staff. On 5 July 1916 Buchan told G. M. Brown, works manager at Nelson's, that he would continue to write the account for post-war publication if the War Office opposed its wartime appearance. This suggestion should modify the assumption that the volumes were wholly propagandist in intention and execution.[81] Buchan added,

The Foreign Office would like me to continue it; as they think it very useful for propaganda work. GHQ agree that it would be useful, but they think that if I wrote it now it would make it official and they don't want that. I have said that I cannot decide on such a case, and that Grey must settle it with Haig.[82]

Seventeen days later he informed Brown that *Nelson's History of the War* would continue; GHQ 'are exceedingly nice and reasonable about it. All that they ask is that I should submit my chapters on the Western Front to the Chief of General Staff'.[83] Such a provision was unnecessary for no note of pessimism existed in his volumes. In December 1916 he reflected on his position and told Captain Liddell Hart 'it would ill become an Officer attached to Headquarters Staff to criticise or to praise the Generals in the field'.[84]

Volume xvi of *Nelson's History of the War* was entitled 'The Battle of the Somme' and was largely written at GHQ. He provided a strategic

[78] H. Rider Haggard to Buchan, 14 May 1915, Buchan papers, Acc. 6975, no. 13.
[79] Lord Haldane to Buchan, 10 June 1915, ibid.
[80] J. Galsworthy to Buchan, 5 Jan. 1918, National Library of Scotland, MF MSS 305 (microfilm of MS at Queen's University, Ontario).
[81] Buitenhuis, *The Great War of Words*, 92-3.
[82] Buchan to Brown, 5 July 1916, Nelson papers, B/6/134.
[83] Buchan to Brown, 22 July 1916, ibid. B/6/152.
[84] Buchan to Liddell Hart, 2 Dec. 1916, Liddell Hart papers, I/124/1.

overview and as a result of his visits to the front the terrain was vividly described, but it was also suffused with striking illustrations of the themes which fascinated Buchan—chivalrous ideals, hero-worship, national characteristics, and pastoral romanticism. Consequently, no sense of the slaughter of 1 July can be found. The battles of the Somme offensive were characterized by 'quiet cheerfulness', 'heroic remnants', 'wild adventures', 'tremendous odds', and usually the 'weather did not favour us'.[85] In the ranks there were 'miners from north England, factory hands from the industrial centres, clerks and shop boys, ploughmen and shepherds, Saxon and Celt, college graduates and dock labourers.'[86] Buchan often listed this rich diversity of backgrounds to highlight the equality of sacrifice by region and trade led, of course, by 'The typical public-school boy [who] proved a born leader of men.'[87] Together 'they had turned the ghastly business of war into something homely and familiar'.[88]

For Buchan the worth of men at the front was far greater than in their civil occupations because he celebrated lives of action, national spirit, and military organization and tended to depict the home front as a potential hindrance to victory. For example, 'elaborate provision had to be made for shelter during raids for the poorer classes who lived in flimsy buildings'.[89] Mention of production and government brought overtones of disharmony. Buchan diminished the context of total war, which provided shells in sufficient number, by focusing on 'the gallant procession who offered their all'.[90] His study of the front brought Buchan great satisfaction. Of his Somme volume Buchan noted, 'I think I may say it will be pretty good for it is written with complete knowledge.'[91]

Buchan not only concentrated heavily on the glory of battle and the interdependence of officers and men, but also on the heavy cost of waging war for privileged social groups while the home front remained ill organized and wasteful of resources. Substantial space was devoted to Buchan's contemporaries at Oxford, notably Raymond Asquith ('debonair and brilliant and brave') and Auberon Herbert ('hero of romance').[92] In emphasizing their deaths and highlighting the mystical, sacrificial quality of the battlefield, Buchan averted the reader's attention from blind material force and the grinding war of attrition. In the closing paragraph of the Somme account he wrote,

[85] Buchan, *Nelson's History of the War*, xvi. (London, 1917), in seq., pp. 71, 33, 158, 68, 77. See also xx. 113.   [86] Ibid. xvi. 32-3.   [87] Ibid. 88.
[88] Ibid. 33.   [89] Ibid. xxi. 224.   [90] Ibid. xvi. 171.
[91] Buchan to Brown, 3 Nov. 1916, Nelson papers, B/6/265.
[92] Buchan, *Nelson's History of the War*, xvi. 120-2, 146.

Fortescue, Conan Doyle, and Buchan 33

The young men who gazed on the world, the makers and the doers who left their tasks unfinished, were greater in their deaths than in their lives. They builded better than they knew for the sum of their imperfections was made perfect, and out of loss they won for the country and mankind an enduring gain. Their memory will abide so long as men are found to set honour before ease, and a nation lives not for its ledgers alone but for some purpose of virtue.[93]

Buchan's prose had sustaining qualities and it comforted military participants and civilian onlookers who needed to be assured that the war was, indeed, noble. In 1921 a former captain in the Royal Warwickshire Regiment wrote to Buchan expressing the hope that the 'beautiful summary of a man's life' at the end of the Somme volume would be reproduced in his revised *History of the Great War* because the 'words so expressed what I often feel and they have really given us great comfort'.[94] He related this passage directly to the memory of six friends present at his 21st dinner in Cambridge twelve years before, who all died on the Western Front.

In the revised *History of the Great War*, published in four volumes in 1921-2, the effect of this comforting passage was heightened still further by slight amendment and relocation to the end of the concluding chapter of the book.[95] In the scale of unaltered material reproduced in the revised volumes, including the tribute to Raymond Asquith[96] and the diverse social origins of British soldiers,[97] the originality and historical integrity of *Nelson's History of the War* can be appreciated. Both editions comprised his observations and personal response to the war and have an intense, if sanitized, understanding of aspects of life at the front. His work cannot be summarily dismissed as propaganda, as if it conspired against actual conditions.[98] *Nelson's History of the War* was not a 'government book', whereas Buchan did use the phrase to describe other volumes on the Somme battles which he wrote for American consumption.[99] It so closely represented Buchan's views on the war that four

---

[93] Ibid. xvi. 172-3.
[94] J. de R. Philip to Buchan, 1 Nov. 1921, National Library of Scotland, MF MSS 305 (microfilm of MS at Queen's University, Ontario).
[95] Buchan, *A History of the Great War*, iv. (London, 1922), 443-4.
[96] Ibid. iii. 196-7.   [97] Ibid. 162.
[98] For an insight into heroic episodes of war whose details Buchan retained, see his scrapbooks, Buchan papers, Acc. 6975, Box 3.
[99] Buchan to Brown, 1 Feb. 1917, Nelson papers, B/7/119. Buchan made clear the separate 'propagandist purposes' of his illustrated edition of *The Battle of the Somme* which was to be published in the United States 'before the new big operations commence at the front', Buchan to Brown, 9 Mar. 1917, ibid. B/7/64a; *Schedule of Wellington House Literature*, Imperial War Museum, 79/492, entry nos. 174, 487, 675.

years after the armistice his description of strategic objectives was still couched in euphemistic vocabulary. In 1922 he wrote, 'Like some harsh and remorseless chemical, the waxing Allied energy was eating into the German waning mass' and 'We had opened the old wound and undermined his *moral* by reviving the terrors of the unknown and the unexpected.'[100] His description of some details altered as German memoirs appeared, but Buchan adhered firmly to the twin principles of reasoned optimism and a morally elevated account of war in which military commanders were not criticized.

Like his study of *Montrose*,[101] Buchan's writings on the war reveal the constancy of his preoccupations. In 1922 his perspective remained unchanged, varying little from the awe and confidence expressed in a letter to G. M. Brown of 5 July 1916, 'I have visited all the conquered villages and seen the bloodiest battlefield I ever dreamed of. Things are going very well however.'[102] Similarly his decision not to challenge the organization of the military war effort was not a temporary expedient. Soon after the war ended Buchan reluctantly declined to write an account of Haig's life. His wife recorded that he 'consoled himself with the knowledge that he had paid a tribute to Lord Haig in "A History of the Great War"'.[103] Buchan admired Haig's 'high military talent'[104] and he wrote an article 'The Victorious General and the Man', which received wide newspaper coverage and in which he reiterated his profound admiration for the 'Scottish hero'.[105] In a letter to Liddell Hart in 1935 Buchan noted Haig's 'real greatness of character' and emphasized their common points of reference, notably 'Oxford, the Borders and the Kirk'.[106] The conclusions Buchan first drew in war remained valid for many years thereafter. In 1922 Field Marshal Sir William Robertson identified Buchan's empathy for military high command and concluded, 'You have most commendably avoided the air of superiority too often assumed by the historian.'[107]

[100] Buchan, *A History of the Great War*, iii. 217, 214.
[101] Buchan to Lord Beaverbrook, 15 Oct. 1928, Buchan papers, Acc. 7006; J. Buchan, *Montrose*, enlarged edn., 1928.
[102] Buchan to Brown, 5 July 1916, Nelson papers, B/6/134.
[103] Lady Tweedsmuir, *John Buchan by his Wife and Friends*, 284; Buchan, *Memory Hold-The-Door*, 172-9.
[104] Buchan, *A History of the Great War*, iv. 438.
[105] Undated article, J. Buchan, National Library of Scotland, MF MSS 317 (microfilm of MS at Queen's University, Ontario).
[106] Buchan to Liddell Hart, 19 Feb. 1935, Liddell Hart papers, I/124/60.
[107] Robertson to Buchan, 18 Sept. 1922, National Library of Scotland, MF MSS 305 (microfilm of MS at Queen's University, Ontario).

Nelson's History of the Great War was faithful to Buchan's pre-war denunciation of the Tolstoyan view that nothing in the world was worth the death of fellow men. In the immediate post-war era the view that an unflinching war of attrition was the only path to victory needed to be consolidated and Buchan's romanticized account in his revised volumes served this purpose. It also dwelt on the American contribution to the Allied war effort and was recommended as a definitive or permanent account by Anglophile reviewers who felt that the bonds of friendship between Britain and the United States would be cemented by Buchan's work.[108]

There were also practical reasons for the close similarities of content between *Nelson's History of the War* and the *History of the Great War*. These are revealed in Buchan's timetables of literary work and correspondence with Nelson's. He worked at a furious pace. In Buchan's list 'Literary work to be done' the revision of his war history had the highest priority of ten projects.[109] His timetable for 1919 indicated that his main work in the months of March to December would comprise the revision of 1,200,000 words on the war, alongside the writing of one novel, the completion of the memorial volume on the Grenfell brothers, and the first stages of his history of the South African forces in France.[110] These tasks were delayed by ill health, his move to Elsfield in Oxfordshire, and the process of extending Nelson's list of publications. Consequently, Buchan started the laborious process of revision in July 1920 but completed 52 chapters or two volumes by April 1921.[111] They appeared in September 1921 and were quickly followed by volumes iii and iv in April and September 1922, at twenty-five shillings per volume. The schedule was so tight that full discussion with expert opinion was usually reduced to hasty reassurances that the account would survive scrutiny. For example, ill health forced Buchan to postpone meetings with Lord Beaverbrook—his political mentor of 1918—who could only advise that the chapter on Lloyd George's rise to the premiership 'represents the truth roughly'.[112]

---

[108] Undated review, Edmund J. Carpenter, ibid. MF MSS 317.

[109] Literary work to be done, undated notebook entry, Buchan papers, Acc. 6975, Box 2; A. C. Turner, *Mr. Buchan Writer* (London, 1949), 70.

[110] Timetable [for 1919], Buchan papers, Acc. 6975, Box 2; Buchan, *The Path of a King* (London, 1921); id., *Francis and Riversdale Grenfell: A Memoir* (London, 1920); id., *The History of the South African Forces in France* (1920).

[111] See Buchan-Nelson correspondence, Jan.-Apr. 1921.

[112] Lord Beaverbrook to Buchan, 17 Nov. 1921, National Library of Scotland, MF MSS 305 (microfilm of MS at Queen's University, Ontario).

Throughout his history writing of 1914-21, Buchan conveyed the sense of great drama as a non-combatant participant and protested that 'The book is indeed the opposite of official history.'[113] In revised form it offered 'civilization' some grounds for hope in an uncertain post-war social context, or in the pastoral imagery of harvest time that 'there is ground for humble confidence that that sowing in unimaginable sacrifice and pain will yet quicken and bear fruit to the bettering of the world'.[114] Buchan's *History of the Great War* conveyed a distaste for pacifistic opinion and the 'primordial fires' of revolutionary unrest.[115] It placed faith in national sentiment rather than governmental direction.

Nevertheless, as a four-volume work, the *History of the Great War* was a book for the political, literary, and military establishment. Buchan informed Nelson's, 'An expensive book of this sort is sold better by talk in cultivated society than by any other means.'[116] He suggested that prospectuses should be issued to high-class booksellers, regimental and divisional headquarters, public schools, and various notable figures. Among those who received the volumes were King George V, A. J. Balfour, Lord Beaverbrook, Lord Grey of Fallodon, Thomas Hardy, Lord Rosebery (who wrote the original preface), General Sir Julian Byng, Field Marshal Lord Haig, and Field Marshal Sir William Robertson. An advertising campaign in newspapers was avoided, but special attention was paid to the libraries of Clubland, Universities, professional societies, banks, and the rural gentry.[117]

On the appearance of the *History of the Great War* the *Spectator* marvelled at Buchan's industry, fairness, and capacity for accurate generalization.[118] The review was written by its editor St Loe Strachey who had long admired Buchan's work and used him as a frequent contributor. In the *Edinburgh Review* Buchan's work was expected to rank with Macaulay's *History of England* and his treatment of Plan 17 was compared very favourably to the Official *History of the Great War*.[119] However, the *Army Quarterly* suggested 'It may be that in the country of the blind the one-eyed man is King.'[120] It emphasized inaccuracies of detail regarding the battles of 1914, while the reviewer in the *Times*

---

[113] Buchan, *A History of the Great War*, i. p. ix.
[114] Ibid. iv. 443. [115] Ibid. 442.
[116] Mr Buchan's memorandum on the selling of 'The History of the War', undated [1921], Nelson papers, B/9/370 a and b.
[117] Mr Scheurmier's note on selling of 'History of the War', undated [1921], ibid. B/9/370 c, d, and e. [118] *Spectator* (12 Nov. 1921).
[119] *Edinburgh Review*, 237/483 (Jan. 1923), 171-4.
[120] *Army Quarterly*, 3/2 (Jan. 1922), 393.

Literary Supplement observed that the narrative excluded 'the more general lessons of the war: the dangers of unpreparedness, the cost of improvisation, the unnecessary waste of life . . .'.[121] These remarks percipiently raised important questions, which later became central themes in historical debate, but Buchan's writing was primarily orientated towards the contemporary imperatives of relief rather than celebration in a 'world over-weary, and not inclined for extreme demonstration'.[122] Furthermore, Buchan wished to preserve his belief that the deaths of his younger brother, Tommy Nelson, Raymond Asquith, and others had not been in vain[123] and he was therefore unwilling to diminish confidence in the direction of the war effort and the virtues of loyalty, patriotism, and endeavour. He wrote a form of history which sought to be objective, but was weighed down by a worship of success, innocence, and youth, symptomatic of his formative years and the age in which he wrote.

Despite its limitations, Buchan's work enjoyed serious consideration in the inter-war years. It was cited by Liddell Hart and Cruttwell in their military histories, the former regarding Buchan as his 'first literary counsellor'.[124] Lloyd George took exception to Buchan's descriptions of army morale and the genesis of Nivelle's offensive plan, and refuted his account at length.[125] Lloyd George also surmised that Buchan's *History of the Great War* was not produced with reference to all relevant documents. By the 1930s the debates on the war, particularly on civil-military relations, were far advanced and Buchan's deficiencies as a historian were evident but in 1922, in entirely different circumstances, his work was apposite because it sought to reassure the nation that its terrible sacrifices had not been in vain.

These early historians were willing volunteers in the enlistment of literature during the war. They served the nation by writing closely observed accounts which developed into personal interpretations of the British war effort which were not, pre-eminently, propagandist in tone. It was a highly engaged form of history in which older men compensated for not serving in the front line and the positive qualities of the war effort

---

[121] *Times Literary Supplement* (14 Sept. 1922). This treatment of the revised volumes contrasts with its description of *Nelson's History of the War* as 'everywhere recognised as the authoritative narrative of the war' (9 Jan. 1919).
[122] Buchan, *A History of the Great War*, iv. 419.
[123] See W. Buchan, *John Buchan: A Memoir* (1982), 9, 73, 92, 138; Turner, *Mr. Buchan Writer*, 59.
[124] Liddell Hart to Buchan, 30 Oct. 1926, Liddell Hart papers, I/124/18.
[125] D. Lloyd George, *War Memoirs* (London, 1938), ii. 1329-30 and i. 887.

were freely asserted.[126] The accounts were constrained by the complexities and scale of the war effort and the problems of contemporary history writing, notably the process of censorship, access to sources, and the moral power which leading participants exerted over the construction of narratives.

However, for all their limitations, the accounts by Conan Doyle and Buchan were definite historical responses and despite their narrow focus on the front, these authors provided insightful narratives and therefore some starting-points for debate. Their responses were conditioned by knowledge of limited wars and the supremacy of British forces in the context of imperial frontier warfare. Consequently, their writings in the years after 1914 suggested that the full implications of total war would take time to unfold. While they acknowledged the feat of organization which had transformed the small British Expeditionary Force of 1914 into the sixty-division army of 1917, they failed to consider its impact on other essential aspects of the war effort. Conan Doyle and Buchan attempted to discuss the war in the vocabulary of mobile, barely mechanized, manœuvres for territorial advantage and in the celebratory mode as had been the custom of British military historians throughout the nineteenth century.

Antiquated notions lingered and much phrasing in the initial military histories was of uncertain value, but the enthusiasm with which the Allied war effort was supported should not be misinterpreted as a craven subservience to the will of the state.[127] The writings of Fortescue, Conan Doyle, and Buchan mythologized war, but they wrote as they felt and they did not consciously propagate myths. Indeed, their publications were the outcome of the interrelationship between their lives and the dominant political, military, and social values of a society at war. Detachment was not a strong ingredient of their books—authors reflect their

[126] See Buchan's address at the Stationer's Hall, 3 Mar. 1916 on 'The Future of the War', National Library of Scotland, MF MSS 317 (microfilm of MS at Queen's University, Ontario).

[127] The central point is not the gulf between fact and the process of mythologizing war in which Buitenhuis supposes propagandists, writing untrue accounts, fuelled war neurosis (Buitenhuis, *The Great War of Words*, 98, 101) but the explanation of war by patriotic writers constrained by the powerful literary conventions of English 'romance' (P. Fussell, *The Great War and Modern Memory* (Oxford, 1975), 137). The failure to objectify was not caused by the deliberate distortion of the conduct of war by writers, but their engagement in the quest for total victory and its accompanying value system, which embraced and mobilized all aspects of national life. On the development of modernity after the war Buchan noted that a 'dull farmyard candour became fashionable' (*Memory Hold-The-Door*, 186). See also D. Hibberd, 'Extravagant and Exhausted Words', *Times Literary Supplement* (28 July 1989).

age as much as they are critics of it—but their work was coherent, enjoyed integrity, and sought to explain the seemingly inexplicable. Buchan, Conan Doyle, and, to a lesser extent, Fortescue grappled with the dilemmas of early history writing on the war and in reading their interpretations we can understand more fully the generation who both fought the war and then had to begin to make sense of it.

2
'The Real War': Liddell Hart, Cruttwell, and Falls
HEW STRACHAN

I

Maurice Genevoix, the permanent secretary of the Académie française, and for discerning critics a far more effective writer about the Great War than his better-known compatriots, Henri Barbusse or Roland Dorgelès,[1] opined on the occasion of the fiftieth anniversary of the armistice:

If it is neither desirable nor good that the professional historian prevail over the veteran; it is also not good that the veteran prevail over the historian. That is why the history of the 1914-18 war remains so hard to write.[2]

All three histories of the First World War under review in this chapter were written by veterans of that war; all three now have the status of textbooks. B. H. Liddell Hart's and C. R. M. F. Cruttwell's volumes, originally published in 1930 and 1934 respectively, were both still in print in 1989. Cyril Falls's book was not, but ought to have been. Although Liddell Hart claimed objectivity, and although Cruttwell and Falls more nearly achieved it, each also could not avoid subjectivity in treating the fundamental experience of his life.

The common denominators of the triumvirate go further. They were products of middle-class English homes (although Falls would protest his Ulster connections) and public school educations. They served as infantry officers on the Western Front. The three therefore belonged to those groups, both in society as a whole and in the army, which suffered disproportionately in the Great War. The middle class, the professions, the

---

[1] Genevoix's best-known book on the war, *Sous Verdun*, was published in 1916; his collected war works were published as *Ceux de 14* (Paris, 1950). For opinions on the worth of Genevoix's books relative to those of others, see Jean Norton Cru, *Témoins: Essai d'analyse et de critique des souvenirs des combattants édités en français de 1915 à 1928* (Paris, 1929), 142-54, 663.

[2] Maurice Genevoix, 'Commentaries on the War: Some Meanings', in George A. Panichas (ed.), *Promise of Greatness: The War of 1914-1918* (London, 1968), 486.

public schools, the universities, contributed more men to the forces relative to their aggregate size than did working-class occupations. Within the services, the greatest absolute losses were incurred by the infantry.[3] Thus, Liddell Hart, Cruttwell, and Falls each belonged to a *milieu* for whom the idea of the 'lost generation' was real enough.[4] Cruttwell went to Rugby in September 1901. The entry that term consisted of ninety-two boys, including Rupert Brooke, the latter's friend Sir Geoffrey Keynes, General Sir James Marshall-Cornwall (who himself turned to military history in his retirement), Frank de Pass VC, and Lieutenant-General Sir Henry Pownall. Two of the ninety-two were foreigners and two died before the war; fifteen did not join the armed services during the war, most of them being engineers or diplomats; of the seventy-three who did serve, twenty-three were killed in action, or 31.5 per cent.[5] This bears a striking contrast with the national average: in the nation as a whole, one man was killed for every eight who served, or 11.76 per cent.[6] Liddell Hart's experience was similar. He went up to Corpus Christi College, Cambridge, in October 1913. He was one of twenty-nine, eight of whom were killed in action during the war: thus, at the lowest computation (since not all may have served), 27 per cent were killed.[7]

But it is not only the 'lost generation' with which Liddell Hart, Cruttwell, and Falls can be identified. In the late 1920s and early 1930s, there appeared a spate of publications, which in their blending of memoir, history, and literature defied rigid categorization, and have thus been best described as 'war books'. Written by those of the 'lost generation' who had not been lost, they expressed the guilt of the living at having survived and commemorated the memory of those who had died. Above all, they aspired to capture the comradeship which the intensity of prolonged active service, the sharing of its adversities and tribulations, had fostered. What they described could only be fully understood by the initiated, by those who had themselves suffered the same experiences. But the war books of the late 1920s were not simply written by former

[3] J. M. Winter, *The Great War and the British People* (London, 1985), 33-7, 65-9. Pilots of the Royal Flying Corps, most of whom were officers, had the highest relative losses of all in the war.
[4] Ibid. 65-99; for attacks on the 'myth' of the 'lost generation', see John Terraine, *The Smoke and the Fire: Myths and Anti-myths of War 1861-1945* (London, 1980), 35-47, and Correlli Barnett, *The Collapse of British Power* (London, 1972), 425-35.
[5] George Higginbotham (ed.), *Rugby School Register*, iv. *1892-1921* (Rugby, 1929), 181-92.
[6] Winter, *The Great War and the British People*, 73, 93.
[7] Corpus Christi College matriculation book.

soldiers for former soldiers. They were also an attempt to explain to those who had not been in the front line what the war meant for those who had been. Young men, taken from school and university, had had their educations completed by the war. Yet on their return they needed to adapt themselves to the trappings of civilian life and peacetime existence. Writing a war book was on the one hand a means of personal reintegration, an exorcism and a rationalization, and on the other an effort to bridge the gulf between the front line and domestic society which the war itself had fostered.[8]

Cyril Falls, in his critical bibliography, *War Books* (1930), regarded Edmund Blunden's *Undertones of War* as 'probably the only single book of its kind we have had in English which really reaches the stature of its subject'.[9] Falls compared Blunden with Rembrandt, called *Undertones of War* a 'masterpiece', and gave it the accolade of three stars in his guide. Blunden was above all a pastoral poet: his book is literary, allusive, even detached; it lacks the heroic modernism of many German accounts, for example those of Ernst Jünger or of Fritz von Unruh; it eschews the gore of Barbusse and Genevoix. In its Englishness, therefore, *Undertones of War* has some right to be seen as the exemplar of the sort of war literature with which not only Falls but others of his generation—including Liddell Hart and Cruttwell—might have identified. *Undertones of War* was published in 1928, a decade after the armistice. It was not Blunden's first attempt to write about the war, but like many others he found it took a long time to assimilate his experience, to give coherent expression to the seemingly inexpressible. He thought that only those who had 'gone the same journey' would understand his book. He also reckoned that he would be 'going over the same ground again . . . until that hour when agony's clawed voice softens into the smilingness of a young spring day'.[10] He was right: his widow recalled that up until his death in 1976 'no day passed in which he did not refer to that war'.[11]

II

Basil Liddell Hart is a clear example of Blunden's point. The First World War was the main force in shaping Liddell Hart's military

[8] The critical literature on the 'war books' is enormous, but see esp. Bernard Bergonzi, *Heroes' Twilight: A Study of the Literature of the Great War* (London, 1965), and Paul Fussell, *The Great War and Modern Memory* (New York, 1975).
[9] Cyril Falls, *War Books: A Critical Guide* (London, 1930), 182-3; also p. x.
[10] Edmund Blunden, *Undertones of War* (2nd edn., London, 1930), pp. v-vi.
[11] *The Times* (9 Nov. 1981).

thought. But its impact was not merely intellectual. Liddell Hart wrote in 1933:

It was the most valuable experience of our lives, offering to the fortunate survivors lessons in life that no substitute could have provided to the same extent, tending to the development of sympathy and understanding, correcting the 'cash nexus' of modern civilisation, and laying the foundations of a philosophy of life for those who chose to build upon them. I know that for my own part I am more glad of that experience than of anything else I have known.[12]

The importance of his war service to Liddell Hart is in large measure attributable to his youth. He was born in 1895, and was not yet 19 when war broke out. Although he was considering a career in the army, he had only just completed his first year at Cambridge after schooling at St Paul's. Both Cruttwell and Falls were older and more mature in 1914 than Liddell Hart: its impact on the latter was therefore that much greater. Fighting, Liddell Hart later emphasized, was the task of young men. For him, the description 'war generation' was also a statement about youth and seniority, and about the claims of the former to the recognition of the latter.[13]

Liddell Hart secured a temporary commission in the King's Own Yorkshire Light Infantry. In January 1915 he was posted to a service battalion, and he went out to France just before the Battle of Loos. That autumn, while serving around Ypres, he was concussed by falling sandbags when a shell exploded above his dugout. However, he was back in France by spring 1916, one of eight subalterns, five of whom were killed in action on the opening day of the Somme, on 1 July, and all of whom were out of the battle by the end of that month. Liddell Hart himself suffered three minor wounds in the Somme fighting, found himself in temporary command of a neighbouring battalion on 1 July itself, and became a company commander in his own battalion. On 16 July he was gassed in Mametz wood, and sent home. Unfit for active service, Liddell Hart spent the rest of the war as an adjutant, first of a Royal Flying Corps squadron, and later of Volunteer Force battalions. His principal task was to train men in minor tactics.[14]

Liddell Hart's direct experience of the First World War was therefore limited. It lasted less than a year, from September 1915 to July 1916.

[12] Liddell Hart's foreword to Sidney Rogerson, *Twelve Days* (London, 1933), pp. xiii–xiv.
[13] B. H. Liddell Hart, *Thoughts on War* (London, 1944), 13; see also the Foreword to Rogerson, *Twelve Days*, p. x.
[14] Liddell Hart, *Memoirs*, 2 vols. (London, 1965), i. 11–33.

Although it included the opening month of the Battle of the Somme, it did not embrace the later stages of that battle nor the years 1917 and 1918 when the British army took on an increasing burden (if not the main burden) in the Entente's war effort. In that short time, Liddell Hart had been wounded both physically and—by the loss of friends and comrades—psychologically. Nevertheless, his attitude remained positive and optimistic. He expressed unqualified praise for British generalship, not least for that of Haig on the Somme; at a personal level, he acknowledged the frightfulness of modern war, but went on—as many others did—to say, 'it has an awe-inspiring grandeur of its own, and it ennobles and brings out the highest in a man's character such as no other thing could'.[15]

Liddell Hart published his first book on the war, *Reputations*, a series of biographical essays on leading generals, in 1928. In 1930 he brought out *The Real War*, a general account which appeared in a revised edition as *A History of the World War, 1914-1918* in 1934. *The War in Outline* (1936) was a potted history, an approach he repeated and combined with his earlier treatment—that of biographical essays—in *Through the Fog of War* (1938). Over the same ten years he also wrote two First World War biographies, *Foch: Man of Orleans* (1931) and '*T. E. Lawrence*' (1934), in addition to half a dozen other books, two of them of major importance. The leading ideas of this enormous output, at least in so far as they affect the First World War, are remarkably constant, even repetitious. Over the decade the criticisms became more critical, the theories more dogmatic, but the general thrust is already clear in *The Real War*, and even in *Reputations*.

It therefore seems reasonable to conclude that the gestation period for Liddell Hart's thinking was the period before 1928. It was in the 1920s, influenced in part by J. F. C. Fuller and in part by his own direct contacts with senior officers, that Liddell Hart developed the disillusionment with British generalship in the First World War that turned him from excessive adulation to extreme criticism. The fact that his unfitness prevented his own career as an army officer continuing beyond 1924 may have sharpened his frustrations.[16] In *Paris, or the Future of War* (1925), he already expressed his conviction that the grand strategy of the war had proved an exercise in futility. Certainly between 1918 and 1928 he developed a sufficient stock of ideas, an intellectual capital, to enable him

---

[15] Brian Bond, *Liddell Hart: A Study of his Military Thought* (London, 1977), 18.
[16] John Mearsheimer, *Liddell Hart and the Weight of History* (London, 1988), 81-3; see also pp. 23-4, 55-9.

to write fluently, at length, and almost without pause between 1928 and 1938.

The timing and manner of this creative process place Liddell Hart's books firmly in the context of the war literature of his generation. And yet this was precisely the bracket which Liddell Hart himself wished to avoid. The title, *The Real War*, especially to a generation of historians influenced by John Keegan's eloquent appeal for attention to the experiences of the individual under fire,[17] suggests an autobiographical account of trench fighting. Liddell Hart declared that the aim implicit in his title was to do exactly the opposite. He announced in his preface:

> The title of this book, which has a duality of meaning, requires a brief explanation. Some may say that the war depicted here is not 'the real war'—that is to be discovered in the torn bodies and minds of individuals. It is far from my purpose to ignore or deny this aspect of the truth. But for anyone who seeks as I seek here, to view the war as an episode in human history, it is a secondary aspect. Because the war affected individual lives so greatly, because these individuals were numbered by millions, because the roots of their fate lay so deep in the past, it is all the more necessary to see the war in perspective, and to disentangle its main threads from the accidents of human misery. Perhaps this attempt is all the more desirable by reason of the trend of recent war literature, which is not merely individualistic but focusses attention on the thoughts and feelings of some of the pawns of war. The war was, it is true, waged and decided in the minds of individuals more than in the physical clash of forces. But these decisive impressions were received and made in the cabinets and in the military headquarters, not in the ranks of the infantry nor in the solitude of stricken homes.[18]

Liddell Hart therefore ruthlessly suppressed any overtly autobiographical element in *The Real War*. Indeed there is no glimpse of action at the battalion or company level. So effective was his apparent distancing from the war that Herbert Read, whose own time as an infantry subaltern was a recurring theme of his writings throughout his life, when reviewing *The Real War* in *Criterion* condemned it as a 'shoddy piece of rhetoric', reminding his readers that 'the whole war was fought for rhetoric'.[19] The criticism was merited, at least in part: Liddell Hart's style was rhetorical and could use verbal dexterity as a substitute for sustained analysis. But the wider point, that Liddell Hart, in eschewing an account of human suffering, had effectively perpetuated an essentially false image

[17] John Keegan, *The Face of Battle* (London, 1976).
[18] Liddell Hart, *The Real War 1914-1918* (London, 1930), 9-10; for similar points see Liddell Hart papers, 9/8/5; Liddell Hart to the editor, *Times Literary Supplement* (6 June 1930); and Liddell Hart, *Through the Fog of War* (London, 1938), 214.
[19] Liddell Hart papers, 9/8/6; *Criterion* (July 1930), 763-9.

of the war, resting on the wartime claims of politicians and of generals, was mistaken in more ways than one.

The Real War is a sustained strategical critique. Thus, it is neither accepting of the phrases of propaganda (as Read implied), nor is it a detached account of the higher control of the war (as Liddell Hart claimed). Despite appearances, *The Real War* is a deeply personal statement. For Liddell Hart, military history was didactic; its purpose was to instruct for the future, to be 'a safeguard against renewing past mistakes'.[20] He therefore devoted far more attention to failures than to successes. The fighting on the Western Front of 1918 was studied for the period up to May, the desperate weeks of the allied defeats, but the second half of the year, culminating with the German request for an armistice, was almost completely ignored. Haig's generalship was analysed in the light of the Somme and Passchendaele, the battles of 1916 and 1917 which his critics have so condemned, not those of 1918, the period on which his claim to greatness must rest. This neglect of 1918 Liddell Hart 'justified, on the practical ground of history, by the fact that there are fewer lessons to be learnt from this period—there is always more to learn from failure than from success'.[21]

By suppressing the culminating battles of the war, Liddell Hart allowed his portrayal of British generals to assume an easy continuum, from incompetence on the Western Front to conservatism in the 1920s and 1930s. On the foundations of this presumption, that British generals had not been and would never be truly able commanders, he was able to construct the leading ideas of his strategy. At the heart of these was the conviction that the British army was not up to continental standards in warfare, and that continentalism was therefore the wrong strategy for Britain. The pre-war creation of a general staff had allowed continentalism to be fostered by the army, and particularly by the director of military operations after 1910, Henry Wilson. Continental influences had stretched from grand strategy to the conduct of operations, and sucked the British into a style of making war that emphasized mass and manpower over psychological effect and the efficient exploitation of new technology. The truer way for Britain to fight a European war, and the way by which she had actually won the Great War, was through naval and economic pressure, and specifically through blockade. Naval supremacy also opened up great opportunities through amphibious operations: neither Gallipoli nor Salonika had been effectively exploited because of

[20] Liddell Hart, *Through the Fog of War*, 9.   [21] Ibid. 173.

the fell hand of continentalism. All these were the main themes of *The Real War*; they constituted the bedrock of Liddell Hart's current strategic arguments in the 1930s; in the basic premiss—their rejection of the operations on the Western Front—they reflected the experiences and suffering of one who had actually fought there.[22]

In essence, therefore, *The Real War* is a book about Britain's role in the war. By the standards to which military historians now aspire, it is a very partial and selective look at the First World War given its claim—and its continuing status—as a general survey. Its organization rests on general narratives for each year, and then specific 'scenes' within that year. These 'scenes' are chosen largely from the Western Front. The major land operations of 1915 took place on the Eastern Front, especially the Gorlice-Tarnow offensive and the great Russian retreat, and on the French sector of the Western Front. The British army was not yet ready to take a major role in the war. Yet Liddell Hart's four scenes for 1915 are the Dardanelles (which take up two scenes), the second Battle of Ypres, and Loos. The 1934 edition attempted to beef up the Eastern Front sections, but the only extra 'scene' which that front merited was Lemberg in 1914.[23]

The Real War is also military history, narrowly defined. Even the air war was only added later, to the 1934 edition. The naval history is brief and superficial. Jutland alone merits a 'scene'. The domestic context, the economic, social and political history of the war, is entirely omitted. The result is that the central argument of the book, that blockade won the war, is asserted in the conclusion but not developed throughout the narrative. No evidence is provided of the blockade's effects on German society or of the economic strain it put on the Central Powers. Thus Liddell Hart does nothing to support his case. Admittedly A. C. Bell's official history of the blockade was not completed until 1937 and not published until 1961. But in this instance Liddell Hart clearly followed too closely his own precept, that of attending to mistakes not successes. His later works do nothing to follow up *The Real War*'s conclusion. *The War in Outline*, published in 1936, makes no mention of the blockade at all. Thus, the bold claim for the centrality of the blockade was never followed through, whether by Liddell Hart the historian or Liddell Hart the strategic theorist.

[22] Mearsheimer, *Liddell Hart*, 6.
[23] I am grateful to Professor Geoffrey Best for giving me his copy of *The Real War*, in which he has marked the differences between it and *A History of the World War 1914-1918* (London, 1934). See also Liddell Hart papers, 9/8/10.

On one level, this is unsurprising. Liddell Hart had little real interest in, or grasp of, naval or economic affairs. The genuine focus of *The Real War*, naturally enough given the history of the development of Liddell Hart's ideas, is command. Liddell Hart's abiding enthusiasm was for 'Great Captains'. It is here that the personal and subjective level of the book becomes most explicit. On 28 November 1914 he had written: 'I worship brilliance and brilliance seems to find its truest and fullest expression in the art of generalship.'[24] In the Liddell Hart papers is what appears to be a list of possible titles for his history of the war: they include 'No Napoleon', 'War of the Blind', 'The Headless Monster'.[25] Thus E. C. Bentley was remarkably astute when he wrote in the *Daily Telegraph* that *The Real War* belonged to the literature of 'distress and disillusionment'.[26]

The consequences of Liddell Hart's personal disappointment in the quality of First World War generalship permeate *The Real War*. A devastating critique in the *American Historical Review* by T. H. Thomas—just how devastating is shown by the efforts to which Liddell Hart went to try to publish a reply—regarded *The Real War* as encumbered with a misleading title, since it was

not a record of what happened but a kaleidoscope of hypothetical contingencies which might have arisen if at every turn the various commanders had followed the various (and contradictory) course suggested in after years by their critics ... In this vast mirage the one clear and constant feature is the *dénigrement* of professional leadership ... [The] book stands out by the dialectical skill with which hostile criticism is presented as a narrative of fact, the adroitness with which each leader's role is whittled away in turn by presenting it in the words of some hostile critic.

Thus, Galliéni is used against Joffre, Ludendorff against Falkenhayn, Hoffmann against Ludendorff. 'While to quash Foch and Haig in a question of strategy the author appeals to the high authority of Major General James T. Dickman, U.S.A.'[27]

However, it is not only its use of hindsight that makes Liddell Hart's criticism of command in the Great War naïve. Liddell Hart completely failed to understand that the skills demanded in the leadership of mass armies in an industrialized age were more managerial than heroic. The fact that he could title his biography of Scipio Africanus *A Greater than*

---

[24] Bond, *Liddell Hart*, 16.   [25] Liddell Hart papers, 11/1930/23.
[26] Ibid. 9/8/6.   [27] *American Historical Review*, 36 (1931), 599-600.

Napoleon (1926) confirms not only that he saw the principles of command as unchanging through time but also that those principles were derived more from the ancient world, from small armies led by personal example, than from the twentieth century. Furthermore, since his own command experience was effectively limited to company level, it tended to confirm the heroic model, not moderate it. In 1920, when discussing infantry tactics, Liddell Hart could write: 'The sector of a platoon is a complete battle in miniature. Within its narrow compass we see the eternal principles of great war fulfilled.'[28]

Thus, high command in the Great War was analysed in the light of his own experience as a subaltern. He wrote: 'The decisions which an army commander had to take in the last war, though great in responsibility, were simple in their technical elements compared with those of a battalion commander.'[29] Rather than an aid to command, staff organizations are seen as clogs in the machinery. Ian Hamilton, the commander-in-chief at Gallipoli, earns—despite his lack of success—Liddell Hart's praise: the problems which he encountered arose through

> the defects of the military system under which he was called on to operate; the system arising from the 'foreign growth' of mass armies and large staff organizations, whereby command ceased to be a direct force and became a distant spring of influence filtering down through intermediary channels.[30]

Sir William Robertson, on the other hand, a representative—by virtue of his position as chief of the imperial general staff—of the mass army and of continentalism, is continuously criticized. Because Liddell Hart rejected continentalism, because he associated that strategy with the general staff, and because a European war demanded a mass army, all three ideas were linked in Liddell Hart's mind. By condemning them, he avoided having to rework his view of command in the light of the dominant military experience of modern times.

Instead, for Liddell Hart command remained personal and individual: the emphasis throughout *The Real War* is on the will of the commander, the psychological effect of his actions on his opponent, the value of surprise. And true command was exercised in campaigns of movement. Allenby in Palestine, by achieving victory through mobility, had restored what Liddell Hart called 'the *normal* conditions of warfare'.[31] But the

[28] Mearsheimer, *Liddell Hart*, 27.
[29] Liddell Hart, *The War in Outline 1914-1918* (London, 1936), p. xii.
[30] Id., *Through the Fog of War*, 104.
[31] Id., *The Real War*, 477 (emphasis added). See also Liddell Hart papers, 9/8/6, 561-2.

greatest paean of praise was reserved for Lawrence, whose small command, led by force of personal example, in a backward society, provided all the conditions for the fulfilment of Liddell Hart's ideal. When he redirected his gaze from the Holy Land to North-West Europe, all Liddell Hart could do was to try to understand the latter campaign in terms of the former. The defeat of the German army in 1918 was, he argued, inflicted in the mind of its command.[32] He could not begin to unravel the processes by which the German army was dismembered, its manpower losses in 1918, its crisis in morale, its material needs.

The battle on the Western Front which possessed an abiding fascination for Liddell Hart occurred not in 1918, but in 1914. The Marne manœuvre was a battle which could be understood in Napoleonic terms —and indeed Liddell Hart saw Galliéni, for him the true victor (not Joffre), as a Napoleon. But his enthusiasm was not reserved solely for the French: the 'might-have-beens' of the Schlieffen plan, the failure of the Germans successfully to execute so ambitious a strategic concept, also played on his imagination. And again, the Marne, for all the massive forces involved, and the scale of the fronts on which they were fighting, was won and lost—according to Liddell Hart—in the minds of its commanders.

Liddell Hart's studies of the Battle of the Marne reveal a remarkable strength for a British writer. Because his interest is in command, his focus is on operations. Unlike his fellow nationals, his writings eschewed both grand strategy on the one hand and personal experience on the other. Operational studies were of course the main province of the publications of the 1920s, of the memoirs and official histories, particularly in France and Germany. They built on a tradition in military historical writing established before 1914 on the continent, but little developed in Britain. The quality of much of what was written is excellent, and remains of analytical value to this day. Liddell Hart is the British author most obviously influenced by this continental output, by Général Palat's *Histoire de la grande guerre sur le front occidental* (1917-29) or by Hermann von Kuhl's *Der Weltkrieg* (1929). But in reality his appreciation and exploitation of these sources only goes so far. His bibliography is very full, particularly strong on foreign-language sources, but often finds little reflection in his text. In practice he must have read scarcely any of it. His French was not as fluent as it ought to have been (given the fact that his father had been a Methodist minister in

---

[32] Id., *The Real War*, 466; see also Liddell Hart papers, 9/8/6, 588, 591.

Paris) and he could not read German. He therefore relied on the précis of foreign-language works published in the *Army Quarterly* and on selective translation. Thus, much of the most important German writing on operations, developed in the context of Germany's battles with France or of the Austro-German war with Russia, was neglected.

Having read selectively and digested partially, Liddell Hart then completed the process with his penchant for simplification. The analysis of the Marne is full of illustrations of this leaning to superficiality. Liddell Hart likened the Schlieffen plan, with its strong right wing and its weak left, to a revolving door—'if a man pressed heavily on one side the other side would swing round and strike him in the back'.[33] There is deep irony in Liddell Hart's accusation against Foch, that he was a phrasemaker.[34] Like recognized like. The revolving-door metaphor was used again and again in Liddell Hart's writings on the war. It is striking, memorable, and evocative. Its clarity goes far to explain Liddell Hart's continuing influence. And yet it is totally misleading. It is the justification for Herbert Read's accusation of rhetoric. The German advance could never have been like a revolving door. Any army composed of hundreds of thousands of individuals, advancing tens of miles a day, over a period of weeks, is prey to a whole host of problems, of supply, of intelligence, of stamina. Liddell Hart made no allowance for the grit in the revolving mechanism—Clausewitz's friction. The easy fluency with which he expressed himself became a substitute for careful argument.

Furthermore, inherent in the revolving-door metaphor is an unresolved aspect of Liddell Hart's analysis of the war. The revolving door is a machine. Liddell Hart's retrospective reputation has rested—admittedly to a greater degree than the facts warrant—on his advocacy of the use of machines in war. Great War commanders were berated for the failure to use tanks properly or in sufficient numbers. And yet the thread running through Liddell Hart's analysis rests not on technology but on morale. Victory in 1918 is explained not in terms of allied material superiority but in terms of psychological effects—surprise, flexibility, the indirect approach. For all his reputation as a radical thinker, for all his apparent modernism, Liddell Hart's analysis never juxtaposed his advocacy of the mechanical and the psychological. One of the fundamental dilemmas of the First World War, the need to integrate new technology and even to

---

[33] Liddell Hart, *History of the World War*, 68-9.
[34] Id., *Foch: Man of Orleans* (Harmondsworth, 1937), ii. 291.

shape doctrine in the light of technological capabilities,[35] was not thought through to a synthesis.

What has been written here is critical of *The Real War*. This is because the book is now read and judged as history. In truth *The Real War* and its related volumes are of course didactic. And this constitutes their strength. The illumination provided by *The Real War* arises from its criticisms; in this sense, it is—as Liddell Hart hoped it would be—instructive. But its style and its simplifications have given its historical judgements greater life than they ever deserved. By being first in the field with an English-language synthesis based on a wide range of sources Liddell Hart set the terms of the debate for far too long thereafter. Still alive in the 1960s, he was able to continue to colour the views and interpretations of a later generation. He took issue with John Terraine over Haig, and over Passchendaele; he received effusive thanks from Alan Clark in the latter's *The Donkeys* (1961), a scathing attack on British generalship in 1915; he was 'military consultant' to the Purnell part-work on the First World War, begun in 1969. Even in the 1980s, although criticism of Liddell Hart has produced greater caution, and although our understanding of British command has been transformed by Dominick Graham and T. H. E. Travers, the shadow of *The Real War* continues to obscure the light. Above all, the operational military history of the other major belligerents has lacked the academic revisionism given to Britain: yet these areas, which were neither Liddell Hart's main concern nor ones in which he was particularly well informed, constitute, at least for the period up until July 1917, the nub of the operational history of the war.

III

C. R. M. F. Cruttwell, himself an example of how Liddell Hart's influence has operated, is best known today as the butt of Evelyn Waugh. Cruttwell was Dean of Hertford College, Oxford, when Waugh was an undergraduate. Waugh detested Cruttwell. The latter has been identified as Sniggs, the Junior Dean of Scone College, who at the beginning of

---

[35] These points are informed by a reading of Michael Geyer, 'German Strategy in the Age of Machine Warfare, 1914-45', in Peter Paret (ed.), *Makers of Modern Strategy from Machiavelli to the Modern Age* (Oxford, 1986); T. H. E. Travers, *The Killing Ground: The British Army, the Western Front and the Emergence of Modern Warfare, 1900-1918* (London, 1987), 250-64.

Decline and Fall relishes the prospect of 'Founder's port' for the fellows for at least a week on the strength of the fines that will be levied from riotously drunk undergraduates. Waugh, on his own testimony, went out of his way to bait Cruttwell. In his autobiography he portrays the Dean as limited in his historical range, physically unprepossessing, frequently drunk, and sexually attracted to dogs. All this he attributes to the war and its consequent effects: 'it was as though he had never cleaned himself of the muck of the trenches'.[36]

Cruttwell was born in 1887, the son of an Anglican priest. After Rugby, he went up to the Queen's College, Oxford, and in 1911 was elected to a fellowship at All Souls. In 1912 he became a lecturer in modern history at Hertford. Thus, unlike Liddell Hart, his career was formed before the war, and was not its product. However, its direction—towards modern military history—was the consequence of the war, and was unusual for an academic historian.

In 1914 Cruttwell was commissioned into a territorial battalion, the 4th, of the Royal Berkshire Regiment. The choice was presumably determined by the fact that his brother George was one of its existing officers. In 1922 Cruttwell wrote *The War Service of the 1/4 Royal Berkshire Regiment (T.F.)*. This is a remarkable account for the period which covers Cruttwell's own service, and it is a pointer to his relative maturity that he was able to recall his war experiences so soon after the events. The battalion went to France in May 1915. After initially serving in Ploegsteert Wood, it was sent south to Artois in July. The whole of 1915 was a relatively quiet year for the battalion. Only one officer was killed, his fellow Rugbeian, R. W. Poulton-Palmer, the outstanding England three-quarter. A great deal of time was devoted to trench construction. Cruttwell's writing, with its attention to the flowers and the countryside, displays the same pastoral concerns as those of Blunden. The Battle of the Somme destroyed both the rural idyll and the homogeneity of the battalion. Cruttwell himself contracted rheumatic fever and was invalided home. He served as a captain in military intelligence in 1918-19, and in the latter year returned to Hertford. He became Principal of the college in 1930.

Not all the characteristics which Waugh attributes to Cruttwell found their origin in the war. Even as a junior subaltern, fresh to his battalion,

[36] Evelyn Waugh, *A Little Learning: The First Volume of an Autobiography* (London, 1964), 174; also pp. 173-5, 177. For a somewhat less vitriolic but contemporary portrayal of Cruttwell by Waugh (albeit unsigned), see *Isis* (5 Mar. 1924), 7-8. I am most grateful to Dr Brian Harrison for this and other references from Oxford magazines, and also to Dr Angus Macintyre.

he seemed to his brother most unlike a don, if also most unsoldierly. 'His apparent cynicism, his extravagant talk, and his blasphemous epithets . . . gained the affection of nearly all'—but clearly not everybody.[37] When the battalion arrived in France, it was somewhat surprised to be told by the local priest that Britain had entered the war for its own selfish ends. Cruttwell replied on the battalion's behalf, telling the *curé* that the French army had run away and that the British had arrived to bolster its morale. His reputation for rudeness, his 'command of picturesque invective'[38] were clearly all in place by 1915. Furthermore, Waugh's reaction, though shared by a minority, was no more the majority in the college than it had been in the battalion. Cruttwell's memory and his command of detail, which Waugh construed as narrow, were seen by others as the launching-pad to greater things. Another of Cruttwell's pupils, Alan Thornhill, remembered that: 'His thinking seemed to bestride the centuries like a Roman aqueduct, planting massive piers of insight into the marshlands of conjecture, and conveying the clear water of truth from the earliest times down to the present day.'[39]

Vera Brittain speaks with some approbation of tutorials in modern history from the Dean of Hertford[40]—thus incidentally confirming as ill-founded Waugh's accusation that Cruttwell was a misogynist.

None the less, it seems clear that Cruttwell's health, and perhaps his psyche, never fully recovered from the war. The effects were progressive rather than immediate. As a don in the 1920s, despite the limp bequeathed him by his rheumatic fever, he continued to play rugger and tennis for the college. He was a keen shot. However, when Thornhill returned to Hertford as the college's chaplain between 1931 and 1936, he found Cruttwell progressively more difficult. The Principal, as perhaps befitted the son of a clergyman, had decided views on hymns. Thornhill recalled: 'If God moves in a mysterious way, so also did Cruttwell. If the hymn chosen was not one to his liking, he would shut the book with a slam, bang on the pew in front of him, snort with disgust and throughout the singing stare at the rafters in moody silence.'[41]

---

[37] From a typescript account of his war service by George Cruttwell, in the possession of the Duke of Edinburgh's Royal Regiment. I am most grateful to Dr Ian Beckett for drawing this to my attention.
[38] Alwyn Williams, in *Dictionary of National Biography 1941-1950* (Oxford, 1959), 190.
[39] Alan Thornhill, *Best of Friends* (Basingstoke, 1986), 77.
[40] Vera Brittain, *Testament of Youth: An Autobiographical Study of the Years 1900-1925* (London, 1978 (first pub., 1933)), 486-88.
[41] Thornhill, *Best of Friends*, 81.

The generosity of spirit, which had lain beneath the apparent rudeness in the 1920s, gave way to bitterness and hatred. Thornhill, like Waugh, attributed the progression to shell shock. Many psychological wounds inflicted by the war took a decade to develop. But Cruttwell's case was clearly not a dramatic change of personality, rather a gradual evolution—albeit in a retrograde direction. Furthermore, he was overtaken by an undiagnosed and clearly distressing physical ailment. In 1937 his last book, *A History of Peaceful Change in the Modern World*, appeared. In 1939 he resigned as Principal. In 1941, after a rediscovery of his Christian commitment, movingly recounted by Thornhill, he died.

Cruttwell's *magnum opus*, *A History of the Great War*, was published in 1934, with a second edition in 1936. A paperback edition was brought out as recently as 1982. Most reviewers welcomed it as a standard textbook, and praised it as balanced and free of chauvinism. The exception was a devastatingly critical reception in the *Journal of the Royal United Services Institute*, which concluded that the book might entertain, but that it should not be regarded as a serious history of the war. The main substance of the criticisms was an insufficient knowledge of the French, German, Italian, and Austro-Hungarian official histories, the account of Jutland with its attack on Jellicoe, and Cruttwell's use of English.[42] Some echo, albeit much fainter, of the same points was to be found in Pierre Renouvin's review. Renouvin's own history of the war—although drier—is far more comprehensive and balanced than Cruttwell's, but he praised the latter nevertheless. His worries revolved around inaccuracies in the sections on Verdun, that it was out of date on 1918, and in its emphasis on Britain and the role of the Royal Navy. He felt that Cruttwell was not a master of the primary sources.[43]

Cruttwell's use of sources is, therefore, crucial to estimates of his book. But unfortunately very little is known of his working methods. Unlike Liddell Hart, he did not include a bibliography. His footnotes are fragmentary, although they do include references to the obvious French and German authorities. However, since he began collecting materials for the book while still serving in intelligence and while working on the history of the peace conference,[44] he presumably began to form his views before the major memoirs and official histories had begun to appear. The book's dedication, to the memory of Charles Fletcher, who died in the year of its publication, may be a further indication as to its genesis.

[42] *Journal of the Royal United Services Institute*, 80 (1935), 456-7.
[43] *Revue d'histoire de la guerre mondiale*, 14 (1936), 72-3.
[44] An obituary by N.R.M., *Oxford Magazine*, 59 (8 May 1941), 278.

Fletcher had been elected a fellow of All Souls in 1881, and was a fellow and tutor at Magdalen College, Oxford, from 1889 to 1906: a stimulating teacher, he has been described as a key figure in the development of the Oxford history school. Like Cruttwell, he was an Anglican and a Tory. The paternal influence which Fletcher may have had on Cruttwell is easy to imagine. But Fletcher's role was probably even more direct. From 1905 until 1927, Fletcher was a delegate of the Clarendon Press, the publishing house responsible for Cruttwell's history of the war. Fletcher himself vigorously promoted the work of authors in modern history. Two of his three sons were killed in action in the war. The blow was grievous, and is in part reflected in Fletcher's own book, *The Great War 1914-18: A Brief Sketch* (first published in 1920), which not only tells its story in an extraordinarily informal style, parading its prejudices with great openness, but also saw the war as a victory for British arms and for freedom (rather than the more egalitarian 'democracy').[45] Fletcher may well have persuaded Cruttwell to undertake the book; certainly Fletcher read all but a few chapters in draft; his hallmarks—the book's breezy style, the frank prejudices—find their reflection in *A History of the Great War*.

Although Cruttwell's volume is more objective and balanced than that of Liddell Hart, it achieves it by being more overtly personal. Cruttwell had won an open scholarship in classics to Queen's. He scattered Greek tags and references throughout the book. The German devastation in the 1917 retreat to the Hindenburg line is compared with the Spartan laying-waste of Attica in the Peloponnesian war; the book closes with lines from Sophocles's *Antigone*. Cruttwell also betrays his xenophobia. He displays contempt for the Slavs, the Russians, and the Romanians. Describing the effect of the 1917 Gotha bombing raids on London, he writes: 'some sections of the population were reduced to panic, especially the poor aliens of the East End'.[46] However, Cruttwell was no purblind reactionary. Although he fought the 1935 election as the Conservative candidate for Oxford University (unsuccessfully), he dubbed Lord Lansdowne—whose letter to the *Daily Telegraph*, published on 29 November 1917, called for a negotiated peace—'a worn-out aristocrat' and

---

[45] The book was reprinted in 1921, and came out in a second edition in 1931. For the impact of his sons' deaths, see pp. x, xi, and also [J. C. Dunn], *The War the Infantry Knew 1914-1919: A Chronicle of Service in France and Belgium* (London, 1987 (first pub., 1938)), 174.

[46] C. R. M. F. Cruttwell, *A History of the Great War* (2nd edn., Oxford, 1936), 498. Dr John Sweetman has suggested that Cruttwell's phrasing is derived from the official history of air operations.

'a disillusioned Conservative who saw the old order falling headlong into ruin'.[47]

But it was of course his own personal experience in the war which most illuminated Cruttwell's book. His description of aircraft enfilading trenches early in 1916 carries the imprimatur of personal observation.[48] Particularly striking is the discussion of the impact on morale of the use of gas:

> In fact there is little to choose in horror and pain between the injuries inflicted by modern war. The extent to which a human body can be mangled by the splinters of a bomb or shell, without being deprived of consciousness, must be seen to be believed. The real explanation of the fury felt by the soldiers, which invested the war with a more savage character, is to be sought elsewhere. In the face of gas, without protection, individuality was annihilated; the soldier in the trench became a mere passive recipient of torture and death. A final stage seemed to be reached in the whole tendency of modern scientific warfare to depress and make of no effect individual bravery, enterprise, and skill. Again, nearly every soldier is or becomes a fatalist on active service; it quietens his nerves to believe that his chance will be favourable or the reverse. But his fatalism depends upon the belief that he has a chance. If the air which he breathes is poison, his chance is gone: he is merely a destined victim for the slaughter.[49]

This passage, in its reflections on the industrialization of war and the impact of that on the individual, contains many of the themes of war literature. Cruttwell explains in a footnote that it was based on personal observation in trenches south of Ypres in April 1915.

Cruttwell carried with him much of the infantry subaltern's contempt for the staff.[50] Writing of Loos, he says: 'The Higher Staffs studied maps and not the ground; they could not believe, sitting in their studies and workshops, that the means of destruction which they had assembled would prove less annihilating in practice than in theory.'[51] The failure of the major offensive in which he himself was the victim, the Somme, was blamed principally on the 4 Army's commander, Henry Rawlinson. However, Haig receives remarkably fair, even generous, treatment. All the standard criticisms of the commander-in-chief—that he was a cavalryman, that he was inarticulate—are there. But, Cruttwell concludes, 'Haig grew with disappointment and disaster, until he stood out in the last few months of the war as a very great general.'[52]

[47] Ibid. 373, 374. [48] Ibid. 262. [49] Ibid. 153-4.
[50] See George Cruttwell's account.   [51] Cruttwell, *Great War*, 164.
[52] Ibid. 169.

Liddell Hart, when attacked for the predominantly military account which he had provided, defended himself by pointing out that Cruttwell had devoted only 16 per cent of *A History of the Great War* to nonmilitary aspects.[53] It is indeed remarkable that an Oxford historian, by training and by profession, should have elected to write what is almost exclusively a narrative of military events. Despite his interest in, and familiarity with international relations, Cruttwell gave little attention to the diplomatic history of the war. He himself confessed that he ignored the causes of war. The bulk of recent history has focused here, and has flowed into the discussion of war aims. The ensuing debate, fuelled by Fritz Fischer, has transformed our understanding of the war, but it finds no prefigurings in Cruttwell. The war aims debate in Germany was the pivot of domestic politics, and yet the internal history of the belligerents —and the link between these and their conduct of war—is also ignored. This distaste for a wider interpretation of the history of the war led Cruttwell to exclude any account of the peripheral campaigns in Africa, the aftermath of the Russian revolution, or the 1916 Easter rising in Ireland. However, all these were constituent elements in a German global strategy, designed to fuel nationalism, socialism, or Islamic fundamentalism in order to weaken the Entente powers from within. Finally, Cruttwell ignores the peace settlement, despite the fact that Versailles came to be the lens through which many of his generation looked back at the war and the question of Germany's responsibility. Cruttwell is candid in acknowledging these omissions, but the fact that he felt such themes could be excluded is enormously indicative of the narrowness of his approach.

Because *A History of the Great War* is also a traditionally conceived military history, and because it was published in the same year as *A History of the World War 1914-1918*, the revised edition of *The Real War*, it followed that Cruttwell and Liddell Hart were in direct competition. Yet the two of them seem to have developed reasonably cordial relations. Admittedly, Liddell Hart, after meeting Cruttwell in 1936, and faithfully (and typically) recording all the latter's vitriolic remarks about military historians and others, concluded that Cruttwell 'has certainly a very good opinion of himself, and is embittered. Suffers from an inferiority complex. I diagnose, too, a streak of jealousy.'[54] But Liddell Hart, like others, underestimated Cruttwell's better side. What is striking in the years after 1934 is how Cruttwell, an infinitely greater

[53] Liddell Hart to Cruttwell, 28 Sept. 1936, Liddell Hart papers 1/20/19.
[54] Ibid. 11/1936/80.

historian, took on and identified with the strategic criticisms made by Liddell Hart.

In 1935, Cruttwell reviewed Liddell Hart's *When Britain Goes to War* for the *Spectator*. Not only was he very flattering about the author, but he also suffused his review with Liddell Hart's thinking and forms of expression. Sentences such as 'The plans of the last war had generally the muscle-bound rigidity of dull mechanical giants' or 'Mass production is so fatally easy and such a potent drug to initiative and vivid thinking'[55] might have been culled straight from the pages of *The Real War*. By 1936 Cruttwell had brought his own previously generous view of Haig into line with that of Liddell Hart. Haig was 'dishonest', 'hypocritical', and not a great captain: in the next edition of his history, Cruttwell told Liddell Hart, he planned to revise the favourable judgement on Haig's command in the latter part of 1918.[56] In the same year he reported very positively to Faber and Faber on Liddell Hart's *War in Outline*.[57]

Most striking of all is Liddell Hart's role in Cruttwell's Lees Knowles lectures, 'The British Share in Allied Strategy 1914-1918', delivered in February and March 1936. These lectures were given against the background of an increasing threat of war in Europe and a demand for rearmament in Britain. Cruttwell, having just fought an election in the Conservative interest, could hardly fail to have aligned himself with the principles of collective security and with the argument for economic stability ahead of military strength. Thus, the views of the two writers on contemporary British strategy produced a convergence which was derived from, and reflected back into, their interpretations of the First World War. Cruttwell asked Liddell Hart to read and comment on his lectures, and stated that he incorporated the criticisms in the published version.[58] In the book, which was entitled *The Role of British Strategy in the Great War*, Cruttwell adopted Liddell Hart's view of the British way in warfare, and in doing so used history didactically: 'History', Cruttwell argued, 'went far to prove that British success in the great continental struggles was due, not to the adoption of any continental model of strategy, but to the deliberate maintenance of her own liberty of action.'[59] Thus, the historian of the war underpinned continental disengagement in the 1930s. When it came to discussing British command

[55] *Spectator* (10 May 1935), 789-90. [56] Liddell Hart papers, 11/1936/80.
[57] Cruttwell to Faber, 27 June 1936, ibid. 1/20/16.
[58] Liddell Hart to Cruttwell, 17 Apr. 1936, ibid. 1/20/14-15, and Cruttwell's reply.
[59] Cruttwell, *The Role of British Strategy in the Great War* (Cambridge, 1936), 3. On Cruttwell's views on contemporary foreign policy, see *Oxford Magazine*, 54 (7 Nov. 1935), 118.

in the war, Cruttwell's sentiments and rhetorical phraseology were pure Liddell Hart: 'The great fault of the directing brains in the West was a kind of mechanical megalomania, pinning their faith to masses of men, masses of guns, masses of shells, masses of transport.' Command, Cruttwell argued, aping Liddell Hart, should have concentrated on 'three of the fundamental and clearly connected principles of all successful war', namely 'surprise, economy of force and elasticity of plan'.[60]

A History of the Great War achieves considerable objectivity given the degree to which its author was personally scarred by that war. The relative maturity, at least in terms of career and age, if less of personality, which Cruttwell had achieved by 1914 provided a point for return when the war ended. The personal insights which the war vouchsafed him were frequently integrated into his academic studies in a telling and effective manner. But *A History of the Great War* is still a flawed book. Moreover, there are signs that, if Cruttwell had kept his fitness sufficiently long to produce the fully revised edition which he had in mind, the result would have reflected Liddell Hart's views to the point where originality might well have been lost.

IV

The war record of Cyril Falls was very different from that of Liddell Hart or Cruttwell, and is probably even more important in our understanding of his work than it is of theirs. Falls was born in 1888, and educated at Bradfield, Portora Royal School in Enniskillen, and London University. When the war broke out, he was a clerk in the Foreign Office. He had already begun writing—he was working on a biography of Rudyard Kipling, the proofs of which he corrected in his tent early in the war.[61] As an Ulsterman, he joined 11 battalion, the Royal Inniskilling Fusiliers, which was part of the 36 Division, a division built round Carson's Ulster Volunteer Force. In 1915 he went with his battalion to France. In May 1916 he became a staff officer as GSO3 with 36 Division, and later with 62 Division. He served as a liaison officer with the French. Like Cruttwell and Liddell Hart, he ended the war a captain; unlike them, he was decorated—being twice mentioned in dispatches and awarded the Croix de Guerre.

[60] Cruttwell, *The Role of British Strategy*, 48-9.
[61] Panichas (ed.), *Promise of Greatness*, 226.

Falls, therefore, served throughout the period 1915-18 on the Western Front, and took part in the 3rd Battle of Ypres and all the battles of 1918. Both Liddell Hart and Cruttwell, by virtue of the wounds which they received on the Somme, did not witness that phase of the war when the British army took on its major burden: Falls did. Secondly, because most of Falls's service was as a divisional staff officer, his perspective on his experience was much wider than that of either Liddell Hart or Cruttwell, both restricted to battalion or even company service. The division was the key command (as Falls recognized)[62] of the Great War: it was a self-sufficient unit of all arms, kept as one, and rotated through corps and army commands, both of which were headquarters formations only. Illustrative of Falls's consequent breadth of outlook is the high praise bestowed in his *War Books* on A. Forbes's *A History of the Army Ordnance Services*, with all its details of supply. Thirdly Falls's liaison work with the French, coupled with his linguistic facility (he could read French, German, and Italian) gave him yet another angle from which to observe the war's events. Thus Falls's war service equipped him far better to write a general history of the war than did that of either Liddell Hart or Cruttwell.

The obvious riposte to this assertion, that as a staff officer he was detached from front-line experience, is only of limited validity.[63] Divisional staffs consisted largely of soldiers whose initial experience (like Falls's) had been with battalions; their tasks included going forward to maintain contact with brigade and battalion headquarters. Later in life, Falls wrote of the frequency with which British divisional commanders and their staffs went into the front line, comparing them favourably both with the received image (which, it could be said, derives from the staff officers of yet higher formations) and with the French army.[64]

What Falls aimed to do in his writing was to integrate the two poles of his experience, to set the front-line and eye-witness accounts in the context of the general picture. He therefore took the opposite direction to that adopted by Liddell Hart. In the preface to his first book on the war, *The History of the 36th (Ulster) Division* (1922), Falls wrote:

A yet greater number of seekers will be demanding with curiosity how men lived in such circumstances, how they reacted to the strain of war, what compensa-

[62] Falls, *War Books*, p. viii.
[63] F. P. Crozier, in *The Men I Killed* (London, 1937), 73-4, is by implication critical of Falls on this count. But the assertions cannot hold water, and Crozier, a fire-eater himself, was given to exaggeration. I am grateful to Gary Sheffield for this reference.
[64] Falls, 'Contacts with Troops: Commanders and Staffs in the First World War', *Army Quarterly*, 88/2 (1964), 173-80.

tions they found. It behoves those who were eye-witnesses to depict it in all its aspects, not to shrink from discovering its horror, indeed, but also not to pretend that it had not a better side. The picture now so often painted, representing the war as a single scene in a torture chamber, whence men emerged physical or mental wrecks, may be good anti-militarist propaganda, but it is false, because incomplete. From those experiences many men have emerged happy and strong. Many knew how to snatch some happiness even from their midst. A far greater number can see, in retrospect, that they played a part in one of the most dramatic, as well as one of the most terrible, tragedies in history. That stands for something of good, amid all its evil, in any man's life.[65]

Falls therefore stated his position early—well ahead of the main spate of 'war books'—and it was to become clearer in subsequent decades. His *War Books: A Critical Guide*, published in 1930, makes judgements which stand up well today and which are remarkable for their wisdom so close to the event. Falls, reflecting his early interest in Rudyard Kipling, had considerable strengths as a literary critic; he had a feel for language and style, a taste that was catholic and yet discerning; he was both cosmopolitan and civilized. In *War Books*, his praise is bestowed on Blunden, Charles Douie, Charles Edmonds (i.e. Carrington), Frederic Manning—all estimates which (with the possible exception of Douie) would be endorsed today. His criticism is for Barbusse and Erich Maria Remarque. He accepted that conditions on the Western Front were awful in a way that only those who served there could appreciate, but he found 'the constant belittlement of motives, of intelligence, and of zeal . . . nauseous'.[66]

Falls's objectivity when assessing the war was helped by his subsequent experience in writing its official history. His account of the 36 Division was widely praised: Michael Howard has said of it, that it 'contains some of the finest descriptions of conditions on the Western front to be found anywhere in the literature of the war'.[67] It convinced James Edmonds, the chief official historian, that he should invite Falls to join the historical section of the Committee of Imperial Defence. Falls's main efforts as an official historian were concentrated on theatres other than the Western Front. He collaborated with Sir George MacMunn in writing the first of two volumes on Egypt and Palestine (published in 1928), and compiled the second (published in 1930) himself. He also had sole responsibility for the two volumes on Macedonia, which appeared in 1933 and 1935.

[65] Id., *The History of the 36th (Ulster) Division* (Belfast, 1922).
[66] Id., *War Books*, p. xii.
[67] Michael Howard, 'Cyril Falls', in *Dictionary of National Biography 1971-1980* (Oxford, 1986), 303.

This experience carried a triple benefit. First, it gave him familiarity with primary sources. Secondly, it widened his outlook on the war once again. Thirdly, he avoided being caught up in the controversy over the volumes on the Western Front in 1917. He took part in the preparation of the first of these, but left the historical section in 1939, when the second and more significant—it dealt with the Battle of Messines and the third Battle of Ypres—was in its early stages.[68]

In 1939 he succeeded Liddell Hart as military correspondent of *The Times*, a post which he held throughout the Second World War. Journalism exploited his facility for writing and the balance in his judgements, but it did not breed in him the need to make an argument or develop a case simply for effect. In 1946 he was elected Chichele Professor of the History of War at Oxford University, and a fellow of All Souls. He retired from these posts in 1953.

Falls's general history of the war was published in the United States in 1959 as *The Great War* and in Britain in 1960 as *The First World War*. It is remarkable that he should have waited so long. But, in doing so, his objectivity and balance grew. By 1959 Liddell Hart's criticisms of command in the Great War had not moderated. Falls on the other hand had become wiser and more detached.

In his preface, Falls stated that he had begun to write without a thesis, but that he had been asked sufficiently often what his thesis was to conclude that he ought to have one. What in practice he then did was to advance not one, but several theses, none of them displaying the dogmatism implicit in the original question. He did not duck the fact that his book was a 'war book'. He both treated the war generation as an initiated group, and wished to explain what the war meant to that group to a wider audience, 'to commemorate the spirit in which those men served and fought'.[69] The comradeship of the trenches and the continued act of remembrance for the dead by those who had survived was embodied in the dedication, 'to friends and companions, those growing old and those to whom long life was denied'.

But he had not forgotten his own precepts. His aim remained consonant with that first expressed in 1922, the imposition of reason and purpose on what his generation had experienced. Pivotal to this approach, and in direct contrast to Liddell Hart and also to the tendencies inherent in Cruttwell, was his anxiety to demonstrate that 'the military

[68] On the problems and deficiencies of the Passchendaele volume, see Travers, *The Killing Ground*, ch. 8.
[69] Falls, *The First World War* (London, 1960), p. xv.

art' had not 'stood still in the greatest war up to date'.[70] Falls accepted that 'the sealing up of the war in France and Belgium' had temporarily baffled the war's leaders, but argued that 'skill and intelligence' were applied to 'loosening it again'.[71] If Liddell Hart's interpretation of Great War command had become the orthodoxy, Falls's balance constituted revisionism. The difference of approach was already evident in the 1930s. Both had written biographies of Foch. Liddell Hart, in 1931, had compared Foch with Napoleon and found the former wanting: he had in other words tried to judge the allied generalissimo not on his own merits and by the standard of his time, but by some notion of absolute excellence derived from a past era.[72] Falls's biography, published in 1939, was far more complimentary, praising Foch not only for his strength of will but also his strategic insight. For Falls, the essence of Foch's conception resided in the centrality of railway communications to twentieth-century warfare; Falls showed that Foch's plans not only for 1918 but even as early as 1915 recognized the objectives whose seizure would paralyse the German army.[73] Falls in other words estimated Foch's ability in the light of the First World War as it was, a war where technology had altered strategy as well as tactics and for whose appreciation mechanization (broadly interpreted) was fundamental.

The fact that Falls had been present in the battles of late 1918 was implicit in his estimate of Foch and of the allied high command in general. The conclusions which he drew were ones which anticipated some of the more strident revisionism of John Terraine, but were expressed in a form that is more sensible because it avoids extremes. Like Terraine, Falls argued that the image of the defensive firepower of the machine gun had obscured the fact that the real killer of the war was artillery: guns *en masse* unlocked the German positions in 1918. Like Terraine, Falls accepted that the earlier battles on the Western Front had played their part in the cumulative erosion of the German army and thus prepared the way for its eventual defeat in the field, but that the triumph of the British army had been reserved until the last weeks of the war, from August 1918 onwards. Unlike Terraine, however, Falls did not fall into the trap of seeing the war solely in the terms of a 'westerner', of out-Haiging Haig. It followed from what he had said already that the blockade was not the primary cause of Germany's overthrow. But Falls still acknowledged the contribution which blockade had made to victory.

[70] Ibid. p. xvi.   [71] Ibid. p. xviii.   [72] Liddell Hart, *Foch*, ii. 468–78.
[73] Falls, *Marshal Foch* (London, 1939), pp. vi–x, 87–8.

Furthermore, Falls cautioned against seeing the war solely in terms of the conditions of trench warfare on the Western Front. Generals in the Great War had not forgotten how to manœuvre. In France and Flanders, for much of 1914 and again in 1918 the war had been mobile, not static. Even more did this apply if the conditions prevailing on other fronts were taken into account. And this Falls did. 1915 in Falls's treatment merited seven chapters: only one of these was devoted to the Western Front. Thus, albeit indirectly, was the limited, Anglocentric perspective of Liddell Hart corrected.

Like Liddell Hart and Cruttwell, Falls was primarily writing military history. He was more self-knowing as he did so; he went further in acknowledging the limitations of what he had undertaken. And, within the remit of military history, his range was much greater and his judgement sounder. Yet Falls's book has not enjoyed the same success as the others: his is not in print, theirs are.

In 1960, Falls's book was unfashionable both in the timing of its publication and in the content of its argument. Falls belonged to the generation of writers, mostly veterans, who had bestridden the historiography of the war in the 1930s; but the period after 1945 was dominated by publications on the Second World War. In the early 1960s interest in the First World War was reawoken, in particular after 1964, and the fiftieth anniversary of the war's outbreak. The authors that led the way in this revival formed a new generation: Leon Wolff's *In Flanders Fields* was published in 1959, Alan Clark's *The Donkeys* in 1961, and John Terraine's *Douglas Haig: The Educated Soldier* in 1963. Their concerns, and those of their public, were with the Western Front and the debate on British generalship. Falls's objectivity and balance on these scores did not make for popular appeal. Furthermore his own consciousness of the relative weight of the other fronts led him in the 1960s away from the Western Front, to a study of the Palestine campaign, *Armageddon 1918* (1964), and to *Caporetto 1917* (1966, and his last book).

One side of the 1960s debate, that critical of the generals, was still orchestrated by Liddell Hart. The clash between his interpretation of command in the First World War and that of Falls had been implicit for some time. But in the 1930s their correspondence had focused on the Palestine campaign, an area where their differences were manageable. Falls was essentially modest, his approach reasoned; Liddell Hart was self-advertising and assertive. And yet in 1946 Falls had got the Oxford chair which Liddell Hart coveted. Thus, differences of temperament were added to differences of judgement. In 1961 Falls wrote an article in *The Times* on the anniversary of Haig's birth, arguing that the 1918 victories constituted the basis for Haig's reputation, but regretting that 'the detractors backed by their carefully coached young "mud-and-blood" myrmidons, have by no means given up the struggle'.[74] He reacted to Leon Wolff and Alan Clark as he had to Barbusse and Remarque. Liddell Hart took exception.[75] However, it would be an exaggeration to say that there was an open breach. Falls was not, after all, taking up a diametrically opposed position, as John Terraine was about to. He occupied in this debate, as he had in *The First World War*, the middle ground. But it was controversy, as Liddell Hart knew well, not balance, that made for good sales. At bottom, Falls had no taste for such verbal battles:[76] *Armageddon 1918* and *Caporetto 1917* represented a form of escape.

Good judgement in a historian can be very easily underestimated. The new case is arresting, the discriminating argument unexciting. Falls has suffered this fate. Perhaps it would have been otherwise if he had been as ardent in his self-advertisement as was Liddell Hart. But Falls was a man of cultivated interests—literature and music as well as racing and riding—too broad to feel obsessive about his own argument and his own reputation. Balance can lead to blandness. It threatens in some of Falls's other works, in *A Hundred Years of War* (1953) and in *The Art of War* (1961). But in *The First World War* balance constitutes a distinct argument of its own. The effect of the 1960s clashes, which thanks to John Terraine has continued to determine far too much of the debate even in the 1980s, was to challenge the orthodoxy laid down by Liddell Hart but not to revise the basic framework within which he operated. Thus, in Britain the main arguments of the First World War became limited—to its conduct on the Western Front, to Haig, to mobile versus static warfare, to the relationship between imagination and command—and they became circular. Falls's strengths, a wider perspective and a more detached judgement, were cast into shadow. They deserve better.

[74] *The Times* (19 June 1961).
[75] Liddell Hart to Falls, 29 June 1961, and reply, Liddell Hart papers, 1/276/51 and 52.   [76] Falls to Liddell Hart, 16 July 1960, ibid. 1/276/48.

3
Sir James Edmonds and the Official History: France and Belgium
DAVID FRENCH

In 1962 Martin Blumenson, a staff historian in the Office of the Chief of Military History of the United States Army, wrote an article in the journal *Military Affairs* in which he posed the question, 'can official history be honest history?' He pointed out that critics of official histories had argued that because they were commissioned by governments they sometimes had to ignore pertinent information and consequently 'It cannot meet the tests of objectivity, balance, and independence of judgement. At best a bland, cautious, diluted version of the truth, official history cannot be honest.'[1] But it was possible to write good official history if three criteria were met. It must be written by professional historians; the authors had to have free access to all the relevant documents; and the end product had to be free from censorship. According to Blumenson, Sir James Edmonds's multi-volume *Military Operations France and Belgium, 1914-1918* which appeared between 1922 and 1948, did not fall into the category of 'honest' official history. As evidence he cited the case of Captain G. C. Wynne, one of Edmonds's collaborators on the volume examining the gestation and conduct of the third Battle of Ypres in 1917. In 1946 Wynne insisted that his name should be removed from the title-page of the volume because he believed that Edmonds was deliberately twisting the truth to protect the reputation of Sir Douglas Haig, the commander-in-chief of the British Expeditionary Force.

Other critics have shared Blumenson's doubts about Edmonds's work. Sir Basil Liddell Hart commented on the volume which examined the British preparations to meet the German spring offensive in March 1918 that 'What one is given in this volume is a purely Trade-Union

---

[1] M. Blumenson, 'Can Official History be Honest History?', *Military Affairs*, 26/3 (1962), 152.

point of view—it is not merely "patriotic" history but parochial history.' It was, according to Liddell Hart, '"official" but not "history"'.[2]

Edmonds was not a professional historian although he had some experience of writing history and a well-deserved reputation for intellectual brilliance before he began to work on the official history. He was born in 1861. He passed into and out of the Royal Military Academy at Woolwich in the top place. In 1881 he was gazetted into the Royal Engineers. After serving in Hong Kong he spent six years as an instructor at Woolwich. This set the pattern for his future career. He never held a major troop command but instead filled a variety of staff posts. In 1895 he entered the Staff College where he was an exact contemporary of Haig, Allenby, and many of the senior officers he was to write about in the *Official History*. It was while he was at the college that he acquired the nickname which was to stick to him for the rest of his life, 'Archimedes'. He found the work so unexacting that he was able to turn his hand to history and, together with his brother-in-law, W. B. Wood, he wrote a history of the American Civil War which was eventually published in 1905 and became an official textbook in the United States Army. A fellow sapper, G. W. Macdonogh, who rose to be Director of Military Intelligence and later Adjutant General at the War Office in the First World War, shared Edmonds's opinion about the demands placed on bright students at the college and spent a good deal of his time in London qualifying as a barrister.[3]

During the Boer War Edmonds served as an intelligence officer in South Africa and returned to intelligence work between 1906 and 1910 when he went to the War Office as head of MO5, a sub-section of the Directorate of Military Operations. It was in that capacity that he did more than anyone else to establish the modern British Secret Service. He also wrote a chapter on the laws and usages of war for the sixth edition of the *Manual of Military Law* in collaboration with L. F. L. Oppenheim.[4] In 1911 he left the War Office and became GSO1 of 4 Division. He accompanied the Division to France in August 1914 but his experience as a senior front-line staff officer was limited. He quickly broke down under the physical strain and was invalided home before the end of the

[2] Liddell Hart to Edmonds, 6 and 13 Nov. 1934, Liddell Hart papers, 1/259/93 and 95.
[3] W. B. Wood and J. E. Edmonds, *A History of the Civil War in the United States, 1861-65* (London, 1905); B. Bond, *The Victorian Army and the Staff College, 1854-1914* (London, 1972), 159-60.
[4] Cyril Falls, 'Sir J. E. Edmonds', *Dictionary of National Biography 1951-60* (Oxford, 1971), 329.

year. Even so, the few months he did spend at a divisional headquarters undoubtedly gave him some useful insights into the practical problems of command in war. After he recovered he spent the rest of the war at GHQ in France where he rose to be one of Haig's two Deputy Engineers-in-Chief. He retired in 1919 as a Brigadier General.

The *Official History* was prepared by the Historical Section of the Committee of Imperial Defence. The CID itself had been established in 1902 to act as a defence planning agency to co-ordinate the strategic policy of the entire British Empire. This was a task which it never effectively fulfilled before 1914 because it was hamstrung at practically every turn by the jealousy of existing government departments concerned with particular aspects of foreign and defence policy. One of the CID's moving spirits, and the founding father of the Historical Section, was Lord Esher. In 1906 Esher was gravely concerned that no systematic efforts were being made by either the General Staff at the War Office or the Admiralty's Intelligence Department to garner lessons from recent history. In putting forward his proposal for a Historical Section for the CID Esher had a propagandistic purpose. He hoped that they would write books which would provide historical and intellectual justification for the maritime strategy which he favoured.[5] (In this respect Edmonds's work must have been a sore disappointment to him.) Although the section was established it made little headway before the war. Both services were jealous of their autonomy and the section was kept very short of funds.

When war broke out a special CID sub-committee was established to collect material for a future history. In August 1915 the military historian Sir John Fortescue, who had given the Ford lectures at Oxford in 1911 on 'British Statesmen of the Great War 1793-1814' was persuaded to write a popular history of the campaign on the Western Front. Edmonds was appointed as the head of the Military History Branch of the Historical Section in 1919. In that capacity he was ultimately responsible for producing histories of operations not just in France and Flanders, but in Egypt and Palestine, Mesopotamia, Italy, Salonika, and the African colonies. He assumed more direct responsibility for the history of the Western Front because he did not like what Fortescue had produced. Like Esher, Edmonds believed that military history should teach lessons. He did not want to produce a popular layman's history. He wanted to write textbooks which could be used in military academies. Fortescue's preliminary narrative was highly inaccurate. His account of

[5] N. D'Ombrain, *War Machinery and High Policy: Defence Administration in Peacetime Britain, 1902-1914* (Oxford, 1973), 216-17.

1914, for example, made no mention of the Schlieffen Plan. The two men probably had little sympathy for each other. In December 1919 Fortescue wrote a critical review in the *Quarterly Review* of Lord French's *1914*. Such behaviour was held to be inappropriate for an official historian and the War Cabinet forced him to resign.[6]

Edmonds himself now took on the task of compiling the history of operations on the Western Front. Initial progress was slow. In 1922 the branch was criticized in the House of Commons for its apparent tardiness. The cabinet responded by appointing the President of the Board of Education, H. A. L. Fisher, himself a distinguished historian, to investigate its work. His impressions were favourable and the Fisher committee recommended in 1923 that a permanent sub-committee on the Control of Official Histories ought to be established as part of the CID to organize the future production of the official history.[7] In Edmonds's defence it ought to be stressed that the Military Branch never consisted of more than a dozen officers and that it was kept on a very tight budget by the Treasury. Edmonds's first volume appeared in 1922. It was not published by HMSO but by Macmillan. The final volume, examining Messines and the third Battle of Ypres, appeared in 1948. Edmonds wrote eleven of the volumes himself and contributed prefaces to another three. He also wrote a lengthy account of the occupation of the Rhineland between 1918 and 1929. Because of Foreign Office objections to some of his remarks about the Germans it was printed by HMSO but was given only a limited official circulation in 1944.[8] The secret of his productivity and longevity—he was 87 years old in 1948—perhaps lay in the fact that he kept himself fit 'by swinging two pound dumbbells and pouring a jug of cold water over his head every morning before breakfast'.[9]

The ostensible purpose of the *Official History* was explained in the preface to the first volume. It was 'to provide within reasonable compass an authoritative account, suitable for general readers and for students at military schools, of the operations of the British Army in the Western

---

[6] S. S. Wilson, *The Cabinet Office to 1945* (London, 1975), 124; Edmonds, 'Memoirs' (ch. 32: 'The Historical Section of the Committee of Imperial Defence, 1919-1949'), 1-3, Edmonds papers, III/16; Fortescue to Edmonds, 8 Apr. 1919, ibid. II/2/95; Fortescue to Maurice, 1 Nov. 1919, Maurice papers 3/5/101.

[7] Wilson, *Cabinet Office*, 125.

[8] Sir James Edmonds, *The Occupation of the Rhineland 1918-1929* (London, 1944). In 1987 a facsimile edition of this book with an introduction by Dr D. G. Baylis was published by HMSO in conjunction with the Imperial War Museum.

[9] *Western Daily Mail* (10 Apr. 1944).

theatre of war in 1914-1918'.[10] But Edmonds had a second and more private purpose which does give some credence to the accusation that he sought to conceal the truth about the high command in France from the lay public. Edmonds had been brought up within the tradition of Victorian naval and military biography in which authors had sought to present their subjects as warrior heroes worthy of imitation. To do so they had sometimes been compelled to treat documents in a somewhat cavalier fashion to protect the dignity of the men whose lives they were writing.[11] Edmonds's work was shorn of the Christian moralizing of many Victorian naval and military biographies. Indeed one criticism which can be made of his work is that he made little or no attempt to delimit the characters of the senior officers whose actions he was discussing. He hoped that no biography of Haig would be written because 'It could only lower his place.'[12] He therefore found nothing unusual in admitting to Liddell Hart in March 1932 that

> I want the young officers of the army who are to occupy the high places later on to see the mistakes of their predecessors, yet without telling the public too much. What one cannot hide—except very occasionally—is that the great ones resented suggestions and ideas, fearing perhaps that if they encouraged such things they might in the end lose their jobs.[13]

During the war his position at GHQ as a middle-ranking staff officer gave Edmonds an excellent platform from which to view the doings of his superiors and left him with few illusions about their intellectual abilities. In March 1916 he wrote to Spenser Wilkinson, the Chichele Professor of the History of War at Oxford, that

> We have not discovered a single good general or staff officer except Sir William Robertson. I believe there is plenty of talent in the army but it does not come to the top. Whenever I look at the list I think of Lincoln [sic] saying 'Well, I don't know what effect they have on the enemy but they terrify me.'[14]

Edmonds had a naturally mordant wit. In private he recounted that Sir Henry Rawlinson was nicknamed 'The Cad' by his contemporaries, that corps commanders like Hunter-Weston and Sir Walter Congreve

---

[10] Brig.-Gen. Sir James Edmonds (ed.), *Official History of the Great War: Military Operations, France and Belgium, 1914* (London, 1922; rev. edn., 1933; repr. Woking, 1984), p. vii. (Hereafter referred to as 'Edmonds, *Official History*'.)

[11] C. I. Hamilton, 'Naval Hagiography and the Victorian Hero', *Historical Journal*, 23/2 (1980), 381-98.

[12] Liddell Hart diary, 13 Sept. 1930, Liddell Hart papers, 11/1930/1b.

[13] Edmonds to Liddell Hart, 8 Mar. 1932, ibid. 1/259/46.

[14] Edmonds to Spenser Wilkinson, 15 Mar. 1916, Edmonds papers, II/1/133a.

were 'inefficient', and that Haig had said of his chief of staff in 1918, Sir Herbert Lawrence, that 'I have to kick him along'.[15] But his most severe criticisms were reserved for Haig. He thought that the former commander-in-chief was above-averagely stupid, knew nothing of artillery or infantry matters, and could not understand anything technical. His career had been dominated by an 'unrelaxing pursuit of his ambition, reinforced by a strong religious sense which made him feel he was called by God to lead the British armies'.[16] He promoted his own favourites and was far too reluctant to sack senior officers who had failed because their dismissal would reflect badly on his own judgement in appointing them.[17]

In 1930 Edmonds admitted to Liddell Hart that he wrote about Haig and his colleagues 'with my tongue in my cheek'. Liddell Hart assumed that he did so partly out of loyalty to Haig and his old friends and contemporaries who were still alive and partly because Edmonds possessed what he himself called the clan prejudices of the professional soldier when faced by civilian critics.[18] Thus, for example, in the very first volume of the series which included an analysis of the retreat from Mons in 1914, he did not mention that Sir John French's Chief of the General Staff, Sir Archibald Murray, had suffered a complete physical collapse. Murray was still alive in 1933 when the revised edition of the book was published and presumably Edmonds did not want to hurt his feelings or reputation.

But this explanation only presents a part of the truth. It does not do justice to Edmonds' complex personality nor to his real abilities and insights as a historian. Edmonds was handicapped by the fact that before joining the Historical Section he had spent his entire adult life living in an institution in which great mystique attached to high rank. Junior officers simply did not criticize their seniors in public and Haig's seniority exerted a powerful influence over him at least until the mid-1930s.[19] It would also be misleading to lay too much emphasis on past friendship as the reason why Edmonds kept his private opinions

[15] Liddell Hart, Talk with Edmonds, 23 Sept. 1929, Liddell Hart papers, 11/1929/15; 24 June 1929, ibid. 11/1929/8a; 31 Oct. 1929, ibid. 11/1929/17; 23 Dec. 1933, ibid. 11/1933/31.
[16] Liddell Hart, Talk with E[dmonds]., 10 Jan. 1935, ibid. 11/1935/58.
[17] Liddell Hart, Talk with Edmonds, 6 May 1929, ibid. 11/1929/7; 23 Sept. 1929, ibid. 11/1929/15; 31 Oct. 1929, ibid. 11/1929/17; 10 Jan. 1935, ibid. 11/1935/58; Talk with General Edmonds—Athenaeum, 5 Feb. 1937, ibid. 11/1937/4; diary 15 May 1930, ibid. 11/1930/1b.
[18] Liddell Hart, Talk with Edmonds, 8 Dec. 1930, ibid. 11/1930/30.
[19] Liddell Hart, Talk with Edmonds, 7 June 1934, ibid. 11/1934/41.

about Haig's limitations as a general to himself. Haig died in 1928 and outwardly their relations remained cordial right up to his death. But in private Edmonds did nurse a grievance against his former commander because he had not extended to him the patronage he felt he deserved. In February 1937 he complained to Liddell Hart that Haig had installed him at GHQ 'as a sort of private adviser and father-confessor, but [he] had never troubled to give him a step up in rank'.[20]

From about 1938 onwards Edmonds exhibited a growing bias in favour of Haig and GHQ. This clearly culminated in 1948 with the publication of the volume on the gestation and conduct of the third Battle of Ypres. But it is slightly misleading to suggest that this represented Edmonds closing ranks with his old comrades in the face of civilian criticism. The most recent analysis of this episode has discovered that the drafts of this book went through no less than four versions between 1939, when work was begun on it by Captain Cyril Falls and Captain G. C. Wynne, and its publication in 1948. Edmonds did try to protect Haig's reputation by insisting that Wynne, who did the bulk of the work on the drafts after Falls had left the Historical Section, should rewrite his analysis. But he only did so to place the blame on to another old comrade, Sir Hubert Gough, the commander of 5 Army. The upshot was a bitter personal row between Wynne and Edmonds. The former, after interviewing and corresponding with Gough and Haig's Director of Military Operations, Sir John Davidson, was not prepared to twist his interpretation to suit Edmonds's wishes. The row between the two men was not terminated until April 1946 when Wynne insisted that his name be removed from the title-page.[21]

Edmonds behaved in this way partly because he was an elderly man determined to get his own way. But it must also be noted that he was preparing the Official History during the 1920s and 1930s when large numbers of polemical and self-justificatory books about the war were being written by former participants. Perhaps inevitably, he could not hold himself aloof from the climate of animosity they created. Foremost amongst these works of self-justification was Lloyd George's *War Memoirs* which appeared between 1933 and 1936. Lloyd George wrote

[20] Liddell Hart, Talk with General Edmonds—Athenaeum, 5 Feb. 1937, ibid. 11/1937/4.
[21] T. H. E. Travers, *The Killing Ground: The British Army, the Western Front and the Emergence of Modern Warfare, 1900-1918* (London, 1987), 203-16; Gough to Edmonds, 2 Feb. 1944, PRO CAB 45/140; 18 Mar. 1944, PRO CAB 103/112. Wynne to N. Brook, 23 Mar. 1945, PRO CAB 103/112. N. Brook to Sir E. Bridges and minute by N. Brook, both 17 Apr. 1946.

them to defend himself against 'a stream of criticism polluted with much poisonous antagonism' and to restore his reputation as the man who won the war.[22] When they were published 'he was very sick that Haig and Robertson were not alive. He intended to blow their ashes to smithereens in his fifth volume. Unfortunately, he could not get at them personally.'[23] He also added a good measure of criticism of Edmonds's volumes. He derided Edmonds's contention that the South African Defence Minister, Jan Smuts, who joined the War Cabinet in 1917, was not a soldier as 'a consummate example of the workings of the professional military mind'. He accused him of perpetrating 'a great deal of nonsense' and committing 'a grotesque *gaffe*' in his discussion of the government's manpower policy in the winter of 1917-18. And he suggested that in discussing the debate on the extension of the British front in the autumn of 1917 that he had made 'a slovenly use of the documents at his disposal'.[24]

One of the few generals to escape Lloyd George's censure was Gough. In 1918 Lloyd George had been happy to see Gough dismissed as the scapegoat for the disaster which befell 5 Army during the March offensive. But in November 1935 Liddell Hart had discovered that both men were anxious to bury the hatchet and brought them together over dinner at the Atheneaum.[25] What brought them together was a common desire to damn Haig's reputation. Gough believed that Haig had ignored the pressing needs of 5 Army for reinforcements during the opening stages of the March 1918 offensive and then sacked him as a scapegoat for the destruction of his army.[26] Lloyd George believed that Haig had been 'brilliant to the top of his army boots' and held him responsible for the heavy losses suffered by the British army on the Western Front in 1916-18.[27] In his *War Memoirs* he exonerated Gough from the blame for Passchendaele, for, according to Lloyd George, 'he had insisted as far back as August [1917] against proceeding with the battle.' And he described Haig's decision to replace him with Rawlinson in 1918 as 'shabby'.[28]

[22] Lloyd George to Hankey, 18 Apr. 1934, Lloyd George papers, Box G/212.
[23] C. Cross (ed.), *Life with Lloyd George: The Diary of A. J. Sylvester 1931-45* (London, 1975), 111-12.
[24] Lloyd George, *War Memoirs*, ii. (London, 1936), 1576, 1590, 1666.
[25] Liddell Hart, Talk with Lloyd George and General Sir Hubert Gough, 28 Nov. 1935, Liddell Hart papers, 11/1935/107.
[26] Gough to Edmonds, 27 May 1945, PRO CAB 45/140; Gough to Edmonds, 29 July 1934, PRO CAB 45/192.
[27] Earl Lloyd George, *Lloyd George* (London, 1960), 148.
[28] Lloyd George, *War Memoirs*, ii. 1330, 1742.

Sir James Edmonds

Some notion of the animus which was generated by Lloyd George's work was indicated by remarks which Haig's biographer, Alfred Duff Cooper, made in an after-dinner speech to the Fleet Street branch of the British Legion in January 1935. Anxious to say some words in Haig's defence 'in view of the shameful attacks that had been made on him in the last twelve months' Duff Cooper reminded his listeners that Haig had been fighting to defend the British Empire in South Africa 'when Mr. Lloyd George was snivelling at pro-Boer meetings . . .'.[29] Edmonds generally welcomed constructive criticism but Lloyd George's invective went beyond that and he reciprocated Lloyd George's feelings towards him in full measure, dismissing him as 'a cad' and describing his account of Passchendaele as being 'entirely fictitious . . .'.[30]

Once publication of Lloyd George's *War Memoirs* had begun, Edmonds seems to have shaped his own work in part at least to be a counterblast to what the ex-Prime Minister wrote. As he informed Liddell Hart in February 1935: 'What ammunition I use will depend on what Ll.G. says in his next volume.'[31] In February 1937 he published an article in the *Journal of the Royal United Services Institute* which denied Lloyd George's account in his *War Memoirs* that Haig and Henry Wilson were responsible for sacking Gough. He quoted a telegram from Lord Derby, then the Secretary of State for War, that the responsibility had been the Prime Minister's.[32] Barely a month later Lloyd George took the opportunity to deny the accusation. Because he was ill he could not attend the annual reunion dinner of the Fifth Army Old Comrades Association but he sent his secretary, A. J. Sylvester, to read a letter exonerating both Gough and his troops for the events of March 1918. He laid the blame on Haig and GHQ and, for good measure, insisted that Edmonds's article was 'ill-conditioned'.[33] Herein lay the root of what Norman Brook called Edmonds's 'strong feelings about General Gough's conduct of this campaign . . .'.[34]

And, finally, an analysis which explains Edmonds's propensity for glossing over the shortcomings of some members of the high command on the Western Front by references to old friendships does less than justice to Edmonds's real qualities as a historian. Paradoxically, it was only by

---

[29] *The Times* (14 Jan. 1935).
[30] Edmonds to Liddell Hart, 9 Nov. 1934, PRO CAB 45/185; Edmonds, 'Memoirs', Edmonds papers, III/16.
[31] Edmonds to Liddell Hart, 4 Feb. 1935, Liddell Hart papers, 1/259/109.
[32] Sir J. E. Edmonds, 'The Fifth Army in March 1918', *Journal of the Royal United Services Institute*, 82 (1937), 17-31.
[33] *The Times* (22 Mar. 1937).   [34] Travers, *The Killing Ground*, 210.

being prepared to connive in some attempts to cover up the truth that he was able to discover it. In 1935 the historian G. M. Trevelyan called Edmonds a historian. Edmonds took umbrage at that description. He insisted that he was 'but a G.S.O. writing a military account of a modern campaign with the assistance of friends'.[35] The friends he referred to were the thousands of correspondents, all former participants in the events he was trying to describe, upon whose co-operation he depended to supplement the official written records.

Edmonds produced several drafts of each book before he dispatched the final typescript to the publisher. He began by reading through all the pertinent documentary evidence, war diaries, surviving operational orders, and any private papers which participants in the events he was analysing had made available to him, he made notes on them, and then produced a first draft. He then checked through his notes once again to ensure that he had omitted nothing of importance. But he was far too good a historian to believe that all the evidence could be found in the documents or for that matter that the documents were necessarily accurate. War Diaries were often written up well after the events they purported to describe and by officers who were not present at the time. 'Reports of operations written immediately after an action', he wrote in 1931, 'are of little value except as a general guide'.[36]

There were also occasions when he discovered that deliberate attempts had been made to tamper with or suppress evidence. During his period as Sir John French's Chief of Staff in 1914, Sir Archibald Murray sometimes falsified the times and dates of orders. But Edmonds was able to detect this because of the date and time stamp which his confidential clerk had placed on the documents in question.[37] One of Edmonds's assistants discovered that Sir Henry Wilson removed copies of operations orders from the GHQ files for August 1914 because they reflected badly on the shaken state of mind of the headquarters staff.[38] In June 1917 Sir Henry Rawlinson's Chief of Staff, Sir Archibald Montgomery-Massingberd, destroyed 4 Army's War Diary for the opening weeks of the Battle of the Somme, probably in the hope of concealing the fact that Rawlinson had been reluctant to follow Haig's order and to seek a quick breakthrough on 1 July. He substituted for it his own narrative of events. But

---

[35] Edmonds to Liddell Hart, 4 Feb. 1935, Liddell Hart papers, 1/259/109.
[36] Edmonds to the secretary of the Historical Section of the CID, 11 Feb. 1931, Edmonds papers, VII/II.
[37] Liddell Hart, Talk with Edmonds, 28 Nov. 1933, Liddell Hart papers, 11/1933/25.
[38] Liddell Hart, Talk with General Pope Hennessey, 27 May 1937, ibid. 11/1937/43.

Edmonds detected this fraud by checking the narrative against the evidence presented in the war diaries of subordinate formations.[39] Efforts were also made to omit evidence which might reflect badly on the commanders in question. Thus the 3 Army war diary contained no mention of a warning that the army had received about an imminent German counter-attack at Cambrai on 30 November 1917. Edmonds also had access to typescript copies of Haig's personal diary and noted that not every entry had been written at the time it purported to have been and that some passages had been inserted later.[40]

The oral and written reminiscences of survivors were vital because they enabled Edmonds to amplify and cross-check the written record. He therefore had copies of his first draft made and circulated them to as many participants as possible. Drafts of the Loos volume were sent to about 700 officers, more than half of whom made suggestions which Edmonds thought it worth while to consider. Drafts of the volume which examined the opening of the German March offensive in 1918, an action which was pre-eminently a soldier's battle, seem to have been sent to just about every commander down to battalion and battery level. Edmonds himself questioned surviving senior officers over lunch. Some followed Haig's example and lent him copies of their diaries or other private records.[41] But Edmonds did not treat the mass of information he gathered in this way uncritically. He understood that memories were apt to lapse after the passage of years and that his respondents might try to put the best possible gloss on their actions. 'It is the duty of the historian to make head against these difficulties with the aid of the documents and the evidence of other witnesses.'[42] Edmonds did any necessary rewriting and produced a second draft incorporating any relevant French, German, or Italian material. That was then sent to the Dominion general staffs and to the Australian official historian, C. E. W. Bean, for their comments. Only then did he prepare a final draft.[43]

The danger of Edmonds's determination to tap every available source of information was that it did lay him open to pressure to doctor his conclusions to suit the wishes of his informants. If he did not do so they

---

[39] Edmonds, 'Memoirs' (ch. 32), 12-14, Edmonds papers, III/16; Liddell Hart, Talk with Edmonds, 24 Oct. 1930, Liddell Hart papers, 11/1930/10; Travers, 'The Hidden Army: Structural Problems in the British Officer Corps, 1900-1918', *Journal of Contemporary History*, 17 (1982), 528-9.
[40] Travers, *The Killing Ground*, 24-6.
[41] Sir H. Lawrence to Edmonds, 24 Nov. 1930, Edmonds papers, II/2/227A.
[42] Edmonds to the Secretary, Historical Section (C.I.D'), 11 Feb. 1931, Edmonds papers, VII/II.   [43] Edmonds, 'Memoirs' (ch. 32), 11-14, ibid. III/16.

might simply refuse further co-operation and the geese which lay the golden eggs might drop dead. Many of his informants were ambivalent about helping him. 'Yes: we all want to know the TRUTH, as you say', Sir Ivor Maxse, a former divisional and corps commander, wrote to him in 1927, 'But who knows where to discover it? and, if discovered, how to reproduce it? or whether it should be *told?*'[44] Some witnesses were undoubtedly concerned about their personal reputations. In lending Edmonds some of his private papers Lawrence asked in return that 'if you are using anything which might be controversial I should like to know what it is'.[45] Others were less concerned about their personal reputations and were more concerned about the effect criticisms of the high command might have upon the willingness of the next generations to submit to military discipline. For example, one former divisional commander, Major-General A. Solly Flood, sent Edmonds a press cutting critical of Haig together with a note saying:

But setting aside all questions of loyalty to our revered chief, articles couched in these terms cause one much anxiety on account of the effect they must have on the minds of the uninformed public and of posterity, which may be called upon in their turn to undertake service on behalf of their King and country.[46]

A third category were worried lest criticisms of the army's conduct might harm Britain's international prestige. In 1929 Sir Arthur Conan Doyle raised the issue of Edmonds's description of the precipitous retreat of 21 Division at Loos in September 1915: 'Very frankly. Could it be toned down into more general terms?' he asked, 'You have to remember that there are fellows of the baser sort in America & elsewhere who will leave out all your compensating paragraphs and simply quote the passages which describe the panic. Then there may be a row.'[47] Similarly, Sir George Macdonogh warned him that it might be unwise to include criticisms of General Pétain's conduct in 1918. 'It has got to be remembered that not merely is he still alive but he is also at present the French Minister of War.'[48] Edmonds generally met his critics at least half-way. He dealt with pressures like these in one of two ways. He confined the text to a bald narrative of events and omitted criticisms or he placed awkward evidence in footnotes or appendices, perhaps on the assumption

[44] Maxse to Edmonds, 16 Jan. 1927, ibid. II/2/163.
[45] Lawrence to Edmonds, 24 Nov. 1930, ibid. II/2/227A.
[46] Solly Flood to Edmonds, 28 Oct. 1934, ibid. II/1/125A.
[47] A. Conan Doyle to Edmonds, 4 Dec. 1929, ibid. II/2/203.
[48] Macdonogh to Edmonds, 26 July 1934, PRO CAB 45/186.

that only those already in the know would bother to read them. In the volume published in 1927 examining the second Battle of Ypres in 1915 he agreed to Sir Arthur Currie's request that he should suppress the fact that three times during the battle he had ordered his Canadians to retreat. When he exposed one of Murray's attempts to change the date and time of a GHQ operations order in August 1914 he did so in a footnote to an appendix. Similarly, when Montgomery-Massingberd complained that the first draft of the volume on the battle of the Somme had been written in a 'captious spirit' he agreed to revise it and tone down the criticisms. Only by turning to the volume of appendices could a reader discover that during the planning stage of the Somme Haig and Rawlinson had disagreed fundamentally about whether 4 Army should attempt to break clean through the German defences on the first day of the battle. In 1937 he informed Liddell Hart that 'In my first draft [of *OH*, ii. (1918)] I took the same view as you do to the "backs to the wall" order (? where was the wall), but found that hundreds of my correspondents in the fighting units were against me and I felt bound to alter it.'[49]

Just occasionally he let himself go when his targets could not retaliate or when the need to stay silent had passed. In the first edition of the volume examining the retreat from Mons, published in 1922, he made no mention of the panic which for a time seems to have gripped the headquarters of Haig's 1 Corps and led to it diverging from Smith-Dorrien's 2 Corps. But in 1933, five years after Haig's death, he published a revised edition in which he described this incident and added that 'Haig momentarily lost his head—a remarkable lapse for so stout hearted a fighter.' There was, as he laconically noted 'a gap in the records' about this incident.[50] Similarly, by 1947 enough had happened to remove any inhibitions he might have felt about criticizing Pétain. In the 'Retrospect' to the final volume in the series he felt free to write that 'After General Pétain was given command of the French Armies on 15th. May 1917, our Allies did very little', and that his refusal to reinforce Gough's 5 Army in March 1918 'very nearly brought about a disaster'.[51]

[49] Travers, 'The Hidden Army', 526; Edmonds to Liddell Hart, 15 Apr. 1937, Liddell Hart papers, 1/259/139; Liddell Hart, Talk with Edmonds, 7 Oct. 1927, ibid. 11/1927/17; Edmonds, *Official History 1914*, i. 517 (append. 14); Edmonds, *Official History 1916*, 69, 72, 82 (appends).
[50] Captain Liddell Hart, 'Revelations in New Official History' (n.d. but *c*.1933), Edmonds papers, VII/10; Edmonds, *Official History 1914*, 135.
[51] Edmonds, *Official History 1918*, v. 603.

Edmonds's work received a mixed reception both from participants and from later historians. Some readers liked what he had written. Haig read and commented upon all the volumes up to and including Loos before he died. 'They are all excellent' he wrote of some draft chapters on Neuve Chapelle, 'and I congratulate you on the way in which you have told the story so accurately, *and yet without attaching blame to anyone* . . .'.[52] More surprisingly this camp also included Field Marshal Lord Wavell, who reviewed several volumes in the *Times Literary Supplement*. In 1949 he described the series as 'the best official military history yet written' possibly because he shared Edmonds's view that many British generals in France and Flanders had believed that they were engaged in 'Open Warfare at the Halt' but in reality 'warfare on the Western Front after 1914 was Siege Warfare and should have been treated as such'.[53]

However, some readers thought that he had gone too far to meet the wishes of his informants and that his books were anodyne. Sir William Robertson read one draft and wrote that 'It leaves the same taste behind it as when one drinks skimmed milk. I suppose he wished to avoid having trouble with anyone as to what he says, and therefore leaves out most of what is worth saying.'[54] And thirdly, there were those like Liddell Hart, whose view of the high command's respect for the truth was very largely soured by the fact that Edmonds often told him what he really believed in private but would not say the same thing in print.[55] Liddell Hart believed that Edmonds's practice of covering up the deficiencies of the high command meant that he was only storing up trouble for the future. 'Any writer of history' he informed Edmonds in June 1934, 'who helps to flatter the "brasshat's" self-delusion as to the respect in which he is held, is preparing the country for a greater disaster'.[56]

His books were a qualified success when measured against the self-imposed task of instructing young officers but concealing the worst mistakes of their seniors. Some of the evidence which Edmonds had concealed remained hidden for a long time. As late as 1952 the publication of Robert Blake's *The Private Papers of Douglas Haig* could still evoke a sense of shock amongst those not already privy to what one

[52] Haig to Edmonds, 6 Aug. 1925, Edmonds papers, II/4/39.
[53] Wavell to Edmonds, 28 Dec. 1949, ibid. II/1/129.
[54] Robertson to Maurice, 1 Dec. 1932, Maurice papers, 3/5/201.
[55] Brian Bond, *Liddell Hart: A Study of his Military Thought* (London, 1977), 82-4.
[56] Liddell Hart to Edmonds, 25 June 1934, Liddell Hart papers, 1/259/84; 7 May 1934, ibid. 1/259/77; J. Luvaas, 'The First British Official Historians', in R. Higham (ed.), *Official Histories: Essays and Bibliographies from Around the World* (Manhattan, Kan., 1970), 494-5.

reader of them called 'the petty jealousies that pervaded high places'.[57] In 1932 Lord Gort told Edmonds that if only the next generation of officers read his books they would avoid some of the worst mistakes of their predecessors. And they were encouraged to do so. When he was Commandant of the Staff College in the mid-1930s Sir John Dill used Edmonds's books as texts for his students.[58]

But whether the proper lessons were or indeed could be drawn from Edmonds's books is open to some doubt. After he resigned from Edmonds's staff Wynne wrote an excellent account of the evolution of German tactical doctrine on the Western Front. He was very critical of Edmonds's failure to criticize British tactical doctrine on the grounds that he believed that during the war British and German tactical doctrines were broadly similar. Wynne thought that they were not and that in hiding that fact Edmonds had deprived the next generation of the army's leaders of knowledge of German doctrine which he argued was vastly superior to that of the British army.[59] It would, of course, be absurd, to place all the blame for whatever shortcomings there were in doctrine and training in the British army between the wars on Edmonds alone. As Professor Bond has demonstrated, the inter-war officer-corps were not inclined to read very many books, although Edmonds's dry style did not do much to encourage them to do otherwise. The ethos and structure of the inter-war officer corps placed some formidable obstacles in the way of any general 'learning process'. After 1918 the regular army was largely geared to regimental soldiering in the empire. Officers were often not given much encouragement to read anything more taxing than the latest regulations and the Army List. The mental horizons of many—although by no means all officers—must have shrunk accordingly. The promotion system kept too many old and tired officers in senior posts for too long and denied their more energetic juniors their opportunity until they, too, were past their prime.[60]

It is possible to point to one precise instance where Edmonds's work did make a positive contribution to the rethinking of doctrine. In 1932

[57] Brig. M. C. A. Henniker to Liddell Hart, 15 Mar. 1952, Edmonds papers, II/2/442.
[58] Gort to Edmonds, 13 June 1932, ibid. II/1/42; Dill to Edmonds, 21 July 1933, ibid. II/1/38.
[59] Captain G. C. Wynne, 'Pattern for Limited (Nuclear) War: The Riddle of the Schlieffen Plan', *Journal of the Royal United Services Institute for Defence Studies*, 103 (1958), 42.
[60] Bond, *British Military Policy between the Two World Wars* (Oxford, 1980), ch. 2, *passim*.

the CIGS, Field Marshal Lord Milne, read Edmonds's volume on the opening of the Somme. He was so shocked at the tactical ineptitude that it exposed that he established a committee under Lieutenant-General Sir Walter Kirke to discover what were the main lessons which could be drawn from the war and to find out whether or not they had been incorporated into current manuals.[61]

The Kirke Committee consisted of nine brigadiers and major generals. The part of their report on the Western Front was written by Major-General A. E. McNamara. He had access to all of Edmonds's volumes up to and including the beginning of the Somme. He interpreted his brief broadly and his recommendations ranged well beyond matters of minor or even grand tactics. He recommended that before war broke out it was necessary to have a complete scheme to train and mobilize the Territorial Army, to raise and train large numbers of new recruits, and to have a sufficiently large cadre of good officers and NCOs to do so. It was also important to prepare a programme to supply these troops with the proper quantities of weapons and munitions. On the outbreak of war the General Staff must remain in London. It must not decamp to the front as it had done in 1914.

The history of the war up to July 1916 indicated that higher headquarters had often been too far back from the fighting and out of touch with what was happening in the front line. Training manuals had to lay more stress on the need for commanders to send forward for information rather than expecting hard-pressed subordinates to send it back to them. When orders had reached the front line their meaning was often obscure and so greater emphasis had to be laid on the need to make them perfectly intelligible. McNamara was very critical of GHQ's insistence that ground should never be given up except under overwhelming pressure. Field Service Regulations ought to stipulate that losses would be reduced if contact with the enemy was maintained by a system of lightly held outposts and if the main defensive position was further to the rear. And, finally, the war had demonstrated that in attack the massing of large numbers of guns to overcome the enemy's defences almost always forfeited surprise and that it was only regained late in the war by the use of the tank. In future tactical breakthroughs would only be achieved by relying on a combination of rapid mobility, a properly worked out fire plan, and the use of fog, smoke, or darkness to conceal the attackers. Current training manuals laid too much emphasis on the break-in phase

[61] Milne to DSD, 6 June 1932, Kirke MS 9; Liddell Hart diary entry, 9 May 1932, Liddell Hart papers, 11/1932/1c.

of the battle and did not point clearly to the need for a separate force of all arms to be on hand to convert the break-in into a break-out.[62]

The Kirke report was completed in 1933. Liddell Hart welcomed many of its specific recommendations but he thought that it was killed off by Milne's successor, Montgomery-Massingberd. But in fact in 1933 at least three officers who were to rise to the highest levels of command in the Second World War, Alexander, Wavell, and Montgomery, organized and took part in training exercises involving night attacks in which they made a serious effort to put into practice some of the lessons Kirke and his colleagues had gleaned from Edmonds. Perhaps, therefore, a small part of the credit for Montgomery's victory in the second Battle of Alamein, may be traced back to Edmonds via the Kirke report.[63]

During the First World War the British army was at a crossroads in its development, torn between a traditional, gentlemanly ideal of soldiering and a technical and functionally competent ideal.[64] Edmonds's history in many ways mirrored that clash. There can be few if any modern professional historians who would condone the way in which he deliberately glossed over the professional defects of some of the senior officers about whom he wrote. His determination to write what were in practice staff college textbooks meant that he failed to reach a wider public and that they did not fulfil the objective laid down for them of being 'suitable for general readers'.[65] Indeed, their appeal was so limited that Macmillan had to be subsidized so that they could make a profit from printing them. He failed in what might be considered to be one of the jobs, albeit one of the most difficult, of an official historian, to educate the lay public in the realities of war.

Edmonds's basic explanation of the heavy losses suffered by the British Army on the Western Front echoed many of the points raised by the General Staff during the war. He stressed the external problems which he believed had handicapped British generals. Because of her reliance on the royal navy to maintain her security before 1914, Britain had neglected her army. The pre-war regular army was too small and unprepared for a continental-scale land war in August 1914. Training and equipping the New Armies took longer than they might have done

[62] 'Lessons of the Great War Committee', 'Report by Maj.-Gen. A. E. McNamara', 'Lessons from the Great War on the Western Front' (Edmonds, *Official History*, i, ii, and iv), Kirke MS 9.
[63] Note by L.H. [n.d.], Liddell Hart papers, 11/1932/70; N. Hamilton, *Monty: The Making of a General 1887-1942* (London, 1981), 228, 230.
[64] Travers, 'The Hidden Army', 525.
[65] Edmonds, *Official History 1914*, i. p. vii.

because no plans had been made before the war for a massive expansion of the army. Everything had to be improvised. That task was made doubly difficult by the heavy losses of trained cadres in the original BEF in 1914-15 and the consequent lack of experienced instructors and staff officers. The army in the field was further handicapped by interfering politicians who constantly denied it enough men. Operations were hampered by bad luck, such as the wet weather at the third Battle of Ypres. Strategic policy on the Western Front was largely controlled by the French for most of the war, leaving Sir John French and Haig little freedom of action.[66] Many of Edmonds's interpretations have been challenged by later historians whose work is discussed in this book but none of them can be dismissed out of hand. And, finally, Edmonds must be given credit for his determination not to trust naïvely to the documents but to try to cross-check the written record by corresponding with or interviewing as many survivors as he could reach. His industry meant that he produced a quarry of facts which historians are still able to mine with profit to this day.

[66] Some of these points were raised in, for example, Robertson to Stamfordham, 1 Oct. 1915, Robertson papers, I/12/5; Rawlinson to Robertson, 8 Apr. 1916, ibid. I/21/11.

II

The Battle of the Memoirs

4
Frocks and Brasshats*
IAN BECKETT

If history in any form rarely comes value-free then autobiography, memoir, and biography are arguably the historical genres most susceptible to conscious (or unconscious) manipulation by their authors. Some may profess to recognize the danger, such as Viscount Grey of Fallodon, whose *Twenty-Five Years* in 1925 was offered with the qualification that 'it must be remembered that the scope of each individual mind is fragmentary', or Leo Amery, who quite openly presented the first two volumes of *My Political Life* in 1953 as having no claim to historical detachment or impartiality: 'I tell it as I felt it and as I still feel it. My heroes remain heroes and my villains remain villains.' None the less, even those who allegedly set out to provide an 'impartial' account—to use Lord Beaverbrook's later claim for his *Politicians and the War*, the two volumes of which appeared in 1928 and 1932—were more often than not seduced by what George Egerton has characterized as the 'powerful latent functions' of memoir as a genre.[1]

Egerton maintains that one such function—and consequence—of memoir and especially memoir on the epic scale of the six constituent volumes comprising Churchill's *The World Crisis* published between

---

* The author gratefully acknowledges the generosity of the following in enabling him to consult and, where requested, to quote from archives in their possession or copyright: Colonel J. A. Aylmer; the trustees of the Imperial War Museum; the trustees of the Liddell Hart Centre for Military Archives; the trustees of the Beaverbrook Foundation; the Clerk of the Records and the House of Lords Record Office; the Bodleian Library; the Master, Fellows, and Scholars of Churchill College, Cambridge; the Guildhall Library.

[1] Viscount Grey of Fallodon, *Twenty-Five Years*, 2 vols. (London, 1925), i. p. xvii; The Rt. Hon. L. S. Amery, *My Political Life*, 3 vols. (London, 1953-5), i. (1953), 14; Lord Beaverbrook, *Men and Power, 1917-18* (London, 1956), p. xli; id., *Politicians and the War, 1914-1916*, i. (London, 1928) and ii. (London, 1932); G. W. Egerton, 'The Lloyd George War Memoirs: A Study in the Politics of Memory', *Journal of Modern History*, 60 (1988), 55-94; Winston S. Churchill, *The World Crisis*, 6 vols. (London, 1923-9), i. *The World Crisis, 1911-1914* (1923); ii. *The World Crisis, 1915* (1923); iii-iv *The World Crisis, 1916-18*, pts. 1 and 2 (1927); v. *The World Crisis: The Eastern Front* (1931); vi. *The World Crisis: The Aftermath* (1929); David Lloyd George, *War Memoirs*, 6 vols. (London, 1933-6), i. and ii. (1933); iii and iv (1934); v and vi (1936).

1923 and 1929 or the six volumes of Lloyd George's *War Memoirs* published between 1933 and 1936 is to shape the popular historical memory of the recent past in its own image. Certainly, there is little doubt of the long-term impact on popular perceptions of the Great War of the memoirs by soldiers and statesmen published during the inter-war years. This is not simply a case of the reputations of individuals. What have been described as the 'enthralling tales of olympian intrigue and ambition' in Beaverbrook's *Politicians and the War*, for example, became sufficiently influential to establish a particular view of the reasons for the fall of the Asquith coalition in December 1916 which long obscured the significance of the munitions crisis in determining events. This was despite the fact that Beaverbrook's concern with the 'peaks' of politics showed his narratives deficient with respect to the workings of parliament and popular politics of which he had little knowledge. Similarly, Keith Grieves has pointed to the misrepresentation of wartime manpower planning policy through overemphasis on personality clashes highlighted in memoirs.[2]

Even more significant in terms of the themes of this chapter, David French has strongly argued that the whole conception of a wartime strategic debate between 'westerners' and 'easterners' so firmly entrenched in the polemical contributions of statesmen like Churchill and Lloyd George on the one hand and soldiers such as Field Marshal Sir William Robertson on the other is a 'caricature' of reality. Thus, he would argue that the actual wartime division was between those like Reginald McKenna and Walter Runciman, who advocated limited liability and an essentially maritime strategy, and those like both Robertson and Lloyd George, who recognized the necessity of raising a mass army for continental warfare. Seen in these terms, the 'westerners' and 'easterners' debate, or the differing interpretations of the meaning of attrition, were about means rather than ends. The familiar signposts along the way such as the Dardanelles expedition, the Somme, the Calais Conference and the Nivelle offensive, Passchendaele, the Supreme War

[2] C. Hazelhurst, *Politicians at War* (London, 1971), 15; R. J. Q. Adams, *Arms and the Wizard* (London, 1978), 31; J. O. Stubbs, 'Beaverbrook as Historian: *Politicians and the War* Reconsidered', *Albion*, 14/3-4 (1982), 235-53; P. Fraser, 'Lord Beaverbrook's Fabrications in *Politicians and the War, 1914-1916*', *Historical Journal*, 25 (1982), 147-66; T. M. McEwen, 'Lord Beaverbrook: Historian Extraordinary', *Dalhousie Review*, 59/1 (1979), 129-43; Austen Chamberlain, *Down the Years* (London, 1935), 106-31; K. R. Grieves, *The Politics of Manpower, 1914-18* (Manchester, 1988), 1-5; id., 'Improving the British War Effort: Eric Geddes and Lloyd George, 1915-18', *War and Society*, 7/2 (1989), 40-55; C. Wrigley, 'The Ministry of Munitions: An Innovatory Department', in K. Burk (ed.), *War and the State* (London, 1982), 32-56.

Council, and the Maurice debate are no less important but the stereotypes have masked the significance of both Imperial necessity and alliance politics in dictating decisions.[3]

Nevertheless, it is the image rather than the reality that is of most concern here and, of course, the particular interpretations advanced by soldiers or statesmen could not be readily challenged by historians who possessed neither first-hand knowledge of events at the highest level nor access to primary sources. Indeed, the public accessibility of corrective documents is of crucial significance and it must be borne in mind that, even when the 50-Year Rule was introduced by the Public Records Act of 1958, it was by no means clear that this would apply to Cabinet papers and memoranda although, in practice, the constraints that the Cabinet secretariat would have wished to maintain could not be sustained.[4] In effect, some papers also became available under an informal 30-Year Rule prior to its introduction under the Public Records Act of 1967 but most official records relating to the Great War were not open to historians until the mid-1960s.

As will be seen later, such restrictions did not generally apply to the participants themselves, the war years being considered in a phrase of Austen Chamberlain much echoed by the long-serving secretary to the Cabinet, Colonel Sir Maurice Hankey, to be *sui generis*. Robertson made the same point in his preface to *Soldiers and Statesmen* in 1926, maintaining that 'the rules and customs which ordinarily govern the disclosure of official information can hardly be held to apply to the special conditions which attended the Great War'. However, statesmen were increasingly not prepared to extend such privilege to lesser mortals. In 1921, for example, Captain Peter Wright had escaped prosecution for revealing the deliberations of the Supreme War Council largely because it was felt that action would also have to be taken against Field Marshal Lord French whose notorious *1914* had appeared while French was still holding office as Lord Lieutenant of Ireland. But, following the successful prosecutions of Compton Mackenzie in 1932 and Edgar Lansbury two years later, for a memoir and a biography respectively, under the Official Secrets Act of 1911 (as amended in 1920), new rules drawn up by

[3] D. French, *British Strategy and War Aims* (London, 1986), pp. x-xii; id., 'Allies, Rivals and Enemies', in J. Turner (ed.), *Britain and the First World War* (London, 1988), 22-35; id., 'The Meaning of Attrition, 1914-16', *English Historical Review*, 103/407 (1988), 385-405.

[4] J. F. Naylor, *A Man and an Institution: Sir Maurice Hankey, the Cabinet Secretariat and the Custody of Cabinet Secrecy* (Cambridge, 1984), 238, 266-7, 290-5; P. Fraser, 'Cabinet Secrecy and War Memoirs', *History*, 70 (1985), 397-409.

Hankey and adopted by the Cabinet in February 1934 specifically prohibited the access to official records of historians merely seeking to write 'better books'. There was, therefore, a certain irony that the publication of Hankey's own memoirs, *The Supreme Command, 1914-1918* completed in 1943, was delayed until 1961 by the application of rules he had himself originated. As late as 1965 the biographer of Allenby, Brian Gardner, referred to being summoned to the Foreign Office 'and (literally) presented with the Official Secrets Act' to prevent him reproducing some documents.[5]

If, to quote Lloyd George's somewhat irrisory comment in 1933 on the subject of Passchendaele to the official historian, Brigadier-General James Edmonds, it was 'vital that the public should have all the facts', the latter could only be derived from what soldiers and statesmen chose to reveal. Since soldiers and statesmen themselves might not always be in possession of the 'facts', each successive publication quoted extensively from those that had preceded it. Indeed, in 1931 Churchill urged his publisher, Thornton Butterworth, to 'tweak' V. W. Germains whose *The Tragedy of Winston Churchill* had quoted from *The World Crisis* without authority. Thus, those volumes earliest into print such as French's *1914* published in 1919 or two books published in 1920— Charles à Court Repington's *The First World War* and Sir George Arthur's *The Life of Lord Kitchener*—had a considerable impact in establishing some of the parameters of the post-war controversies.

Churchill, of course, was also relatively quick into print, while certain other later volumes were equally influential, either like Robertson's *Soldiers and Statesmen* because of the importance of the author's wartime position or like Major-General Sir Charles Callwell's 1927 biography, *Field Marshal Sir Henry Wilson: His Life and Diaries*, Beaverbrook's *Politicians and the War*, Edward Spears's *Liaison 1914* (1930), and Lord Riddell's edition of his own diaries (1933) because of the candid nature of their revelations. In fact, it is instructive to chart the frequency with which certain volumes such as those mentioned are cited not only by other biographers or memorialists in the 1930s—a particular example is the third volume of Ian Colvin's biography of Edward Carson

[5] Hankey to Churchill, 8 Dec. 1944, University of Cambridge, Churchill College Archives Centre (hereafter CAC), HNKY 25/1; Field Marshal Sir William Robertson, *Soldiers and Statesmen*, 2 vols. (London, 1926), i. p. xiv; Hankey to Lloyd George, 8 Apr. and 17 Oct. 1933, Lloyd George MSS, G/212; P. Wright, *At the Supreme War Council* (London, 1921); Naylor, *A Man and an Institution*, 211-27; S. Roskill, *Hankey: Man of Secrets*, 3 vols. (London, 1972-4), iii. (1974), 587-90, 616-21; Lord Hankey, *The Supreme Command, 1914-18*, 2 vols. (London, 1961); B. Gardner, *Allenby* (London, 1965), p. xviii.

covering the war years, which appeared in 1936—but also by popular historians in the 1950s and 1960s.[6]

That the reading public was anxious for revelation is reflected in the sales figures not only of the more controversial volumes but also of even the relatively mundane reminiscences from the peripheries of power offered them in the inter-war years. This is the more impressive given an average retail price of about £1. 5s. 0d. for a single volume and two guineas for a two-volume set at a time of some economic difficulty. Success was not therefore guaranteed. Beaverbrook, for example, sold 9,000 copies of the first volume of *Politicians and the War* in 1928 against the competition from Asquith's *Memories and Reflections* but apparently insisted on such a low retail price of 7s. 6d. that the book made a loss and he had to establish his own publishing imprint for the second volume which was delayed until 1932: it sold only 2,700 copies. Asquith's *The Genesis of War* had not sold well in 1923 and even Churchill found a lukewarm reception for his volume on the Eastern Front in 1931, *The Times* declining to serialize it because it judged that readers were 'responding less and less to War History'.

Nevertheless, despite occasional publishing difficulties there was never really any discernible slump in sales and competition between publishing houses was keen. In the case of Maurice Brett's edition of the journals and diaries of his father, Lord Esher, Sir John Murray, Thornton Butterworth, and Ivor Nicolson all pursued the author between 1931 and 1933 notwithstanding Murray's belief that Esher was not well known to the public. Similarly, the leading London literary agent, A. P. Watt, who had already represented authors such as Grey, Callwell, and Major-General Sir Frederick Maurice for his *The Life of Lord Rawlinson of Trent*, published in 1928, solicited Brett's custom and another of Watt's clients, Lord Mottistone, the former J. E. B. Seely, whose *Adventure* had appeared in 1930, also approached Brett on Watt's behalf.[7]

---

[6] Lloyd George to Edmonds, 28 Dec. 1933, Lloyd George MSS, G/211; M. Gilbert, *Winston S. Churchill*, companion volume, v. pt. 2 (London, 1981), 337-8; Field Marshal Lord French, *1914* (London, 1919); C. à C. Repington, *The First World War*, 2 vols. (London, 1920); Sir George Arthur, *The Life of Lord Kitchener*, 3 vols. (London, 1920); Maj.-Gen. Sir Charles Callwell, *Field Marshal Sir Henry Wilson: His Life and Diaries*, 2 vols. (London, 1927); E. L. Spears, *Liaison 1914* (London, 1930); Lord Riddell, *War Diary, 1914-18* (London, 1933); E. Marjoribanks and I. Colvin, *The Life of Lord Carson*, 3 vols. (London, 1932-6), iii. (1936).

[7] A. J. P. Taylor, *Beaverbrook* (London, 1972), 250-1, 310-12; The Earl of Oxford and Asquith, *Memories and Reflections*, 2 vols. (London, 1928); R. Jenkins, *Asquith* (London, 1964), 494-5; The Rt. Hon. H. H. Asquith, *The Genesis of War* (London,

All the major memoirs and biographies were also serialized prior to publication in the national press and while Sir John Murray feared that it discouraged subsequent sales, there is little evidence that this was the case. While Lord Esher remarked that all Churchill's 'purple passages' had already appeared in *The Times* before publication of the first volume of *The World Crisis* and that serialization of Margot Asquith's *Autobiography* had led to many of her statements being taken out of context, it was equally said of French's *1914* that 'no book of modern times has been so extensively discussed in advance of its appearance'. None of these suffered from the advanced publicity while the publication in 1934 of Lloyd George's controversial fourth volume dealing with Passchendaele not only received a leader in *The Times* but also banner headlines in the *Daily Express*: 'Lloyd George's Appalling War Revelations. Why 400,000 Died in the Mud of Passchendaele. "Impossible" Battle. Vital Facts Cabinet Never Knew. Haig Indicted. Would Not Admit Error.'[8]

Given such publicity and the continuing interest in memoirs and biographies, sales of the genre as a whole were generally good. Thus, even the two-volume edition of the diary of Britain's wartime ambassador in Paris, Lord Bertie, prepared by Lady Gordon-Lennox and published in 1924, and which was described by Cyril Falls in his classic 1930 bibliography, *War Books*, as needing to have been 'purged of its dross before being presented to the public', had sold 2,706 copies in Britain and 600 overseas out of 3,450 printed in less than a year. The better known the individual the greater were the sales. General Sir Hubert Gough's 1931 memoir, *The Fifth Army*, had sold 3,168 copies by March 1932 from its total print run of 4,240 copies while Lord Haldane's *Autobiography* sold 5,269 copies in Britain and Canada in its first year of publication in 1929 and a further 2,528 copies in 1930. Grey's *Twenty-Five Years* had sold 11,690 copies by March 1926.[9]

1923); Smith to Churchill, 7 and 10 July 1931, Gilbert, *Churchill*, companion volume, v. pt. 2, 330-1; Murray to Brett, 3 Feb. 1931 and 8 and 27 Dec. 1933, CAC, ESHR 22/3; Butterworth to Brett, 9 Aug. 1932, ibid.; Watt to Brett, 4 July, 15 Sept., and 16 Dec. 1933, ibid.; Mottistone to Brett, 9 July 1933, ibid.; Maj.-Gen. Sir F. Maurice, *The Life of Lord Rawlinson of Trent* (London, 1928); Maj.-Gen. the Rt. Hon. J. E. B. Seely, *Adventure* (London, 1930).

[8] Murray to Watt, 15 Dec. 1933, CAC, ESHR 22/3; M. Brett (ed.), *The Journals and Letters of Reginald, Viscount Esher*, 4 vols. (London, 1934-8), iv. (1938), 267-8, 287; Margot Asquith, *The Autobiography of Margot Asquith*, 2 vols. (London, 1920-2); *The Times* (23 June 1919 and 27 Nov. 1934); *Daily Express* (26 Oct. 1934).

[9] Lady Algernon Gordon-Lennox, *The Diary of Lord Bertie*, 2 vols. (London, 1924); Cyril Falls, *War Books* (London, 1930), 35; Hodder & Stoughton Ledgers for Gordon Lennox, Gough, Grey, and Haldane, Guildhall Library MS 16312, vols. 18-20; General Sir Hubert Gough, *The Fifth Army* (London, 1931); R. B. Haldane, *An Autobiography* (London, 1929).

Yet, even Grey's success was dwarfed by those of Churchill and Lloyd George. Churchill's first volume was reprinted twice within a month of publication in April 1923 to attain a print run of 11,380 copies in Britain alone while the two parts of his third volume covering the years 1916 to 1918 was again reprinted twice within a month of publication in March 1927 and had sold 12,894 copies by the end of the year. Lloyd George's sales were even more extraordinary with his six volumes collectively selling 54,237 copies in Britain alone by February 1937. In addition, both Churchill and Lloyd George sold well in United States editions and foreign editions were also an option for some other authors, Spears's *Liaison 1914* selling 1,950 copies in its French edition.

Many copies in the original print runs of the major memoirs would have been purchased by the circulating libraries and this would have enabled a far wider readership to gain access to the historical controversies without the need to purchase what were still relatively expensive books. However, there were also popular cheaper editions such as the 'People's Library' editions of Haldane and Grey, of which 4,000 and 9,000, priced at 7s. 6d., and 5s. 0d., were printed respectively in 1932 and 1936. In fact, Grey's book did badly, only selling a derisory 162 copies in its first year, but Margot Asquith claimed to have sold 150,000 of the cheap Penguin 6d. edition of her autobiography by 1943, while Churchill certainly did well with the various cheaper, abridged, and weekly part-work versions of *The World Crisis* between 1933 and 1940. There was even a limited 'Sandhurst' edition in 1933 which Liddell Hart claimed had been deliberately sponsored to replace his own *The Real War*, 'being less likely than that of a detached critic as mine is, to impress on the young soldiers the fact that the version of the so-called amateur . . . was superior to the version of professional authority'. Lloyd George also sold 286,429 individual copies of the two-volume cheaper 1938 edition of his *War Memoirs* by 1944.[10]

Consequently, pecuniary rewards for memoirs and biographies could be significant and should not be ruled out altogether as a contributory factor in motivating authors. Hubert Gough first showed interest in

[10] Gilbert, *Churchill*, v. (London, 1976), 6-7; id., *Churchill*, companion volume, v. pt. 2, 741 n.; Egerton, 'Lloyd George Memoirs', 55-94; Spears correspondence with Gaston Gallimard, CAC, SPRS 2/19; Hodder & Stoughton Ledgers, Guildhall Library MS 16312, vols. 19-20; Countess of Oxford and Asquith, *Off the Record* (London, 1943), 11; Hart to Churchill, 4 Aug. 1932, Liddell Hart papers 1/171/18. Liddell Hart variously alleged that the CIGS, Sir George Milne, and a new chief instructor at Sandhurst had suppressed his book—see 'Some Odd Notes for History' Liddell Hart papers, 11/1933/35, and J. Luvaas, *The Education of an Army* (Chicago, 1965), 391.

publishing his account of his wartime command after learning that Major-General Sir George Aston had earned £2,000 for his *pre-war* memoirs, while those who acutely felt that their financial situation compelled writing included both Asquith and the former Minister of Munitions, Christopher Addison, whose work on the vivid *Politics from Within* followed the loss of his parliamentary seat in 1922. Addison published another two-volume work, *Four and a Half Years*, in 1934 largely echoing Lloyd George's view of 'the perverse limitations of the military mind'. Lloyd George similarly wrote in 1922 that after seventeen years in office he had 'retired a poor man, and it is absolutely imperative that I should return to writing as a means of livelihood'. Churchill, whose own tenure of office was equally elusive during the inter-war years, was also highly dependent upon his pen.[11]

Accordingly, Gough secured a £1,000 advance for his memoirs while Grey received a royalty of £5,860. 15*s*. 8*d*. in 1926 and Haldane a posthumous £1,555. 1*s*. 3*d*. in 1929. Churchill received £16,500 in non-returnable advances for his first volume and, with additional American advances, this rose to £27,000 before a single copy had been sold, the 'half-a-crown a word' reward certainly arousing the interest of Asquith. In effect, the second volume enabled Churchill to complete work on his home at Chartwell with an additional six to seven months' income from the surplus. There was a £2,000 advance for the third volume and this also earned an almost immediate £4,874 in royalties. When he first contemplated writing his memoirs in 1922, Lloyd George signed contracts for the British and US rights which would have brought him a record £90,000 before royalties and, had this initial project come to fruition, total advance earnings might have exceeded £132,000. The sum aroused so much controversy that Lloyd George was compelled to indicate that he would give the money to war charities. In the event, he was unable to pursue the project at that time and, following court proceedings on a contractual dispute over American serial rights, Lloyd George returned his £5,500 advance in 1925. His renewed interest in completing his memoirs instituted another lively publishing race in

[11] A. H. Farrar-Hockley, *Goughie* (London, 1975), 352; Maj.-Gen. Sir George Aston, *Memories of a Marine* (London, 1919); J. A. Spender and C. Asquith, *The Life of H. H. Asquith, Lord Oxford and Asquith*, 2 vols. (London, 1932), ii. 314; Jenkins, *Asquith*, 494–5; K. Morgan and J. Morgan, *Portrait of a Progressive* (Oxford, 1980), 163–4; Rt. Hon. C. Addison, *Politics from Within*, 2 vols. (London, 1924); id., *Four and a Half Years*, 2 vols. (London, 1934); Review of Addison, Edmonds papers, VIII/16; F. Owen, *Tempestuous Journey* (London, 1954), 701; Gilbert, *Churchill*, companion volume, iv. pt. 3 (London, 1977), 1706–7.

1932 with no question on this occasion of charitable gifts. Although the talk of film rights did not manifest itself in any eventual Hollywood production, it is estimated that Lloyd George still made £65,000 from his memoirs.[12]

But, if gain was one factor stimulating the production of memoirs in the inter-war years, personal vindication was a far more important one, Churchill disposing neatly of the relative weight of consideration in a letter to his wife in December 1921: 'It is a great chance to put my whole case in an agreeable form to an attentive audience. And the pelf will make us v[er]y comfortable.' Occasionally, an author seemed genuinely diffident towards his own reputation. General Sir Charles 'Tim' Harington claimed that he had only been persuaded to commit pen to paper by his friends, and his memoirs published in 1940 were generally low-key in approach in the same way that his biography of his old chief, Plumer, five years earlier had equally eschewed wider wartime controversies. The circumspection of Field Marshal Lord Birdwood's *Khaki and Gown* in 1941 on similar matters was sufficiently marked to be especially mentioned by Churchill, who contributed the foreword.

There was even a handful of leading participants such as the former Master-General of the Ordnance, Sir Stanley von Donop, who deliberately chose to keep their silence but this was not the usual course. Indeed, it was sometimes the case that individuals apparently uninterested in presenting a public defence of their actions were privately active in their own cause or that of others. As David French has demonstrated, Haig was a prime example of the former, while the latter included Major-General Sir Wyndham Childs, whose *Episodes and Reflections* in 1930 omitted anything 'which could even remotely hurt the feelings of those who figure therein or their relatives or friends'. None the less, Childs was appalled by the account in Duff Cooper's biography of Haig in 1935 of the intrigues against French and communicated privately with Lloyd George on the understanding that his assistance should not be revealed.[13]

[12] Hodder & Stoughton Ledgers, Guildhall Library MS 16312, vols. 18-20; Gilbert, *Churchill*, iv. (London, 1974), 751-4; ibid. v. 12, 229; M. G. Fry, *Lloyd George and Foreign Policy, 1890-1916* (Montreal, 1977), 2-4; Owen, *Tempestuous Journey*, 699-701, 724-5; Egerton, 'Lloyd George's War Memoirs', 55-94; Note by Sylvester on talks with MGM Studios, 6 June 1934, Lloyd George MSS, G/214.

[13] Churchill to Clementine Churchill, 29 Dec. 1921, Gilbert, *Churchill*, companion volume, v. pt. 3, 1706-7; General Sir Charles Harington, *Tim Harington Looks Back* (London, 1940); id., *Plumer of Messines* (London, 1935), pp. xiii-xvi; Field Marshal Lord Birdwood, *Khaki and Gown* (London, 1941), 7; von Donop to Edmonds, 7 Mar. 1925, Edmonds papers, II/1/126a; Maj.-Gen. Sir Charles Callwell, *Experiences of a Dug-out, 1914-1918* (London, 1920), 195-7; D. French, 'Sir Douglas Haig's Reputation,

However, for the most part, memorialists or biographers had a clear intention. A number of works were little more than hagiography including Chapman-Huston's and Rutter's biography of General Sir John Cowans in 1924, Frederick Maurice's biography of Haldane, proclaiming him the 'greatest Secretary of State for War England has ever had', and Dewar's and Boraston's *Sir Douglas Haig's Command* in 1922. As Richard Holmes's essay in this volume will later make clear, a significant number of early authors were protagonists on one side or another of the debate over the reputations of Kitchener, French, and Smith-Dorrien but some, such as Callwell's two biographical contributions, *Experiences of a Dug Out* in 1920 and *Stray Recollections* three years later, were also personal vindications—in this case of his role as Director of Military Operations. Some other contributions to the Kitchener or French debates, such as V. W. Germains's *The Truth About Kitchener* in 1925 or one of the Hon. Gerald French's attempts to retrieve his father's reputation, *French Replies to Haig*, in 1936 actually ranged widely over post-war controversies. In seeking to defend Kitchener, for example, Germains denigrated both Robertson and Lloyd George as lacking his genius and knowledge, claiming that 'we are entitled to deduce from all this that a Battle of the Somme fought by Lord Kitchener in 1916 would have been a blow similar to that struck by Ludendorff almost on the same ground in 1918'. With a foreword by Lloyd George, Gerald French's volume was an extended commentary on Duff Cooper's biography of Haig.[14]

Some authors had a highly individual cause to plead like General Sir Aylmer Haldane whose *A Soldier's Saga* in 1948 specifically refuted allegations about his conduct of attacks in 1915 made in Philip Gibbs's *The Realities of War* published in 1920 or Major-General J. F. C. Fuller and Major-General Sir Ernest Swinton who were equally concerned to record their own contribution to the development of the tank. Swinton clearly found the whole experience of setting his thoughts down cathartic,

1918-1928: A Note', *Historical Journal*, 28/4 (1985), 953-60; Maj.-Gen. Sir Wyndham Childs, *Episodes and Reflections* (London, 1930), p. vii; Childs to Lloyd George, 23 Sept. and 2 Oct. 1935, Lloyd George MSS, G/211; Duff Cooper, *Haig*, 2 vols. (London, 1935-6).

[14] D. Chapman-Huston and O. Rutter, *General Sir John Cowans: The Quartermaster-General of the Great War*, 2 vols. (London, 1924); Maj.-Gen. Sir F. Maurice, *Haldane of Cloan*, 2 vols. (London, 1937-9); G. A. B. Dewar and J. H. Boraston, *Sir Douglas Haig's Command, 1915-18*, 2 vols. (London, 1922); Maj.-Gen. Sir Charles Callwell, *Stray Recollections*, 2 vols. (London, 1923); V. W. Germains, *The Truth About Kitchener* (London, 1925), 219, 228, 240, 262-3; The Hon. G. French, *French Replies to Haig* (London, 1936).

writing to Liddell Hart in December 1931 that each successive draft had enabled him to eradicate 'personal bitterness or peevish bleating' since 'the passage of the years has acted like a carpenter's plane on my soul and shaved off the grooves dug in it by events'. But if Liddell Hart had failed to detect any bitterness, Hankey reported to Swinton in May 1932 that one reader in the War Office had concluded the manuscript of *Eyewitness* to be the work of a man with a grievance.[15]

Those who had been dismissed from office or command had an even stronger motive for presenting a public defence. Lord Haldane, who had been effectively hounded from office for allegedly pro-German views when the Asquith administration fell in May 1915, began privately circulating a 'dossier' in April 1916 to demonstrate the perspicacity of his pre-war ideas on foreign policy and his creation of the British Expeditionary Force. The dossier and subsequent newspaper articles became the basis for *Before the War* in 1920. Both this and his posthumously published autobiography were written, in the words of Edward Spiers, with 'every advantage of hindsight' and were 'sedulously compiled for the benefit of posterity'. Without doubt, they succeeded in restoring Haldane's reputation, the *Times Literary Supplement* greeting the autobiography in 1929 as by 'one of the half-dozen men who, above all others, made possible the ultimate defeat of the Germans'.

But the principal victim of the establishment of the coalition in May 1915 had been Churchill. The later volumes of *The World Crisis* went beyond memoir in covering events in which Churchill had had no direct role but, as indicated by the letter already quoted, the first two volumes were a formidable defence of his time at the Admiralty and of his advocacy of the Dardanelles expedition. Indeed, it was Churchill who had been instrumental in persuading the Cabinet in January 1922 to allow ministers the right to use official documents in their own cause following the publication of passages critical of him in Esher's *The Tragedy of Lord Kitchener*. When Lloyd George's successor as premier, Andrew Bonar Law, appeared to put a different construction on access to Cabinet records in February 1923 in answering Commons questions on Churchill's use of official telegrams in the first volume of *The World Crisis*, Churchill again vigorously asserted his right to defend himself. Singling out the personal criticism he detected in both Julian Corbett's official naval

[15] Gen. Sir Aylmer Haldane, *A Soldier's Saga* (Edinburgh and London, 1948), 303-4; Philip Gibbs, *The Realities of War* (London, 1920), 22-36; Maj.-Gen. J. F. C. Fuller, *Memoirs of an Unconventional Soldier* (London, 1936); Maj.-Gen. Sir Ernest Swinton, *Eyewitness* (London, 1932); Swinton to Hart, 1 Dec. 1931, Liddell Hart papers, 1/670; Hankey to Swinton, 5 May 1932, ibid. 1/352/228 (also Swinton papers, C).

history of the war and C. E. W. Bean's official Australian history, Churchill declared that 'it would appear unfair and unreasonable that a Minister should be the only person debarred from stating his own case in regard to war matters in which he has been held responsible'.[16]

Among soldiers, Hubert Gough was ultimately successful in clearing his name following his dismissal from the Fifth Army in March 1918. Assisted by the publication of W. Shaw Sparrow's *The Fifth Army in March 1918* in 1921 and by Lord Birkenhead's *The Turning Points of History* in 1930, Gough made his case in both his memoir in 1931, the separate publication of its relevant chapters as *The March Retreat* three years later, and in periodic forays into the national press. Gough blamed Lloyd George for his dismissal but, after his critique of Lloyd George's fourth volume of memoirs was reported in the *Sunday Chronicle* and other newspapers in March 1935, Liddell Hart effected reconciliatory meetings between the two, culminating in Gough's collaboration on Lloyd George's sixth volume and a public letter of apology from Lloyd George in April 1936.[17]

Less successful in his post-war campaigning was Frederick Maurice, whose public condemnation of Lloyd George in the press on 7 May 1918 was long to remain a touchstone of the subsequent civil-military controversies interpreted according to taste—be it as the act of 'gross insubordination' depicted by Leo Amery in 1953 or the act of 'great moral courage' described by Spears in 1972. Maurice himself circulated an account of the affair in May 1918 and wrote a series of articles in the *Westminster Gazette* in June 1922 which were then issued as a pamphlet,

---

[16] R. B. Haldane, *Before the War* (London, 1920); E. M. Spiers, *Haldane: An Army Reformer* (Edinburgh, 1980), 11-28, 187; *Times Literary Supplement* (21 Feb. 1929); Lord Esher, *The Tragedy of Lord Kitchener* (London, 1921); Naylor, *Man and an Institution*, 117-18; Churchill to Bonar Law, 3 Mar. 1923, Gilbert, *Churchill*, companion volume, v. pt. 1 (London, 1979), 32-6.

[17] Gen. Sir Hubert Gough, *Soldiering On* (London, 1954), 211-23, 255; id., *The March Retreat* (London, 1934); Farrar-Hockley, *Goughie*, 350-9; W. Shaw Sparrow, *The Fifth Army in March 1918* (London, 1921); Liddell Hart papers, 1/323/1, 22, 26-9; Gough to Lloyd George, 3 May and 3 Oct. 1936 and Sylvester to Gough, 13 June 1936, Lloyd George MSS, G/215; Capt. B. Liddell Hart, *The Memoirs of Captain Liddell Hart*, 2 vols. (London, 1965), i. 367. For Gough's duels with the official historian, Edmonds, see T. H. E. Travers, *The Killing Ground: The British Army, the Western Front and the Emergence of Modern Warfare, 1900-1918* (London, 1987), 203-49. For the official history generally, see D. French, 'Official but not History: Sir James Edmonds and the Official History of the Great War', *Journal of the Royal United Services Institute for Defence Studies*, 131/1 (1986), 58-63 and J. Luvaas, 'The First British Official Historians', in R. Higham (ed.), *Official Histories: Essays and Bibliographies from Around the World* (Manhattan, Kan., 1970), 488-96.

Intrigues of the War, with Maurice's former GSO1, the Duke of Northumberland, taking formal responsibility for publication so that he could demand trial by his peers if a prosecution was brought by government. Maurice also mounted a major assault on Lloyd George's memoirs while, earlier, he had assisted Robertson in the preparation of *Soldiers and Statesmen*, Robertson writing appreciatively in January 1926: 'I have adopted *all* your suggestions and think they were necessary, and are an improvement.' However, it was not until the publication of extracts from Frances Stevenson's diary relating to the 'burnt paper'—a recollection from her work on Lloyd George's memoirs in October 1934—by Beaverbrook in *Men and Power* in 1956 that Lloyd George's own duplicity during the Maurice debate on 9 May 1918 became widely known. Nevertheless, it took even longer for the almost universal assumption that Lloyd George had deliberately held back troops in Britain in the winter of 1917/18 to be discredited as a fabrication of Maurice and other military opponents of the prime minister.[18]

The charge of withholding men from the mobilized reserves in Britain was not one levelled against Lloyd George by Robertson but, of course, both *From Private to Field Marshal* in 1921 and *Soldiers and Statesmen* five years later were skilfully constructed statements of the 'westerner's' case. They also portrayed Robertson's resignation as CIGS in February 1918 as a consequence of his putting duty to country before duty to ministers. In unemotional terms which continued to attract praise for his moderation, Robertson's books advanced what became a familiar charge echoed by Asquith, Grey, and others that Lloyd George should not have sought second opinions to supplement that of his principal military adviser. If Lloyd George had no confidence in Robertson or Haig then, it was reasoned, he should have had the courage to dismiss them. Cyril Falls detected in the somewhat difficult thematic composition of *Soldiers and Statesmen* 'a certain inelasticity both of thought and of temper, which to a small extent justified the impatience of statesmen while being instructed', while in 1933 Liddell Hart provided Lloyd George with a

---

[18] Amery, *My Political Life*, ii. 154; E. L. Spears, 'Introduction', in Nancy Maurice (ed.), *The Maurice Case* (London, 1972), 3–56, which also reproduces *Intrigues of the War* (pp. 171–5) and other documents; Robertson to Maurice, 12 Jan. 1926, Maurice papers, 3/5/158; press cuttings on Maurice's reaction to Lloyd George's memoirs, ibid. 4/1/3; Beaverbrook, *Men and Power*, 262–3; A. J. P. Taylor (ed.), *Lloyd George: A Diary by Frances Stevenson* (London, 1971), 281–2; D. Woodward, *Lloyd George and the Generals* (Newark, Del., 1983), 236–7; id., 'Did Lloyd George Starve the British Army of Men Prior to the German Offensive of 21 March 1918?', *Historical Journal*, 27/1 (1984), 241–52.

detailed critique of Robertson's military assumptions as revealed by the same book. None the less, Robertson's reputation was enhanced by his publications at least until the appearance of Lloyd George's memoirs.[19]

Certainly, Robertson's charges and those of other soldiers and politicians including Asquithian Liberals like the MP for Pembrokeshire, W. F. Roch, in 1920 and Sir Charles Mallet in 1930 weighed heavily on Lloyd George, who was delayed from beginning serious work on his memoirs until 1932—a certain amount of preparatory work had been undertaken by Swinton acting as principal research assistant between 1922 and 1925 and some of Swinton's drafts were eventually included without substantial alteration. As early as 30 November 1918 A. G. Gardiner's article, 'Mr Lloyd George and Unity of Command: A Legend and the Truth' in the *Daily News* had challenged the view that the prime minister was 'the man who won the war'. In 1922 the publication of Boraston's and Dewar's *Sir Douglas Haig's Command* had been rushed forward in an attempt to do damage to Lloyd George in the November general election campaign. While the final stimulus appears to have been Hankey's own declared intention to start a memoir, a pivotal event in Lloyd George's decision to press ahead with his memoirs after the various delays was Callwell's biography of Henry Wilson. Writing in the *Daily News*, Lloyd George attempted to counter Wilson's version of his conversations with the prime minister: 'I need hardly add that I never uttered many of the observations, some of them extremely foolish, attributed to me in these diaries.' At the same time, he told Hankey, 'I must publish my story.'

With the continuing attacks from other authors in the intervening period, Lloyd George's frustration was apparent in his violent reaction in April 1933 to the King's reported displeasure with his manuscript: 'Why should the King be against my book? Was he against Arthur's book on Kitchener, or against the book [by Charteris] on Haig? No, he was not. He raised no objection to what was said about me, yet when I am about to defend myself he does not like it. He can go to Hell!' When his first volume appeared in September 1933 the preface indicated that Lloyd George's shelves 'groan under the burden of war autobiographies' and he used the same imagery in a letter to Hankey in April 1934: 'My shelves groan under their mutilated, bowlderised, distorted

---

[19] Field Marshal Sir William Robertson, *From Private to Field Marshal* (London, 1921), 255, 328, 383-6; id., *Soldiers and Statesmen*, ii. 300-2; Asquith, *Memories and Reflections*, ii. 150-5; Cooper, *Haig*, ii. 435; Sir Sam Fay, *The War Office at War* (London, 1937), 115-39; Falls, *War Books*, 73-4; Hart to Lloyd George, 19 May 1933, Lloyd George MSS, G/212; Liddell Hart papers, 15/2/25 (also 11/1933/14).

quotation. I must in all justice not to myself but to public and posterity, tell the whole truth.'

Clearly, Lloyd George did not intend to spare those he considered either 'skunks' or 'charlatans' and, in the words of *The Times*, he had 'not forgotten, still less forgiven, a single acidulated reference in recent first-hand narratives of the War to the most energetic and effective of those whom Sir Henry Wilson was accustomed to disparage as "frocks".' The fourth volume was a massive assault on the reputations of Haig and Robertson, *The Army, Navy and Air Force Gazette* commenting that, if true, the charges robbed the two soldiers 'of any right to the public esteem in which they have been held up to the present, for they show them as lying, dissembling and misleading the ministers responsible for the conduct of the War in order that the offensive they had planned should not be interfered with'. The volume provoked predictable outrage from soldiers like Maurice and Major-General Sir Charles Gwynn, who devoted a series of articles to the charges in the *Morning Post* in September and October 1934.

But Lloyd George's belated literary revenge was still not sated, his secretary, A. J. Sylvester recording in the latter month that Lloyd George 'was very sick that Haig and Robertson were not alive. He intended to blow their ashes to smithereens in his fifth volume. Unfortunately, he could not get at them personally.' In his sixth volume published in November 1936 Lloyd George returned in full measure criticisms of his earlier volumes, maintaining in the light of the revelations in Duff Cooper's biography of Haig that the living also had rights since Haig's own diary comments 'must silence the reproof directed against my memoirs on the absurd grounds that they occasionally express adverse opinions on the strategy of Generals who have now passed away'. Lloyd George made further capital from the publication of his Passchendaele chapters in a separate pamphlet, *The Campaign of the Mud*, while he also added a 22-page appendix of soldiers' letters in support of his case to the abridged two-volume edition of his memoirs in 1938. Almost the last of the major statements by leading participants, Lloyd George's memoirs were certainly crucial in establishing a particular image of Passchendaele as one of 'the most gigantic, tenacious, grim, futile and bloody fights ever waged'—Churchill had chosen to concentrate on the Somme—and in general they were, to echo the conclusion of George Egerton, 'a success judged by all criteria of intentional functions'.[20]

[20] W. Roch, *Mr Lloyd George and the War* (London, 1920); Sir Charles Mallet, *Mr Lloyd George* (London, 1930); Fraser, 'Cabinet Secrecy', 397–409; Egerton, 'Lloyd

But if many memoirs or biographies served to enhance or rescue a reputation, others failed in their object. A few reviewers of Beaverbrook's *Politicians and the War* like Robert Donald writing in the *Evening Standard* in May 1928 may have believed that the book was 'not handicapped by a motive', but most rightly recognized its unqualified praise of Bonar Law. But Bonar Law was an unacceptable hero to contemporaries and it was not until the publication of a single-volume edition in 1960 that Beaverbrook found himself hailed by A. J. P. Taylor as 'Tacitus and Aubrey rolled into one'. Worse were those books which actually succeeded in destroying the reputation of author or subject. Primarily, this was a fate of the more candid accounts. Margot Asquith paid the price for breaking new stylistic ground in her irreverent autobiography, which was savaged by the press. Repington's *The First World War*, which drew heavily on his frank diaries, made money but, according to Edmonds, the gossip and intrigues thus laid bare lost Repington his 'social position'. From the evidence of the diaries, Cyril Falls adjudged Repington 'an elderly thruster living in the greatest comfort, dining and wining with all the prettiest and most charming ladies, and from the vantage of Hampstead continually calling for more sacrifices . . .'. There was also a merciless spoof in *Punch* of 'War to the Knife (and Fork)': 'Spent the morning in the War Office, showing everyone how the work there ought to be done. Then to Downing Street to put things right there. Lunched at Claridge's with six leading Ladies, all of them cheery souls.'[21]

However, the most damaging biography of all was Callwell's two volumes on Henry Wilson, which did lasting harm to Wilson's reputation through extensive quotation from the contentious diaries. Even now, in the words of Keith Jeffery, Wilson seems an 'overambitious, self-serving monster, with such violent passions and prejudices as to appear at times actually unbalanced'. F. S. Oliver declined Lady Wilson's offer

George's War Memoirs', 55-94; Woodward, *Lloyd George and the Generals*, 9; French, 'Sir Douglas Haig's Reputation', 953-60; Fry, *Lloyd George and Foreign Policy*, 3-4; C. Cross (ed.), *Life with Lloyd George: The Diary of A. J. Sylvester, 1931-45* (London, 1975), 94, 111-12 quoting entries for 18 Apr. and 3 Oct. 1934; Brig.-Gen. J. Charteris, *Field Marshal Earl Haig* (London, 1929); Lloyd George, *War Memoirs*, i. p. vii; Lloyd George to Hankey, 18 Apr. 1934, Lloyd George MSS, G/212; *The Times* (27 Nov. 1934); Lloyd George, *War Memoirs*, iv. 2110 and vi. 3373; *Army, Navy and Air Force Gazette* (1 Nov. 1934). A useful collection of press cuttings on Lloyd George's memoirs can be found in Liddell Hart papers, 1/450.

[21] *Evening Standard* (17 May 1928); Chamberlain, *Down the Years*, 107; Taylor, *Beaverbrook*, 645; M. Bonham-Carter (ed.), *The Autobiography of Margot Asquith* (London, 1962), pp. xi-xxix; Luvaas, *Education of an Army*, 327; Falls, *War Books*, 227; *Punch* (27 Oct. 1920).

to write the biography for fear of 'being tied by the leg by the widow' and it was generally supposed that Callwell had decided upon publication of lengthy extracts against the advice of friends through Lady Wilson's 'reverence' for the diaries. Callwell was aware of the likely public impact, writing to Boraston in April 1926 that they were 'extremely outspoken, and very critical of most soldiers on the British side'. He had resolved, therefore, to 'present the position as regards our soldiers reasonably impartially and not to accept all that H.W. says without comment'. Nevertheless, there was little apparent qualification of Wilson's views in the published biography and, in any case, Callwell had decided that 'as far as I am concerned, the politicians must take their chance'.

A devastating attack, which was in itself something of a *succès de scandale*, was launched on Wilson by the professor of the history of medicine at McGill University and a well-known Canadian literary figure, Sir Andrew Macphail, in *Three Persons* in 1929. For Macphail, it was rare indeed for 'a friend to publish the writings of a friend, and thereby exhibit him as a public spectacle' while Wilson himself stood revealed as an 'inhuman figure, calculating, callous without a single generous sentiment or kind word'. Asquith and Churchill were equally appalled by the revelation of what the latter termed Wilson's 'nightthoughts' and, just as publication was a considerable stimulus to Lloyd George's memoirs, it also marked a critical turning-point in Liddell Hart's view of the war and the true beginning of his disillusionment with the generals. Prior to 1927, Liddell Hart had seen Wilson as a 'genius' but now, 'Never has any man so condemned himself'.[22]

One subsidiary function of some of the memoirs and biographies was also to serve the national interest in terms of the presentation of Britain's case for entering the war and the blame to be attached to Germany for its outbreak. Thus, Asquith and Grey or, more specifically, J. A. Spender acting for Grey, received Foreign Office assistance in the compilation of *The Genesis of War* and *Twenty-Five Years* respectively. The same

[22] K. Jeffery, 'An Introduction to the Papers of Field Marshal Sir Henry Wilson', *Imperial War Museum Review*, 4 (1989), 12-21; Author interview with Mrs Beatrix Rabagliati (née Oliver), 18 Dec. 1985; B. Collier, *Brasshat* (London, 1961), 13-14; Callwell to Boraston, 24 Apr. 1926, Imperial War Museum, Boraston papers, 71/13/2 Folder A (I am grateful to Dr Jeffery for bringing this letter to my attention); B. Ash, *The Lost Dictator* (London, 1968), pp. v, 51; Falls, *War Books*, 55; Sir A. Macphail, *Three Persons* (London, 1929), 3-99; Asquith, *Memories and Reflections*, ii. 155; Winston S. Churchill, *Great Contemporaries* (London, 1937), 229; Luvaas, *Education of an Army*, 391 quoting Hart to Scammell, 22 Mar. 1932; Brian Bond, *Liddell Hart: A Study of his Military Thought* (London, 1977), 21, 54; Roskill, *Hankey*, ii. 533; Basil Liddell Hart, *Through the Fog of War* (London, 1938), 125-85.

facility was also extended to Churchill, not only for his first volume but also for his last volume, *The Aftermath*, published in 1929, Sir William Tyrrell authorizing the Foreign Office's historian, Professor James Headlam-Morley, to continue helping Churchill in December 1927: 'By all means. Give him all the help you can without stint. The more you give him the better it will be & he deserves it thoroughly.' Churchill maintained that he really needed information that 'fills the gaps of my memory and confirms the conclusions of my judgement' but he often incorporated Headlam-Morley's notes in their entirety. In fact, it had already been widely recognized abroad that Grey's account was 'bound to be read with high expectations for the truths they tell us in regard to the origins of the war' and it had been attacked by German apologists. Even before the war, some Foreign Office officials had begun to advocate opening archives for historians' inspection in Britain's cause and the process culminated in the decision in 1924 to launch an official series of *British Documents on the Origins of the War*, the first appearing in December 1926.[23]

While the Foreign Office had relented to some extent in terms of access to its records, this was not true of the War Office and, of course, Hankey was determined on establishing and maintaining the secrecy of Cabinet records. However, as already noted, the Cabinet Office was effectively forced to treat the period of the Great War as an exception to its fledgling rules and authors such as French, Arthur, Robertson, Callwell, Boraston, and Dewar freely reproduced official memoranda and documents in their possession. To the despair of his legal adviser, Beaverbrook was especially prone to quoting letters without clearing copyright and also highly acquisitive in the matter of documents, even securing one of Churchill's October 1914 telegrams from Antwerp of which Churchill himself had no copy. It seems possible Beaverbrook obtained the telegram from the former War Office Secretary, Sir Reginald Brade to whose papers he had access, and he also drew on Bonar Law's papers and the private letters sent by Asquith to Venetia Stanley. By the time he wrote *Men and Power* in 1956 Beaverbrook had accumulated even more papers including those of Lloyd George.[24]

[23] Asquith, *Genesis of War*, p. vii; K. Robbins, *Sir Edward Grey* (London, 1971), 366-7; Tyrrell to Headlam-Morley, 7 Dec. 1927 and Churchill to Headlam-Morley, 6 Dec. 1921 and 16 Jan. 1923, CAC, HDLM Box 48; H. Lutz, *Lord Grey and the World War* (London, 1928), 10; K. A. Hamilton, 'The Pursuit of Enlightened Patriotism: The British Foreign Office and Historical Researchers during the Great War and its Aftermath', *Bulletin of the Institute of Historical Research*, 61/146 (1988), 316-44.

[24] Gilbert, *Churchill*, companion volume, v. pt. 1, 32-9; Hankey to Lloyd George, 8 Apr. 1933, Lloyd George MSS G/212; Withers to Doidge, 2 Oct. 1928, Beaverbrook

None the less, most authors had relatively limited access to such documents—even Robertson was compelled to ask Maurice for his recollections of the conclusions of the War Policy Committee in May 1917 because he could not remember and had no record. Thus, more often than not, even authors like Beaverbrook, Churchill, and Lloyd George had to turn to others for assistance. In any case, it was the custom of all three of the latter to circulate widely typeset or proofed drafts for comment. In this way Lloyd George's sounding-board included Sir Eric Geddes, Austen Chamberlain, Lord Lee, Sir Alfred Herbert, Vice-Admiral R. G. H. Henderson, Rear-Admiral Mark Kerr, and Captain Peter Wright, while Beaverbrook consulted Churchill, Brade, Robertson, Austen Chamberlain, Birkenhead, Lloyd George, and McKenna's widow. However, he did not always act on their advice, telling Churchill in 1930 that 'If I went on cutting out passages in the book there would be nothing left but praise of everybody for everything.' The other drawback was that Beaverbrook tended to put his own gloss on drafts prepared for him by collaborators such as J. L. Garvin or the chief political leader writer of the *Daily Express*, Maurice Woods, to the extent of inventing conversations and much else.[25]

Churchill also depended upon a wide number of collaborators besides Headlam-Morley and other Foreign Office or Committee of Imperial Defence Staff like Desmond Morton who assisted on the final volume. Naval chapters, for example, were read by Rear-Admiral Jackson, Sir Graham Greene, Roger Keyes, and Admiral of the Fleet Earl Beatty, a member of whose staff, Vice-Admiral Kenneth Dewar, was largely responsible for the sections on submarine warfare. Both Sir Ian Hamilton and the official historian, Aspinall-Oglander, supplied information on military operations at the Dardanelles while one of Churchill's most imaginative acts was to enlist Haig's assistance on the second part of the third volume, which he generally saw as balancing the criticism he had

papers, G/8; Withers to Beaverbrook, 18, 19, and 25 Feb. 1929, ibid. G/9; Churchill to Beaverbrook, 23 Mar. 1927, Gilbert, *Churchill*, companion volume, v. pt. 1, 970-1; Taylor, *Beaverbrook*, 104-5; copies of the correspondence of Venetia Stanley, Beaverbrook papers, G/8; and Brade's diary, ibid. G/9.

[25] Robertson to Maurice, 30 Jun. 1925, Maurice papers, 4/5/77; Stephens to Sylvester, 4 and 20 Dec. 1932, Lloyd George MSS, G/211; for Lloyd George correspondence with Lee, Herbert, Henderson, and Kerr, ibid. G/213; Wright file, ibid. G/215; proofs submitted to Birkenhead, Lloyd George, Churchill, and Brade, Beaverbrook MSS, G/6; Mrs McKenna to Beaverbrook, 5 July 1928, Robertson to Beaverbrook, 30 Aug. 1928 and 27 Feb. 1929, Beaverbrook to Churchill, 25 Dec. 1930, ibid. G/8; Stubbs, 'Beaverbrook as Historian', 235-53; Fraser, 'Lord Beaverbrook's Fabrications', 147-66.

directed at the generals in the first part dealing with the Somme. On occasions, Churchill did change his narrative as when modifying criticism of Bonar Law at Beaverbrook's request, but his work remained highly partial towards friends like Beatty, Hamilton, or Rawlinson and highly disparaging to selected victims such as Admirals Milne, Troubridge, de Robeck, Jellicoe, and Evan-Thomas. His narratives also showed little interest in technical matters, dwelled on minor successes, and, more often than not, characterized failure as the working of the fates.[26]

Many authors turned to Hankey or to Edmonds for assistance. Among those to whom Edmonds supplied information were Charteris, Duff Cooper, Gough, Smith-Dorrien, Swinton, Spears, Churchill, and Lloyd George. In the case of Churchill, it would appear that Edmonds, who specifically asked that his help should not be acknowledged publicly, used *The World Crisis* to project views regarding the conduct of the Somme battle that he did not feel free to put forward in the official history. However, it must also be said that Edmonds did not agree with Churchill's statistical conclusion that the British suffered casualties in the ratio of 3:2 to those of the Germans, the calculation of the 'blood test' lying at the heart of Churchill's critique of the Somme strategy. Churchill's figures were also challenged by Sir Charles Oman but it would appear that they were generally more accurate than those paraded by Edmonds. One of Edmonds's former assistants, Lieutenant-Colonel Charles Hordern, was later appointed by Churchill to work as researcher for the Eastern Front volume. Hankey was also not keen that his assistance to 'old pals' should be acknowledged. Indeed, he initially declined to help Spears in the preparation of *Prelude to Victory*, an account of the Nivelle offensive and its consequences published in 1939, but eventually relented and supplied details of the Calais Conference from his own diary.[27]

---

[26] Gilbert, *Churchill: The Wilderness Years* (London, 1981), 17; id., *Churchill*, v. 298-9, 311, 318-19. This paragraph largely draws on R. Prior, *Churchill's World Crisis as History* (London, 1983), which is a penetrating analysis of Churchill's historical judgement.

[27] Edmonds papers, II/1/43 (Gough), 111a (Smith-Dorrien), 162 (Spears), 239 (Gough), 243 (Charteris), 288-9 (Duff Cooper); Swinton correspondence with Edmonds, ibid. II/5/1-22; Hart to Edmonds, 17 May 1934 and Edmonds to Hart, 23 May 1934, Liddell Hart papers, 1/259/77 and 78; Lloyd George to Edmonds, 28 Dec. 1933, Lloyd George MSS, G/211; Churchill, *World Crisis*, iii. pt. 1, 36-62; Prior, *Churchill's World Crisis*, 176-7, 212-14; Sir Charles Oman, 'The German Losses on the Somme', in Lord Sydenham, *et al.*, *The World Crisis by Winston Churchill: A Criticism* (London, 1927), 40-65; M. J. Williams, 'The Treatment of the German Losses on the Somme in the

It was also Hankey who had to police the compilation of memoirs by former Cabinet ministers under the evolving rules formulated after 1919. It was a demanding task on top of Hankey's other duties, the Cabinet Secretary apologizing to Spears in June 1934 for not returning proofs earlier due to the 'gruelling business' of checking Lloyd George's manuscript simultaneously with Lady Blanche Dugdale's biography of A. J. Balfour. Indeed, earlier in October 1933 Hankey had also apologized to Churchill for not spotting an error in the account in his first volume of the celebrated meeting of the War Council on 5 August 1914: 'I always have to give a warning to the author that time does not permit me to check the different points, and that it is only where doubt is aroused in my mind, or on special request, that I do so.'

Churchill's use of supporting documents—Hankey was later to point out that just one chapter of Churchill's first volume had contained twenty-five quotations for January 1915 alone—was extensive. Indeed, when faced with Churchill's refusal to allow him to publish his own account in 1945—the wartime coalition had again resolved to exempt its own future memoirs from restriction—Hankey was astonished by the 'affrontery' of one who was 'practically the first to publish all the inner secrets of his rows with Fisher, and so many intimate and confidential letters'. In fact, Churchill was not averse to omitting key sections from the documents he used, a point noted by *The Times* in reviewing the second volume in October 1923. But the controversy surrounding the use of official memoranda in Churchill's first volume and Churchill's claim that he had received the consent of the former prime minister, Asquith, to publish documents relating to his administration actually established the precedent of seeking prime ministerial authority prior to publication given the seeming ineffectiveness of the Privy Councillor's oath of secrecy. Thus, Churchill's later volumes were cleared through the agency of Hankey, who succeeded in modifying some of Churchill's criticism of others. It was also Hankey who suggested that Churchill extend his account into the post-war period. However, Churchill's later volumes posed less of a threat since, as Churchill himself wrote to Beaverbrook, 'Nothing can obscure the fact that I was a much less important person in this period than in the former one.' By far the

British Official History', *Journal of the Royal United Services Institute for Defence Studies*, 111/641 (1966), 69-74; Gilbert, *Churchill*, v. 363; id., companion volume, v. pt. 2, 349; Spears to Hankey, 1 Feb. 1933, CAC, SPRS 1/159; Hankey to Spears 3 Feb. 1933, 29 Apr., and 30 Sept. 1935, Spears papers, 2/3/57-9; Hankey to Spears, 25 Oct. 1939, ibid. 6/2/3; E. L. Spears, *Prelude to Victory* (London, 1939).

greater problem, therefore, was posed by Lloyd George, who also sought to establish his case through extensive documentation.[28]

Like Churchill and Addison, Lloyd George declined to return any Cabinet documents in his possession when the attempt was made—albeit on somewhat dubious legality—following the Lansbury prosecution to secure all post-1919 papers from former ministers or their executors. In effect, there was little that could be done to prevent Lloyd George publishing what he wished although Ramsay Macdonald had successfully added the necessity to secure the King's permission for publication to that of the prime minister and Lloyd George agreed to allow Baldwin—acting as Lord President—and Hankey to act as arbiters. Hankey did his best to tone down Lloyd George's comments on individuals since, as in the case of Churchill's earlier work, he believed that it was undesirable for 'our national heroes' to be 'hauled off their pedestals'. The King in particular objected to Lloyd George's treatment of wartime Labour leaders such as Macdonald and Snowden now in government but the most that Lloyd George was prepared to do was to modify his comments on Churchill and Balfour and, in deference to the King, to remove a chapter on the wartime discussion of the 'Tsar's future residence' which reflected badly on the King.

Lloyd George could simply not be persuaded by Hankey that 'the more exacerbation you display, the greater will be the temptation of opponents and critics to say that you are partisan and a prejudiced witness'. Similarly, Lloyd George rarely took much note of the corrections to his military narratives by Liddell Hart, who had been secured as military adviser at Hankey's suggestion in April 1933. Liddell Hart's papers contain the most detailed comments on Lloyd George's drafts. On the chapter in the fifth volume entitled 'Wilson Turning Prophet', for example, Liddell Hart noted in May 1936, 'The argument in this chapter needs very careful handling—in order to avoid exposing yourself to the charge that you condemn the generals for the immoderation of their estimates in 1917, and then condemn them again because they tend to become sanely cautious in 1918'. However, in April 1934 Liddell Hart had commented to Hankey that while Lloyd George was

---

[28] Hankey to Spears, 4 June 1934, CAC, SPRS 1/159; Lady Blanche Dugdale, *A. J. Balfour*, 2 vols. (London, 1936); Hankey to Churchill, 13 Oct. 1933, CAC, HNKY 5/1; Hankey to Bridges, 15 May 1945, ibid. 25/1; Hankey to Jones, 28 Feb. 1945, ibid. 25/2; Gilbert, *Churchill*, v. 14; J. H. Plumb, 'The Historian', in *Churchill: Four Faces and the Man* (London, 1969), 119-51; Prior, *Churchill's World Crisis*, *passim*; Gilbert, *Churchill*, companion volume, v. pt. 1, 32-9, 888-9 (Churchill to Beaverbrook, 27 Nov. 1926); Roskill, *Hankey*, ii. 534.

ready to listen to suggestions, 'one notices that the points remain as they were in the next draft'. Thus, after pointing out a number of errors in the chapter on 'The Nivelle Affair' in the third volume, Liddell Hart lamented to Sylvester in May 1934 that Lloyd George's revisions did 'not appear to be very extensive'. Hankey clearly recognized the essential weakness of his position when noting in July 1936 that Lloyd George declined to be kinder to Haig: 'but as we have already discussed this and you remain adamant, I do not propose to pursue the matter further'. Moreover, it had already been agreed in April 1934 that Lloyd George could use his large accumulation of Cabinet documents providing paraphrasing and other suitable devices were employed 'so as to reduce to a minimum the impression that they are in fact quotations'.[29]

Liddell Hart maintained that Lloyd George's access to the facts was 'far superior to that of his critics' but there was no escaping that, as Liddell Hart wrote in reviewing the fifth and sixth volumes, 'the book is the man'. Indeed, while the drafts had been worked over by secretaries like Sylvester, Stevenson, and Malcolm Thomson and reworked by Norman Collins of the *News Chronicle*, Lloyd George remained very much in control at all stages of production. For all its copious documentation, therefore, Lloyd George's memoirs could not be other than another polemic. Only Hankey really rivalled Lloyd George's mastery of the facts but, of course, his account was not published until almost the moment when the public archives were opened. When it did appear, *The Supreme Command* had been purged of many of Hankey's more revealing diary entries and was not the book it might once have been.

Some of the inter-war memoirs and biographies have remained useful where, as in the case of Plumer or General Sir Nevil Macready, personal papers have not survived, but the majority have been exposed to the corrective of public accessibility to official records or the personal papers on which they were based. The distorting effects of the 'battle of the memoirs' on the historiography of the Great War has thus become apparent. In 1927 Lord Sydenham complained of *The World Crisis* that, 'The very attractiveness of Mr Churchill's writing of itself constitutes a danger; for the layman may well be led to accept facile phrase and

---

[29] Naylor, *Man and an Institution*, 206-9, 216-22; Hankey to Lloyd George, 30 Mar. 1933, 16 Apr. 1934, and 15 June 1936, and Lloyd George to Hankey, 18 Apr. 1934, Lloyd George MSS, G/212; Liddell Hart, *Memoirs*, i. 360-5; Hart to Lloyd George, 2 Mar. 1934 and 27 May 1936, and Hart to Sylvester, 2 May 1934, Liddell Hart papers, 1/450; Hart to Hankey, 28 Apr. 1934, ibid. 1/352/33; Hankey to Lloyd George, 21 and 26 Apr. 1934 and 16 July 1936, Lloyd George MSS, G/212.

seductive argument for hard fact and sober reasoning.'[30] At least for the historian, that danger grows increasingly less and the contributions of Churchill, Lloyd George, and the others can be more properly judged as outstanding examples of a distinctive literary genre.

[30] Liddell Hart, *Memoirs*, i. 361; id., review for *London Mercury* (Oct. 1936), Liddell Hart papers, 1/450; id., *Through the Fog of War*, 155-74; Egerton, 'Lloyd George's War Memoirs', 55-94; Roskill, *Hankey*, iii, 619-21; General Sir Nevil Macready, *Annals of an Active Life*, 2 vols. (London, n.d. [1925]), which is actually not very informative; Sydenham, *World Crisis of Winston Churchill*, 6.

5
Sir John French and Lord Kitchener
RICHARD HOLMES

The lines of battle between French and Kitchener were drawn long before the dispute between them burst into print. The seeds of the clash lay in character. French was a lively cavalry officer whose amorous exploits were legendary; Kitchener a dour engineer of monkish proclivities. French welcomed publicity, and counted journalists and press barons amongst his friends. Kitchener shunned it, and once greeted a group of expectant journalists with the cry: 'Get out of my way, you drunken swabs.'[1] French was an inspiring speaker: Kitchener was gruffly reticent. Kitchener was a high church Anglican: French had spiritualist leanings. Kitchener was imposingly tall, with upswept moustache, unblinking gaze, and outward calm: French was short, with a mercurial temperament which could not conceal pleasure or disapproval.

All this would not have mattered if the accidents of very different careers had not buffeted the men together. They first met in South Africa. In September 1899 the British government sent out an army corps under Sir Redvers Buller, who chose French to command his cavalry. Shortly after his arrival French won the little battle of Elandslaagte, making his reputation at a stroke. But reverses elsewhere caused the government to replace Buller with Lord Roberts, and with him came his chief of staff, Horatio Herbert Kitchener, Lord Kitchener of Khartoum, hitherto commander-in-chief of the Egyptian army and governor-general of the Sudan.

Kitchener and Roberts developed a plan for advancing on Bloemfontein and relieving the besieged town of Kimberley. French got wind of it when he was summoned to Cape Town in January 1900 to discuss another matter, and began to suspect that Roberts and Kitchener might have someone else in mind to command the cavalry. Although there was no evidence to support this, it was not an unreasonable fear, for French

[1] Philip Magnus, *Kitchener: Portrait of an Imperialist* (London, 1958), 133-4.

was a Buller man, and his patron had fallen from grace. He soon had doubts about Roberts' military ability, and clashed with Kitchener over a scheme to centralize transport. The operation itself developed well. French led the striking force around the Boer position on the Modder River, and burst through defences at Klip Drift to relieve Kimberley on 15 February, in an action that added fresh lustre to his reputation.[2]

The relief of Kimberley was followed by the pursuit of the main Boer army under Cronje. Roberts was ill, and sent a message saying that Kitchener's orders were to be regarded as his own: invested with this authority, Kitchener ordered an attack on the Boer laager at Paardeberg. The assault produced the heaviest losses in any single day's fighting in the war, and earned Kitchener the nickname 'K of chaos'.[3] When Roberts arrived he ordered the cessation of attacks, and Cronje surrendered a week later. Paardeberg strained relations between French on the one hand, and Kitchener and Roberts on the other, and a misunderstanding over fodder widened the rift. Worse still, French, whose views on shock action by cavalry were coloured by Elandslaagte and Klip Drift, was disturbed to find that Roberts favoured mounted infantry and mistrusted the *arme blanche*.[4]

Defeated in the field, the Boers embarked upon an increasingly bitter guerrilla war. Roberts returned to England in December 1900, leaving Kitchener in command. French was pleased by the change, for Kitchener did not preach heresy on cavalry tactics and seemed to have a sounder operational grasp than his predecessor. Kitchener, for his part, 'spoke in the highest terms' of French to the future King George V, and wrote to Roberts that he was 'quite first rate, and has the absolute confidence of all serving under him, as well as mine'.[5] French spent the remainder of the war in the eastern Transvaal and Cape Colony, where his slow progress disappointed Kitchener. 'French has not done much lately in the colony,' he told Roberts, 'I cannot make out why, the country is no doubt difficult but I expected more.'[6] But as Ian Hamilton, Kitchener's

[2] L. S. Amery (ed.), *The Times History of the War in South Africa* (London, 1900-9), iii. 394-5; Erskine Childers, *War and the Arme Blanche* (London, 1910), 67, 107; Maj.-Gen. Sir F. Maurice and Capt. H. M. Grant, *Official History of the War in South Africa* (London, 1906-10), ii. 36.
[3] Maurice and Grant, *Official History*, ii. 143-4.
[4] French diary, 5 Apr. 1900, Department of Documents, Imperial War Museum.
[5] Kitchener to Roberts, undated, in Sir George Arthur, *The Life of Lord Kitchener* (London, 1920), iii. 24; Sir Harold Nicolson, *King George V* (London, 1953), 71.
[6] Kitchener to Roberts, 17 Jan. 1902, Roberts papers, National Army Museum, 7101-23-30.

chief of staff, observed, French was: 'one of the very few men that Kitchener had trusted to do a job on his own'.[7]

French and Kitchener sailed for England after peace terms were agreed in the summer of 1902: they did not meet again until 1914. In the interim, French commanded 1 Corps till 1907, when he became inspector-general of the forces. In 1912 he succeeded Sir William Nicholson as chief of the imperial general staff, but resigned over the Curragh affair in 1914, though he remained commander-in-chief designate of the British Expeditionary Force. Kitchener went to India as commander-in-chief. Promoted field marshal on relinquishing the appointment in 1909, he narrowly failed to secure the post of Viceroy. Sent instead to govern Egypt, he was on leave in England when war came in 1914.

Kitchener hoped that war in Europe would not become his concern, and sought to return to Egypt. But the secretary of state for war had resigned, alongside French, as a result of the Curragh affair, and the prime minister, Asquith, held the office on a temporary basis. There was wide agreement amongst senior Liberals and Conservatives that Kitchener should go to the War Office, and on 3 August Lieutenant-Colonel Charles Repington, military correspondent of *The Times*, urged that his talents should not be wasted. Kitchener was already aboard the boat train for Calais when a message from the prime minister ordered him back to London. He was appointed secretary of state for war two days later.

Asquith regarded Kitchener's appointment as 'a hazardous experiment'.[8] He had initially favoured using Lord Haldane to do the work while he retained the seals of office himself. Haldane went to the War Office on 4 August, and told Ian Hamilton that he had done so precisely to keep Kitchener out of it.[9] The press clamour in favour of Kitchener and against the 'pro-German' Haldane helped persuade Asquith to opt for Kitchener, and the cross-party support enjoyed by the field marshal also contributed to his decision.

Both Asquith's initial reluctance to send Kitchener to the War Office, and the public ferment urging him to do so, are relevant to what followed. Asquith recognized that Kitchener's background made him unsuited for close association with politicians, a point with which Kitchener concurred.[10] Haldane believed himself a better prospect at the War Office

[7] Quoted in Maj. A. H. Farrar-Hockley, *The Commander* (London, 1957), 133.
[8] H. H. Asquith, *Memories and Reflections* (London, 1928), ii. 24.
[9] Diary of Lady Hamilton, 5 Aug. 1914, quoted in George H. Cassar, *Kitchener: Architect of Victory* (London, 1977), 175.
[10] Sir Percy Girouard to Joseph Chamberlain, 9 Dec. 1929, Chamberlain papers, quoted Cassar, *Kitchener*, 177.

than Kitchener, because soldiers would find it easier to work with him than with the autocratic field marshal.[11] That this should be the case was scarcely surprising, for Kitchener had no experience of the central organs of national defence, and his proconsular habits fitted uncomfortably into the tight departmental world of the War Office. He was so secretive that cabinet and military colleagues often found him difficult to deal with. Although used to hard work, he found the pressures of his post extremely wearing: Sir Archbibald Murray, who served under him at the War Office, felt that he was 'quite unfit to hold high office at a period of acute strain'.[12] He found it hard to delegate, and expended energy in matters better left to subordinates. In late 1914 he told French that he had ordered snow shoes from Canada for the army—a perfect illustration of misplaced organizing zeal.[13] If Kitchener's vices were known to the few, his virtues were a matter of public record. George Cassar, his most perceptive biographer, notes the importance of the press in creating the Kitchener legend. Although Kitchener had a low regard for journalists, he did look favourably on G. A. Steevens, whose *With Kitchener to Khartoum* and vigorous *Daily Mail* articles painted a picture of an 'inhumanly unerring' figure, a one-man military machine before whom ordinary mortals were helpless. The scale of his achievements abroad, allied, in a curious way, to his personal disregard for publicity, fostered the image of the almost godlike warlord.

Kitchener did indeed have great qualities. His energy and determination were awesome, and his recognition that the war would be a long one set him apart from most of his contemporaries. In his maiden speech in the Lords on 25 August he envisaged an army of thirty divisions within six or seven months, and refused to place an upper limit on the size of Britain's armies or measures necessary to maintain them.[14] The New Armies were his creation. His appeal, published on 6 August, conjured them into being, and his steely gaze stared out from recruiting posters. He mistrusted the Territorial Force, and raised the New Armies through the adjutant-general's branch of the War Office. Volunteers rushed to respond. He had his first hundred thousand by 12 September, over a million men had volunteered by the end of the year, and in all thirty New Army divisions were raised. Kitchener was conscious that the New Armies were his own. 'I have held up my finger and men are

[11] Stephen E. Koss, *Lord Haldane: Scapegoat for Liberalism* (London, 1968), 115-16.
[12] Stephen Roskill, *Hankey: Man of Secrets* (London, 1970), i. 161.
[13] Kitchener to French, 25 Nov. 1914, French papers.
[14] *The Times* (26 Aug. 1914).

flocking to me in thousands,' he was fond of remarking.[15] They were widely known as 'Kitchener's Armies', a fact which was little comfort to Sir John French, haunted by the spectre of Kitchener's armies marching to France with their founder striding purposefully at their head.

The events of early August 1914 came as no surprise to French. He had long believed in the high risk of European war, and had been intimately involved in the army's war plans, though their details were largely the work of the francophile gadfly Henry Wilson. French and Kitchener got off on the wrong foot when they attended Councils of War at 10 Downing Street on 5 and 6 August. At the first meeting French presented the staff's plan for a concentration around Maubeuge on the French left. He suggested that as British mobilization would now lag behind that of France, the Amiens area might be safer, but in any event the British Expeditionary Force should go to France as soon as possible. He then showed brief enthusiasm for a scheme for operating from Antwerp against the German right flank, much to the alarm of Wilson. There was agreement that the staff plan was sound, and on the morning of the 6th the cabinet agreed to send the BEF to France. At the Council of War that afternoon Kitchener, now formally installed as secretary of state, warned of a long conflict and advocated caution. French, who believed in a short war, pressed strongly for the immediate dispatch of five divisions. He lost the argument: the BEF was initially to comprise only four infantry divisions and a cavalry division.

French suspected, very early on, that Kitchener intended to meddle with the appointment which he regarded as the apogee of his military career. And Wilson, now sub-chief of the general staff in the BEF, clashed with Kitchener over disclosure of mobilization plans to the French. Wilson had far more influence on French than the well-meaning but fragile Archie Murray, the BEF's chief of the general staff, and the fact that he would now fuel suspicion of Kitchener boded ill. On 12 August French and Wilson persuaded Kitchener that the BEF should indeed concentrate around Maubeuge, though Kitchener's warnings of danger north of the Meuse pointed to a sound instinctive grasp of German planning.

The final plank of the springboard of mistrust from which Sir John plunged to war was laid by Kitchener's formal instructions to him as commander-in-chief of the BEF. These informed Sir John that his force was to collaborate with the French, but added that he should ensure 'the

[15] Trevor Royle, *The Kitchener Enigma* (London, 1985), 261-2.

minimum of losses and wastage', and take care in 'forward movements where large bodies of French troops are not engaged and where your Force may be unduly exposed to attack'. French was left in no doubt that 'your command is an entirely independent one and you will in no case come under the orders of any Allied general'.[16] John Terraine has rightly observed that the wording of the instructions was 'in places necessarily vague and even contradictory'.[17] Sir John was to co-operate with the French, but was to avoid heavy losses in doing so; he was warned of the danger of offensive operations, although he knew that the French war plan was offensive in character and that the BEF was expected to conform with it. Sir John was told that he was not under French command, but both the French War Minister and Joffre, the French commander-in-chief, had received what Lord Esher called *'quite the contrary impression.'*[18]

Sir John crossed to France on 14 August, met Joffre on the 16th, and on the following day he visited Lanrezac, commander of the French 5 Army on the BEF's right. The meeting was not a success, with Lanrezac joking at the expense of Sir John's schoolboy French, but giving him the impression that the 5 Army was indeed going to attack as planned. The truth was more sombre. Lanrezac was suspicious of German strength to his front, and already had doubts as to the wisdom of the offensive. He did not communicate these to Sir John, who arrived at GHQ at Le Cateau, confident that the offensive would take place as planned.

Bad news awaited him. Sir James Grierson, commander of 2 Corps, had died of a heart attack on his way to the concentration area. French immediately wired Kitchener, asking for Sir Herbert Plumer as a replacement. Instead he received Sir Horace Smith-Dorrien, an officer whose history of bad relations with French was a matter of common knowledge in the army. Smith-Dorrien believed that French nursed 'great jealousy of and personal animosity' towards him: French was infuriated by having his preference ignored.[19] Matters were not improved when Smith-Dorrien reported for duty on 20 August and told French that the King had asked him to report directly on the doings of 2 Corps.

[16] French's copy is in the French papers: the instructions are quoted in full in Sir James Edmonds (ed.), *Official History of the Great War: Military Operations, France and Belgium, 1914*, 2 vols.*(London, 1922-5), i. 444-5.
[17] John Terraine, *Mons: The Retreat to Victory* (London, 1960), 37.
[18] Esher to French, 3 Apr. 1915, French papers (original emphasis).
[19] Gen. Sir Horace Smith-Dorrien, *Memories of Forty-Eight Years' Service* (London, 1925), 375; French diary, 17 Aug. 1914.

The BEF advanced on 21 August, unaware of the worsening situation in Alsace-Lorraine, and of the might of the German armies swinging down upon it. On the 22nd GHQ learnt that Lanrezac had no intention of attacking, and that there were at least three German corps to the BEF's front. The advance was halted, and on the 23rd the BEF gave battle at Mons. It was not until midnight that French gave up hope of continuing to fight on the ground he still held. A liaison officer brought news that Lanrezac intended to withdraw, and it was clear that the BEF must conform.

The retreat from Mons is one of the best-polished feats of British military history. Two points merit discussion here. The first, which was to affect Sir John's imminent meeting with Kitchener, concerns the mercurial mood of the commander-in-chief. Confident in the French offensive and his own role in it, he was downcast by what he regarded as Lanrezac's betrayal. Thereafter he found it difficult to trust the French, and, influenced by the tone of Kitchener's instructions and the chilling experience of near-defeat, began to favour pulling out of the line altogether. Secondly, Smith-Dorrien's decision to fight at Le Cateau on the 26th further strained the relationship between French and the commander of 2 Corps. The affair was to lead to a battle of the memoirs in its own right. Although its details lie outside the compass of this chapter, it should be noted that the evidence favours Smith-Dorrien. Fudged staff-work at GHQ had made the retreat less than efficient, and in the small hours of the 26th Smith-Dorrien was faced with formally giving battle or being caught piecemeal as the German advance guards came up: he determined to stand and fight. French's dispatch paid tribute to his 'rare and unusual coolness, intrepidity and determination,' but Sir John later told Haig, commander of 1 Corps, that he regretted not court-martialling Smith-Dorrien for disobedience. In his book *1914* French was to maintain that the dispatch was written before the full facts were available, and condemned Smith-Dorrien for fighting an unnecessary battle which cost 14,000 men and 80 guns.[20] This was a gross overstatement, and the Official History gives the real casualties of the battle at 7,812 men and 38 guns. Nevertheless, coming as they did upon the casualties of Mons, also borne by 2 Corps, these losses were serious enough to persuade French, Murray, Wilson, and Haig that Smith-Dorrien's corps had been irreparably damaged, and this too helped persuade French to withdraw from the line.

[20] Visc. French, *The Despatches of Lord French* (London, 1917), 10-11; Diary of Sir Douglas Haig, 30 Apr. 1915, National Library of Scotland; French, *1914* (London, 1919), 79-80.

On the 30th French told Joffre that he proposed to take the BEF out of the line to refit. Kitchener heard of the plan obliquely, and at once asked for an explanation. French replied first by telegram, and then by a longer letter, saying that his confidence in the French high command had waned, and that withdrawal was dictated by the spirit of Kitchener's instructions as well as by common sense.[21] French's decision whipped up a storm of protest. Joffre begged him to change his mind, pointing out that the Germans had begun to shift troops to the east; Kitchener urged him to adhere to Joffre's plans, and Sir Francis Bertie, British ambassador in Paris, relayed a message begging French to 'fill the gap'. Sir John told Kitchener that he could not do anything until he had refitted, and, though he would do his best to stay in the line if the French held their present positions, he concluded: 'I think you had better trust me to watch the situation and act according to circumstances.'[22]

After an informal meeting with other ministers, Kitchener set off for Paris, and met Sir John in the British embassy. French was not at his best. He later complained that he had been taken away from his headquarters when he was needed there, and was nettled by the fact that Kitchener was in field marshal's uniform. As Lieutenant-Colonel Maurice Hankey, secretary of the Committee of Imperial Defence, observed, Kitchener 'lived in uniform at the time' and it had probably not occurred to him to change into plain clothes.[23] The sight of Kitchener in uniform inflamed French's worst fears, and matters were not improved when Kitchener announced his intention of inspecting the BEF. Huguet, French liaison officer at GHQ, thought that the two field marshals presented a sharp contrast. Kitchener was 'calm, balanced, reflective', while Sir John was 'sour, impetuous, with congested face, sullen and ill-tempered in expression'.[24] When it became clear that the conversation was getting nowhere, Kitchener suggested that they withdraw into an adjoining room. The only account of what followed is French's. He wrote in his diary that 'we had a rather disagreeable time. I think K found he was making a mistake.'[25] In *1914* he added that he had told Kitchener that while he welcomed advice, he could not tolerate 'interference with my executive command and authority,' and that 'an amicable understanding' had been reached.[26] Its nature was demonstrated in a telegram sent by Kitchener to the Cabinet: the BEF would remain in the

[21] French to Kitchener, 30 Aug. 1914, French papers.
[22] French to Kitchener, 31 Aug. 1914, ibid.
[23] Lord Hankey, *The Supreme Command* (London, 1961), i. 191.
[24] General V. Huguet, *Britain and the War* (London, 1928), 84.
[25] French diary, 1 Sept. 1914.   [26] French, *1914*, 100.

line. This message was copied to Sir John, and a rider added: 'in any case, until I can communicate further in answer to anything you may wish to tell me, please consider it as an instruction'.[27]

The meeting exorcized the spectre of unilateral British withdrawal and, if Sir John's collaboration with the French over the next weeks was less than wholehearted, the BEF played its part in stemming the German tide on the Marne and the follow-up to the Aisne. In later September French gained Joffre's approval to shifting the BEF to the allied left, and in mid-October GHQ was established in the little town of Saint-Omer.

In the mean time the Kitchener–French relationship had taken on the character it was to retain until Kitchener's death. There was outward politeness, and sometimes real affection, especially after the field marshals met face to face. In October French declared: 'I never for a moment supposed you wished to interfere with my operations, and I know perfectly well that I have your confidence and that the same mutual understanding exists between us now as always. Don't think that I forget South Africa so easily.'[28] Kitchener told French frankly of the difficulties he faced. In early 1915 he wrote that: 'my position now is not a very happy one owing to all these W[inston] C[hurchill] freaks. I have told the PM that I should much prefer that he took over the WO as he is making my position impossible here.'[29]

Beneath this ran a strong undercurrent of mistrust on French's part. He complained repeatedly of Kitchener's ignorance and propensity for interfering. He fired his first salvo after the Paris meeting, asking Churchill to:

add once more to all the many and great kindnesses you have done & *stop this interference* with field operations. Kitchener *knows nothing* about European Warfare. Of course he's a fine organiser but never was and never will be a commander in the field.[30]

His diary betrayed increasing peevishness. In early 1915 he complained of 'one of K's worrying letters. They might be written by an old woman,' and later lamented that Kitchener was 'ignorant of the conditions under which modern war is conducted'.[31]

[27] Kitchener to French, 1 Sept. 1914, French papers.
[28] French to Kitchener, 13 Oct. 1914, ibid.
[29] Kitchener to French, 18 Feb. 1915, ibid.
[30] French to Churchill, 6 Sept. 1914, M. Gilbert, *Winston S. Churchill*, iii. *1914-1916* (London, 1971), 61-2 (original emphasis).
[31] French diary, 6 Mar. 1915.

Friends strove to pour oil on the troubled waters. Churchill wrote several letters urging French to trust Kitchener. In September 1914 he stressed that 'K is your friend and [is] loyal and staunch beyond description', and in March 1914 pronounced that good relations between the two were worth a corps. He wrote: 'The world looks on Kitchener as a ruthless crafty terribly efficient strategist & soldier; whereas he is a good and simple man, up to big issues & with much personal address but not strategist administrator or business man.'[32] In May 1915 Haldane told French that: 'you and K being men of strong individuality easily misinterpret each other . . . I am convinced K does not mean to be difficult. It is the old story of expression and manner.'[33] Lord Selborne identified what he saw as the government's problem:

The two men are not mutually sympathetic and never have been, but F is indispensable with the fighting army and K is indispensable in the UK, and each man must be supreme in his own sphere, and when the two spheres touch A[squith] must settle it.[34]

There were three major areas of friction, linked so as to apply intolerable strain to the relationship. The first concerned the strategic direction of the war. Despite the initial debate at Downing Street, there was a general assumption that it was to the Western Front that Britain's military strength should be bent. But as the fluid battles of the summer and early autumn hardened into trenchlock, doubt grew in Kitchener's mind. On 2 January 1915 he sent what French called 'another incomprehensible letter', suggesting that a stalemate might have been reached on the Western Front, and fresh troops might be better employed elsewhere.[35] French replied that, given sufficient men and munitions, he was sure of breaking the German line, and warned against diverting resources to attack Turkey. He sent Murray to England with his memorandum on the subject, and a copy was shown to Asquith. Kitchener protested that communications between French and the prime minister should pass through the secretary of state, and French riposted with a sarcastic apology that it was easy to overlook such details 'when one's mind is engaged with the command of ¼ million men in war'.[36]

French's request for 50 New Army or Territorial battalions, and enough ammunition to give his field guns fifty rounds a day for at least

[32] Churchill to French, 6 Sept. 1914, French papers.
[33] Haldane to French, 16 May 1915, ibid.
[34] Selborne MS 92, Bodleian Library, Oxford.
[35] Kitchener to French, 2 Jan. 1915, French papers.
[36] French to Kitchener, 8 Jan. 1915, ibid.

ten days was turned down by the War Council. Kitchener told French of the decision, observing that the plan suggested—an attack on Zeebrugge in co-operation with the fleet—would be unacceptably costly, and in any case resources were not available. He added that while the Western Front should retain primacy for the time being, alternative areas of operation should be considered if stalemate set in.

Alternative projects had already been proposed, amongst them the forcing of the Dardanelles by an unsupported naval attack. This plan, in essence Churchill's, was regarded as impracticable by many: Kitchener thought that it would take 150,000 troops to take the Gallipoli peninsula. Churchill's scheme, which made much of the ability of modern battleships to reduce forts, gained momentum, although when French came to London to press his case in mid-January he was close to success when Churchill unleashed his project, and the War Council concluded in favour of a naval expedition. French was to receive some reinforcements, although fewer than he had hoped for, and the news encouraged him to proceed with projects for a joint offensive. Evolution of plans for the attack on Turkey eventually persuaded Kitchener to withhold the regular 29 Division, initially expected by French, and to replace it by a Territorial division. This led to an acrimonious exchange between French and Kitchener, and forced the former to modify his plans. He was unable to relieve a sector of the French line as had been agreed, and the French, regarding the 29 Division as a symbol of future intent, professed themselves unable to participate in the offensive. Thus, the Battle of Neuve Chapelle, originally intended to be an Allied attack, ended as an all-British affair.

Failure at Neuve Chapelle convinced Kitchener that French was not up to his job, and on 18 March Asquith noted that: 'K spoke to me *very confidentially* about French. He says he is not a really scientific soldier; a good and capable leader in the field; but without adequate equipment or expert knowledge for the huge task of commanding 450,000.'[37] On 29 March an Allied conference at Chantilly discussed strategy. Kitchener agreed to send two more divisions to France, and when French said that he hoped that no more troops would be sent to the Dardanelles, the secretary of state implied that Hamilton, the land force commander, had enough already. Two days later Kitchener gave French a frank warning that he and Joffre were on trial. If they could make a substantial advance in the next month or five weeks, Kitchener would ensure that they were

[37] Asquith, *Memories and Recollections*, ii. 66 (original emphasis).

backed with all available troops: otherwise the government would look elsewhere. The first landings on Gallipoli took place on 25 April, just inside the trial time allocated by Kitchener, and, in an effort to break the stalemate that soon gripped the peninsula, a second landing was launched on 6 August. It too failed, and Allied troops eventually evacuated Gallipoli in December 1915 and January 1916.

French was well disposed to the Gallipoli project as long as it did not involve any troops. In February he told his mistress Winifred Bennett: 'I hope the Navy will get on quickly with that Dardanelles business. It will make an enormous difference and settle old Constantinople for good and all.'[38] In mid-May he was less sanguine, declaring: 'We have certainly made a hideous mistake in getting mixed up there at all. I was *dead against it* but they wouldn't listen to me.'[39] A month later he was convinced that: 'We were absolutely mad to embark upon the infernal Dardanelles expedition. It is the very thing the Germans would have wished us to do. Certainly if we win this war it will not be on account of our Great Strategic combinations.'[40]

Joffre joined French in resenting the drain on resources which might have been better employed on the Western Front. At Chantilly on 24 June they affirmed their belief in offensive operations in the West, condemned the Dardanelles project, and agreed to press their respective governments to ensure that all available British reinforcements were sent to France. At Calais on 6 July a compromise was achieved between Joffre, who wanted the heaviest possible offensive in the West, and Kitchener, who opposed such an attack. From this agreement grew the Allied offensive, planned over July and August, and fought in late September by the French in Artois and the British at Loos. French had considerable reservations about attacking into the industrial hinterland around Loos, and believed that he lacked adequate artillery ammunition. He eventually decided to co-operate fully for two main reasons. First, he felt that his own position depended on retaining Joffre's confidence. Secondly, he believed that the French had come to doubt Britain's commitment: failure to introduce conscription, strikes, and the diversion of resources to other theatres had created a danger that the French might conclude a separate peace.[41]

The strategic debate helped persuade French to embark upon plans which he regarded as operationally unsound. It is simplistic to attribute

[38] French to Winifred Bennett, 25 Feb. 1915, French papers.
[39] French to Winifred Bennett, 18 May 1915, ibid.
[40] French to Winifred Bennett, 10 June 1915, ibid.
[41] French diary, 29 July 1915.

French's opposition to the Dardanelles to the mere desire not to see his own command reduced in importance, although this played its part. He still had flashes of genuine confidence in achieving a breakthrough. Even when it should have been clear that Loos had ground to a halt in mud and blood, he told Foch that if he was overall Allied commander: 'I should put every available man in just N of Hill 70 and "rush" a gap in the enemy's line. I should feel quite confident of success.'[42] What is abundantly clear is that French, wrestling with problems which he had decreasing confidence in solving, and worn down by the deaths of many of his friends, personalized the strategic debate. He did not appreciate that Kitchener was the prey of conflicting forces in London, and interpreted the secretary of state's interventions as tiresome meddling. The extent to which personalities influenced French may be gauged from the fact that he remained on good terms with Churchill, author of the Dardanelles expedition, but gave Kitchener little credit for his profound reservations about sending troops to Gallipoli.

The second major area of friction concerned ammunition. As the lines had solidified along the Aisne in September 1914 French wrote perceptively to the King about the advent of trench warfare and the importance of heavy artillery.[43] During the first Battle of Ypres in October the supply of artillery ammunition caused him concern, and he pressed so vigorously on the point that Kitchener felt bound to assure him that he was not keeping ammunition back deliberately. Shortages were a feature of early 1915, and Sir William Robertson, then quartermaster general, and later to take over from Murray as CGS, told the master-general of the ordnance that it was difficult to plan operations with confidence if there were massive shortfalls in ammunition supply.[44]

The question of ammunition assumed crisis proportions in the spring of 1915. In his report to Kitchener, French blamed inability to sustain initial success at Neuve Chapelle on 'the fatigue of the troops, and, above all . . . the want of ammunition'.[45] In fact Sir John realized that this was a half-truth, and that failure also reflected shortcomings in planning and execution. Given his fears about his own tenure of command, however, it was attractive for French to blame forces beyond his control for his inability to achieve and exploit a breakthrough. But the shells crisis was not manufactured by pure self-interest: French saw Neuve Chapelle as

[42] Ibid. 28 Sept. 1915.
[43] French to King George V, 2 Oct. 1914, Royal Archives RA GV Q832/72.
[44] Robertson to Maj.-Gen. Sir Stanley von Donop, 23 Jan. 1915, Robertson papers, 1/4/19.   [45] French to Kitchener, 22 Mar. 1915, French papers.

part of a sustained 'Battle of Lille' which would enable his army to grind its way through the Germans facing it, and lack of ammunition made this plan impossible.

Intending to mount a successful offensive so as to prevent the dispatch of further resources to the Dardanelles, French attacked at Aubers Ridge on 9 May. He had discussed ammunition with Kitchener, who had passed on to Asquith Sir John's assurance that 'the ammunition will be all right'.[46] It was demonstrably not, and lack of high explosive was a fatal obstacle to success. French's position was now extremely difficult: he had failed to produce the victory which would persuade Kitchener to give primacy to the Western Front, and on 10 May, when he was already depressed by watching his infantry cut to pieces by German machine-guns, he returned to his headquarters to find a telegram from the War Office ordering him to send 2,000 rounds of 4.5 inch howitzer ammunition and 20,000 18-pounder shells to the Dardanelles. The latter ammunition was replaced rapidly, but the former took longer to arrive, and the incident exasperated French.

Charles Repington of *The Times* was staying with French at the time, and on 12 May he told his paper that lack of shells was 'a fatal bar to our success'. It later became evident that French had provided him with his information. Sir John also sent two of his personal staff to London with instructions to show a memorandum, containing the material disclosed to Repington, to David Lloyd George, a cabinet minister who was far from satisfied with Asquith's leadership, and to the opposition leaders Balfour and Bonar Law. Repington's article appeared on the 14th. It blamed the limited success of British attacks on shortage of shells, and in so doing cast doubt on the credibility of both prime minister and secretary of state, for on 20 April Asquith, using information supplied to him by Kitchener, had publicly stated that the supply of ammunition was equal to the army's needs.

The cabinet could probably have weathered the storm. But it coincided with the resignation of Lord Fisher as first sea lord, and Asquith decided to form a coalition government under his own leadership. Lloyd George became minister of munitions, Reginald McKenna replaced Churchill at the Admiralty—and Kitchener stayed on at the War Office. The Northcliffe press continued its attacks, and on 21 May the *Daily Mail* told its readers of 'The Shells Scandal: Lord Kitchener's Tragic Blunder' and suggested that Kitchener should go. Northcliffe himself was bitterly

---

[46] Kitchener to Asquith, 14 Apr. 1915, Asquith MS 14, Bodleian Library, Oxford.

hostile to Kitchener and shared French's view of the supremacy of the Western Front, but such was the wave of reaction in Kitchener's favour that even Lloyd George warned Northcliffe that the campaign was proving counter-productive.

There can be no doubt that French had leaked the information on shortage of ammunition. He later claimed that he had done so to 'destroy the apathy of a Government which had brought the Empire to the brink of disaster', knowing that the consequences would be serious.[47] At the time, however, he strove to retain Asquith's support, thanking him for his 'unfailing sympathy and encouragement'. But he went on to tell the Prime Minister that Kitchener had been *'overbearing* and *unfair'*, and that his continued presence at the War Office was 'most detrimental to the successful conduct of operations as long as I remain in command'.[48] The evidence suggests that Kitchener, not Asquith, was his real target. His papers betray little hostility towards Asquith until December 1915, when he was 'driven out of France by Asquith at the instigation of Haig', and his allegations in *1914* should be seen in this context.[49] It is also clear that the furore became more generalized than French had expected. Some damage was probably done by the American railway magnate George Moore, whose house at 94 Lancaster Gate was shared by French. He was, as Brinsley Fitzgerald of Sir John's staff told Selborne: 'a mad enthusiast about French and equally mad in his bitterness against Kitchener, and being an American wouldn't have the same ideas about the Press as you or I have'.[50]

From the point of view of French and his supporters the issue was, yet again, personalized. French had made no secret of the fact that the supply of artillery ammunition was fundamental to success, and British tactical doctrine was evolving towards a solution which favoured the massive and methodical use of artillery.[51] Not attacking at all was an option French considered, quite specifically because there was too little ammunition—and yet such reluctance would both weaken his position with Joffre, and discourage Kitchener from sending more troops to the Western Front. Not only did French genuinely believe that Kitchener was largely responsible for the paucity of ammunition supply, he also hoped that the removal of Kitchener would reduce the likelihood of more troops being

---

[47] French, *1914*, 357–61.
[48] French to Asquith, 20 May 1915, Asquith MS 26 (original emphasis).
[49] French to Esher, 7 Sept. 1918, French papers.
[50] Fitzgerald to Selborne, 17 May 1915, Fitzgerald papers.
[51] *Military Operations*, 1915, ii. 51.

sent to the Mediterranean. He failed to recognize the enormous difficulties facing those responsible for the manufacture and supply of ammunition, and gave no credit to Kitchener for his success in inspiring a nineteenfold increase in supply during the first six months of the war.

The third source of friction was the question of command. Sir John was chronically unsure of his position, and the 1 September 1914 meeting left him feeling that he was on probation, vulnerable should the French press for his replacement. On 1 November, with Sir John heavily preoccupied with the first Battle of Ypres, Kitchener visited Dunkirk to meet Joffre. The meeting centred upon the arrival of the New Armies, and although Kitchener promised to have one million men on French soil within 18 months, Joffre favoured having fewer men sooner. In the course of the discussion Kitchener offered to replace French with Ian Hamilton, but Joffre said that he worked 'well and cordially' with French. Foch, commander of the Northern Group of Armies, passed this news on to Wilson, who told French. Sir John sent strong protests to Asquith and Churchill, and was not mollified by assurances that there was no truth in the story. Aware that he had been saved only by Joffre's support, he took care not to turn down French requests for co-operation, and thus mounted a number of operations in which he had limited confidence, with the battle of Loos in September 1915 as the most terrible case in point. Just before it he told Winifred Bennett that: 'I have little fear of defeat or disaster, but it might be little better or no better than previous attempts. Whatever happens I shall have to bear the brunt of it and in cricket language they may "change the bowler".'[52]

It was a prescient statement. The late commitment of the reserve corps rapidly became a key issue. Haig, who had lacked confidence in Sir John's ability from the outset, ensured that the papers on the affair were seen by the King. He also corresponded secretly with Kitchener.[53] By late 1915 French's position was impossible, and the acrimony following failure at Loos made his replacement inevitable. It is ironic that Kitchener was away in the Mediterranean on a fact-finding mission when the damage was done. French fell because he had lost the confidence of the King, most of the Cabinet, and that of several of his senior subordinates, notably Haig and Robertson, who had replaced Archie Murray as CGS. Kitchener, as we have seen, also felt that Sir John was out of his depth, but his absence meant that he played no part in the deft hatchet-work

[52] French to Winifred Bennett, 18 Sept. 1915, French papers.
[53] Haig diary, 14 July 1915.

that went on at GHQ and in London in December 1915. French was persuaded to resign, and Haig took over on 18 December.

French had always seen Kitchener, not Haig, as the real threat. Kitchener had certainly considered becoming commander-in-chief of British and Imperial forces at home and abroad in May 1915. When the coalition government was formed there were demands that Kitchener, his authority blunted by failure at the Dardanelles and the shells scandal, should give up the War Office. The commander-in-chief option was one way out of the impasse, although Kitchener rejected it, partly because he believed that his relations with French were so bad that the arrangement would break down within a week. As French was to observe from his side of the Channel, Kitchener's status had been visibly weakened, and with his own dismissal imminent Sir John wrote that: 'it is generally believed that K will not return to the WO. He may well take command in the Near and Middle East'.[54] Kitchener survived though French did not, and was still in office when he perished when HMS *Hampshire*, taking him to Russia, struck a mine off Orkney in June 1916. French, then a viscount and commander-in-chief of Home Forces, spoke to the motion of condolence in the House of Lords on 'poor K's sad death'.[55]

The historian writing at the close of the twentieth century has ample evidence of the failings of both Kitchener and French, and these can easily blind him to what their contemporaries regarded as great qualities. Kitchener's lack of political feel, propensity for interfering, and inability to see the need for a proper general staff can veil his immense vision and massive public authority. French's quarrelsomeness and jealousy may prevent us from acknowledging the real fire of leadership which was apparent to men as different as Churchill and Robertson.

But it was precisely these personal qualities which lent bitterness to the battle of the memoirs. Kitchener died without writing memoirs, and most early biographies—like Walter Jerrold's *Earl Kitchener of Khartoum* (1916) and E. S. Grew's *Field Marshal Lord Kitchener* (1916) were pure hagiography. In 1920 Sir George Arthur, Kitchener's private secretary, produced a massive and well-proportioned biography of his former chief which was altogether more serious. It was based upon thorough research in the field marshal's papers, and remains a most useful source. Arthur's closeness to Kitchener made objectivity difficult: there could be no doubting where his sympathies lay. In 1917 he had written to French, asking why, if French's assurances of 'lively and

[55] Ibid. 20 June 1916.   [54] French diary, 4 Nov. 1915.

grateful regard' for Kitchener were true, he had recently criticized Kitchener in the press. French replied that he could not enter into lengthy correspondence, but had spoken to the press to praise Lloyd George's work on munitions, not to denigrate Kitchener's.[56]

This gave an early foretaste of what was to come, for while Arthur was at work on his book French's *1914* appeared, containing an outspoken attack on Kitchener. This no doubt encouraged Arthur to bend his own evidence in Kitchener's favour. His version of the instructions given by Kitchener to French in August 1914 omitted the sentence affirming that French's command was an independent one.[57] Huguet, no friend of French's, argued that this was deliberate, for it encouraged the reader to infer that French believed himself to be under Joffre's command, and was thus entirely in the wrong at the 1 September meeting.[58] Arthur saw Kitchener as a gigantic figure, out of proportion to the petty men surrounding him. He ended by comparing the field marshal's death with that of King Arthur, as if somewhere those piercing eyes and upswept moustache still waited to inspire another generation to fresh sacrifice. For Sir George Arthur, Kitchener joined Sir Francis Drake and Frederick Barbarossa in that pantheon of once and future heroes. It was the apotheosis of the Kitchener of the recruiting posters, Kitchener the man writ larger than life.

Lord Esher, too, had known Kitchener, but had not fallen under his spell, and in *The Tragedy of Lord Kitchener* (1921), he found Hamlet a more appropriate model than King Arthur. His tragedy was: 'the consciousness of his own irresolution . . . as he realized that the qualities of mind and character which had served him well through life were under these entirely new conditions out of place.'[59] George Cassar found this 'a dishonest book, evidently written for the sake of sensationalism'.[60] Yet it does throw useful light on the Kitchener–French relationship, and Esher's personal knowledge of the leading actors in the drama means that his evidence should not be ignored. Indeed, he comes near the heart of the relationship:

There was no doubt that Sir John, highly-strung and sensitive, was sore and angry at Lord K's telegrams and letters, written hastily and unsympathetically expressed; while Lord K, irritable and overworked, had spoken injudiciously to

[56] Arthur to French, 17 Sept. 1917; French to Arthur, 19 Dec. 1917, French papers.
[57] Arthur, *Kitchener*, iii. 26.   [58] Huguet, *Britain and the War*, 43.
[59] Lord Esher, *The Tragedy of Lord Kitchener* (London, 1921), 214.
[60] Cassar, *Kitchener*, 483.

Generals, who had repeated his blunt criticisms to the Commander-in-Chief. Easily swayed by personal prejudices, Sir John's violent dislikes rarely placed fatal obstacles in the way of a saner judgement. When not goaded or exasperated, he grew calm, and time after time he would return from an interview with Lord K with admiration for his old chief re-established. On the other hand, he was ever ready to scan the written word with a perverse desire to find cause of offence...[61]

French survived to write his memoirs or, more accurately, to do so with the assistance of Lovat Fraser, a *Times* journalist. French spent a great deal of time with Fraser in 1917, and the eventual book was very much a co-production. There are some portions of manuscript in the field marshal's own hand in the French papers, but there is also a note reading: 'This is written as though you dictated it in a conversational way (as indeed you did). LF'. Sir James Edmonds, the official historian of the war, was approached early in 1919 by 'a clean and tidy widow' who was helping Fraser. 'I gathered from the officers of French's staff', wrote Edmonds, 'that the field-marshal sat in an armchair and talked to his ghost and was questioned by him, a shorthand writer taking down what was said.'[62]

1914 was a belt of ammunition fired at French's enemies in general rather than a sniping shot at Kitchener in particular. Smith-Dorrien was certainly one target. Asquith noted in November 1915 that Smith-Dorrien was 'disposed to be obsessed with his grievance against Sir John French'.[63] In a *Weekly Dispatch* interview of February 1917 Smith-Dorrien gave his own account of the retreat from Mons. Major A. Corbett-Smith, a special reserve gunner, wrote *The Retreat from Mons*, which appeared the same month and took a pro-Smith-Dorrien line over Le Cateau. Corbett-Smith was commanding a battery in England, and was thus under French's command when his book appeared. French set his adjutant-general on to the matter, and the ensuing investigation revealed that Smith-Dorrien had worked on the proofs: French immediately detected a conspiracy.

One of the aims of *1914* was, therefore, to drive home the case against Smith-Dorrien. The Le Cateau casualty figures were exaggerated, and French declared that 'there is not a semblance of truth' in Smith-Dorrien's statement that his decision to stand and fight received the tacit support of GHQ. The effect of the battle was 'to make the subsequent

---

[61] Esher, *Tragedy*, 127.
[62] Sir James Edmonds, 'Unpublished Autobiography', Edmonds papers, 111/16.
[63] Asquith, *Memories and Recollections*, ii. 110.

conduct of the retreat more difficult and arduous'.[64] Asquith was criticized by implication, for it was he who had presided over a government which had not taken proper steps to ensure the supply of ammunition. Thus, the leaking of information to the press, an admission which surprised many of French's friends who did not believe that he had really been behind it, was justified as: 'the only way if we were to continue with success the great struggle which lay before us . . .'.[65]

Yet Kitchener was the main target. French stressed that he 'deeply resented' being summoned to Paris for the 1 September meeting while his army was in action, and declared that Kitchener had 'assumed the air of a Commander-in-Chief'.[66] 'Lord Kitchener', he continued, 'did not make things easy for me. Keenly desirous to influence the course of operations, his telegrams followed one after the other each containing 'directions' regarding a local situation of which, in London, he could know very little.'[67] Then, in a section entitled 'Evils of Divided Command', French attacked what he saw as Kitchener's attempt to combine what should have been the distinct role of cabinet minister and commander-in-chief. He did so because only 'a plain statement of fact' might save Britain from a similar error in future war.[68] 'Divided counsels', he declared, 'lead to half measures and indecisive action. Such counsels always had, and always will have, the most detrimental and disadvantageous effect on any vigorous prosecution of a war, great or small.'[69]

The book was not wholly one-sided. French was prepared to admit that the differences between him and Kitchener 'may have been to some extent my own fault', and spoke of 'a certain mistrust of one another' which clouded their relations. He persisted in the assertion that he had 'always loved and revered' Kitchener in his capacity as a soldier—it was Kitchener as politician that he found hard to tolerate.[70]

1914 first appeared in serial form in the *Daily Telegraph*, and at once drew a hail of fire. Lord Stamfordham wrote to say that the King was 'much concerned' by the articles, and there was a chilly audience after which French admitted that: 'I don't think I made things much better.'[71] Bonar Law, the acting Prime Minister, summoned French to point out that *1914* should not have been published while French was actively employed as Lord Lieutenant of Ireland. He could not undertake to defend the book if it was debated in the Commons, but would not ask

[64] French, *1914*, 80.   [65] Ibid. 361.   [66] Ibid. 99.
[67] Ibid. 177.   [68] Ibid. 177-8.   [69] Ibid. 319.   [70] Ibid. 333.
[71] Stamfordham to French, 8 May 1919, French papers; French diary, 9 May 1919.

French to resign unless compelled to do so by a vote of the House.[72] Lord Bertie helpfully pointed out that French's account of the 1 September meeting was inaccurate, and Lord Midleton who had previously supported French most warmly, begged him not to venture into print again without getting his work vetted by some independent authority.[73]

French tried to repair the worst of the damage. His official apology to the prime minister maintained that he had not been employed in a military capacity when the articles appeared: other field marshals had published once their active command was over. This was not a strong point, for he had previously made it clear that he regarded himself as 'a military viceroy', and habitually wore uniform in Ireland. 'If I have erred', he concluded, 'I can only plead inexperience of Government official life and express regret.'[74]

Smith-Dorrien wished to protest at the book's inaccuracies, but the Army Council dissuaded him from doing so. However, in the *Quarterly Review* of October 1919 Sir John Fortescue pronounced *1914* 'one of the most unfortunate books ever written'. He accused its author of 'misstatements and misrepresentations of the most ludicrous kind', and fumed that: 'No accumulation of titles, batons, grants, orders or decorations' could ever fit French to stand in the company of great British soldiers. Fortescue's steel was winged by more than a little personal interest. French had dismissed his brother from command of a brigade in France, and Sir James Edmonds thought that this might partially explain the vitriol: moreover, Fortescue was, as Smith-Dorrien admitted, an 'old friend' of his.[75]

Asquith quickly entered the lists. He defended his government against accusations of lack of energy in munitions production in a speech at the Connaught Rooms on 3 June 1919, and published the speech in pamphlet form as *The Great Shell Story*. In his *Memories and Reflections* (1928) he announced that: 'His [French's] statements teem with unpardonable inaccuracies. Some of them, which are in flat contradiction to the contemporary documents, I felt bound, as they appeared, in justice to Lord Kitchener's memory, to expose.'[76] Some felt that it was simply humbug for Asquith to take up the cudgels on Kitchener's behalf. Ian Hamilton suggested to French that Asquith had ensured that the

---

[72] French diary, 9 May 1919.
[73] Bertie to French, 10 May 1919; Midleton to French, 6 July 1919, French papers.
[74] French to Bonar Law, 10 May 1919, French papers.
[75] Smith-Dorrien, *Memories*, 482.
[76] Asquith, *Memories and Recollections*, ii. 76.

Dardanelles Commission, which enquired into that unfortunate episode, contained a personal enemy of Kitchener's.

Asquith aspires to play the role of defender of K's memory. You have an answer straight and deadly as a sword thrust—if you like to deliver it. Who put that bloodhound Nick [Field Marshal Lord Nicholson], K's bitterest enemy, on to the Dardanelles commission? . . . K would have needed no defence if Asquith had not put on Nicholson in order to try and saddle K's memory with all the sins of the old gang.[77]

A second edition of *1914* corrected some of the worst errors, but the book is best seen as part propaganda and part reflection of what French *believed* to be the truth. The latter point is important: French sent the proofs of the final chapter to Brigadier-General Sir Edward Spears, an impartial witness, for whom he had the highest regard, scarcely an action he would have taken had he consciously twisted the truth. None the less, *1914* was a milestone as far as the war's historiography was concerned because it made Kitchener's reputation a public issue, and was the first major example of a senior protagonist publicly criticizing higher direction of the war.

In contrast, Smith-Dorrien's *Memories of Forty-Eight Years Service* (1925) was a measured account of his career. It was restrained over Le Cateau, suggesting that at the time 'the Chief did not altogether disapprove of the decision I had taken . . .'. Smith-Dorrien also testified to the poor relations between French and himself: his last official letter to the field marshal complained that: 'I have had more to fear from the rear than from the front.'[78] As is often the case, biographers hit harder than their subjects: A. J. Smithers' *The Man who Disobeyed: Sir Horace*

---

[77] Hamilton to French, 17 May 1919, French papers.
[78] Smith-Dorrien, *Memories*, 403, 480. The relationship between French and Smith-Dorrien deserves a chapter of its own. The weight of evidence, including Smith-Dorrien papers recently acquired by the Imperial War Museum, points to the correctness of the decision to fight at Le Cateau, and there can be no doubting 'Smith Dorrien's' appeal to the rank and file. But his defenders often skate over the general's spectacularly savage temper. It was so alarming that he was not appointed commander-in-chief of the Indian army because of this lack of self-control, and during the battle of Mons his chief of staff, Forrestier-Walker, left his post with the intention of resigning his commission, having had enough of his general's foul temper. Smith-Dorrien was happily married and moral; French had a succession of mistresses. Smith-Dorrien was an infantryman with a high regard for firepower; French a cavalryman with lasting affection for the *arme blanche*. The two men were on bad terms, and Kitchener was ill-advised to appoint Smith-Dorrien to command 2 Corps on the death of Grierson. Plumer, French's choice, would have been a wiser selection: not only did he get on well with French, but he was to establish himself as one of the most reliable British senior commanders of the war.

Smith-Dorrien and his Enemies (1970) contained a sharp attack on French, described as 'the wild beast'.

After French's death the cudgels were taken up on his behalf by his second son Gerald, whose spirited defence of his father's reputation owed not a little to a Frenchian temperament which scented conspiracy everywhere, and sought, perhaps, to compensate for a relationship which had often been difficult when the field marshal was alive. His *The Life of Field-Marshal Sir John French* (1931), written with access to the field marshal's diaries and papers, was no less uncritical than George Arthur's work on Kitchener, and was even more selective in its use of sources. In *French Replies to Haig*, published in 1936 after the appearance of Duff Cooper's *Haig*, Gerald French accused Haig of flagrant disloyalty, and made much of his 'treachery' in corresponding with Kitchener. He also persuaded Lloyd George to write the introduction, giving that gentleman an opportunity to take a swipe at Haig, who he described as: 'efficient, courageous, and within the measure of his abilities a thoroughly competent general. But he had not that breadth of instinct or military vision which Lord French possessed.'[79] In 1937 Gerald edited his father's papers to produce a volume of *War Diaries, Addresses and Correspondence*, and this too was characteristically selective. There was no reference to the 1 September meeting, but a diary entry noting that Smith-Dorrien had been given a 'strongly worded' rebuke because of his army's unpreparedness to meet the German gas attack at the second Battle of Ypres was quoted in full.

Gerald's final salvo was *The Kitchener–French Dispute: A Last Word* (1960), an attempt to resolve the argument in French's favour, which said more for its author's loyalty than for his critical or literary ability. His father's contemporaries and recent historians alike received a brisk fire. Kitchener's 'formidable opposition' had made Sir John's task harder, and the Haig-Kitchener correspondence was nothing less than 'shameless duplicity'. John Terraine was attacked for writing in *Mons: The Retreat to Victory*, that: 'Joffre struck back on the Marne'. 'A certain Sir John Elliot', who had reviewed *Mons* in the *Sunday Times* had had the culpable temerity to describe French as 'harassed'. It was filial loyalty of an almost obsessive sort.

Kitchener and French were inevitably spattered by the debris thrown up by other people's memoirs and biographies. General Huguet, French liaison officer at GHQ in 1914-15, published *Britain and the War* in

---

[79] Maj. the Hon. Gerald French, *French Replies to Haig* (London, 1936), 10.

1928. It contained a bitter attack on British post-war perfidy, and the Sandhurst copy bears the furious marginal notations 'rubbish', 'bosh', and 'rot' in three different hands. Huguet announced that French had squabbled with Joffre, and that his replacement had been regarded with 'undisguised satisfaction' at GQG.

With Lord Kitchener also, the disagreements with Sir John French were continual and arose over every possible question . . . His animosity towards Sir John French had never waned since the interview of 1 September . . . in spite of occasional heartfelt emotion which softened its bitterness, it only grew as a result of these continual disagreements.[80]

He paid tribute to French's 'warm and generous heart', but saw this counterbalanced by an impulsive nature and the tendency to judge men wrongly. Kitchener's great strength, in contrast, was his rock-solid recognition that the war would be a long one. Huguet dedicated his book to Henry Wilson, who, of course, had taken a properly Francophile view of strategy.

Field Marshal Sir William Robertson had worked for both French and Kitchener, and felt that: 'the achievements and foresight of Lord Kitchener place him in a class entirely by himself; and they justify the conclusion that no man in any of the Entente countries accomplished more, if as much, to bring about the final defeat of the enemy'.[81] He set French on a lower scale, but argued that his ability as a leader was indispensable. No other general could have held the BEF together as French did, at a time when the war was new and strange, the BEF at its weakest and the enemy at his strongest.[82] When he published his statesmanlike *Twenty-Five Years* (1925) Lord Grey, as Sir Edward Grey, Asquith's foreign secretary, saw 'sideshows' as the war's chief strategic error, and deeply regretted that he had not supported Kitchener in his opposition to them.[83]

Winston Churchill had also worked with both men, though he made no secret of the fact that his association with French was far warmer than that with Kitchener.[84] Churchill included French in *Great Contemporaries* (1937), but excluded Kitchener. Although he did not go into details of the dispute, he implied that its roots lay in French's long-standing

[80] Huguet, *Britain and the War*, 157.
[81] Field Marshal Sir William Robertson, *From Private to Field Marshal* (London, 1921), 289-99.
[82] Field Marshal Sir William Robertson, *Soldiers and Statesmen* (London, 1926), i. 71.
[83] Grey of Falloden, *Twenty-Five Years* (London, 1925), ii. 74-5.
[84] Churchill, *Great Contemporaries* (London, 1937), 79.

ambition to command the British army in a major war, and the way in which this ambition turned to ashes in 1914-15. Repington was more partisan. In *The First World War* (1920) he maintained that he had himself played a major part in bringing down the Asquith government, and repeated the accusation that Kitchener did not understand the importance of artillery.[85] Brigadier-General C. R. Ballard's *Kitchener* (1930) was the last biography of either protagonist to emerge before the Second World War. It was better-balanced than previous studies of Kitchener, and strove to do justice to French, acknowledging that he had some right to be preoccupied with events elsewhere at the 1 September meeting.

By the time that Ballard's book appeared the general tide of historiography ran strongly against French and Kitchener alike. The war was increasingly seen in terms of duck-boards and parapets, with its heroes as private soldiers and regimental officers, not the allegedly château-bound generals and their staff. The trend continued after the Second World War, with Alan Clark's *The Donkeys* and Leon Wolff's *In Flanders Fields* as striking examples of a literary genre which depicted generals as mindless butchers. Kitchener's first modern biography, Philip Magnus's *Kitchener: Portrait of an Imperialist*, appeared in 1958. It was written with access to the Salisbury Papers, and strove to catch the lights and shades of its subject. But Magnus concluded that:

> Kitchener's thoroughness constrained him to swing his boot into any system of administration and to rend in pieces any established chain of command. His system was, in reality, the negation of any system, and his drive prompted him inexorably to centralise every species of authority in himself.[86]

George Cassar detected an 'almost contemptuous depreciation of Kitchener and his work'.[87] Magnus was far less impressed by Kitchener than was Cassar, but it seems to the present author that Cassar overstates his case against Magnus. Indeed, given the mood prevailing when Magnus wrote, the book was even-handed, and in his portrayal of Kitchener as what Cassar calls more 'a figure out of mythology than a human being', Magnus was reflecting the towering stature accorded to Kitchener by his contemporaries. Of more recent biographies, Philip Warner's *Kitchener: The Man Behind the Legend* (1985) was a robust popular study, while Trevor Royle's *The Kitchener Enigma*, published the same year, was a more scholarly attempt to explore the man's strengths and weaknesses.

[85] Lt.-Col. C. à C. Repington, *The First World War*, 2 vols. (London, 1920), 37.
[86] Magnus, *Kitchener*, 361.   [87] Cassar, *Kitchener*, 483.

The doyen of Kitchener biographies is George Cassar's *Kitchener: Architect of Victory* (1977). As its title might suggest, the book concludes that 'Kitchener's record of assessing military prospects was far better than that of any other leading politician or soldier in the land.'[88] It acknowledges his intellectual limitations, but endorses Robertson's judgement that no man did more, if as much, to ensure Allied victory. It is exhaustively researched, applying the best of modern scholarship to Kitchener for the first time, and though its comprehensive character and heavy prose makes it anything but an easy read, it is unlikely to be bettered. Cassar sided unequivocally with Kitchener in the Kitchener-French dispute, describing Sir John's 'childish tantrums' on 1 September, and laying much of the blame for the shells scandal squarely at his door.

French had to wait for a full biography until 1981, when my book *The Little Field-Marshal* appeared. This was written with unrestricted access to French's papers, many of which had not been available previously. It concluded that Brian Bond's verdict in *The Victorian Army and the Staff College*—'a brave fighting general who proved to be out of his professional depths'—was by no means wide of the mark. French was professionally ill-equipped and temperamentally unsuited for command of the BEF in 1914-15, but, as Robertson acknowledged, his inspirational qualities enabled him to hold the army together as no other general could. The book admitted that French was not a success in France, but agreed with Churchill that: 'French, in the sacred fire of leadership, was unsurpassed . . .'.[89] The book did not attempt a total rehabilitation of French, but, as Ronald Lewin observed in a *Times* review, it managed 'to revive the almost irrecoverable something which commended him to acute men like Haldane, Esher and Churchill'.

And there the battle might have ended, with each of the major protagonists having been the subject of a biography which had placed him firmly in context. But in 1985 Cassar published *The Tragedy of Sir John French*, its title a clear reference to Esher's work on Kitchener. Admittedly no full-dress biography, it dealt chiefly with French's time in command of the BEF. It was an unnecessary final shot, for it ended by affirming, unoriginally, that: 'French could inspire the men in the field as few commanders could . . . French was a fine cavalry officer, dedicated, brave, and able to elicit the intense devotion of his troops. He was, however, out of his depths in the conditions of 1914-15.'[90] The book

[88] Cassar, *Kitchener*, 488.
[89] Repington, describing a conversation with Churchill (*First World War*, 192).
[90] George Cassar, *The Tragedy of Sir John French* (London, 1985), 292.

stands little comparison with the same author's *Kitchener*, and perhaps its chief motivation was to round off the case against French over the shells scandal.[91]

The fact that the battle of the memoirs rumbled on no less than seventy years after the main *casus belli* is a tribute to the ability of both men to arouse emotion long after their deaths. That they should have attracted biographies whose titles included the word tragedy is not unreasonable, for both were ultimately tragic figures, men whose reputations were made and attitudes forged in the nineteenth century, and who, in their different ways, ultimately found the realities of twentieth century war beyond their competence.

[91] This case is most fully explored by David French in 'The Military Background of the "Shell Crisis" of May 1915', *Journal of Strategic Studies* (Sept. 1979). See also Chris Wrigley, 'The Ministry of Munitions: An Innovatory Department', in Kathleen Burk (ed.), *War and the State* (London, 1982). Wrigley argues that Kitchener had abundant foresight, and was flexible in his approach to getting adequate supplies: but he failed to control his department adequately, and adopted the drill-sergeant approach to both his government colleagues and the industrial community.

6
The Reputation of Sir Douglas Haig
KEITH SIMPSON

When in 1973 Michael Howard reviewed James Marshall-Cornwall's *Haig as Military Commander*, he wrote,

It is probably as difficult for an Englishman (or even more a Scotsman) over the age of fifty to write a dispassionate book about Haig, as it is for an American under fifty to write one about Lyndon B. Johnson. Passchendaele, like Vietnam, is one of those memories that drives reason from her sovereign throne.[1]

From the time of his appointment as Commander of the British Armies in France Haig has been a central, controversial figure of the First World War. Ridiculed by many as a stupid and insensitive general who fought a series of attritional battles which destroyed a generation of British youth, his image became a caricature in the hands of Sir John Mills in the film '*Oh! What a Lovely War*'. But Haig has been stoutly defended both by his former brother officers and by revisionist historians who have argued that he fought and won a war with a largely inexperienced army grappling with new technology and constrained by the limits of coalition warfare. By the time of the armistice in 1918 Haig commanded an army of nearly 1.8 million men, the largest army Britain had ever and has ever deployed, and that army under Haig's command played a decisive role in defeating the German army and winning the war for the allies.

Haig personified British generalship in the First World War, and around his character and command a debate has raged unceasingly. The bitter argument with Lloyd George over the direction of the war and the strategy to be pursued; the conduct of operations on the Somme in 1916 and Flanders in 1917; the responsibility for the collapse of the 5 Army in March 1918. All these issues combined with the clash of personalities and interests continued during and after the war in official documents, in the press, and in the pages of memoirs, biographies, and histories. Haig never wrote his memoirs or published his diaries and papers, but in his

[1] *Sunday Times* (2 Sept. 1973).

lifetime he made sure that his account of the conduct of operations and who had really won the war would be available to form the basis of a record that would confound his critics.

Haig had been an inveterate diarist all his life. Throughout the war Haig wrote up his diary usually on the evening of the day of the events related, although occasionally a few days elapsed before he brought it up to date. Haig's diary for the war is of an impressive length, and probably consists of at least three-quarters of a million words. He wrote his diary in a field service notebook, and after several days sent the carbon pages by King's Messenger to his wife in England. The diary is full of day-to-day details about administration, training, operations, and his personal routine. But it also contains Haig's comments about the conduct of the war, leading political and military personalities, and his relations with allies. Certainly Haig was not alone amongst senior British generals to keep such a diary. Field Marshal Sir Henry Wilson had been a compulsive diarist throughout his life and his indiscreet and emotional comments when published in an edited form after his death in 1927 did little to sustain his reputation. Henry Rawlinson was another general who kept a diary, and extracts appeared in Sir Frederick Maurice's biography of him published in 1928.

Complementing the diary are Haig's regular letters to his wife which aside from discussing family business frequently supplemented issues referred to in his diary. Through Lady Haig's connections with the Royal Family, extracts from Haig's diaries were forwarded to Clive Wigram, King George V's Assistant Private Secretary. On 28 April 1915 Haig wrote to his wife:

As regards sending copies of my diary to Wigram—use your own judgement in this and send him of course whatever *you think necessary* but I hope you will limit these extracts to *past* events and *not to future plans*. With this exception send him what you like—and if there is anything about which he wishes information of course tell him.[2]

In this way Haig's critical view of the conduct of operations on the Western Front and Sir John French's exercise of command was brought to the attention of the King. But Haig was not alone in writing directly or indirectly to the King, and as he commented laconically to his wife in November 1915, 'I gather from what the King has told me that all kinds of Generals write to Stamfordham [the King's Private Secretary],

---

[2] Haig to Lady Haig, 28 Apr. 1915, Haig papers, 141, National Library of Scotland, Edinburgh (original emphasis).

Wigram etc. for the King's information.'[3] After the war Haig began to sort out his diaries and papers, a task that Lady Haig was to continue following his death. The diary was typed out and bound into thirty-eight volumes which included many official papers, letters, and other documents. According to Robert Blake who edited Haig's private papers in 1952, 'there is no doubt that he intended these volumes to be his personal account of the war and it is clear from his will that he expected them or parts of them to be published eventually, though not in his lifetime.'[4] Although when revising his diary Haig did make some changes, Robert Blake was satisfied that these were not significant. But both Brigadier-General Sir James Edmonds, the Official Historian, and Basil Liddell Hart suspected that not all the diary entries had been written up at the time, and that some things were inserted later. Certainly Lady Haig was anxious after Haig's death that 'passages hurriedly written at the front which may not read well' should be put right.[5] Critics believe that in contrast to the strong feelings expressed in his letters to Lady Haig, the final version of the diary is rather 'cool'. Taken together, however, the diaries and letters provide substantial documentation for historians and biographers, and any doubts concerning details can be checked from the wide range of official and private collections of papers now open to public scrutiny.

As soon as his diary had been typed out Haig made a copy available to Brigadier-General Sir James Edmonds, the Director of the Military Branch, Historical Section, Committee of Imperial Defence, whose task it was to edit, and in many cases write, the volumes of the Official History of Military Operations in Belgium and France. Thus, Haig made sure that his account of the war formed a significant and indispensable source for the official historians. Haig and Edmonds had been contemporaries in the army, with Edmonds intellectually much the cleverer of the two. But in 1914 Edmonds had suffered a nervous collapse whilst a divisional staff officer and Haig had found him a less stressful appointment at GHQ. Edmonds could be very critical of Haig and had an ambivalent attitude about his personality and conduct of operations during the war, something which came out in his conversations with Liddell Hart. Nevertheless he repaid Haig's loyalty and preserved his reputation during the compilation of the Official History. Indeed Haig,

[3] Haig to Lady Haig, 10 Nov. 1915, Haig papers, 142.
[4] Robert Blake (ed.), *The Private Papers of Douglas Haig 1914-1919* (London, 1952), 13.
[5] Quoted in T. H. E. Travers, *The Killing Ground: The British Army, the Western Front and the Emergence of Modern Warfare, 1900-1918* (London, 1987), 25-6.

like many other senior officers, corrected and commented on the early draft chapters of the Official History.

Apart from making his diaries and papers available to the Official Historian, Haig was indirectly involved in two other publications relating to his period of command during the war. Haig was determined to defend his reputation from two sources of criticism—Sir John French and David Lloyd George.[6] In 1919 French published his memoirs *1914* which gave an inaccurate and biased account of his period of command in 1914-15, to which Haig took exception. But Lloyd George was a far more formidable critic, and Haig had been affronted at the obvious attempts to censor his dispatch dealing with the March Offensive of 1918 and then Lloyd George's subsequent claim that he had won the war. In 1919 Haig's Private Secretary, Lieutenant-Colonel J. H. Boraston, edited a complete collection of Haig's dispatches and the censored passages were indicated by a row of asterisks.[7]

Haig's final dispatch, dated 21 March 1919, was a closely argued case outlining his conduct of operations. Haig sought to establish that during the four and a half years of the war the operations in Belgium and France had been a single continuous campaign which had been fought through the four stages of manœuvre, the preparation or wearing out battle, the decisive attack and the cavalry exploitation. Haig believed that these operations had the same general features as all the conclusive battles of history. What distinguished operations on the Western Front from other campaigns was their duration, and this had been determined by factors beyond Haig's control—the unpreparedness of the British for a war of such magnitude, the subsequent delay of two years before Britain's armies were able to intervene in strength, the situation in theatres other than that of the Western Front, problems of Allied co-operation, and restrictions on manœuvre because of the continuous battle front in the West. As long as the opposing forces at the outset were approximately equal in numbers and morale and there were no flanks to turn, then it was obvious that a long struggle was inevitable and this meant increased casualties. Haig had thought through all the arguments that would be marshalled against his conduct of operations and by arguing that his strategy was based on the principles of war and had to be considered as a

[6] See David French, 'Sir Douglas Haig's Reputation, 1918-1928: A Note', *Historical Journal*, 28/4 (1985), 953-60.
[7] Lt.-Col. J. H. Boraston (ed.), *Sir Douglas Haig's Despatches, December 1915-April 1919* (London, 1919).

Sir Douglas Haig

whole, he made it difficult for those who wished to criticize the individual parts—

> To direct attention to any single phase of that stupendous and incessant struggle and seek in it the explanation of our success, to the exclusion or neglect of other phases possibly less striking in their immediate or obvious consequences, is in my opinion to risk the formation of unsound doctrines regarding the character and requirements of modern war.[8]

In 1920, determined to safeguard his reputation for posterity, Haig asked his former chiefs of staffs, Lieutenant-General Sir Launcelot Kiggell and General Sir Herbert Lawrence to write a 'Memorandum on Operations on the Western Front, 1916-1918'. A number of copies were made and deposited with trusted friends and colleagues such as Boraston and Edmonds, and the trustees of the British Museum, with the instruction that they were not to be published until 1940. Finally, in 1921, Haig gave tacit approval to Boraston to collaborate with G. A. B. Dewar, a journalist and former war correspondent, in writing *Sir Douglas Haig's Command, December 19th 1915, to November 11th 1918*. Haig had been alarmed at the widespread political and industrial unrest following the armistice and feared that many ex-servicemen would be involved in left-wing politics. Haig was convinced that Lloyd George's behaviour during the war, including his attack on the military high command, had eroded traditional authority and caused the collapse of moral standards. Dewar and Boraston rushed through the publication of this volume to coincide with the General Election in November 1922 which saw the overthrow of Lloyd George.

By the time of his death in January 1928 Haig had neither written his memoirs nor published his diaries, but he had established a literary legacy which had been deployed in the defence of his reputation and that of the British High Command and which could be used by official historians and future biographers. Since Haig's death there have been more than a dozen biographies of him and yet none of them is really satisfactory—he remains an enigmatic figure who appears to have eluded the authors. For the historian, it is not only important to establish the motive of the biographer but the context in which he wrote. By the time that the first biographies of Haig appeared in 1928, the controversies concerning the political and military conduct of the war and the clash of personalities had already been addressed in a number of books. Field Marshal Sir William Robertson had published in 1921 his memoirs,

[8] Ibid. 320.

From *Private to Field Marshal*, and then in 1926 his formidable critique of civil-military relations, *Soldiers and Statesmen*. In both works Robertson was very reticent about his relationship with Haig and his reservations about Haig's conduct of operations from 1916 to 1918. Winston Churchill had published the first volumes of *The World Crisis 1911-1918* and had consulted Haig about the early drafts. Churchill was a critic of Haig's strategy, but he was to write in 1937 in *Great Contemporaries*, that although Haig was unequal to the prodigious scale of events no one else was thought his equal or his better. Major-General Sir Charles Callwell's injudicious decision to publish extracts from the diaries of Field Marshal Sir Henry Wilson had dramatized the clash of personalities and the petty intrigues which appeared to have been as prevalent amongst the military as amongst the politicians. And the first volumes of the Official History had been published and avoided controversies by relegating them to footnotes and appendices.

Sir George Arthur's *Lord Haig* and Ernest Prothero's *Earl Haig* were both published in 1928 within a few months of Haig's death, and were thin memorial volumes. In the same year Captain Basil Liddell Hart published *Reputations Ten Years After*, a study of ten not-so-great captains of the First World War, including an essay on Haig. *Reputations* was a transitional assessment in Liddell Hart's study of military commanders during the First World War. Liddell Hart had served as a temporary officer during the war and had been wounded in 1916. As Brian Bond has noted, 'It is important to establish that during his actual service Basil Hart was very much the conventional, ultra-patriotic ex-public-school officer whose admiration for the High Command bordered on adulation.'[9] In September 1916 Liddell Hart wrote a short book entitled *Impressions of the Great British Offensive on the Somme* in which he described Haig as 'the greatest general Britain has ever owned'.[10] By the end of the war Liddell Hart had begun to study tactics and in the 1920s established a reputation as a writer on military affairs, including both military history and on contemporary British Army doctrine and tactics. In *Reputations* Liddell Hart gave a critical but not ungenerous assessment of Haig, writing that as an executive commander there had hardly been a finer defensive general, whilst as an offensive general none perhaps had made worse errors. Liddell Hart concluded that Haig's mind was dominated by the instinct of method rather than the instinct of surprise, but that he was 'a great gentleman' who would

[9] Brian Bond, *Liddell Hart: A Study of his Military Thought* (London, 1977), 17.
[10] Ibid. 18.

stand out in the Roll of History as *'chevalier sans peur et sans reproche'*.[11] Liddell Hart's assessment of Haig and the British High Command evolved from the uncritical adulation of the war years to his bitter criticism of the 1930s. This evolution was a consequence of Liddell Hart's growing disillusionment through studying the increasing amount of information that was becoming available about the war; his conversations with many of the participants; and his belief that the same wartime military establishment was resisting new ideas in the 1930s. By 1935 Liddell Hart was describing Haig in his diary as

> a man of supreme egoism and utter lack of scruple—who, to his overweening ambition, sacrificed thousands of men. A man who betrayed even his most devoted assistants as well as the Government which he served. A man who gained his ends by trickery of a kind that was not merely immoral but criminal.[12]

Liddell Hart's increasingly critical view of Haig and the British High Command can be documented in the principal books and articles which he was to write over the next thirty years.[13] His case against Haig and the British High Command was that at an operational and tactical level they were incompetent, having replaced the element of surprise with stalemate and attrition; they had failed to exploit new military technology such as the tank; and they had been unwilling to divert military resources to operational theatres beyond the Western Front. Liddell Hart's significance as a critical contributor to the debate about Haig and the British High Command during the First World War was not only a consequence of his considerable reputation as a military historian, but through his complementary work in the 1930s as a distinguished military correspondent and his influence on a whole generation of writers and military historians, particularly after 1945.

Brigadier-General John Charteris published in 1929 his biography of *Field Marshal Earl Haig*.[14] Charteris had served on Haig's staff before

---

[11] B. H. Liddell Hart, *Reputations: Ten Years After* (London, 1928), 123.

[12] Quoted in John J. Mearsheimer, *Liddell Hart and the Weight of History* (Ithaca, NY, 1988), 60.

[13] See his *The Real War 1914-1918* (London, 1930); revised and enlarged as *A History of the World War 1914-1918* (London, 1934); id., *The War in Outline 1914-1918* (London, 1936); id., *Through the Fog of War (London, 1938)*; id., 'The Basic Truths of Passchendaele', *Journal of the Royal United Services Institute for Defence Studies* (1959); and id., *History of the First World War* (London, 1970). His editorship and contributions to the weekly part magazine *Purnell's History of the First World War* published in the late 1960s should not be underestimated for its impact on a mass market.

[14] In 1933 Charteris wrote an abridged version entitled *Haig* which appeared in a 'Great Lives' series.

and during the First World War and could claim to have been Haig's friend. Charteris was able to write a very personal book about Haig and his conduct of operations, but any critical assessment was tempered by loyalty and an element of self-justification. Charteris had been Haig's controversial head of intelligence and was believed to have misled Haig about the strength and morale of the German army during the Battles of the Somme in 1916 and Flanders in 1917. Charteris's sources were limited to his own letters and papers, which in 1931 were to form the basis of his book *At GHQ*; to his observations, and to the reminiscences of Haig's friends and former colleagues. Charteris did not have access to official papers, and Lady Haig refused to allow him to use her husband's. No friend of Charteris, Lady Haig regarded him as a dirty and vulgar man. She was offended not only by his indiscretions concerning political and military affairs, but for revealing personal details about her husband.

No man is a hero to his valet, and Haig's former orderly, Sergeant Secrett, did little to enhance his master's reputation with his account of *Twenty-Five Years with Earl Haig* published in 1929. Writing for money, Secrett revealed Haig's meanness and showed Haig as a conservative, authoritarian figure, who had mastered his emotions by rigorous self-control. Lady Haig was determined that her husband's reputation should be defended against the criticisms appearing in some of the many books about the war that were published in the early 1930s. A suitable biographer was to be found who would have access to Haig's diaries and papers. The executors of Haig's estate approached Sir Frederick Maurice, Edmonds, Boraston, John Buchan, and G. M. Trevelyan, all of whom had declined the honour for a variety of reasons, although the hovering presence of the redoubtable Lady Haig was a significant factor. In March 1933 Haig's executors approached Alfred Duff Cooper, author of the widely acclaimed biography of Talleyrand, and a junior minister at the War Office. Although Duff Cooper was not really interested in military affairs and had no great empathy with Haig, he accepted the commission as it was a great opportunity to write a book of significance. Duff Cooper stipulated that he should have access to all Haig's papers and the right to publish what he wanted, but he soon found himself at odds with Lady Haig. She attempted to prevent him from using the copy of Haig's diary lodged with Edmonds—it took the personal intervention of Sir Herbert Creedy, Permanent Under Secretary at the War Office, and one of Haig's trustees, before Edmonds relented—and then she attempted to rush out her own biography of her husband before Duff Cooper and it took legal proceedings by Duff Cooper's

Sir Douglas Haig 149

publishers to prevent this from happening. It is unclear exactly how Duff Cooper had upset Lady Haig, although it may have been his quite legitimate intention to write about Haig's early life and his family.[15]

Despite these difficulties, the first volume of *Haig* was published in 1935, and the second in 1936. (Today in an age of almost professional politicians any junior minister who appeared to have the time to undertake such a task would be viewed with a great deal of suspicion by the Prime Minister, his parliamentary colleagues, and his constituents.) Duff Cooper had written an acceptable if unexceptional biography of Haig which was muted in its critical analysis. Duff Cooper believed that Haig had been a moral giant and that it would be difficult in history to find a better man. But as far as genius was concerned, he concluded that there was no action Haig had taken, no sentence he had written, nor word he had spoken 'bearing the hallmark of that rare quality which puts certain men in a separate category, dividing them by a thin but unmistakable line from those who possess the highest talents.'[16] Duff Cooper's restraint was not only a consequence of his difficulties with Lady Haig, but reflected his sensitivity to contemporary political events and the impact his biography could have on civil–military and Anglo-French relations. Fifteen years later Duff Cooper told Robert Blake that he had omitted many of Haig's strident criticisms of the French because in 1935–6 it would have been irresponsible for a member of the British government to damage Anglo-French relations at a time of European instability.[17]

Duff Cooper had written his biography of Haig against the background of Lloyd George's *War Memoirs* appearing volume by volume between 1933 and 1936. In his *War Memoirs* Lloyd George defended his reputation and political judgement during the war, whilst attacking and denigrating the reputation and military judgement of certain British generals, including both Haig and Robertson. Lloyd George consulted Liddell Hart and whilst the latter gave the former his professional assessment of British generalship during the war, the former reinforced the latter's growing criticisms of the military high command. Despite claiming that his differences with the generals was not due to any personal or political motives, Lloyd George revealed in his *War Memoirs* a deep, emotional, and personal antagonism towards both Haig and Robertson.

[15] For the background to the Duff Cooper–Lady Haig dispute see John Charmley, *Duff Cooper: The Authorised Biography* (London, 1986), 72–3 and Gerard J. De Groot, *Douglas Haig 1861–1928* (London, 1988), 408.
[16] Duff Cooper, *Haig*, ii. (London, 1936), 441.
[17] Charmley, *Duff Cooper*, 74.

In the index of his *War Memoirs* under 'Haig' can be found emotive and biased entries such as 'his refusal to face unpleasant facts', 'his limited vision', 'viciously resists Lloyd George's attempts to get Unity of Command', and 'prefers rather to gamble with men's lives than to admit an error'. Although Duff Cooper's biography appeared before the final volumes of *War Memoirs* were published, Lloyd George preferred to wait until the concluding chapter of his sixth volume in 1936 before replying to what he referred to as 'Lord Haig's "Diaries"'. Lloyd George was dismissive of Haig's diaries writing that the extracts were 'not only meagre but remarkably sterile and undistinguished'.[18] Lloyd George cast aspersions on the editing of the diaries inferring that a lot had been left out. He also cast doubt on Haig's motives in keeping such a diary during the war, writing 'I certainly had no time or inclination amidst the labour and anxiety of the war for sitting down every evening to write for the enlightenment of posterity the tale of my accomplishments during the day.'[19] Lloyd George claimed that his *War Memoirs* were based on the most careful official diary of current events—the minutes kept by Sir Maurice Hankey.

Lloyd George insisted, somewhat ingenuously, that during the war he had made no public attack on Haig's personal fitness to command, nor had he ever concealed from his colleagues his opinion that he believed Haig was intellectually and temperamentally unequal to his responsibilities as Commander of the British Armies in France. Claiming that Duff Cooper's conclusions were similar to his own, Lloyd George criticized Haig for being a *bon général ordinaire* who 'lacked those highest qualities which were essential in a Great Commander in the greatest war the world has ever seen.'[20] Lloyd George's *War Memoirs* failed to provide any judicious assessment of Haig, and with his own highly selective approach towards the evidence and his emotional criticisms, Lloyd George failed to impress either Haig's supporters or any objective reader.

In 1936, within a few months of the publication of the second volume of Duff Cooper's biography, Lady Haig published *The Man I Knew*. Lady Haig's original biography was much longer and more detailed but was never published, although the manuscript is contained in the Haig Papers at the National Library of Scotland. Lady Haig's biography might have been more aptly entitled, 'The Man I Didn't Know'. She wrote that her husband had always hoped she would write a biography of him.

[18] David Lloyd George, *War Memoirs*, 6 vols. (London, 1933-6), vi. (1936), 3374.
[19] Ibid. 3375.   [20] Ibid. 3380.

Sir Douglas Haig 151

In her foreword Lady Haig explained that she had intended to publish extracts from his letters and diaries with chapters on his personal life. She had kept Haig's pre-1914 diaries, despite his explicit instruction to destroy them in 1914 as they were of no value. But she had found them very interesting because 'all who know Douglas will know of his extraordinary reserve (true to Scots type) and he had told me very little of what he had done before I married him'. Lady Haig claimed that her biography 'has also been the cause of much anxiety. The barriers against publication have now, however, been removed'. *The Man I Knew* shows a devoted, loyal wife, who worked in the shadow of her famous husband and, unintentionally, reveals the relationship between husband and wife and the strengths and defects of Haig's character.

After the Second World War, Haig's son Dawyck asked Robert Blake to edit selections from his father's diaries. In his preface to *The Private Papers of Douglas Haig 1914-1919* (1952) Blake made clear that it was 'not another biography of Haig'.[21] Blake considered Duff Cooper's *Haig* to be the standard biography. These extracts from Haig's private papers, principally his diary, were to present the most important political and military events of the First World War as they appeared through the eyes of one of the principal participants. Out of some three-quarters of a million words Blake extracted about one-fifth for publication. Although Blake had made it clear that his volume was not a biography of Haig, he did find it necessary to write a forty-page introduction, which included Haig's biographical details before 1914, a short survey of the political history of the war, Haig's relations with the French, and a comparative assessment of the politics of the two World Wars. In his introduction Blake gave a favourable portrait of Haig and his period of command during the First World War. For the next thirty years *The Private Papers of Douglas Haig* was to become an important source for those writing about the war.

In 1953 Major General Sir John Davidson published *Haig: Master of the Field*. Davidson had been Haig's Director of Military Operations at GHQ during 1915-18, and his book was based upon notes he had kept at the time. His account was a defence of Haig's strategy in 1917-18, particularly the offensive in Flanders. Davidson wrote that he had waited thirty years before the publication in 1948 of the volume of the Official History dealing with the third Battle of Ypres. Davidson believed that Haig would have been satisfied with the Official History but he had decided, nevertheless, to publish his own account.

[21] Robert Blake, *Private Papers*, 11.

John Terraine's *Douglas Haig: The Educated Soldier*, published in 1963, is considered by many to be the definitive modern biography of Haig. Certainly John Terraine has become, in the words of Alan Clark, 'the official custodian of Haig's reputation'.[22] Yet Terraine made it quite clear in his preface that it was 'not meant to be a biography of Field-Marshal Earl Haig; it is an attempt at a study of him as a soldier, and in particular, as a Commander-in-Chief'.[23] As far as Terraine was concerned those who wished for more biographical material could turn to the biographies written by Sir George Arthur, Brigadier-General Charteris, and Duff Cooper. As Terraine has explained, when he first began seriously to study the First World War in the late 1930s he approached Haig in what he claims was the fashion of the period, thinking him 'an unimaginative "slogger", imbued with absurd and unreal optimism, fatally detached from battlefield realities.'[24] His lack of detailed knowledge about the war led him, he believes, to miss the significance of large portions of Haig's diary when he read the Duff Cooper biography shortly after its publication. For Terraine, his real awakening to the significance of Haig and his role in the war came with the publication of Robert Blake's *The Private Papers of Douglas Haig*. Terraine was amazed by Lord Beaverbrook's comment following the publication that it was equivalent to Haig committing suicide twenty-five years after his death. Terraine in a letter of protest to the *New Statesman and Nation* wrote:

> We may not like the psychological basis of Haig's imperishability. We may condemn the system that moulded him. But it could not have been a 'small' man who bore that massive responsibility, and worked out his behaviour by the creed of a world in whose destruction he himself was taking, unwittingly, a major part.[25]

But Terraine did acknowledge certain reservations about Haig in an article in the *Spectator* in 1958 to commemorate the fortieth anniversary of 1918, the year Terraine considered to be 'Haig's vindication'. On the debit side of Haig's balance sheet Terraine noted

> that he was no restless seeker after new techniques of conducting war. Neither, of course, was Wellington... It is impossible not to connect the slogging matches into which so many of Haig's battles developed with his missionary persistence of purpose. Persistence so often took on the features of pure obstinacy, as though

[22] Alan Clark in a letter to *History Today* (1960), 67.
[23] John Terraine, *Douglas Haig: The Educated Soldier* (London, 1963), p. xv.
[24] Id., *The Western Front 1914-1918* (London, 1964), 205.   [25] Ibid.

Haig had accepted the martyrdom of his army and the hazard of his own reputation as part of the necessary sacrifices upon the altar of the God of Victory.[26]

Despite some reservations, Terraine's robust championing of Haig's command during the First World War came to the attention of the second Earl Haig, who mentioned to Sir Robert Lusty of Hutchinson that Terraine would make a good biographer of his father. In 1960 Terraine wrote a study of *Mons* in which Haig was predominantly mentioned. As Terraine began to read Haig's diaries and papers in preparation for writing his study, he continued his public defence of Haig and went over to the offensive against those he regarded as 'instant historians'. Terraine was scathing about the new generation of historians who were writing highly critical accounts of British generalship in the First World War. He considered that Leon Wolff's *In Flanders Fields*, an account of 1917, had been responsible for a new turn in writing about the First World War, a new cynicism which was quite different in tone and value from the disillusionment felt by those who had actually fought in the war. Terraine saw Wolff's book as a model for other writers who 'desire the same cheap advantage'. He was to cross literary swords with Alan Clark whose book *The Donkeys*, published in 1961, was a critique of British generalship in the first eighteen months of the war.[27] For Terraine, Alan Clark's book symbolized the 'bloody fools' interpretation of British generalship.

In 1961 Terraine wrote a short article commemorating the centenary of Haig's birth outlining his thesis that Haig should be considered as one of the great British military commanders.[28] Over the next thirty years, in both articles and books, Terraine would extend and refine this thesis.[29] Terraine argued, paraphrasing Haig's final wartime dispatch, that it was wrong to consider the Battles of the Somme in 1916 and Flanders in 1917 in isolation, and that it was only possible to consider them as parts of a continuous campaign. Terraine rejected the charge made by others that Haig was a cavalry-minded general who was insensitive, unreceptive, obstinate, and unimaginative. He cites four examples to show that Haig was capable of what he defined as 'grand scale imagination'—that before the war he had recognized the need for a Citizen Army, that during the initial stages of the war he recognized the need for

---

[26] Ibid. 206.
[27] Id., 'Instant History', *Journal of the Royal United Services Institute for Defence Studies* (1962), 140-5.
[28] Id., 'Haig: 1861-1928' ibid. (Nov. 1961), 491-6.

Britain to take over the burden of the war on the Western Front from the French, that in 1918 he was the first allied leader to perceive the imminence of victory, and, finally, during the war he had addressed the problem of what was to be done to help ex-servicemen after the war, something which eventually was to become a physical reality in the form of the British Legion.[30] At an operational and tactical level Terraine believed that Haig had grasped the opportunities for exploiting new technology, including artillery bombardments and tanks, had demonstrated the value of surprise in warfare, and had been instrumental in employing civilian experts on the staff of the British Armies in France. Terraine acknowledged that Haig was associated between 1916 and 1918 with bloody 'slogging matches', but suggests that these were a consequence of Haig's style of command—a reluctance to interfere with his subordinates once he had issued his orders—and Britain's total lack of preparation or experience of fighting a continental war on a modern scale. Finally, Terraine suggests that no other general, either in Britain or any of the other belligerent countries, was able to avoid the stalemate and the heavy casualties. For Terraine, Haig was certainly no worse, and in many instances far superior, to every other senior military commander in the First World War.

In *Douglas Haig: The Educated Soldier*, Terraine was to argue that 'such a study can only have meaning through careful attention to the context in which the subject's career was made',[31] but in fact he was not concerned with the development of Haig's personality and character or the influence of his family except within a very narrow context. As Terraine saw it

neither Haig's career nor his personality lent themselves to gossip-mongering or petty anecdote. His private life was private indeed; all that need concern us is that

---

[29] Id., *Douglas Haig: The Educated Soldier* (London, 1963); id., *The Western Front 1914-1918* (London, 1964); id., *The Great War* (London, 1965) reissued as *The First World War 1914-1918* (London, 1983); id., *Impacts of War 1914 and 1918* (London, 1970); id., 'Haig', in Michael Carver (ed.), *War Lords* (London, 1976); id., *The Road to Passchendaele: The Flanders Offensive in 1917: A Study in Inevitability* (London, 1977); id., *To Win a War: 1918, The Year of Victory* (London, 1978); id., foreword to the repr. of the 1919 edn. of *Sir Douglas Haig's Despatches* (London, 1979); id., *The Smoke and the Fire* (London, 1980); id., *White Heat: The New Warfare 1914-1918* (London, 1982); id., 'Field Marshal Haig', in *Stand To!, Journal of the Western Front Association* (Summer 1989), 9-12; id., 'Douglas Haig 1861-1928—A Review Article', in *British Army Review* (Aug. 1989), 41-2; id., *Douglas Haig: The Educated Soldier* (London, 1990) a repr. of the 1963 edn. with a new foreword.

[30] By 1979 Terraine had added a fifth example of Haig's 'grand-scale imagination'—in victory magnanimity to be shown to a defeated Germany. Foreword to *Sir Douglas Haig's Despatches* (p. viii). [31] Terraine, *Douglas Haig* (1963), p. xv.

it contained no disturbances likely to affect his handling of public affairs. In this respect he affords a remarkable instance of concentration and single minded devotion.[32]

'Educated soldier' is defined by Terraine to mean 'an officer who takes his work seriously, who studies it from all aspects, who (above all) has the mind, as well as the aspiration, to think issues through for himself'.

In 1990 Terraine's study of Haig was reprinted with a new introduction. Although Terraine had written numerous articles and books over the intervening twenty-seven years, he appears not to have thought it necessary to alter his original thesis. In 1963, shortly after the publication of *Douglas Haig*, Terraine did admit to being dissatisfied with parts of his book, believing that he might have helped perpetuate some injustices, in particular that he had not written enough about Haig's victories in 1918.[33] Presumably over the years Terraine had read the various publications about Haig and almost every aspect of the First World War based in many cases on newly released official papers and private collections of documents. But these appear to have had little impact on Terraine apart from reinforcing him in his own convictions about Haig. To his surprise he still finds that Haig is viewed as a controversial figure. He is convinced that Haig is viewed with some distaste because of an emotional revulsion from the unprecedented slaughter of the First World War, with which Haig's name is identified; to the misunderstanding about Britain's role in the war; the 'disenchantment' of the post-war years; a misunderstanding about the level of casualties in the Second World War where the overall figures were greater, but Britain's smaller; and the anti-war revulsion of the 1960s and 1970s.[34]

Terraine has been genuinely puzzled by what he has seen as the hostility shown towards Haig. As far as Terraine is concerned he did not write books about the First World War in a certain way 'because of my view of Haig; I wrote about Haig in a certain way because I saw that the War demanded it.'[35] Those who have criticized Haig do so, according to Terraine, with mean motives; the shuffling off of responsibilities; with doctrinaire conceit; with injured self-esteem and with plain jealousy and spite.[36] Terraine has seen it as his historical duty to defend Haig and to proclaim what he considers were Haig's undoubted virtues, but in doing so Terraine himself has become within the historical debate almost as controversial a figure as Haig.

[32] Ibid.
[33] Id., *The Western Front*, 207.
[34] Id., *Douglas Haig* (1990), p. xiii.
[35] Ibid.
[36] Ibid.

Apart from Terraine's *Douglas Haig*, 1963 had been a year of publications about the First World War as writers and publishers prepared to exploit the fiftieth anniversary of the outbreak of war. Victor Bonham Carter wrote a biography of Robertson based on his private papers which presented the traditionally accepted portrait of the relationship between Robertson and Haig.[37] Correlli Barnett's *The Swordbearers: Studies in Supreme Command in the First World War*, mentioned Haig only in the context of other commanders, and although Barnett criticized some of Terraine's defence of Haig's strategy in 1917, in general terms he was to support and would continue to support Terraine's interpretation of Haig and his conduct of operations during the First World War. A. J. P. Taylor's highly popular, and very populist, illustrated history of the First World War tended to caricature Haig and the British High Command and give Lloyd George the benefit of the doubt. Taylor concluded that Haig had no more idea than Sir John French on how to win the war, but he was sure he could win it. Yet Taylor was forced to admit that Haig's strategic judgements were sound within the framework of the Western Front, although until the summer of 1918 he appeared to have no more success than French.[38]

Haig's religious beliefs and his conviction that he was 'sustained by the Great Unseen Power'[39] were explored in G. S. Duncan's *Douglas Haig as I Knew Him*, published shortly after the author's death in 1966. George Duncan had been a young Church of Scotland chaplain who Haig happened to hear preaching near St Omer in January 1916. We know from Haig's diary entries that he was profoundly impressed by Duncan's earnest approach to religion which reinforced his own religious convictions. On succeeding Sundays Haig returned to St Omer to listen to Duncan preaching, and when he moved GHQ to Montreuil Duncan was posted there as the Presbyterian chaplain to GHQ troops, but effectively as the commander-in-chief's personal chaplain. Haig regularly attended Duncan's services throughout the war, and until Haig's death in 1928 they kept up a correspondence. Duncan wrote his book as a contribution to a better understanding of Haig's 'greatness both as a man and as a commander'.[40] Duncan had access to Haig's diaries and papers and received encouragement and advice from John Terraine.

[37] Victor Bonham Carter, *Soldier True: The Life of Field Marshal Sir William Robertson* (London, 1963).
[38] A. J. P. Taylor, *The First World War: An Illustrated History* (London, 1963), 81-2.
[39] Letter from Haig to G. S. Duncan in *Douglas Haig as I Knew Him* (London, 1966), 122. [40] Ibid. preface.

Two military biographies of Haig were written in the 1970s. General Sir James Marshall-Cornwall had worked as a junior staff officer for Charteris at Haig's GHQ in 1916–17. A prolific writer of books on military history, Marshall-Cornwall's *Haig as Military Commander*, published in 1973, was in the same style in the same publisher's series, as his biographies of *Napoleon*, *Foch*, and *Grant*. Marshall-Cornwall had the advantage of having worked on Haig's staff and knowing many of the leading personalities at first hand. He had access to Haig's diaries and papers and wrote a military biography of Haig attempting to show that, like Ulysses S. Grant, he had been misrepresented. He was particularly scathing towards some of Haig's critics, writing that few of them 'can be regarded as competent military judges'.[41] Marshall-Cornwall's conclusions were similar to Terraine's, except that he emphasized Haig's faulty judgement in the selection of some of his subordinates, including Charteris, who had failed to provide him with correct information. Marshall-Cornwall considered that it was unfortunate that Haig was a cavalryman and therefore obsessed with the belief that cavalry would achieve the final breakthrough, and he acknowledged that Haig protracted his offensives unnecessarily.

In 1976 General E. K. G. Sixsmith wrote *Douglas Haig*, as he believed that previous biographies were out of print and because 'it cannot be said that the last word on Haig has been written'.[42] Sixsmith was also aware that although in 1961 Haig's diaries and papers had been deposited in the National Library of Scotland other collections of private papers had become available which provided new source material to study Haig and the British High Command during the First World War. Sixsmith's short, judicious study gave Haig the benefit of the doubt, although he was critical of Haig's intellectual ability and concluded that Haig was not a master of the weapons and tactics of his day, and the absence of that one characteristic 'must forfeit for him a place among the great Captains of History'.[43]

Marshall-Cornwall and Sixsmith both wrote favourable and sympathetic military biographies of Haig, perhaps rather old-fashioned and restricted in their approach, very much in the 'Great Captains' school of military history, but with the advantage of having been written by two former generals who knew something of the strain and stress imposed on a commander in war.

[41] James Marshall-Cornwall, *Haig as Military Commander* (London, 1973), 290.
[42] E. K. G. Sixsmith, *Douglas Haig* (London, 1976), p. ix.
[43] Ibid. 164.

In the same year as General Sixsmith's military biography of Haig appeared, Dr Norman Dixon published *On the Psychology of Military Incompetence*. Dixon rejected the 'bloody fools' interpretation of military history and sought explanation for the behaviour and success or failure of military commanders through psychological and pathological analysis. Dixon cited Haig as a classic example of authoritarian personality—that is someone who is driven on by the need for achievement which is motivated by a fear of failure. According to Dixon, Haig was ultra-conservative, conventional, and ethnocentric. Haig's diaries and papers suggested to Dixon that Haig was unemotional and not a person to reflect upon his own motives, that he lacked compassion towards others, that he was a confirmed believer in the direction of events by supernatural powers, that he was reserved to the point of being verbally almost inarticulate, and that he was obstinate, orderly, and mean. Naturally aggressive and self-willed, Haig encountered strong opposition from his mother. The Church of Scotland appealed to him with its authoritarian, puritan concepts, including the belief in hard work, the inevitability of punishment for wrong-doing and a preoccupation with the concept of discipline. Not surprisingly, Dixon's assessment of Haig was controversial both from a psychological and historical point of view.

In terms of the historiography of the First World War, the 1970s and 1980s saw the emergence of a post-Second World War generation of professional military historians who had the advantage of being at a distance from both world wars and who had virtually unlimited access to a wide range of source material. Brian Bond, Richard Holmes, Shelford Bidwell, Dominick Graham, David Woodward, Keith Jeffery, David French, Tim Travers, and Ian Beckett produced first-class scholarly analyses of the British Army as a social institution, its attempts to absorb new technology and doctrine, the practical difficulties of military operations, and a more subtle interpretation of the personalities and issues.[44]

The role of Haig and the performance of the British High Command on the Western Front were seriously addressed by the Canadian military

---

[44] Brian Bond, *The Victorian Army and the Staff College 1854-1914* (London, 1972) and *Liddell Hart: A Study of his Military Thought* (London, 1977); Richard Holmes, *The Little Field Marshal: Sir John French* (London, 1981); Shelford Bidwell and Dominick Graham, *Fire-Power: British Army Weapons and Theories of War 1904-1945* (London, 1982); David R. Woodward, *Lloyd George and the Generals* (Newark, NJ and London, 1983) and id. (ed.), *The Military Correspondence of Field Marshal Sir William Robertson, Chief of the Imperial General Staff December 1915-February 1918* (London, 1989); Keith Jeffery (ed.), *The Military Correspondence of Field Marshal Sir Henry Wilson 1918-1922* (London, 1985); David French, *British Strategy and War Aims 1914-1916* (London, 1986); Travers, *The Killing Ground*; Ian Beckett, *Johnnie Gough* (London, 1988).

Sir Douglas Haig

historian Tim Travers, first in a series of articles between 1978 and 1983, and then in 1987 in his book *The Killing Ground*. Travers contended that two major British Schools of thought had developed in an attempt to address the controversies surrounding the British experience on the Western Front. The critical school, which has included both Lloyd George and Liddell Hart, has tended to stress internal factors, usually the incompetence of Haig, GHQ, and senior military commanders. The second major school of thought, which has included both Brigadier-General Edmonds and John Terraine, has stressed external factors, including the pre-war British inexperience and lack of preparation, the problem of adapting to new technology, the fighting power of the German Army, restraints imposed by coalition warfare, and political interference. Travers suggested that few studies, apart from *Fire-Power* by Shelford Bidwell and Dominick Graham, have taken a balanced view between the internal and external arguments. In *The Killing Ground* Travers argued that he had attempted to take a balanced judgement, but with greater emphasis on internal factors and with his analysis commencing well before the war and based upon a wide range of sources, including official and private papers. Travers stressed five major themes, beginning with an attempt to unite intellectual history with the raw material and the events of the war. He was convinced that it was only by considering patterns of thought in conjunction with the behaviour of senior British officers could one really understand why events occurred in the way they did. Second, he emphasized the persistence of pre-war ideas throughout the war and that this was not just a combination of old ideas and new weapons, but that a particular pre-war image of warfare continued throughout the war. In this sense he argued that there was not a revolution in military thinking before the war, in fact quite the reverse, and he stressed the enduring legacy of the Napoleonic experience and the cult of the offensive spirit. His third theme concerned the pre-war 'personalized' army structure, whereby the hierarchical and personality-influenced officer corps proved inflexible in meeting the challenges of the war. A fourth and related theme was the underlying conflict going on within the British officer class during and after the war and which involved personalities, differences over doctrine and tactics, and the attempts to write up history to an individual's personal advantage. Travers's fifth and final theme concentrated on the way in which British generals regarded warfare as ordered and regulated, and sought to re-emphasize that order if the battlefield showed signs of confusion. To Travers, Haig personified much of what was wrong with the British Army, and this was explored in his central chapters on 'Douglas Haig, the Staff College, and the Continuity of Ideas' and 'The Personality of Douglas Haig and the Role of GHQ'. Travers's scholarship undoubtedly influenced Gerard J. De Groot when he wrote his biography of Haig in 1988.

In the introduction to his biography, *Douglas Haig 1861-1928*, De Groot revealed that his fascination with the First World War had begun ten years earlier. His original intention had been to study British intelligence during the war, particularly the relationship between Haig and Charteris. An American undertaking postgraduate research at the University of Edinburgh, De Groot was advised by his supervisor to look at the Haig papers in the National Library of Scotland. As a consequence, De Groot abandoned his original plan and wrote a doctoral thesis on the pre-war life and military career of Haig.[45] This was to form the core of De Groot's critical biography of Haig which was based on a study of the Haig Papers, and a wide range of official and private papers. According to De Groot, Haig has become 'the piltdown man of military history'[46] with his papers and diaries being mined to support the users' preconceptions. De Groot argued that there was room for a new study of Haig, and his development at each stage of his life had to be examined in relation to the previous stages, not in relation to the First World War or any preconceptions concerning his character. Haig was, according to De Groot, a product of his Victorian and Edwardian class background and these values and attitudes helped determine his behaviour as a military commander. De Groot challenged Terraine's contention that Haig was not a narrow-minded cavalry general. De Groot sought to establish by a carefully documented study of Haig's service before 1914 and his military writings that Haig's military thinking was dominated by his very conservative views about the role of cavalry on the modern battlefield. He does not deny that Haig was an administrative reformer within the army or that he had striven for efficiency, but he suggests that this was combined with tactical and doctrinal conservatism. De Groot concurs with Travers that Haig went to war in 1914 with a simple military doctrine learnt at the Staff College which he did not significantly alter throughout the war.

De Groot's own ambivalent attitude to Haig is revealed when he writes that 'although it was impossible to deny that in the end Haig won

[45] Gerard J. De Groot, 'The Pre-War Life and Military Career of Douglas Haig', Ph.D. Thesis (Edinburgh, 1983) and id., 'Educated Soldier or Cavalry Officer? Contradictions in the pre-1914 Career of Douglas Haig', *War and Society*, 4/2 (Sept. 1986), 51-69. [46] Id., *Douglas Haig 1861-1928* (London, 1988), 5.

the war his victory should not be interpreted as a vindication of his methods or an exoneration of his character'.[47] Not surprisingly, Terraine was highly critical of De Groot's biographical interpretation of Haig. Terraine reiterated his belief that the only way to understand and assess Haig was in the context of the First World War and the political and military restraints that were imposed on him. De Groot's approach he contemptuously dismissed, claiming that he had used techniques already well displayed by earlier detractors, such as 'suppression of contrary evidence, elimination of context, *a priori* judgement impervious to new thought, steeped in malice and fortified by ignorance of history, which suffers serious damage in this process'.[48] Whilst Terraine's criticism is emotionally driven and very exaggerated, De Groot's prejudices are apparent, although he claimed to have written a balanced biography of Haig. De Groot's biography also suffers from the fact that, whilst the period of Haig's life before 1914 is well documented and seems to have been written at a leisurely pace, the wartime years are rushed through and seem little more than a chronology of events based on Haig's diaries and letters. It may be that the author faced restrictions imposed by the publishers on the time available for research and writing, and on the length of the book.

Out of the thirteen books specifically written about Douglas Haig since 1928, nine are biographies with certain limitations or are personal memoirs. Sir George Arthur and Ernest Prothero wrote slim, memorial volumes; Sergeant Secrett a series of anecdotes based on personal service; Lady Haig a wife's devoted memoir; Robert Blake a biographical essay; Major-General Davidson an operational military study of 1917-18; the Reverend Duncan a memoir of Haig and his religious beliefs; and Generals Marshall-Cornwall and Sixsmith military biographies. Only four of the thirteen can be reasonably considered full biographies, and even then three have limitations. Charteris wrote a full and very personal biography of Haig but his sources were limited as he had access neither to Haig's papers and diaries nor to official documents. Duff Cooper wrote the official biography with his own self-imposed restrictions, particularly his decision to modify Haig's views about the French. John Terraine is regarded by many as the definitive modern biographer, but he made it quite clear in his introduction that he had not written a biography of Haig but a study of him as a soldier. Nevertheless, despite his own

[47] Ibid. 6.
[48] Terraine, 'Douglas Haig 1861-1928—A Review Article', *British Army Review* (Aug. 1989), 42.

caveat, Terraine's study has all the hallmarks of a biography. Gerard J. De Groot has written the most recent full-length biography of Haig, based on a wide range of sources, which attempts to study him both as a man and as a soldier and put him into the wider context of Victorian and Edwardian society but which is marred by the author's obvious dislike of his subject. Haig has been portrayed by some of his biographers as an honest, loyal, professional soldier who beat the German army, despite making some errors of judgement and in spite of restraints imposed by external factors. Others have viewed him as a man of contradictions who in public was generous, but who in private could be petty and malicious; loyal to his subordinates but disloyal to his superiors; as a professional soldier who was an odd mixture of administrative progressivism and tactical conservatism. It is impossible to write a biography of Haig outside the context of the society in which he lived and the army in which he served, and Haig still personifies all that was both good and bad about the British army in the era of the First World War.

Since going to press a new, and what will undoubtedly be seen as a very controversial study of Haig has been published. Denis Winter's *Haig's Command: A Reassessment* (Viking 1991) is the result of the author spending ten years researching through unpublished material in Britain, the USA, Canada and Australia. Winter has previously published two well received studies on the First World War.[49] In *Haig's Command* he attempts nothing less than an historical demolition job on the reputation of Haig, those who have written about him, and the departments of state responsible for the safeguarding of public documents relating to the British Army and the Western front. Basing his thesis upon sources largely outside Britain Winter argues that Haig carefully edited and rewrote his own papers, that the Government subsequently supported him by instructing Edmonds to massage the official history, and then carefully weed those documents that were eventually placed in the public domain. Winter then dissects Haig's reputation as a military commander and concludes that previous historians have failed to discover the truth. *Haig's Command* is a stimulating reassessment of the subject and Winter has assiduously searched for new documentary material, but many will question his selective use of evidence and his subjective analysis. So Haig still remains an enigma and his reputation a matter of heated controversy.

[49] *Death's Men: Soldiers of the Great War* (London, 1978) and *The First of the Few: Fighter Pilots of the First World War* (London, 1982).

III
Indirect Approaches

7
Gallipoli*
EDWARD SPIERS

The Gallipoli campaign, wrote Alan Moorehead, proved 'a mighty destroyer of reputations'.[1] Indeed it did; as Brian Bond observed, it 'destroyed Hamilton's reputation, undermined Kitchener's and eclipsed Churchill's'.[2] Yet the assessment of the campaign, not least the merits of the Eastern strategy, would be significantly influenced by the way in which it was reviewed and reconsidered at different times and from different perspectives. Assessments of the campaign and of its three major personalities would ebb and flow as commentators recurrently grappled with two basic questions: was the project strategically sound and why did the expedition founder? These assessments will be examined in four basic periods: the war and its immediate aftermath when writing was influenced by the reports of the Dardanelles Commission; the subsequent reaction begun by Churchill's *World Crisis* and largely sustained by the Official History; the post-war reappraisal, dominated by the writings of or about Lord Hankey; and the subsequent reconsideration of the roles of Churchill and Kitchener.

The early wartime writings were rarely clinical and dispassionate. In the immediate aftermath of the campaign, correspondents like Sydney Moseley and Granville Fortescue and the Poet Laureate, John Masefield, who was writing to impress a neutral American audience, alluded to the spectacle of the Hellespont, evoked classical and crusading imagery, and dwelt upon the heroism of the participants and the 'tragedy' of the enterprise.[3] This emphasis was none too surprising; as John North

* I should like to thank Brian Bond, Bryan Ranft, Alex Danchev, Brian Holden Reid, Peter Simkins, and Keith Simpson for their helpful comments on an earlier version of this chapter.

[1] A. Moorehead, *Gallipoli* (London, 1956), 361.
[2] Brian Bond, *The First World War* (*The New Cambridge Modern History*, xii, Cambridge, 1968), 183.
[3] S. A. Moseley, *The Truth about the Dardanelles* (London, 1916), 14, 196; G. Fortescue, *What of the Dardanelles: An Analysis* (London, 1915), 27, 49; J. Masefield, *Gallipoli* (London, 1916), 5-9, 25.

subsequently recalled, there was 'no magic in the soil of France for the men who fought there', whereas Gallipoli, by virtue of its setting and its tragedy, lent itself 'to retrospective sentimentality'.[4] Cyril Falls would even claim that

> No episode of the war is more poignant than the effort to force the Dardanelles. As pure tragedy it may not equal the Somme, yet the tragedy of missed chances, the might-have-been, often strikes the imagination even more forcibly than a human holocaust.[5]

In their descriptive campaign studies and strategic assessments, the wartime commentators were, perforce, writing about the campaign in isolation and with little documentary evidence. The Royal Commission, appointed in 1916, did little to mitigate this shortcoming. Having interviewed all the major figures involved, with the exception of Lord Kitchener who had drowned on 5 June 1916, it simply issued highly critical reports without publishing any evidence. Arguing that the losses outweighed the modest achievements of the campaign (the diversion in favour of Russia, delaying the adhesion of Bulgaria to the Central Powers, and immobilizing a large body of Turkish troops), it criticized Churchill for advocating the 'ships alone' attack 'on a certain amount of half-hearted and hesitating expert opinion'; Kitchener for his costly prevarications in February and March 1915, his failure to use the General Staff, and his fears of the consequences of abandoning the Gallipoli peninsula; and Hamilton for deficiencies in the planned attack upon Suvla, and for failing to appreciate the tenacity of the Turkish resistance.[6]

Writing in the wake of the Commission's reports, commentators either tended to develop its findings, often referring extensively to them, or to challenge the conclusions or aspects of them. In a balanced and perceptive account of the campaign, Henry W. Nevinson, an eyewitness, praised the expedition as 'a strategic conception surpassing others in promise', but he also agreed with the Commissioners that the idea was essentially Churchill's, and that the latter 'was carried away by his sanguine temperament and his firm belief in the success of the undertaking which he advocated'.[7] Nevinson attributed the failure to the premature naval attacks, which removed any element of surprise, the

---

[4] J. North, *Gallipoli: The Fading Vision* (London, 1936), 15, 20.
[5] Cyril Falls, *The First World War* (London, 1960), 107.
[6] Dardanelles Commission, *First Report*, Cd. 8490 (1917-18), x. 41-3 and *The Final Report of the Dardanelles Commission*, Cmd. 371 (1919), xiii. pt. 1, 84-5, 87-8.
[7] H. W. Nevinson, *The Dardanelles Campaign* (London, 1918), pp. vii, 21, and 39.

Gallipoli 167

attack by ships alone, the delay in concentrating military forces for the land attack, and the tactical mistakes of the two landing operations.[8]

Criticism of Churchill's impulsiveness, 'amateurish strategy', and the blunder of a 'ships alone' attack emanated from the pens of Viscount Esher, H. W. Wilson, Lord Wester-Wemyss, and Sir Charles Callwell, the former Director of Military Operations.[9] They corroborated the doubts of Lord Fisher and Sir Arthur Wilson about the wisdom of the 'ships alone' attack, which the Commission had mentioned, and which Lord Fisher had confirmed in his memoirs: as Sir Julian Corbett observed, this was 'serious opposition . . . from the best British naval opinion, with the First Sea Lord at its head'.[10] Callwell stressed, too, that the project of attacking the Dardanelles had already been rejected by the Committee of Imperial Defence in 1906, but that this paper was not considered by the War Council until May 1915. Finally, he defended his former department over the Commissioners' criticisms about the lack of maps, plans, and inadequate logistical arrangements by reiterating, quite reasonably, that the General Staff had never been allowed to exercise its proper functions under Kitchener.[11] This line of criticism was perhaps most succinctly summarized by Charles E. W. Bean, the author of the immensely detailed official Australian history of the campaign: 'nothing', he concluded, 'could justify the initiation of the enterprise by means which could not attain its goal'.[12]

Inevitably those who had been criticized sought to explain their actions and to redress the balance of opinion. Sir George Arthur, the former secretary of Lord Kitchener, proffered a stout defence of Kitchener in the third volume of his hagiography. Kitchener, he argued, was not opposed to an Eastern initiative (and had favoured a landing in the Gulf of Eskandroon at Alexandretta) but, in January 1915, he lacked the 150,000 men necessary for 'a serious naval and military attack upon the Dardanelles'.[13] When Kitchener subsequently offered and then withdrew the services of the 29 Division in February 1915, he did so, argued

[8] Ibid. 407–8.
[9] Reginald Viscount Esher, *The Tragedy of Lord Kitchener* (London, 1921), 92; H. W. Wilson, 'Mr Churchill and Lord Fisher at the Admiralty', *National Review*, 81 (May 1923), 379; Sir C. E. Callwell, *The Dardanelles* (London, 1919), 26.
[10] Callwell, *Experiences of a Dug-Out* (London, 1920), 92; Dardanelles Commission, *First Report*, 42; Lord Fisher, *Memories* (London, 1919), 67–9; Sir J. Corbett, *Naval Operations* (London, 1921), ii. 105.
[11] Callwell, *Experiences of a Dug-Out*, 87–9, 95.
[12] C. E. W. Bean, *The Story of ANZAC* (Sydney, 1921–4), ii. 909.
[13] Sir G. Arthur, *Life of Lord Kitchener*, 3 vols. (London, 1920), iii. 104.

Arthur, because he perceived the interrelationship between the fronts in Europe, and feared that recent Russian reverses could compound Allied problems in the West—'the front vital to us'—by the switching of large numbers of German forces from the East to West. Only when he thought it prudent would Kitchener countenance the dispatch of the 29 Division.[14]

In the same year, 1920, Sir Ian Hamilton published his two-volume diary which was effectively a memoir in diary form.[15] Hamilton claimed that he had received meagre instructions, about half of the troops which the Greeks had thought necessary, and derisory information on which to base his plans. 'The Dardanelles and Bosphorus', wrote Hamilton, 'might be in the moon for all the military information I have got to go upon'.[16] An ardent believer in the Eastern strategy, he argued that if the fleet had got through, Constantinople would certainly have fallen, echoing, thereby, the views of two American diplomats who served in the Turkish capital during the hostilities.[17] Once it was clear that the Navy was not willing to renew its assault after 18 March, Hamilton explained how he had had to move his base from the utterly inadequate island of Lemnos to Alexandria, nearly 600 miles away, and to organize his heterogeneous units, without an adequate administrative staff, for an invasion one month hence. He defended his choice of landing places and his reluctance to interfere with the actions of subordinate commanders in the landing of 25 April. He castigated the War Office for the subsequent delays in sending artillery ammunition and reinforcements and for failing to send 'young and up-to-date Generals' to lead the second invasion. Nevertheless, he insisted that the expedition could still have prevailed if only the government had accorded it priority and had deferred the Loos offensive of September 1915.[18]

In *The World Crisis*, Winston Churchill proffered an even more vigorous defence of the Gallipoli operation. He maintained that the War Council was overwhelmingly in favour of an Eastern initiative in January 1915, and that the 'ships alone' attack, though not an ideal method, was the only practical scheme in the absence of military support. In its 'genesis' and 'elaboration', he argued, it was a 'purely naval and

[14] Sir G. Arthur, *Life of Lord Kitchener* (London, 1920), iii. 110-13.
[15] R. R. James, *Gallipoli* (London, 1965), 52-3 n.
[16] Sir Ian Hamilton, *Gallipoli Diary*, 2 vols. (London, 1920), i. 14.
[17] Ibid. 10; L. Einstein, *Inside Constantinople* (London, 1917), pp. xii-xiv; Ambassador Henry Morgenthau, *Secrets of the Bosphorus* (London, 1918), 124, 149-50.
[18] Hamilton, *Gallipoli Diary*, i. 95-7, 132-3, 141, 147, 232-3; ii. 12, 95, 183-4.

professional' concept; indeed 'right or wrong, it was a Service plan', and it proposed the risking of ships which were largely 'valueless for any other purpose'.[19] Churchill was trenchantly critical of Kitchener. The latter, he asserted, was utterly dominating on the one hand (having 'absorbed the whole War Office into his spacious personality' and having left the General Staff 'completely in abeyance'), but utterly indecisive on the other hand. He had succumbed in the conflict between the Eastern and Western factions, lapsing 'into a state of most painful indecision between them'. Churchill disputed the rationale for this indecision, doubting that the Germans could have switched troops rapidly from the Russian to the Western Front, and questioning whether the retention of a single division—the 29—could have affected the issue significantly even if they had done so. Above all, he deprecated the delay in February 1915 as it had prevented the Allied forces from exploiting the vulnerability of the small Turkish garrison which was then on the peninsula.[20]

Overall, Churchill depicted the operation as one of glittering strategic promise foiled by 'a long chain of missed chances'. Despite the losses of 18 March, the naval attacks should have continued and could have swept the minefields while exhausting the limited supplies of Turkish ammunition; 'not to persevere', argued Churchill, 'that was the crime'.[21] Had there been no initial delay, or had the government responded more promptly to Hamilton's request of 17 May for more troops and ammunition, the Turks could have been attacked before they were able to double the strength of their Army. Even so, Churchill contended that there were still tactical and local opportunities to redeem these shortcomings, but that these too were wasted at the battle of Suvla Bay. 'The story of the IXth British Corps and of the whole Suvla landing', he observed, 'would be incredible if it were not true'.[22] The outcome, he concluded, left nothing but a 'war of exhaustion—not only of armies but of nations', with victory proving 'only less ruinous to the victor than to the vanquished'.[23]

The World Crisis proved a watershed in the historiography of Gallipoli. Henceforth a reaction set in with more and more writers defending the strategic concept, if not the tactics, of the Dardanelles operation. This impact derived not simply from the vigorous advocacy of Churchill nor even from its subsequent endorsement in large measure by the Official

---

[19] W. S. Churchill, *The World Crisis 1915* (London, 1923), 97, 121-2, 166-7.
[20] Ibid. 173, 175, 181-2, 213, 275.   [21] Ibid. 169, 515-16.
[22] Ibid. 272, 275-6, 516.   [23] Ibid. 515.

History of the campaign[24] but from the timing of these publications. Churchill's work pre-empted, and the Official History coincided with, the war book boom which erupted after 1928; their defence of an Eastern strategy chimed with the increasing wave of revulsion against the carnage and futility of the tactics pursued over several years on the Western Front.

Several of Churchill's former Cabinet colleagues spearheaded the defence of the Gallipoli expedition. Viscount Grey, the former Foreign Secretary, agreed that Churchill had been unfairly criticized and that the operation was a collective responsibility of the War Council. 'The real defence of it', he added, 'is that it very nearly did succeed as planned.'[25] Asquith and Lloyd George also sprang to Churchill's defence, with the latter endorsing Churchill's criticisms of Kitchener, especially his reluctance to release troops earmarked for the Western Front.[26] The publication of some German memoirs confirmed further aspects of Churchill's account, particularly the state of alarm in Constantinople at the approach of the fleet, the premonitions of defeat, the initial shortage of troops, arms, and ammunition on the peninsula, and the vital importance of time for the enhancement of the Turkish defences. Liman von Sanders, who had commanded the Turkish forces on the peninsula, even stressed the tactical advantages of Hamilton: his degree of initiative, artillery support, extensive means of transportation, and the constraints upon the Turks, who had to guard against a host of eventualities and who could only concentrate gradually against specific Allied attacks. 'In the three crises' (the naval attack of 18 March and the landings of April and August), he observed, 'the decision often hung on a knife edge'.[27] Although there may have been an element of special pleading in these comments to emphasize the resourcefulness of Sanders' command (for example, the naval guns, despite their power and range, lacked the most suitable trajectory for suppressing fire from the Turkish entrenchments),[28] his comments and impressions were widely quoted, not least by the British Official historian.

[24] Brig.-Gen. C. F. Aspinall-Oglander, *Military Operations Gallipoli* (London, 1929-32), i. 57, ii. 479-80.
[25] Visc. Grey of Falloden, *Twenty-Five Years 1892-1916* (London, 1925), ii. 77.
[26] The Earl of Oxford and Asquith, *Memories and Reflections 1852-1927* (London, 1928), ii. 89-90; David Lloyd George, *War Memoirs*, 6 vols. (London, 1933-6), i. (1933), 223-4, 390-1, 395.
[27] Liman von Sanders, *Five Years in Turkey* (Annapolis, Md., 1928), 63-6, 71, 87-9; Hans Kannengiesser Pasha, *The Campaign in Gallipoli* (London, 1927), 73, 267; Maj. E. R. Prigge, *Der Kampf um die Dardanellen* (Weimar, 1916), 32; C. Muhlmann, *Der Kampf um die Dardanellen 1915* (Berlin, 1927), 74.
[28] Sir F. Maurice, *British Strategy* (London, 1929), 134.

Nevertheless, the critics of Churchill and of the Gallipoli operation were far from silenced. In *The Uncensored Dardanelles*, Ellis Ashmead-Bartlett was fiercely critical of Hamilton for his strategy and tactics, of Kitchener for trying to run the war 'as a one-man job', and of Churchill for his impulsiveness. Although he absolved Churchill from any blame for the conduct of the naval or military operations, and praised the 'brilliant scheme' of 'his far-seeing mind', he doubted that Churchill had 'ever carefully weighed what forces were necessary to ensure victory or weighed the consequences of failure'.[29] Several writers, especially those still wedded to the Western Front strategy, agreed that Churchill's contribution had proved amateurish and impulsive. Sir Gerald Ellison's critique of the 'ships alone' strategy, Churchill's disregard of naval experts, and his enthusiasm for an impractical naval attack was appropriately entitled, *The Perils of Amateur Strategy*.[30] The military historian, Sir Frederick Maurice, though willing to recognize the merits of the Dardanelles campaign as a strategic concept, still reckoned that it had been launched precipitately before the Allies had the resources 'to make the Western Front safe'.[31]

Sir William Robertson wrote the most skilful defence of the Western Front priority. Switching fronts, he argued, was inherently risky, especially as 'the decisive front was fixed for us by the deployment of the enemy's masses in France and Belgium'.[32] He asserted, too, that the Dardanelles expedition, however potentially attractive, could not have achieved anything useful without the assistance, sooner or later, of troops. As these were not available initially, the scheme was simply impractical on the basis of a 'ships alone' attack. If Kitchener erred, claimed Robertson, it was not in temporarily withholding the 29 Division but in departing from his first instinct that sufficient troops for the new venture could not be found, even if the Allies adopted a strictly defensive posture on the Western Front. Taking up Churchill's point about the significance of the 29 Division, he insisted 'that there must have been something wrong with the main project from the first, otherwise the employment of a single division would not have become so important a matter as Lord Kitchener found it to be'.[33] Ultimately he contended that the means were not available and so the project was inherently impractical.

[29] E. Ashmead-Bartlett, *The Uncensored Dardanelles* (London, 1928), 13-15, 20-1.
[30] Sir G. Ellison, *The Perils of Amateur Strategy* (London, 1926), 23, 45, 52, 68-70, 111. [31] Maurice, *British Strategy*, 81-2, 101.
[32] Field Marshal Sir William Robertson, *Soldiers and Statesmen 1914-1918* (London, 1926), i. 74-5. [33] Ibid. 88, 103-4, 147.

Robertson's critique was soon followed by the second major defence of the expedition, the two-volume Official History written by Brigadier-General C. F. Aspinall-Oglander. The prize, it asserted, was worth the effort:

> There is little doubt to-day that the idea of forcing the Straits with a view to helping Russia, eliminating Turkey from the war and rallying the Balkan States to the side of the Entente, was one of the few great strategical conceptions of the World War.[34]

Moreover, it maintained that the prize could have been secured with more careful planning to exploit the Turkish vulnerabilities. Indeed, the History quoted liberally from the various Turkish and German accounts of the campaign to recount the fears and weaknesses of the Turks, and their surprise that the British did not invest more resources and take more risks to force the Straits.[35] Even in the absence of a carefully planned joint naval and military attack, it emphasized that the issue hung in the balance on at least three occasions.[36] Sir Ian Hamilton, it concluded, despite his formidable handicaps, had been entrusted with a feasible undertaking; he had failed partly on account of his own defects, especially his excessive confidence in an untried subordinate at the Suvla Bay landing, his optimistic assessment of the task confronting him, and his reluctance to ask for more than the minimum of reinforcements. His innate optimism and buoyant spirits, which had sustained the Expeditionary Force during the summer of 1915, had compounded his difficulties at critical moments.[37]

In several works, including his history of the Great War, Basil Liddell Hart powerfully endorsed the rehabilitation of the Gallipoli strategy. Compared with 'the dark and barren prospect in France',[38] he argued, Gallipoli was 'a sound and far-sighted conception, marred by a chain of errors in execution almost unrivalled even in British history'.[39] Although he believed that the belated land attack, despite its many difficulties, could have succeeded, Liddell Hart was fairly restrained in his comments upon Hamilton, mainly criticizing his failure to provide for a 'floating' reserve in his initial landing. He ascribed the failure of the second landing to the inexperience of the troops and to the inertia of the

---

[34] Aspinall-Oglander, *Military Operations Gallipoli*, ii. 479; see also i. 58.
[35] Ibid. i. pp. ix, 17-21, 31-8, 79-80, 105-7, 153-63; ii. 480, 482.
[36] Ibid. i. p. viii.   [37] Ibid. ii. 387-8.
[38] B. H. Liddell Hart, *The Decisive Wars of History: A Study in Strategy* (London, 1929), 199.
[39] Id., *A History of the World War 1914-1918* (London, 1934), 188.

local commanders.⁴⁰ Nevertheless, he praised the overall strategy as an example of the 'indirect approach' and reasonably asserted the outcome might have been different had the troops 'ultimately expended in driblets' been concentrated for action at the outset.⁴¹

If the strategy of Gallipoli was now increasingly endorsed, the naval and military tactics still occasioned fierce debate. While some naval writers condemned the preparatory naval bombardments and the 'ships alone' attack, Sir Roger Keyes stoutly defended Churchill. He insisted, as he had done in April 1915, that the Fleet could have forced the Straits, with far fewer losses than those suffered by the Army, and that its appearance in the Sea of Marmora would have produced a decisive victory.⁴² Bean, in the preface to the third edition of his official Australian history, questioned the merit of retrospective speculation. Magnifying the chances of success, he surmised, was a tendency which developed as the events in question receded into the past. He believed, too, that this approach lost sight of the difficulties which had bedevilled the operation. Indeed, he maintained that 'The initiation of the attempt to force the Dardanelles with ships alone, and the launching, when this failed, of the well-advertised land-campaign, appear as rash to-day as they did, to those who bore the consequences, in 1915.'⁴³ The publication of the letters of one Australian who had endured those consequences, Colonel (later General Sir) John Monash, corroborated this point of view. As he had noted on 18 July 1915, 'we have dropped the Churchill way of rushing in before we are ready, and hardly knowing what to do next . . .'.⁴⁴

The controversy over the land attack persisted, none the less. Compton Mackenzie, in his illuminating and incisive memoirs, defended his former commander-in-chief as a man who had looked, acted, and sounded like a leader in April 1915. Although Mackenzie applauded Hamilton's commitment to the strategic enterprise, he thought that he had been too optimistic about the potential of the second-best forces with which he had been entrusted and too deferential in his dealings with Kitchener, thereby tacitly accepting that the campaign would remain as a 'sideshow'.⁴⁵ Orlo Williams, formerly the chief cipher officer on Hamilton's

---

⁴⁰ Ibid. 187, 227-42.
⁴¹ Id., *Strategy: The Indirect Approach* (London, 1974), 195 and id., *The Decisive Wars of History*, 198.
⁴² Adm. Sir R. Keyes, *Naval Memoirs* (London, 1934), 186, 275-7, 523; Lord Wester-Wemyss, *The Navy in the Dardanelles Campaign* (London, 1924), 256-7, 260-1, 266; E. Keble Chatterton, *Dardanelles Dilemma* (London, 1935), 53-5.
⁴³ Bean, *The Story of ANZAC*, preface to 3rd edn. (1934), p. xli.
⁴⁴ F. M. Cutlack (ed.), *War Letters of General Monash* (Sydney, 1935), 59.
⁴⁵ C. Mackenzie, *Gallipoli Memories* (London, 1929), 362-4.

staff, endorsed these impressions. Based upon his knowledge of the telegram traffic, Williams maintained that Kitchener had made fundamental errors of judgement, imposing desperate burdens upon Hamilton, but that the latter had compounded his difficulties by diluting 'cogently crafted reports with literary palliatives and comforting trimmings that were justified less by facts than by his own personal convictions'.[46] Sir George MacMunn described some of Hamilton's administrative problems in greater detail, especially the improvisation of lines of communication from the island of Lemnos,[47] while others either regurgitated criticisms of Hamilton or defended him by castigating the indecision of Kitchener.[48]

Major John North, though, demonstrated that it was still possible to deliberate perceptively upon the strategic and tactical issues of the campaign. In *Gallipoli: The Fading Vision*—probably the best of the inter-war commentaries—North scrutinized the strategic options, largely favouring the Churchillian approach, and analysed the difficulties of Sir Ian Hamilton, particularly in his dealings with the War Office. North observed that had Hamilton dwelt upon all his difficulties in his dispatches, he would have provided opponents of the campaign with firsthand evidence of its impracticality; in other words, the reports may have reflected an element of calculation and not simply excessive optimism or deference towards Lord Kitchener.[49] North fully examined the many handicaps of Hamilton but still concluded that he had failed to impose his will on subordinate commanders at critical moments in the campaign.[50]

By the late 1930s, the first wave of historiographical revisionism was complete. Even so, the doubts about the wisdom of the enterprise and Churchill's strategic judgement persisted; indeed, as Alex Danchev has demonstrated, they recurred during the Second World War as a complicating factor in Anglo-American planning. During the heated debates of July 1942, copies of Robertson's critique circulated widely as the Americans feared that the British were trying to divert them from their *idée fixe* of a cross-Channel crossing: 'history', noted US Secretary of

[46] O. Williams, 'The Gallipoli Tragedy: Part One', *The Nineteenth Century and After*, 106 (July 1929), 82-94.
[47] Sir G. MacMunn, 'The Lines of Communication in the Dardanelles', *Army Quarterly*, 20/1 (Apr. 1930), 52-63 and id., *Behind the Scenes in Many Wars* (London, 1930), 120-91.
[48] Lt. Col. C. O. Head, *Glance at Gallipoli* (London, 1931), 200-1; E. Delage, *The Tragedy of the Dardanelles* (London, 1932), 66-70, 72-3, 235.
[49] North, *Gallipoli: The Fading Vision*, 54-60, 78-9, 83, 88-99, 249.
[50] Ibid. 318.

State Henry Stimson, 'is certainly repeating itself . . .'.[51] In fact, history would not repeat itself as the Allies, utilizing the massive industrial and military power of the United States, eventually mounted a highly successful amphibious operation in the D-Day landings.

Post-Second World War interest in the Gallipoli operation was largely revived by Alan Moorehead's lively account of the campaign, which was based mainly upon secondary sources. Moorehead defended the strategic concept as one of the most imaginative of the First World War, even arguing that the 'ships alone' attack could have precipitated the fall of Constantinople. Having consulted a wide range of Turkish and German sources, Moorehead proffered some interesting insights on Turkish attitudes. He claimed that the abortive naval attack of 18 March not only warned the Turks of the approaching invasion and gave them time to fortify the peninsula, but that it also served as a powerful political and psychological boost for the Turks, their first significant victory for many years.[52]

Moorehead's work would soon be followed by a series of more critical reappraisals. J. F. C. Fuller and Philip Magnus severely criticized the contributions of the three major figures. Churchill's idea, argued Fuller, may have been 'brilliant' as pure strategy, but launching an attack upon Constantinople without the support of a powerful army was essentially amateurish: 'the inadequacy of the means', wrote Fuller, 'never disturbed his vision'.[53] He also dismissed any defence of Hamilton based upon ill-luck; Hamilton, he insisted, was a product of the pre-Boer War army when wars were fought as 'gentlemanly affairs': hence his optimism, his lack of drive, and his reluctance to leave the general headquarters at critical moments.[54] Magnus, though willing to accept that Kitchener had to heed the representations of Sir John French and of the French government in January 1915 about the need to concentrate resources on the Western Front, still castigated his willingness to believe in the viability of a 'ships alone' attack, his failure to make any contingency plans, and his reluctance to confer with others. He confirmed, too, that Kitchener's persistent indecision, even 'crippling irresolution', left him without a policy on the Dardanelles and with diminishing credit in the

---

[51] A. Danchev, *Very Special Relationship: Field Marshal Sir John Dill and the Anglo-American Alliance 1941-44* (London, 1986), 34-5.

[52] Moorehead, *Gallipoli*, 40-1, 95-6, 363, 365.

[53] Maj.-Gen. J. F. C. Fuller, *The Decisive Battles of the Western World and their Influence upon History* (London, 1956), iii. 234-5.

[54] Ibid. 239, 255, 262-3.

government: by December 1915, Kitchener was merely 'a passenger in a feeble team'.[55]

The next major addition to the Gallipoli literature was the publication of several works in the 1960s, using the diaries, reports, and correspondence of Lord Hankey who had acted as secretary to the War Council during the Gallipoli campaign. His two volumes, *The Supreme Command 1914-1918*, published in 1960, provided the most extensive account hitherto of the deliberations of the War Council. The account was a fiercely damning indictment, made more striking by the fact that many of the retrospective criticisms of the supreme command had been made at the time by Hankey but had simply been swept aside. Hankey described how the meetings under Asquith's premiership were conducted on an *ad hoc* and often informal basis, with relatively few written memoranda or staff appraisals. In the absence of any co-ordinated direction, or support from naval/military technical committees, or continuous reviews, departmental preferences prevailed. As a consequence, some Council decisions, like those of 13 January, largely reflected a compromise between those concerned, and policy tended to drift towards an ever deeper involvement in a major campaign on the peninsula. The catalytic impulse often came from external events (like the reaction to the bombardments of 18 February, which convinced the War Council that it had to see the operation through, despite its earlier belief that the attacks could easily be terminated if unsuccessful) or from individual initiatives (such as Kitchener's authorization of a military landing in his instructions of 23 March to Hamilton, which was made without the knowledge or approval of the Cabinet or War Council). War, argued Hankey, could not be departmentalized; nor, at the highest level, could it be based upon obsessive secrecy and a chronic lack of staff preparation.[56]

Hankey's book was doubly depressing since he had clearly warned Asquith and the other members of the War Council of the dangers which could befall a poorly planned and uncoordinated venture. Given his incisive grasp of the requirements of an amphibious operation, he had warned Asquith that unless the details were thought through 'a serious disaster may occur'.[57] He had pleaded for the creation of a naval and military technical committee to avoid a repetition of the naval fiasco of 18 March, and, on 6 April, had warned of the 'extraordinary difficulty'

[55] P. Magnus, *Kitchener: Portrait of an Imperialist* (London, 1958), 313, 317-18, 343, 357, 368-9.
[56] Lord Hankey, *Supreme Command 1914-1918* (London, 1961), i. 264-7, 281-4, 291-5, 320-9, 338-45, 406-12. [57] Ibid. 292.

of Hamilton's landing. Churchill, apparently, had 'remarked that he could not see that there was any difficulty at all'.[58] Hankey depicted Churchill as the motive force of the Dardanelles enterprise—the man who had skilfully swayed the War Council on 13 January, who had pressed ahead with the 'ships alone' attack despite the objections of Admiral Fisher and Vice Admiral Sir Henry Jackson, and who had then enthusiastically backed a military assault without realizing 'the extreme difficulties of the operation'. Hankey reckoned that Asquith and Kitchener had also underestimated the hazards of a military landing, but admitted that everyone had underestimated the tenacity of the Turkish resistance.[59]

In the second volume of *From Dreadnought to Scapa Flow* (1965), Arthur Marder expanded upon this critique. Using a wide array of naval manuscript sources, the papers of Lord Esher, and Hankey's volumes, he wrote an authoritative work on the formulation of naval policy. He confirmed that Churchill did not override his expert advisers, that important questions relating to the operation were discussed at War Staff Group meetings with subsequent decisions embodied in the minutes, and that senior officers, including Rear-Admiral Henry F. Oliver, the Chief of the Admiralty War Staff, had endorsed the proposed naval assault on the Turkish forts. Yet Marder still described that professional support as 'perfunctory', with some officers lukewarm or doubtful about particular points, if not openly opposed to the naval attack. Accordingly, he criticized Churchill for giving the War Councils of 13 and 28 January the impression that he represented 'the considered opinion of the Board of Admiralty as a whole'. He deprecated the idea that the Navy alone could 'take' the Peninsula and a city of one million people, using naval guns with their flat trajectory against land defences, but endorsed Churchill's view that the delay in sending the 29 Division was critical: 'had Kitchener acted boldly at the end of February and bent every effort towards preparing a large and well-organized amphibious operation, the Peninsula probably could have been taken'.[60]

Marder conceded that Churchill had always favoured a joint attack and had repeatedly pressed for the dispatch of troops to the Dardanelles, but insisted that this did not absolve Churchill from the error of believing that the Fleet alone could have succeeded. Even if Asquith and Kitchener, for their own reasons, were inclined to agree, Churchill was the decisive

[58] Ibid. 293-5, 300.   [59] Ibid. 265-7, 299-306.
[60] A. J. Marder, *From the Dreadnought to Scapa Flow* (Oxford, 1965), ii. 236; see also ii. 206-7, 214-18, 260-1.

voice: his 'impetuosity, eloquence, and doggedness carried the day'.[61] He also blamed Churchill for not consulting his professional advisers more regularly, even though the War Staff lacked a Plans Division until 1917. Nevertheless, he endorsed the conclusion of Hankey (and before him of Admiral Wemyss) that the real blame lay not with individuals but with the system of government—the lack of co-ordinated naval/military planning, the War Council's preoccupation with policy ends, and the failure to elicit professional advice.[62]

In *Gallipoli*, another major study of the campaign as a whole, Robert Rhodes James sustained the critical reappraisal of the 1960s. Based upon an extensive knowledge of the secondary literature and some primary source material, he put forward an interpretation which differed sharply from Moorehead's in several key respects. Moreover, he used the historiographical debate as a basis for some of his own assessments; he severely contested Churchill's claim that the 'ships alone' attack had been a Service plan and followed Hankey in his criticism of the staff work, or the lack of it, and of Kitchener's unilateral initiatives. But he reserved his sharpest attacks for Hamilton, deriding his planning as too ambitious and rigid, his tendency to cross the border between optimism and wishful thinking, his imperfect grasp of detail, his over-confidence in battle and his lack of an iron will or dominating personality.[63]

Rhodes James unfolded an even more strident critique of Churchill in his subsequent work, *Churchill: A Study in Failure 1900–1939* (1970). He conceded that Churchill could not bear the full responsibility for the campaign, and that the War Council, lacking any strong leadership, had compounded his difficulties, but he still maintained that Churchill was 'to a very real extent deeply responsible'. Indeed, he disputed Marder's assertion that the three-week delay had proved crucial, claiming that Churchill never appreciated 'at the time or subsequently' the immense problems of an amphibious landing. He also contested Liddell Hart's belief that a chain of errors in execution had marred a far-sighted strategy. 'The errors in execution', he argued, had 'stemmed directly from the fundamental fallacies in the original conception', which was, in effect, 'a wholly illegitimate war gamble'.[64]

Stephen Roskill was also critical, albeit in more measured prose, in his biography of Hankey. Using a wide array of correspondence and Cabinet

[61] A. J. Marder, *From the Dreadnought to Scapa Flow* (Oxford, 1965), ii. 213, 261.
[62] Ibid. 262–3; Wester-Wemyss, *The Navy in the Dardanelles Campaign*, 283.
[63] James, *Gallipoli*, 31, 53–4, 69, 91–3, 318–20.
[64] Id., *Churchill: A Study in Failure 1900–1939* (London, 1970), 91, 96–9.

papers to amplify the secondary literature, he largely corroborated Hankey's reputation as one of the few advisers who understood the requirements of an amphibious operation. Roskill doubted whether Churchill or Kitchener ever perceived the risks or the demands involved in undertaking an opposed landing. He reiterated the familiar criticisms of Hamilton and quoted extensively from the letters written by Hankey during and immediately after his visit to Gallipoli. He quoted Hankey as observing that the most serious mistakes were those inherent in the British military system: 'the regimental officers and the rank and file', wrote Hankey, 'never knew enough of what is expected of them, and what they have before them'. Until the system was radically reformed, the gulf between the staff which planned operations and the men who had to carry them out would persist, so perpetuating, in Roskill's words, 'one of the greatest weaknesses in the British military system in World War I'.[65]

In this post-1945 period there was also a multitude of works about Hamilton. They generally repeated the well-known arguments. Hamilton and his apologists reviewed his many difficulties, and his purported fate as 'the scapegoat for the politicians', without adducing any further extenuating evidence. Hamilton's nephew even dismissed *Gallipoli* by Robert Rhodes James because it dwelt 'unduly on dismal stories'.[66] Hamilton's critics focused upon his failings of personality, planning, secrecy, and belated initiatives. Alan Wykes noted that critics had often observed that if the invasion had been planned with a fraction of the care and co-operation invested in the evacuation under Sir Charles Monro's leadership, it might have succeeded. As Wykes conceded, that was a somewhat glib comparison but it had some justice in it:[67] at the very least it punctured the assumption that British staff officers were fundamentally incapable and unable to establish an effective liaison with the officers and men who had to implement their plans. Although there were

[65] S. Roskill, *Hankey Man of Secrets*, i. *1877-1918* (London, 1970), 157, 162-5, 213-14.
[66] I. B. M. Hamilton, *The Happy Warrior* (London, 1966), 461; Gen. Sir I. Hamilton, *Listening for the Drums* (London, 1944), 252-61; Maj. A. Farrar-Hockley (ed.), *The Commander by General Sir Ian Hamilton* (London, 1957), 16-24, 139-43.
[67] Maj.-Gen. E. K. G. Sixsmith, *British Generalship in the Twentieth Century* (London, 1970), 148-56; J. Hargrave, *The Suvla Bay Landing* (London, 1964), 29; Brig.-Gen. S. L. A. Marshall, 'Suvla Bay', *Military Review*, 43/11 (Nov. 1963), 60-8; Maj. T. A. Gibson, 'Eyeless in Byzantium: The Tragedy of Sir Ian Hamilton', *Army Quarterly*, 91/1 (Oct. 1965), 82-96; A. Wykes, 'First Landings at Gallipoli', *Purnell's History of the First World War*, 2/12 (1970), 761-73; D. Schurman, 'Suvla Bay', ibid. 3/6 (1971), 1048-59; Wykes, 'Gallipoli Evacuation and Withdrawal', ibid. 3/9 (1971), 1135-6.

further criticisms of Hamilton by Cyril Falls and Sir Llewellyn Woodward in their major histories of the First World War,[68] most commentators regarded the lack of forethought and planning, particularly the misunderstandings about the proposed function of the Mediterranean Expeditionary Force, as ultimately responsible for the failure of the entire campaign.[69]

The next major watershed in the historiography of Gallipoli was the publication of Martin Gilbert's *Winston Churchill*, iii. *1914-1916*, shortly followed by the companion volume of documents. Having consulted seventy-three collections of papers, Gilbert provided the most detailed account hitherto of the policy-making process until Churchill's exclusion from the Coalition Government in May 1915. He disposes of some myths about Churchill's behaviour, including the belief that he was obsessed about an attack on Turkey in the early days of the war. As Gilbert indicates, Churchill was not the first to press for an attack on Turkey at the Dardanelles; in fact, he had preferred, and had repeatedly pressed for, an attack on the north German coast.[70] Gilbert also questions whether the bombardment of 3 November 1914 rashly alerted the Turks, as the latter 'needed no warning from the Allies of where the major attack was likely to come'.[71] He stresses that no one at the Admiralty questioned the main assumptions of the bombardment, namely that naval guns could demolish land forts, and emphasizes that Churchill had insisted from the outset (25 November 1914) that any assault on the Dardanelles should involve a large military force. Only the Russian appeal of 1 January 1915, and Kitchener's wish to respond but without committing any military forces, persuaded Churchill to consider 'the very plan which until then he had believed to be impossible'. Even so, as Gilbert confirms, Churchill continued to request the support of a large military force and to complain bitterly over Kitchener's procrastination.[72]

Some of Gilbert's assertions are debatable (notably his claim that Callwell once regarded an attack on the Dardanelles as justifiable[73]

---

[68] Falls, *The First World War*, 110, 115; Sir L. Woodward, *Great Britain and the War of 1914-1918* (London, 1967), 74.
[69] P. Guinn, *British Strategy and Politics 1914 to 1918* (Oxford, 1965), 61; T. Higgins, *Winston Churchill and the Dardanelles* (London, 1963), 187; Woodward, *Great Britain and the War of 1914-1918*, 95.
[70] Gilbert, *Winston Churchill*, iii. *1914-1916* (London, 1971), 180-1, 237, 246-7.
[71] Ibid. 218. [72] Ibid. 219-21, 232-3, 260, 292, 300-4, 310-11, 314.
[73] Ibid. 203. See also J. Gooch, *The Plans of War: The General Staff and British Military Strategy c. 1900-1916* (London, 1974), 331 n. 37.

Gallipoli

which has to be placed in a broader context) and his contention that every aspect of the naval attack was examined[74] (which has to be compared with Marder's account), but his insights on Churchill are certainly instructive. He acknowledges that Churchill sincerely believed that once the Dardanelles were forced, naval power alone could defeat the Turks. He agrees, too, that Churchill's powerful advocacy of the 'ships alone' attack contributed to the War Council's self-deception. Moreover, by persisting in the advocacy of this attack, despite believing that military support was necessary, Churchill had to be responsible for the disaster he forecast.[75] Gilbert confirms that Churchill remained sanguine about the campaign—willing to risk a second naval attack after 18 March, confident of a successful military landing in April, and a champion thereafter of the need to reinforce Hamilton.[76] Gilbert refers to the perceptive correspondence of Clementine Churchill which addressed the critical question of why Churchill often created distrust when he sought approval.

She saw clearly that the ideas which he produced with such extraordinary energy and conviction were seen by others as lacking in judgement; and that the more fiercely he pressed forward with a course of action, the more lacking in perspective he appeared to colleagues without whose support he could not act.[77]

Churchill could still be persuasive at times. In his authoritative account of the French involvement in the Dardanelles, George Cassar explains that it was Churchill's eloquence and vision of the military and political benefits which converted the French Minister of the Marine against his own judgement and the scepticism of his professional advisers. As Cassar indicates, the French reluctantly joined the naval phase, even abdicating their right to choose a naval commander-in-chief, and subsequently sent troops, because they were not prepared to let Britain dismember the Ottoman Empire on her own. Thereafter two French decisions had a critical bearing upon the campaign: General Joffre's insistence that he must be allowed to launch an autumn offensive on the Western Front and the dispatch of reinforcements, formerly destined for Gallipoli, to Salonika. Throughout the campaign, inter-allied politics had frustrated the prospects for co-ordinated endeavour. Cassar concludes, quite reasonably, that 'the political aims of the Entente

---

[74] Gilbert, *Winston Churchill*, iii. 249, 255-6. See also A. J. Marder, *From the Dreadnought to Scapa Flow*, ii. 262-3.
[75] Gilbert, *Winston Churchill*, iii. 249, 311.
[76] Ibid. 377, 390-6, 433, 471, 497-8.   [77] Ibid. 825.

Powers prevented them from using adequate military means for their military ends'.[78]

In the wake of Gilbert's work, several authors renewed the debate over the 'ships alone' attack. Some, like Jeffrey Wallin and Captain Bush, defended the decision as a legitimate gamble, with Wallin even disputing the modest criticisms of Gilbert.[79] Marder, in an interesting review of the naval attack, claimed that there was at least 'a 50-50 chance' that another attack could have forced the Straits and compelled the Turks to sue for peace.[80] Roskill remained unconvinced. In *Churchill and the Admirals*, he reiterated his belief that the Navy by itself could not possibly have taken Constantinople, that Churchill did not consult his advisers properly, that he exaggerated the effects of naval gunnery, and that he prematurely launched the naval operations.[81] Finally, the publication of Asquith's highly indiscreet letters to Venetia Stanley confirmed Clementine Churchill's comments upon the impression which Churchill could make on his colleagues. After the War Council meeting of 26 February 1915, Asquith wrote 'Winston was in some ways at his worst—having quite a presentable case. He was noisy, rhetorical, tactless & temperless—or—full'.[82]

The lack of any new major works or newly discovered manuscript material has not inhibited commentators from further writing on Hamilton. In several works, the judgements have become ever more harsh. 'The fundamental responsibility for the overall strategic failure', writes Monick (not merely in the landings but also the 'fatal and futile' offensives in Helles during June and July) 'must rest with Hamilton's lack of decisive leadership'.[83] Peter Liddle argues that Hamilton 'lacked both the capacity and the will to lead the expedition at every stage of its planning and execution', while John Laffin dismisses him as a 'Commander-in-Chief in name only'.[84]

[78] G. H. Cassar, *The French and the Dardanelles* (London, 1971), 248; see also pp. 54-80, 181-205, 238-47.
[79] J. D. Wallin, *By Ships Alone: Churchill and the Dardanelles* (Durham, NC, 1981), 5, 7, 133-5; Capt. E. W. Bush, *Gallipoli* (London, 1975), 1-32.
[80] A. J. Marder, *From the Dardanelles to Oran* (Oxford, 1974), 1-32.
[81] S. Roskill, *Churchill and the Admirals* (London, 1977), 41-53.
[82] M. Brock and E. Brock (eds.), *H. H. Asquith Letters to Venetia Stanley* (Oxford, 1982), 449; see also V. Bonham Carter, *Winston Churchill as I Knew Him* (London, 1965), 355-7.
[83] S. Monick, 'Gallipoli: The Landings of 25 April 1915', *Military History Journal*, 6/4 (Dec. 1984), 121.
[84] P. Liddle, *Men of Gallipoli* (London, 1976), 276; J. Laffin, *Damn the Dardanelles* (London, 1980), 202.

Liddell Hart, though, in 'Gallipoli Judgement' made several interesting points about Hamilton—'the military leader who comes out best, if by no means unscathed' from the campaign. Despite his many handicaps, argued Liddell Hart, Hamilton achieved a real tactical surprise in April and August, securing a potentially decisive superiority at the critical points. Even if nine out of ten chances went begging success was still sure, but his subordinates bungled ten out of ten. The failure, asserted Liddell Hart, was not so much that of individuals as of a military system 'which chose leaders by seniority and preferred safe men to men who were bold in thought and action'.[85] Liddell Hart agreed that Hamilton did not exert his authority sufficiently and impose his will on his subordinates, but claimed that 'his influence was cramped by the nature of war at that time'.[86] Whether Hamilton was compelled to stay back at Imbros seems debatable, but Liddell Hart's comparison between Hamilton and the Western Front commanders is perhaps more perceptive. 'Hamilton erred', he suggested, 'in pursuing aims, which his plans had made possible, after they had become impossible', whereas the latter had persisted, at far greater cost, in pursuing aims that had never been possible.[87]

Kitchener, also, became the subject of several studies. Some scholars, particularly those writing on the General Staff, focused on his 'chronic and even pathetic indecisiveness over the Dardanelles campaign'.[88] John Gooch emphasizes that Kitchener not only dominated the War Office and ignored the General Staff, but that he effectively left Hankey as the prime source of strategic advice for the War Council. 'Without the professional advice of the General Staff, functioning through the medium of government', writes Gooch, 'the result was a haphazard and irresolute selection of objectives which doomed a military operation to disaster'.[89]

In *The Continental Commitment* (1972) and a subsequent lecture, 'The British Way of Warfare', Michael Howard began the reappraisal of Kitchener or at least of his strategic insights. He defends Kitchener's commitment of British resources to the Western Front in August 1915, arguing that there was no other way of sustaining France and of relieving

---

[85] Liddell Hart, 'Gallipoli Judgement', *Purnell's History of the First World War*, 3/9 (1971), 1140.   [86] Ibid.   [87] Ibid.

[88] Brian Bond, *The Victorian Army and the Staff College 1854-1914* (London, 1972), 302; see also A. Wykes, 'Gallipoli Evacuation and Withdrawal', *Purnell's History of the First World War*, 3/9 (1971), 1132; P. Simkins, 'Kitchener and the Expansion of the Army', *Politicians and Defence: Studies in the Formulation of British Defence Policy 1845-1970*, ed. Ian Beckett and J. Gooch (Manchester, 1981), 95.

[89] Gooch, *The Plans of War*, 309, 311-16.

pressure on the Eastern Front. The flexibility of sea power had been tried and found wanting; the Dardanelles campaign, however 'flawless' as a strategic concept, had 'met the fate of virtually every British amphibious operation since the Age of Elizabeth . . . all brilliant in conception, all lamentable in execution'. British amphibious assaults, he states, would not become a major tool of strategy until buttressed by American military and industrial muscle to ensure a local superiority, by land, sea and air.[90]

George Cassar's biography of Kitchener develops the reappraisal of Kitchener's contribution. He attributes Kitchener's oscillation between the 'Eastern' and 'Western' viewpoints to a belief in the primacy of the Western Front but not at the expense of further futile offensives, especially if the latter involved his new Armies which would not be ready until the spring of 1915. As diversionary attacks in secondary theatres might thin the German line in France, Kitchener was willing to support such ventures, particularly if they could also help the Russians quickly without involving British troops. Hence the political and strategic attractions of the 'ships alone' attack, which had further merit inasmuch as it could supposedly be abandoned if unsuccessful, without any serious loss of prestige. Cassar ascribes Kitchener's subsequent reluctance to commit the 29 Division to his continuing concern about events on the continent and his non-use of the General Staff 'to the same single-handed methods that had carried him through the Sudan and South Africa'. He regards Kitchener's meagre instructions to Hamilton as reflecting a lingering belief that the Army would only be required in a limited and subordinate role.[91]

Cedric Lowe and Michael Dockrill had already drawn attention to Kitchener's dilemma on 24 February, namely his uncertainty about what Churchill wanted the troops for and the rationale for requesting the 29 Division.[92] Once the troops were committed in April, argues Cassar, Kitchener became extremely pessimistic about the feasibility of the undertaking. He doubted that Hamilton, even with reinforcements, could do more than cut the waist of the peninsula in a second attack. After the second abortive assault in August, he became even more depressed but was reluctant to evacuate lest it damage British prestige in the East and entail a heavy loss of life. Ultimately Cassar agrees that

[90] M. E. Howard, *The British Way in Warfare* (London, 1974), 19-20 and id., *The Continental Commitment* (London, 1972), 57.
[91] Cassar, *Kitchener: Architect of Victory* (London, 1977), 270-1, 283-5, 293-5, 311-12.
[92] C. J. Lowe and M. L. Dockrill, *The Mirage of Power* (London, 1972), ii. 189.

Kitchener's secrecy and personal methods 'bred confusion and error', but he still maintains that Kitchener was the only member of the government who viewed the war as a whole.[93]

Keith Neilson carries the revisionism still further, by contending that Kitchener's decisions were neither capricious nor vacillating but reflected a 'sophisticated understanding of the two-front nature of the war' and a shrewd assessment of the relative strengths of the Allies, especially Russia. Kitchener, he claims, was deeply concerned about the viability of both fronts. He feared that a stalemate in the East could enable the Germans to transfer massive numbers of troops to the West, thereby precipitating the defeat of France and the invasion of Britain. He was always ready to buttress the Russian war effort, either by supporting the Dardanelles venture as a prompt, positive, but essentially limited response to the plea of the Grand Duke Nicholas at a time when the New Armies were being raised, or, in a more substantive manner, by holding large German forces in the West. As he believed in the primacy of the Western Front (to protect Britain and sustain her Allies), he would only countenance a limited involvement in the Mediterranean. Neilson asserts that it was the changing nature of the military situation in Russia, and its effect upon Kitchener's thinking, which made his advice seem inconsistent to his colleagues. By the end of July 1915, Kitchener was not only doubtful about the prospects of the Gallipoli operation, but he was also deeply concerned about the deteriorating political situation in France and Russia. A new offensive in France had to have priority over further reinforcements for Hamilton 'to relieve pressure on Russia and keep the French Army and people steady . . .'.[94] Neilson concludes that Kitchener failed to clarify his views in the War Council partly because of his instinctive secrecy and well-founded suspicions about the indiscretions of his colleagues, and partly because of his reluctance to reveal too much of his information about the Russian situation. His premature death, finally, denied him an opportunity of fully presenting his case.[95]

Neilson amplifies this thesis in a subsequent work, *Strategy and Supply* (1984), providing a detailed account of Kitchener's concerns about the issue of reinforcing the Dardanelles at a time of fluctuating fortunes on the Eastern Front.[96] If this is the best defence of Kitchener's strategic judgement, it hardly answers the many other criticisms: his

[93] Cassar, *Kitchener*, 376-7, 417, 442.
[94] Draft of Kitchener to Asquith, 17 Aug. 1915, Kitchener MSS, WO 159/7, repr. in K. Neilson, 'Kitchener: A Reputation Refurbished?' *Canadian Journal of History*, 15 (1980), 222.   [95] Neilson, 'Kitchener', 209-27.
[96] Id., *Strategy and Supply* (London, 1984), 90-7.

ready acceptance of the plausibility of the 'ships alone' attack, his failure to use the General Staff and his failure to authorize any contingency planning. Even minor operations have to be carefully planned, particularly if they are amphibious in character and involve opposed landings: Hankey's insights on these issues still seem more impressive than those of Kitchener.

How far the Straits Agreement of November 1914[97] influenced the planning of the Gallipoli expedition is not entirely clear. Sir Edward Grey had certainly consulted Asquith and King George V before making his secret promise over the Straits and Constantinople and, in William Renzie's assessment of fairly ambiguous evidence, Grey may have sought the advice of Churchill and Kitchener, too.[98] But Gregory Paget makes a bolder claim, asserting that the campaign was only sustained and expanded in March 1915 because of the November 1914 Agreement, and that the satisfaction of Russia had become much more important than the swaying of the Balkan states to the cause of the Entente. Although it is certainly true that the War Council of 10 March was prepared to meet Russia's more specific requests over Constantinople, Paget fails to explain how Hankey's memory is faulty over the Council meeting of 24 February, held before the receipt of any Russian requests, when the Council agreed that the naval bombardments of 18 February had committed the government to seeing the operation through.[99]

In another review of the decision-making process, David French maintains that even the wholesale reform of the administrative machinery would not necessarily have ensured a successful operation. Any small cabinet committee and its professional advisers, he claims, would have had to 'rid themselves of the erroneous assumption that the Turks were not a serious enemy who would surrender the moment the fleet appeared off Constantinople'.[100] This article and his subsequent book, *British Strategy and War Aims* (1986) break new ground in their reassessment of the assumptions of British policy-makers. He effectively develops the

---

[97] C. Jay Smith, 'Great Britain and the 1914-1915 Straits Agreement with Russia: The British Promise of November 1914', *American Historical Review*, 70/4 (1965), 1015-34; W. A. Renzie, 'Great Britain, Russia and the Straits, 1914-1915', *Journal of Modern History*, 42/1 (1970), 1-20; V. H. Rothwell, *British War Aims and Peace Diplomacy 1914-1918* (Oxford, 1971), 24-5.

[98] Renzie, 'Great Britain, Russia and the Straits', 7-8.

[99] G. Paget, 'The November 1914 Straits Agreement and the Dardanelles Gallipoli Campaign', *Australian Journal of Political History*, 33/3 (1987), 253-60; Hankey, *The Supreme Command*, i. 283.

[100] French, 'The Origins of the Dardanelles Campaign Reconsidered', *History*, 68 (1983), 224.

contention of Don Schurman that the positions of the 'Easterners' and 'Westerners' were 'not as firmly taken as subsequent writers have suggested'.[101] Indeed he argues that all were 'Easterners' in the sense of wishing to preserve the Empire and help Russia, while most were 'Westerners' in their recognition that the Entente had to be preserved on the Western Front. The real division, he suggests, was between those who wished to follow what they believed had been their predecessors' policy during the Napoleonic War, that is, basically an economic and naval support for a long war effort, and those who believed that only active military intervention on the Continent would prevent either a German victory or an indecisive peace.[102] The latter view prevailed partly, as A. L. Macfie states, because the Allies possessed surplus forces in 1915 by virtue of the deadlock on the Western Front and their command of the sea, so enabling them to make the 'demonstration' which Kitchener had promised.[103]

Tuvia Ben-Moshe makes a similar point in his reassessment of Churchill's strategy. He argues that Churchill recognized the interrelationship of the fronts, and that he never discounted the importance of the Western Front—'the main theatre' as he called it. Nevertheless, he believed that if a successful assault could be launched upon the Balkan front, it could turn the latter into 'the decisive theatre'. In view of the limited prospects for a feasible or inexpensive breakthrough in the West, Ben-Moshe accepts Churchill's definition of the Gallipoli move as 'a legitimate war gamble'. He adds, however, that gamblers should know when to stop, especially when they are losing, and that Churchill's opposition to the evacuation of Gallipoli reflected a loss of strategic judgement.[104]

What then, if anything, still needs to be written about Gallipoli? First, Sir Ian Hamilton certainly warrants a proper biography, one which avoids the extremes of hagiography or glib criticism. If it could be written on the scale and in the style of Geoffrey Serle's biography of Sir John Monash,[105] it would be eminently readable, but, if written by a professional military historian, it might shed some light on Hamilton's

[101] D. Schurman, 'Easterners versus Westerners', *Purnell's History of the First World War*, 2/10 (1971), 712.
[102] French, *British Strategy and War Aims 1914-1916* (London, 1986), pp. xii–xiii.
[103] A. L. Macfie, 'The Straits Question in the First World War 1914-18', *Middle Eastern Studies*, 19/1 (1983), 69.
[104] T. Ben-Moshe, 'Churchill's Strategic Conception during the First World War', *Journal of Strategic Studies*, 12/1 (Mar. 1989), 9.
[105] G. Serle, *John Monash: A Biography* (Carlton, Victoria, 1982).

opportunities and handicaps in Gallipoli. Secondly, the enigma of Kitchener could be probed further; neither Cassar's biography nor Neilson's strategic rationalizations seem to answer all the questions about this complex personality. Finally, the process by which Asquith's government embarked on this operation could serve as a useful case study within a broader analysis of military policy-making in the United Kingdom.

8
Allenby and the Palestine Campaign*
JONATHAN NEWELL

> I do not think I should over do, if I were you, the fact of Allenby being so very wonderful in every way. This ... rather makes him out an altogether superman and, as you know very well, he had his very human aspects as well.
>
> Field Marshal Sir Philip Chetwode to Archibald Wavell
> 17 February 1939, Allenby papers, 6/VIII/31

When General Allenby walked into Jerusalem on 9 December 1917 he entered not only one of the most famous and revered cities in the world but also the collective imagination of a generation. In part this was due to careful planning by the British government, which achieved a propaganda triumph that looks impressive even in our age of the mass media and sophisticated techniques of manipulation. Each aspect of the ceremony during which Allenby accepted the surrender of the Holy City and declared Britain's future intentions in the region was delicately stage-managed for the maximum possible effect. As early as 21 November the Foreign Office in London had already drafted the general's official proclamation, thereby allowing sufficient time for Allenby himself to make any suggestions or modifications that he might consider necessary.[1] That Allenby avoided entering Jerusalem on horseback but 'walked rather self-consciously'[2] was a deliberate ploy designed to contrast British humility with the apparent pre-war arrogance of the Kaiser, as Allenby himself explained to his wife a few days later: 'we walked into

---

* I would like to thank the Trustees of the Liddell Hart Centre for Military Archives and Lord Robertson of Oakridge, and the Trustees of the Imperial War Museum and Mr Alisdair Murray, for permission to quote from material for which they hold the copyright. The staff of all four depositories where I consulted papers from which I have quoted or to which I have referred were unfailingly courteous and helpful, and I would like to thank them also.

[1] Hardinge to Robertson, 21 Nov. 1917, Robertson papers, I/21/78/1; draft proclamation for capture of Jerusalem, ibid. I/21/79/2.
[2] K. Robbins, *The First World War* (London, 1985), 71.

the Holy City—because the Kaiser rode in. It was said, then, that a better than he had walked. He had a gap made in the wall for him. I went in through the Jaffa gate; not through the gap, though within 20 yards of it.'[3] Even this calculated act of humble reverence, emphasized as it was by the fact that no Allied flag was flown in the city while the ceremony took place, concealed still deeper subtleties and complexities on the part of the British. At first it had been hoped to arrange for Allenby to make his way into Jerusalem through another entrance—the Golden Gate, which had been walled up since the Crusades of the Middle Ages—as 'there was a prophecy that the conqueror who entered by the Golden Gate again would hold Jerusalem for ever. Unfortunately you had to go through a Muslim graveyard and the area of the Mosque of Omar, so it was dropped.'[4] The general himself was under strict orders from London concerning the declaration of the capture of the Holy City because Lloyd George wanted the news kept secret until he could announce it personally in the House of Commons to an expectant nation.[5] Consequently Allenby actually refrained from mentioning anything about the fall of the city in his letters to his wife until 11 December, although he wrote to her on both the 9th and the 10th![6]

All this hard work and meticulous planning was not wasted. The news that the 'thousand-year-old objective', Jerusalem, had been taken 'had a moral value far in excess of the material effect' because of the general gloom that had descended upon the British nation after over three severe years of war.[7] Nor was it only Lloyd George's electorate which was impressed, for the events at Jerusalem on 9 December had a more far-reaching impact than even the (Welsh) Prime Minister could have expected: 'Austere and humble as it was, the ceremony caught the imagination of the world, and when much else was forgotten about the First World War its memory remained, clear and undefiled.'[8] Ever since, Allenby's name has been linked with the seizure of the Holy City and all the historical, religious, and romantic connotations that this inevitably includes. This very fact has exercised a profound influence upon almost everything written about him since December 1917, as is demonstrated in this comment by one of his biographers: 'Israelite, Assyrian, Greek,

[3] Allenby to wife, 14 Dec. 1917, Allenby papers, 1/8/33. The very fact that many people today are aware that Allenby did walk into Jerusalem testifies to the success of this action. [4] Chetwode to Wavell, 17 Feb. 1939, Allenby papers, 6/VIII/31.
[5] Allenby to wife, 11 Dec. 1917, ibid. 1/8/32.
[6] A. P. Wavell, *Allenby: A Study in Greatness* (London, 1940), 231.
[7] B. H. Liddell Hart, *The War in Outline 1914-1918* (London, 1936), 192.
[8] J. Connell, *Wavell: Soldier and Scholar* (London, 1964), 132.

Roman, Jew, Arab, Crusader, Turk had entered Jerusalem as conquerors before the British. None of these nations can have been represented by one more impressive or worthier of his race than was Allenby, physically or morally.'[9]

The temptation to see the general's triumph at Jerusalem as the final revenge of the medieval Crusaders has proved too much for many subsequent chroniclers of these dramatic events. Within a few years of the Great War's conclusion there emerged books with titles such as *The Romance of the Last Crusade: With Allenby to Jerusalem*, *The Last Crusade*, *The Deliverance of Jerusalem*, *Khaki Crusaders*, and *Temporary Crusaders*.[10] Most of these were based on the personal reminiscences of men who had served under Allenby in Palestine and they did all they could to emphasize the romance of the entire campaign in Palestine in order, no doubt, to improve the sales of their books. Consequently the British commander was presented to the reader as a victorious crusader whose chief aim in coming to the Holy Land was to seize Jerusalem: 'At last Jerusalem was in our hands! In all the ten crusades organised and equipped to free the Holy City, only two were really successful—the first led by Godfrey de Bouillon, and the last under Edmund Allenby.'[11] Since Allenby is portrayed as the most successful of all the Crusaders it becomes inevitable that his military standing must be shown to be second to none. So we are told that every order issued by the commander-in-chief was executed 'with exactitude and enthusiasm' because no army had 'such complete confidence in its leader'.[12] Nor has the parallel between Allenby, the conqueror of Jerusalem, and Richard the Lion-Heart, perhaps the most romantic figure of all the Crusaders, escaped the attention of many writers. Thus we find Allenby's prestige enhanced still further at Richard I's expense:

Many before Allenby had failed in these harsh hills; Saladin had broken Christian hearts among them and Richard Cœur de Lion had stood on a commanding peak and turned his back on Jerusalem out of anguish at his impotence. But in mist and rain . . . Allenby's infantry struggled on their bitter way . . . until they came dour and implacable over the skyline and saw the city.[13]

[9] Wavell, *Allenby*, 230.
[10] V. Gilbert, *The Romance of the Last Crusade: With Allenby to Jerusalem* (London, 1923); D. Maxwell, *The Last Crusade* (London, 1920); E. W. G. Masterman, *The Deliverance of Jerusalem* (London, 1918); F. H. Cooper, *Khaki Crusaders* (Cape Town, 1919); C. Sommers, *Temporary Crusaders* (London, 1919).
[11] Gilbert, *The Romance of the Last Crusade*, 171.   [12] Ibid. 224.
[13] J. Lord, *Duty, Honour, Empire: The Life and Times of Colonel Richard Meinertzhagen* (London, 1970), 333-4. Lord's account of the march on Jerusalem has almost

Lavish descriptions such as this, loaded with references to the past, make it plain of whom the Mayor of Jerusalem was thinking when he called Allenby a 'roaring lion' and T. E. Lawrence when he alluded to the British general as 'our Lion'.[14]

In connection with the capture of Jerusalem Allenby's name has also been linked, quite deliberately, with various ancient prophecies that add to the mystique of his career in the Middle East. It has even been suggested, in fact, that the field marshal could be seen as 'a prince of the West' who, according to a prophecy recorded in the *Book of Sir John Mandeville*, would win the Holy Land.[15] And there were other prophecies that various writers have gleefully recorded. The best known was based on the 'bizarre coincidence', as one author put it,[16] that the Arab population called General Allenby 'Al Nebi', which, in Arabic, means 'the prophet'. The significance of this coincidence rested on an Arab saying that was by 1917 already over two hundred years old and yet which seemed to some accurately to describe what took place in December of that year, for it ran, 'When the Nile flows into Palestine, then shall the prophet from the West drive the Turk from Jerusalem'. The argument concerning the dramatic relevance of the prophecy went something like this—Allenby was the prophet, for this was what the contemporary Arabs called him, while the waters of the Nile actually had begun to flow into Palestine, because the British had constructed a water pipeline from Kantara across the Sinai Peninsula to provide their troops with adequate drinking water, and, just before the Holy City fell, this very water was being pumped from Egypt into Palestine, north of Gaza, at the rate of a thousand gallons a day, and from there being transported by camels to the front-line soldiers fighting for Jerusalem![17] Somewhat ironically, given later developments, the same prophecy and its apparent fulfilment 'added to the conviction in many Arab minds that Britain had

---

certainly been influenced by the attitude of Meinertzhagen, Allenby's Field Intelligence Officer, who wrote in his diary on 31 Oct. 1917: 'We enter on this the Seventh Crusade, once and for all to evict the Turk from the sacred places of Christianity.' See R. Meinertzhagen, *Army Diary, 1899-1926* (London, 1960).

[14] R. Storrs, *Orientations* (London, 1943), 321; T. E. Lawrence, *The Seven Pillars of Wisdom* (London, 1935), 427.

[15] B. W. Tuchman, *Bible and Sword: How the British Came to Palestine* (London, 1984), 343-4.

[16] N. Bethel, *The Palestine Triangle: The Struggle between the British, the Jews and the Arabs, 1935-1948* (London, 1979), 14-15.

[17] Gilbert, *The Romance of the Last Crusade*, 177-8. The similarity between the prophecy recorded in the *Book of Sir John Mandeville* and the Arab suggests that they might both have come from the same source.

come to Jerusalem to restore the holy places of Islam to their rightful Arab ownership'.[18]

Remarkably there was yet another 'astonishing coincidence'[19] which appeared to link Allenby's entry into Jerusalem with the past. This, too, has been emphasized by writers and historians determined to accentuate the importance of this event for whatever reason. A quotation from Major Pirie-Gordon's semi-official account of the operations in Palestine demonstrates how this additional coincidence has influenced descriptions of the capture of Jerusalem:

> On this same day 2,082 years before, another race of conquerors, equally detested, were looking their last on the city which they could not hold, and . . . it was fitting that the flight of the Turks should have coincided with the national [Jewish] festival of the Hanukah, which commemorates the recapture of the Temple from the heathen Seleucids by Judas Maccabaeus in 165 BC.[20]

With so many historical parallels surrounding the surrender of the Holy City to Allenby one can understand why even the Official History of the Palestine campaigns describes it as 'one of the most dramatic incidents of the war' which 'made an extraordinary impression upon all men's minds'.[21]

Interestingly enough, Allenby became extremely irritated by the romantic manner in which his operations in Palestine were being portrayed after the war and in a public lecture given in 1933 he tried to redress the balance:

> Our campaign has been called 'The Last Crusade'. It was not a crusade. There is still a current idea that our object was to deliver Jerusalem from the Moslem. Not so. Many of my soldiers were Moslems. The importance of Jerusalem lay in its strategical position. There was no religious impulse in this campaign. The sole object of every man in my army was to win the war.[22]

Nor was Allenby the only participant in the Holy Land campaigns to point out the 'lack of logic' in calling them a 'crusade' since, as Liman von Sanders—the commander of the forces opposing the British in Palestine in 1918—asserted, many of the Arabs supported Allenby and

---

[18] Bethel, *The Palestine Triangle*, 14-15.
[19] H. M. Sachar, *A History of Israel* (New York, 1979), 113.
[20] Quoted by M. Gilbert, *Jerusalem: Illustrated History Atlas* (London, 1977), 63.
[21] Cyril Falls, *Military Operations Egypt and Palestine*, ii. (London, 1930), 252, 256. Hereafter referred to as Official History.
[22] Notes from a lecture given by Allenby at YMCA, Jerusalem, 19 Apr. 1933, Allenby papers, 6/VIII/70.

they were Muslims also.²³ There remains, nevertheless, much that is not logical in the published accounts of the Palestine operations in the First World War and Allenby's role in them. Moreover, as we have already seen, the field marshal himself was not being entirely frank with his audience in 1933 when he claimed that Jerusalem's importance lay in its 'strategical position', for he knew only too well of the 'political' significance of the city for his civilian masters in London in 1917.

Allenby was mistaken when he stated that there was 'no religious impulse' in the campaign. On the contrary, it is a well-documented fact that he, perhaps as much as any other participant, consistently turned to the Bible as his forces advanced across Palestine. Thus we find one of his companions writing, 'the historical lore contained in the books of Judges and Kings were at his finger-tips, and often, as we drove along, he would say: "You see that hill over there? That is where such and such a thing happened—it's in the second book of Chronicles."' ²⁴ Indeed, his devotion to the Scriptures could even lead him to take a close interest in what to many of his staff must have seemed like minor religious matters. When Chaim Weizmann, then a member of the Zionist Commission in Palestine, was approached by some strictly orthodox Jews asking for his assistance in obtaining myrtles for the Feast of Tabernacles, for example, Weizmann himself was reluctant to take up such a matter with the British authorities while they were engaged in the final advance against the Turks in September 1918. Nevertheless, when Weizmann went to bid farewell to Allenby, the commander-in-chief amazed him by suddenly exclaiming,

By the way, about those myrtles! . . . You know it is an important business; it's all in the Bible; I read it up in the Book of Nehemiah last night. Well, you'll be glad to hear that . . . a consignment of myrtles will get to Palestine in good time for the Feast of Tabernacles! ²⁵

Of course, Allenby was not alone in drawing upon his biblical knowledge. In the England of the First World War the average citizen had a far more detailed grasp of the Authorized or King James Version of the Bible than today; indeed, we might go so far as to say that it was almost a part of the popular consciousness of the time—a fact that we overlook at our peril if we wish to understand much of the literature of the period. No doubt later writers deliberately emphasized this feature of the

---

²³ L. von Sanders, *Five Years in Turkey* (Annapolis, Md.: US Naval Institute translation, 1927), 35.   ²⁴ W. F. Stirling, *Safety Last* (London, 1953), 78.
²⁵ C. Weizmann, *Trial and Error* (London, 1949), 288-9.

campaign in order to heighten the drama and romance of their accounts but, on the other hand, it seems unlikely that they could have entirely fabricated such instances as the following, if only because it appears almost incredible to us today:

> The first things we bought after the capture of Jerusalem were Bibles. . . . We used the Bibles as guide books. . . . It was no uncommon sight to come across cockney soldiers out under the stars when they should have been sleeping, arguing about some incident in the Bible because of a place or event in the day's march that made the Biblical pages live again.[26]

Aware of such intense religiosity amongst the ranks, the Official History found it necessary to admit that the troops 'could not be indifferent to the sacred memories of the soil which they trod' because of its 'spiritual and historical traditions'.[27]

The image of Allenby presented to the reading public was bound to be distorted by these biblical influences upon almost every aspect of the campaigns. We find the field marshal mentioned, therefore, in the same breath as Samson, the great judge and strong man of ancient Israel, because he captured Gaza, 'the town of Samson's tragic triumph'.[28] Allenby's achievements, moreover, bore a striking resemblance to those of Joshua, for he led his men to victory and the conquest of the 'Promised Land' after his predecessor, Sir Archibald Murray, whose name was linked to that of Moses, had crossed the Sinai but failed to enter the 'Land of Canaan', just like Joshua's great predecessor, Moses.[29] Allusions such as these are not hard to find, but they are perhaps at their densest in connection with Allenby's final offensive of September 1918. Even a generally respected history of the First World War such as that by Cruttwell suddenly appears to lose all objectivity in its examination of this particular campaign, as if the author has been overwhelmed by a multitude of biblical references and allusions all at once: 'The battle was appropriately called Megiddo, the modern version of "the place which is called in the Hebrew tongue Armageddon", where John saw in a vision all the nations gathered together to battle.'[30] So strong is the influence of Scripture at this point that Cruttwell decided he needed a footnote to explain that he was referring to Revelation 16: 16 and that it was possible

---

[26] Gilbert, *The Romance of the Last Crusade*, 180.
[27] Official History, 647.
[28] Tuchman, *Bible and Sword*, 320. See Judg. 16: 21-31.
[29] Col. Watkins to Murray, 25 Jan. 1929, Murray papers, 79/48/3. See Deut. 34: 1-8; Josh. 1-5.
[30] C. R. M. F. Cruttwell, *A History of the Great War, 1914-1918* (Oxford, 1936), 621.

to argue that this very prophecy had been fulfilled because, if one included a West Indian detachment, it could be said that all five continents of the world were represented in the battle.[31] It need not be stressed here, but whoever commanded the victorious forces on such an occasion was, by implication at least, doing God's work and even accelerating the return of Christ, or so many avid Bible-readers might have concluded at the time.[32] Certainly, he was no ordinary general!

Mention of Megiddo brings us to the second most influential event in Allenby's career, at least in so far as the creation of his public image was concerned. The very fact that his full title after the war was Field Marshal Viscount Allenby of Megiddo and Felixstowe indicates how closely his name became linked to this great military triumph. There can be little doubt that the Megiddo campaign was a remarkably successful operation in which not only were the opposing forces largely eliminated but also cavalry was used in a daring manner to exploit initial hard-won victories by the infantry. The 'apocalyptic' connotations from the Bible, however, combined with the success of covering hundreds of miles for such small casualty lists compared to the engagements in France, have helped to distort descriptions of the battle. Influences such as these can be seen in references to the encounter as Allenby's 'climactic autumn offensive' or as 'a battle of annihilation'.[33] The impression is given, moreover, that the actual plan was 'executed without fault' so that Megiddo became 'the best kind of victory—it was achieved with comparatively little fighting'.[34] For these reasons the military historian and theorist, Liddell Hart, seized upon Megiddo as an example of what he had for so long been asserting—that great battles could be won 'by strategic means, with fighting playing a minor part'.[35] As far as he was concerned, therefore, Megiddo was 'one of history's masterpieces' and the success achieved by Allenby needed to be emphasized because, he argued, there had been no 'Clausewitzian blood-bath' which could lead other authors to play down Megiddo's significance.[36] But Megiddo was

---

[31] C. R. M. F. Cruttwell, *A History of the Great War, 1914-1918* (Oxford, 1936), 621. See Rev. 16: 12-16.

[32] See Rev. 19: 11-21. I have refrained from making the most obvious of all comparisons for according to Revelation it is Christ who defeats the armies of the world in a final cataclysmic battle! For those contemporaries with eschatological interests what happened in Palestine during the First World War was of enormous significance.

[33] Sachar, *A History of Israel*, 115; Cruttwell, *A History of the Great War*, 619.

[34] V. H. Rothwell, *British War Aims and Peace Diplomacy, 1914-1918* (London, 1971), 190; Robbins, *The First World War*, 80.

[35] Liddell Hart, *History of the First World War* (London, 1973), 553.

[36] Ibid. 553-4.

also attractive for other reasons. After all, did it not seem to demonstrate that 'the days of cavalry were not over—anyhow not quite'?[37] Those writers searching for practical military lessons to be learnt from these operations, such as Archibald Wavell, who wrote the standard military textbook on the Palestine campaigns in the 1920s and about whom we will have more to say later, were quick to grasp this feature of Megiddo and so argued that it proved once and for all the value of mobility in warfare, at both the strategic and the tactical level.[38] In fact, the entire offensive seemed to many to have restored an element of 'boyish fun' to war that 'inspired and delighted' the troops and offered a stark contrast to the British Army's experiences on the Western Front.[39]

It seems likely that later accounts of Allenby's final campaign have been influenced by the sheer amazement felt by his political masters in London as the news filtered through to them that British forces in Palestine had scored a major victory far in excess of anything they could have expected. Published sections of the diary of Sir Henry Wilson, who was the Chief of the Imperial General Staff at the time, reveal how news of the victory was received by the War Cabinet: as each day passed, fresh information reached the CIGS concerning Allenby's achievements which he then relayed to the politicians. For example, on 23 September 1918 Wilson recorded in his diary that 'the news from Allenby to-night is 25,000 prisoners' while on the following day he mentions that he told the War Cabinet about the capture of three important towns in Palestine; on 25 September, however, he informed the Cabinet that the latest news from Palestine was that Allenby now had '40,000 prisoners and 265 guns and booty', but by 28 September the estimates had to be altered again, as the CIGS explains in a somewhat laconic entry that shows just how accustomed he had become by this stage to regular news of still greater successes in Palestine and Syria: 'No further news ... nor of Allenby, except that his prisoners are now 50,000'.[40] Something of the heady atmosphere of success that must have filled the corridors of Whitehall during these days in September 1918 has been absorbed by the various writers trying to describe the Megiddo campaign; consequently, at times, one is left with the impression that they are straining for the most dramatic adjectives available in an attempt to compete with

[37] Falls, *The First World War* (London, 1960), 378.
[38] A. P. Wavell, *The Palestine Campaigns* (London, 1928), 235-6.
[39] J. Masters, *Fourteen Eighteen* (London, 1965), 161; Falls, *The First World War*, 378.
[40] C. E. Callwell, *Field Marshal Sir Henry Wilson: His Life and Diaries*, ii. (London, 1927), 126-7.

an earlier author's account. Lest this be thought a fanciful assessment the reader is directed to the Official History's version of the battle which concludes with the following: 'The thoroughness of the Turkish defeat is almost without a parallel in modern military history.'[41] Quite naturally the 'official' narrative of the campaign has been the starting-point for most subsequent writers seeking to chronicle its major features, so their accounts have taken a similar approach. As a result, we discover that the strategic handling of cavalry in these operations has been described elsewhere as 'unrivalled in British military history',[42] for instance, while Megiddo has also been called 'one of the most quickly decisive campaigns and the most completely decisive battles in all History'[43] and 'the greatest exploit in history of horsed cavalry'.[44]

Megiddo's influence upon Allenby's reputation as a military commander has been massive. His name has been adorned with it in the titles of such books as *Allenby of Armageddon* and *Allenby's Final Triumph*.[45] Moreover he has been unanimously accorded almost total credit for the plan behind the campaign. Once again we must turn to the Official History, where it is claimed that 'the offensive was in origin and conception the result of the Commander-in-Chief's own cogitations'.[46] Later writers have concurred.[47] Since Allenby has been given sole credit for the plan, he has necessarily received most of the credit for the very successful development of the campaign. He is described as having devised and executed 'a battle that went according to plan', thus justifying his being named in the same breath as such great commanders as Napoleon and Alexander the Great.[48] One of the most important writers upon Allenby's career in Palestine has been Cyril Falls. He was responsible for the Official History[49] and later became 'one of the foremost British military historians'[50] who, from his Oxford Chair, continued his

---

[41] Official History, 617.   [42] Cruttwell, *A History of the Great War*, 610.
[43] Liddell Hart, *History of the First World War*, 553.
[44] Wavell, *Allenby*, 245.
[45] R. Savage, *Allenby of Armageddon* (London, 1925); W. T. Massey, *Allenby's Final Triumph* (London, 1918).   [46] Official History, 447.
[47] See e.g. Cruttwell, *A History of the Great War*, 619; Wavell, *Allenby*, 223-5; B. Gardner, *Allenby* (London, 1965), 178.
[48] Masters, *Fourteen Eighteen*, 164; Gardner, *Allenby*, 178; Wavell, *Allenby*, 246.
[49] Falls also wrote the first volume of the Official History of the operations in Egypt and Palestine, covering the period between Aug. 1914 and June 1917 (up to the departure of Gen. Murray), jointly with G. MacMunn. See MacMunn and Falls, *Military Operations Egypt and Palestine*, i. (London, 1928).
[50] V. J. Esposito (ed.), *A Concise History of World War I* (London, 1964), p. vi.

Allenby and the Palestine Campaign

writing on the First World War and so helped to perpetuate, partly by repetition, the Official History's version of events.[51] Probably his most significant contribution to the subject, however, was his final book, which he devoted entirely to the Megiddo operations and entitled *Armageddon 1918*.[52] In it he provides what has been called an 'excellent account of Allenby's final campaign'[53] and he was by this stage undoubtedly the leading expert on the subject, having seen many War Office documents for himself during his time as an official historian. But the Allenby of *Armageddon 1918* is a general totally in command both of his army and the situation in which he finds himself; at the same time he seems to overflow with self-confidence and to be absolutely certain about what he intends to achieve. Thus Falls tells us that Allenby 'knew his men and their respective virtues', inspiring his force 'superbly' partly through his own 'physical strength and endurance', on occasion exercising remarkable 'moral influence' over exhausted troops, and that he even won the 'trust and admiration' of his Australian units, although he was a 'strict disciplinarian'. He describes Allenby's Megiddo plan as 'daring, grandiose', and dismisses its having emanated from a staff suggestion by posing the rhetorical question, 'What staff officer would put up such a plan, involving the certainty that the cavalry would run away from its transport and have to live on the country, a country which, as has been pointed out, was thought to be more barren than was in fact the case?'[54]

This emphasis upon Allenby's triumphs during the Megiddo campaign has distorted our picture of him and has even led to the earlier phase of his career being presented in the light of his 1918 victories—a most unsatisfactory state of affairs for any historian who wishes, for example, to uncover the progress of his career before Palestine. The problem is, in reality, even more serious than this suggests, for the account of Megiddo that has been offered to the reading public is itself open to criticism. It is simplistic and misleading to state so categorically that the plan was solely Allenby's creation; on the contrary, there is strong evidence that it was not drawn up in some kind of vacuum but rather under the influence of earlier assessments of how most effectively British forces could be

[51] See e.g. ibid. 218. Falls wrote the chapter on the Middle East theatre of war in this work. His own general account of the war also continues to present the same arguments on Megiddo and Allenby's role in it; see Falls, *The First World War*, 376, 379.
[52] Falls, *Armageddon 1918* (London, 1964).
[53] Esposito, *A Concise History*, 383.
[54] Falls, *Armageddon 1918*, 51, 181.

advanced to complete the conquest of Palestine and Syria.[55] What is more, there has been some controversy over the extent to which Allenby kept the final version of his plan—with its apparently very ambitious aim of seizing Damascus by daring cavalry thrusts—from his senior officers and staff until the last minute.[56] This is, of course, an important element in the available published accounts because it seems to lend weight to the argument that the battle was all Allenby's doing, from beginning to end. Finally, and perhaps most significantly of all, Allenby's own letters reveal that although he may have convinced both his men and later historians of his absolute confidence in the original plan and his army's ability to execute it the actual extent of his successes amazed him.[57]

The extent to which Megiddo and the capture of Jerusalem overshadow the rest of Allenby's career is hard to over-emphasize. His two raids across the Jordan in March and the end of April 1918, both of which failed, for example, have received scant attention, largely because they have been 'sandwiched' between Jerusalem and Megiddo—yet there is much about these operations that suggests the commander-in-chief was still finding his way in Palestine and was able to learn from what were very real mistakes at the time.[58] It has nevertheless been blandly asserted that the two raids were not failures since they distracted the enemy's attention from the coast where Allenby's final blow would

---

[55] Early in Feb. 1918 Allenby entertained a mission from London headed by Gen. Smuts which included Leo Amery. The 'Smuts Mission', as it became known, had been assigned the task of examining how best to co-ordinate British efforts in the Middle East with the aim of knocking Turkey out of the war. Although the deliberations of the Mission were largely overtaken by the German offensives on the Western Front in March 1918 Allenby must have remembered the discussions and various operations that were considered—especially one that recommended a 'bold cavalry push' and became a serious plan devised by Amery. The significance of this proposed operation lies in the number of similarities it displays with Allenby's final offensive. See Amery to Wavell, 27 Mar. 1939, Allenby papers, 6/IX/5. This letter includes extensive notes on the Smuts Mission as well as extracts from Amery's own diary which he kept at the time. The matter can also be pursued in the published version of Amery's diaries; see L. S. Amery, *My Political Life*, ii. (London, 1953).

[56] The reader should be aware that Wavell, Allenby's biographer, and others who had served alongside Allenby, disagreed with the Official History when it suggested that the commander-in-chief suddenly revealed Damascus as the objective to his startled senior officers; see Official History, 449. For criticism of this view see Bartholomew to Wavell, 2 Jan. 1939, Allenby papers, 6/IX/11 and Wavell to Falls, 8 May 1938, ibid. 6/IX/22.

[57] Allenby to wife, 24 Sept. 1918, Allenby papers, 1/9/6.

[58] e.g. Chetwode to Wavell, 28 Mar. 1939, ibid. 6/IX/18. The second raid is the more interesting of the two as the British tried to co-operate directly with Arab forces. This feature of the operation was a fiasco but may have given Allenby the necessary lesson in Arab unreliability before his Megiddo campaign in which he assigned the Arabs a major role.

be delivered months later.[59] On the other hand, the claim has been made that if Allenby had struck at the Turks more firmly in April they would have broken just as they did in September.[60] Deliberate attempts appear to have been made, moreover, to shift the responsibility for the failure of the second operation from Allenby's shoulders.[61]

The real problems caused by this over-emphasis upon Jerusalem and Megiddo appear if one tries to re-examine features of Allenby's career before December 1917. This detrimental influence can be discerned in even the standard accounts of the third Battle of Gaza, because the battle itself and the ensuing advance are described in the light of the capture of the Holy City as 'a most brilliant campaign'.[62] But this is misleading. It is possible, in fact, to find veiled criticisms of the planning and direction of this battle and the subsequent operations. Falls, for one, admits that Allenby's achievements at this time 'may not seem remarkable' when one remembers that he had odds of well over two to one in his favour in infantry and eight to one in cavalry, and that during the battle itself he enjoyed 'unmerited good fortune'.[63] It seems that Falls had begun to alter his views, for in the Official History—which was published long before his later writings on the Great War—the third Battle of Gaza is referred to as Allenby's 'great coup'.[64] However, private letters of both Falls and Liddell Hart reveal that they had begun to doubt whether Allenby's plan and strategy in the autumn and winter of 1917 was really as praiseworthy as they had originally concluded. Both men had been impressed by the arguments of a certain Colonel Garsia, who had challenged the orthodox interpretation that the move to break the Turkish line by outflanking it at Beersheba was truly the most suitable option open to the British. Garsia had been a staff officer with the Egyptian Expeditionary Force and in 1934 he contacted Liddell Hart

[59] For a classic example of this see Official History, 392.
[60] See statement by Hauptmann Simon-Eberhard quoted in appendix to the chapter entitled 'The Passage of the Jordan and the Raid on Amman', Official History, 328.
[61] This is in connection with the attempt to co-operate with Arab units. According to Falls both Liddell Hart and Graves in their books on T. E. Lawrence 'try to shovel the blame for the incident on to Bols [Allenby's Chief of Staff], as if he would have taken such a decision without reference to Allenby!' Falls to Wavell, 10 May 1938, Allenby papers, 6/IX/25. See R. Graves, *Lawrence and the Arabs* (London, 1927) and Liddell Hart, *T. E. Lawrence—in Arabia and After* (London, 1934). Wavell added a detailed footnote on this subject in his biography; see Wavell, *Allenby*, 212-13. The Official History places all the blame for the failure upon the Arabs, whose resolutions are, it declares with considerable bitterness, 'as shifting and unstable as their own sands', Official History, 391. [62] Wavell, *Palestine Campaigns*, 167.
[63] Falls, *The First World War*, 308; see also Esposito, *A Concise History*, 213.
[64] Official History, 95.

because he felt his published version of the battle gave an inordinate degree of praise to a plan which, in his opinion, had been basically flawed. So strongly did he feel on this matter and so sure was he of his ground that he decided to publish his views in a book that has been almost totally ignored, and yet contains much that is of considerable value to the historian of the Palestine campaigns. Garsia's book, *A Key to Victory: A Study of War Planning*, is not exclusively about the third Battle of Gaza but uses it as an example of how the planning system in an army can break down.[65] His basic thesis is that if Allenby had concentrated his attack on the Gaza flank of the enemy line he could have slipped his cavalry through between the town and the sea and prevented a Turkish retreat to a line above Jerusalem—a retreat that did occur when the actual battle took place because, according to Garsia, the plan adopted could never ensure Allenby the knock-out blow that a thrust at Gaza could provide. Liddell Hart admitted that he had 'modified' his views after hearing from Garsia while Falls, to whom Liddell Hart had written about the matter, expressed himself similarly: 'While I do not go all the way with him [Garsia] I must say it [his argument] impressed me considerably.'[66] One of Garsia's complaints had been that the Official History barely mentioned this alternative plan even though it had been suggested by a number of Allenby's senior officers before the battle.[67] Perhaps Falls felt a little guilty about this omission from the official account because he advised Wavell in 1939 to consider the Garsia thesis —or the 'Gaza school' as it was called—in the biography of Allenby that he was then near to completing.[68] Wavell, however, ignored this suggestion and makes no mention whatsoever of the 'Gaza school' in his

---

[65] C. Garsia, *A Key to Victory: A Study of War Planning* (London, 1940). The book's relevance to any study of the Palestine campaigns is heightened by the fact that it also considers the previous two battles of Gaza, while its foreword is written by Field Marshal Chetwode, who was one of Allenby's corps commanders and also one of the men behind the plan to attack the enemy line at Beersheba. Garsia had actually been GSO1 in the 54 Division, part of the EEF.

[66] Liddell Hart to Lloyd George, 25 June 1934. Enclosed notes on Lloyd George's Memoirs, 'The Struggle with the Turk', Liddell Hart papers, 1/450/File I. Falls to Wavell, 2 Jan. 1939, Allenby papers, 6/VIII/53. The precise sequence of events by which Garsia influenced these two prominent writers seems to have been as follows: Garsia wrote to Liddell Hart who then wrote to Falls recounting what Garsia had written while, either from Garsia himself or through Liddell Hart, Falls received the MS of Garsia's book before it was published. See Liddell Hart to Falls, 12 May 1934, Liddell Hart papers, 1/276/6 and Falls to Wavell, 2 Jan. 1939, ibid. 6/VIII/53.

[67] Official History, 33.

[68] Falls to Wavell, 2 Jan. 1939, Allenby papers, 6/VIII/53. The first volume of Wavell's biography of Allenby was published in 1940.

final text, where he describes the appreciation behind the Beersheba plan which Allenby and his staff refined at a series of conferences as 'one of the shrewdest . . . made during the War!'[69] The implication, of course, is that the conqueror of Jerusalem could not possibly have made such a grave error as to have chosen only the second-best of the options open to him at the end of October 1917, for such a line of reasoning led to the conclusion that 'if Allenby had made his real push up the coast he would have had the Turkish Army in the bag in 1917'.[70] Jerusalem and Megiddo had too powerful an influence for such a conclusion ever to enter an Allenby biography.

While we are largely concentrating upon Allenby's tenure of command in Palestine it is nevertheless revealing to note that the influence of Megiddo and Jerusalem extends beyond the Near East where the field marshal's career is concerned. Indeed, at times one cannot help feeling that anyone writing about Allenby prior to June 1917 and his arrival in Egypt does so with one eye on the future. Take, for example, this reference to his command of the British cavalry at Le Cateau in 1914: 'Allenby's handling of the cavalry in covering the retreat was a foretaste of the imaginative daring of his later triumphs in Palestine.'[71] In reality, of course, Allenby's time in France was not without its failures and disappointments and he seems to have spent much of it in the shadow of Haig, whom he found most uncommunicative whenever they met.[72] To contemporary observers who did not fully understand the personal dynamics behind the relationship between the two men Allenby appeared a somewhat enigmatic figure without Haig's energy. In the light of hindsight, even this simple observation can become an implied criticism of the observers themselves rather than of Allenby, in the hands of an author who is looking beyond France: 'There were not many in 1916 who were able to tell correctly which was the military genius and which

[69] Wavell, *Allenby*, 158, 170. It was clearly Wavell's intention to stress Allenby's involvement in the plan that was actually adopted in order to allow his subject to gain some of the credit for the success it achieved. Consequently he was reluctant to admit the existence of such a serious criticism of the Beersheba plan. An extract reveals that this was the way in which Wavell's mind was working: 'The details of the plan were developed at a series of conferences. Allenby presided at these and made his qualities as a commander very evident. He had a complete grasp of all sides of the plan, strategical, administrative, and tactical, and gave any decision required with authority and without hesitation' (p. 170).
[70] Liddell Hart to Falls, 12 May 1934, Liddell Hart papers, 1/276/6.
[71] Sir F. Sykes, *From Many Angles: An Autobiography* (London, 1942), 135.
[72] To be fair to Haig, he found he had precisely the same problem with Allenby! The truth was that they were both extremely uncomfortable in each other's presence.

was not; the self-assured, sprightly Haig, or the slow-moving, inarticulate Allenby.'[73] It is unlikely that these examples are deliberate attempts to rewrite history: rather, they are the result of an undue emphasis upon future developments to the detriment of an objective examination of the event the author is seeking to describe. Such instances, however, have certainly helped to distort our picture of Allenby prior to Palestine. Perhaps most seriously of all they have distracted the attention of many historians from lesser-known but more balanced assessments of the illustrious commander during this period. In fact, it does not take too much work to find, for instance, that Allenby's favourite nickname 'The Bull' was not the only one he won for himself in France, as one of his junior officers recounted: 'The Army Commander, Allenby, has gone to Egypt. He is not popular—no stories of his little ways are in circulation, and he is quite unknown to regimental officers and men. The Army calls him "Tin-hat"; its Upper Circles call him "The Bull"!'[74] There are also published accounts in existence by senior officers who observed Allenby at closer quarters in France, and they are not necessarily all complimentary. General Gough, for one, actually describes Allenby as 'mentally somewhat lazy', 'not always sure of what he did want', and a leader who 'never suggested anything' but who was prepared to take responsibility for major decisions and accept suggestions rapidly from his staff.[75]

Although it is true to say that much of the distortion of Allenby's career that has crept into the literature of the Great War has not been largely the result of deliberate manipulation, this is not exclusively the case. Indeed, there has been a concerted effort on the part of a select group of writers and historians to single him out for praise. In part this may have been to a certain extent inevitable. Liddell Hart—a writer who, we have already noted, is not entirely objective in his assessment of Allenby—pointed out most perceptively that his own brief 'outline' of the war was a little misleading: 'It does not attempt to weigh men, but only such of their thoughts and actions as decisively influenced history. It may thus tend to give a better or worse impression of an individual

[73] B. Gardner, *The Big Push* (London, 1961), 31-2.
[74] Capt. J. C. Dunn, *The War the Infantry Knew, 1914-1919* (repr. with new introd., London, 1987).
[75] Gen. Sir H. Gough, *Soldiering On* (London, 1954), 95-6. Gough compares Allenby most unfavourably with Haig, and ascribes his success in Palestine to first-rate staff officers and other senior men who already knew the region and provided him with the advice that he was not afraid to accept and act upon.

Allenby and the Palestine Campaign

than would appear in a just biographical balance.'[76] This is an important statement so far as Allenby is concerned. His battles give the impression of having 'decisively influenced history' and he and they usually receive the sort of attention in the standard general accounts of the First World War that certainly create a better image than would 'a just biographical balance' if only because limitations of space restrict such descriptions to the most simplistic of explanations for his successes: and there is a certain simplicity to Allenby's victories.[77]

But this is only part of the story. Much more significant is what certain authors tell us about their intentions. Cyril Falls, for example, lets slip the real aim of his *The First World War* in a most revealing paragraph: 'I wanted to do all I could to demolish a myth as preposterous as it is widely believed. For the first time in the history of war, we are told, the military art stood still.'[78] And how does Falls intend to correct this mistaken assumption? By simply demonstrating that the war did in fact throw up leaders 'notable for skill and character'—one of whom, according to Falls, was Allenby.[79] Allenby becomes, therefore, not only a successful general but one through whom Falls would prove his point that there were first-class exponents of the military art in the Great War. To a certain extent, therefore, Allenby is a 'pawn' in Falls's grand scheme: he ceases to function as a purely historical figure. Other writers have adopted a similar approach, albeit for different reasons. Lloyd George presents us with a classic example. His *War Memoirs* are nothing if not forthright in their evaluation of many of the military leaders with whom he had to deal, and Allenby is no exception. But Allenby falls into a special category. He is one of a select few on whom the wartime Prime Minister decided to lavish praise as he explained in the preface to his memoirs: 'I have dwelt on the successes of Generals like ... Allenby ... whose triumphs lit up the dismal narrative of military ineptitude displayed by a few others.'[80] Elsewhere he confesses that Allenby, along with T. E. Lawrence and others, was one 'whom I have sought out for laudation'.[81] We cannot expect Lloyd George to offer us an objective portrait of Allenby, therefore, especially since he

---

[76] Liddell Hart, *The War in Outline*, pp. vii–viii.
[77] This point could be developed further; suffice it to say here that Allenby's two great campaigns, Jerusalem and Megiddo, were both based upon strategic planning that does appear remarkably simple at one level, and which lends itself to sweeping, generalized descriptions.   [78] Falls, *The First World War*, p. xvi.
[79] Ibid. p. xvi.   [80] Lloyd George, *War Memoirs*, i. (London, n.d.), p. xi.
[81] Ibid. ii. p. vii.

was assisted in the writing of his memoirs by Liddell Hart, whose interest in the field marshal we have already commented on.[82]

Of course, Lloyd George's reasons for seeking to emphasize the achievements of General Allenby were not solely to render his memoirs more readable. Like Falls, he had his own axe to grind, although he went about this in a far less subtle manner. What he intended was to widen the debate that had erupted after 1918 as to whose strategy on the Allied side had been the right one. This was, in itself, a reflection of what one historian claims became a 'personal duel' during the war between the Prime Minister and Sir William Robertson, the Chief of the Imperial General Staff.[83] The tendency has been to simplify this debate and so to distort the arguments of the protagonists—especially Robertson's—so we must at least make brief mention of some of the issues involved here since they are of crucial importance to our subject.[84] Lloyd George was a keen advocate of operations in Palestine and, as a result, saw in their final success the vindication of his views, which at times during the war were bitterly opposed by Robertson, who tended to see undue emphasis upon Palestine as a dangerous distraction of forces from the main theatre of the war—the Western front. In his memoirs, consequently, Allenby becomes one of Lloyd George's champions.

Since Allenby was a key figure in this wartime debate that was continued in the publications of the main participants long after 1918 he has, to some extent, become linked with a series of controversies. For example, in more recent times it has beeen claimed that he was implicated in a deliberate plot to deceive Lloyd George by working hand-in-hand with Robertson in order to frustrate the Prime Minister's strategy in Palestine.[85] Allenby's own opinions on the entire acrimonious debate have never been sought. It might well surprise many that in 1931 he wrote in a private letter on the very subject of the notoriously named 'Easterners' versus 'Westerners' dispute, 'I think that the success obtained in the East justified the risk in the main theatre'.[86] Allenby himself was therefore no neutral figure in the controversy.

The author of the field marshal's most influential biography—Archibald Wavell (soon to be Field Marshal Earl Wavell of Cyrenaica)—was a

---

[82] See e.g. Liddell Hart to Lloyd George, 25 June 1934, enclosed notes on Lloyd George's Memoirs, 'The Struggle with the Turk', Liddell Hart papers, 1/450/File I.

[83] Rothwell, *British War Aims*, 174.

[84] One of the aims of both sides in this dispute, of course, was to simplify and thereby ridicule their opponents' arguments.

[85] D. R. Woodward, *Lloyd George and the Generals* (Newark, NJ, 1983), 199, 206, 231. [86] Allenby to Murray, 23 Dec. 1931, Murray papers, 79/48/3.

key personality associated with the Robertson–Allenby–Lloyd George triangle. Robertson appointed Wavell his liaison officer to Allenby from July 1917 until after the capture of Jerusalem. This was a shrewd move by the CIGS who wanted to have his finger on the pulse of events in Palestine; it also meant, however, that he had to explain very carefully the precise role of this new officer to Allenby in order to assure him that he was 'in no way a spy' but rather that his duty would be 'to help you and to help me'.[87] Lieutenant-Colonel Wavell, as he was then, found himself in a unique position, for it was his job to explain the intentions of Allenby to Robertson and even those of Robertson to Allenby if necessary. Wavell's involvement with the higher strategy behind the Palestine campaigns continued when, in January 1918, the CIGS placed him on General Sir Henry Wilson's staff at the Supreme War Council. This was not a happy time for Wavell: he gained a poor opinion of the higher direction of the war and disagreed with Wilson's desire for a major offensive in Palestine.[88] In fact, Wavell wrote a memorandum criticizing Wilson's aim of an advance to Damascus and Aleppo which the Official History of the campaign actually quotes from and then comments on in a manner that clearly demonstrates where its sympathies lay on the issue: 'Possibly, discovering to his astonishment that there was at Versailles no conception of the difficulties of an advance . . . he [Wavell] deliberately laid stress on the obstacles and causes of probable delay as a corrective to roseate optimism.'[89]

As a result of his experiences Wavell gained a high regard for Robertson's abilities and strategic acumen.[90] In his private correspondence after the war he often defended some of Robertson's views and decisions. To Liddell Hart he expressed his strongest feelings on the matter, since he believed that the military theorist had been unfair in his assessment of Robertson:

You are wrong about Robertson, he wasn't by any means a rigid and inflexible pedant. I dealt very closely with him as liaison officer between him and Allenby . . . and I know. He was probably always at his worst with L.G., whom he didn't trust. An unhappy combination.[91]

[87] Robertson to Allenby, 4 July 1917, Robertson papers, I/32/61.
[88] Connell, *Wavell*, 135.   [89] Official History, 296.
[90] Connell, *Wavell*, 126-7.
[91] Wavell to Liddell Hart, 4 Feb. 1935, Liddell Hart papers, 1/733/40. See also Wavell to Liddell Hart, 15 Mar. 1934, ibid. 1/733/25.

These firm opinions of Wavell's inevitably found their way into his biography of Allenby. Firstly he informed the reader that Lloyd George's strategy was basically mistaken:

> He [Lloyd George] overlooked the fact that her [Germany's] allies were in no sense the 'props' of Germany (in fact, the converse was the truth), and was also inclined to disregard geographical differences of communications, distances and climate.[92]

Next, he set about bringing Allenby into the grand debate. According to Wavell, therefore, Allenby remained aloof from these unhappy arguments amongst the upper echelons of command in London because he was the epitome of the loyal professional soldier, interested solely with getting on with the job to hand.[93] Since this was Allenby's attitude to the entire affair, in Wavell's view, Robertson could be shielded from Lloyd George's most vicious attacks as well: 'There was, of course, no question of collusion between him [Allenby] and Robertson to frustrate the Prime Minister's plans.'[94] What the Official History described as reminiscent of scenes from a Greek drama—namely the clash between the War Office and Lloyd George during the war—has, therefore, left its indelible mark upon the portrait available to us today of the victor of Jerusalem and Megiddo.[95]

If some writers have tried to manipulate the figure of Allenby for a variety of motives, others have found themselves, usually unawares, unduly influenced by the man himself. Everyone agrees that Allenby's physical appearance was striking. General Smith-Dorrien, for example, remembered the impact that Allenby's presence made on him in 1901: 'I was much impressed with Allenby as a fine specimen of an Englishman: he looked twenty-four instead of nearly forty.'[96] Others described him as a Cromwellian figure who simply looked 'like a winner'.[97] Contemporaries were often struck, in addition, by the sheer size of the man. This combination of immaculate appearance, striking military bearing, above-average height, and general burliness of figure caused some writers to integrate the physical and the spiritual in Allenby so that Amery, for one, described him on their first meeting as 'a big man, in character as well as physique'.[98] It is as if Allenby's size and appearance were synonymous with his character which, of course, is usually inter-

[92] Wavell, *Allenby*, 238-9.   [93] Ibid. 239.
[94] Ibid. 205.   [95] Official History, 297.
[96] Gen. Sir H. Smith-Dorrien, *Memories of Forty-eight Years' Service* (London, 1925), 291.   [97] Lord, *Duty, Honour, Empire*, 323, 324-5.
[98] Amery, *My Political Life*, ii, 141.

preted in terms of the highest moral integrity, as it is in this example: 'At a time when British good faith was being freely impugned by the politicians and people of the Middle East, Allenby's massive integrity and straightforwardness shone forth with a brightness which neither nationalist resentments nor British mistakes could dim.'[99] In part it would seem that Allenby deliberately went out of his way to foster a definite image of himself among his contemporaries and that later writers have therefore been victims of this elaborate role-playing. General Edmonds was with Allenby at Staff College and watched his subsequent development with some interest: 'When . . . Allenby became a general, to our great amusement, he tried to play what he thought was the part and assumed a roughness of manner and abruptness of speech which were not natural to him—and became "The Bull".'[100] But what has generally been overlooked about Allenby's appearance and his assumption of this title, 'The Bull', is that both were two-edged swords. While he was leading his troops to success after success in Palestine the image of the impeccably military, austere, determined, solid 'Bull' seemed to inspire his men with confidence in his ability. On the other hand, if all were not going well and there was frustration with the commander, these very traits could be seen in a different light. In fact, Allenby's appearance might lead an observer to almost precisely the opposite conclusions under less auspicious circumstances. Thus, one author has described him as 'a heavy, awkward man, looking like a human caricature of a traditional soldier'.[101] His nickname of 'The Bull' is often referred to as if it was evidence of the ranks' affection for the general or proof that he was a determined leader, but it could be used as a term of intense dislike and even ridicule, for when all was not quite as Allenby wished it to be his temper could be 'revolting'.[102] Wavell personally experienced this side to 'The Bull' when he found him unhappy over a report he had compiled: 'He was an alarming person when angry, and though I was not afraid of him and argued the point, I found myself at the end of it pouring with perspiration though it was not a warm evening.'[103] The very name 'The Bull' conjured up in many minds the picture of a stupid animal always attacking yet never inflicting serious damage upon its enemy. Such a use of the term can be

[99] J. Marlowe, *Anglo-Egyptian Relations, 1800–1956* (London, 1965), 275.
[100] Unpub. memoirs by Edmonds, ch. 14, 'The Staff College', Edmonds papers, III/2/14. [101] Gardner, *The Big Push*, 31.
[102] Evans to Wavell, 11 Feb. ?1938, Allenby papers, 6/VIII/49.
[103] Quoted by Connell, *Wavell*, 133.

found in Lloyd George's *War Memoirs*. Obviously ignorant of the irony behind what he had written Lloyd George described the Somme campaign as 'this bullheaded fight' while in the same book praising 'The Bull' in Palestine![104] Indeed, it is hard not to believe that before Allenby was transferred to the Middle East he was the very embodiment of all that the Prime Minister despised about the military. That Allenby could convey this impression to civilians is revealed in the effect he seems to have had on C. S. Forester. In *The General* the novelist created a fictitious Corps and Army commander called General Wayland-Leigh, whose nickname was 'The Buffalo' and who is undoubtedly intended to represent Allenby. Although Wavell claimed that Forester's portrait was 'a grotesque caricature of the man' he admitted that it was 'no more than a slightly exaggerated picture of him as he appeared to those who knew him by reputation only'.[105] Forester drew upon what he saw and heard of Allenby before the latter's departure for Egypt and appears to have remained uninfluenced by the dramatic Palestinian victories.[106]

Another writer who created a very definite, if distorted, image of Allenby was T. E. Lawrence. His *The Seven Pillars of Wisdom* remains an extremely popular narrative of the author's experiences in Arabia and Palestine during the Great War. His portrayal of Allenby, therefore, has exerted considerable influence upon later writers and the general public because the book and its author still fascinate many people today. Lawrence's presentation of Allenby is both extravagant and unique: Allenby is 'clean-judging', 'the image we worshipped', and a man in whom Lawrence admitted he had 'dreamlike confidence'; he is also 'morally so great that the comprehension of our [i.e. the Arab forces'] littleness came slow to him', as well as having 'an acute sense of style' and being a leader with 'indisputable authority'.[107] Taken together these statements appear absurd, and yet as part of the text of *The Seven Pillars of Wisdom* they help to create a vivid picture of a general who is completely in command of the whole campaign, including his Arab allies on the right flank. But it is not only Lawrence's text that has been important in the creation of a patriarchal and near-omnipotent Allenby, since he supplemented it with portraits of the main characters. We have already seen how striking was Allenby's physique, or in this case his profile; in a stylized portrait by a well-known artist the effect could be

[104] Lloyd George, *War Memoirs*, i. 321. There is an additional level of irony here, because Allenby criticized the plan behind the Somme battles.
[105] Wavell, *Allenby*, 158-9.
[106] C. S. Forester, *The General* (London, 1936).
[107] Lawrence, *The Seven Pillars of Wisdom*, 321, 383, 565, 527, 84.

emphasized. And this was the intention behind these mini-portraits, for 'they are pictures of heroes and paladins, exemplars of loyalty and chivalry, in drawing which Kennington was entirely influenced by what Lawrence wrote'.[108] While we might not wish entirely to agree with a leading Middle Eastern historian who has argued that *The Seven Pillars of Wisdom* is really 'a work of the imagination in which events are transmuted into myths', it seems possible that Lawrence had begun to 'transmute' his image of Allenby into an almost mythical figure.[109] This impression is certainly strengthened by the author's perspective: he is on the flank of Allenby's armies and so the general himself is often presented as being over the hills on the horizon, whence can be heard the roar of gunfire and at night the flashes of his heavy artillery are seen. At this distance, far removed from the Arab forces, Allenby's decisions nevertheless influence the fortunes of Lawrence and his men. And when the author does come face to face with his commander it is as a suppliant seeking favour from his master. There is an element of detachment in the author's presentation of Allenby, therefore, and Lawrence actually tells the reader that he was afraid to get too close to his 'idol' in case he discovered he had 'feet of clay'.[110]

Lawrence's memoirs—if we can so describe *The Seven Pillars of Wisdom*—also influenced the various dramatic presentations of his career that necessarily prominently featured Allenby. Terence Rattigan's play *Ross* presents both Lawrence and Allenby as 'one consummate duellist to another' in order 'to illuminate a situation which is extraordinary and characters who are exceptional'.[111] The powerful if overlong film *Lawrence of Arabia* clearly drew its image of Allenby from *The Seven Pillars of Wisdom* also, because he is played quite brilliantly by Jack Hawkins as the only officer able to deal with and even manipulate Lawrence—a resolutely self-confident Allenby in full command of the situation.[112]

Allenby's name and reputation have, therefore, been linked with Lawrence's. As Lawrence's post-war popularity increased so did

---

[108] E. Kedourie, 'The Capture of Damascus, 1 October 1918' in id., *The Chatham House Version and other Middle Eastern Studies* (London, 1970), 33.

[109] A. Hourani, 'The Arab Awakening Forty Years Later', in id., *The Emergence of the Modern Middle East* (London, 1981), 195. Of course, the recent appearance of the authorized biography of T. E. Lawrence has helped to clear up many of the 'myths' surrounding Lawrence himself and will remain the standard reference work on all things Lawrentian for many years to come. See J. Wilson, *Lawrence of Arabia* (London, 1989).

[110] Lawrence, *Seven Pillars of Wisdom*, 659.

[111] Kedouri, 'The Capture of Damascus', 34. [112] Ibid. 34.

Allenby's, though his image was also more and more distorted by the 'bonanza of romance in the person of Lawrence of Arabia, the fabulous young Englishman who led the Arab revolt in the war of the desert', as the son of the man who first popularized Lawrence—Lowell Thomas—put it.[113] And later when Aldington's critical biography of Lawrence appeared Allenby was used by Lawrence's supporters as a witness in the 'defence' of their hero and, somewhat perversely, as a witness for the 'prosecution' by Aldington himself while the Lawrence legend was subjected to a burst of revisionism.[114] The close connection between Lawrence and Allenby meant that the field marshal was to a certain degree overshadowed by the famous Arabist.[115] Wavell was clearly unhappy at this and felt it necessary to redress the balance in his biography: 'Lawrence had great courage, versatility, and quickness of mind, but Allenby was unquestionably the stronger and greater character of the two outstanding figures in this campaign.'[116]

If Allenby has been overshadowed by Lawrence, the field marshal's predecessor in Egypt, General Sir Archibald Murray, has been almost forgotten by virtue of the lavish praise heaped upon Allenby. Lawrence and Allenby must both bear some of the responsibility for this neglect. *The Seven Pillars of Wisdom* shows Murray as a weak and jealous man partly, no doubt, to accentuate those qualities in Allenby that Lawrence especially admired—namely, his moral authority and extreme generosity to the Arab cause.[117] The influence of this assessment of Murray ought not to be dismissed lightly, since at least one writer found himself reminded of it in April 1941 whilst waiting, most disconsolately, for the British expedition to Greece: 'Morbidly I remembered Lawrence writing in his *Seven Pillars of Wisdom* of a moment in the last war that seemed unpleasantly like this: "Meanwhile I had heard of Allenby's excellence and of the last tragedy of Murray, that second attack on Gaza which

---

[113] L. Thomas, Jun., *Out of This World* (London, 1951), 18.
[114] R. Aldington, *Lawrence of Arabia: A Biographical Enquiry* (London, 1955). It is one of Aldington's points that what is significant about Allenby's few public statements concerning Lawrence is what he does not say. For an example of how Allenby was used to defend Lawrence see Stirling, *Safety Last*, 84. Here Stirling argues that Lawrence must have been a remarkable man because 'three of the greatest men in England'—Allenby, Admiral Wemyss and Churchill—thought so.
[115] A remarkable example of this is that Gardner's biography of Allenby, which is here simply entitled *Allenby*, was published in the United States as *Lawrence's General*.
[116] Wavell, *Allenby*, 286.
[117] Lawrence, *The Seven Pillars of Wisdom*, 110, 321. For an example of Lawrence's deliberate attempt to emphasize Allenby's generosity to the Arabs, see p. 527: 'It was an immense, a regal gift; the gift of unlimited nobility'.

London forced on one too weak or too polite to resist . . .".'[118] Allenby's responsibility for the disservice that has been done to Sir Archibald by history is still more direct. Privately the new commander-in-chief of the Egyptian Expeditionary Force was happy to acknowledge that 'it was Murray's preparations that made his success possible' but publicly he said nothing to this effect.[119] Watching events from England, Murray became exasperated that Allenby made no mention whatsoever of his own efforts in Egypt and Palestine in the dispatches he issued.[120] In the end the unfortunate Murray had to wait precisely two years before Allenby referred to his predecessor's 'brilliant campaign in Sinai' and acknowledged his 'indebtedness' to the man who 'laid the foundation for the subsequent advances'.[121]

Even after this belated acknowledgement of his achievements in Sinai and Palestine Murray discovered that he was not at liberty to publish his own final dispatch from the campaign of 28 June 1917. The reasons for this prohibition were largely political, although at first the government asserted that the dispatch could not be issued in its original form during the war because it contained information that could be of value to the Turks.[122] However, when the military arguments for deferring publication of the dispatch lost much, if not all, of their validity after Allenby had defeated the enemy in November 1917 and forced them back to new positions, Murray's dispatch remained unpublished. The problem now was not a military one at all; rather it concerned what Murray had written about the various alterations in the War Cabinet's policy in Palestine before his final battle at Gaza and his subsequent recall. Robertson put his finger on the difficulties with this part of the dispatch as far as the government was concerned when he noted, 'It is almost entirely of a

[118] A. Moorehead, *African Trilogy* (London, 1944), 144.
[119] Browne to Wavell, 4 Apr. 1939, Allenby papers, 6/VIII/28. See also Earl Winterton MP, 'The Genius of Allenby', *Daily Telegraph* (15 May 1936) for a similar comment.
[120] 'Notes on Four Despatches from Egypt, 1916-17' by Murray, Murray papers, 79/48/3.
[121] Extracts from Allenby's dispatch of 28 June 1919 quoted by A. Murray, *Sir Archibald Murray's Despatches* (London, 1920), p. vii.
[122] Robertson seems to have been behind the initial decision to delay publication of the dispatch because, he explained, its publication in October of 1917 while Allenby was preparing to strike at the enemy might be 'highly detrimental to the military situation'. However, once Allenby had attacked the Turks in November and defeated them Murray raised the matter again and this time the CIGS promised to get the dispatch printed as fast as possible since it was 'no longer being delayed by the General Staff'. See Robertson to Dawson, 12 Oct. 1917, Robertson papers, I/36/25; Murray to Robertson, 4 Nov. 1917, ibid. I/36/63; Robertson to Murray, 15 Nov. 1917, ibid. I/36/64.

political character'.[123] The CIGS was correct, for the Lloyd George government was not prepared to allow the issuing of a dispatch to the general public which gave such a critical assessment of its military policy in Palestine. Consequently the dispatch achieved publication—privately—in 1920 only after the War Office had compelled Murray to add its own statement to the dispatch by which it sought to vindicate the government's 'various changes in policy' by stressing that they ought to be seen in the context of the whole war then being waged in France, Russia, and the Balkans as well as in Palestine.[124] In reality, however, the reasons for continuing to muzzle Sir Archibald had, by 1920, been overtaken rather ironically by still more pressing political arguments in favour of allowing the general to have his way, since there was now the possibility that he might start 'accusing the Government of deliberate suppression of unpalatable facts'.[125] The history of Murray's final dispatch is important, because it helps to explain why Murray has barely been remembered by the generation that fought in the First World War and because it illuminates why Lloyd George found it so convenient in his *War Memoirs* both to praise Allenby lavishly and simultaneously to denigrate Murray. By so doing he was able to combine two objectives: the destruction of the latter's reputation, thereby neutralizing Murray's trenchant criticisms of his government's policy in Palestine, while boosting Allenby's image in comparison with that of his luckless predecessor. The text of the *War Memoirs*, however, gives one the impression that Lloyd George was unable to detach himself sufficiently from the matter in order to render such a strategy entirely successful, for his allusions to Murray are, at times, almost laughably hostile and redolent with bitterness:

In Egypt, Sir Archibald Murray had been instructed to pursue a mainly defensive policy. He was a General well adapted to the faithful conduct of a timorous policy. Such a message from the War Office read by him on the balcony of his hotel at Cairo would be as welcome as a cool breeze in the sultry desert air.[126]

---

[123] CIGS note for Secretary, 23 Aug. 1917, PRO WO 32/5131. Robertson himself was indirectly criticized by the dispatch since he had been involved in the alterations in strategic policy in Palestine before the second Battle of Gaza.

[124] Murray, *Sir Archibald Murray's Despatches*, pp. v-vi: official letter by H. J. Creedy of the War Office.

[125] Extract from draft conclusion of a conference held at 10 Downing Street, 3 Feb. 1920, by H. Creedy, PRO WO 32/5134.

[126] Lloyd George, *War Memoirs*, ii. 1075.

Under Murray, according to Lloyd George, the Palestine campaign had been conducted 'with a flabbiness and lack of nerve' which contrasted dramatically with the atmosphere once Allenby took over:

> A new Commander had been appointed and he a man of high courage and resolution, and that made all the difference. He raised the spirit of the Army by his presence and the inspiration of his personality . . . He introduced an element of imagination into his tactical arrangements.[127]

But Lloyd George was actually assisted in his design by Murray, who refused to defend himself publicly once he had managed to get his final dispatch into print; as one of Allenby's biographers has quite rightly pointed out, he has ever since 'been somewhat unfairly treated by history as a result of Lloyd George's published strictures'.[128] Another reason why Lloyd George was able to succeed in what was little more than a piece of character assassination lies in the nature of the campaign before Allenby arrived in Egypt. Much of Murray's tenure of command had been spent behind his front lines seeing to it that his forces were adequately supplied as they traversed the arid Sinai Peninsula. Such mundane activities, however important they may have been, are not the stuff to enthuse authors and their readers, for 'the part played in a great victory by organization and preparation . . . seldom receives proper recognition in military history, which is apt to concern itself with the more spectacular movements and clashes of the campaign itself'.[129]

The temptation to elevate Allenby by unduly criticizing Murray has been too strong for other writers besides Lloyd George. Wavell seems to have fallen into this trap in the first draft of his biography, for it received a lukewarm response from some of those to whom he circulated it. General Bartholomew, for example, was most unhappy with the way in which Wavell had portrayed Murray and his staff:

> Are you not a little cruel about the 'shaken staff' . . . even to Murray I would not be too cruel and you do later pay tribute to him. I think you can bring out Allenby's character just as well without hitting the staff quite so hard . . . Murray was in a very difficult position . . . I am no lover of Murray at least I wasn't in the war . . . and in spite of that I draw your attention to this. He is alive too and may say or feel something.[130]

---

[127] Ibid. 1922, 1923.   [128] Gardner, *Allenby*, 119.
[129] Wavell, *Allenby*, 261. Wavell also added the following in a generous footnote: 'Thus . . . Sir Archibald Murray, has never received full credit for his great work in reorganization, in the spring of 1916 of the troops evacuated from Gallipoli.'
[130] Bartholomew to Wavell, n.d., Allenby papers, 6/VIII/23.

216   Indirect Approaches

Another of Wavell's correspondents, General Sir Richard Howard-Vyse, seconded Bartholomew's misgivings and recommended that 'in one or two places the references to Murray might be toned down'.[131] Wavell's reaction to these comments, however, was to defend his text and he stuck to his original picture of Murray.[132] The Official History also came under similar criticism from Murray's ex-Chief of Staff, Lynden-Bell, when he read its account of the transfer of command in Palestine: 'I think that . . . there is perhaps a little too much rejoicing at the departure of Sir A.M. and the arrival of Sir E.A. Could this be toned down a bit—as it stands the opening page of the chapter seems to me . . . a little like hitting a fellow when he is down.'[133] Of course, it was particularly in the interest of Allenby's various biographers to emphasize the dramatic effect that his arrival supposedly had in Egypt and Palestine. Raymond Savage—not one to miss the opportunity to break into purple prose—described the new general's impact thus:

> But with the coming of Allenby all this changed in a remarkable manner, and within one month an amazing transformation had taken place. There was a curious stiffening of purpose which was felt not only in the firing line, but in Egypt itself. It was as though some giant beast was awakening from torpor and, throwing off its lethargy, was cleaning itself and preparing at last for definite action.[134]

Another biographer, Gardner, writing years later, seems to have been influenced by Savage, for he refers to the same affair as 'a remarkable event' that left 'a lasting impression'.[135] Wavell was clearly thinking along similar lines when he described the Egyptian Expeditionary Force as 'becalmed and dispirited' and in need of 'the wind of Allenby's tremendous personality to fill the sails and give it steerage-way'.[136]

One method of intensifying the seemingly extraordinary effect that Allenby exercised upon the EEF was to concentrate on his decision to move his Headquarters—which under Murray had been in Cairo—into the Sinai and so closer to the front. This action by Allenby has been

[131] Maj.-Gen. R. Howard-Vyse to Wavell, 17 Mar. 1939, ibid. 6/VIII/60.
[132] Wavell to Bartholomew, 2 Feb. 1939, ibid. 6/VIII/24.
[133] Lynden-Bell to MacMunn, 15 Nov. 1925, PRO CAB 45/78. MacMunn seems to have been far more accommodating in his attitude towards this criticism than was Wavell.
[134] Savage, *Allenby*, 176.
[135] Gardner, *Allenby*, 116. The impression that Gardner is drawing upon Savage is strengthened by the fact that Gardner also makes mention of something else that Savage refers to at this point—the grievance among the ranks caused by the large number of decorations awarded to the staff in Egypt: see Savage, *Allenby*, 176 and Gardner, *Allenby*, 117.   [136] Wavell, *Allenby*, 189.

Allenby and the Palestine Campaign 217

presented as if it revolutionized the army overnight. To strengthen this interpretation various writers have marshalled phrases and a particular vocabulary in order to win sympathy for Allenby's decision. We are informed that Murray's staff had become 'accustomed to the fleshpots of Egypt', that they were 'living in luxury on the fat of the land', in the 'affluent stewpot of Cairo', and so on.[137] Such emotive language proved effective, for the decision to leave Egypt was now viewed not only as a military but also as a moral necessity, and Allenby's moral stature was thereby emphasized. This is not to say that much was not made of the move in military terms; the consensus, in fact, would probably be that far too much weight was placed on this decision from a military perspective. The standard view strongly argued by all Allenby's biographers is that the new commander's presence in the desert, closer to his troops and away from Cairo's luxuries, instilled new enthusiasm into the EEF and allowed Allenby to concentrate upon the destruction of the Turk from a viewpoint that enabled him more successfully to grasp the true nature of the task facing his army.[138] But the reality was not so simple. For one thing, Murray himself had not wanted to locate his Headquarters in Cairo, but the pressure from his political advisers had become so intense that he had felt constrained to move in order to maintain a firm grip on the situation in Egypt. It is one of the great ironies of Allenby's career that his decision to move to the desert meant that his army and staff grew increasingly isolated from the Egyptian scene, with the result that the Egyptians felt alienated and so resented the EEF's demands that when the war ended their frustration boiled over into a political upheaval, which Allenby himself was called in to manage as the new High Commissioner.[139] Nor should the move necessarily be seen as a courageous act by a determined man; on the contrary, there is evidence to suggest that it had something to do with the fact that Allenby simply did not like Cairo or its climate.[140] Finally, undue emphasis on the incident not only distorted history but also caused problems for generals in similar circum-

---

[137] Ibid. 187; Savage, *Allenby*, 176; Connell, *Wavell*, 125. The term 'fleshpot' or 'stewpot' appears to be the standard way for military writers to describe Egypt between the wars and after. Connell was, of course, influenced by what Wavell wrote but others used the same term for experiences in the Second World War. See e.g. R. Farran, *Winged Dagger: Adventures on Special Service* (London, 1950), 20: 'Like most of the young officers in Cairo at the beginning of the war . . . we overspent our incomes with a reckless, gay abandon in the cabarets and fleshpots of Cairo.'

[138] See Lloyd George, *War Memoirs*, ii. 1090 for a good example of this.

[139] For the negative effect of the transfer of GHQ which has frequently been ignored see P. G. Elgood, *Egypt and the Army* (London, 1924).

[140] 'June-December 1917', notes by Dick Andrew, Allenby papers, 6/VIII/12.

stances looking for inspiration during the Second World War. For example, according to Alan Moorehead, Auchinleck wanted to get his entire Headquarters under canvas 'the way Allenby had done . . . so that the staff men should be less distracted by the baubles of Cairo, and able to devote more time to their jobs'.[141] Unfortunately for Auchinleck, however, he picked precisely the wrong time to initiate such a move for the commotion it created was the last thing he and his staff needed at a time of crisis. Interestingly enough, in 1942, amidst all the debates then running concerning Britain's military policy in the Middle East, Murray wrote to Raymond Savage stressing that it was misleading to lay too much emphasis on the transfer of the EEF's Headquarters in 1917:

The comparison you draw between Allenby and myself does not do justice to the actual facts. He had a clear cut job to conquer Palestine . . . and no worry about sending the bulk of his troops to France or Mesopotamia, no railway or pipe lines to build, no Western Desert problem, no Macedonian problem to solve; no Soudan and Arabian problems necessitating daily meetings with Sultan and High Commissioner.[142]

Perhaps British strategists might have benefited more from this kind of comment than from slavishly assuming that the Allenby solution was always the answer. It is certainly true that some younger British officers who served in the Second World War felt that their seniors, who had experienced the Great War as well, were often to be found 'a good deal farther forward than was strictly necessary' because of the fear that they would become like the 1914–18 generals who had, they believed, 'stayed in the rear, and eventually, toddled home to die in bed'.[143]

So successful have Allenby's supporters been in the elevation of their hero at the expense of his predecessor that in some instances it is almost as if General Murray has disappeared from the historical account altogether. Take, for example, this brief extract from a general work on the history of the Arabs:

Seeking to outshine his illustrious rival Khalid, in 639 Amr ibn-al-As with 4,000 riders took the beaten track from Palestine along the coast trod by Abraham, Cambyses, Alexander, Antiochus, the Holy Family—and later Napoleon and Allenby. It was the international highway of the ancient world.[144]

[141] A. Moorehead, *The Desert War* (London, 1965), 192-3.
[142] Murray to Mr Savage, 10 July 1942, Murray papers, 78/48/3.
[143] J. Masters, *The Road Past Mandalay* (London, 1967), 281.
[144] P. K. Hitti, *The Arabs: A Short History* (London, 1965), 51.

Allenby could hardly have been placed in better company! Strictly speaking, however, it is Murray who should have been named along with these great figures of the past, since it was he, not his successor, who led his army along that international highway of the ancient world —for when Allenby reached the Middle East the EEF was already in Palestine, having left the Egyptian frontier and the Sinai Peninsula. It is not hard to find the assumption that Allenby led his troops from Egypt to Jerusalem and beyond. An Israeli history of the War of Independence with the Arabs draws parallels with Allenby's experiences in the same region and then states by way of explanation that all this took place in the First World War 'when he [Allenby] moved north from Egypt to conquer Palestine'.[145] Most remarkably of all, however, in a recent dictionary of biography Allenby's entry includes the statement, 'In April 1917, Allenby replaced General Dobell in Egypt and quickly reorganized British forces and command structure.'[146] Aside from the date (Allenby succeeded to the command in June) the entry unfortunately substitutes Dobell (whom Murray appointed to command the operations in Sinai and Palestine after the transfer of Headquarters to Cairo)[147] for Murray himself. The error is symptomatic of the effect that the systematic destruction of Sir Archibald's reputation has exercised.

The major reason for the almost total neglect of Sir Archibald Murray has been the intense admiration that those who have written about Allenby have felt for their subject. In fairness it ought to be emphasized that not all the criticism of Murray that emerged was part of a premeditated attempt to glorify Allenby at his expense: much of it sprang from a strong personal attachment to Allenby the man. This tendency can be traced in all the biographies of the field marshal and in Liddell Hart's sketch in *Reputations*.[148]

The longest and by far the most influential of the Allenby biographies is Wavell's. The title of his first volume, *Allenby: A Study in Greatness*, indicates the author's opinion of his subject. It was published in September 1940, when undoubtedly it touched a chord in the hearts of the English reading public, as its author had hoped: 'The military career

[145] Lt.-Col. N. Lorch, *The Edge of the Sword: Israel's War of Independence 1947-1949* (Jerusalem, 1968), 96.
[146] A. Briggs, A. Isaacs, and E. Martin, *Longman Dictionary of Twentieth Century Biography* (London, 1985), 9.
[147] Dobell was sent home after the second British failure at Gaza in Apr. The entry could, of course, ironically be understood to mean that Allenby succeeded Dobell as Murray's subordinate commander in Palestine!
[148] Liddell Hart, *Reputations* (London, 1930).

of one of the greatest soldiers of the last war, whose courage and will to victory never faltered, may perhaps be of more interest and value during the present conflict than at a later time.'[149] Wavell's wish was fulfilled—the volume had been reprinted four times by December 1941.[150] In 1943 Wavell issued a second volume, which was also rapidly reprinted, entitled *Allenby in Egypt*, covering his subject's career as High Commissioner after the war.[151] Finally, in 1946 he was able to complete what he had always intended to do but had been prevented from achieving by the interruption of war—he published the biography as a single volume, now called *Allenby: Soldier and Statesman*.[152]

Allenby had a profound effect upon Wavell's life and career. His own biographer records that Wavell took an instant liking to Allenby when he first caught sight of him in 1905 and thereupon decided that this was the officer he wanted to serve under.[153] And when Wavell was sent to Palestine as Robertson's liaison officer Allenby received him so warmly that he gained Wavell's 'deep and abiding gratitude'.[154] Wavell served alongside the field marshal while he himself was in his mid-thirties and his own military thinking was still developing, so it proved a significant period for the younger officer and the experience left a lasting impression upon him: 'He believed with all his heart that Allenby was a great man, and that he himself had been lucky to serve him.'[155] Those who knew Wavell during the Second World War referred to Allenby as 'his old master', while a more recent writer has called him 'his guiding hero'.[156] Wavell was certainly much struck by his mentor's character. He included a prologue in his biography on this subject, and an assessment of the work has described it as 'a fine character study'.[157] This may not be without a certain significance, for Wavell affirmed in a letter to Liddell Hart that 'character is worth more than brains in war'.[158] We have it on reliable evidence that he wrote his first volume on Allenby in what seemed to be 'the most unpropitious circumstances' and that he composed all his books and articles in similar fashion: 'They were ... brought forth in a welter of daughters borrowing three-ha'penny stamps, and puppies chewing at the boot-laces, and a series of bulletins

---

[149] Wavell, *Allenby*, 7.
[150] It was reprinted almost immediately in Sept. 1940, again in Dec., and in Mar. and Dec. 1941.   [151] Wavell, *Allenby in Egypt* (London, 1943).
[152] Id., *Allenby: Soldier and Statesman* (London, 1946).
[153] Connell, *Wavell*, 64.   [154] Ibid. 124.   [155] Ibid. 145.
[156] Moorehead, *African Trilogy*, 79; B. Gardner, *The Wasted Hour: The Tragedy of 1945* (London, 1963), 279.   [157] Esposito, *A Concise History*, 383.
[158] Wavell to Liddell Hart, 30 Oct. 1931, Liddell Hart papers, 1/733/16.

about what was happening in the stables and who couldn't come to luncheon.'[159] In fact, on his own admission, Wavell was able to 'spare little time for writing' from 1938 and part of *Allenby in Egypt* was written 'during my frequent aeroplane journeys' while he commanded in the Middle East during the first two years of the Second World War.[160] It seems likely, therefore, that what we have in Wavell's biography of Allenby is not an objective, factual account of his career, but rather a general impression of the man's character and the way in which it influenced those around him. Needless to say, criticisms that Wavell had made Allenby into 'an altogether superman' who was 'so very wonderful' and that he deliberately ignored certain evidence naturally resulted.[161]

Savage's biography has tended to be ignored because, despite its inclusion of some useful information, its journalistic style, with its conspiratorial claims to authoritative personal sources—such as Savage's reference to Lloyd George and the assertion that 'I have it on his own authority' that military opinion in London opposed Allenby's plans in Palestine[162]—is hard to take seriously. Savage goes out of his way to claim that he is writing at a sufficiently 'distant time' after the events he is recording—actually 1925—but his text reveals that he cannot detach himself from what he is recounting.[163] In part the lack of objectivity is due to Savage's own role in the campaign as Allenby's deputy Military Secretary.[164] By virtue of this position he would have seen Allenby in action at close quarters and, like Wavell, gradually developed that strong admiration for his commander-in-chief which so colours his biography. He opens his account by stating, 'I believe [Allenby] to be the most outstanding and distinguished public man which the British Empire possesses today' and continues in similar vein until he concludes:

As a soldier Lord Allenby will always be remembered with glowing admiration for his daring qualities, and as the leader of always victorious armies he will be counted among the greatest of those who have served the Empire, while for all

[159] B. Fergusson, *Wavell: Portrait of a Soldier* (London, 1961), 38.
[160] Wavell, *Allenby: Soldier and Statesman*, 5.
[161] Chetwode to Wavell, 17 Feb. 1939, Allenby papers, 6/VIII/31; unpub. memoirs by Edmonds, Edmonds papers, III/2/15.
[162] Savage, *Allenby*, 174. Incidentally this example clearly demonstrates that Savage had little idea of the true nature of the relationship between Allenby and Lloyd George and their respective roles in British military policy in Palestine.
[163] Ibid. 175.
[164] Sachar, *A History of Israel*, 105. Savage's rank was captain.

time he will be associated with Jerusalem and the deeds which culminated in its capture and freedom from centuries of notorious misrule.[165]

We have already seen how Liddell Hart had good reason to emphasize Allenby's achievements. His personal papers show that he had an intense interest in the field marshal, for he collected and preserved numerous press-cuttings after Allenby's death in 1936.[166] His assessment of Allenby in *Reputations*, as with Wavell and Savage, reflects a genuine attachment of the author to his subject. Thus he states that 'it is doubtful whether any other leader, if sent to Palestine, would have been Allenby's equal in boldness of conception and extent of success', and continues:

In Palestine he was a supreme war-lord, not merely one of the 'Barons'—as the Army Commanders in France were somewhat aptly styled. And there is little doubt that he was cast by nature for an independent role, better and bigger in carrying out his own plans than in executing the orders of others; for, although not insubordinate, subordination cramped and irked the free play of his genius and the full development of his powers. Experience and the change of conditions, both material and moral, combined to improve and expand him, not only as a General, but as a leader of men, to make him less of a martinet and more of a magnet, less intolerant and more understanding, less obstinate but no less resolute—in fact, to humanize 'the Bull', whose coming many had feared, without diminishing, but rather refining, his inborn strength of character and purpose.[167]

But Liddell Hart was prepared to accept that criticisms of Allenby were permissible. He managed to anger Wavell and provoke a letter from him after he criticized Allenby elsewhere for not having an alternative to his Megiddo plan available if the necessity arose.[168] He also recognized that the field marshal had made mistakes concerning other aspects of the Palestine campaigns—but these acknowledgements were often confined to private letters and did not always find their way into print.[169] It seems, therefore, that Liddell Hart's military knowledge and sharp intellect allowed him a certain degree of objectivity as he approached Allenby, but that this was ultimately clouded by his admiration for the man, combined with his need to use Megiddo to prove a theoretical point.

[165] Savage, *Allenby of Armageddon* (Indianapolis, 1926), 16, 352.
[166] See Liddell Hart papers, 1/11 for the various cuttings.
[167] Liddell Hart, *Reputations*, 251, 261-2.
[168] Wavell to Liddell Hart, 5 Jan. 1935, Liddell Hart papers, 1/733/35.
[169] Liddell Hart to Lloyd George, 25 June 1934, ibid. 1/450/File I. Here Liddell Hart criticizes both the plan for the third Battle of Gaza and the two attacks that Allenby ordered across the Jordan in spring 1918.

Perhaps the most objective evaluation of Allenby in a biographical format is Gardner's *Allenby*. As this is the most recent work, published in 1965, we might have expected it to have broken free from the heady romanticism and passionate loyalty of earlier writers. And yet Gardner's biography is disappointing. As a professional military historian Gardner seems to have approached Allenby by way of books about the Somme and the operations in German East Africa during the Great War.[170] Both these previous works are of significance and probably had a bearing on his biography. In his coverage of the Somme, for instance, Gardner came upon Allenby and noted, with what must have been some admiration, that he disliked the official plan for the operation and made his misgivings known.[171] As he pursued his research for the actions in Africa, moreover, he encountered Colonel Richard Meinertzhagen, whom he praised in his final text and upon whose personal reminiscences of the campaign he clearly drew heavily.[172] This is important, for Meinertzhagen was later transferred to Palestine and became Allenby's Intelligence Officer and his memoirs, published as *Army Diary, 1899-1926*, include his time with the EEF.[173] Gardner used Meinertzhagen's diary extensively in his biography of Allenby: the colonel played a crucial role in the third Battle of Gaza by helping to deceive the Turks as to the true direction of the British attack.[174] But Meinertzhagen's own account is not always entirely reliable. He arrived in Egypt late in May 1917 towards the very end of the Murray regime and rapidly adopted a hostile attitude to Sir Archibald. He subsequently claimed that 'no member' of the EEF was sorry to see Murray leave—a sweeping generalization by a man who had been in Egypt less than a month and which can be easily refuted.[175] Meinertzhagen admired Allenby and considered him a great improvement on Murray (whose wife also came in for some criticism in his diary for her poor sense of humour!).[176] Meinertzhagen's unreserved opinions helped to distort Gardner's biography.

[170] Gardner, *The Big Push*; id., *German East* (London, 1963).
[171] Id., *The Big Push*, 21, 31.
[172] Id., *German East*, 2. Meinertzhagen also seems to have personally assisted Gardner by providing him with some photographs.
[173] For details see n. 13 above. [174] See Official History, 30.
[175] Meinertzhagen, *Army Diary*, 213. For an example of an officer being sorry to see Murray go see letter by W. Deedes, n.d. (but probably June 1917), Deedes papers, DR 588.4. Deedes was also in Intelligence, but he was in the Political Section while Meinertzhagen was in Field Intelligence.
[176] Meinertzhagen, *Army Diary*, 219, 247.

The life of Allenby by Gardner owes much to Wavell's work. Before *Allenby* was published he had already committed himself in print to the belief that Wavell had been 'a man of outstanding character and great talents'.[177] What is more, given Gardner's fairly rapid output of books in the first half of the 1960s it is unlikely that he had time to complete much research for *Allenby*. Indeed, apart from his use of some of Allenby's letters there is little that is new in his book.[178] Nevertheless he leaves us with no doubt that Allenby was a great man whom he admires.[179]

It may surprise the reader that three biographies, none of them entirely satisfactory, a chapter by Liddell Hart, and some articles here and there are really all that constitute the literature exclusively concerned with Allenby.[180] Of course, he appears frequently in many general works, as we have seen, and in those devoted to the Palestine operations themselves, but even here one can be disappointed, for the Official History and Wavell's own *The Palestine Campaigns*, with which he made his name, still largely remain the standard texts.[181] Such paucity of material may perhaps be the result of the seemingly straightforward nature of the British campaign in Palestine when compared with, for example, the Gallipoli operations, which have attracted so many more writers, together with the climactic events on the Western Front. But there is another element to this neglect. One of the most curious features of Allenby's career is that his tenure of office as Egyptian High Commissioner has attracted more serious attention than has his time as commander of the EEF. The main reason for this surprising situation lies with the nature of the modern Middle East. Since the establishment of the British mandate in Palestine, the rise of Arab nationalism, and the creation of the state of Israel historians have sought to identify the causes of these events. Consequently Allenby appears more important as a political figure than as a soldier.[182] Moreover, since Allenby 'liberated' the land that is now Israel and administered it for a while after the war

[177] Gardner, *The Wasted Hour*, 279.
[178] Id., *Allenby*, 157. There is some mystery as to where Gardner got hold of these letters, which now reside in the Liddell Hart Centre for Military Archives.
[179] Ibid. 154, 178-9.
[180] Wavell wrote an article for *Army Quarterly* in 1936, for example; the MS is in Allenby papers, 1/14/36.
[181] Fergusson, *Wavell*, 13: 'The first time I met Wavell I had barely heard of him, except as the author of *The Palestine Campaigns*.'
[182] This impression has been intensified in Britain by the 1956 Suez Crisis which led many to seek the causes behind the rise of Nasser and the reasons for Egyptian hostility towards Britain. Thus, Allenby's time as High Commissioner seemed more important.

ended he has even become a significant figure in the contemporary Arab-Israeli dispute that has been taken up by historians. Thus, the charge has been laid that he and his senior staff were 'openly hostile to Zionism' and were even prepared to advocate the 'abandonment' of the newly conquered territory of Palestine.[183] On the other hand, Arab leaders have seen him in almost precisely the opposite light:

> It was England and France that attacked this region under the name of the Crusades, and the Crusades were nothing else but British-French imperialism . . . It was no accident at all that General Allenby said on arriving in Jerusalem: 'Today the wars of the Crusades are completed.'[184]

So Allenby remains a crusader—even today! The problem with this kind of thing is that it reduces the military operations in Palestine during the First World War to mere adjuncts of the political developments at the time so that interest in them for their own sake has been sadly lacking in recent years. Contemporaries did not see them in this way at all. As Sir Henry MacMahon admitted in September 1916 it was the military who pulled all the strings, even when it came to British involvement with the Arabs—surely the most politically contentious issue of the whole campaign: he wrote, 'It was the most unfortunate date in my life when I was left in charge of this Arab movement and I think a few words are necessary to explain that it is nothing to do with me: it is a purely military business.'[185]

A new generation of military historians needs to rediscover Allenby and his triumphs and mistakes—for there were some—in Palestine. There is much that can be learnt from Allenby the commander rather than Allenby the crusader or Allenby the moral giant. Surely it is now possible to view him with objective detachment. Of course, such an approach may not lead to big sales or popular acclaim, but it might achieve something more important—something that Thucydides, perhaps the greatest military historian of all, did achieve:

> And with regard to my factual reporting of the events of the war I have made it a principle not to write down the first story that came my way . . . And it may well be that my history will seem less easy to read because of the absence in it of a

---

[183] Sachar, *A History of Israel*, 168; J. Peters, *From Time Immemorial: The Origins of the Arab-Jewish Conflict over Palestine* (London, 1985), 274. Ironically enough it was Meinertzhagen who made this second charge.

[184] Speech by President Nasser of Egypt, 20 Mar. 1958, quoted by J. Laffin, *The Arab Mind* (London, 1975), 157.

[185] Quoted by E. Kedourie, 'Cairo and Khartoum on the Arab Question', in id., *The Chatham House Version*, 14.

romantic element. It will be enough for me, however, if these words of mine are judged useful by those who want to understand clearly the events which happened in the past and which (human nature being what it is) will, at some time or other and in much the same ways, be repeated in the future. My work is not a piece of writing designed to meet the taste of an immediate public, but was done to last for ever.[186]

[186] Thucydides, *History of the Peloponnesian War*, trans. R. Warner (Harmondsworth, 1965), 24-5.

9
T. E. Lawrence and his Biographers*
BRIAN HOLDEN REID

The influence of the mass media on our treatment of heroes has been profound. The attention they lavish on the famous is frequently so undiscriminating as to require the drawing of a distinction between the heroes thrown up by historical change and the great mythology that their fame has spawned. In many cases, great men have transcended their reputations to such a degree that the relationship between their legends and the objective reality of their careers has become somewhat strained. In almost all cases, the growth of these fantastic legends has been the product of the spread throughout the nineteenth century of mass-circulation newspapers. Hence the growth of the enduring, self-serving, or didactic Napoleonic legend in France and the nationalistic legends surrounding George Washington, Andrew Jackson, and Abraham Lincoln in the United States. Colonel T. E. Lawrence was the first figure in British history to become the subject of such a legend. Of course, the British Empire has had many heroes and heroines: Queen Elizabeth I, Wolfe, Clive, Nelson, Wellington, Florence Nightingale, and Kitchener, but they have not spawned a self-generating mythology. Kitchener was the subject briefly of massive press attention and inspired some extraordinary legends, but by 1918 he was largely a forgotten and discredited figure.

Lawrence was the most glamorous figure thrown up by the last years of the Great War. His glamour shone the more brightly because of the brutal and indecisive character of the First World War which shattered the romantic illusions cherished by so many in 1914. Interest in Lawrence's seemingly romantic achievements in an exotic part of the world increased as revulsion with the slaughter and horror of the trenches increased. It also coincided with a general, romanticized interest in the Middle East. ('Arabia' was a generic term favoured at the time for

---

* I am grateful to the Trustees of the Liddell Hart Centre for Military Archives for permission to quote from copyright material.

the Middle East which should not be confused with Saudi Arabia.) This was manifest in the films of such screen heroes as Rudolph Valentino and the 'Sheik of Araby'. It is significant that this curiosity was reinforced by Hollywood, which added a new dimension to press interest. The interest in Lawrence's career was almost as strong in the United States as in Britain, and would provide the initial impetus for the growth of the Lawrence legend.[1]

The literature on Lawrence and the Arab Revolt is so vast that this essay can only concentrate on the most important and representative of the many biographies completed since his death in 1935. There have been about 30 biographies. Those considered in detail here will only be works which began a trend in writing about him, or opened up a new line of inquiry. No attempt has been made to survey all the books written, a task which has been undertaken by a number of recent bibliographies.[2] This essay will also consider how the Lawrence legend has influenced the reactions of historians to his career. The legend in its fullest sense was the progeny of journalists rather than historians or participants in the Arab Revolt. Here the American journalist, Lowell Thomas, was especially influential. It was his picture show, 'With Allenby in Palestine and Lawrence in Arabia' which began showing in London in August 1919 that drew an enormous audience and framed the terms of reference for the ensuing legend. (References to Allenby had been dropped by 1922.) Thomas's picture show was based on photographs taken on a very brief visit (no more than a fortnight) to the Middle East in 1918. In 1922 Thomas turned his 'hard copy' into a bestselling book, illustrated by a number of photographs of Lawrence in Arab dress striking romantic and picturesque poses, which was eventually published in England in 1924. Lawrence wrote of Thomas to his confidante, George Bernard Shaw's wife, Charlotte, that he was 'the American who made my vulgar reputation; a well intentioned, intensely crude and pushful fellow. He has been threatening this book about me for years. I fear it will be awful: and

---

[1] For a sampling of the kind of mythology that grew up in the United States in the nineteenth century, see Marcus Cunliffe's introduction to his edition of Mason L. Weems, *The Life of Washington* (Cambridge, Mass., 1962); John William Ward, *Andrew Jackson: The Symbol for an Age* (New York, 1955); David Donald, *Lincoln Reconsidered* (2nd edn., New York, 1961); and Dixon Wecter, *The Hero in America* (New York, 1973).

[2] Jeffrey Meyers, *T. E. Lawrence: A Bibliography* (New York and London, 1975); P. M. O'Brien, *T. E. Lawrence: A Bibliography* (Boston, 1988). For an earlier survey see Elie Kedouri, 'Colonel Lawrence and his Biographers', in *Islam in the Modern World and other Studies* (London, 1980).

yet I can't imagine it beastly enough to make me publish the truth.'³ The latter phrase is a reference to *The Seven Pillars of Wisdom* which though unpublished would also be a profound influence on some of the earlier biographies of T. E. Lawrence.

With Lawrence in Arabia, for all its errors and omissions, is an important book because it establishes the framework for future discussion of Lawrence in a number of ways. Interestingly, Thomas, in his foreword, remarked on the likelihood of the growth of an anti-myth. 'Unhappily', he wrote, 'no matter how much unselfish work a man does for his country, and no matter how modest he is, there are always people hovering about on the sidelines ready to tear his record to pieces'. His acquaintance with Lawrence had lasted no longer than a few days. But in praise of that record Thomas struck the religious note that is so marked a feature of the early literature. On meeting Lawrence, 'My first thought . . . was that he might be one of the younger apostles returned to life. His expression was serene, almost saintly, in its selflessness and repose.' This was linked, too, with the certainty that he was 'one of the most picturesque personalities of modern times, a man who will be blazoned on the romantic pages of history with Raleigh, Drake, Clive and Gordon'. Yet this modest hero would say nothing about himself, only commend the achievements of comrades in the desert, like Newcombe, Joyce, Dawnay, and Stirling among others. Later he was equally forthright about the contribution of Arab leaders. 'Like children', Thomas commented, 'those doughty old warriors were not at all reticent about accepting it, and, of course, from then on they were Lawrence's sworn friends.'⁴

The third feature that Thomas observed was Lawrence's impatience with formalities of military discipline. 'His aversion to saluting superiors, for instance, and his general indifference to all traditional military formalities did not exactly increase his popularity with some of the sterner warriors of the old school.' Departing from established military practice, Lawrence evolved his own theory of guerrilla war, a technique which Thomas described as, 'not to hunt out his enemy and fight it out to the finish, but to stalk his prey as a hunter stalks his game'.⁵ As regards Lawrence's methods, Thomas's account was a medley of utter nonsense

---

³ T. E. Lawrence to Charlotte Shaw, 19 Mar. 1924, British Library Add. MSS 45903. The details of Thomas's visits to the Middle East are taken from Jeremy Wilson, *Lawrence of Arabia: The Authorised Biography* (London, 1989), 493.
⁴ Lowell Thomas, *With Lawrence in Arabia* (New York, 1924), pp. x, 5-6, 107.
⁵ Ibid. 77, 82, 123.

and some sense. Apparently, 'Blue eyes terrify the average Arab. Lawrence possesses two that are bluer than the waters of the Mediterranean, and so the Bedouins decided there was something superhuman about him.' But his account, finally, of Lawrence's leadership was rather less fanciful. He noted how Lawrence would delegate when he thought an Arab was capable of carrying out the task. He also grasped how successful Lawrence was in handling men. 'The gallant old brigands who had roamed freely all their lives over the vast stretches of Arabia . . . were not to be commanded or conscripted; they had to be gently cajoled into the bigger war and made to feel the sense of their importance.' Lawrence's sense of humour was an inestimable asset. 'Make an Arab laugh and you can persuade him to do most things.' In short, Thomas claimed, Lawrence's success could be put down to 'the faculty of mastering the unexpected with some inspired improvisation'. He was a 'consummate actor' who had acquired more influence with the Arabs than any other Westerner. 'Lawrence, recognising generosity to be a cardinal virtue with the Arabs', Thomas wrote, 'made it a point to excel them in this as well as in bravery, physical endurance, and nimbleness of wit, which they so much admire'. Touching on the thorny question of Lawrence's motives, he declared that his 'sole motive' was the defeat of the Germans and Turks 'and at the same time to help his friends the Arabs win their freedom'—a note likely to appeal to his North American readers, though not perhaps to Lawrence himself.[6]

This early book lays down the first layer of encrustation of the legend of 'Lawrence of Arabia'. It obscures more than it reveals about Lawrence. Yet it is not difficult to appraise. The book is over-written, adorned with adjectives, sentimental imagery, and yarns about the natives. Travelogue is mixed up with biography and war commentary. *With Lawrence in Arabia* enshrined Lawrence as the 'man of mystery': the leader as romantic inspiration; an inspiration for future generations as much as for the Arabs he led. For all its excesses and inaccuracies, the majority of Lawrence's earlier biographers were to follow Thomas on this desert trail. Thomas's book was the first attempt at a biography and therefore, for all its foolishness, not insignificant. Lawrence once wrote, 'A man gets carried away and says brave things . . . but if you take him away . . . and lend him your pocket-mirror he will recant.' Thomas got carried away but did not recant, and the result was that in transforming Lawrence into a 'star' an important step was taken in casting the style of the Lawrence

[6] Lowell Thomas, *With Lawrence in Arabia: The Authorised Biography* (London, 1989), 124, 155, 168, 195, 346, 357, 366.

legend. At this point it remained style rather than substance, for the legend should not be confused with the historiography. There is a marked difference between press tittle-tattle and a view propounded in a serious book, no matter how romantic. As views about Lawrence changed, it was common for later authors to attack their predecessors as myth-makers. Criticism of the legend requires a sense of proportion. More substantial books may add to or detract from it, but it is assumed here that the authors selected have sufficient integrity to be taken seriously, however mistaken their portraits of Lawrence might be. Thomas's book here falls into both camps because so much of it is purely imaginary; yet certain aspects have been given serious attention because they preface features of later, more substantial books.[7]

This substance was to be provided by two books, published by Lawrence's friends, Robert Graves and Captain B. H. Liddell Hart. These quite different writers did not meet until after Lawrence's death in 1935. 'He [Lawrence] never mentioned you to me', Graves wrote, 'or that you were writing a book about him. To you he showed almost wholly his military historian side: you were to him "military historian". As Augustus John was "painter" and I was "poet". All so damn water-tight his compartments.' Robert Graves was to come increasingly to see Lawrence as a guru—indeed one resembling Jesus Christ (the religious overtones spilling over from his campaigns in Palestine seemed to effect even those who were not religious). Graves was Lawrence's literary and Liddell Hart his military 'disciple'.[8]

Graves and Liddell Hart were to write the two most important books about Lawrence. To be understood adequately they must be related to the intellectual climate of the inter-war years, especially the increasingly bitter criticism of the British conduct of the First World War along the Western Front that prevailed amongst educated opinion. It is no coincidence that Lawrence's finest early biographers were themselves eloquent and sardonic critics of the British military effort. Graves in *Good-bye to All That* (1929) and Liddell Hart in a series of books on the First World

---

[7] T. E. Lawrence to Charlotte Shaw, 26 March 1924, Add MSS 45903. For an example of the absurd yarns that circulated about Lawrence, see F. H. Croseley to Liddell Hart, 25 Jan. 1933, Liddell Hart papers, 9/13/8: 'I do know that he was present at the British Legion Tattoo, Belle Vue, Manchester on Saturday, October 8, 1932 and he led off the musical ride of the 5th [Royal] Inniskilling Dragoon [Guard]s . . .'.

[8] Robert Graves to Liddell Hart, 12 Dec. 1935, ibid., 9/13/14, quoted in Brian Holden Reid, 'T. E. Lawrence and Liddell Hart', *History*, 70 (June 1985), 227; Liddell Hart's account of his friendship with Lawrence is in his *Memoirs* (London, 1965), i. 339-56.

War, culminating in his *History of the World War 1914-1918* (1934). Both Graves and Liddell Hart were to a greater or lesser extent members of a liberal intellectual circle that T. E. Lawrence himself entered in the 1920s. Though Liddell Hart did not share their political concerns he did sympathize with their broader intellectual and idealistic values. One aspect of these was the increasing reputation that Lawrence enjoyed in liberal and left-wing circles as a romantic hero. As the Communist writer Ralph Fox put it, he was the only hero 'the English ruling classes have produced in our time, a hero who in his own lifetime gathered about him all the legendary atmosphere of the hero'. One important aspect of this appeal was Lawrence's renunciation of wealth and fame and his decision to seek what amounted to exile in the ranks of the Tank Corps and the RAF. He was a new kind of hero; the agonizing, somewhat neurotic intellectual who had transformed himself into a man of action by an act of will. Christopher Isherwood once described him as a figure who 'suffered in his own person, the neurotic ills of an entire generation'. Certainly this insight catered to the varying idealistic appetites of Graves and Liddell Hart who seemed to feed off Lawrence's achievements and air of worldly wisdom. Samuel Hynes has expressed this very well, when he writes of Lawrence's 'two personalities'—the brooding, self-conscious intellectual and the thrusting man of action. 'For young men of Auden's generation, these lives were parables of their own problems solved. "How shall the self-conscious man be saved?" The answers in these cases had nothing to do with politics, but everything to do with action and with self-knowledge.'[9]

This symbolic significance of Lawrence for critics of the British war effort in the First World War can be traced in the diary of Graves's friend, Siegfried Sassoon. On seeing Lawrence leave a friend's house in July 1923 he was not impressed. He espied 'a queer little figure in dark motor overalls, his brown and grimy face framed in a fur-lined cap'. Once he had been introduced by Graves and exposed to the power of Lawrence's personality, Sassoon succumbed. Reading *The Seven Pillars of Wisdom* in draft, Sassoon wrote,

> his book has impressed him on me as one of the most intensely real minds in my experience. He is an ascetic. And his attitudes are superb, the way he hacks his way down to reality, never sparing himself. My admiration for him grows steadily

[9] Reid, 'T. E. Lawrence and Liddell Hart', 220; Liddell Hart described him in his *Memoirs* (i. 356), as 'in combination of personality and intellect, of capacity for action and reflection, he surpassed any man I have met'. See also Samuel Hynes. *The Auden Generation: Literature and Politics in England in the 1930s* (London, 1976), 189-92.

as I plough through his double-columns of small print, which are like a physical experience.

When meeting Lawrence he began to behave like a bashful schoolboy, even though Sassoon had been no mean man of action himself. He confessed that 'While reading his book I saw him [Lawrence] as an infallible superman, and myself as an inveterate shambler.' When Lawrence paid him a call unexpectedly, Sassoon was overawed. 'I blurted out questions and assertions, mainly about his book and his present health and existent projects.'[10]

Both Graves and Liddell Hart hero-worshipped Lawrence. Of these two disciples, Lawrence had known Graves the longer. They had first met at a guest night at All Souls College, Oxford in March 1920. Graves had been very flattered to discover that Lawrence had not only read but liked his poetry. Flattery soon turned to worship. Lawrence was an older man in whom he could confide and argue—but fundamentally agree. This pattern replicated itself later when he met Liddell Hart in 1929. These younger friends were inspired not only by his great and youthful achievements but by his *wisdom*, to which they could aspire but could not emulate. Martin Seymour-Smith has pointed out that by this date:

Graves had already become exhausted by the difficulties created by his own idealism and conventional moral rectitude, by his struggle to reconcile a rigid personal morality with a growing hatred and distrust of conventional morality (the 'morality' which produced the war). He compensated by indulging in a robust opposition to the Establishment, in which Lawrence—an accepted figure —also shared.

A similar moral quest, though with different roots, motivated Liddell Hart. But what strikes the reader is how fundamentally similar their approach to Lawrence was. Their works tell us more about their idealism, aspirations, and moral struggles than they do about Lawrence's motives; indeed their two books form a *glossa ordinaria* on them.[11]

There was also a more mercenary reason why Graves began work on his biography, *Lawrence and the Arabs*. He was (not for the first nor the last time) in financial difficulties. In September 1935 Graves revealed to Liddell Hart that Lawrence 'felt that what I was doing in poetry was

[10] Siegfried Sassoon, *Diaries, 1923-1925*, ed. Rupert Hart-Davies (London, 1985), 52-3, 66, 69 (entries for 28 July, 26 Nov, 9 Dec. 1923); *T. E. Lawrence to his Biographer Robert Graves* (2nd edn., London, 1963), 3-4.
[11] Brian Bond, *Liddell Hart* (London, 1977), 80, 82; Reid, 'T. E. Lawrence and Liddell Hart', 228-9; Martin Seymour-Smith, *Robert Graves: His Life and Work* (London, 1982), 30, 84-5.

important and that I should be financed for doing it—this was the real reason for letting me write *Lawrence and the Arabs'*. The original scheme was for a children's book, but this was undercut by Lowell Thomas. So alarmed was the publisher, Jonathan Cape, that another enterprising author might scoop the market, that Graves was given only six weeks to finish it. Lawrence was relaxed about the task he had set Graves. He thought him 'a decent fellow, does not know too much about me: will think out some psychologically plausible explanation for my spiritual divagations: and will therefore help to lay at rest the uneasy ghost which seems to have stayed in England when I went abroad'. The spirits haunting Lawrence were those of illegitimacy. Lawrence was also conscious that Graves would do his bidding. 'Graves is smaller than I am, and so will do mainly what I have asked him.'[12]

Graves soon realized that he would have to expand the book by something like three times the original projected length. Lawrence agreed that three quarters of this would perforce consist of a substantial paraphrase of *The Seven Pillars of Wisdom*—though not material that was omitted from the abridged version of that book, *Revolt in the Desert*. Charlotte Shaw refused Graves permission to see Lawrence's correspondence with her, and *Lawrence and the Arabs* was based on a narrow range of sources. After it was completed, Lawrence wrote to Graves complaining that 'The thing that was really important was for you to do yourself really well, and I don't feel it's up to the level of your other prose.' And to Charlotte Shaw he criticized the degree to which Graves had relied on *The Seven Pillars of Wisdom*, 'I do not think it was quite right to make so free with another's work.' This was characteristic of Lawrence's pandering to Charlotte Shaw's possessiveness towards him (and he would make similar critical comments about Liddell Hart's biography). He had hoped that

> If Doran and Cape [the publishers] had financed you to go round and see some of these [Arab leaders and other witnesses] and collate their stories with the reports of the *Arab Bulletin* . . . then you'd have produced that most valuable thing, a cross check on my accuracy or inaccuracy. A history of the Arab Revolt would have been definitive. Whereas a 'life' of me cannot be.

Lawrence was quibbling and his scheme impracticable. He consoled himself that it 'might have been done 5,000 times worse by someone merely sensation-hunting'. Under the circumstances Graves had done a

---

[12] Robert Graves to Liddell Hart, 14 Sept. 1935, Liddell Hart papers, 9/13/14; Wilson, *Lawrence of Arabia*, 792, 794-6.

creditable job. His prose was strong, sinewy, and graphic. His account was accurate—or as accurate as the limited sources at his disposal would allow. Graves had made the money he needed (he had got an advance of £500) and the book sold well. In December 1927 it was selling 10,000 copies per week; in 1934 a concise edition appeared, and in 1940 a school edition. The book had fulfilled everybody's expectations save his subject's. Graves did not appear very concerned; Lawrence always fussed in this way when books were completed.[13]

Graves began his absorbing account with a detailed biographical survey (which was, for Lawrence, pleasingly vague about his origins). This amply fulfilled Lawrence's hope that Graves would concoct some philosophical theory about him while remaining ignorant of the full truth. The initial two chapters were by far the most interesting in the book. He began by noting Lawrence's 'two conflicting selves':

> the Bedouin self always longing for the bareness, simplicity, harshness of the desert—that state of mind of which the desert is a symbol—and the over-civilized European self . . . These two selves are mutually destructive, so Lawrence has finally fallen between them into a nihilism which cannot find, in being, even a false god in which to believe.

He also put his finger on another recurring theme, which would engage Liddell Hart's attention, namely that Lawrence regarded knowledge as a tool for achievement:

> the impression of omniscience that he conveys is due rather to a faculty of forgetting what he calls utterly useless knowledge such as higher mathematics, classroom metaphysics and theories of aesthetics, and of fitting together harmoniously what he does know. . . . he despises mere knowledge, though he accumulates it and stores it carefully from old habit. He despises it because it is imperfect, because he sees *knowledge* as the opposite of *wisdom*.

The result of this wisdom was that 'He, a foreigner and an unbeliever, inspired and led the broadest national movement of the Arabs that had taken place since the great times of Mohammed . . . and brought it to a triumphant conclusion.'[14]

Graves recognized that the very magnitude of this achievement presented an obstacle to understanding it. He deplored 'a cosmic joke in the worst taste' that 'the legend of "The Uncrowned King of Arabia" has become popularly entangled with a novelist's myth of the "Sheik of

---

[13] Wilson, *Lawrence of Arabia*, 796, 800-3; Seymour-Smith, *Graves*, 142-3; *T. E. Lawrence to his Biographer Robert Graves*, 46-7.
[14] Robert Graves, *Lawrence and the Arabs* (London, 1927), 21-2, 24-5, 49-50.

Araby". Booksellers have wasted a good deal of time in explaining that "Revolt in the Desert" is not a sequel to "The Son of the Sheik"'. After the first two chapters (which rely heavily on Graves's own observations of Lawrence's personality), the book becomes dependent on *The Seven Pillars of Wisdom* and its passages are recognizable to readers of that book. Graves's account of Lawrence's first brush with military discipline and its arcane formalities would recur constantly in later books. The opinions of a mere civilian were treated with disdain. 'The General Staff disliked history and suspected a joke.' The former is probably true but not the latter. Lawrence resembled

a small grinning second-lieutenant, with hair of unmilitary length and no belt, hiding behind a screen in the Savoy Hotel with another equally unmilitary colleague, softly counting 'One, two, three, four!' ... through a hole in the screen. They were counting generals. An important conference was going on in the room, for generals only. His colleague swears to me that Lawrence counted up to sixty-five. He himself only made it to sixty-four, but one of the Brigadier-Generals may have moved.[15]

Once he had joined the Arabs and was free of the strait-jacket of conventional military thinking, he made a rapid appraisal of both the influence of terrain and the character of the Arab forces at his disposal for campaigning in the Middle East. Most of Lawrence's admirers were impressed by the rapidity and clarity of his thought. Graves emphasized, too, how much Lawrence learned from studying the patient, persuasive, cajoling, rather than hectoring, methods of the Emir Feisal. Lawrence soon understood that the norms of military discipline could not be applied to the Arabs. 'In mass they were not dangerous: in fact their use in battle lessened as their numbers increased.' Graves stressed a point made earlier by Lowell Thomas that

The Arabs were not pressed men accustomed to be treated as cannon-fodder like most regular soldiers. The Arab army was composed rather of individuals, and its losses were not reckoned merely by arithmetic. And because kinship is so strong a force in the desert, twenty men killed meant a far wider range of mourning than a thousand names in an European casualty list.

The oblique parallels that Graves made here to European warfare, with its acceptance of systematized killing are striking, and he would return to them. The Arab Revolt was a form of warfare in which the human element was paramount—not the dehumanized methods of machines.[16]

[15] Robert Graves, *Lawrence and the Arabs* (London, 1927), 57, 82-3, 84.
[16] Ibid. 109-10, 121, 132, 141.

Central to Graves's account of Lawrence as a strategist, was his acceptance of Lawrence's reasoning in *The Seven Pillars of Wisdom*: namely, that the Turks should be encouraged to store up useless strength by holding the great cities of the south, like Medina, while the Arabs moved into the desert spaces and wore this force down by striking at its supply lines. Moreover, Lawrence intended to switch the centre of political gravity of the Arab Revolt northwards, so that the Arabs could co-operate with the right flank of the Egyptian Expeditionary Force. Hence the true significance of the fall of Wejh in January 1917, which opened up a line of communication with Allenby. Lawrence was determined to avoid pitched battles which the Arabs could not win. Thus, he advocated not a direct approach on Medina, but an indirect approach on Akaba from the land. 'There was need for true epic action', Graves applauded, 'if Akaba was to be taken, for it was a feat beyond the scope of unheroic twentieth century soldiering'. Once the strategy was agreed, then Lawrence could apply his diplomatic skills to building up a 'ladder' of sympathetic Syrian tribes (previously riven by feuds and rivalries) over which the Arab forces could move.

Once more the tactics should be tip and run, not the regular advance of an organised army, and for this the eastern desert was most convenient. One might look on it as a sort of sea in which to manœuvre with camel-parties instead of ships . . . From the war in the south Lawrence had learned that the best tactics were to use the smallest raiding parties on the fastest camels, and to strike at points widely separated with the most portable weapons of destruction.

The Arabs could seize the initiative and hold it because thanks to their excellent intelligence-gathering service, they could predict with reasonable accuracy Turkish movements. 'So the Arabs could always decide in time whether to fight or avoid fight.'[17]

In elucidating Lawrence's methods so convincingly, Graves did not fail to note his dependence on Allenby, or his dislike of combat. He quoted him as saying that 'I love the preparation, and the journey, and loathe the physical fighting.' At Tafileh, Graves suggested, 'This was the one occasion in the War that Lawrence abandoned his principles of irregular mobility and fought a real battle, as a sort of bad joke, on the ordinary text-book lines.' But Graves's analysis of an original strategist rested less on his appreciation of the skill with which Lawrence persuaded others to adopt his methods, as on his sustained exploration of Lawrence's basic insight into the irregular dimension of the Arab Revolt.

[17] Ibid. 149-51, 161, 224-5, 254-5.

Lawrence was, after all, a soldier (though admittedly a temporary one) who had enjoyed no previous experience of guerrilla warfare. He had developed 'a whole modern theory of War', one which rejected contemporary notions of strategy and tactics—and by implication the methods used on the Western Front.

The obvious comment to be made on his strategy is that it enabled the Arab Revolt in the sphere of politics, as in the sphere of war, to assume a much larger share of influence and attention than its material importance justified ... [Lawrence insisted], with a repetition that conveys the painfulness of his problem, upon the extreme economy of means necessary.

Graves concluded that Lawrence 'does not like wars in which the individual is swallowed up in the mass'; the Arab Revolt was so unlike the 'civilized' war that had prevailed in France, 'and so romantically appealing, that it is perhaps fortunate that Siegfried Sassoon, Wilfred Owen, Edmund Blunden, and the other poets who got badly involved in the war were all infantrymen in France'.[18] The implication here was that if these poets had served in Arabia rather than in France, they would not have become so passionately anti-war.

Graves lacked the military knowledge to develop a theory of war out of these insights. The military writer who did share some of his romantic ideals and who could develop such ideas didactically was Liddell Hart. Liddell Hart's book was shaped by many of the same factors that framed Graves's. Among Liddell Hart's motives for writing it was a desire to hold up Lawrence as an object lesson in how commanders, by serious thought and study, could become sagacious men of action. Lawrence, too, encouraged him in this endeavour. 'So please', he wrote 'if you see me that way and agree with me, do use me as a text to preach for more study of books and history, a greater seriousness in military art'. The second was to inveigh against one of Liddell Hart's bugbears, the mentally cramping effect of a military system whose commanders were obsessed with turn-out and dress. In *T. E. Lawrence in Arabia and After*, he recorded how Lawrence began work in the Geographical Section of the General Staff in 1914. He wandered into General Rawlinson's office dressed in casual clothes, blissfully unaware of military rituals, to show him the new maps of Belgium. Rawlinson ' "nearly had

---

[18] Robert Graves, *Lawrence and the Arabs* (London, 1927), 301, 333, 355, 412-13, 417. The romantic appeal of the desert landscape serves as a counterpoint to the aesthetic appeal of English landscape in the work of those poets, and as a contrast to the horrors and destruction inflicted by industrialized war on the French countryside. See Correlli Barnett, *The Collapse of British Power* (London, 1972), 430.

a fit when he saw me" and exclaimed "I want to talk to an officer"'. Liddell Hart continued, 'Those professional soldiers who were in his immediate circle, men who recognised his value, who had a sense of humour, learnt to tolerate his jests at their profession and even enjoyed the smarting ring of truth.' But there was a duller, more pompous breed of officer who resented Lawrence 'correcting their prose style, on paper, and their ignorance, over the telephone'.[19]

But in terms of strategy, Lawrence, in Liddell Hart's opinion, had developed the 'first scientific theory of irregular warfare'. This theory, he argued, was based on the assumption that war was diffuse in time and space. Thus it rested on *dispersion*. 'In fulfilment of theory his idea was to spread the infection of revolt over as wide a space as possible.' Economy of force was fundamental to the theory's application. Here the fall of Akaba was an object lesson. Economy of force was important not only because of the Arab's dread of casualties, but because direct confrontation with the Turks was inimical to Lawrence's theory. This was indirect. Lawrence refused to permit the Arabs to charge the Turks at Minifir in November 1917 merely to achieve 'a success that was superfluous to their mission of pure distraction'. Hence Liddell Hart's assertion that 'In such a war, ideas that gradually evolved into a changed *state* had a more decisive significance than any particular act.' In a long conversation in 1933 Lawrence urged on Liddell Hart two main points. That armies should 'Pass around obstacles, but don't branch the main stream', and secondly, the importance of distractions, but leave 'an air space between them and the main stream—to prevent ruffling'. This emerging theory, Liddell Hart was convinced, would 'with slight adaption' be suitable for armoured forces in regular warfare. Lawrence's main contribution to the victory of 1918 was in destroying Turkish *organization*, paralysing them from the rear. Lawrence's drive on Damascus was 'Decisive not in itself but because it alone made possible the decision.'[20]

This analysis in itself would have been sufficient to draw Liddell Hart towards Lawrence. But increasingly he was fascinated by 'Lawrence's uncanny detachment', his 'historical understanding' and 'that quiet but resistless air of assurance which all who know him know so well'.

[19] Reid, 'T. E. Lawrence and Liddell Hart', 218-21; T. E. Lawrence to Liddell Hart, 26 June 1933, Liddell Hart papers, 9/13/5; Liddell Hart, *T. E. Lawrence in Arabia and After* (London, 1934), 95, 102.
[20] Liddell Hart, *T. E. Lawrence*, 59, 128-30, 182-3, 198, 207, 340-1, 349; Talk with T. E. [Lawrence], 1 Aug. 1933, Liddell Hart papers, 9/13/21.

Lawrence became for Liddell Hart a symbol of truth, a seer, a man with 'an intellectual equipment such as no other commander of his time possessed'.

The blend of wisdom with knowledge would restrain men from contributing to this endless cycle of folly [of war], but only understanding can guide them towards positive progress.

T.E. is rare among great men in adjusting his opinions to his knowledge . . . He is rarer still in avoiding abuse of the power that knowledge brings, in freeing himself from the desires that commonly direct this power into channels harmful to other men's gifts and growth.

He came increasingly to see Lawrence 'as a spiritual force'—'He is the Spirit of Freedom, come incarnate to a world in fetters.'[21]

The Christ-like imagery employed by Liddell Hart is striking. In the early 1930s, for the only time in his life, he began to read the Scriptures. This mystical element added a further dimension to his study. 'From personal experience', he commented to Robert Graves, 'he was certainly less mystery-making in the last year or two than when he first came back from India in 1928-29.' But this mysterious air predominated just at the date when Liddell Hart and he first became fast friends. As Lieutenant-Colonel W. F. Stirling observed, 'Lawrence is undoubtedly the most difficult man in the world to explain.' Their friendship dates from 1929, and Liddell Hart only became a member of Lawrence's intimate circle in these last years. In his eagerness to identify strongly with Lawrence and lavish youthful idealism in his direction, it is tempting to view Lawrence's friendship with Liddell Hart as a repeat performance of his relationship with Robert Graves. Lawrence was eight years older than Liddell Hart, and their friendship waxed while that with Graves waned. It is interesting to speculate whether, had Lawrence lived, they would have remained on such intimate terms after 1935, or whether a cooling of mutual regard might also have occurred.[22]

Paradoxically, the more idealistic the rhetoric that Liddell Hart indulged in, the more Lawrence objected to the emphasis on his singular achievement. Liddell Hart replied

that his remonstrance was rather late, in two senses—for the real time to rectify this was sixteen years before. I had found by examining the evidence and the

[21] Liddell Hart, *T. E. Lawrence*, 356, 359, 368-9, 436, 446-8.
[22] Liddell Hart to Robert Graves, 3 June 1935, ibid. 9/13/14; Seymour-Smith, *Robert Graves*, 254-7; l.t.-Col. W. F. Stirling to Liddell Hart, n.d., ibid. 9/13/8.

witnesses, that his predominant part in the Arab Revolt was historical fact, and it was inevitable that it had to be treated proportionately.

Liddell Hart's book was based on a much wider study of the sources and participants than Graves's book, although he too relied heavily on *Revolt in the Desert* and *The Seven Pillars of Wisdom*.[23] Liddell Hart was anxious, however, that his book should not be viewed as an uncritical eulogy. He included a long account of the origins of the Arab Revolt which George Bernard Shaw thought distracting. Liddell Hart retorted that 'The campaign was sired by opportunism and damned by confusion . . . There was a long period of chaos, and then out of this chaos T.E. emerged—the problem is to show this without wearying the reader.' In this effort Liddell Hart was laying out his objectivity for the reader's inspection. At this time he had a veritable obsession for seeking out 'the truth'. For instance, Vyvyan Richards, an old friend of Lawrence, assured him that 'Reviewers—even Graves—seem to have axes of their own to grind so often: you struck me . . . to be really concerned with objective truth.' But this search after truth was guided by passionate conviction and vigorous idealism. 'He is too serious', Lawrence told Charlotte Shaw. 'His book on me is very interesting where it is military, and *awful* . . . where it deals with me as a human being.' Lawrence could not resist deflating occasionally his more earnest prognostications. One evening leaving the Savage Club, after Liddell Hart had shown Lawrence the passage in which he was hailed as the 'Spirit of Freedom', Liddell Hart recorded that 'As we came away into the Strand I happened to be talking of my desire to get at the root of things, and T.E. pointing to a match-seller, remarked—"If you let your passion for truth grow upon you like this, you'll finish by selling matches in the Strand."' [24]

Liddell Hart was candid in admitting that in *'T. E. Lawrence'* he had given his subject the benefit of the doubt perhaps too frequently. 'That effect, of generosity over critical sense, was reinforced because the more I poked into the *reasons* which guided his actions in the war, the more I found them to coincide with my own critical philosophy . . . he served as the almost perfect example of that philosophy of war.' Some

[23] Talk with T. E. [Lawrence], Sept. 1933, *T. E. Lawrence to his Biographer Liddell Hart* (London, 1963), 171; for an assessment of the sources, see Reid, 'T. E. Lawrence and Liddell Hart', 220.
[24] Liddell Hart to George Bernard Shaw, 16 Dec. 1933, Liddell Hart papers, 9/13/7; Vyvyan Richards to Liddell Hart, 24 Mar. 1936, ibid. 9/13/69; T. E. Lawrence to Charlotte Shaw, 29 June 1934, British Library Add. MSS 45904; Talk with T. E. [Lawrence], 14 Dec. 1933 (Savage Club), Liddell Hart papers 9/13/21; *T. E. Lawrence to his Biographer Liddell Hart*, 202.

correspondents, like Eric Kennington and Robert Graves, thought that Liddell Hart's book was too didactic. By pouring so much of himself into the book he obscured Lawrence. John Brophy reassured him that 'I can't see that there is any danger at all of people thinking you have put too much of yourself into it . . . my verdict is all in favour of showing T.E.'s mind and opinions clashing on yours.' But a cost over the long term would be exacted. By identifying Lawrence with an idealistic vision of truth and freedom, Liddell Hart offered hostages to fortune. When later writers contemplated sceptically his vision of this protean, almost omniscient figure—a philosopher king, a lost leader—they forgot the conditions, especially the post-1929 disillusion and fears of another great war, that had inspired it. None the less, by the diligence of his research, the fluency of his style, and the incisiveness of his military analysis, Liddell Hart produced one of the most significant of all Lawrence biographies. It still remains, over half a century after its publication, the only serious study in English of Lawrence's leadership of the guerrilla war in the desert.[25]

The basic interpretative framework for books about Lawrence for the next two decades was laid down by Graves and Liddell Hart. Later books, composed mainly by other friends, filled out the details of his life. Vyvyan Richards, for instance, identified the mysterious 'S.A.', the dedicatee of *The Seven Pillars of Wisdom*, as Sheik Ahmed, or Dahoum.[26] Sir Ronald Storrs provided his memories of Lawrence in *Orientations*, which in 1940 was turned into a short paperback. This account was checked by Liddell Hart.[27] There was, in addition, Churchill's famous chapter in *Great Contemporaries*, a collection of essays by friends edited by his brother Arnold, a limited edition of *T. E. Lawrence to his Biographers, Robert Graves and Liddell Hart* (which included most of the material they had collected in writing their biographies, though not their correspondence), published in 1938, and in the same year David Garnett's edition of his letters. All these books were devoted to Lawrence's memory and were either essentially memoirs or source

[25] Final Queries about T.E. [Lawrence], 20 May 1935, Liddell Hart papers, 9/13/22; John Brophy to Liddell Hart, 1 Nov. 1935, ibid. 9/13/9.
[26] Vyvyan Richards, *A Portrait of T. E. Lawrence* (London, 1936), 244-50; *T. E. Lawrence* (London, 1939), 32. See also under this heading, Edward Robinson, *Lawrence: The Story of his Life* (London, 1935) and R. H. Kiernan, *Lawrence of Arabia* (London, 1935).
[27] Ronald Storrs, *Orientations* (London, 1937), repr. as *Lawrence of Arabia: Zionism and Palestine* (Harmondsworth, 1940); Storrs to Liddell Hart, 20 Nov. 1936, Liddell Hart papers, 9/13/63.

material upon which they were built rather than critical biographies.[28] Probably the most interesting book produced in these years was by Charles Carrington, under the pseudonym 'Charles Edmonds'. Carrington was a veteran of the Western Front and author of *A Subaltern's War*. The older he got the more critical he became of the view of the First World War popularized by Sassoon and Graves. He defended regular officers more stoutly than either Graves or Liddell Hart and wrote of the Lawrence legend in a sardonic tone. The world of Lowell Thomas was 'a world of wish fulfilment where gallant young subalterns contrived, dared and triumphed . . . here was a Romance of War, a tale of Jack the Giant-killer, the right tonic for men devitalised by the unheroic mass-murder of the Western front battles.' As for Lawrence himself: 'Lawrence was the archetype of the Lost Generation, the men who would have been in the prime of life, if they had not been killed or maimed or silenced by the shock of the Great War.' But Carrington's picture of Lawrence did not differ fundamentally from that of either Graves or Liddell Hart.[29]

The book which changed the direction of writings about Lawrence was Richard Aldington's *Lawrence of Arabia: A Biographical Enquiry*. This was dedicated to the proposition that 'much he [Lawrence] reports of himself—including and especially his Arabian experiences—was heightened, exaggerated, faked, boastful, and sometimes entirely without foundation'. Aldington was indignant 'that such a man should have been given the fame and glory of the real heroes of 1914-18.'[30] Aldington's was the most controversial book ever published about Lawrence, and the controversy was pursued in newspaper articles, letters to the press, and articles in journals. The martial figure leading the counter-attack was Captain Liddell Hart.[31] Aldington himself was a minor litterateur who had written a famous war book, *The Death of a Hero*, some volumes of poetry, and a number of biographies, including one of Wellington which has stood the test of time well, and whom he liked more than he had anticipated. The reverse was true of his biography

---

[28] Winston S. Churchill, *Great Contemporaries* (London, 1937), A. W. Lawrence (ed.), *T. E. Lawrence by his Friends* (London, 1937), *T. E. Lawrence to his Biographers, Robert Graves and Liddell Hart* (London, 1938); David Garnett (ed.), *The Letters of T. E. Lawrence* (London, 1938).
[29] Charles Edmonds, *T. E. Lawrence* (London, 1935), 115, 164, 188-9.
[30] Richard Aldington, *Lawrence of Arabia: A Biographical Enquiry* (London, 1955), 381. The French edn. was entitled *Lawrence L'Imposteur* (Paris, 1954).
[31] In Liddell Hart's papers there are two boxes devoted to the Aldington controversy alone—not counting his correspondence with individuals.

of Lawrence. By comparison with the ambitious goals he had set himself, and certainly when compared with his youthful promise, Aldington's life had been frustrating and disappointing. He was a bitter, spiteful, and venomous individual, convinced that the world had conspired to thwart his talents. He tended to be patronized by various literary circles.[32] Although Graves believed that the origins of Aldington's hatred was a slighting reference that Lawrence had once made to him in a letter, it was rather the symbolic Lawrence on which Aldington vented his spleen. Aldington was horrified by the ease with which Lawrence had seduced and been accepted by the Establishment, while his own more substantial talents had been overlooked. Certainly this book tells us more about Aldington's psychological state than it does about Lawrence's. In this, at least, he shared something with earlier authors.[33]

Why such a debunking book appeared in the mid-1950s rather than in the 1920s, when such writing was in vogue, has more to do with Aldington's quirky bitterness than any profound historiographical trend. Early in 1954 Colonel Newcombe warned Liddell Hart that 'Aldington is clearly writing a novel designed to sell to a sensational public.'[34] The role of Lawrence's comrades-in-arms in this campaign is significant and undercuts Aldington's most poisonous charge—that he deliberately obscured their role in a calculated campaign of self-advertisement. Liddell Hart acquired a proof copy (by dishonest methods Aldington later claimed).[35] He was appalled by what he read. He branded the book 'by a long way the most dishonest one I have ever read'.[36] He was so angered by the numerous misquotations (especially from '*T. E. Lawrence*') that he considered legal action. After his temper had cooled he dismissed this course of action. As he wrote to Charles Carrington, 'At one time I thought Aldington would do great harm to historical truth by creating an anti-Lawrence myth as fantastic as the Lowell Thomas myth . . . But his book is so bad and so dull . . . that I think he has over-reached himself and will produce the contrary effect.' In this Liddell Hart was mistaken, for Aldington was to etch a design for future books.[37]

[32] See Leonard Woolf, *Downhill All the Way: An Autobiography of the Years, 1919-1939* (London, 1975), 133, who thought him 'disgruntled' and 'prickly' but while Woolf was editor of *The Nation* he was 'a godsend' because he could be relied upon to 'write me a good review of almost any book which I sent him—never a very good and never a bad, always a good review'.
[33] Seymour-Smith, *Robert Graves*, 496; Aldington, *Lawrence of Arabia*, 388.
[34] Newcombe to Liddell Hart, 30 Jan. 1954, Liddell Hart papers, 9/13/61.
[35] This annotated copy can now be found ibid. 9/13/44.
[36] Liddell Hart to John Lehman, 18 Feb. 1955, ibid.
[37] Liddell Hart to C. E. Carrington, 8 Feb. 1955, ibid. Robert Graves had counselled against legal action. 'The libel on T.E.'s memory is nothing—T.E. would get a kick out

Aldington, in his paranoid way, believed that Liddell Hart and another of Lawrence's old comrades, Lord Winterton, had conspired to stop the book being published. There is nothing in this charge. The only former friend who suggested this was Lady Astor, who also considered legal action.[38] Liddell Hart did enlist the support of the Prime Minister, Winston Churchill, before publication to scotch Aldington's attempt to prove that Lawrence was 'a boastful liar' by reference to his supposed claim that he had been offered the post of High Commissioner of Egypt in 1922 and again in 1925. Liddell Hart, whose relations with Churchill were not good at that time, asked him to make a public statement that such a claim was not fictional. Churchill was in bad health and could not remember the details distinctly, but did issue a general statement. Aldington he rightly considered a 'mediocrity hoping to gain a reputation as a debunker'.[39]

What stung Liddell Hart more than anything else was Aldington's suggestion that the legend was inspired by Lawrence himself ('a watchful and clever adventurer') and then accepted uncritically by credulous friends and admirers (the 'Lawrence Bureau'). All previous writers but Aldington had been 'taken in. It must be wonderful to have such a conceit of one's own unique detective powers', he wrote.[40] As Liddell Hart observed to Churchill, 'it is absurd to imagine that you (and all the others who worked closely with him) would have been taken in by "a charlatan"'.[41] Aldington's portrait of Lawrence was contradictory. He devoted great energy to exposing his chicanery and self-serving boasting. 'Everything he did was conscious, deliberately planned and willed, except when fate or accident tripped him up, or at least so he would have us believe.' Yet he was a young man with his head in the clouds, full of self-indulgent 'roseate idealism', listless and idle. According to Aldington, throughout his life Lawrence maintained an 'objection to hard work'. Fundamentally, he was a perpetual adolescent with dreams

of it were he alive, and even offer to go into the witness box on Aldington's behalf.' Graves to Liddell Hart, 25 Apr. 1954, ibid.

[38] Charles Doyle, *Richard Aldington* (London, 1989), 276; Nancy Astor to Liddell Hart, 4 Oct. 1954, Liddell Hart papers, 9/13/44.

[39] Liddell Hart to Churchill, 18 Feb. 1954, Churchill to Liddell Hart, 2 Feb. 1954, ibid. 1/171/43-4, ibid. 1/171/52, but this response to inaccuracies is far from forming a conspiracy to stop its publication.

[40] Aldington, *Lawrence of Arabia*, 12, 13, 18, 32, 35, 103, 109-10, 188, 277-95; 'T. E. Lawrence, Aldington and the Truth', *London Magazine* (Apr. 1955), 9.

[41] Liddell Hart to Churchill, 25 Jan. 1854, Liddell Hart papers, 1/171/42. Interestingly, it was Liddell Hart who on the strength of the Lawrence connection introduced his distant relative, Wingate, to Churchill in 1938. See Liddell Hart to Churchill, 11 Nov. 1938, ibid. 1/171/32.

beyond his true capacity. Aldington in his passion to denounce Lawrence at every turn failed to distinguish between *how* the Lawrence legend began and *why* it developed. The reasons behind its growth cannot be put down simply to the manipulations of one unscrupulous individual. If Lawrence was as lazy as Aldington suggested, then the mental effort required to carry off such a campaign of dissimulation would have been enormous and beyond him. In any case, Lawrence could not possibly have *known* what the effect of such a campaign would have been. Aldington is guilty of assigning too much conspiratorial connivance to what was essentially an unplanned and spontaneous burst of enthusiasm for a media hero. Aldington, moreover, fails conspicuously to discern any motive for this effort but vanity. Lawrence made no money out of his writings. As Aldington was the first to admit, after some very nasty passages on *The Seven Pillars of Wisdom*, Lawrence 'preferred to be known as the writer of a mysterious unprocurable masterpiece rather than to have it read'. Without readers there were no royalties.[42]

Probably the most noteworthy aspect of his book, which set a trend for other writers, was the comparative neglect of the Arab Revolt. Of his 388 pages, only 130 deal with the main reason for Lawrence's historical significance. Much space was devoted to his early life, which included revealing Lawrence's illegitimacy.[43] It also began that fascination with Lawrence's psychopathology which so intrigued later biographers. But one need not be a great admirer of either Graves's or Liddell Hart's books to notice that Aldington's account of the Arab Revolt was not only misleading but ignorant. As a 'debunker' he lacked the subtlety and feline wit of Lytton Strachey. His vitriol provokes sympathy for Lawrence, as Harold Nicolson observed, not hatred. The only aspect of his account which the modern historian finds interesting is his impatience with the disproportionate attention devoted to the Arab Revolt at the expense of Allenby's campaigns. This 'begs the question as to who really defeated the Turks in 1918?' To which one may retort that Aldington's highly personalized approach did nothing to redress the balance. On the contrary, it continued to focus attention on Lawrence at the expense of Allenby. Aldington insisted that the Arabs played no important part in the seizure of Jerusalem, and this revealed

> enough to show up this Arab nonsense and Lawrence's pretentious theorising about winning wars without fighting or having casualties . . . Of course you can

[42] Aldington, *Lawrence of Arabia*, 12, 27, 71, 90, 111, 328.
[43] Ibid. 23, 349-53. Many of Lawrence's friends, especially Graves, thought this in appalling taste while his mother was still alive. Robert Graves to Liddell Hart, ?Mar. 1954, Liddell Hart papers, 9/13/44.

fight without casualties, if you confine yourself to tip-and-run and hasty demolitions and ambuscades of small isolated enemy units, while somebody else holds up the enemy's real fighting force and does all the dirty work.

Here Aldington appeared to concede that Lawrence did have individual ideas rather than claiming other people's as his own. His indictment of Lawrence was inconsistent. Was he a fraud, or was he just wrong? Aldington could never make up his mind. When Graves and Liddell Hart dilated in their books on bloodless fighting one is reminded of a speech by Xenophon when he claimed, 'No one has ever died in battle through being bitten by a horse; it is men who do whatever gets done in battle.' In Aldington's book can be heard the shrill, twisted, and belated howl of protest of a veteran of the Western Front.[44]

Aldington made four specific points in defence of his view of the Arab Revolt. He argued that Lawrence's own self-serving account (*The Seven Pillars of Wisdom* he described as 'a work of the imagination') was not to be trusted. Lawrence, moreover, had after 1918 either exaggerated or invented his role in the fall of Erzerum, the planning for an assault on Alexandretta, and the seizure of Wejh.[45] The other two issues he explored were Lawrence's part in the fall of Akaba and in the attacks on the Hejaz railway. The first of these inspired some of Aldington's more ferocious invective. He denounced as 'pretentious strategic theorising' Lawrence's thinking on these strategic problems, which were, furthermore, irrelevant 'in the face of the fact that the Arabs couldn't take Medina'—although this was by no means a guarantee that they would have not wasted their resources on trying to take it. Much of Aldington's account is riddled with this kind of retrospective certainty. He also overlooked that the real value of Akaba was not just access to the sea, but control of the passes on the landward side, 'the strategic gateway to the interior'.[46]

In some ways his treatment of the Hejaz railway was even more illuminating because it reveals the contradiction inherent in his form of

---

[44] Aldington, *Lawrence of Arabia*, 137, 203-5. The quotation is taken from the English translation of the *Cyropaedia: The Persian Expedition* ed. Rex Warner (Harmondsworth, 1961), 108.

[45] Aldington, *Lawrence of Arabia*, 131-5, 170-6.

[46] Ibid. 178, 186-90; 'T. E. Lawrence, Aldington and the Truth', *London Magazine* (Apr. 1955), 5-7; see also 'Richard Aldington's Reply and Captain Liddell Hart's Comment', ibid. (Aug. 1955). These two essays are devastating in their criticism; never had Liddell Hart's powers as a controversialist been shown to better effect. The first is reprinted substantially as Liddell Hart's Foreword to the new edition of David Garnett, *The Letters of T. E. Lawrence* (London, 1964), 26-30.

anti-biographical special pleading. Aldington commented sarcastically that attacks on the Hejaz railway 'which has been celebrated with such gorgeous rhetoric' failed to destroy it. Indeed it 'managed to survive so many attacks and thereby assisted Medina to hold out the entire war'.[47] Then switching his attention to Thomas, who neither Graves nor Liddell Hart would have considered a very reliable authority, Aldington claimed that attacks on the railways by others were ignored by later writers. Passing over the obvious error that the aim of the strategy was not to destroy the line but rather to permit the Turks to continue to reinforce Medina, an idea which Colonel Newcombe insisted was Lawrence's, Aldington failed to answer an equally obvious question: if the Arab Revolt was so unimportant why did it matter if the other attempts to destroy the Hejaz railway received little attention? It mattered to Aldington because it involved Lawrence; but his indignation seems to cast little credit on his sense of historical perspective *if* these were the fantasies of a charlatan. Aldington's account, therefore, leaves more than a doubt in the mind of the reader as to his reliability as a critic.[48]

Of all the members of the 'Lawrence Bureau', Robert Graves took the most relaxed view of Aldington.

I think that . . . it had better be published, *because* it is perverse and sneering and contains all the muck that an industrious rogue could rake together . . . and should certainly not be corrected or modified by you or anyone else to modify its nastiness, but left to its critical fate.[49]

The book is now widely regarded as a curiosity piece. Its prime assumption, that the release of papers in the Public Record Office and elsewhere, would confirm Aldington's view that Lawrence was a poseur and a liar has proved unfounded. It remains, even after a generation of 'psychobiography', one of the most unpleasant books ever written about a public figure. It can only be excused on the grounds that it attacks the Lawrence legend, although these swipes are frequently spurious and undiscriminating. One measure of its unpleasantness is the unprincipled accusation of homosexuality thrown at Lawrence. This issue is one of the utmost insignificance; it has no historic weight one way or the other, unless the moral climate is such that an author calculates that it will defame his subject. There can be little doubt that Aldington had made such a

[47] Aldington, *Lawrence of Arabia*, 180-3.
[48] Notes on Major N. N. E. Bray's book *Shifting Sands: The True Story of the Arab Revolt* by S. F. Newcombe (Nov. ?1934), Liddell Hart papers, 9/13/61. Bray's book was one of the very few by a participant in the Arab Revolt which was hostile to Lawrence.
[49] Robert Graves to Liddell Hart, ?Mar. 1954, Liddell Hart papers, 9/13/44.

calculation. The much-publicized defection of Burgess and Maclean and a sustained legal witch-hunt of homosexuals organized by the Home Secretary, created the background in the early 1950s against which Aldington mounted his hypocritical and unprincipled attack. It is no small measure of Lawrence's substance as a public figure that his reputation survived this intemperate onslaught.[50]

His attack prompted the publication of two further books, which were essentially throw-backs to earlier themes. Flora Armitage, wrote of her biography, *The Desert and the Stars*, that 'It has been a labour of love in the aesthetic and spiritual sense of the word; I wanted to show the beauty of Lawrence's life as I saw it, as well as the seeming terrible waste of his later years.' She was appalled by 'the malice and vindictiveness' of Aldington's book, 'and even where the facts are correct the twisted and stupid interpretation of these facts leaves one wondering whether the author is quite rational'. She was concerned at the possible effect this might have on her own book. Despite some rather florid prose, her biography is accurate and, on the whole, was well received. It is to some degree a refutation of Aldington, though it only restates the traditional, somewhat romantic view.[51] The other book was by Jean Beraud Villars, *T. E. Lawrence, or the Search for the Absolute*, which also returned to an earlier theme—the tension in Lawrence's character between the man of thought and the man of action. 'To be an artist', Villars explained, 'is to be an egocentric, to be a soldier is to sacrifice and forget self. Two philosophies so contradictory within the same man can but produce anomalies and heartbreaks.'[52]

Despite these attempts to defend Lawrence's reputation from Aldington's diatribe, his book had a lasting impact on Lawrence historiography out of all proportion to its scholarly weight and objectivity. This was felt mainly in the attention which biographers gave to Lawrence's *motives*, because it was in discovering these that further revelations could be made. These, in turn, could cast doubt on the portrait of Lawrence painted by earlier writers. Such an approach led to the

[50] H. Montgomery Hyde, *The Other Love* (London, 1970), 213-14, 220; Peter Parker, *The Old Lie: The Great War and the Public School Ethos* (London, 1986), 175, has some interesting observations on Aldington, especially that he was married to a bisexual woman. On the basic unimportance of the homosexual issue, see B. Ifor Evans, 'Straightening the Record', *Truth* (27 Apr. 1956).

[51] F. A. Armitage to Liddell Hart, 25 Jan. 1954, 17 Feb. 1955, Liddell Hart papers, 9/13/44; Flora Armitage, *The Desert and the Stars: A Biography of T. E. Lawrence* (New York, 1955).

[52] Jean Bernard Villars, *T. E. Lawrence, or the Search for the Absolute* (London, 1958 (first pub. in France, 1955)), p. xi.

appearance of several superficial books based on thin research, as exemplified in Anthony Nutting's book, *Lawrence of Arabia: The Man and the Motive*.[53] Suleiman Mousa's book, *T. E. Lawrence: An Arab View* was unusual in devoting so much attention to his military career. At certain points he was at pains to argue that 'I was not intent on minimising the services he [Lawrence] rendered to the Arabs. . . . My main concern was to shed new light on the whole story, by providing an honest and fair representation reflecting my findings on the subject.' Nevertheless the tone of his analysis belied this intention. 'Lawrence was an imaginative adventurer, driven by his historical studies to achieve something of note . . . Deep within himself, Lawrence knew that the greater part of his fame was based on fraud.' This book, despite a disclaimer to the contrary, followed Aldington's path of denigration. Lawrence's claims concerning his role at Erzerum and Alexandretta were dismissed as 'incredible'. Where Lawrence had contributed to the strategic planning of the Revolt, it was to help implement designs already fashioned by Arab commanders, such as Auda's plan for the fall of Akaba. Lawrence is portrayed as an efficient liaison officer, with skill in obtaining supplies, money, and technical help. He was 'an ordinary British officer who liked the Arabs' but nothing more than this. Mousa conceded that Lawrence's strategic design before Akaba 'held water, but it is doubtful whether this was a view that he actually developed at Wejh in April 1917'. His schemes as they appeared in the biographies of the inter-war years were the retrospective elaborations of a fertile imagination. A case in point, in Mousa's view, was the Battle of Tafileh. He claimed that Lawrence did not command here, but merely witnessed the battle. The account in *The Seven Pillars of Wisdom* was based on a visit he paid to the ground in 1921.[54]

If Mousa had pursued this theme consistently, namely that Lawrence was a glorified guerrilla quartermaster, then the overall effect of the book would be more persuasive. But like Aldington, Mousa could not make up his mind whether to treat Lawrence as a fraud or as simply mistaken—and the temptation to criticize could not be resisted because it added weight to the indictment, but served to treat Lawrence as a serious

---

[53] Anthony Nutting, *Lawrence of Arabia: The Man and the Motive* (London, 1961). See also Robert Payne, *Lawrence of Arabia: A Triumph* (New York, 1962) and Victoria Ocampo, *33171 T.E.: Lawrence of Arabia* (London, 1963). A Swedish view can be found in Eric Lonnorth, *Lawrence of Arabia: An Historical Appreciation* (London, 1956), whose ch. 4 is entitled 'The Secret Motives'.

[54] Suleiman Mousa, *T. E. Lawrence: An Arab View* (Oxford, 1966), 11-12, 49, 51-2, 62, 80-5, 139-40, 278, 287.

figure. The amount of space devoted to proving that Lawrence was never in command was wasted. Lawrence himself in the 'Twenty-Seven Articles' (a document that excited little comment from Mousa) had stressed repeatedly 'Never give orders to anyone . . . Your place is advisory, and your advice is due to the commander alone.'[55] The Arab sources he relies upon do not amount to very much. Though Mousa criticizes *The Seven Pillars of Wisdom* as a very partial account, he himself relies on memoirs, such as those of King Abdullah, which are not only very partial but were written almost half a century after the events they describe. Mousa relies, moreover, on witnesses who were criticized in *The Seven Pillars of Wisdom*, such as the Emir Zeid (who was then a youth of 19) and they exacted their revenge.[56] Mousa detailed with pride the achievements of the Arab Revolt but at the same time this required a downgrading of Lawrence's contribution.

Without the Arab Revolt Lawrence and the Lawrence legend would not have seen the light of day. The Arab Revolt therefore ought to be regarded as the root and Lawrence as the offshoot, whereas the imagination of Western writers has reversed the picture, portraying the Revolt as of his making.[57]

It was inevitable that an Arab author would seek some 'semblance of justice' in redressing the balance of attention given to Lawrence. But, as with Aldington, the attempt to achieve this by denigration only served to ensure that the spotlight remained on Lawrence. Mousa does not illuminate how the irregular and regular forces were knitted together,[58] and there is little mention of Allenby. Mousa's book is perhaps the most interesting of a series of belittling books published during the post-war years—interesting in that he devotes most of his space to the Arab Revolt. At least this interest springs from a consideration of Lawrence's historical significance rather than from the tensions within his personality.

A book of a rather more sensational nature was Phillip Knightley and Colin Simpson, *The Secret Lives of Lawrence of Arabia*, published three years later, which explored Lawrence's personality in clinical detail. There are a number of 'Aldingtonian' aspects to this book. The first is

[55] Wilson, *Lawrence of Arabia*, 960, append. 4: 'Twenty-Seven Articles' by T. E. Lawrence, Aug. 1917.
[56] Mousa, for instance (*T. E. Lawrence*, 84), criticizes *Seven Pillars* and then writes enigmatically that 'Information available to us [i.e. Zeid] indicates that King Hussein was personally distrustful of Lawrence, as if he intuitively sensed an unhealthy attitude in this double-dealing, bragging officer.' Very few accounts characterize Lawrence thus at the time. [57] Ibid. 186-7, 208-9, 257.
[58] The phrase is taken from Richards, *T. E. Lawrence*, 43.

that Lawrence's career is treated as a source of revelation rather than study. This was in part Lawrence's own fault, though he had private reasons for his mystery-making. Knightley and Simpson observe at the outset in a rhetorical passage:

from the new material uncovered by our researches there emerges a picture of Lawrence of Arabia no less remarkable than the legend, though almost the antithesis of it. It is now clear that, far from having a deep emotional attachment to the Arabs, as a race Lawrence did not care for them. Far from devoting himself to uniting their divided tribes . . . he believed that it was in Britain's interests to keep the Middle East divided. Far from furthering the cause of Arab freedom and independence, he was intent on making them part of the British Empire.

In a period when ridiculing 'imperialism' was fashionable, Lawrence was held up as an imperialist agent. Lawrence's new role in the Arab Revolt was not as a soldier but as a 'political officer attached to Feisal with the object of influencing him and so ensuing the success of British policy'. In a book of 276 pages of text, a mere 50 were devoted to the Arab Revolt itself—a pattern set by Aldington. Lawrence was not only the archetypal hero of his time and class, as Aldington claimed, 'but also of the policy and tactics adopted by an imperial power to protect its interests. It is in this role that history will judge him'.[59]

Knightley and Simpson devoted a lot of attention to Lawrence's formative experiences. It was here that they developed another controversial aspect. As the 1960s were the heyday of the 'secret agent', so, they claimed, Lawrence was recruited while a young archaeologist into the circle around D. G. Hogarth, the Keeper of the Ashmolean Museum at Oxford. Lawrence had always spoken kindly of Hogarth as his mentor; but to Knightley and Simpson, Hogarth was transformed into a figure resembling the sinister Sillery in Anthony Powell's novel, *A Question of Upbringing*. He recruited intelligent and able young men into what was 'unofficially, Hogarth's Political Intelligence Service'. Such claims tended to be qualified, doubtless because of lack of evidence, by the disclaimer: 'This is not to suggest that Hogarth or any of his young men were formally on any intelligence department's payroll.' Whereas Aldington was scornful of Lawrence's military reading, mainly on the grounds that few books on military subjects were to be found in his library at his death (which is no more of a guide as to what is actually *read* than the books found in a library), Knightley and Simpson envisaged

[59] Phillip Knightley and Colin Simpson, *The Secret Lives of Lawrence of Arabia* (London, 1969), 4-6.

his early reading as part of Hogarth's training. It is not clear how a reading of Creasy, G. F. R. Henderson, or A. T. Mahan helped prepare Lawrence for secret intelligence work. Indeed all these references to a 'secret Lawrence', so appealing to readers of the day, were strong on assertion and weak on supporting evidence—mainly because evidence of such activities does not exist.[60]

By attempting to draw strong links between Lawrence's pre-war, wartime, and post-war career, Knightley and Simpson developed various themes that were implicit in Aldington's approach. Although their account is more accurate in regard to Lawrence's role in the fall of Erzerum and Kut, and the evolution of his methods, the main reason for Lawrence's significance—the Arab Revolt—received scant attention. Instead, they focused on the sincerity or otherwise of Lawrence's motives in 'controlling the tide' of the Arab Revolt and his 'dream of an Arab dominion in the Empire'. And, finally, by revealing Lawrence's masochistic compulsions, they confirmed a trend by which Lawrence's psychopathology rather than his historical significance became the touchstone of interest for biographers. Liddell Hart was surely justified in claiming that 'There is certainly a "Lawrence myth" but it is of a psychological rather than a historical nature.'[61] Writing of this more than thirty years later to Lawrence's brother, Arnold, he remarked,

I can all too well understand how the attitude of so many of the present generation of writers to the evidence about T.E. 'baffles and depresses' you. So it does me. Presumably the cause is that nothing really new and important can be said about T.E. without adopting the debunking attitude.[62]

Not all books published about Lawrence after *The Secret Lives of Lawrence of Arabia* were debunking, though several were belittling. But whatever their standpoint, many do confirm a trend started by Aldington and followed by Knightley and Simpson, namely, that little space is allotted to the Arab Revolt. Increasing attention was devoted to Lawrence's life in the ranks in the Tank Corps and the RAF.[63] Other

[60] Aldington, *Lawrence of Arabia*, 120-1; Knightley and Simpson, *Secret Lives*, 20-2, 26-7. Significantly, Christopher Andrew, *Secret Service* (London, 1986), does not even mention Lawrence.
[61] Liddell Hart to C. E. Carrington, 30 Sept. 1935, Liddell Hart papers, 9/13/23.
[62] Liddell Hart to A. W. Lawrence, 8 Feb. 1967, ibid. 9/13/57.
[63] Stanley Weintraub, *Private Shaw and Public Shaw: A Dual Portrait of Lawrence of Arabia and GBS* (London, 1963) and H. Montgomery Hyde, *Solitary in the Ranks: Lawrence of Arabia as Airman and Private Soldier* (London, 1977). Also of interest here is J. M. Wilson's introduction to his edition of Lawrence's anthology, *Minorities*, with a preface by C. Day Lewis (London, 1971).

254 *Indirect Approaches*

books were devoted to a study of Lawrence's writings.[64] In the mid-1970s two illustrated biographies were published, one which reflected the psychoanalytical predilections of biographers of this period,[65] the other a straightforward and reliable account shorn of much of the pretentious theorizing which disfigures so many books of this period.[66] A substantial book published in the mid-1970s, like a similar biography published in the mid-1980s, reflected many of the characteristics of post-Knightley and Simpson works. Both attach a great deal of significance to explaining Lawrence's psychological state and dwell on sexual matters; they rely on old sources to belittle Lawrence's role— especially in connection with that old favourite of Lawrence's critics the fall of Erzerum; they stress the importance of Arab sources which seem fragmentary and not very illuminating. Both occasionally display some insights into the creation of the Lawrence legend but in attempting to 'get at the man behind the legend' (like Knightley and Simpson) their revelatory technique often obscures as much as it reveals. Fundamentally, these books do not increase our understanding of Lawrence's role in the Arab Revolt.[67]

One book, which does exhibit some of these characteristics, but deserves praise, is John E. Mack's *A Prince of our Disorder: The Life of T. E. Lawrence*. Mack is a distinguished psychiatrist and his analysis of Lawrence's complex personality is not only stimulating but authoritative, minus the tedious speculation and unwarranted extravagances of earlier writers. It is a model of how a 'psychobiography' should be written. Mack is sympathetic towards Lawrence and makes discriminating use of a wide range of sources, including Lawrence's letters to Charlotte Shaw. When writing the book, his intention was 'not in any way to reduce Lawrence or to show him in a bad light but to complete my own picture'. It is perhaps ironic, but not very surprising in this field, that a psychiatrist should display a better grasp of historical technique than many historians. 'I have hopes that it [*A Prince of our Disorder*] may be a contribution that will clarify rather than clutter the field.'[68] In

---

[64] Jeffrey Meyers, *The Wounded Spirit: A Study of the Seven Pillars of Wisdom* (London, 1973), and *Homosexuality and Literature, 1880-1930* (London, 1977), esp. pp. 114-30; Andrew Rutherford, *The Literature of War* (London, 1978), 38-63; Stanley Weintraub and Rodelle Weintraub, *Lawrence of Arabia: The Literary Impulse* (Baton Rouge, 1975).   [65] Peter Brent, *T. E. Lawrence* (London, 1975).

[66] Richard Perceval Graves, *Lawrence of Arabia and his World* (London, 1976).

[67] Desmond Stewart, *T. E. Lawrence* (London, 1977); Michael Yardley, *Backing into the Limelight: A Biography of T. E. Lawrence* (London, 1985).

[68] John E. Mack to Liddell Hart, 8 July 1965, 2 Aug. 1967, Liddell Hart papers, 9/13/60. For Mack's writings on Lawrence, see 'T. E. Lawrence: A Study of Heroism

this endeavour Mack succeeded. The most significant aspect of Mack's book was that by shrewd psychoanalysis and basic historical sense devoid of the revelatory zeal of the many journalists that have written about Lawrence, Mack convincingly demonstrates that most of the insights of his friends like Graves and Liddell Hart were not mere myth-making; that they were far more than the mere dupes of a confidence trickster. Mack employs psychoanalytical techniques to explain Lawrence rather than to denigrate him. He shows how Lawrence consciously prepared himself for some as yet undefined quest. He has much of sense to say about Lawrence's penchant for spinning yarns and the historical reliability of *The Seven Pillars of Wisdom*. Admitting that 'Lawrence had a compelling need to tell stories, which grew in part out of his deep doubts about his self-worth', Mack none the less arrives at the conclusion that far from being a rogue and a liar, Lawrence's accounts of the Arab Revolt and much else 'were largely accurate and, if anything, he would customarily leave out information that was to his credit . . . I have not found Lawrence to be a liar'. This confirms Liddell Hart's view that Lawrence 'was usually very careful, and accurate, when it came to a matter of putting anything on record himself'. Indeed the distortions in *The Seven Pillars of Wisdom* arise more from striving for artistic effect rather than playing fast and loose with the historical records; by comparison with other memoirs, say those of Metternich or Bismarck, Lawrence's book is a model of historical balance and objectivity.[69]

Though Mack's biography was thorough and had much of interest to say, especially on the process by which Lawrence transformed his personality by 'an effort to perfect the self, a shaping of his personality into an instrument of accomplishment, example and change', he does concentrate on psychological factors and his book is not a measured narrative.[70] Despite the enormous literature on Lawrence, a scholarly biography based on a detailed study of manuscript sources had yet to be written, and this was a task ably discharged by the 'authorized biography' which eventually appeared in 1989. It is a massive work of scholarship. By comparison with the flights of romantic rhetoric proclaimed by earlier biographers and the scorn and denigration of his later critics, the tone of *Lawrence of Arabia: The Authorised Biography* is restrained and rather

and Conflict', *American Journal of Psychiatry*, 125 (1969), 'Psychoanalysis and Biography', *Journal of the American Psychoanalytic Association*, 19 (1971), and *A Prince of our Disorder: The Life of T. E. Lawrence* (London, 1976).

[69] Mack, *A Prince of our Disorder*, 49, 58, 74, 86, 177, 222, 459; Liddell Hart to L. S. Amery, 26 Jan. 1954, Liddell Hart papers, 9/13/44.

[70] Mack, *A Prince of our Disorder*, 454.

matter-of-fact. It is modelled consciously on Winston Churchill's biography of his father, Lord Randolph. The massive, perhaps excessive documentation, reminds the reader of Martin Gilbert's biography of Churchill. Great chunks of documents are quoted, sometimes without comment, and problems and issues in Lawrence's life are relegated to discussion in the footnotes. Of course, Wilson was right in thinking that there have been a good many previous 'critical' biographies based on a rudimentary study of the documents. It is pleasing to see the mastery with which Wilson interprets the sources, and note how carefully this interpretation has been weighed. None the less, the very act of selecting a document is itself an act of historical judgement. History cannot, and does not, live on documents alone. The weight of documentation, however, is crucial to Wilson's view of Lawrence. After years of study,

I have found that Lawrence was not as Aldington claimed a habitual liar, and that *Seven Pillars* is remarkably accurate on questions of fact. Those who wished in the 1950s to show that Lawrence was pathologically dishonest hoped that the contemporary documents would eventually demonstrate that they were right. In the event, the documents have done exactly the opposite.[71]

The vast array of contemporary reports, memoranda, and correspondence utilized by Wilson serves as a check, not only on Lawrence and *The Seven Pillars of Wisdom* (as Lawrence himself asked of Graves), but on the accuracy of his earlier biographers. As to his general role and motives in the First World War, Wilson's work demonstrates that Lawrence was an important and influential figure—indeed the mainspring—of the Arab Revolt, and that so much of the self-righteous, indignant, and denunciatory language directed at his career is utterly misguided. Wilson points out that Lawrence often alienated very able officers unnecessarily; but his view of his personality is very favourable. Lawrence was shocked by the arrogant manner of Anglo-Indian imperial administration in Mesopotamia and believed that the Arabs deserved self-determination. Wilson reveals that Lawrence took Feisal into his confidence concerning the implications of the Sykes–Picot agreement without revealing its precise terms. This accounted for the northern emphasis of Lawrence's strategy, because unless the Arabs took Homs, Hama, Damascus, and Aleppo, the Arabs would gain nothing from their military adventure.[72] He also rightly points out that Lawrence gained such an ascendancy over the Emir Feisal because of the very extent of his

---

[71] Jeremy Wilson, *Lawrence of Arabia: The Authorised Biography* (London, 1989), 1084. [72] Ibid. 246, 309, 313.

commitment to the Arab cause, which was not shared by other British officers. Lawrence gained influence, whether he was formally in command or not, because of Feisal's confidence in him and his pivotal importance (acknowledged by Mousa) in sustaining the Arab Revolt with gold and other supplies. No wonder Lawrence wrote home, 'the position I have is such a queer one—I do not suppose that any Englishman before ever had such a place'.[73]

Wilson also illuminates a number of the controversies that have exercised the imaginations of Lawrence's biographers. On Erzerum, Lawrence did provide the Russians with valuable information; his role was not the fantasy denounced by Aldington and Mousa. As for the debate over the strategy prefacing the fall of Akaba in 1917, Wilson shows that the Arabs were thinking in terms of a landing at Akaba on the lines of Wejh, rather than the indirect approach overland advocated by Lawrence. Lawrence was also conscious of the need to hold the Turks at Medina because if they withdrew their forces northwards, they would inevitably reinforce the Turkish army opposing Allenby's Egyptian Expeditionary Force. Hence the need to harry their supply lines to keep them distracted without actually cutting them. Wilson concludes, with Lawrence looking northwards:

> Above all, Akaba was vital to the progress of Feisal's campaign: without it, the Arab Revolt might be confined to the Hejaz for the duration of the war. Lawrence concluded that it must be taken as soon as possible, without warning, and without British help.[74]

Finally, on the vexed question of Tafileh, Wilson in a cool, relaxed way emphasizes Lawrence's 'key role' in the battle 'overturning Jaafar Pasha's original idea of moving from the village to a defensive position further south. After some indecision, Zeid had put his weight behind Lawrence's plan.' He has some harsh words on Mousa's technique of relying on very elderly eyewitnesses whose memories were somewhat selective.[75]

Wilson's sober and scholarly treatment tends to confirm the earlier portrait of Lawrence presented by Graves and Liddell Hart without their extravagances. There is more substance to their accounts than allowed for by later debunkers. Indeed, on examining trends in Lawrence historiography there appears something perverse in writers who, while simul-

[73] Ibid. 278, 331, 355-6, 359, 1058-9.
[74] Ibid. 365-78, 398-400, 1055-6.
[75] Or had something to hide. See ibid. 1089, on Zeid's appropriation of £30,000. Lawrence's report on the battle is in WO158/634.

taneously attempting to reveal the 'real' Lawrence, fail signally to treat Lawrence as a historical figure like any other. The writings of debunkers, as Andrew Rutherford suggests, 'imply that vices are, in some unexamined sense, more real than virtues—that vanity, hypocrisy and self-deception . . . somehow constitute a truer reality than altruism, self-sacrifice and heroism, *even when these are known to have existed*'. By bringing both the positive and negative features of Lawrence's personality into focus sympathetically, Wilson is able to draw more convincing conclusions about the nature of Lawrence's achievement. His etching may be more mundane than the luxuriant texture and bright colours of earlier literary artists, but it is more realistic. Also the Arab Revolt is given the proper degree of attention that it warrants, which reverses Wilson's earlier thinking that too much attention had been accorded this in other books.[76]

That Lawrence biographies have now turned a full interpretative circle must prompt some further thoughts on the relationship between the historiography and the 'legend'. Very few writers actually define what they mean by this term. Clearly it would include fanciful travelogue, pulp fiction, and other forms of invention such as the film *Lawrence of Arabia* (which should be viewed as a cinematic historical novel), press tittle-tattle, and Lawrence's appearance in boys' comics and adventure stories. Some of this may be based on fact, and therefore Norman Mailer's inelegant category of 'factoid' appears appropriate to categorize it. All legendary figures, even those as revered as Abraham Lincoln, generate an anti-myth—an age-old journalistic technique. The anti-myth tends to form a mirror image of the myth. Thus, early romantic images are matched by the mean-spirited debunking of Aldington, damnation with faint praise in Mousa's nationalistic apologia, and the exposure of psychological inadequacies in Knightley and Simpson's sensational book. The extreme statements of both sides tend to merge into one rather ridiculous caricature in which historical perspective has been abandoned.

In attacking the romantic vision of Lawrence advanced by Graves and Liddell Hart, their critics tended to overlook the possibility that these two skilful writers may not have been as gullible as they had anticipated. They also tended to blur an important feature of biographical method. A version of the events of a major personality's life which is proved

---

[76] Rutherford, *Literature of War*, 3. See J. M. Wilson, 'Sense and Nonsense in the Biography of T. E. Lawrence', *T. E. Lawrence Studies*, 1 (Spring 1976), 3. It is to be regretted that no further issues of this promising journal have yet appeared.

incorrect is not sheer fantasy; also, this version may not be wholly wrong. Here the assaults on later attempts at 'myth-making' in more recent wars is instructive. For example, R. W. Thompson's *The Montgomery Legend* (London, 1967), is a criticism of a version of events that the author considered incorrect after serious, if limited, study. It is not an attack on colourful yarns, speculation or press gossip. None the less, the substitute version may be deemed no less inadequate by later writers. Obviously, our definitions of what is meant by 'myth-making' needs to be precise. They also require standards of historical proportion and scholarly detachment not always met by many journalistic writers.

Lawrence, because of his great fame, will always be the victim of works by writers who are more concerned with selling books than with displaying scholarly technique. This is as true of those biographers sympathetic to Lawrence, like Graves, as those, like Aldington, who were not. This literary market is sustained by Lawrence's symbolic significance, which may be of greater historical importance than Lawrence himself. T. E. Lawrence symbolized hopes and romantic dreams in some circles, and the distaste for these dreams in others, and will continue to do so. As John E. Mack has written,

Schoolboys who dream of performing heroic deeds, even perhaps of leading an oppressed people out of bondage, are not unusual. What is unusual and perhaps unique in Lawrence's case is the particular confluence of personal history, psychological need, extraordinary capabilities and historical opportunity that made it possible for these dreams to be enacted in reality.

It is this fundamental ambiguity that has appealed to the many biographers that have written about Lawrence over the last fifty years, and which will provoke the curiosity of the many that will undoubtedly follow.[77]

[77] Mack, *A Prince of our Disorder*, 37. I have borrowed this notion of the importance of ambiguity to heroes of folk-lore from Donald, *Lincoln Reconsidered*, 18.

IV
The Great War Rediscovered

10
'Bunking' and Debunking: The Controversies of the 1960s*

ALEX DANCHEV

In the early 1960s four disparate enterprises were afoot which conjoined to reanimate public interest in the Great War and revitalize its study. Each according to its means achieved instant popular acclaim, a degree of influence, and a certain sort of enduring renown. Each was immediately and deliberately controversial. In each case the controversy, like the éclat, lingers on—not least because, for a variety of reasons, each has enjoyed a remarkably long life. There was, firstly, the phenomenon of A. J. P. Taylor in his heyday. In 1961, with the historical community reeling from the shock of *The Origins of the Second World War*, Taylor delivered an electrifying series of TV lectures on the earlier war. His 'illustrated history', *The First World War*, was published in 1963 and has never been out of print. It is now almost certainly the most widely read historical work on the war as a whole in the English language.[1] Two years later Taylor produced *English History 1914-1945*, another mammoth seller, encompassing Britain's part in the conflict in its first 150 pages. Secondly, there was the central figure of John Terraine, whose first book, *Mons*, appeared in 1960. In 1963 Terraine hoisted a standard emblazoned *Douglas Haig* under which he campaigned continuously for a quarter of a century. A large-format, lavishly illustrated volume on *The Great War* followed in 1965, reissued in 1983 shorn of the illustrations.[2] Thirdly, there was the epic twenty-six part TV series, *The Great War*, first shown on the fledgling BBC2 during the summer

---

* I should like to thank Brian Bond, David French, John Keegan, Peter Simkins, Keith Simpson, Hew Strachan, and John Sweetman for their help and advice.

[1] Total sales of *The First World War* (hereafter, to avoid confusion, the illustrated history) are difficult to establish. Penguin Books estimated c.250,000 by 1989—a prodigious figure.

[2] *The First World War* (London, 1983; in paperback, 1984). Paperback sales c.7,000 by 1989 (information from Macmillan Publishers).

of 1964 and hastily repeated on BBC1 over the following winter.[3] Lastly, there was the most memorable stage treatment of the Great War since *Journey's End* (1928): the Theatre Workshop production of *Oh! What a Lovely War*, which opened at the Theatre Royal, Stratford, London, in March 1963 and transferred to Wyndham's Theatre in June 1963. Richard Attenborough's subsequently more familiar film version, involving as it seemed the entire British acting profession, came out in 1969.[4]

These enterprises, though arguably the most important then and since, were by no means the only ones to come to fruition in the early and mid 1960s. Before examining them in greater detail, it is appropriate to ask why, quite suddenly, after a long fallow period, it had become fashionable to work on the First World War rather than the Second. To do both was then uncommon. It smacked of popularization or cleverness (both terms of abuse) in Taylor's case; careerism or caricature in Alan Clark's.[5] As *The Economist* noted in October 1962, 'the fashion is easier to date—Mr Alan Moorehead was the pioneer in *Gallipoli* [1956]—than to explain'.[6] There is a clear consensus about the stimulus and challenge provided by Moorehead's book. Its 'dispassion yet passion' was still recalled thirty years later by Alistair Horne, whose beautifully written elegy on Verdun, *The Price of Glory* (1962), became the standard work on 'the Mill on the Meuse'. More prosaically, but perhaps more significantly, Moorehead had apparently found a market. Of those who came after, Clark for one was much concerned with commercial success, while the impulsion of 'public demand' was frankly acknowledged at the time by Barrie Pitt, whose subdued and careful reconstruction of 'the last act', *1918*, also came out in 1962.[7]

This analysis was powerfully reinforced by the appearance in Britain in 1959 of an American work, very much in the vanguard of fashion, Leon Wolff's evocation of 'Passchendaele', *In Flanders Fields* (1958), which took its title from John McCrae's iconic poem ('In Flanders fields the poppies blow | Between the crosses, row on row . . .'). In a laudatory

[3] I am indebted to the Department of Film at the Imperial War Museum for allowing me to view the whole series, and for making available the original programme synopses and other related material.

[4] The play script is published (London, 1965); the full 'official' film synopsis (1 Nov. 1968) is in the Reference Library of the British Film Institute (BFI), London.

[5] Cf. *The Donkeys*, *The Fall of Crete*, and *Barbarossa* (London, 1961, 1963, and 1965). [6] 'Our Fathers' War', *The Economist* (27 Oct. 1962).

[7] Interviews with Alistair Horne and Alan Clark, 14 June and 6 July 1988; B. Pitt, 'Writers and the Great War', *Journal of the Royal United Services Institute for Defence Studies*, 109 (1964), 247.

introduction embodying his own characteristically pungent reflections on the subject, none other than J. F. C. Fuller underlined the vivifying quality of a book that was 'much more than a military history'. The author's reconstruction of what he called 'the pathetic, almost fabulous reality of 1917', his extraordinary success in appearing to recreate the atmosphere of the time, especially the casual heroism and fragile hold on life at the Front, plainly touched a public nerve. In several ways, Wolff's book was a prototype and a portent.[8]

The most conspicuous of these was its highly developed dramatic sense. Wolff himself remarked, in an understated preface, 'I have tried, but without avail, to avoid saying that it [the battle] unrolled with the inevitability of a Greek tragedy.'[9] Inescapably, for this writer, it did. The narrative drive, the atmospheric richness, the tragic undertone: these were the cardinal elements in many of the most commercially successful books that followed—above all one by another American, Barbara Tuchman, whose *August 1914* (1962) provided an object lesson in sheer readability and consequent popularity. In method and style, also, Wolff was influential. He drew on an older tradition, best exemplified by Cecil Woodham-Smith's famous treatment of Lord Raglan's 'finest thing ever done', the Charge of the Light Brigade, in *The Reason Why* (1953).[10] Following this tradition, Wolff, like Tuchman after him, painted word pictures. As Charles Carrington noted in an unfavourable review, much of the word-painting was 'a pastiche of the popular war books which everyone was reading twenty-five years ago [that is, in the 1930s], and of which the names are still remembered, though no one now reads the books'. Wolff's explanatory reference notes tend to confirm this impression. As well as Churchill, Liddell Hart, and to a lesser extent Lloyd George, the pages teem with the names of Conan Doyle, Philip Gibbs, even H. G. Wells. The background to the opening of the British offensive, for example, is drawn almost exclusively from Conan Doyle's *The British Campaign in France and Flanders* (iv. (1920)), Gibbs's *The Struggle in Flanders* (1919), and the British official history (*Military Operations, France and Belgium, 1917*, (ii. (1948)). Both British and Australian official histories are quarried exhaustively. Bernard Shaw, *Blackwood's Magazine*, and the *Britannica* make occasional appearances.[11] Incipient nostalgia is hard to resist. For

[8] L. Wolff, *In Flanders Fields* (London, 1979), 11, 332. [9] Ibid. 24.
[10] Wolff had read Woodham-Smith with care. See ibid. 329.
[11] C. Carrington, 'Passchendaele battlepiece', *Daily Telegraph* (27 Feb. 1959); Wolff, *In Flanders Fields*, 328-44.

the journeyman writer of the 1950s, however, nostalgia was a luxury he could not afford. These were virtually the only English-language sources then available (particularly in the United States). There were also French and German official histories, which Wolff did not use; though in mitigation his perspective was exclusively British in focus, unlike that of Tuchman, still less of Horne, who did make extensive use of both French and German sources, published and unpublished. Tuchman for her part was one of the first to try to utilize Gerhard Ritter's fundamental revisionist work on the Schlieffen Plan, only recently translated into English.[12]

Wolff's recourse to that galaxy of well-remembered names and their unremembered books was unavoidable. What his skilful 'pastiche' helped incidentally to accomplish was the smuggled transmission of an earlier generation of Great War writing to a new generation of readers and writers in their turn. Correlli Barnett (born 1927) prefaced *The Swordbearers* (1963) with the thought that the Great War

> has a fascination beyond the historical insights it gives. It is the fascination of events, of sentiments, as near as one's father's youth and yet as remote as the crusades: lances of the *Garde Ulanen* scratching the summer sky of 1914; the guns of Jellicoe's thirty-four capital ships firing the valedictory salute to British sea-power into the mists of Jutland; horizon blue and field grey; the Motherland, the Fatherland, *La Patrie*.[13]

Ironically, the historian who probably accomplished most by way of inter-generational transmission was John Terraine, whose early work—collected in *The Western Front* (1964)—coincided almost exactly with the appearance of *In Flanders Fields*. Aptly described as 'chief censor' of what he called the 'instant history' modelled on Wolff's book, Terraine himself relied on the published edition of the Haig Papers, buttressed by German memoirs and official histories.[14] Yet he too leaned very heavily, and continued to lean, on those same evanescent published sources so vividly summoned up by Wolff. In part, this was a considerable strength. At once more traditional and less derivative than the books he sprang to

---

[12] B. Tuchman, *August 1914* (London, 1962), 428-78; A. Horne, *The Price of Glory* (London, 1962), 353-64; G. Ritter, *The Schlieffen Plan* (Munich, 1956; London, 1958). Taylor was especially alert to the impact of Ritter's work. See his reviews: 'The Schlieffen Plan', *Manchester Guardian* (13 Nov. 1956); 'Death of a Legend', *Observer* (25 May 1958); 'When everyone was wrong', *Observer* (3 June 1962).

[13] C. Barnett, *The Swordbearers* (London, 1963), 11.

[14] J. P. Campbell, 'Refighting Britain's Great Patriotic War', *International Journal*, 26 (Autumn 1971), 700; J. Terraine, 'Instant History', *Journal of the Royal United Services Institute for Defence Studies*, 107 (1962), 140-5.

censure, Terraine's fundamentalist output insistently reasserted the important continuities in Great War writing, and the abiding interest and genuine scholarship of earlier work. Evanescence need not imply obsolescence. It is difficult to think of any recent Great War historian who has exploited the official histories and quasi-official memoirs as fully —or relentlessly—for his chosen purpose, at least until the archival excavations of Tim Travers in the 1980s.[15]

Terraine's standpoint was, of course, diametrically opposed to that of Wolff. His scathing denunciation of 'the new cynicism' testified to the cumulative impact of Wolff's work and pointed towards its principal theme. 'It is the onlooker's snigger', wrote Terraine, 'which makes one feel, as one turns almost every page, how silly everything was, how ridiculous that no one saw what is obvious to ourselves, how clumsy, how unperceptive they all were.' This was to burlesque; Terraine seemed sometimes to identify so closely with the war as to take on the protective colouring of its surroundings. He himself used Robertson's habitual retort, 'I've heard different,' for example. His distinguishing brand of archaic language and euphemism ('a warm corner', 'a bad business', 'a terrible baptism of fire') would make an interesting study in itself.[16] Nevertheless it is true that the tragedy as reconstructed by Wolff appeared less inevitable than predictable, and hence avertible. If a tragedy had taken place which could or should have been averted, but was not, someone was clearly culpable. It remained only to make a positive identification. From Wolff's standpoint—and again it was an influential one—there could be no doubt. Though his writing was in fact notably restrained, it came from a deep well of indignation. The book was born of 'a violent adolescent prejudice', as he put it disarmingly in a later edition. 'The campaign was a caricature of war . . . It was unfairly and brutally conducted up to the highest level.'[17]

It was the well-remembered name and mischievous pen of Robert Graves that succinctly encapsulated the theme as 'the Butcher and the Cur' (Haig and Lloyd George). 'We used to wonder in the trenches', he ruminated knowingly,

[15] *To Win a War* (London, 1978) shows very clearly Terraine's continuing dependence on earlier published work, even after the release of documents over the previous decade. *The Road to Passchendaele* (London, 1977) has an interesting note on his ubiquitous 'Author's Papers' (p. xi). The argument of the book, 'a study in inevitability', relies to an astonishing degree on questionable or variously interpretable German evidence (pp. xxi, 336-42).

[16] Terraine, 'Instant History', 141; letter to *Journal of the Royal United Services Institute for Defence Studies*, 131 (1986), 80; *Douglas Haig* (London, 1963), 86, 87, 159.   [17] Wolff (1963), pp. xiv-xv.

whether the real dirt on our bugbears, the generals and the politicians, would ever come out while we were still alive. It seemed improbable, and when the guns stopped, the church bells rang, and bugbears were exalted to heaven, it seemed positively impossible. Yet here is a shocking shovelful of dirt at last, presented to us with excellent documentation and as little display of passion as a generous nature can achieve in the circumstances.

Momentously, at Wolff's hands it was the Butcher who came off worst. As Liddell Hart observed without compunction in an introduction even more laudatory than Fuller's, 'the story amounts to a tremendous indictment of the High Command, and particularly of Haig'.[18] The debunking had begun in earnest.

The cry of 'unfairness' was taken up again and again in the years to come. It was adopted as the premiss of Alan Clark's much inferior evocation of 1915, *The Donkeys* (1961), a book whose notoriety owed much to the assiduous personal sponsorship of Lord Beaverbrook, for his own vindictive purposes.[19] Clark's essential theme was the unfairness of what the soldier lions, subject to the officer donkeys, had been made to endure on the Western Front when golden opportunities glistened in the East if only donkeys were capable of appreciating them. His view was that most officers above the rank of captain were 'grossly incompetent for the tasks which they had to discharge and that Haig, in particular, was an unhappy combination of ambition, obstinacy and megalomania'.[20] For Robert Kee, widening the argument, the issue of unfairness helped to explain the current 'almost obsessional fascination' for 'the truth' about the Great War. In 1962, he reflected,

we are still spellbound by the appearance of this gigantic swindle by which the top politicians and generals preserved their status—even waxing more powerful and prosperous—and society maintained its decency, at the expense of the sufferings of millions of brave men in a hell comparable with nothing we know, though in some ways analogous to the concentration camps indispensable to Nazi Germany.[21]

---

[18] R. Graves 'The Butcher and the Cur', *Observer* (1 Mar. 1959); Liddell Hart, introduction to Wolff (1963), pp. xvii–xxii.

[19] Clark interview, 6 July 1988; C. Douglas-Home, 'The Donkeys', *Daily Express* (15 July 1961); M. Gilbert, *Winston S. Churchill*, viii. (London, 1988), 1326. Beaverbrook recruited Clark on the strength of his artful trailer, 'The dismissal of Sir John French', *History Today* (Sept. 1960).

[20] Clark, *The Donkeys, passim*; letter to *Daily Telegraph* (20 Mar. 1965). P. A. Thompson, *Lions Led by Donkeys* (London, 1927), unlike Clark, wrote a scrupulous 'apologia' for the title (p. v).

[21] R. Kee, 'How the Lights Went Out', *Spectator* (1 June 1962).

'Bunking' and Debunking 269

The concentration camp analogy retains its capacity to shock. Kee's assorted essays and reviews, like the occasional writings of John Keegan in a slightly later period, offer a penetrating commentary on the history and historiography of the Great War. Both men were somehow able to think freshly about the war, crystallizing their thinking in an expressive phrase. Kee's work is uncommonly rich, but because of its journalistic provenance regrettably ephemeral.[22]

In his reflections on the persisting British fascination with the Great War, Kee returned repeatedly to the persuasive idea of a deep national trauma, as yet unexorcized. From that perspective it would be tempting to interpret the tremendous release of emotion, variously directed, at the time of the fiftieth anniversary in August 1964 as a kind of catharsis. The audience reaction to some episodes of *The Great War* on TV certainly bears such an interpretation. 'There are no words to express my depth of feeling' was a typical response to the climacteric of the Somme, or Passchendaele.[23] The principal scriptwriter of that series, John Terraine, abetted by Correlli Barnett, several times took up the idea of a trauma to explain the deep-seated and in his view irrational hostility occasioned by the 'quasi-symbolic' figure of Haig—and by his own work on that subject. Barnett's indelicate characterization of the Great War as the British 'wooden leg', apropos of the debilitating effects of a 'lost generation', partook of the same spirit.[24] And yet, as historical writing so often reminds us, anniversaries have profound commercial as well as psychological significance. In this instance the significance was enhanced by the bandwagon effect of recent spectacular publishing successes and by the very fact of making the BBC TV series, with all its attendant publicity. Reviewing Barnett's *Swordbearers* in November 1963, Robert Blake conjured up the wondrous spectacle of publishers who, 'even at this belated hour, scuttle cap in hand from one military historian to another imploring them for a book on something, anything, to do with this popular and already not untilled field'.[25]

[22] See e.g. Kee's 'Haig the Unhero', ibid. (26 Apr. 1963); and Keegan's discussion of trench warfare in issue 21 of *Purnell's History of the First World War* (London, 1969-71).
[23] Quoted in BBC Audience Research Report VR/64/461, 11 Sept. 1964, BBC Written Archives Centre, Caversham Park, Reading. I am grateful to Gwyniver Jones of the WAC for help in locating and analysing BBC data.
[24] J. Terraine, 'Exorcising the Trauma', *Spectator* (10 May 1963); *The Smoke and the Fire* (London, 1980), 35 (quoting Barnett in *Sunday Telegraph* magazine (7 Nov. 1968)).
[25] R. Blake, 'Correlli Barnett's Four Commanders', *Eastern Daily Press* (8 Nov. 1963).

Nor did the outflow diminish markedly after 1964-5. At the end of the decade Michael Howard could be found giving thanks for the continued popularity of military history in general and Great War history in particular.[26] There was plenty of scope for a veritable creeping barrage of fiftieth anniversaries, with November 1968 a particularly attractive target. Much more important was the documentary revolution which took place between 1968 and 1972, a revolution started by the Public Records Act of 1967. At a stroke the new act reduced from fifty to thirty years the moratorium on public inspection of the records of government departments. Moreover it was accepted that the strict chronological rule would not be enforced if it had the effect of arbitrarily separating clearly connected records. Thus, records bearing on the Great War were made available in 1968; on the Second World War likewise in 1972. As is well known, this did not mean that all the records were now open. Certain documents from both wars, especially the Second World War, continued to be withheld (and are still withheld) under the capacious section 3(4) of the Public Records Act of 1958, often because they were thought to contain 'highly sensitive information relating to national security', but also for 'special reasons' usually unspecified.[27] 'Original documents,' A. J. P. Taylor remarked, 'are much too dangerous for beginners. They are often too dangerous for most historians, who do better to copy from their predecessors.'[28]

However many precautions were taken, this was a real revolution. Under the new regime the Cabinet Office was induced to temper somewhat the zeal with which it pursued errant public records in private collections. As the thaw was seen to continue, so more private papers also emerged for public scrutiny. In the event, the last substantial pre-revolutionary works appeared in 1965: Paul Guinn's *British Strategy and Politics*, Robert Rhodes James's *Gallipoli*, and Taylor's volume of *English History*. To compare the sources available to Guinn with those of David French's *British Strategy and War Aims* (1986), both model monographs of their time, is to take the measure of the change that had been brought about.[29] Exceptionally, Rhodes James was given the 'right

---

[26] M. Howard, 'The Demand for Military History', *Times Literary Supplement* (13 Nov. 1969).

[27] Public Records Acts 1958 and 1967; 'Access to Public Records', PRO Information sheet 37 (Sept. 1986).

[28] Taylor, 'Playing the Party Game', *Observer* (23 Aug. 1970). Cf. his *English History* (London, 1975), 729-30, 751.

[29] P. Guinn, *British Strategy and Politics* (Oxford, 1965), 322-32; D. French, *British Strategy and War Aims* (London, 1986), 250-67.

of inspection', but not publication, of closed public records. He was allowed to see the crucial evidence to the Dardanelles Commission, due for release in 1970. A scrupulous historian, steeped in the traditions and actual practice of high politics, Rhodes James was a cautious debunker. Indeed, the subjects and tone of his biographical output tend to suggest a natural but careful 'bunker'.[30] The semi-privileged circumstances of *Gallipoli*'s creation accord well with this picture. The end product, for all its scholarship, is heavy with the weight of the author's self-restraint. We are aware that Rhodes James knows more than he tells. He is vigilant for the truth; but he is also guarded.

No one could accuse A. J. P. Taylor of being guarded—except perhaps *The Times*, which pronounced his illustrated history of the war 'competent but pedestrian', a description as inappropriate as any to be found. Taylor was *sui generis*, as others have been driven to remark. The bestselling *First World War*, with the chatter of its epigrams, its love of paradox and delight in chance, its compression, its hyperbole, its mischief, its range and clarity, was in many ways quintessential Taylor: 'a style and manner of presentation unequalled in his own time', as Arthur Marwick has underlined, 'but very much of his own time'.[31] Style, it has been said, is the physiognomy of the soul. The illustrated history surely bares its author's soul. Sir John Elliot, himself a veteran of 5 Army, encapsulated it best as 'a bitter book, penetrating, prejudiced and altogether brilliant'. Elliot also noted wisely that it was Taylor's 'mischievous and often mordant wit that puts him apart from other historians', a comment on the famous caustic (in Taylor's word 'light-hearted') captions to the book's plenitude of diverting photographs: 'Sir John French in training for the retreat from Mons'; 'Lord Kitchener with his keeper, Sir William Robertson'; 'He relied on divine help, became an earl and received £100,000 from Parliament: Field Marshal Sir Douglas Haig'.[32]

Like his historical favourites, Taylor has paid a high price for his incorrigible troublemaking. Ostensibly undermined, discredited even, his work is freely disparaged. Terraine, for example, referred to his 'sly' illustrated history of the war. It has always been necessary to make a

---

[30] See *Lord Randolph Churchill* (London, 1959); *Lord Rosebery* (London, 1963); and esp. *Anthony Eden* (London, 1986). *Churchill: A Study in Failure* (London, 1970) is a partial exception.

[31] 'Fifty years on', *The Times* (7 Nov. 1963); A. Marwick, *The Nature of History* (London, 1970), 191.

[32] Sir John Elliot, review in *Sunday Times* (17 Nov. 1963); Taylor, illustrated history, pp. 28, 105, 108. Cf. Taylor's *A Personal History* (London, 1983), 242-3.

point of taking Taylor seriously.[33] Of course there were mistakes in *The First World War*. There would have been more but for a meticulous 'vetting' by Liddell Hart, a regular correspondent and something of an admirer since 1957. 'All I ask is to be saved from glaring faults,' requested Taylor. These were remarkably few. Like Macaulay, Taylor sought literally to vulgarize, but never to violate. He insisted on Haig's alleged 'recruiting' of Jellicoe to urge that Ostend and Zeebrugge must be taken as an anti-submarine measure, as a boost to Haig's own strategic designs for 1917, but otherwise adopted the bulk of Liddell Hart's suggestions. 'I shall not thank you in the book,' Taylor wrote when it was finished, 'so that you may be free to attack or even praise it.'[34]

The force of the book stems from Taylor's argument, constantly reiterated, that the war had a damning simplicity: it was senseless.

No one asked what the war was about. The Germans had started the war in order to win; the Allies fought so as not to lose. Of course the French hoped to recover Alsace and Lorraine; the British were determined to liberate Belgium. But these were not enough in themselves; they were the symbols of victory, not the reason why it was being pursued.

By 1916, when both sides at Verdun fought 'literally for the sake of fighting', the reductive case was virtually closed. Haig's long-cherished strategy received short shrift. 'Third Ypres was the blindest slaughter of a blind war.' Who was culpable? Taylor proved less uncompromising than might be supposed from his known sympathy for the roguish 'ranker' Prime Minister. 'Haig bore the greatest responsibility. Some of the Flanders mud sticks also to Lloyd George, the man who lacked the supreme authority to forbid the battle.' He put the last point more exactly in his original review of Wolff's book: 'the story loses much of its sense unless Lloyd George's precarious political position is made clear. Rightly or wrongly—probably wrongly—he dared not overrule Robertson and Haig until they had discredited themselves by bloody failure.'[35]

---

[33] Terraine, *Road to Passchendaele*, p. xxi. Significantly, Michael Howard always did. See the review-essay, 'Reflections on the First World War', *Encounter* (Jan. 1964), repr. in his *Studies in War and Peace* (London, 1970), 99-109.

[34] Taylor to Liddell Hart, 13 Feb. and 29 May 1962, Liddell Hart to Taylor, 22 Nov. 1963, Liddell Hart papers, 1/676. Marwick, who also made a point of taking him seriously, quotes Taylor himself on 'vulgarization' (p. 190). The illustrated history and his valedictory lecture at Oxford were dedicated to Joan Littlewood, director of *Oh! What a Lovely War. Personal History*, 243; *Daily Telegraph* (31 May 1963).

[35] Taylor, illustrated history, 62, 126, 194; 'The battle in the mud', *Manchester Guardian* (27 Feb. 1959). Cf. 'Lloyd George: Rise and Fall', 1961 Leslie Stephen Lecture, Cambridge, printed in his *Essays in English History* (London, 1976), 254-82.

Even at the discreditable expiration of 1917 Haig, if not Robertson, remained out of reach.

'Winning the war was the end in itself.' There was no point to it, though it did have enormous social and political significance: the perfect Taylorian paradox. *The First World War* revealed, not 'a good war' like the Second, but an utterly senseless one—debunking, according to some, on a grand scale.[36] Yet Taylor, typically, dissented from the prevailing orthodoxy. Taking issue with 'lions led by donkeys', he concluded firmly: 'this character was not confined to the British, or to soldiers. All the peoples were in the same boat. The war was beyond the capacity of generals and statesmen alike.' He had earlier written to Liddell Hart, 'you will be shocked to hear that, on reflection, I have become a cautious "westerner". That is, the war could only be won in the west; though it could not be won there with the existing weapons and tactics.' In the book he was correspondingly severe on side-shows. 'They were "dodges" in a double sense. They were ingenious; and they were designed to evade the basic problem—that the German army could be beaten only by an antagonist of its own size.'[37] Terraine himself could scarcely have put it better.

Among British military historians John Terraine colonized the territory of the Great War in a uniquely personal fashion. The war, above all the Western Front, became his preserve. His name, like the names of the battles themselves, had to be protected; his reputation, like the generals', reclaimed; his credentials, like Haig's, established and then re-established. Terraine (born 1921) was brought up, as he has said himself, 'in the shadow of the war'. His father fought throughout, was severely wounded, never spoke of the war, and died when Terraine was six. His earliest explorations began with the apprehension of a disparity between the comfortable wisdom purveyed by his female relatives and the less comfortable wisdom of Liddell Hart's *Foch* (1931). Many years later in 1958, as he was in the process of cutting that umbilical cord, Terraine wrote:

For the first time the Great War assumed for me an intelligible shape. I have come to disagree with you on various matters since then, but I shall not forget

---

[36] Taylor, illustrated history, 11, 62-4; *The Second World War* (London, 1976), 234, a verdict foreshadowed in an earlier review: 'somehow it must be conveyed to them [the younger generation] that it was that rare, perhaps unique, thing: a good war'. 'Two wars in One', *Observer* (2 July 1972).

[37] Taylor, illustrated history, 287, 68-71; to Liddell Hart, 4 Oct. 1962, Liddell Hart papers, 1/676.

this debt that I owe you for first dispelling the intense obscurity of those events.[38]

Robert Kee (born 1919) gave eloquent voice to such feelings in a meditation on the Great War written in 1962. A resonant passage on the middle-aged, 'brought up in the years after 1918 in a curious atmosphere of light and shade about what happened', continued:

Only very slowly, as one grew older, did one begin to suspect that the truth lay in the shade, made deeper and more impenetrable by the glare of national self-congratulation and piety in which the war was officially bathed. No one who experienced a school Armistice Day in the 1920s is likely to forget its compelling air of tribal solidity. We had beaten the Germans. The retreat from Mons had been a wonderful thing. Angels had appeared there for us. We had won the Battle of the Somme. Sir Douglas Haig was a great hero. Men, rather larger than life-size, like the bronze figures on the Artillery memorial at Hyde Park Corner, had laid down their lives finely that we might live.

One can imagine the young Terraine thinking about this fineness, as did the young Kee, 'hard and self-reproachfully' during the two minutes' silence; and then clamouring to know 'what it was like' in the war.

The schoolmasters who had been in it talked of Jerry and Wipers and Plug Street. One turned to the illustrated *History of the War*, brooding over the murky tin-hatted figures struggling about in that awful landscape of mud that was somehow so respectable. Later one read Sassoon, Blunden, Owen, Graves, Aldington, turned pacifist for a week, fought in a new war, voted Labour, anti-Labour, but always 'The Great War' remained at the back of one's mind, obscurely unfathomed.[39]

Terraine's own trajectory bears fascinatingly, though ambiguously, on the process of remembrance depicted by Kee. He too was immersed in post-war piety. As late as 1933 he received as a school prize a book called *The Crown of Honour*. Tiring of its stories of 'Heroism, Gallantry, Magnanimity, and Devotion', he reacted even more strongly against the 'distortion' of 'disenchantment'. He quotes approvingly Sidney Rogerson's sour commentary on the charade 'war of the sewers, in which no one ever laughed, those who were not melancholy mad were alcoholically hysterical, and most of the action took place in or near the crude latrines of the period'.[40]

---

[38] Interview with John Terraine, 11 July 1988; Terraine to Liddell Hart, 14 Oct. 1958, Liddell Hart papers, 1/683 (quoted to the same effect in R. Pocock, 'Liddell Hart', *Listener* (28 Dec. 1972)).
[39] R. Kee, 'How the Lights Went Out', *Spectator* (1 June 1962).
[40] Terraine, *Smoke and Fire*, 13-14.

Most ambiguous was Terraine's mature response to the litany of long ago. In 1960 he devoted a book to the retreat from Mons, in fact 'the retreat to victory', wonderful indeed, and 'one of the finest sustained endeavours in the Army's story'. Disappointingly, angels appeared only as 'myths and legends' in a later work on that theme, *The Smoke and the Fire* (1980).[41] He came very close to saying that we *had* won the Battle of the Somme. It was admittedly 'a human disaster'; but it was also 'an unquestionable Allied victory, mainly a British one, because it laid the essential foundation for the final defeat of the Germans in the field'. The Somme, it emerged, was 'the turning-point'. In it could be discerned 'the first dim harbingers of the still far distant victories of 1918'. For Terraine, it was an absolutely necessary battle. In his favourite quotation from Haig, 'we cannot hope to win until we have defeated the German Army'.[42] Much of his argument proceeded backwards from the consoling and irrefutable fact that we did win, in spite of all. His final response to Kee's remembrance was to shift the emphasis. *We* had beaten the Germans. It was very largely a British feat of arms. The French were too tired, the Russians too unreliable, and the Americans (in strength) too late. In hindsight, Terraine warranted Haig's claim that he himself had devised a strategy and stuck to it, on the Somme in 1916, in Flanders in 1917, on the Somme again in adversity in 1918. It was a strategy of attrition—a slippery concept. Ultimately it paid off. Haig, the self-confessed instrument of Providence, was able to compensate for French fatigue and capitalize on American absence. 'I ask thee for victory, Lord,' he prays in *Oh! What a Lovely War*, 'before the Americans arrive.'[43]

Terraine's massive study of the providential commander-in-chief (1963), discussed in detail by Keith Simpson, was the supreme act of bunking in a generally debunking decade. His Haig was simpler and greater than the one disclosed in his subject's diaries in 1952, the occasion of Beaverbrook's classic remark about Haig committing suicide twenty-five years after his death. In the face of appalling difficulties, Terraine's Haig remained unperturbed. He more than anyone mastered events—demonstrably so, for he won the war. He was irreducibly heroic. Kee underscored the conscious justification in a prescient review which

---

[41] Id., *Mons*, subtitle and p. 217; *Smoke and Fire*, 17-21.

[42] Id., *Haig*, 229-30, 482; *Smoke and Fire*, 125.

[43] *Oh! What a Lovely War* play script (London, 1967), 96. Attrition is not too slippery for David French, 'The Meaning of Attrition', *English Historical Review*, 103 (Apr. 1988), 385-405; or T. H. E. Travers, *The Killing Ground* (London, 1988).

drew indiscriminate covering fire from the author. Terraine, he wrote astutely,

> does some disservice to Haig in this book, otherwise so thorough, conscientious and indispensable that it might have been the product of his master's voice itself. For it is a book to praise Haig not to bury him, when what Haig requires is that he should be set without emotion in the context of his abilities, his limitations and his time, and left there.

Somewhat like Taylor, Kee cast Haig as the 'unhero', neither hero nor anti-hero, as much in thrall to events beyond his control as 'the unheroic dead who fed the guns'. The unheroic Haig 'did the only job he could do in the circumstances unspectacularly well'—in principle an argument which might have commended itself to Terraine, who was developing a powerful case for the Western Front as the inescapable predicament of the war. Regretting the encumbrance of the book's heavy emotional baggage—a signature recognizable on all Terraine's work—Kee offered the penetrating comment that 'Haig was not the father-figure Mr Terraine yearns to make him.'[44]

There can be no doubting Terraine's genuine commitment to the long-sustained effort to rehabilitate Haig. His emotional investment in the eponymous book is reminiscent of nothing so much as a first, skin-shedding, autobiographical novel. After 1963 his concern widened to embrace collectively 'that hideously unattractive group, the British generals of the first world war', in John Keegan's graphic phrase, 'whose diaries reveal hearts as flintlike as the textures of their faces'.[45] Terraine was easily stung by criticism but wrote contentiously, with increasing stridency. In return he was corrected, castigated, insulted, pilloried. Not untypical was denunciation of 'the fantastic philistinism of John Terraine—who has made a historical career out of trying to suggest that the generals who presided over the demolition of a whole British generation were something more respectable than idiots'.[46] The abuse stuck like a banderilla. More wounding still was Keegan's irreverent

---

[44] Kee, 'Haig the Unhero'. See also Terraine's overheated response, 'Exorcising the Trauma', and Kee's letter of rejoinder, *Spectator* (10 and 17 May 1963). Cf. Liddell Hart to Horne, 18 May 1963, Liddell Hart papers, 1/380.

[45] J. Keegan, 'Whole Stunt Napoo', *New Statesman* (17 Nov. 1978). Cf. Terraine's 'The Generals', *Stand To! Journal of the Western Front Association* (founder-president J. Terraine), 7 (Spring 1983), 4–7.

[46] B. Page, 'The Gunner's Story', *New Statesman* (24 Aug. 1979), citing A. Rutherford, *The Literature of War* (London, 1979); logged by Terraine, *Smoke and Fire*, 36.

treatment of his *œuvre* on the publication of *To Win a War* (1978). 'It's good to have a line from John Terraine again,' Keegan wrote sportively.

We have *received no letter from him lately/for a long time*. We feared he might *have been admitted to hospital/sick/wounded*, perhaps not *going on well/hoping to be discharged soon/sent down to base*. We have been expecting *a letter/card/ telegram to follow at first opportunity* to say that he was *quite well*.

There was no cause for alarm.

Here he comes now, swinging down the duckboards in the gloaming from the support line, marching easy, tin hat slung, cap comforter over his ears, Woodbine on ... There is mud on his ammunition boots ... dirt has worked its way into his medal ribbons, so that one peers to make them out. Can the first be the Star for *Mons* ... Has he been out that long?[47]

Indeed he had. Wounds or no, Terraine was out for another ten years or more. He remained equally sensitive and argumentative. With time, the extraordinary intensity of his commitment became the touchstone, not only of his own work, but of the interpretation he had come to represent.

The essence of it was identified by Terraine himself in an article deliberately entitled 'Big Battalions', in 1962. 'The question continues to be asked: was the bloodbath on the Western Front inevitable? Was there no other way? My own view will have become apparent by now: that there was not.'[48] The Germans were the main enemy. They perched vulture-like on the shoulder of every Frenchman, perilously close to the Parisian jugular. A decision had to be sought in France and Flanders. After 1915, quite apart from political and diplomatic imperatives, without any obliging German offensives the requisite attrition could be achieved only by British ones. Hence the 'necessity' of the Somme, the 'inevitability' of Passchendaele and the crowning 'simplicity' of the Great War according to Terraine: 'between 1916 [and] 1918, the task of engaging the main body of the main enemy in a continental war fell upon the British Army, for the only time in its history, and it carried out that task at very heavy cost with ultimately decisive effect'. In consequence, it was 'unprofitable to look for the causes of loss very far beyond the quality of the enemy who inflicted it and the technical character of the war itself'.[49]

[47] Keegan, 'Whole Stunt'.
[48] Terraine, 'Big Battalions', *History Today* (June 1962), repr. in *The Western Front* (London, 1964), 202. Cf. the concluding sentence of *Haig*, 482.
[49] Terraine, new introduction (Spring 1983) to *First World War*, p. x; *To Win a War*, 99 (cf. p. 31).

Consistently supported by a staunch friend, Shelford Bidwell, and skilfully propagated by a growing convert and brilliant ally, Correlli Barnett, this interpretation has made a considerable impact on Great War historiography.[50] Its remorseless reiteration by Terraine in the course of ten books sounded the passing of the Churchill–Lloyd George interpretation of the war, an interpretation shaped and advanced by the Sage of Great War scholarship, Liddell Hart, whose long reign and tentacular patronage extended deep into the bunking and debunking of generals which afforded him such pleasure.[51] Terraine's viewpoint, stripped of its rhetorical excess and forfeit of its emotional charge, served to reorientate the historian's mental map of the war. As even persistent critics were driven to concede, 'the "futility" of the Western Front now seemed less self-evident'. Terraine incited and, progressively, influenced military historians for three decades, and perhaps beyond. His work elicited the uncomfortable tribute of the most searching critiques, notably by Robert Kee in the 1960s, John Keegan in the 1970s, and Hew Strachan in the 1980s.[52] Keegan, in serious vein, caught what was at once distinctive and provocative about Terraine in a dazzling portrait, antipathetic yet tinged with reluctant admiration, of 'the Enoch Powell of British military historians',

> not only deeply patriotic but fiercely nationalist and unashamedly imperialist, dedicated to a belief in the military unity of the British Empire, convinced still of the rightness of the decisions of August 1914, morbidly suspicious of alliances and allies, whether they are Frenchmen trying to fight to the last Tommy or Americans brashly usurping his place in the victory parade, endlessly contemptuous of liberal politicians, of whatever party, who fail to understand the harshness of life and the inevitability of struggle, totally unmoved by modern

[50] Interviews with Correlli Barnett and Shelford Bidwell, 10 and 11 June 1988; Terraine, *Right of the Line* (London, 1985), p. xv. Barnett, *Swordbearers*, 105; letter to *New Statesman* (1 Dec. 1978); *The Great War* (London, 1979), 74-87, 123-4. Bidwell, letters to *Journal of the Royal United Services Institute for Defence Studies*, 105 (Feb. 1960), 110-11, and *Journal of the Society for Army Historical Research*, 60 (Spring 1982), 54-5.

[51] R. Prior, *Churchill's 'World Crisis' as History* (London, 1983); G. W. Egerton, 'The Lloyd George *War Memoirs*: A Study in the Politics of Memory', *Journal of Modern History*, 60 (Mar. 1988), 55-94. 'Sage' is Michael Howard's perfect epitaph on Liddell Hart, *Encounter* (Apr. 1970). Liddell Hart's 'bunking' was confined mainly to pre-Great War generals (Sherman) or lesser figures (Monash).

[52] Kee, 'Haig the Unhero' and 'Haig Trauma'; Keegan, 'Whole Stunt'. H. Strachan, review-essay in *Journal of the Society for Army Historical Research*, 59 (Autumn 1981), 177-80, and subsequent corr., 60 (Spring 1982), 50-6; 'The British Way in Warfare Revisited', *Historical Journal*, 26 (June 1983), 453-5 (quotation p. 454); 'Strategies of Attrition', *Times Literary Supplement* (9 Mar. 1984).

distaste for the upstairs–downstairs world of hierarchy and obedience in which he seems to feel so much at home.[53]

To his chagrin, the impact of Terraine's interpretation on the popular conception of the war has by no means equalled the impact on its historiography. He was given the opportunity to find a wider audience in 1963, immediately after the appearance of *Douglas Haig*, when approached by the BBC producer Tony Essex to act as scriptwriter (and eventually associate producer) on what became the biggest documentary series ever made in Great Britain, *The Great War* (1964).[54] This seminal production was the making of many reputations. It led to more military telehistory of quality—providing the model for *The World at War*—and involved some of the best-known military historians of the period, most prominently Terraine himself and Correlli Barnett, but also including Victor Bonham-Carter, Alistair Horne, Robert Kee, Barrie Pitt, and John Williams, with Liddell Hart as consultant 'military adviser'. Though the twenty-six-part series conformed very much to Essex's original design, often the film was cut to fit the script, reversing the normal procedure and allowing the writer an unusual degree of influence on the final product.[55] Without question *The Great War* had an immensely powerful effect on the viewing public. Its mass popularity exceeded all expectations. When it was repeated on BBC1 even as the final episodes were still running on BBC2, each programme was watched by almost one-fifth of the entire population: some eight million people on average—figures which rivalled such contemporary household gods as the glossy-lipped Kathy Kirby or the imperishable Likely Lads. On both channels the BBC's audience reaction index (sampled by questionnaire) reached heights exceeded only by the well-primed collective rapture of cup finals or, at the very apogee of enchantment, royal weddings.[56]

Not everyone was equally impressed. The series was seen in some quarters as a clear case of cultural overkill. John Connell penned an elegant, ironic epitaph.

Platoons of earnest researchers have been employed; old men have recalled, with poignant precision, engagements in which they took part when they were boys of

[53] Keegan, 'Whole Stunt'.
[54] Terraine interview, 11 July 1988; *First World War*, p. vii.
[55] Barnett, Horne, and Terraine interviews, 10 June, 14 June, and 11 July 1988; J. Isaacs, 'How to Make History', 1988 Huw Weldon Lecture, Channel Four, 17 May 1988; *Great War* script synopses, Dept. of Film, Imperial War Museum. Terraine alone scripted 12 episodes and co-scripted 3 others.
[56] BBC Audience Research Reports; figures from BBC Audience Barometer, BBC Written Archives Centre.

nineteen; and the golden voices of great actors have keened over the holocaust of a generation. A great deal of noble platitudes have been uttered, and a great deal of flapdoodle.

War, noted Connell, 'has become big business for the communicators.'[57]

There was a lot at stake for the aspiring telehistorian—an experiment in cross-breeding which promised more in the early 1960s than it later delivered. Correlli Barnett has talked of the 'cabinet crises' among the historians on *The Great War*, necessitating virtually a replay of the war itself, episode by episode, as the historian-generals refought each battle in its proper time and place, now constrained by the new and ferocious discipline of television's unchangeable requirement to win on schedule.[58] Alistair Horne experienced for himself 'the clash of personalities about the issue of the High Command' throughout the series, alluding to 'those who now appear dedicated to whitewashing Haig and company at any price'. Horne was not the only one to notice some 'inconsistency' between the marked reluctance to appraise British generals in the Somme and Passchendaele programmes (both scripted by Terraine) and the free criticism of foreign generals, Nivelle, for example, in other programmes. Passchendaele was especially hard-fought; on the very eve of its first transmission Liddell Hart, who had not been shown the script and therefore feared the worst, demanded that his name be removed from the credits. 'I think Captain Liddell Hart has taken a certain view over a long period', commented Terraine aptly, 'and has pushed this view forward in a number of ways. It is not my view.'[59]

There is, then, some suggestion that key episodes of *The Great War* were themselves intended to promote 'a certain view', a view encompassing beneficent British generalship, the primacy of the Western Front, and the unavoidability of penal casualty-rates; most importantly, a certain view of the outcome of the war—in Foch's plangent phrase—which 'won the gratitude of posterity'. In the final episode of the series this phrase was carefully used to fix in the mind's eye, if not a good war, then at least a necessary one. But what did the populace in fact conclude? Audience Research Reports persistently dwelt upon one theme. In the words of an anonymous housewife, 'this series should be seen by *all* to bring home the horrors of war and the dreadful waste of young man-

---

[57] J. Connell, 'Writing about Soldiers', *Journal of the Royal United Services Institute for Defence Studies*, 110 (1965), 222. Cf. John Brophy, 'TV "errors" in Great War Series', *Daily Telegraph* (12 Dec. 1964).   [58] Barnett interview, 10 June 1988.
[59] Horne to Liddell Hart, 4 Sept. and 13 Nov. 1964, Liddell Hart papers, 1/380; 'TV War', *Sunday Express* (20 Sept. 1964).

'Bunking' and Debunking 281

hood'. BBC analysis of the production's total effect emphasized precisely the 'myth' which John Terraine adjudged the most pernicious of all: 'the horror of trench warfare', the 'appalling and needless slaughter of innocent people'. Here was a rich irony. The new audience had not swallowed 'the old lie'. In the end the message the series actually communicated was as unexpected as the scale of its success. It was the utter futility of the war.[60]

Many of those who watched the BBC's *The Great War* may have been reeling still from their exposure to an avowedly entertaining work, also hugely popular, *Oh! What a Lovely War* (1963), a Theatre Workshop group production under the direction of Joan Littlewood, with the chameleon presence of George Sewell and the monstrously inventive Victor Spinetti among others in the original company.[61] The stage play had its origins in the anabasis of Charles Chilton, deviser and producer of individualistic BBC radio programmes, and himself a 'war orphan'. In 1958 Chilton yielded to his grandmother's request for a photograph of his father's grave at Arras. Only on arrival did he discover the bitter truth. His father had no grave.

Instead his name was inscribed upon the wall along with those of '35,942 officers and men of the forces of the British Army who fell in the battle of Arras and who have no known grave.' What could have possibly happened to a man that rendered his burial impossible? What horror could have taken place that rendered the burial of 35,942 men impossible and all in one relatively small area?

Chilton returned home. The questions would not leave him. He began work on a new version of his broadcasting trademark, a web of reflection spun around soldiers' songs of the period, some forty in all, seeking to catch the spirit of what did happen to the common man on the Western Front throughout the war. The result was a small masterpiece. 'The Long, Long Trail' was first heard on the BBC Home Service in December 1961. With Chilton's active participation it became the model and prime source (along with authentic atmosphere and dialogue from *The Wipers Times*) for Joan Littlewood and her managerial consort, producer Gerry Raffles.[62]

[60] BBC Audience Research Reports, VR/64/461 and 624, 11 Sept. and 28 Dec. 1964, BBC Written Archives Centre; Terraine, *Smoke and Fire*, 205 ff.
[61] *Oh! What a Lovely War* play script, 7.
[62] Interview with Charles Chilton, 8 Aug. 1988; Chilton, note on provenance of *Oh! What a Lovely War*, 1963, Chilton private papers; Raffles and Chilton, *Oh! What a*

Littlewood and Raffles had an additional collaborator whose importance has been rather obscured, perhaps by his billing as 'military adviser'. This was the journalist and military historian Raymond Fletcher, subsequently Labour Member of Parliament for Ilkeston in Derbyshire. Fletcher, a warm-hearted man with something of the autodidact about him, was a self-styled pupil, fan, and inevitably a correspondent of Liddell Hart's, and an inveterate and unashamed propagandist for his passionately held beliefs.[63] His great weakness as a military historian was his inability to 'get out of the trenches', as he put it. He railed against any 'whitewashing' of the generals by 'the Terraine brigade', commenting appropriately to Liddell Hart that it 'smacks of the systematic denigration of Lloyd George—the target of the whole school'. The consequential debunking of Lloyd George was very much a feature of the time, most pronounced in what Fletcher called 'writing at the salute', a biting reference to Victor Bonham-Carter's life of Robertson, unpromisingly titled *Soldier True* (1963). Fletcher himself had no truck with saluting. He would have scorned Correlli Barnett's striving to see 'inside the commander's skull'. His only interest was 'the ordinary soldier'.[64] This chimed exactly with the musical inspiration and inquisitive roots of Chilton's original conception; but Chilton's work was neither as ideologically committed nor as didactic. It was Fletcher's fixity of purpose which supplied *Oh! What a Lovely War* with its precepts and its strong socialist undertow, always appealing to its inimitably 'vulgarian' director. Littlewood herself forged the weapon of what she called a 'clownerie', a fusion of music hall, *commedia dell'arte*, and Brechtian epic theatre. Fletcher made the bullets for the cast to fire—and delighted in so doing. Very early in the play's evolution he delivered to the assembled Theatre Workshop an overview lecture designed to give the war some recognizable shape: a marathon three-hour session memorably described by the lecturer as 'one part me, one part Liddell Hart, the rest Lenin!'[65]

Lovely War souvenir programme notes, 1963; 'The Long, Long Trail', script for transmission on 27 Dec. 1961, BBC Written Archives Centre; *The Wipers Times* (1916-18) (fac. edn., London, 1973). 'Long Trail' was repeated with Bud Flanagan as narrator on 21 Feb. and 11 Nov. 1962.

[63] Fletcher interview, 13 June 1988; Fletcher-Liddell Hart correspondence, Liddell Hart papers, 1/288. Fletcher reviewed military history for *Tribune*; his plug for Liddell Hart's republished *Sherman* on 6 Nov. 1959 triggered their intensive correspondence.

[64] Barnett and Fletcher interviews, 10 and 13 June 1988; Fletcher to Liddell Hart, 28 Oct. 1963, Liddell Hart papers, 1/288.

[65] Chilton and Fletcher interviews, 8 Aug. and 13 June 1988; P. Gardner, 'Joan Littlewood: Call me a Vulgarian', *New York Times* (27 Sept. 1964). There was a brief

Fletcher had another message to deliver, 'a message for the sixties'. For him the Great War had an urgent contemporary relevance. 'Our world resembles that of August 1914,' he wrote in a review of Tuchman's book of that title, anticipating the rediscovery in the 1980s of the inherent danger of 'war by miscalculation' or accident, and the perils of a nuclear 'July crisis'. He was much influenced by his reading of Herman Kahn, whose wonderfully fertile mind so dominated the strategic thinking of the early 1960s, most profoundly by Kahn's heretical *On Thermonuclear War* (1960), once described as 'a moral tract on mass murder' but treated by Fletcher with surprising reverence. 'The works of Herman Kahn' took their place as some of the more unusual source material for Theatre Workshop sessions.[66] Fletcher's thinking was also affected by the amazing spectacle of the Cuban Missile Crisis (1962), a fevered melodrama whose realization on the public stage was apt to quicken all his old fears. In the world of Doctor Strangelove *Oh! What a Lovely War* carried to a new generation a message about the holocaust of a previous one, a message at once universal and immediately applicable. As Raymond Fletcher saw it, there was always the chance of war. Joan Littlewood's 'musical entertainment' was a cautionary tale in more senses than one.[67]

A new and more durable entertainment opened at the resplendent Paramount Cinema, Piccadilly, in 1969. With the passage of time and the aid of television, Richard Attenborough's film treatment of *Oh! What a Lovely War* has inexorably eclipsed the original production in the public mind. Like the play, the film caused an immediate sensation. On general release it had a tremendous worldwide reception; it was shown at international film festivals in New York, Osaka, and Barcelona; it still rivals the inextinguishable *Sound of Music* as the perfect TV extravaganza.

---

possibility that Spike Milligan would collaborate on the stage adaptation. Though 'very interested', he preferred to fulfil commitments in Australia. Chilton to Raffles, 27 Mar. 1962, Chilton private papers.

[66] Fletcher interview, 13 June 1988, and 'Europe's Old Order', *Tribune* (15 June 1962); J. R. Newman, review in *Scientific American*, 204 (Mar. 1961), 200; *Oh! What a Lovely War* play script, 110-11. Littlewood was notorious for borrowing freely from published sources. Borrowings for *Oh! What a Lovely War* included portions of Clark's *Donkeys* (he sued), Tuchman's *August 1914* (she acquiesced) and, most in keeping, Jaroslav Hasek's unfinished masterpiece *The Good Soldier Svejk* (complete English edn., London, 1973).

[67] Fletcher interview, 13 June 1988. In the climate of the late 1960s, the contemporary resonance was noted more by film reviewers, British and American. e.g. M. Hinxman, 'A Lovely War for British Films', *Sunday Telegraph* (6 Apr. 1969); P. Kael, 'Off with the Statues' Heads!', *New Yorker* (11 Dec. 1969).

The credits read like a gazetteer of the British stage, sporting more titles than GHQ.[68] The casting was deliberately stylized or gloriously eccentric, according to taste. Among many: Jack Hawkins was Franz Joseph; John Gielgud, Berchtold; John Mills, Haig; Laurence Olivier, a splendidly harrumphing French ('Tell me, Douglas, what d'you think of this fella Kitchener?'); Michael Redgrave, the mellifluous narrator of *The Great War*, Wilson; Ralph Richardson, the spectral voice of Haig in the BBC production, Grey. In style, tone, and premiss, the film remained broadly true to its origins. Littlewood's inspired use of a pierrot show ('the Merry Roosters') to present the war was replaced by Attenborough's clever framing device of Brighton Pier, with all its fairground and music hall appurtances. 'The front' could be easily identified not far away on the Sussex Downs.

The film was not without cinematic progenitors. Attenborough's work was as distinctive as Leon Wolff's, but like the writer he followed in a well established tradition. He appears to have benefited also from the involvement of Len Deighton—no mean military historian—as uncredited scriptwriter and, through his production company, godfather to the whole project.[69] Just as Wolff had Cecil Woodham-Smith's *The Reason Why*, Attenborough had Tony Richardson's film of the same subject, *The Charge of the Light Brigade*, with many of the cast in common; Richard Lester's anarchic *How I Won the War*; and Joseph Losey's finely etched *King and Country*. A parallel with Noël Coward's celebratory *Cavalcade* (1933) has even been proposed—by Pauline Kael, doyenne of American film critics—a deflating, blasphemous contemporary equivalent, 'a swollen, hollow anti-*Cavalcade*' for the satirical sixties.[70] Satire was certainly crucial to *Oh! What a Lovely War*, but selectively targeted. Commentators as diverse as Kael and Michael Howard have noted that although accepted as anti-war, the film was more emphatically anti-authority, specifically upper-class authority. It was, in a word, anti-officer. It presented a Great War run only by officers. The war was a disaster because these asses ('too absurd to be classified as a donkey', A. J. P. Taylor once wrote of Wilson) managed to combine homicidal imbecility with vainglorious ambition. At this level of explana-

[68] *Oh! What a Lovely War* material, BFI.

[69] There is controversy about the proper attribution of the scriptwriter/adaptation credit, carefully omitted on the film itself. Deighton's close involvement is an open secret; differences with Attenborough apparently led to his abrupt departure in the final stages of filming. Duffy to Whitaker, 21 Aug. 1984, *Oh! What a Lovely War* material, BFI; P. Houston, 'Through the Pierglass', *Spectator* (18 Apr. 1969); Taylor, *Personal History*, 243; private information.   [70] Kael, 'Off with the Statues' Heads!'.

tion, war was made by the officer-class, and made badly. The losses suffered by that 'class' were virtually ignored, especially in the purer stage version. Officers were by definition completely impervious to the fate of their men. 'The other ranks don't seem to mind so much.' Classless military professionals on both sides were immune from this treatment, as Michael Howard pointed out; but such sociologically admirable specimens (Rommel, Slim) have always been harder to identify in the Great War than in later conflicts.[71]

One notable absence from *Oh! What a Lovely War* was immediately trumpeted by Barnett and Terraine. There were butchers aplenty, but no Cur: Lloyd George did not appear in the production at all. 'What next?' asked Barnett with a suitably theatrical flourish. 'The rottenness of the State of Denmark blamed on Rosencrantz and Guildenstern, or Polonius, in a film without Hamlet or the King? What a pity such filmic brilliance should have been devoted to propagating ignorance and prejudice.'[72] Even Liddell Hart admitted that 'in some respects it is too devastating an indictment of the "powers that were"', though he quickly sought to make amends with the suggestion that the Haig character, for instance, should be seen as 'the quintessence of the High Command attitude, on all sides, rather than as an individual portrait'—a return to Terraine's 'quasi-symbolic' Haig from a different point of view. Raymond Fletcher confirmed that the 'stage' Haig at least was not intended to be 'an accurate portrait of the man but rather a personified attitude, taking in Charteris and all the other red tabs'. This was an interesting notion, perhaps too little explored, but the fact remained that both play and film seemingly 'laid the blame for the slaughter solely on the shoulders of the High Command', as Barnett claimed.[73] If only officers appeared, only officers could be charged. Their guilt could be established from their class: debunking made simple. *Oh! What a Lovely War* was the greatest exercise in debunking for forty years—debunking the generals, debunking the Western Front, debunking the war itself.

Its makers intended, and for many imparted, something more. In this respect the film stands or falls on its solemn and audacious final sequence, as described by the broadcaster Philip French.

[71] Ibid.; Howard, 'Military History', *Times Literary Supplement* (13 Nov. 1969); Taylor, 'Diaries Bring Doom', *Observer* (23 July 1961); *Oh! What a Lovely War* play script, 100. Cf. Connell, 'Writing about Soldiers', 223.
[72] Barnett, letter to *Observer* (20 Apr. 1969).
[73] Liddell Hart, comment for *Observer* (20 June 1963), and Fletcher to Liddell Hart, 24 July 1963, Liddell Hart papers, 3/119 and 1/288; Barnett, letter to *Observer* (6 Apr. 1969). Cf. Taylor's critical notice of the play, ibid. (23 June 1963).

Here the surviving Smith soldier goes into battle on the eve of the Armistice. Following a red guide tape to the attack start-line, he finds himself alone in swirling smoke. A control sergeant . . . escorts him through a blockhouse which leads into the conference hall where busy politicians are signing peace documents. Silently he follows the red tape around the room and out the other side to emerge on the Sussex Downs and join his dead relatives, who are reclining on the grass beside the family's picnicking female survivors.

At this point the sound returns. Smith's small daughter asks the ever-present question, 'what did daddy do in the war?' The slow, sad Great War parody of Jerome Kern's 'They Wouldn't Believe Me' rises in answer on the soundtrack. The men dissolve into white crosses. The camera soars away into the sky to reveal the four living Smiths marooned in a sea of crosses, those neat, clean, anonymous, familiar rows of crosses, which gradually fill the screen. In the cinema, this effect is overwhelming. Philip French was not alone in experiencing an infinite sense of waste, 'a feeling of impenetrable sadness, of unassuagable grief'.[74]

'Some of *Oh! What a Lovely War* is trying to cut through to the common denominator in this easy but dangerous mood of emotional association,' wrote one critic thoughtfully. 'Much more is parody, fun, mockery, the bitter taste of futility . . . mixed up with something still of that hazardous and vicarious nostalgia' in which the generations so helplessly indulged.[75] The contemporary associations of the war were impossible to dispel. It was these associations that explained its 'peculiar attraction' for journalists, or 'journalists-in-history' in Robert Rhodes James's rather condescending terminology. A. J. P. Taylor, as so often, anticipated the coming fashion. 'Like all journalists,' he wrote in 1953 of Luigi Albertini's *Origins of the War of 1914*, 'he studied the past in order to discover how it led to the present.'[76] This was true of the fashion's original inspirator, Alan Moorehead. It was equally true of two very different gentleman scholars turned journalists, the greatly respected Alistair Horne and the much reviled Alan Clark—who was forthrightly accused of 'monkeying with the evidence' by one of his self-confessed victims, Bernard Fergusson.[77]

[74] P. French, '*Oh! What a Lovely War*', *Sight and Sound*, 38 (Spring 1969), 94.
[75] Houston, 'Through the Pierglass'.
[76] R. Rhodes James, 'Soldiers and Biographers', *Journal of Contemporary History*, 3 (Jan. 1968), 100 (and 'Thoughts on Writing Military History', *Journal of the Royal United Services Institute for Defence Studies*, 111 (May 1966), 103); Taylor, review in *English Historical Review*, 68 (Jan. 1953), 113-15.
[77] B. Fergusson, 'Sniping at the 1914 Generals', *Daily Telegraph* (21 July 1961). Clark's *Donkeys* received similarly scorching reviews from Howard (*Listener* (3 Aug. 1961)) and Taylor (*Observer* (23 July 1961)), among others.

Such motivation produced some high-class entertainment, and not only in the theatre. If plot and character tended to be stereotyped, it proved an exceptionally popular genre: the historian's version of 'the whodunit', as Geoffrey Barraclough wrote in rebuke.[78] Similarly derived, there developed also an urge to proselytize, or at least to instruct; a sense of mission, salutary and on occasion revelatory, but ultimately self-defeating. This *déformation professionnelle* became gradually more pronounced in the work of John Terraine, whose constant theme was that 'disenchantment with the war bred distrust of all things military':

> disarmament . . . became the great quest of the post-war years, and nowhere was it pursued more whole-heartedly than in Britain, where dread of military commitment was linked to the dread of military expenditure, and both were excused by constant reference to the 'futility of war'.

The word 'futile', he was brought to write, 'has helped to warp professional reappraisal, twist political intentions, rot national morale and confuse international relations'.[79] The same urge was clearly evident in Correlli Barnett's dauntless pursuit of the roots of Britain's national decline, an odyssey traceable through the use of a phrase he made his own, 'the audit of war', which occurs in his work as early as 1963.[80]

There was a final twist. In the end, all the 'bunking' and debunking of the period was subsumed in the overpowering effect of renewing, and so perpetuating, the decisive impression made on the public by the spate of classic personal trench reminiscences produced in 1928-31. The generational ghosts were rattling their chains in the 1960s—once more through the incantatory names of the villages and rivers and battlefields, the numbers of dead and the dates now flashing a garish reminder on the screen. The war acquired a patina of verisimilitude, with newly available photographs, interviews, archive and feature film. Its pictorial image was restored to popular consciousness. 'The unknown soldier was the hero of the First World War. . . . He lives again in the photographs,' Taylor wrote in his illustrated history. The enormity of the event was the ruling concern. The great drama of the war was brilliantly done. Few 'troubled themselves overmuch with the minds and spirits of the men involved', lamented John Connell in 1965. The theatre of war reverted to music

---

[78] G. Barraclough, 'Goodbye to All That', *New York Review of Books* (14 May 1964).   [79] Terraine, *Smoke and Fire*, 205.

[80] Barnett, *Swordbearers*, 11; *The Collapse of British Power* (London, 1972), ch. 1; *The Audit of War* (London, 1986).

hall. The modern master of ceremonies, as if to ape the military historian, wore a mortar board. 'Milords, ladies and gentlemen, may we perform for you the ever-popular War Game!'[81]

[81] Taylor, illustrated history, 11; Connell, 'Writing about Soldiers', 222; *Oh! What a Lovely War* play script, 9, 11.

11
Everyman at War: Recent Interpretations of the Front Line Experience
PETER SIMKINS

If the late 1920s and early 1930s constituted a 'golden age' of writing about the First World War, the period since 1964 has been even more remarkable, at least in Britain, for the quantity of books published on the subject. This second, and more prolonged, surge of interest was undoubtedly stimulated by the fiftieth anniversary of the Great War, which led not only to a host of new books but also to the outstanding BBC television series *The Great War* and to a major part-work publication, *Purnell's History of the First World War*.[1] At the same time, serious study of the subject here was greatly helped by the opening for research of the bulk of the British official records of the conflict and by the increasing respectability of military history as an academic discipline. As yet, the present tide of popular interest in First World War topics shows no sign of abating. Evidence of the hold which the war continues to exert on scholars and the general public alike may be seen in the growing numbers visiting the battlefields of Flanders and Gallipoli each year; in the founding of specialist organizations such as the Western Front Association, with its own regular and occasional journals *Stand To!* and *Gun Fire*; and in the frequent appearance of new feature films and television dramas and documentaries with a First World War setting.[2]

[1] The television series *The Great War* was produced in 1964 and helped to launch the BBC2 channel that year. The many letters written by First World War veterans to the producers of the series following a nationwide appeal in 1963 are now held by the Department of Documents of the Imperial War Museum. *Purnell's History of the First World War*, edited first by Barrie Pitt and then by Brigadier Peter Young, was produced by Purnell and Sons Ltd. for BPC Publishing in 128 weekly parts between 1969 and 1971.
[2] *Gun Fire* is an occasional journal produced by members of the Western Front Association and issued from the York Educational Settlement. Recent films with a First World War theme include *Oh! What a Lovely War* (1969); the remake of *All Quiet on the Western Front* (1979); *Gallipoli* (1981); and *The Lighthorsemen* (1987). Among the

One of the principal features of the works published in Britain and in Commonwealth countries since 1964 is that collectively, if not always individually, they give far greater prominence than was previously the case to the views and experiences of junior officers and other ranks.[3] Such a shift in historiographical fashions may simply be a reaction to the increasingly 'stale debate on generalship' which has long absorbed military historians.[4] In some respects the change of emphasis mirrors the corresponding social history boom, which is apparent not only in publications but also in museums and in the unparalleled public appetite for heritage sites. It certainly owes something to political changes and the creation of a more egalitarian social climate with the blossoming of 'pop' culture in the 1960s. The rise of women's studies is a further manifestation of the same general trend. The shift towards social history has not yet fully extended into the field of First World War military studies, although the work of such scholars as J. M. Winter, Tony Ashworth, and David Englander has, in different ways, done much to bring the disciplines closer together over the past decade or so.[5] John Keegan's arguments in favour of a stronger emphasis on the direct experiences of soldiers in battle have both reflected and accelerated the change of approach. Thus, historians of the Great War are now liable to ask, or be asked, 'What was it like?' as frequently as 'What happened?' or 'Why did it happen?'[6]

Three factors, in particular, have combined to encourage the emergence of popular works about 'everyman's' experience of the First World War, including what one Canadian historian describes as 'group

television drama series with a 1914-18 setting have been *The Anzacs* (1985) and *The Monocled Mutineer* (1986).

[3] It is not within the province of this chapter to survey the many new personal experience accounts or First World War diaries and letters that have been published during this period. Good examples of books in this overall category are: George Coppard, *With a Machine Gun to Cambrai* (London, 1969); P. J. Campbell, *The Ebb and Flow of Battle* (London, 1977), and id., *In the Cannon's Mouth* (London, 1979); Edwin Campion Vaughan, *Some Desperate Glory: The Diary of a Young Officer, 1917* (London, 1981); and Reginald H. Roy (ed.), *The Journal of Private Fraser, 1914-1918: Canadian Expeditionary Force* (Victoria, BC, 1985).

[4] See the review by Ian Beckett of Charles Messenger's 'Terriers in the Trenches', in *Journal of the Royal United Services Institute for Defence Studies*, 127 (1982), 70; also id., 'The Nation in Arms, 1914-18' in id. and Keith Simpson (eds.), *A Nation in Arms: A Social Study of the British Army in the First World War* (Manchester, 1985), 2.

[5] See e.g. J. M. Winter, *The Great War and the British People* (London, 1986); Tony Ashworth, *Trench Warfare, 1914-1918: The Live and Let Live System* (London, 1980); David Englander and James Osborne, 'Jack, Tommy and Henry Dubb: The Armed Forces and the Working Class', *Historical Journal*, 21/3 (1978), 593-621.

[6] John Keegan, *The Face of Battle* (London, 1976), esp. pp. 27-54 and 62-78.

memoirs'.[7] First, the mass media, especially television, have contributed to a heightened public awareness of the intrinsic as well as the monetary value of historical material, so improving its chances of being brought to light and properly preserved. Secondly, wider recognition of the worth of this material has facilitated the assembly of superb collections of relevant private papers—themselves rich in diaries, letters, and unpublished accounts—at institutions such as the Imperial War Museum and by dedicated individuals like Peter Liddle.[8] Thirdly, the advent of new technology, notably the portable cassette tape-recorder, suddenly made it possible for almost anyone to interview and record the oral testimony of men who had seen active service in the British Army between 1914 and 1918. The technology came just in time to permit a 'smash and grab raid on history' while there were still sufficient veterans of the First World War left alive to make the recording projects worth while.[9]

The process has been a cumulative one in the last twenty years. While some British and Commonwealth historians in this field, such as Tony Ashworth and Peter Charlton, have based their books largely upon known published and unpublished sources, other writers on 'everyman' at war—including Martin Middlebrook and Lyn Macdonald in Britain, Pierre Berton in Canada, and Patsy Adam-Smith in Australia—have more deliberately sought to interview, or correspond with, First World War veterans. During the preparation of *The First Day on the Somme*, for example, Martin Middlebrook traced over 500 former British soldiers who fought on 1 July 1916 and who were willing to tell him of their personal experiences.[10] Hence, even if these writers unearthed, recorded,

[7] O. A. Cooke, 'Canada's Historiography and the First World War', in Jurgen Rohwer (ed.), *Neue Forschungen zum Ersten Weltkrieg* (Koblenz, 1985), 233.

[8] Peter Liddle's 1914-18 Personal Experience Archives were formerly housed at Sunderland Polytechnic. The Liddle Collection, as it is now known, has been at the University Library, Leeds, since 1988.

[9] The phrase 'smash and grab raid on history' is used by the New Zealand author Maurice Shadbolt in his book *Voices of Gallipoli* (Auckland, 1988), 11. According to Shadbolt, there were fewer than 200 New Zealand survivors of Gallipoli left by 1982, when he was working with Christopher Pugsley on a television documentary about the campaign. The Department of Sound Records at the Imperial War Museum has conducted, since 1972, over 330 interviews with veterans of the First World War, most of whom served on the Western Front or Gallipoli.

[10] Ashworth, *Trench Warfare, 1914-1918*, 225-58; Peter Charlton, *Australians on the Somme: Pozières 1916* (London, 1986), 312; Martin Middlebrook, *The First Day on the Somme* (London, 1971), 353; id., *The Kaiser's Battle: 21 March 1918, The First Day of the German Spring Offensive* (London, 1978), 9-11; Lyn Macdonald, *They Called it Passchendaele* (London, 1978), p. xiii, ead., *The Roses of No Man's Land* (London, 1980), 11-13, 308-310, and ead., *Somme* (London, 1983), pp. xiii-xvi, 351-7; Pierre

and collected such material for their own studies in the first instance, they have none the less made a useful addition to the existing body of evidence about the 1914-18 conflict. The popularity of their books has, in turn, helped to persuade publishers to bring out more new autobiographical accounts by ex-soldiers, swelling the available sources still further.

Not surprisingly, oral history has its critics. Some question the value of people's recollections of events which occurred fifty or more years ago. A. J. P. Taylor has declared: 'In this matter I am an almost total sceptic . . . Old men drooling about their youth—No'.[11] The horizon of junior officers and other ranks in the First World War was undeniably limited and they were all too often ignorant of the wider context and significance of operations in which they took part. One should not rely upon the oral testimony of 1914-18 veterans for precise details of troop movements, statistics, and dates, and few witnesses are able to resist a natural tendency to present themselves in a favourable light. Conversely, it is arrogant in the extreme to assume that anything the old soldier remembers in later life is valueless to the historian. Men can clearly recall going into battle for the first time, being wounded, or seeing a close comrade die beside them. They can also comment usefully on such general topics as food, equipment, recreation, leave, morale, front-line conditions, and officer-man relationships. In describing his own methodology when interviewing New Zealand Gallipoli veterans, Maurice Shadbolt claims that, pinned to particulars, 'they often revealed total recall of Gallipoli's landscape, and the hellish lives they lived there'. Lyn Macdonald, in her book on Passchendaele, similarly argues that people do have vivid memories of intense personal experiences, quoting Bill Fowler, who served as a stretcher-bearer in the 13 Battalion, the Rifle Brigade: 'In a way I lived my whole life between the ages of nineteen and twenty-three. Everything that happened after that was almost an anti-climax.'[12] Inevitably, much of the value of the oral history interview hinges upon the way in which it is structured and upon the objectivity, sensitivity and scholarship of the interviewer. It should be pointed out, in addition, that those who have incorporated oral testimony in their books on the front-line soldier's experience in the Great War have, in most cases, applied stringent tests

Berton, *Vimy* (Toronto, 1986; Harmondsworth, 1987), 313-14; Patsy Adam-Smith, *The Anzacs* (London, 1978), pp. vi-viii.

[11] A. J. P. Taylor, quoted in Brian Harrison, 'Oral History and Recent Political History', *Oral History*, 1/3 (1972), 46.
[12] Shadbolt, *Voices of Gallipoli*, 12; Macdonald, *They Called it Passchendaele*, p. xiii.

to this evidence, cross-checking it, before use, against a whole range of other sources.[13]

Proponents of oral history assert that, at its best, it can add colour, body, and feeling to written records; that it 'opens up' history to 'ordinary' people, giving a voice and a more central place in history to working-class men and women who are unlikely to leave behind private papers; that it is a good, if by no means unique, method of studying or recreating a multiplicity of standpoints; and that it allows non-professionals to collaborate and so helps to break down barriers between chroniclers and their audience.[14] In short, as one leading advocate puts it, oral testimony brings one back from 'the grand patterns of written history to the awkwardly individual human lives which are its basis'.[15] Other sources, indeed, have their own pitfalls. Letters written by soldiers on active service were censored and the writer may well have underplayed conditions at the front to avoid alarming his family. Newspapers too were subject to censorship or could be made to reflect the views of their editors and proprietors. Officers did not always give the unit war diary the highest priority at times of crisis, so entries were often completed at a later date, while published regimental histories, like autobiographies, are rarely the most objective of accounts. What should be remembered is that oral history is just one skein in the tapestry. Employed properly, it can usefully 'complement and supplement' documentary records.[16]

Even without recourse to oral testimony, there is ample evidence available for the student of the front-line soldier's viewpoint. As Denis Winter observes, the successive Education Acts after 1870 made it more likely that British soldiers of the Great War would be abler writers than their counterparts in earlier conflicts.[17] Most were at least literate if not literary. Considering the unprecedented size of the British army in the

---

[13] See e.g. Middlebrook, *The Kaiser's Battle*, 11-12; also Sidney Allinson, *The Bantams: The Untold Story of World War I* (London, 1981), 277; Liddle, *Men of Gallipoli: The Dardanelles and Gallipoli Experience, August 1914 to January 1916* (London, 1976), 19-20.

[14] The case for oral history is most cogently and persuasively presented by Paul Thompson in *The Voice of the Past* (2nd edn., Oxford, 1988).

[15] Ibid. 10.

[16] Review by Keith Simpson of Lyn Macdonald's *Somme* in *Journal of the Royal United Services Institute for Defence Studies*, 128 (1983), 70. For recent discussions of the strengths and weaknesses of different types of evidence see Thompson, *The Voice of the Past*, 101-49, and Arthur Marwick, *The Nature of History* (2nd edn., London, 1981), 136-51.

[17] Denis Winter, *Death's Men: Soldiers of the Great War* (London, 1978), 16-17.

latter half of the First World War, it is no surprise that surviving personal records of the 1914-18 period are abundant nor that they come from a wider cross-section of society than hitherto. Peter Liddle suggests that educational differences as well as the social habits of writing letters, keeping diaries, and saving personal papers may mean that a disproportionate amount of this evidence stems from commissioned officers.[18] Nevertheless, the quantity of written records of NCOs and private soldiers which has found its way into British and Commonwealth archives is far from negligible. One of the most important achievements of military historians during the past twenty years is that, despite the daunting nature of the task, they have at last begun to make a serious attempt to mine this rich vein of material.

Several writers and historians have bravely chosen to take an overview of British and Dominion soldiers on active service rather than analyse their attitudes and experiences from the perspective of a particular battle or campaign. A good example of this type of work is Denis Winter's *Death's Men*, based on a wide range of published personal accounts as well as unpublished diaries and memoirs in the Imperial War Museum. Winter examines how recruits progressed from enlistment and training in Britain to the front line and, ultimately, battle—an experience which, in itself, 'qualified men for the world's most exclusive club'. He also looks in some detail at the routine of trench warfare, at rest and recreation, home leave, the treatment of the wounded, and British soldiers' attitudes to the Germans or to the war as a whole. Almost at the beginning of the book Winter stresses that any event involving millions of men cannot be expected to provide a consensus and that, when set against the enormous diversity of individual experiences, the limits of any generalization are all too obvious. Variations in intelligence and temperament may, for instance, lead to radically different evaluations of an apparently simple event or situation. Much also depended upon the phase of the war in which the soldier saw the bulk of his active service. In late 1914 and early 1915, he remarks, there was a degree of improvisation which would have astounded the Kitchener men arriving at the front in 1916, by which time trench warfare had become much more highly organized. Even so, Winter adds that when all allowances are made for the diversity of men and the changing circumstances of the conflict, one is left with the impression that the factors uniting the soldiers of the First World War outweighed those dividing them.[19]

[18] Liddle, *The Soldier's War, 1914-1918* (London, 1988), 215-16.
[19] Winter, *Death's Men*, 17-20.

Denis Winter's observations on the multi-faceted nature of the front-line soldier's service are echoed by Tony Ashworth, who contends that no 'typical' or 'average' experience existed, but rather 'a number of diverse, sometimes inconsistent experiences, each formed by the particular mix of sectors and units which characterized a soldier's war career'.[20] Dr Ian Beckett has added scholarly support to those who argue against the concept of a 'war generation' and the idea of a 'universality of experience linking officers and men in a common community of spirit bred in the trenches'. He points out that there were divisions between British, Anzac, and Canadian troops, between Regulars, Territorials, Kitchener men, and conscripts, between front and rear echelons and, in reality, between officers and men. Differences were also present between 'holding' and 'assault' formations or between ordinary infantry and specialists such as trench mortar detachments. Beckett concedes that distinctions between Regulars, Territorials, and New Army troops became less clear-cut as the war progressed and drafts were no longer sent to units from their own traditional recruiting areas, but he underlines the view that no one battalion was quite like any other and that the reactions of an individual to the front-line situation were primarily determined by the unit in which he actually served.[21]

John Ellis, in *Eye-Deep in Hell*, and Malcolm Brown, in *Tommy Goes to War*, cover similar ground to Denis Winter, although both make much greater use of photographic evidence, a resource all too often undervalued by modern historians. Ellis goes further than Winter in comparing British, French, and German experiences while Brown, who describes his work as 'something of an anthology', concentrates chiefly on the infantryman's war but incorporates substantial extracts from diaries, letters, and unpublished memoirs. All three deal at length with the horrors and discomforts of front-line life, the aspects and images which still shape the collective folk-memory of the First World War: the mud, cold, lice, and rats; poison gas; the intense, mind-numbing artillery bombardments; and the terrrible wounds inflicted by shell fragments.

---

[20] Ashworth, *Trench Warfare*, 21-2.
[21] Beckett, 'The British Army, 1914-18: The Illusion of Change', in John Turner (ed.), *Britain and the First World War* (London, 1988), 107-110; see also id., 'The Nation in Arms', 21-2; and Richard Bessel and David Englander, 'Up from the Trenches: Some Recent Writing on the Soldiers of the Great War', *European Studies Review*, 11/3 (1981), 387-95. Similar views to Beckett's are contained in the excellent short survey by Keith Simpson, 'The British Soldier on the Western Front', in Peter H. Liddle (ed.), *Home Fires and Foreign Fields: British Social and Military Experience in the First World War* (London, 1985), 135-58.

Yet, equally, these studies each help to correct some popular misconceptions, re-emphasizing, amongst other points, that soldiers did not spend all their time in the fire trenches, that artillery caused more casualties than machine guns, and that, at times, more men were admitted to hospital with venereal disease than with trench foot, frostbite, and pneumonia combined.[22]

Recent work, moreover, has indicated how far front-line soldiers were able to make their daily lives more tolerable by controlling, or trying to control, the level of aggression on their sector of the front when no major battle was in progress. Malcolm Brown and Shirley Seaton have looked closely at the Christmas Truce of 1914, while Dr Tony Ashworth, in his detailed and perceptive analysis of the tactics and sociology of trench warfare, maintains that the 1914 truce was not an isolated occurrence but merely the best-known manifestation of the unofficial 'live- and let live' policy which could be found in operation on the Western Front, in one form or another, throughout the conflict. Ashworth brings out clearly the differences between 'active' and 'quiet' or 'cushy' sectors. Some 'élite' units remained aggressive whereas others acquiesced in tacit, indirect truces with the Germans, whereby both sides confined themselves to ritualized, predictable, and relatively harmless actions. These unspoken background assumptions in quiet sectors, shared and recognized by seasoned troops, persisted even when the British high command institutionalized aggression in 1916 by adopting a more systematic raiding programme. Not the least thought-provoking of Ashworth's conclusions, however, is that the scale and frequency of raiding from 1916 played a significant role in the general policy of constant attrition which, Haig later insisted, had fatally weakened the Germans by the latter half of 1918. Raids 'not only contributed to the wearing out process but also prevented the disintegration of war into peace' by stopping 'live and let live' from getting out of hand. It is, in fact, highly debatable whether raids really had a beneficial influence on morale, and some even argue that they had the contrary effect. Never-

---

[22] John Ellis, *Eye-Deep in Hell: The Western Front, 1914-18* (London, 1976), 28-9, 61, 153; Malcolm Brown, *Tommy Goes to War* (London, 1978), 63-89, 237-9; Winter, *Death's Men*, 81-2, 99, 113-19, 150-1; see also John Terraine, *The Smoke and the Fire: Myths and Anti-Myths of War, 1861-1945* (London, 1980), 130-41; Peter Simkins, 'Soldiers and Civilians: Billeting in Britain and France', in Beckett and Simpson, *A Nation in Arms*, 185-6; Martin Stephen (ed.), *Never Such Innocence: A New Anthology of Great War Verse* (London, 1988), 297-8.

theless, Ashworth's sociological approach to questions of battlefield performance has, in many respects, pointed the way forward.[23]

Few historians have given more attention than Peter Liddle has to the nature of active service in the Great War. In contrast to Ashworth, who relies heavily on published sources, Liddle's works are based principally on the 1914-18 Personal Experience Archives which he has built up with such determination and devotion in recent years. He does not always share the opinions of his fellow historians in the field, declaring, for example, that the prevalence of the 'live and let live' system should not be exaggerated. He also challenges those who overstate the gulf between officers and other ranks. The letters and diaries of men 'on both sides of the divide between leaders and led', Liddle writes, 'conclusively refute such an interpretation'. Unlike Winter, Ellis, and Ashworth, who all deal largely with the Western Front, Liddle takes a broader view and, in *The Soldier's War*, surveys conditions in several other theatres, including Gallipoli, Mesopotamia, Salonika, Egypt, Palestine, and Italy. His *Men of Gallipoli*, which focuses on one campaign, is a particularly useful guide to the differences, as well as the similarities, between trench warfare on the Peninsula and that in France and Belgium. There was little on the Western Front to match the 'sheer concentrated ferocity' of the combat at Quinn's or Courtney's Post in May 1915 or the close-quarter fighting at points where sandbag barricades were all that separated the two sides. Leave and proper recreation were virtually unknown in the Gallipoli campaign, and sickness reached levels only paralleled or surpassed in Salonika or East Africa. In an area of military history which has tended to become dominated of late by the Anzac perspective, Liddle's works offer a timely reminder that British troops had to suffer the same miseries of the Peninsula as did Australians and New Zealanders. He is anxious to counter the well-known Australian accusation that New Army troops performed badly at Suvla Bay partly because they were stunted by urban and industrial conditions in Britain. After pointing, with some justice, to the long training and high morale and optimism of the Kitchener volunteers, Liddle insists that the charges levelled at

[23] Malcolm Brown and Shirley Seaton, *Christmas Truce: The Western Front, December 1914* (London, 1984); Ashworth, *Trench Warfare*, 22-47, 99-128, 153-75, 177-83, 185; Simpson, 'The British Soldier on the Western Front', 142, 149-50; Lt.-Col. J. H. Boraston (ed.), *Sir Douglas Haig's Despatches, December 1915-April 1919* (London, 1979), 319-21. For doubts about the value of trench raids as a means of raising morale see James Brent Wilson, 'The Morale and Discipline of the BEF, 1914-1918', MA thesis (New Brunswick, 1978), 118-57, 238.

British troops at Suvla—namely that they were over-cautious on landing, unsteady under fire, and had 'neither the physical adequacy nor the mental readiness for the fighting'—do not withstand serious scrutiny. Instead he follows the British official history in attributing the failure at Suvla mainly to the unnecessary secrecy of Hamilton and his staff, the lack of proper briefing at all levels, and the excessive age and dearth of initiative of divisional, brigade, and battalion commanders.[24]

Analysis of casualty rates is, of course, crucial in any discussion of the experience and impact of battle. Here the work done by Dr J. M. Winter has been invaluable. From the statistics of both voluntary recruiting and conscription, Dr Winter deduces that British levels of military participation varied by occupation and that the higher a man was on the social scale, the more likely it was that he 'would serve from early in the war and that he would do so in a combat unit'. According to the figures he presents, over 70 per cent of those who died were under the age of 30 while casualty rates were markedly higher among officers, particularly subalterns, than among other ranks. Since so many junior officers came from well-to-do families and had passed through public schools and universities, Dr Winter reasons that the disproportionate share of casualties suffered by the middle and upper classes was a 'direct consequence of the social selection of the officer corps'. In this respect, the idea of a 'lost generation' of British youth can be supported—a classic case of scholarly research confirming conventional folk-wisdom.[25]

[24] Liddle, *The Soldier's War*, 62, 80, and id., *Men of Gallipoli*, 20-2, 190-2; Brig.-Gen. C. F. Aspinall-Oglander, *Military Operations: Gallipoli* (London, 1932), ii. 140. For early comments by C. E. W. Bean on the physical condition of British troops, see Kevin Fewster (ed.), *Gallipoli Correspondent: The Frontline Diary of C. E. W. Bean* (Sydney, 1983), 155. Other contemporary Australian views can be found in Bill Gammage, *The Broken Years: Australian Soldiers in the Great War* (Canberra, 1974), 85-7.

[25] J. M. Winter, *The Great War and the British People*, 65-99, 281-2, 305; see also his article 'Britain's Lost Generation of the First World War', *Population Studies*, 31/5 (1977), 449-66. Winter is careful to add that numerically, if not proportionately, the working class bore the brunt of British losses as, for every officer killed, twenty men of lower ranks died. With scarcely a family left untouched by the death in battle of someone close, the war truly scythed a bloody path through the whole of British society. The loss of potential leaders and poets was just one aspect of the collective sacrifice. For other recent work on recruiting patterns and the social composition of the British Army in the 1914-18 period, see J. M. Osborne, *The Voluntary Recruiting Movement in Britain, 1914-1916* (New York, 1982); Clive Hughes, 'Army Recruitment in Gwynedd, 1914-1916', MA thesis (University of Wales, 1983); Peter Simkins, *Kitchener's Army: The Raising of the New Armies, 1914-16* (Manchester, 1988); P. E. Dewey, 'Military Recruiting and the British Labour Force during the First World War', *Historical Journal*, 27/1 (1984), 199-224.

The wider aspects of British morale and discipline on the Western Front were not seriously studied by scholars until the mid-1970s, when James Brent Wilson and others began to address the subject. Wilson detects crises of morale in the BEF in the winters of 1914-15 and 1917-18, the latter crisis being the longer-lasting. Figures for courts martial, sickness, and shell-shock were, he suggests, not wholly reliable as a guide to the spirit of the troops and led senior officers to misjudge the state of morale. This, coupled with the concentration of authority in higher echelons at the expense of battalion officers, often obstructed the dissemination upwards of tactical lessons, increasing the isolation of the staff and inducing them to issue unrealistic or contradictory orders. In Wilson's view, trench raiding, far from instilling fighting spirit, was basically ineffective and injurious to morale.[26]

Britain's new citizen army was never entirely docile in the face of authority, even during its initial training period in England. However, as Gloden Dallas and Douglas Gill have shown, the more dramatic outbreaks of collective indiscipline, particularly the mutiny at the Etaples base camp in September 1917, happened in the latter part of the war, when early enthusiasms had evaporated.[27] The writings of Dallas and Gill on the Etaples mutiny provide a valuable corrective to some of the more fanciful treatments of the topic which have appeared in recent years.[28] Dallas and Gill refer to the former camp adjutant's opinion that a prime cause of discontent was the forcing of men who had already served in the trenches to undergo the same strenuous training at the infamous Etaples 'Bull Ring' as was imposed on drafts fresh from the United Kingdom. Regimental links between officers and men were largely missing at Etaples while the presence there of both Scottish and Anzac troops proved a volatile mixture. The effects of the mutiny were contained and most British troops in France were still committed to seeing the war through, but 'the spirit of the Old Army had not survived three years of war intact'.[29]

[26] J. Brent Wilson, 'The Morale and Discipline of the BEF', 67-117, 121-57, 212-62, 310-13.

[27] For examples of unrest in England during the training period, see Simkins, *Kitchener's Army*, 200-1, 243-4; also Gloden Dallas and Douglas Gill, *The Unknown Army: Mutinies in the British Army in World War I* (London, 1985), 40-5.

[28] William Allison and John Fairley, *The Monocled Mutineer* (London, 1978), contains no source notes but includes hearsay evidence and is inaccurate in several key details. The BBC television drama series of the same title, and based partly upon the book, was produced in 1986.

[29] Dallas and Gill, *The Unknown Army*, 63-83, 139-40; see also their 'Mutiny at Etaples Base in 1917', *Past and Present*, 69 (1975), 88-112.

Notwithstanding the fact that the files relating to capital courts martial have remained closed to the general public, a handful of books have investigated the individual fates of 346 men, including three officers, who were shot by the British Army for desertion, cowardice, mutiny, or other offences during the 1914-18 war. The author of one such book, Judge Anthony Babington, was permitted to look at the relevant documents, so long as he refrained from naming the soldiers concerned or from precisely identifying their units. Though denied similar access to the records, Julian Putkowski and Julian Sykes, following much diligent detective work, have recently decided to disclose most of the names and units in question. The evidence presented by these writers is certainly disturbing as, in nearly every instance, the Army's court martial procedures seem to have hampered the chances of a fair trial. An adequate defence for the accused was rare and insufficient account was taken of the effects of shell-shock or the strain of prolonged trench warfare on the conduct of some soldiers whose behaviour had otherwise been exemplary. Conversely, it is difficult to accept that *all* were 'victims' of an unforgiving military system. A number were executed for murder and others were previous offenders who had clearly stretched Army tolerance to the limit. Even Putkowski and Sykes, who press for the complete exoneration of the executed men, repeat John Terraine's reminder that 90 per cent of the 3,080 death sentences passed between 1914 and 1920 were commuted. The strength of Babington's arguments is weakened by his use of a curious collection of secondary sources for background information. These are seen by Terraine as selective and outdated and Babington's approach as being in the 'emotional manner of the Disenchantment school of writers' of the 1930s. None of the recent works on capital courts martial satisfactorily correlates the detailed story of those who were executed to the overall question of morale and discipline in the BEF and a major study which knits together the precise and the general aspects is still awaited.[30]

Various explanations have been offered as to why, despite disturbances and indiscipline, the British Army managed to avoid the sort of collapse that afflicted the armies of most of the other major belligerents in the

---

[30] See in particular Anthony Babington, *For the Sake of Example: Capital Courts Martial, 1914-1920* (London, 1983); Julian Putkowski and Julian Sykes, *Shot at Dawn* (Barnsley, 1989). William Moore's *The Thin Yellow Line* (London, 1974) fails to utilize much relevant material which is available in the Public Record Office. For comments on Babington's book see Keith Simpson's invaluable annotated bibliography of the British Army, 1914-18, in *A Nation in Arms*, 252, and John Terraine's review in *Journal of the Royal United Services Institute for Defence Studies*, 129 (1984), 81-2.

First World War. Liddle, for one, rejects the idea that every soldier reacted with 'automatically triggered outrage' to the horrors of war or that disillusionment was universal. Naïve early enthusiasm was succeeded by a stoic, if grudging, readiness to 'stick it out' in the hearts and minds of the majority of British soldiers by 1917-18. Liddle is probably right to infer that the front-line soldier, with his restricted horizon, was not generally concerned with the 'great issues' but rather with making the conditions of his daily existence marginally less unpleasant. Food, drink, warmth, security, links with home, and the respect of one's pals were the things which preoccupied the average soldier.[31] Beckett summarizes the principal characteristics of the British working-class civilian soldier of the period as being 'a phlegmatic acceptance of fate or sheer bloodymindedness' mixed always with sardonic humour. A discernible sense of duty and loyalty motivated many, while the British regimental system, from which men drew a robust feeling of local as much as national identity, was undeniably a key element in upholding morale. None of this is to underplay the value of leadership, especially at company and platoon level, which is seen by John Keegan as perhaps 'of higher quality and greater military significance in the First World War, at least in the British army, than before or since'.[32] Given that the social composition of the officer corps had widened somewhat, albeit temporarily, under the impact of casualties by 1918, one recent study submits that the officers themselves were sustained throughout by the ideals and notions of leadership taught by the public schools. The stress of war may have caused some to become sceptics, but the majority of young officers held on to their beliefs: 'The schools and their ethos exacted a loyalty which seems to have been virtually unshakeable.'[33]

Whatever their line of approach, British military historians are in broad agreement that the nature of British society in 1914-18 provided a bedrock of social cohesion which prevented the BEF from total collapse, even during the crisis of March and April 1918. There may be some truth in the view that the huge network of welfare facilities—including canteens and YMCA and Church Army huts—as well as the provision of concert parties and organized sports, offered the British soldier

[31] Liddle, *The Soldier's War*, 206-7, 216.
[32] Beckett, 'The Nation in Arms', 24-5; Simkins, *Kitchener's Army*, 64, 317; Keegan, *The Face of Battle*, 272; see also John Baynes, *Morale: A Study of Men and Courage: The Second Scottish Rifles at the Battle of Neuve Chapelle, 1915* (London, 1967), 253-4.
[33] Peter Parker, *The Old Lie: The Great War and the Public School Ethos* (London, 1987), 283-4.

comfortingly familiar recreational and cultural outlets which were not enjoyed to the same extent by men of other armies.[34] Dr. J. M. Winter postulates that the comparative stability of the British Army stemmed from the fact that it was largely manned by what was probably the most highly disciplined industrial labour force in the world. His namesake, Denis Winter, finds the explanation in the habits of 'sturdy and cheerful deference' which were, he claims, features of Edwardian England. Acceptance of fate by 'a relatively static, tradition-oriented people' was, he proclaims, a vital source of strength to the British Army.[35]

Battle and campaign studies have always been recognized as a point of entry for those wishing to examine the front-line soldier's experience. In this category, John Keegan's *The Face of Battle* and Martin Middlebrook's *The First Day on the Somme* are arguably two of the most popular and—in different ways—influential books on First World War topics to have been published since the mid-1960s. Keegan's chapter on the Somme forms only one section of a much wider survey, which also covers Agincourt and Waterloo, but, like Middlebrook, he chooses to concentrate on 1 July 1916, the bloodiest day in the British Army's history. Keegan offers a masterly analysis of the tactics and motivation of the British divisions which attacked on that day, while Middlebrook—in what Keegan himself describes as 'a truly heroic effort of historical fieldwork'—draws on the personal experiences of 526 British soldiers and twenty Germans to produce an account which possesses both power and sensitivity. Admittedly most of Middlebrook's evidence comes from junior officers and other ranks who had a limited perspective and grasp of events on the day itself. Yet the many individual stories he quotes are skilfully threaded together to yield a much more rounded picture of Britain's citizen soldiers of 1916 than most previous historians had presented. He is perceptive enough to question the inaccurate but lingering popular impression that the New Army divisions were all merely bands of 'uniformed innocents', as even Keegan calls them. After noting that the 18 and 36 Divisions, two of the most effective on 1 July, had *not* conformed blindly to the Fourth Army's Tactical Notes, Middlebrook adds: 'It is possible that the intelligence of the New Army men proved, on this occasion, more successful than the blind obedience of the Regulars.'[36]

[34] Beckett, 'The Nation in Arms', 25.
[35] J. M. Winter, *The Experience of World War I* (London, 1988), 159; Denis Winter, *Death's Men*, 229, 234.
[36] Keegan, *The Face of Battle*, 204-84, particularly pp. 215-25 and 257-8; Middlebrook, *The First Day on the Somme, passim*. For Middlebrook's remarks about the initiative shown by the 18 and 36 Divisions see p. 279.

Middlebrook employs the same methodology in *The Kaiser's Battle*, his book on the first day of the German offensive in March 1918. Again he concentrates on the experiences of individuals and small units but here—to an even greater extent than in his study of the Somme—the evidence he has garnered plainly exposes the limitations of the British unit war diaries and published histories as source material. As one of several cases in point, he reminds us that the regimental history of the Royal Inniskilling Fusiliers describes the 2 Battalion's action at Boadicea Redoubt on 21 March in terms of an epic last stand, in which there were 'very few of the defenders left alive and unwounded'. In reality, Middlebrook maintains, the garrison filed out of the redoubt after a negotiated surrender, at least 16 officers and 500 men of the battalion being captured. He concludes that the 'hybrid' British Army of March 1918 was indeed 'tired and war weary', and that it did collapse prematurely in many places, its 'threshold of resistance' having been eroded.[37]

The main problems with Middlebrook's approach are that his First World War studies dwell on British disasters and defeats rather than victories, and deal primarily with one day of battle. Illuminating and highly readable as they are, the books leave fellow historians wishing that the author had opted for slightly wider terms of reference as he has in one or two of his later works.[38] John Terraine, for example, has been at pains to show that the 'true texture' of the Somme lies not in the story of the first day but in the remaining four and a half months, when some 330 counter-attacks irretrievably blunted the cutting-edge of the German army.[39] Similarly, it is frustrating that Middlebrook has not used his undoubted historical talents to explain how the 'war-weary' veterans and raw conscripts of March 1918 came to play such an important part in the defeat of the Germans on the Western Front after August of that year.

Along with Middlebrook, Lyn Macdonald can justly claim to have played a leading part in re-awakening popular interest in the Great War. Her canvas is always broader than Middlebrook's and, although she generally adopts a less analytical or argumentative stance, she is adept at providing a straightforward narrative framework within which individual participants in the First World War are allowed, as far as possible, to relate their own experiences. Apart from her books on Passchendaele, the Somme, and the 1914 campaign, she has tackled a long-neglected

[37] Middlebrook, *The Kaiser's Battle*, 326-39.
[38] See e.g. Middlebrook's study of a phase of the strategic bombing offensive against Germany in *The Berlin Raids: RAF Bomber Command, Winter 1943-44* (London, 1988).
[39] Terraine, *The Smoke and the Fire*, 111-25.

aspect of the war in *The Roses of No Man's Land*, a sympathetic study of British casualties and the men *and women* who tended them. Lyn Macdonald has done as much as any author to reveal the many-sided nature of the front-line experience. It is not hard to see why her books have a large circulation, for the soldiers' own oral and written reminiscences which she uses obviously have an immediacy and a direct appeal for general readers, who can often identify more closely with the originators of such testimony than with other sources of evidence.[40]

A welcome sign of the depth of the fresh wave of interest is the publication of a number of new divisional and battalion histories, most of which have been produced by non-professional historians. On the divisional front, Colin Hughes has gone a long way towards rebuilding the reputation of the 38 (Welsh) Division, which was unfairly criticized for its performance at Mametz Wood between 7 and 9 July 1916.[41] Philip Orr's work on the 36 (Ulster) Division bravely questions the traditional explanation that the unit's achievements on 1 July 1916 were entirely the product of political and religious fervour and a unique *esprit de corps*. Orr argues that even the most highly motivated troops cannot always succeed in the face of a storm of bullets and shells. What counted most was the decision at Divisional Headquarters to send the men out into no man's land before the barrage lifted.[42] A remarkable series of books on individual 'Pals' battalions of the 31 Division has also been published since 1986. The three produced to date all deal with battalions of the 94 Brigade which was involved in the ill-fated attack on Serre on 1 July 1916. Each gives an extremely detailed picture of the raising and training of the battalions concerned and each contains a mass of newly discovered evidence, testifying to the assiduous research of the respective authors.[43] Unfortunately, they succumb to the tyrannical

[40] Besides those works by Lyn Macdonald already mentioned in the text or in n. 10, above, see also her *1914* (London, 1987). Philip Warner's *The Battle of Loos* (London, 1976) reconstructs the story of this long-neglected battle largely through the words of participants. It contains much previously unpublished material, most of the evidence being in the form of reminiscences in letters written to Warner following his appeal in the press in 1975. However, although Warner provides a fairly brief survey of the battle at the beginning of the book, there is no linking narrative in the body of the work. The author's remarks on the fighting between 27 Sept. and 14 Oct. 1915 are restricted to four short paragraphs and there is little real operational analysis. A definitive work on Loos is still to be written.

[41] Colin Hughes, *Mametz: Lloyd George's 'Welsh Army' at the Battle of the Somme* (Gerrards Cross, 1982).

[42] Philip Orr, *The Road to the Somme: Men of the Ulster Division Tell their Story* (Belfast, 1987), esp. pp. 129-32, 181-2, 200-1.

[43] Jon Cooksey, *Pals: The 13th and 14th Battalions, York and Lancaster Regiment* (Barnsley, 1986); William Turner, *Pals: The 11th (Service) Battalion (Accrington), East*

hold which July 1916 is now beginning to exert on British First World War studies—possibly the least desirable consequence of the trend-setting works of Keegan and Middlebrook. William Turner, for example, covers the post-Serre operational experiences of the Accrington Pals in sixteen out of over two hundred and fifty pages, and Orr devotes only eight pages to the story of the 36 Division after the Somme.[44] Another battalion study confined very largely to the Somme period is Alex Aiken's *Courage Past*, which looks at the operations of the 1/9 Highland Light Infantry (Glasgow Highlanders) at High Wood on 14 and 15 July.[45] John Baynes, himself an Army officer until 1972, has contributed a stimulating analysis of the factors affecting the morale and performance of the 2 Battalion of his own regiment—the Scottish Rifles—at Neuve Chapelle in 1915. One of the few unit-orientated studies with a wider scope is Sidney Allinson's book on the British and Canadian 'Bantam' formations. This incorporates some fascinating new material, including many personal accounts relating to the battlefield performance of the 35 and 40 Divisions, and helps to clarify why the authorities were unable to sustain the original Bantam concept as the supply of recruits of the requisite physical quality declined. Last, but by no means least in this category, is the scholarly research done by Gary Sheffield into the history of the 22 Battalion of the Royal Fusiliers, a New Army unit raised in Kensington. Sheffield establishes that this battalion placed greater reliance than many British units on self-discipline and informal officer-man relationships and, in this regard, resembled Australian and Canadian battalions rather than British Regular formations.[46]

The lengthy shadow of C. E. W. Bean continues to fall across much Australian writing on the Great War. So far as that conflict is concerned, Bean, the editor of the Australian official histories and the author of the Gallipoli and Western Front volumes, can perhaps be described as the creator and greatest exponent of the 'everyman at war' approach, with his emphasis on the tactical side of operations and the inclusion of

---

Lancashire Regiment (Barnsley, 1987); Ralph Gibson and Paul Oldfield, *Sheffield City Battalion: The 12th (Service) Battalion, York and Lancaster Regiment* (Barnsley, 1988).

[44] Orr, *The Road to the Somme*, 202-9; Turner, *Pals*, 169-84.

[45] Alex Aiken, *Courage Past: A Duty Done* (Glasgow, 1971).

[46] Baynes, *Morale*, 3-10, 165-6, 253-4; Allinson, *The Bantams*, esp. pp. 105-29, 142-74, 226-76; G. D. Sheffield, 'The Effect of War Service on the 22nd Royal Fusiliers (Kensington), with special reference to Morale, Discipline and the Officer-Man Relationship', MA thesis (Leeds, 1985); see also Sheffield and G. I. S. Inglis (eds.), *From Vimy Ridge to the Rhine: The Great War Letters of Christopher Stone DSO, MC* (Marlborough, 1989), 14-16.

personal details about individual participants. Convinced that the success of Australian troops derived from the unique Australian character—itself a product of 'bush' values and egalitarianism—Bean resolved to celebrate the deeds of the front-line soldiers of the AIF. In this way, as Peter Dennis and Jeffrey Grey note in a recent survey, Bean propagated the 'digger myth' that has since been 'a potent force in the development of an Australian consciousness'.[47] Jane Ross, who has examined the main components of the 'myth' without actually seeking to measure its truth, comments that the rowdy, laconic Australian private soldier, contrasted to the 'stiff' British officer, has become a national stereotype. According to Dr Ross, the essential qualities of the 'digger' embraced a deep dependence on 'mateship'; dash and aggression in battle; a desire to know the reason for orders; impatience with orthodox military discipline and 'spit and polish'; the lack of social divisions between officers and men; and a conviction that authority should be based on competence. The fact that British methods were often unsuccessful and proved unsuitable for Anzac social conditions and customs led Australians to be more confidently nationalistic in their military style, tactics, and discipline by the end of the war. Moreover, the speed at which the Anzac experience was mythologized seems to reveal Australian eagerness for confirmation of their national identity.[48] Both Bean and Dr Ross receive some backing from Suzanne Welborn, whose study of Western Australia at war not only suggests that the best soldiers did indeed come from the country areas, but also that—even during the war—Western Australians at least were acting out a stereotype role which they clearly already wanted to believe.[49]

Not all Australian historians have allowed Bean to remain unchallenged. In the early 1970s, L. L. Robson demonstrated that Bean's statements about the rural origins of some members of the AIF were inaccurate. Robson shows, in addition, that the highest single occupational and state group in the AIF consisted of industrial workers from New South Wales, and that in Victoria, the next biggest source of recruits, significantly few men were engaged in farming. Statistical evid-

[47] Peter Dennis and Jeffrey Grey, 'Australian and New Zealand Writing on the First World War', in Rohwer (ed.), *Neue Forschungen zum Ersten Weltkrieg*, 2.
[48] Jane Ross, *The Myth of the Digger: The Australian Soldier in Two World Wars* (Sydney, 1985), 11-12, 19-20, 24-5, 34-5, 44. See also K. S. Inglis, 'The Anzac Tradition', *Meanjin Quarterly*, 24/1 (1965), 25-44; Geoffrey Serle, 'The Digger Tradition and Australian Nationalism', *Meanjin Quarterly*, 24/2 (1965), 149-58.
[49] Suzanne Welborn, *Lords of Death: A People, A Place, A Legend* (Fremantle, 1982), *passim*.

ence similarly indicates that Australian officers were not so democratic in origin and character as Bean leads us to imagine.[50] It would appear, however, that the impact of Robson's research has been relatively limited. Bill Gammage's *The Broken Years*, published in 1974, is one of the most widely acclaimed of all recent Australian books on the First World War. Based primarily on the diaries and letters of over one thousand soldiers of the AIF, the book vividly portrays the experiences and attitudes of Australians on active service but, in most respects, diverges little from the path laid down by Bean.[51] In *The Anzacs*, Patsy Adam-Smith is refreshingly prepared to strip away some of the more romanticized elements of the Anzac legend.[52] Peter Charlton's work on the Australians at Pozières in 1916 differs from Bean in as much as Charlton dates Australian disillusionment with British methods and command from that time rather than from the fighting at Anzac Cove a year earlier. Charlton also tries to place the Australian achievements at Pozières in the context of a coalition war: 'to treat it as solely an Australian victory is to ignore the very substantial British contribution in this sector of the Somme before 23 July 1916'.[53] But, in the opinion of Peter Dennis and Jeffrey Grey, a comparative approach is still sorely needed to test many of the cherished beliefs about Australian military performance 'and to examine critically the Bean thesis, so central to Australian perceptions'.[54]

Reviewing Charlton's book in 1987, Dr David French made the important point that the Australian divisions, unlike the British, usually fought together under the same Corps Headquarters and so had greater opportunities to learn from their own mistakes and mould their experiences into a common doctrine.[55] These remarks can also be applied to Canadian units, as Desmond Morton and Stephen Harris affirm in

[50] L. L. Robson, 'The Origin and Character of the First AIF, 1914-18: Some Statistical Evidence', *Historical Studies, Australia and New Zealand*, 15/61 (1975), 737-49; see also Robson, *The First AIF: A Study of its Recruitment, 1914-1918* (Carlton, 1970).

[51] Gammage, *The Broken Years, passim*; Dennis and Grey, 'Australian and New Zealand Writing on the First World War', 3.

[52] Patsy Adam-Smith, *The Anzacs*, esp. pp. vii-viii, 122-7. For example, when discussing John Simpson Kirkpatrick, the 'Man with the Donkey' on Gallipoli, Patsy Adam-Smith remarks that many may wish she had not written of him as 'a boozer, a brawler, a rowdy stoker-type larrikin. But that is what he was. He was never the delicate, aesthetic visionary the artists and eulogists have recorded'. Simpson was, in fact, an Englishman from South Shields.   [53] Peter Charlton, *Pozières 1916*, 311.

[54] Dennis and Grey, 'Australian and New Zealand Writing', 5.

[55] David French, review of Peter Charlton's *Pozières 1916*, in *Journal of the Royal United Services Institute for Defence Studies*, 132 (Mar. 1987), 86-7.

articles which highlight the changing relationship of the Canadian Expeditionary Force, and its principal component—the Canadian Corps —to the British Army of the First World War.[56] Harris contends that the CEF was helped by the country's militia tradition. Less governed by inappropriate lessons from past campaigns than the British, he argues, the officers and men of the Canadian units in France and Belgium had freer rein for their native talents and abilities to solve problems and overcome obstacles. Acceptance of common sense and initiative encouraged Canadian officers to embrace the idea that detailed information about operational objectives should be passed on to other ranks.[57]

The storming of Vimy Ridge in April 1917 inevitably looms large in Canadian First World War studies. Two of the most readable accounts of the battle to have been published in recent decades are those by Alexander McKee and Pierre Berton, both of whom make considerable use of oral history interviews in relating the experiences of those who took part in the assault. Berton's bestselling book on the subject is marred, however, by his tendency to snipe at the British Army whenever an opportunity arises. References to haughty and 'stiff-necked' British officers, for example, are liberally scattered throughout the text.[59] Berton also seems to have much in common with Bean, particularly in the manner in which he describes the citizen-soldiers of his blossoming nation. He states that, to a very large extent, the men who fought at Vimy had worked on the land and were accustomed to hard work and rough conditions. A good proportion had known what it was like to sleep in the open, eat cold food in the wilderness and, 'in many cases, to knock over a deer with a rifle'. He does concede, on the other hand, that men of British birth or descent were heavily represented in the Canadian Corps at Vimy Ridge.[60] Research carried out by Brown and Loveridge reinforces this latter point. Nearly half of the men of Canada's First

---

[56] Desmond Morton, 'Junior but Sovereign Allies: The Transformation of the Canadian Expeditionary Force, 1914-1918', *Journal of Imperial and Commonwealth History*, 8 (1979), 56-67; Stephen Harris, 'From Subordinate to Ally: The Canadian Corps and National Autonomy, 1914-1918', *Revue internationale d'histoire militaire*, 51 (1982), 109-30. See also Cooke, 'Canada's Historiography and the First World War', in Rohwer, *Neue Forschungen*, 229-41.

[57] Harris, 'From Subordinate to Ally', 118-25. See also Kenneth C. Eyre, 'Staff and Command in the Canadian Corps', MA thesis (Duke, 1967); William Stewart, 'Attack Doctrine in the Canadian Corps, 1916-1918', MA thesis (New Brunswick, 1982).

[58] Alexander McKee, *Vimy Ridge* (London, 1966); also Pierre Berton, *Vimy*, (Harmondsworth, 1987).

[59] See Berton, *Vimy*, 49-50, 61, 63, 160-1, 236-7, 298.

[60] Ibid. 27-8.

Contingent were recruited in the western provinces, where the depression troubling the country in 1914 was most severe. The number of single British-born male immigrants in these provinces was also significantly higher than in the east. Thus, unemployment and the patriotic response of British settlers together account for the extraordinarily large contribution of the western provinces to the early phases of the Canadian voluntary recruiting campaign. Brown and Loveridge observe that almost 60 per cent of the First Contingent had been born in the British Isles. Where they give a different impression to that created by Berton is in their well-documented evidence that more than 60 per cent of the recruits in the First Contingent were raised in urban areas, nearly one-third of the men coming from industrialized Ontario. Even during the second phase of recruiting, which began even before the First Contingent reached England, well over half of those joining up in the western provinces enlisted in battalions which recruited exclusively in urban areas.[61]

Of all the Dominion contributions to the Allied cause in the First World War, that of New Zealand was second to none. By the Armistice, New Zealand had sent 19.4 per cent of her men, compared to 13.5 per cent from Canada and Australia and 11.1 per cent of white South African males. Proportionately, New Zealand also suffered the heaviest casualties.[62] Bean regarded the New Zealanders as colourless, although the early recruits, according to one historian, were, as a group, 'a bit wild, as indiscipline in Dunedin; drunkenness and lechery in Wellington; thieving and looting in Samoa; and venereal disease and (consequent) rioting in Cairo all testify'.[63] Robert Rhodes James claims that, on Gallipoli, New Zealanders saw themselves as the pick of the Dominion contingents, combining the dash of the Australians with 'the meticulous professionalism of the British troops'. Despite the rigours of Gallipoli, the subsequent demands of the Western Front, and the exacerbation of social divisions at home by the conscription issue, the New Zealand Division was probably the only Allied division at full strength at the Armistice.[64] For all this, only two interrelated books on the front-line

[61] Robert Craig Brown and Donald Loveridge, 'Unrequited Faith: Recruiting the CEF, 1914-1918', *Revue internationale d'histoire militaire*, 51 (1982), 53-79.
[62] Paul Baker, *King and Country Call: New Zealanders, Conscription and the Great War* (Auckland, 1988), 138; Dennis and Grey, 'Australian and New Zealand Writing', 2, 6; Shadbolt, *Voices of Gallipoli*, 122.
[63] Baker, *King and Country Call*, 17; Fewster, *Gallipoli Correspondent*, 39.
[64] Robert Rhodes James, *Gallipoli* (London, 1965), 172; Ross, *The Myth of the Digger*, 50; Baker, *King and Country Call*, 137.

experience of New Zealand soldiers have emerged in the past decade or so, and both deal only with the Dardanelles campaign. Christopher Pugsley, a professional officer in the New Zealand Army, offers a balanced and well-researched treatment of his countrymen's role on the Gallipoli Peninsula, and concludes that 8 August, the anniversary of the fleeting New Zealand success on the heights of Chunuk Bair in 1915, would be a more fitting date for celebration and commemoration in New Zealand than the more familiar Anzac Day on 25 April.[65] An altogether angrier book has been produced by Maurice Shadbolt, who worked closely with Pugsley on a television documentary about New Zealanders on Gallipoli. As the author himself warns, those 'who wish for a dispassionate account of the Gallipoli campaign of 1915 had best look elsewhere'.[66] Shadbolt's own commentary on the campaign is certainly written in the embittered style of the 'Donkeys' school of military historians of the early 1960s, but anyone who doubts the value of oral history should sample the reminiscences of the twelve veterans featured in the book. It is difficult to find more vigorous and moving evocations of front-line combat or the ravages of sickness than those presented here, even if criticisms of British troops and commanders permeate each individual testimony.

New Zealand's contribution may have received scant attention, but other contingents have fared worse. Although two general surveys of the Indian Army include some coverage of the First World War, published work on the history of the Indian Corps on the Western Front appears to be restricted to a brief article dealing with the British high command's policy on the issues of cross-racial contacts.[67] The role of the South African Brigade, which fought as part of the 9 (Scottish) Division on the Western Front, has been more generously treated of late with the publication of Ian Uys's book *Delville Wood*. The brigade began the action at Delville Wood on 14 July 1916 with 121 officers and 3,052 other ranks: it came out six days later with two wounded officers and 140 other ranks. Uys gives a detailed description of each day's savage fighting in turn, from Brigade Headquarters down to battalion and company level. This method permits him to incorporate the personal

[65] Christopher Pugsley, *Gallipoli: The New Zealand Story* (Auckland, 1984), 21.
[66] Shadbolt, *Voices of Gallipoli*, 7.
[67] Philip Mason, *A Matter of Honour: An Account of the Indian Army, its Officers and Men* (London, 1974); T. A. Heathcote, *The Indian Army: The Garrison of British Imperial India, 1822-1922* (Newton Abbot, 1974); Jeffrey Greenhut, 'Race, Sex and War: The Impact of Race and Sex on Morale and Health Services for the Indian Corps on the Western Front, 1914', *Military Affairs*, 45/2 (1981), 71-4.

stories of many of the individuals involved, but the accounts of the fighting are weakened by the repetitive nature of much of the evidence and by the overall lack of editorial discipline and analysis.[68]

Whereas the capture of Vimy Ridge is remembered by Canadians as a landmark in their national history, British popular perceptions of the First World War are still stuck fast in the mud of Passchendaele or coloured by the bloody ordeal of Kitchener's Army on the Somme. Bungling generals and futile attacks in Flanders are the images which, to this day, almost immediately take shape in the minds of most British people whenever the Great War is mentioned. One would never, of course, seek to underplay the recurrent tragedies and horrors of the front-line soldier's experience during the war. Nevertheless, defeats and disasters have a remarkable fascination for the British. Apart from students of military history, probably not more than one or two British citizens in every ten thousand could name the year in which the Battles of the Canal du Nord and St Quentin Canal or the Battle of the Selle took place, let alone discuss their significance. Thus—the herculean efforts of John Terraine notwithstanding—Field Marshal Sir Douglas Haig remains in the British folk-memory as the 'villain' of the Somme and Passchendaele rather than as the victor of the 'Hundred Days'. Nor is this historical masochism and ignorance necessarily restricted to the proverbial man or woman on the Clapham omnibus. Even during the great attrition battles of 1916 and 1917 there were both small- and large-scale British successes on the Western Front other than those at Vimy Ridge and Messines Ridge. One could point, for instance, to the tactical initiative and flexibility displayed by the Royal Naval Division at Beaucourt and Gavrelle; to the consistently high level of performance of the 18 Division, under Major-General Sir Ivor Maxse, throughout the Battle of the Somme; or to the 3½-mile advance of 17 Corps towards Fampoux on 9 April 1917, the deepest penetration on the Western Front in one day since 1914. Yet, while the achievements of the Australian and Canadian Corps are widely acknowledged, these operations have barely attracted a second glance from the majority of British military historians in recent years.

Part of the explanation for this state of affairs lies in the way that teachers of First World War history, particularly at secondary school level, continue to approach the subject in Britain. The most familiar view from the trenches is still that depicted by Graves, Sassoon, Owen,

[68] Ian Uys, *Delville Wood* (Johannesburg, 1983). For the casualty statistics quoted here, see pp. x, 274-87.

and other soldier-poets and novelists. Theirs is the 'voice of outraged middle-class protest' which we most commonly hear.[69] Theirs is the 'cry of disillusion' which gives much Great War literature 'its impetus, its power, its poignance and its dominant mode of irony'.[70] But, as several recent commentators have emphasized, Graves, Sassoon, and their ilk were nearly all officers from an educated class with an awareness of literature. To regard them as typical of the majority of men who served in the British Army between 1914 and 1918 is probably quite misleading.[71] The legacy of the literature of disillusionment is that, because of our inherited guilt and revulsion, we go on seeing the First World War as we think it ought to have been, not as it actually was.

Professional military historians must bear some of the responsibility for the current imbalance of British First World War studies. It is perhaps appropriate to note that approximately half of the works covered by this chapter—and *most* of the books which have reached a general, rather than a specialist, readership—have been produced by writers and historians based outside universities, museums, or the war studies departments of military academies. Although the pattern is undoubtedly changing, research on the high command, strategy, organization, doctrine, and civil-military relations still tends to hold sway over battle studies. As a result, the great personal experience archives assembled in the past two decades are virgin territory for many postgraduates working on the First World War, and all too few military historians in this country possess *intimate* knowledge of the tactical and sociological factors affecting the conduct of units in battle.

[69] Martin Stephen, *Never Such Innocence*, 6.
[70] Parker, *The Old Lie*, 27. See also Paul Fussell, *The Great War and Modern Memory* (Oxford, 1975), 18-35. An interesting general study, which examines aspects and consequences of combat from French, German, and American standpoints as well as British, is Eric J. Leed's *No Man's Land: Combat and Identity in World War I* (Cambridge, 1979). Almost wholly based on published sources, it looks at some of the central and common features of the front-line experience, such as comradeship, death, separation from home, and the shattering of most conventions and codes of normal life. The author highlights the contrast between the ideals of the generation of 1914 and the realities of the modern industrialized war awaiting them. However, more recent research suggests that, in Britain at least, the motivation of those who went to war or volunteered in 1914 was far more varied, and certainly not always as innocent or romantic, as previously assumed. Here too there is room for doubt as to whether Leed's sources are drawn from a sufficiently wide spectrum to represent the great mass of soldiery on either side of No Man's Land.
[71] Beckett, 'The British Army, 1914-18', in Turner (ed.), *Britain and the First World War*, 100, 107; Winter, *The Great War and the British People*, 284, 289-304; Stephen, *Never Such Innocence*, 9-11; Parker, *The Old Lie*, 25-6; Simpson, 'The British Soldier on the Western Front', 135, 153-5.

The study of strategy, grand tactics, and command decisions will not illuminate all the issues raised by First World War battles. Research on the experience of front-line soldiers is also crucial to any analysis of the reasons for variations in battlefield performance. What motivates a unit to do well, or causes it to do badly, in a particular battle? What are the effects of continuity or changes of command at divisional, battalion, or company level? How far were other ranks briefed about their objectives or allowed to rehearse operations? What was the quality of a unit's officers and NCOs? Did the unit have good or sufficient equipment? What part did regimental tradition play in battlefield morale? Did the unit have social cohesion? If so, was this based on a shared occupational or geographical background among its citizen soldiers? How was the unit affected by casualties? How often did a particular battalion successfully carry out its orders? These, and many similar questions can be answered just as easily—and often more fully answered—from personal experience sources. The clues may not always be found in individual letters, diaries, unpublished memoirs, or oral history recordings but rather by what Dr Paddy Griffith has called 'tactical snippeting', the painstaking analysis of sometimes minute detail in a whole range of such sources.[72] Unless scholars in Britain and elsewhere brace themselves to undertake the necessary comparative research and produce more operational histories and studies of battlefield performance, many of the current myths and half-truths about the First World War are likely to prevail.

[72] Paddy Griffith, *Rally Once Again: Battle Tactics of the American Civil War* (Marlborough, 1987), 193-6.

INDEX

Compiled by Andrew Orgill

AIF, see Australian Imperial Forces
Abdullah, King 251
Adam-Smith, Patsy 291
  Anzacs, The 307
Addison, Christopher:
  Four and a Half Years 96
  Politics from Within 96
Adventure (Seely) 93
Aiken, Alex:
  Courage Past: a Duty Done 305
Akaba, fall of 237, 239, 247, 250, 257
Albertini, Luigi:
  Origins of the War of 1914 286
Aldington, Richard 4, 212, 252, 257, 259
  Death of a Hero, The 243
  Lawrence of Arabia: a Biographical Enquiry 212 n., 243-9, 258
Alexander, Field Marshal Earl 85
Alexandretta, proposed landings at 247, 250
Allenby, General Edmund (later Field Marshal Viscount) 4-5, 50, 70, 189-225, 228, 246
  capture of Jerusalem by 189-94
  character of 204, 208-10
  and T. E. Lawrence 211-12
  at Le Cateau 203
  and Archibald Murray 213
  religious impulses of 194
  reputation of 215-25 *passim*
  and third battle of Gaza 198-9
Allenby (Gardner) 216, 223-4
Allenby: a Study in Greatness (Wavell) 215, 219-20
Allenby in Egypt (Wavell) 220, 221
Allenby of Armageddon (Savage) 198, 221-2
Allenby: Soldier and Statesman (Wavell) 220
Allenby's Final Triumph (Massey) 198
Allinson, Sidney:
  Bantams, The 305
Amery, Leo 100, 200 n., 208
  My Political Life 89
Anzacs, The (Adam-Smith) 307

Arab Revolt 236-7, 246, 247, 251, 252, 253, 256
Armageddon 1918 (Falls) 66, 67, 199
Armitage, Flora:
  Desert and the Stars, The 249
Army Diary 1899-1926 (Meinhertzhagen) 223
Art of War, The (Falls) 67
Arthur, Sir George 106, 167-8
  Life of Lord Kitchener 92, 129-30, 167
  Lord Haig 146, 161
Ashmead-Bartlett, Ellis
  Uncensored Dardanelles, The 171
Ashworth, Tony 290, 291
  Trench Warfare 1914-18 295, 296
Aspinall-Oglander, Brig.-Gen. C. F. 107
  Military Operations Gallipoli 169-70, 172
Asquith, Herbert (later Earl of Oxford) 23, 96, 126
  and appointment of Kitchener at the War Office 115
  defence of Churchill by 170
  and French-Kitchener dispute 122, 125, 127, 133-4
  and Gallipoli 177, 186
  Genesis of War, The 93, 105
  Great Shell Story, The 133
  Memories and Reflections 93, 133
  and the War Council 176
Asquith, Margot:
  Autobiography 94, 95, 104
Asquith, Raymond 32, 33, 37
Aston, Maj.-Gen. Sir George
  Memoirs of a Marine 96
Astor, Lady 245
At GHQ (Charteris) 148
Attenborough, Richard 283
  see also *Oh! What a Lovely War* (film)
Auchinleck, Field Marshal Sir Claude 218
August 1914 (Tuchman) 265, 266, 283
Australian Imperial Forces (AIF) 306-7, 309
autobiographies, see memoirs

Autobiography (Asquith, M.) 94, 95, 104
Autobiography (Haldane) 7, 94, 95, 96
BBC 263, 279, 281
BEF, *see* British Expeditionary Force
Babington, Anthony
  For the Sake of Example 300
Backing into the Limelight (Yardley) 254
Balfour, A. J. 36, 126
Ballard, Brig.-Gen. C. R.:
  Kitchener 137
Bantams, The (Allinson) 305
Barbusse, Henri 41, 43, 63
Barnett, Correlli 269, 278, 279, 280, 282, 285, 287
  Swordbearers, The 156, 266, 269
Barraclough, Geoffrey 287
Bartholomew, General 215-16
Battle of Loos, The (Warner) 304
Baynes, John:
  Morale 305
Bean, C. E. W. 79, 100, 305-6, 307
  Story of Anzac, The 167, 173
Beatty, Admiral of the Fleet Earl 107, 108
Beaverbrook, Lord 30, 106, 268
  and access to official sources 5-6
  on Buchan's portrayal of Lloyd George 35
  on Haig 275
  Men in Power 101
  Politicians and the War 89, 90, 92, 93, 104
Beckett, Ian 158, 295, 301
Before the War (Haldane) 99
Bell, A. C.:
  Blockade of the Central Empires 1914-18, The 48
Ben-Moshe, Tuvia 187
Bennett, Winifred 124, 128
Bentley, E. C. 49
Bertie, Lord 120, 133
  Diary of Lord Bertie, The 94
Berton, Pierre
  Vimy 308
Bidwell, Shelford 158, 278
  Firepower 159
biographies:
  motives for writing 97-9
  sales of in the inter-war years 7, 93-5
  value of to historians 111-12

Birdwood, Field Marshal Lord:
  Khaki and Gown 97
Birkenhead, Lord 107
  Turning Points in History, The 100
Bismarck, Prince Otto von 255
Blake, Robert 143, 149, 161, 269
  Private Papers of Douglas Haig, The 82, 151, 152
Blockade of the Central Empires 1914-18, The (Bell) 48
Blumenson, Martin 69
Blunden, Edmund 63, 238
  Undertones of War 43
Boer War 22, 113-15
Bonar Law, Andrew, *see* Law, Andrew Bonar
Bond, Brian 83, 138, 146, 158, 165
Bonham-Carter, Victor 279
  Soldier True: the Life of Field Marshal Sir William Robertson 156, 282
Boraston, Lt.-Col. J. H. 106, 148
  Sir Douglas Haig's Command 1915-18 98, 102, 145
  Sir Douglas Haig's Despatches 144
Brade, Sir Reginald 107
Brent, Peter:
  T. E. Lawrence 254
Brett, Maurice:
  Journals and Letters of Reginald Viscount Esher 93
Britain and the War (Huguet) 135-6
British Broadcasting Corporation, *see* BBC
British Butchers and Bunglers of World War One (Laffin) 11 n.
British Campaigns in Flanders 1690-1794 (Fortescue, J.) 17
British Campaigns in France and Flanders, The (Conan Doyle) 22, 23, 25-7, 28-9, 265
British Documents on the Origins of the War 106
British Expeditionary Force (BEF) 20, 38, 86, 119, 120, 138
  dispute over size of 117
British Strategy and Politics (Guinn) 270
British Strategy and War Aims (French, D.) 10 n., 90, 186-7, 270
Brittain, Vera 55
Broken Years, The (Gammage) 307
Brooke, Rupert 42
Brown, G. M. 31

Brown, Malcolm:
  Christmas Truce 296
  Tommy Goes to War 295
Brown, Robert Craig 308-9
Buchan, John 15, 29-37, 38, 148
  as a historian 16
  History of the Great War 33, 35, 36-7
  Montrose 34
  Nelson's History of the War 7, 29, 30-3, 35
  on the Somme 31-3
  'Victorious General and the Man' (article) 34
Buller, General Sir Redvers 113, 114
Bush, Captain E. W.:
  Gallipoli 182
'Butcher and the Cur' (article by Robert Graves) 11, 267-8
Butterworth, Thornton 92, 93
By Ships Alone (Wallin) 182
Byng, General Sir Julian (later Viscount) 36

CEF, *see* Canadian Expeditionary Force
CID, *see* Committee of Imperial Defence
Cabinet Office 106, 270
Callwell, Maj.-Gen. Sir Charles 93, 106, 167, 180
  Experiences of a Dug Out 98
  Field Marshal Sir Henry Wilson: His Life and Diaries 92, 104-5, 197
  Stray Recollections 98
Cambrai, battle of 79
Campaign in the Mud, The (Lloyd George) 103
Canadian Expeditionary Force (CEF) 308-9
Caporetto 1917 (Falls) 66, 67
Carrington, Charles 63, 244, 265
  Subaltern's War 243
  T. E. Lawrence 243
Cassar, George 116, 130, 137
casualty rates 42, 108, 298
Cavalcade (Coward) 284
censorship 24-5, 91-2, 144, 293
Chamberlain, Austen 91, 107
Chapman-Huston, D.:
  General Sir John Cowans 98
Charge of the Light Brigade (film) 284
Charlton, Peter 291
  Pozières 1916 307

Charteris, Brig.-Gen. John 108, 157, 285
  At GHQ 148
  Field Marshal Earl Haig 147-8, 161
Chetwode, Field Marshal Sir Philip 189, 202 n.
Childs, Maj.-Gen. Sir Wyndham
  Episodes and Reflections 97
Chilton, Charles 281
Christmas Truce (Brown) 296
Churchill, Lady Clementine 181, 182
Churchill, Sir Winston 129, 256
  on Aldington 245
  and collaborators for his books 107-8
  and the Dardanelles and Gallipoli 123, 166, 167, 168-70, 174, 177-82 *passim*, 184, 186, 187
  earnings from books by 96-7
  and the French-Kitchener dispute 121-2, 136
  and V. W. Germains 92
  Great Contemporaries 136, 146, 242
  use of official papers by 5-6, 109
  World Crisis, The 6, 89-90, 93, 94, 95, 99, 106, 146, 165, 168-70
Churchill: a Study in Failure 1900-1939 (Rhodes James) 178
Churchill and the Admirals (Roskill) 182
Clark, The Hon. Alan 8, 67, 152, 264, 286
  Donkeys, The 6, 9, 53, 66, 137, 153, 268
  on the futility of WWI land campaigns 11
Colvin, Ian:
  Life of Lord Carson, The 92-3
Committee of Imperial Defence 19, 63, 64, 71
Conan Doyle, Sir Arthur 15, 22-9, 38, 80
  access of to official papers 23-5
  British Campaigns in France and Flanders, The 22, 23, 25-7, 28-9, 265
  as a historian 16
  To Arms 23
  'Victrix' (poem) 27-8
  Visit to Three Fronts, A 25
  War in South Africa, The 22
Congreve, Sir Walter 72
Connell, John 279, 287
Continental Commitment, The (Howard) 183

Cooksey, Jon:
  Pals: the 13th and 14th Battalions
  York and Lancaster Regiment 304-5
Cooper, A. Duff 108, 148-9
  Haig 97, 98, 149, 150, 161
Cooper, F. H.:
  Khaki Crusaders 191
Corbett, Sir Julian 19, 99
Corbett-Smith, Major A.
  Retreat from Mons, The 131
Courage Past: A Duty Done (Aiken) 305
courts martial 300
Cowans, General Sir John 98
Creedy, Sir Herbert 148
Crown of Honour, The 274
Crozier, F. P.:
  Men I Killed, The 62 n.
Cruttwell, C. R. M. F. 3, 41-3, 53-61, 62, 64, 66
  academic career of 54-5
  on Haig 58
  History of Peaceful Change in the Modern World, A 56
  History of the Great War 1914-18, A 29, 41, 56-61, 195
  and the Lees Knowles Lectures 60
  portrayal of by Evelyn Waugh 53-4
  Role of British Strategy in the Great War, The 60
  War Service of the 1/4 Royal Berkshire Regiment, The 54
Currie, Sir Arthur 81

Dallas, Gloden:
  Unknown Army, The 299
Damn the Dardanelles (Laffin) 182
Danchev, Alex 174
Dardanelles campaign 165-88 *passim*, 310
  see also Gallipoli
Dardanelles Campaign, The (Nevinson) 186-7
Dardanelles Commission 134, 165, 166, 271
Davidson, Maj.-Gen. Sir John:
  Haig: Master of the Field 151, 161
Dawnay, Alan 229
De Groot, Gerard J.:
  Douglas Haig 1861-1928 160-1, 162
de Pass, Frank 42
Death of a Hero (Aldington) 243
Death's Men (Winter) 294, 302
Deedes, W. 223 n.

Deliverance of Jerusalem, The (Masterman) 191
Delville Wood (Uys) 310-11
Dennis, Peter 306, 307
Desert and the Stars, The (Armitage) 249
Dewar, G. A. B. 106
  Sir Douglas Haig's Command 1915-18 98, 102, 145
Dewar, Vice-Admiral Kenneth 107
Diary of Lord Bertie (Gordon-Lennox) 94
Dill, Field Marshal Sir John 83
discipline 299-301
Dixon, Norman:
  On the Psychology of Military Incompetence 158
Dobell, Lt.-Gen. Sir Charles 219
Dockrill, Michael:
  Mirage of Power, The 184
Donkeys, The (Clark) 9, 53, 66, 137, 153, 268
Donop, Sir Stanley von 97
Dorgelès, Roland 41
Douglas Haig (Sixsmith) 157, 161
Douglas Haig as I Knew Him (Duncan) 156, 161
Douglas Haig 1861-1928 (De Groot) 160-1, 162
Douglas Haig: the Educated Soldier (Terraine) 66, 152-3, 154-5, 275-6, 287
Douie, Charles 63
Duncan, G. S.:
  Douglas Haig as I knew Him 156, 161

EEF, see Egyptian Expeditionary Force
Earl Haig (Prothero) 146
Earl Kitchener of Khartoum (Jerrold) 129
'easterners and westerners' dispute 65, 90, 101, 187, 206
Edmonds, Charles (pseudonym), *see* Carrington, Charles
Edmonds, Brig.-Gen. Sir James 19, 27, 63, 69-86, 131, 148, 159
  on Allenby 209
  and assistance to other writers 6, 108
  and Conan Doyle 24
  History of the Civil War in the United States 70
  influence of on British Army doctrine 83-4, 85

Index

loyalty of to Haig 69, 74, 143
Manual of Military Law 70
Military Operations France and
  Belgium 69-75 passim, 143-4, 265
  and the Official History 3-4, 71-5,
    77-8
  and his use of source material 78-9
Egerton, George 89, 103
Egyptian Expeditionary Force (EEF)
  216-17, 218, 257
Elandslaagte, battle of 113
Elliott, Sir John 271
Ellis, John:
  Eye-Deep in Hell 295
Ellison, Sir Gerald:
  Perils of Amateur Strategy, The 171
Englander, David 290
English History 1914-45 (Taylor) 263
Episodes and Reflections (Childs) 97
Erzerum, fall of 247, 250, 253, 254,
  257
Esher, Viscount 71, 94, 118, 167, 177
  Journals and Letters of Reginald
    Viscount Esher 93
  Tragedy of Lord Kitchener 99, 130-1
Essex, Tony 279
Etaples Mutiny 299
Experience of World War I (Winter, J.)
  302
Experiences of a Dug Out (Callwell) 98
Eye-Deep in Hell (Ellis) 295
Eyewitness (Swinton) 99

Face of Battle, The (Keegan) 302
Falls, Cyril 3, 5, 41-3, 61-7, 101, 180,
  198
  Armageddon 1918 66, 67, 199
  Art of War, The 67
  background of 61-2
  Caporetto 1917 66, 67
  First World War, The 41, 64-7
  on Gallipoli 166
  History of the 36th Ulster Division,
    The 62, 63
  Hundred Years of War, A 67
  Military Operations Egypt and
    Palestine 193, 195, 198-9, 201,
    205, 207, 208, 216, 224
  and the Official History 63-4, 75
  on the third battle of Gaza 201, 202
  War Books 43, 62, 63
Feisal, Emir 236, 252, 256, 257
Fergusson, Bernard 286

Field Marshal Earl Haig (Charteris)
  147-8, 161
Field Marshal Lord Kitchener (Grew)
  129
Field Marshal Sir Henry Wilson
  (Callwell) 92, 104-5, 197
First World War: an Illustrated History,
  The (Taylor) 156, 263, 271-3
Fischer, Fritz 59
Fisher, H. A. L. 72
Fisher, Lord 167, 177
Fifth Army, The (Gough) 7, 94, 95-6
Fifth Army in March 1918, The
  (Sparrow) 100
Firepower (Bidwell) 159
First Day on the Somme, The
  (Middlebrook) 291, 302
First World War, The (Falls) 41, 64-7
First World War, The (Repington) 11,
  92, 104, 137
Fitzgerald, Brinsley 127
Flanders 153, 275, 311
Fletcher, Charles 56-7
  Great War 1914-18: a Brief Sketch,
    The 57
Fletcher, Raymond 7, 8, 282-3, 285
Flood, Maj.-Gen. A. Solly 80
Foch, Marechal Ferdinand 52, 65, 125,
  280
Foch: Man of Orleans (Liddell Hart) 45,
  273
Foot Guards, The (Fortescue, J.) 17
For the Sake of Example (Babington) 300
Forbes, A.:
  History of the Army Ordnance
    Services, A 62
Forester, C. S.:
  General, The 210
Fortescue, Granville:
  What of the Dardanelles? 165
Fortescue, The Hon. Sir John 15,
  16-21, 38
  British Campaigns in Flanders
    1690-1794 17
  on Conan Doyle 28-9
  Foot Guards, The 17
  on French's 1914 133
  History of the British Army 16, 19,
    20
  and the Official History 18, 21, 71-2
Four and a Half Years (Addison) 96
Fowler, Bill 292
Fox, Ralph 232

Fraser, Lovat 131
French, David 97, 158, 307
British Strategy and War Aims 10 n.,
  90, 186-7, 270
French, The Hon. Gerald:
  French Replies to Haig 98, 135
  Kitchener-French Dispute: the Last Word, The 135
  Life of Field Marshal Sir John French 135
French, Field Marshal Sir John (later Earl) 86, 113-39 *passim*, 175
  and access to official papers 106
  and the Boer War 113-15
  and Conan Doyle 23, 24
  and disputes with Kitchener 113-29
  1914 (memoirs) 72, 91, 92, 94, 119, 120, 130-4, 144
  and the 'shells scandal' 126-8, 139 n.
  and Smith-Dorrien 118, 119, 131, 134 n.
  War Diaries, Addresses and Correspondence 135
French, Philip 285-6
French and the Dardanelles (Cassar) 181-2
French Replies to Haig (French, G.) 98, 135
From Dreadnought to Scapa Flow (Marder) 177
From Private to Field Marshal (Robertson) 101, 146
From the Dardanelles to Oran (Marder) 182
Fuller, J. F. C. 4, 45, 99, 175, 265, 268
  Memoirs of an Unconventional Soldier 99
Fussell, Paul 2, 8 n.
  Great War and Modern Memory, The 1
  Wartime 1 n.

Gallipoli 4, 6, 47, 50, 123-4, 125, 165-88 *passim*, 297
  New Zealand troops at 309-10
Gallipoli (Bush) 182
Gallipoli (Masefield) 165
Gallipoli (Moorehead) 175, 264
Gallipoli (Rhodes James) 178, 179, 270-1
Gallipoli Diary (Hamilton) 168
Gallipoli Memories (Mackenzie) 173

Gallipoli: the Fading Vision (North) 174
Gallipoli: the New Zealand Story (Pugsley) 310
Galsworthy, John 31
Gammage, Bill:
  Broken Years, The 307
Gardiner, A. G. 102
Gardner, Brian 92
  Allenby 216, 223-4
Garnett, David:
  Letters of T. E. Lawrence 243
Garsia, Colonel C. 201-2
  Key to Victory 202
Garvin, J. L. 107
  Key to Victory: a Study in War Planning 202
gas warfare 58
Gaza, third battle of 201-3, 223
Geddes, Sir Eric 107
General, The (Forester) 210
General Sir John Cowans (Chapman-Huston) 98
Genesis of War, The (Asquith, H.) 93, 105
Genevoix, Maurice 41
George V, King 36, 110, 118, 125, 132, 186
Germains, V. W.:
  Tragedy of Winston Churchill, The 92
  Truth about Kitchener, The 98
Gibbs, Sir Philip:
  Realities of War, The 98
  Struggle in Flanders, The 265
Gibson, Ralph:
  Sheffield City Battalion York and Lancaster Regiment 304-5
Gilbert, Martin:
  Winston Churchill 180-1, 256
Gilbert, V.:
  Romance of the Last Crusade, The 191
Gill, Douglas:
  Unknown Army, The 299
Gooch, John 183
Good-bye to All That (Graves, R.) 2, 231
Gordon-Lennox, Lady Algernon:
  Diary of Lord Bertie, The 94
Gort, Field Marshal Viscount 83
Gough, General Sir Hubert 27, 75, 76, 77, 108
  on Allenby 204

Fifth Army, The 7, 94, 95-6
March Retreat, The 100
Soldiering On 100
Graham, Dominick 53, 158
Firepower 159
Graves, Richard Perceval:
Lawrence of Arabia and His World 254
Graves, Robert 231-8 *passim*, 241, 242, 257, 259
on Aldington 248
'Butcher and the Cur, The' (article) 11, 267-8
Good-bye to All That 2, 231
and his influence on public perception of the war 311-12
Lawrence and the Arabs 7, 231, 233-8, 258
T. E. Lawrence to His Biographers 242
Great Contemporaries (Churchill) 136, 146, 242
Great Shell Story, The (Asquith, H.) 133
Great War, The (television series) 7, 263, 279-81, 289
Great War, The (Terraine) 263
Great War and Modern Memory, The (Fussell) 1
Great War and the British People, The (Winter, J.) 298
Great War 1914-18, The (Fletcher) 57
Greater than Napoleon (Liddell Hart) 49-50
Grew, E. S.:
Field Marshal Lord Kitchener 129
Grey of Falloden, Viscount (formerly Sir Edward Grey) 36, 93, 170, 186
Twenty-Five Years 7, 89, 94, 95, 96, 105-6, 136
Grey, Jeffrey 306, 307
Grierson, Lt.-Gen. Sir James 118
Grieves, Keith:
Politics of Manpower 1914-18, The 90
Griffith, Paddy 313
Grigg, John 10
Guinn, Paul:
British Strategy and Politics 270
Gun Fire (journal) 289
Gwynn, Maj.-Gen. Sir Charles 103

Haggard, Sir H. Rider 31
Haig, Lady Dorothy (Countess) 142, 143, 148-9
Man I Knew, The 150-1, 161
Haig, General Sir Douglas (later Field Marshal Earl) 26, 27, 34, 36, 47, 81, 86, 119, 129, 268, 272-3, 296
and Allenby 203
and his assistance to Churchill 108
criticism of by Lloyd George 150
diaries and letters of 142-3, 150
on Sir John French 128
portrayal of in *Oh! What a Lovely War* 285
religious beliefs of 156
reputation of 9, 11, 53, 58, 60, 67, 69, 73, 74-5, 76, 141-62 *passim*, 275-6, 311
and the Somme 275
Haig (Cooper) 97, 98, 149, 150, 161
Haig as a Military Commander (Marshall-Cornwall) 157, 161
Haig: Master of the Field (Davidson) 151, 161
Haig's Command: a Reassessment (Winter, D.) 162
Haldane, General Sir Aylmer:
Soldier's Saga, A 98
Haldane, R. B. (later Viscount) 31, 115, 122
Autobiography 7, 94, 95, 96
Before the War 99
Haldane of Cloan (Maurice) 92
Hamilton, General Sir Ian 107, 115-16, 123, 133, 187
and Gallipoli 166, 169-76 *passim*, 184
Gallipoli Diary 168
praised by Liddell Hart 50
Hankey, Sir Maurice (later Lord) 91-2, 102, 106, 120, 150, 178, 179, 183
assistance of to other writers 6, 108-11
and Gallipoli 176-9
Supreme Command, The 92, 111, 176-7
Hankey: Man of Secrets (Roskill) 179
Hardy, Thomas 36
Harington, General Sir Charles 'Tim':
Tim Harington Looks Back 97
Harris, Stephen 307-8
Hawkins, Jack 211, 284
Headlam-Morley, Sir James 106, 107
Hejaz railway 247-8
Henderson, Vice-Admiral R. G. H. 107

Herbert, Sir Alfred 107
Herbert, Auberon 32
Histoire de la Grande Guerre sur le Front Occidental (Palat) 51
History Men, The (Kenyon) 2
History of Peaceful Change in the Modern World (Cruttwell) 56
History of the Army Ordnance Services, A (Forbes) 62
History of the British Army (Fortescue, J.) 16, 19, 20
History of the Civil War in the United States (Edmonds) 70
History of the Great War (Buchan) 33, 35, 36-7
History of the Great War 1914-1918, A (Cruttwell) 29, 41, 56-61, 195
History of the 36th (Ulster) Division, The (Falls) 62, 63
History of the World War 1914-18, A 29, 45, 48, 232
Hogarth, D. G. 252
Holmes, Richard 158
　Little Field Marshal: Sir John French, The 138
Hordern, Lt.-Col. Charles 108
Horne, Alistair 279, 280, 286
　Price of Glory, The 264, 266
How I Won the War (film) 284
Howard, Michael 9, 63, 141, 270, 284-5
　Continental Commitment, The 183
Howard-Vyse, General Sir Richard 216
Hughes, Colin:
　Mametz: Lloyd George's 'Welsh Army' at the Battle of the Somme 304
Huguet, Général M. 120, 130
　Britain and the War 135-6
Hundred Years of War, A (Falls) 67
Hunter Weston, Lt.-Gen. Sir A. G. 73
Hynes, Samuel 232

Imperial War Museum 10, 291
Impressions of the Great British Offensive on the Somme (Liddell Hart) 146
In Flanders Fields (Wolff) 66, 137, 153, 264-6, 267
Indian Army 310
Intrigues of War (Maurice) 101
Isherwood, Christopher 232

Jackson, Vice Admiral Sir Henry 107, 177
Jeffery, Keith 104, 158
Jellicoe, Admiral of the Fleet Earl 108, 272
Jerrold, Walter:
　Earl Kitchener of Khartoum 129
Jerusalem, capture of 205 n., 246
　and British propaganda 189-92
　religious imagery in descriptions of 193-6
Jeudwine, Maj.-Gen. H. 24-5
Joffre, Maréchal Joseph 118, 120, 121, 123, 124, 128, 181
Journals and Letters (Esher) 93
Journey's End (Sherriff) 264
Joyce, Colonel P. C. 229
Junger, Ernst 43
junior officers 290, 292
　casualty rates of 298
　see also officers

Kael, Pauline 284
Kahn, Herman
　Thermonuclear War 283
Kaiser's Battle, The (Middlebrook) 303
Kee, Robert 8, 9, 268-9, 274, 275-6, 278, 279
Keegan, John 9, 46, 269, 291, 301
　Face of Battle, The 302
　on Terraine 276-7, 278-9
Kennington, Eric 242
Kenyon, John:
　History Men, The 2
Kerr, Rear Admiral Mark 107
Key to Victory (Garsia) 202
Keyes, Sir Roger:
　Naval Memoirs 173
Keynes, Sir Geoffrey 42
Khaki and Gown (Birdwood) 97
Khaki Crusaders (Cooper) 191
Kiggell, Lt.-Gen. Sir Launcelot 145
Killing Ground, The (Travers) 10 n., 159-60
King and Country (film) 284
Kirke, Lt.-Gen. Sir Walter 84
Kirke Committee 84-5
Kitchener, Field Marshal Lord 18, 113-39 *passim*, 166, 227
　in the Boer War 113-15
　and the Dardanelles and Gallipoli 166, 169-80 *passim*, 183-6

and deployment of the BEF 117
and his relationship with French
117-29
and the 'shells scandal' 126-8, 139 n.
at the War Office 115-16
Kitchener (Ballard) 137
Kitchener: Architect of Victory (Cassar)
138, 139, 184-5
Kitchener Enigma, The (Royle) 137
Kitchener-French Dispute: the Last Word
(French) 135
Kitchener: Portrait of an Imperialist
(Magnus) 137, 175
Kitchener: the Man Behind the Legend
(Warner) 137
Kitchener's Army (Simkins) 10 n.
Knightley, Philip:
*Secret Lives of Lawrence of Arabia,
The* 251-3, 258
Kuhl, Hermann von:
Weltkrieg, Der 51

Laffin, John:
*British Butchers and Bunglers of
World War One* 11 n.
Damn the Dardanelles 182
Lanrezac, Général 118, 119
Lansbury, Edgar 91
Lansdowne, Lord 57-8
Last Crusade, The (Maxwell) 191
Law, Andrew Bonar 99, 104, 106, 126, 132
Lawrence, A. W. 253
T. E. Lawrence by His Friends 242
Lawrence, General Sir Herbert 145
Lawrence, T. E. 4, 51, 80, 205, 212, 227-59
on Allenby 192, 210-11
on Lowell Thomas 228
military thought of 239
Revolt in the Desert 234, 241
Seven Pillars of Wisdom, The 210-12, 229, 232-3, 234, 241, 242, 246, 247, 250, 251, 255, 256
'Twenty-Seven Articles' 251
Lawrence and the Arabs (Graves, R.) 7, 231, 233-8, 258
Lawrence of Arabia (film) 6, 211, 258
*Lawrence of Arabia: a Biographical
Enquiry* (Aldington) 212 n., 243-9, 258
Lawrence of Arabia and his World
(Graves, R. P.) 254

*Lawrence of Arabia: the Authorised
Biography* (Wilson) 4, 255-8
*Lawrence of Arabia: the Man and His
Motive* (Nutting) 250
Le Cateau, battle of 18, 24, 119, 131, 134, 203
Lee, Lord 107
Leed, Eric J.:
*No Man's Land: Combat and Identity
in World War I* 312 n.
Lester, Richard 284
Letters of T. E. Lawrence (Garnett) 243
Lewin, Ronald 138
Liaison 1914 (Spears) 92, 95
Liddell Hart, Sir Basil H. 31, 34, 43-53, 64, 66, 73, 159, 220, 224, 235, 243, 278, 282
on Aldington 244-5
on Allenby 222
Army career of 44-5, 62
background of 41-2
on Buchan 37
and Cruttwell 59-61
on Edmonds' Official History 69-70, 82
Foch: Man of Orleans 45, 273
on Gallipoli 172-3, 178
and *The Great War* (television series) 280
Greater than Napoleon 49-50
on Haig 146-7
on Hamilton 183
and historiography of WWI 6-7
History of the World War 1914-18, A 29, 45, 48, 232
*Impressions of the Great British
Offensive on the Somme* 146
and the Kirke Committee report 85
and T. E. Lawrence 231, 233, 240, 253
and Lloyd George 100, 110-11
on the battle of Meggido 196, 222
on *Oh! What a Lovely War* 285
on the Palestine Campaign 201-2
Paris or the Future of War 45
Real War, The 41, 45, 46-53 *passim*
Reputations: Ten Years After 7, 45, 146, 219, 222
T. E. Lawrence in Arabia and After 45, 231, 234, 238-42, 257, 258
T. E. Lawrence to His Biographers 242
and A. J. P. Taylor 272, 273

324 Index

Liddell Hart, Sir Basil H. (*cont.*)
 Through the Fog of War 45
 War in Outline, The 45, 48, 60
 When Britain goes to War 60
  on Sir Henry Wilson 105
  on Wolff's *In Flanders Fields* 268
Liddle, Peter 10, 291
 Men of Gallipoli 182, 297-8
 Soldier's War 297, 301
Liddle Collection 291 n., 297
Life of Field Marshal Sir John French (French, G.) 135
Life of Lord Carson, The (Colvin) 92-3
Life of Lord Kitchener (Arthur) 92, 129-30, 167
Life of Lord Rawlinson of Trent, The (Maurice) 93, 142
literacy 293-4
Little Field Marshal, The (Holmes) 138
Littlewood, Joan 281-2, 283, 284
Lloyd George, David 25, 107, 126, 141, 144, 145, 159, 272
  on Allenby 205, 210
  and Buchan 37
  Campaign in the Mud, The 103
  defence of Churchill by 170
  and his earnings from books 96-7
  and Gough 76
  and Haig 76, 135, 149-50
  and Jerusalem 190
  and the 'Maurice debate' 100-1
  on Archibald Murray 214-15
  and Passchendaele 92
  reputation of 98, 101, 102-3, 283
  strategy of criticized by Wavell 208
  use of official papers by 5-6, 110
  War Memoirs 7, 11, 75-7, 90, 95, 101, 103, 149, 205-6, 210, 214
Loos, battle of 27, 48, 58, 80, 124, 125
Lord Haig (Arthur) 146, 161
Lords of Death (Welborn) 306
Losey, Joseph 284
'lost generation' 42, 298
Loveridge, Donald 309
Lowe, Cedric:
 Mirage of Power, The 184
Lusty, Sir Robert 153
Lynden-Bell, Maj.-Gen. Sir A. L. 216

Macdonald, Lynn 291, 303
 Roses of No Man's Land, The 304
 They Called it Passchendaele 292

Macdonogh, Lt.-Gen. Sir George 70, 80
Macfie, A. L. 187
Mack, John E.:
 Prince of our Disorder: the Life of T. E. Lawrence 254-5, 259
McKee, Alexander:
 Vimy Ridge 308
McKenna, Reginald 90, 126
Mackenzie, Compton 91
 Gallipoli Memories 173
MacMahon, Sir Henry 225
MacMunn, Sir George 63, 174
McNamara, Maj.-Gen. A. E. 84
Macphail, Sir Andrew:
 Three Persons 105
Magnus, Philip:
 Kitchener: Portrait of an Imperialist 137, 175
Mallet, Sir Charles 102
Mametz (Hughes) 304
Man I Knew, The (Haig) 150-1, 161
Man Who Disobeyed, The (Smithers) 134-5
Manning, Frederic 63
Manual of Military Law (Edmonds) 70
March Retreat, The (Gough) 100
Marder, Arthur 178
 From Dreadnought to Scapa Flow 177
 From the Dardanelles to Oran 182
Marne, battle of the 51
Marshall-Cornwall, General Sir James 42, 141
 Haig as a Military Commander 157, 161
Marwick, Arthur 271
Masefield, John:
 Gallipoli 165
Massey, W. T.:
 Allenby's Final Triumph 198
Masterman, E. W. G.:
 Deliverance of Jerusalem, The 191
Maurice, General Sir Frederick 100-1, 103, 148, 171
 Haldane of Cloan 92
 Intrigues of War 101
 Life of Lord Rawlinson of Trent, The 93, 142
Maxse, Maj.-Gen. Sir Ivor 80, 311
Maxwell, D.:
 Last Crusade, The 191
Meggido, battle of 195-203 *passim*, 222
Meinertzhagen, Colonel Richard:
 Army Diary 1899-1926 223

Index

memoirs:
  motives for writing of 97-9
  profit from 96-7
  sales of in the inter-war years 7, 93-5
  value of to historians 111-12
Memoirs of a Marine (Aston) 96
Memoirs of an Unconventional Soldier (Fuller) 99
Memories and Reflections (Asquith) 93, 133
Memories of Forty-Eight Years' Service (Smith-Dorrien) 134
Men I Killed, The (Crozier) 62 n.
Men in Power (Beaverbrook) 101
Men of Gallipoli (Liddle) 182, 297-8
Metternich, K. Furst von 255
Middlebrook, Martin 5, 10
  First Day on the Somme, The 291, 302
  Kaiser's Battle, The 303
Midleton, Lord 133
Military Operations Egypt and Palestine (Falls) 193, 195, 198-9, 201, 205, 207, 208, 216, 224
Military Operations France and Belgium (Edmonds) 69-75 *passim*, 143-4, 265
Military Operations Gallipoli (Aspinall-Oglander) 169-70, 172
Mills, Sir John 141, 284
Milne, Field Marshal Lord 84
Mirage of Power (Dockrill) 184
Monash, General Sir John 173
Monick, S. 182
Monro, Sir Charles 179
Mons, battle of 81, 119
Mons: the Retreat to Victory (Terraine) 135, 153, 263, 275
Montgomery, Field Marshal Viscount 85
Montgomery Legend, The (Thompson) 259
Montgomery-Massingberd, Sir Archibald 78, 81, 85
Moore, George 127
Moorehead, Alan 165, 218, 286
  Gallipoli 175, 264
morale 58, 299-301
Morale (Baynes) 305
Morton, Sir Desmond (Government official and friend of Churchill) 107
Morton, Desmond (Canadian historian) 307-8

Moseley, Sydney:
  Truth about the Dardanelles, The 165
Mottistone, Lord, *see* Seely, J. E. B.
Mousa, Suleiman:
  T. E. Lawrence: an Arab View 250-1, 257, 258
Murray, General Sir Archibald 116, 117, 119, 122, 195
  falsification of records by 78, 81
  reputation of 74, 212-19 *passim*, 223
Murray, Sir John 93, 94
My Political Life (Amery) 89
Myriad Faces of War, The (Wilson, T.) 10 n.
Myth of the Digger, The (Ross) 306

Naval Memories (Keyes) 173
Neilson, Keith 185, 188
  Strategy and Supply 185
Nelson, Thomas 37
Nelson's History of the War (Buchan) 7, 29, 30-3, 35
Neuve Chapelle, battle of 82, 123, 125
Nevinson, Henry:
  Dardanelles Campaign, The 166-7
New Armies 116-17, 185, 302
New Zealand Division 309-10
Newcombe, Colonel S. F. 229, 244
Nicolson, Harold 246
Nicolson, Ivor 93
1918: the Last Battle (Pitt) 264
1914 (French, J.) 72, 91, 92, 94, 119, 120, 130-4, 144
1914-18 Personal Experience Archives, *see* Liddle Collection
Nivelle, Général R. 280
No Man's Land (Leed) 312 n.
North, Major John 166
  Gallipoli: the Fading Vision 174
Northcliffe, Lord 126-7
Nutting, Anthony:
  Lawrence of Arabia: the Man and the Motive 250

officers:
  casualty rates of 298
  image of 284-5
  motivation of 301
  personal papers of 294
  see also junior officers
Official Histories (Australian):
  Bean as editor of series of 79, 100, 305-6, 307
  Story of Anzac, The (Bean) 167, 173

Official Histories (British):
  Blockade of the Central Empires, The (Bell) 48
  Edmonds as editor of series of 3-4, 71-5, 77-8
  Falls' work on 63-4, 75
  Fortescue's work on 18, 21, 71-2
  Military Operations Egypt and Palestine (Falls) 198-9, 201, 205, 207, 208, 216, 224
  Military Operations France and Belgium (Edmonds) 69-75 *passim*, 143-4, 265
  Military Operations Gallipoli (Aspinall-Oglander) 169-70, 172
  Wynne's work on 69, 75, 83
'official' history (as a concept) 16, 21, 69
official papers 91-2, 270-1, 289
  Conan Doyle's lack of access to 23-5
Official Secrets Act (1911) 91-2
Oh! What a Lovely War (film) 9, 141, 264, 283-6
Oh! What a Lovely War (play) 7, 264, 275, 281-3
Oliver, F. S. 104
Oliver, Henry F. 177
On the Psychology of Military Incompetence (Dixon) 158
Oppenheim, L. F. L. 70
oral history 10, 79, 292-3
Orientations (Storrs) 242
Origins of the Second World War (Taylor) 263
Origins of the War of 1914 (Albertini) 286
Orr, Philip:
  Road to the Somme, The 304
other ranks 285, 290
  private papers of 294
  see also casualty rates; discipline; morale
Owen, Wilfred 238
  influence of on perceptions of WWI 331
Oxford and Asquith, Earl of, *see* Asquith, Herbert

Paardeberg, battle of 114
Paget, Gregory 186
Palat, Général:
  Histoire de la Grande Guerre sur le Front Occidental 51

Palestine campaign 189-206 *passim*
Palestine Campaign, The (Wavell) 197, 201-2, 203 n., 224
'Pals' battalions 304
Pals: the 11th Service Battalion (Accrington) East Lancashire Regiment (Turner) 304-5
Pals: the 13th and 14th Battalions York and Lancaster Regiment (Cooksey) 304-5
Paris or the Future of War (Liddell Hart) 45
Passchendaele, battle of 47, 53, 73, 94, 103, 280, 311
Perils of Amateur Strategy, The (Ellison) 171
Petain, Général (later Maréchal) H. P. 80, 81
Pirie-Gordon, Major H. 193
Pitt, Barrie 279
  1918: the Last Act 264
Plumer, General Sir Herbert (later Field Marshal Viscount) 111, 118, 134 n.
Politicians and the War (Beaverbrook) 89, 90, 92, 93, 104
Politics from Within (Addison) 96
Politics of Manpower, The (Grieves) 90
Portrait of T. E. Lawrence, A (Richards) 242
Poulton-Palmer, R. W. 54
Powell, Anthony 252
Pownall, Lt.-Gen. Sir Henry 42
Pozières 1916 (Charlton) 307
Prelude to Victory (Spears) 108
Price of Glory, The (Horne) 264, 266
Prince of our Disorder (Mack) 254-5, 259
Prior, Robin 10, 11
private papers:
  as historical sources 293-4
Private Papers of Sir Douglas Haig (Blake) 82, 151, 152
Prothero, Ernest:
  Earl Haig 146, 161
Public Records Act (1958) 91, 270
Public Records Act (1967) 91, 270
Pugsley, Christopher:
  Gallipoli: the New Zealand Story 310
Purnell's History of the First World War 53, 289
Putkowski, Julian:
  Shot at Dawn 300

Index

Raffles, Gerry 281-2
Rattigan, Terence:
  Ross 211
Rawlinson, General Sir Henry (later Lord) 58, 73, 76, 78, 81, 142, 238-9
  reputation of 11
Read, Herbert 46, 52
Real War, The (Liddell Hart) 41, 45, 46-53 *passim*
Realities of War, The (Gibbs) 98
Reason Why, The (Woodham-Smith) 265
Renouvin, Pierre 56
Repington, Charles à Court 115, 126
  character of 104
  First World War, The 11, 92, 104, 137
Reputations: Ten Years After (Liddell Hart) 7, 45, 146, 219, 222
Retreat from Mons, The (Corbett-Smith) 131
Revolt in the Desert (Lawrence, T. E.) 234, 241
Rhodes James, Robert 286, 309
  Churchill: a Study in Failure 1900-39 178
  Gallipoli 178, 179, 270-1
Richards, Vyvyan 241
  Portrait of T. E. Lawrence, A 242
Richardson, Tony 284
Riddell, Lord:
  War Diary 1914-18 92
Ritter, Gerhard:
  Schlieffen Plan, The 266
Road to Passchendaele, The (Terraine) 267 n.
Road to the Somme, The (Orr) 304
Roberts, Field Marshal Earl 113
Robertson, Field Marshal Sir William 11, 24, 36, 90, 125, 149, 156, 267, 272-3
  access of to official papers 106, 107
  on Buchan 34
  and the Dardanelles 171
  and French 128, 129, 136, 138
  From Private to Field Marshal 101, 146
  on Kitchener 136
  and Lloyd George 206, 208
  and Murray's final despatch from Palestine 213 n.
  on the Official History 82

and the Palestine campaign 207, 214
  reputation of 50, 98-102
  Soldiers and Statesmen 91, 92, 101, 146, 171, 174
Robson, L. L. 306-7
Roch, W. F. 102
Rogerson, Sidney 274
Role of British Strategy in the Great War, The (Cruttwell) 60
Romance of the Last Crusade, The (Gilbert) 191
Roseberry, Lord 30, 136
Roses of No Man's Land, The (Macdonald) 304
Roskill, Stephen:
  Churchill and the Admirals 182
  Hankey: Man of Secrets 179
Ross, Jane:
  Myth of the Digger, The 306
Ross (Rattigan) 211
Royal Military College Sandhurst 95
Royle, Trevor:
  Kitchener Enigma, The 137
Rugby School 42, 54
Runciman, Walter 90
Rutherford, Andrew 258
Rutter, O. 98

Safety Last (Stirling) 212 n.
Sanders, Liman von 170, 193
Sandhurst, *see* Royal Military College Sandhurst
Sassoon, Siegfried 232-3, 238, 311-12
Savage, Raymond 216, 218
  Allenby of Armageddon 198, 221-2
Schedule of Wellington House Literature 18 n., 23
Schlieffen plan 51, 52, 72, 266
Schlieffen Plan, The (Ritter) 266
Schurman, Don 187
Seaton, Shirley:
  Christmas Truce 296
Secret Lives of Lawrence of Arabia, The (Knightley) 251-3, 258
Secrett, Sergeant T.:
  Twenty-Five Years With Earl Haig 148, 161
Seely, J. E. B. (later Lord Mottistone):
  Adventure 93
Selborne, Lord 122, 127
Serle, Geoffrey 187
Serre, attack on 304

328   Index

Seven Pillars of Wisdom, The (Lawrence, T. E.) 210-12, 229, 234, 241, 242, 246, 247, 250, 251, 255, 256
Sewell, George 281
Seymour-Smith, Martin 233
Shadbolt, Maurice:
   Voices of Gallipoli 291 n., 292, 310
Shaw, Charlotte 228, 234, 241
Shaw, George Bernard 241, 265
Sheffield, Gary 305
Sheffield City Battalion (Gibson) 304-5
Sherriff, R. C.:
   Journey's End 264
Shot at Dawn (Putkowski) 300
Simkins, Peter 1, 10
   Kitchener's Army 10 n.
Simpson, Colin:
   Secret Lives of Lawrence of Arabia 251-3, 258
Sir Douglas Haig's Command 1915-18 (Boraston) 98, 102, 145
Sir Douglas Haig's Despatches (Boraston) 144
Sixsmith, General E. K. G.:
   Douglas Haig 157, 161
Smith-Dorrien, General Sir Horace 16, 108
   on Allenby 208
   and French 118, 119, 131, 133, 134 n.
   Memories of Forty-Eight Years' Service 134
Smithers, A. T.:
   Man Who Disobeyed, The 134-5
Smoke and the Fire, The (Terraine) 275
Smuts, Jan 76, 200 n.
Soldier True (Bonham-Carter) 156, 282
Soldiering On (Gough) 100
Soldiers and Statesmen (Robertson) 91, 92, 101, 146, 171, 174
Soldier's Saga, A (Haldane, A.) 98
Soldier's War, The (Liddle) 297, 301
Solly Flood, Maj.-Gen. A. 80
Somme, battle of the 24, 31-2, 33, 44, 45, 47, 54, 58, 78, 81, 84, 148, 155, 275, 280, 303, 311
   casualty figures for 108
Sommers, C.:
   Temporary Crusaders 191
South African Brigade 310
Sparrow, W. Shaw:
   Fifth Army in March 1918, The 100
Spears, Brig.-Gen. Sir E. L. 100, 108, 134

   Liaison 1914 92, 95
   Prelude to Victory 108
Spender, J. A. 105
Spiers, Edward 99
Spinetti, Victor 281
Spring, Howard 30
Staff College Camberley 83
Stamfordham, Lord 132, 142
Stand To! (journal) 289
Stanley, Venetia 182
Steevens, G. A.:
   With Kitchener to Khartoum 116
Stevenson, Francis 101
Stewart, Desmond:
   T. E. Lawrence 254
Stimson, Henry 175
Stirling, Colonel W. F. 229, 240
   Safety Last 212 n.
Storrs, Sir Ronald:
   Orientations 242
Story of ANZAC, The (Bean) 167, 173
Strachan, Hew 278
Strachey, St Loe 36
Straits Agreement (1914) 186
Strategy and Supply (Neilson) 185
Stray Recollections (Callwell) 98
Struggle in Flanders, The (Gibbs) 265
Subaltern's War (Carrington) 243
Supreme Command, The (Hankey) 92, 111, 176-7
Suvla Bay, landings at 169, 172, 297-8
Swinton, Maj.-Gen. Sir Ernest 98-9, 102, 108
   Eyewitness 99
Swordbearers, The (Barnett) 156, 266, 269
Sydenham, Lord 111
Sykes, Julian:
   Shot at Dawn 300
Sylvester, A. J. 77, 103

T. E. Lawrence (Brent) 254
T. E. Lawrence (Carrington) 243
T. E. Lawrence (Stewart) 254
T. E. Lawrence: an Arab View (Mousa) 250-1, 257, 258
T. E. Lawrence and His Friends (Lawrence, A. W.) 242
T. E. Lawrence in Arabia and After (Liddell Hart) 45, 231, 238-42, 258
T. E. Lawrence or the Search for the Absolute (Villars) 249

T. E. Lawrence to His Biographers Robert Graves and Liddell Hart 242
Tafileh, battle of 237, 250, 257
Taylor, A. J. P. 6, 8, 104, 263, 270, 286
  English History 1914-45 263
  First World War: an Illustrated History, The 156, 263, 271-3
  on oral history 292
  Origins of the Second World War, The 263
  on Sir Henry Wilson
Temporary Crusaders (Summers) 191
Terraine, John 7, 8-9, 65, 118, 152-6, 159, 271, 285
  on Babington 300
  background of 273-4
  defence of Haig by 53, 161, 275-8
  Douglas Haig: the Educated Soldier 66, 152-3, 154-5, 263, 275-6, 287
  Great War, The 263
  Mons: the Retreat to Victory 135, 153, 263, 275
  Road to Passchendaele, The 267 n.
  Smoke and the Fire, The 275
  on the Somme 303
  To Win a War 267 n., 277
  and his use of sources 266-7
  Western Front, The 266
  and his work on *The Great War* television series 269, 279, 280
Theatre Workshop, The 281, 282
  see also *Oh! What a Lovely War* (play)
Thermonuclear War (Kahn) 283
They Called it Passchendaele (Macdonald) 292
'*They Wouldn't Believe Me*' (song) 286
Thomas, Lowell 4, 212, 228, 243
  With Lawrence in Arabia 228-31
Thomas, T. H. 49
Thompson, R. W.:
  Montgomery Legend, The 259
Thornhill, Alan 55, 56
Three Persons (Macphail) 105
Through the Fog of War (Liddell Hart) 45
Thucydides 225-6
Tim Harington Looks Back (Harington) 97
To Arms (Conan Doyle) 23
To Win a War (Terraine) 267 n., 277
Tommy Goes to War (Brown) 295

total war 16, 18, 32
Tragedy of Lord Kitchener (Esher) 99, 130-1
Tragedy of Sir John French, The (Cassar) 138-9
Tragedy of Winston Churchill, The (Germains) 92
Travers, Tim 10, 53, 158, 267
  Killing Ground, The 10 n., 159-60
trench warfare 281, 294, 296
Trench Warfare 1914-18 (Ashworth) 295, 296
Trevelyan, G. M. 78
Truth About Kitchener, The (Germains) 98
Truth About the Dardanelles, The (Moseley) 165
Tuchman, Barbara:
  August 1914 265, 266, 283
Turner, William:
  Pals: the 11th (Service) Battalion (Accrington) East Lancashire Regiment 304-5
Turning Points in History, The (Birkenhead) 100
Twenty-Five Years (Grey) 7, 89, 94, 95, 96, 105-6, 136
Twenty-Five Years with Earl Haig (Secrett) 148, 161

Uncensored Dardanelles, The (Ashmead-Bartlett) 171
Undertones of War (Blunden) 43
Unknown Army, The (Dallas) 299
Unruh, Fritz von 43
Uys, Ian 310-11

Villars, Jean Bernard:
  T. E. Lawrence or the Search for the Absolute 249
Vimy (Berton) 308
Vimy Ridge (McKee) 308
Visits to Three Fronts, A (Conan Doyle) 25
Voices of Gallipoli (Shadbolt) 291 n., 292, 310

Wallin, Jeffrey:
  By Ships Alone: Churchill and the Dardanelles 182
War Books (Falls) 43, 62, 63
War Council 181, 182, 183, 186
  criticized by Hankey 176-7

War Diaries 78, 303
War Diaries, Addresses and Correspondence (French) 135
War Diary 1914-18 (Riddell) 92
War in Outline, The (Liddell Hart) 45, 48, 60
War in South Africa, The (Conan Doyle) 22
War Memoirs (Lloyd George) 7, 11, 75-7, 90, 95, 103, 149, 205-6, 210, 214
War Office 28, 31
  access to records of 23-4, 106
War Propaganda Bureau 23, 30
War Service of the 1/4 Royal Berkshire Regiment, The (Cruttwell) 54
Warner, Philip:
  Battle of Loos, The 304
  Kitchener: the Man Behind the Legend 137
Wartime (Fussell) 1 n.
Watt, A. P. 93
Waugh, Evelyn 53-4
Wavell, Field Marshal Earl 85, 200 n., 206-8, 216
  on the Official History 82
  Palestine Campaign, The 97, 201-2, 203 n., 224
Weizmann, Chaim 194
Wejh, capture of 237, 247, 257
Welborn, Suzanne:
  Lords of Death: a People, a Place, a Legend 306
Weltkrieg, Der (Kuhl) 51
Wester-Wemyss, Admiral Lord 167, 178
Western Front, The (Terraine) 266
Western Front Association 289
What of the Dardanelles? (Fortescue, G.) 165
When Britain Goes to War (Liddell Hart) 60
Wigram, Clive 142
Wilhelm II, Kaiser 189-90
Wilkinson, Spenser 73
Williams, John 279
Williams, Orlo 173-4
Wilson, Sir Arthur 167
Wilson, H. W. 167
Wilson, Field Marshal Sir Henry 11, 47, 77, 78, 103, 119, 136, 142
  and deployment of the BEF 117
  diaries of 6, 197
  and the Palestine campaign 207
  reputation of 104-5
Wilson, J. Brent 297 n., 299
Wilson, Jeremy:
  Lawrence of Arabia: the Authorised Biography 4, 255-8
Wilson, Lady 104-5
Wilson, Trevor 10, 11
  Myriad Faces of War, The 10 n.
Winston Churchill (Gilbert) 180-1, 256
Winter, Denis 293
  Death's Men: Soldiers of the Great War 294, 302
  Haig's Command: a Reassessment 162
Winter, J. M. 290
  Experience of World War I, The 302
  Great War and the British People, The 298
Winterton, Lord 245
Wipers Times, The (journal) 281
With Kitchener to Khartoum (Steevens) 116
With Lawrence in Arabia (Thomas) 228-31
Wolff, Leon 6, 67
  In Flanders Fields 66, 137, 153, 264-6, 267
Wood, W. B. 70
Woodham-Smith, Cecil:
  Reason Why, The 265
Woods, Maurice 107
Woodward, David 158
Woodward, Sir Llewellyn 180
World Crisis, The (Churchill) 6, 89-90, 93, 94, 95, 99, 106, 146, 165, 168-70
Wright, Captain Peter 91, 107
Wykes, Alan 179
Wynne, G. C. 69, 75, 83

Xenophon 247

Yardley, Michael
  Backing into the Limelight: a Biography of T. E. Lawrence 254
Ypres, second battle of 81

Zeid, Emir 251, 257

Printed in the United Kingdom
by Lightning Source UK Ltd.
9713000001BD

For Lucy & James,
let your passions take you wherever they guide you.

CONTENTS

FOREWORD SERGE VALENTIN	5
INTRODUCTION	8
Chapter 1: WHY CAMPBELTOWN?	20
Chapter 2: THE LAST DISTILLERY	36
Chapter 3: BARNARD VISITS	55
Chapter 4: TRADITIONS	88
Chapter 5: THE GREENLEES BROTHERS	105
Chapter 6: SHOCKWAVES	129
Chapter 7: THE GREAT WAR	149
Chapter 8: UNWANTED GOUT IN THE TEEN YEARS	165
Chapter 9: RATES, RANTS & RUPTURES	186
Chapter 10: TEETERING	206
Chapter 11: EPILOGUE	225
APPENDIX A: Distillery Histories	237
APPENDIX B: 'Origin & Romance' 1923	313
APPENDIX C: 'Reminiscences of a Gauger' 1873	332
APPENDIX D: Contract of Reid & Colville, Dalintober Distillery	335
APPENDIX E: Article 'Scotch Whisky' 1903	337
APPENDIX F: Lochhead & Lochruan Distillery Production 1923	343
APPENDIX G: Early 19th Century Distillers in Kintyre	347
APPENDIX H: Table of production, stock dispatched and in bond	350
APPENDIX I: Table of Springbank production 1905 - 1937	351
APPENDIX J: Springbank Distillery by Hedley G. Wright 1963	355
Endnotes	360
Bibliography	367
Image sources	369
Acknowledgements	370

INTRODUCTION

"The habit that distilleries have of crowding into a few closely-defined areas whose natural conditions have been proved by centuries of experience to be most suitable for distilling, is well illustrated by the Campbeltown malt whiskies. The whole of this important group of distilleries is found in or around the town of Campbeltown on the peninsula of Kintyre, which juts southward from Argyllshire to within a few miles of Northern Ireland. Within the few square miles which make up the whole of this, the smallest of the four whisky areas, a spirit is produced which differs widely from any of the other types of Scotch whiskies.

"The Campbeltowns are the double basses of the whisky orchestra. They are potent, full-bodied, pungent whiskies, with a flavour that is not to the liking of everyone. Indeed the market for these whiskies is largely confined to Scotland and the western part thereof. So masterful and assertive are they that the marrying of them to obtain a smooth, evenly-matched blend is an extremely difficult business. Yet, if the full repertoire of whisky is not to be irremediably impoverished the Campbeltowns must remain. As might have been expected in an age when the standardised, anaemic grain-plus-malt are triumphant, Campbeltown distilling has been somewhat under a cloud in recent years. This district has suffered more severely than the others from trade depression."

'Whisky' by Aeneas MacDonald
(George Thomson), 1930

FOREWORD

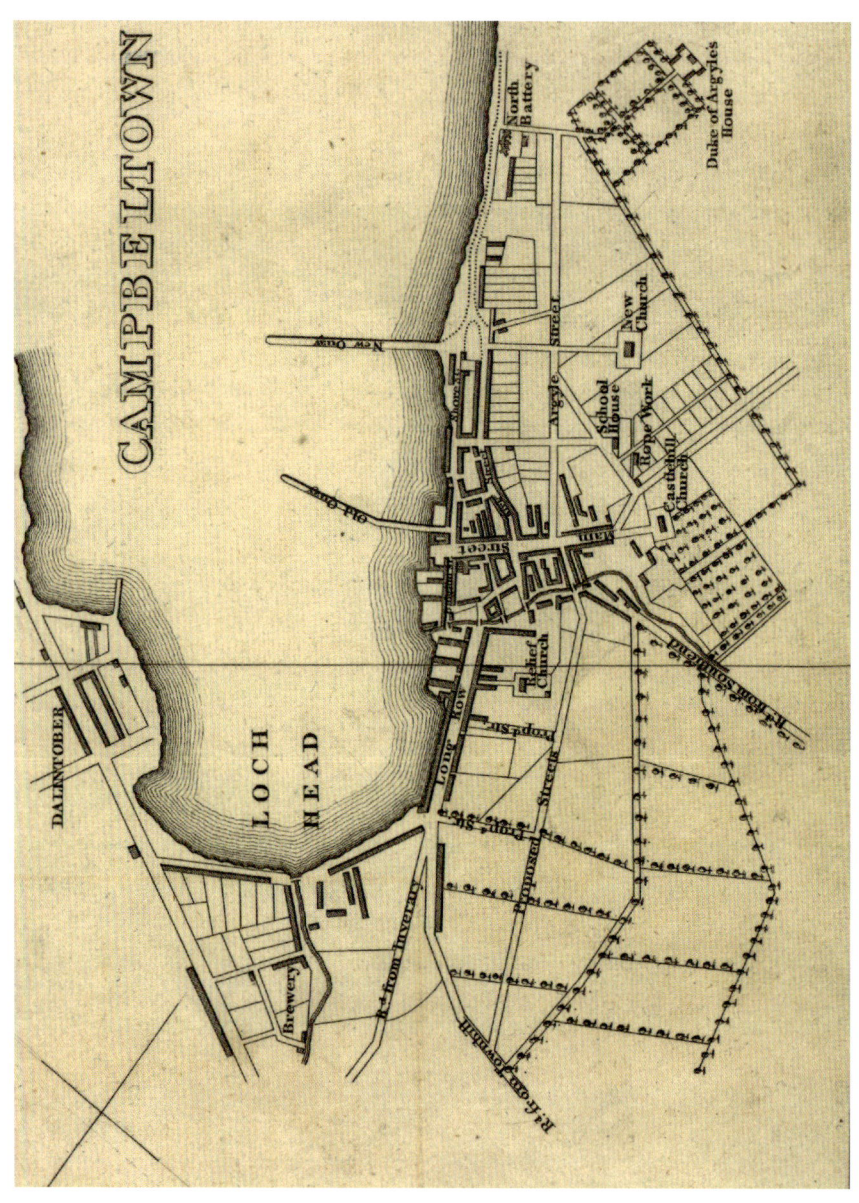

1824 survey of Campbeltown showing proposed streets.

the release of the first 'Local Barleys' and 'West Highland Malts' - it was that endearing resistance to innovation that always struck us as, paradoxically, the most profound form of innovation. To the mantra 'Innovation is good!' the brilliant Dilbert retorted, 'Sure, you go first!' That could well have been Springbank's motto. I am convinced that the shattered casks and piles of rotting staves scattered around the distillery were intentionally left there to drive the point home. And oh, the whiskies indeed!

That said, Glen Scotia at the time, was at the opposite end of the spectrum. The distillery's output largely ended up in hypermarkets, especially in our always-thirsty France, sold under own-brand labels at bargain-basement prices. In hindsight, I think we greatly underestimated Glen Scotia back then, but how things have changed - and for the better!

As for the rest, even though I made an impromptu visit just recently, I'll have to return to the 'Wee Toon' soon to revisit Springbank, of course, but also to see the newer distilleries. Imagine - I haven't even visited Glengyle yet!

FOREWORD

SERGE VALENTIN
Creator of Whiskyfun.com
Keeper of the Quaich

Any serious whisky enthusiast will have visited Campbeltown at least once in their life. As for me, I've been there several times, the first being in the early 2000s when the town still exuded an atmosphere akin to a Ken Loach film - very post-Thatcherite and somewhat similar to the mood lingering in the south of Islay, particularly in the small town of Port Ellen. There were displaced communities, mass unemployment or, close to it, old Morris Marinas lining the streets, but also a palpable charm, almost documentary-like. In the pubs, you could still hear Dexys Midnight Runners or Bonnie Tyler playing. Cigarette butts still littered the floors of Springbank, and the washbacks at Glen Scotia - who had seen better days - had been painted a garish blue some thirty years prior, their thick, stubborn rust peeking through in patches.

Yet even the smallest ray of sunshine felt like a divine apparition, celebrated as it should be at the Ardshiel Hotel, where the whisky bar was so vast the charming waitresses couldn't possibly reach the top shelf. We had to help ourselves, naturally - though, of course, we were more than happy to oblige, especially since the finest bottles always seemed to reside at the very top. I recall that during one visit, the Springbank 25-year-old 'Frank McHardy' had just been released, and, as you can imagine, we gave it the attention it deserved.

Campbeltown, however, always felt like a stopover en route to Islay - or rather, an unmissable detour. A magical place, untouched by modernity, where whisky seemed to be crafted as best as it could, without a single commercial consideration, in keeping with the old adage that 'the best soups are made in old pots'. Beyond the unquestionable quality of its whiskies - especially following

INTRODUCTION

Circa 1890. New warehouses would change this view in the next 10 years.

WHISKYOPOLIS

In December of 2001, I made my inaugural journey down the A83, the main road along the Kintyre Peninsula, to Campbeltown. Unless you are one of the five per cent of Scots living north of the junction at Tarbet – where the A82 meets the A83 – you are heading north before heading south to get to Campbeltown.[1] I vividly recall how, on entering the town, it struck me as a memory of past glories – a graveyard to a once thriving distilling industry. I was in Campbeltown by pure serendipity, having secured a job with J. & A. Mitchell. Whilst not suggesting any superiority of vision or precognition (being just 25), I was ever so slightly ahead of the curve as I began my journey into Scotch whisky - especially when considering what the future had for single malt Scotch whisky. As I spent many a day walking around Campbeltown, it struck me that within the streets, walls, roofs, and (hopefully) living memories was a story: an incredible story – and one quite unique to the town.

Imagine an island off the west coast of New England, America – perhaps an island close enough for a suspension or road bridge. On that island, now conjure a small hamlet of folk making enough beer to keep the entire six states of 19th century New England content. Campbeltown, a small town strung out on Europe's most prominent peninsula, was doing just that with whisky. Single malt Scotch whisky: malted, mashed, fermented, distilled, and (latterly) matured before being shipped to the great blending houses in Glasgow, Leith and London.

I was not a historian when I entered Campbeltown all those decades ago. In spite of reading every whisky-related book I could get my hands on, I was not much of a history buff and had little idea about research, sources or interpretation. Frankly, I still feel like an imposter to those who are classically, or at least structurally, trained to research, interpret, and portray history. In the last decade, I have read (and listened to) more history articles, books, podcasts and essays than in the first 30-plus years of my life. I have learned that history, and its retelling, is not a monopoly for those with doctorates, master's degrees, PhDs, or double-barrelled surnames. Sure, the research, writing and publishing are much easier for those with deep pockets, private

INTRODUCTION

incomes and parents who can magically open doors, but if left to the elite, the wider story often remains untold.

What I perhaps had on my side back in 2003 when I decided to research 'The Distilleries of Campbeltown – The Rise and Fall of the Whisky Capital of the World' was youthful confidence and a complete lack of concern about what a 'history' book was – or should be. Occasionally, being entirely out of your depth allows an opening of a groove on an otherwise untouched surface. And so it was with my book. I was very fortunate that a publisher, sadly no longer in operation, persevered through my inadequacies and produced something that became the only guide to Campbeltown's once-thriving industry. My book was mightily rudimentary to any educated, trained historian – but not from lack of trying.

The simple and overriding issue was a dearth of data. Naively, perhaps, I had assumed that the townsfolk – families that went back well beyond the period I was researching – would have attics, offices, carrier bags and folders full of letters, ledgers, news clippings and ephemera from the distilleries (silent or otherwise) that surrounded them as they grew up. This proved as fruitful as energy from crystals or offerings to gods. I placed ads in the local paper and held local tastings, including one for the Rotary Club (if any group in the town would have information, surely it was the Rotary Club?) and came up empty-handed.

Due to this, my book (published in 2005 and now out of print) became a collection of anecdotes, news clippings, odd letters, and other random pieces. What was missing was a narrative – a story. And, frankly, up until a few years ago, I had no intention of revisiting my initial foray. Had it not been for three extraordinary releases, I would likely have enjoyed most of 2024 by catching up on casual reading rather than researching this project.

The first release was from exhaustive research by James Eadie & Co., who stumbled across a prolonged series within 'The Wine & Spirit Trade Record', beginning in 1922 and concluding in 1929. This chance discovery within the British Library led to 'The Distilleries of Great Britain & Ireland 1922-29' being released in 2022. This was the first significant evidence of new material that I had seen relating to the Campbeltown distilleries since my research in 2004. This meant that along with Alfred Barnard's 'The Whisky Distilleries of the United Kingdom', released in 1887, there now existed two great surveys of the Campbeltown distilleries - separated by 30 or so years.

However, this still did not offer me what I wanted – a narrative. I wanted to tell a fuller story – with as much first-hand testimony as possible. This was made more achievable by two additional releases that were also unavailable to me when I wrote my initial book. Both are now part of the British News Archive: 'The Distillers Magazine and Spirit Trade News' (1897 – 1905) and the 'Campbeltown Courier' (1873 to present day). Had these digital sources been available when I researched my first book, I may have avoided some of the inevitable criticism.

The 'Distillers Magazine', launched in April 1897, included a periodically printed section that was an update from Glasgow, Leith, The Highlands, Campbeltown, Dublin and later Belfast. This provided a significant personal account of the goings' on within Campbeltown and the distilleries. Coupled with the digitisation of the 'Campbeltown Courier' I could finally research and reveal a glimpse into what the Victorian period - and frankly the most successful (and interesting) period of Campbeltown's distilling era - was like.

There are still frustrations with the writing of this new edition. One obviously is that there are no living witnesses. The period in question would require a newborn to be over 100 years old – and would hardly make a suitable witness to the whisky industry – or any industry. As I reasoned in my first book, being born into, growing up and living in Campbeltown during the 19th century meant that distilleries were not a 'special' occurrence - nothing worthy of much attention, record or remembrance. I have always likened it to growing up near modern supermarkets or distribution hubs – no archivist or hobbyist records details and opinions on these industrial blocks. It simply wouldn't enter into anyone's consciousness to do so.

And so it was with Campbeltown and its numerous distilleries. Anyone born into the region was not thinking twice about the

INTRODUCTION

belching, burping, and discharging factories of Uisge Beatha (Gaelic for Water of Life – Uisge is where the name Whisky is derived from). As distilleries closed, families moved out of the town or moved on with their lives; records, ledgers, memories and memorabilia were discarded and lost. Auctioneers claim that personal memorabilia, on average, lasts for a maximum of three generations. We are well beyond that now from the heyday of the Campbeltown whisky era.

This is summed up by an article submitted to the 'Campbeltown Courier' and published in May 1930. Titled 'Campbeltown in the Nineties – I Remember', it is a series of reminiscences (one can reasonably assume from the same author) printed over several months. Despite living through the incredible height of the distilling period for the town (and through the collapse), the author has only the following comments on the whisky industry:

"Campbeltown, in the latter part of last century, perhaps reached the zenith of its industrial supremacy. Fishing was prosperous and regular. The fishermen could depend on shoals appearing at regular dates on recognised grounds. The shipbuilding yard was constantly in activity, launches being regular red-letter days in the lives of the townspeople. How many remember the splendid turret-decked ships constructed at the now desolate Trench – the 'Yik-Sang', the 'Cato' and many others built for British, Norwegian, Spanish and other companies? How the rattle of the riveters could be heard all over the town. How the naphtha flares [early form of lighting] burned so brightly on winter mornings and evenings! How the black squad so merrily trooped to and from the yard, and how mothers and children used to go with the dinners! Oh! What a pleasant task it was for so many loving wives to make up 'the pieces' for their bread-winners!

"Distilling was regularly carried on every season in more than twenty distilleries. Although the individual 'stills' gave employment to comparatively few men, and although the value of the output was very great in comparison with the number

employed, yet at least 200 men could depend upon getting work during the winter and spring months. This was also reflected on increased activity at the harbour in the importation of the barley and necessary coal, and on the export of the whisky. What a week it was when the 'grainers' lay along the quay front, and how the surface of the quay and of the roads leading to it from the distilleries were churned into mud by the many carts which were then employed in taking the barley to the distilleries. How the empty carts used to race along the Kinloch Road or across the Esplanade! How the winches used to rattle as the tubs of barley were deftly taken from the holds to be weighed by the expert porters! How the contents were then skilfully tilted into the two hundred-weight bags, which were then carried along the planks to the carts! I wonder how many of these carriers who used 'to walk the plank' are still alive?

"I remember the London boats 'Eva', 'Edith' and others of the same company: the Falmouth boats 'Trevelyan', 'Trefusio', etc, the Greek boats 'Alexandros Michelinos', the 'Aphrodite', and others: and the 'Head' liners. I wonder what our present generation would say if they saw the front of the quay taken up by one of these boats discharging barley into the many carts on one side, and into lighters for the Islay distilleries on the other. Then, in addition to this activity, we had the Drumlemble pit going at full swing. We had the primitive 'Chevalier' and 'Pioneer', drawing loads of coal in the small buggies, and Argyll Street knew then what coal traffic meant as the carts – these were the pre-motor and pre-railway days – trundled slowly along with their loads either to the distilleries or to the ships at the quay for export to Ireland.

"The result of all this was that our native town had an air of business which was gratifying to see and which was in marked contrast to its present funereal outlook. The citizens were light-hearted, as all hard-working people should be, for nothing is better for the human race than constant work. If any had said at that time, 'This town is done', he would have been considered

INTRODUCTION

a fit subject for Lochgilphead or for Morningside. There were no 'croakers' then: the 'dole' was unknown: peace and plenty reigned. This was reflected on the satisfactory trade carried on by the merchants, and by the constant employment of tradesmen. Full cargoes of foodstuffs and of manufactured goods were carried inwards by the 'Kintyre', the 'Kinloch', the 'Davaar' and the 'Pirate', and outwards we had the whisky and 'draff' of the distilleries, the coal of Drumlemble, fish and farm produce.

"I remember the races made by the 'draff' schooners on the run to Belfast or Larne. When bad weather prevailed, sometimes three or four of our schooner fleet, which comprised, amongst others, the 'Mary Ann', 'Jessie Ann', 'Bengullion', 'Benmore', 'Campbeltown', 'William and Leigh', 'Lavinia', 'Sovereign', 'Mary, Isabella Stuart', lay in the loch, or alongside the quay waiting for a 'slant'. As soon as a windlass or a rope was touched on one, the others would do likewise, and a race across the Channel to get unloaded first was the result. What an exciting time it was – what a change from the present somnolent state of the harbour!"

The discovery of the 'In Campbeltown' section published in 'The Distillers Magazine and Spirit Trade News' has provided the most significant insight into the true heyday of the Campbeltown distilling industry and its effect upon the town. These letters appeared from the first edition in April 1897; the last one being published in September 1904. Frustratingly, although perhaps due to the nature of the journal, these letters are submitted anonymously. Knowing which member of the distilling fraternity within Campbeltown was the contributor would be illuminating. At times, the letters are highly critical of elements within Campbeltown and quite often, especially when we get to the infamous Pattison crash episode in 1898/99 of the wider whisky industry. So much is drawn from this one source that I have marked all comments with an '*' or 'OMIC' (Our Man In Campbeltown).

I have also taken the liberty of reinterpreting the visit of Alfred

Barnard in his seminal 'The Distilleries of The United Kingdom' and the writer(s) from 'The Wine and Spirit Trade Record' 1922-29 rather than attempting to reproduce them verbatim. Both books are commonly available, although, perhaps due to their size and content, they are only suitable for the most ardent researcher in the whisky industry.

Alfred Barnard took two years to compile his exhaustive and, at times, pedantic encyclopaedia. Perhaps, despite how famous this book has become within whisky circles (and in reality, that has been due to the shortage of pre-1900 information on the UK whisky industry), Barnard's most remarkable feat was in convincing his bosses at 'Harper's Weekly Gazette', a journal for the wine and spirit trade, to cover the costs of such a mammoth undertaking.

The banality of the writing may have been part of the gig. Even today, trade journals often demand that personal whims, fancy, and opinions are not part of the delivered message.

Unfortunately, Barnard was rather apt to get numbers wrong. In his defence, he does state in his Preface: *"I earnestly bespeak the leniency of the Distillers, who will doubtless see faults and technical errors in my description... The book makes no pretension to literary merit of any sort, and should not be judged by any such standard."* A proclamation all writers make when allowing their finished text to be scrutinised. I have tried, wherever possible, to correct original quotes and facts. I have also added as many of the lithographs produced by Messrs. Walker & Boutall as possible - they are invaluable pieces of visual history.

Likewise, I have attempted to provide a more historical narrative to 'The Wine & Spirit Trade Record' coverage of the 1920s. Again, we do not know the author (despite being attributed to the editor). I hope I have managed to take the shine off of what was clearly trade journal hyperbole of a crumbling distilling industry.

At times, this book does not follow chronologically, occasionally dipping into topics or quotes from the past. This is due, in part, to the chapters requiring the story of an issue to be told in its entirety within the context of the narrative of that

INTRODUCTION

chapter.

When considering the Campbeltown distilling industry, it is a natural supposition to expect to find a 'smoking gun'. As someone once said to me, 'The demise of the Campbeltown distilleries is the greatest 'whodunnit' that this industry has ever known'. Indeed, the acorn, or spark, that first made me want to research the burgh's past was just that – 'How does an industry that thrived for a century suddenly just perish?' Was it attributable, as in the case of the Irish distilling industry, to the activities of one large company? Or was it an implosion? Did the Campbeltown distillers fight it out until only a few, the fittest, survived? Or was it a nuanced multitude of factors? Unlike a good Agatha Christie novel, you cannot turn to the last page to find the murderer. Hopefully, this book goes some way to explain how, from the height of 21 distilleries working in 1885, only two would survive the 1930s.

I have omitted certain aspects and side stories from the complete picture. As Angus Martin states in his superbly-researched, 'Campbeltown Whisky: An Encyclopaedia', an entire book could be written on the Customs and Excise of the burgh. Another volume could be written on the illicit distilling and yet another on the supplementary industries such as the coal mines, shipping and raw materials such as peat and barley. Another book could look at the industry as a whole, incorporating Campbeltown's whisky into the bigger picture (which I have partly covered), instead of that two or three-line sentence in nearly every whisky book that goes something like 'Campbeltown once had [insert a number between 21 and 37] distilleries but due to [insert a reason] now has two'. It is likely that someone will one day write a comprehensive book of how the Speyside whisky region stole the blender's heart, but for this book, I have concentrated on the Campbeltown industry, its triumphs, trials, tribulations and return to triumph. And I still live in hope of that cupboard full of discarded and forgotten files, photos, ledgers and logbooks turning up.

As I write, the malting floors are full at Springbank, the

stills at Glen Scotia are bubbling away, and Glengyle is being prepared for the next distilling season. The Witchburn Distillery and Machrihanish Distillery builders are battling the elements (and earth) to build their distilleries. The race is on to see who will have the first independently built distillery in Campbeltown since 1879. I am again reminded of my first trip to Campbeltown when just the faintest of embers were still glowing from the kilns at Springbank Distillery. It is from that ember and stubbornness of belief, passion and determination that the survival and revival of Campbeltown as a Scotch whisky destination par excellence has been possible. Any traveller to Campbeltown is now spoilt should they partake of a glass of Scotch.

From my window on Hall Street, I watch as the raindrops fall into Campbeltown Loch. Behind me, the Crosshill Reservoir is slowly being fed. After all, 'today's rain is tomorrow's whisky', as the saying goes. Surrounded by the remnants, whispers and ghosts of what made this small town celebrated as 'Whiskyopolis', I can think of nothing more appropriate than a glass of Springbank whisky - the distillery that somehow clawed its way to worldwide fame from the jaws of ignominy.

Come to think of it, that phrase does not do justice to the turnaround.

What a sight this town must have been.
What a destination it is now.

David Stirk, Campbeltown, 2025

INTRODUCTION

Author's notes:

There are several words and phrases that are repeated, requiring some explanation. All references to 'pure malt', 'all malt', or 'self-whiskies', are in reference to what we now term single malt whisky. When applied to whisky, and before the latter part of the 19th century, the term 'silent' referred to grain whisky. The term later came to mean those whiskies with less pungency or strength of flavour.

The word 'whisky' was intermittently spelt with or without an 'e' and without any nod to heritage or national difference. Likewise, the name of Colville was continually spelt with and without the 'e' – it is the same name and can be seen to change within families or from one generation to the next. I have not attempted to paint a family tree, thereby demonstrating how closely related so many of the Campbeltown distilling dynasties were. I recommend Angus Martin's 'Campbeltown Whisky: an Encyclopaedia' for more information on the links between individuals and their families.

Wherever possible, I have offered my source but must add caution, certainly regarding facts and figures (and some dates), that you read these with discretion. For instance, I don't believe I found a single source quoting the exact same number of gallons of whisky dispatched each year from Campbeltown (unless they were, in turn, quoting the same source). I'm not sure minor errors will take anything away from the narrative.

CHAPTER 1

WHY CAMPBELTOWN?

"This [distilling] business is undoubtedly gainful to a few individuals but extremely ruinous to the community. It consumes their means, hurts their morals, and destroys both the undertakings and their health. Were it not for preventing the temptation of smuggling, a duty next to a prohibition would be mercy."
'Statistical Account on Kintyre'
Reverend John Smith, 1794

"What the spirit dealers call fine whisky (Islay or Campbeltown) is at present very scarce."
'Glasgow Chronicle' 1823

WHY CAMPBELTOWN?

In January 1923, one hundred years after the great Excise Act that would revolutionise the Scotch whisky industry, Duncan Colville presented a paper to the Kintyre Antiquarian Society titled, 'The Origin & Romance of the Distilling Industry in Campbeltown'. Colville was a descendant of a distilling dynasty, being the son of David Colville, who, along with his brother (also named Duncan), owned and operated the Dalintober Distillery. In his paper, Colville asked, *"How has it come about that so many distilleries are located in Campbeltown?"*

There are always two uppermost questions for those with just a passing interest in the area: 'Why were there so many distilleries in Campbeltown?' and, 'Why are there now so few?' Sadly, and despite Colville being a contemporary in the period of mass closures, his paper is delivered just before the Grim Reaper for distilleries scythed a way through (almost) an entire centuries-old industry. Lacking any indications to the latter question, Colville does, at least, present us with eight points, by way of conclusion, as to what prompted the mass integration of distilleries in the small burgh: -

1. *There existed in Kintyre, prior to the seventeenth century, a knowledge of the art of distilling aquavitae, although little light can now be thrown on this remote period, the product having been used for domestic rather than commercial purposes.*
2. *An influx of Lowland settlers in the seventeenth century, not only created an additional demand for whisky produced locally, but provided new capital and enterprise to gradually develop its manufacture.*
3. *The natural situation of Campbeltown resulted in its use as a centre of smuggling operations in connection with the importation of rum, brandy, and wine in the eighteenth century, thus familiarising the inhabitants with the Customs and Excise regulations, and perhaps at the same time creating an increase in the local demand for and consumption of alcoholic liquor.*
4. *The population of the parish (New Statistical Account)*

rose from 4,597 to 9,539 between the years 1775 and 1841, during which period the fishing industry assumed very large proportions locally. This created a still further local demand for spirits, and as in the course of time the smuggling of rum, brandy, and wine was gradually suppressed, so the people came to drink the local whisky in place of these foreign products. Distillation was then, as now, found to be a remunerative occupation in winter when fishing was slack.

5. *The withdrawal of the herring fishing bounty, with the consequent decrease in the size and number of boats in the local fishing fleet, resulted to some extent in capital being transferred from the fishing to the distilling industry.*
6. *Rigid Excise Regulations and corresponding licenses and duties had the ultimate effect of centralising the industry into the large type of distillery with which we are now familiar.*
7. *The heavy rainfall of this district ensured a plentiful water supply. Many of the large distilleries, before improved facilities were available, used the water obtained from wells sunk within their own premises.*
8. *A good market for whisky existed in the Lowlands (or Low Country as it was then generally termed) in the first half of the 19th century, thus encouraging increased production of whisky here.*

Each point can be argued one way or the other. For instance, take point number one: the knowledge of distillation. There are references to aquavitae being made in several other parts of Scotland, and no single centre of distillation can lay any claim to mastering the skill before another. Likewise, Campbeltown and the entire Kintyre peninsula, whilst at times an absolute hive of illicit distilling, has no extraordinary claim to the practice over parts of the Highlands and Islands (and possibly the Lowlands). The fishing industry was prevalent wherever the coastline of Scotland permitted it, and local towns saw their population boom from the trade (points two and five). The Excise Regulations (point six) were not localised to Campbeltown, and, whilst Argyllshire experiences a lot of rainfall, it is difficult to argue that many places in Scotland suffer greatly from drought. Regarding getting the product to markets (point eight), Kintyre is hardly the most accessible destination.

As a recipe for success, however, Colville's points lay out a possible 'perfect storm' for distillers. Campbeltown's remoteness, links to Ireland and beyond, influx of Lowlanders, natural advantages and capitalist drive all mesh together to the point where no one knows (exactly) how many distilleries have come and gone. Colville's paper also highlights that the townsfolk were ideally placed to take advantage of the changes in law and excise due to a flourishing legal (and often illegal) industry. Moss & Hume remark in their seminal book 'The Making of Scotch Whisky':

"At Campbeltown, on the Mull of Kintyre, a region well-known for illicit distilling, at least twenty-seven distilleries were established between 1823 and 1837, taking advantage of a number of favourable factors. It was the only place in the West Highlands with workable coal deposits. It had a sheltered natural harbour and was only a short sea voyage from the rich grain markets of Ireland and southwest Scotland, where demand for whisky was also strong. It had a well-established malting industry with over twenty maltings,[2] drawing their grain from the surrounding countryside."

Until the early part of the 19th century, much of the distilling was carried out to supply local needs, particularly those working in the flourishing herring fishing industry, coal mine, inns, and merchants throughout what is now known as Argyllshire and Ayrshire. The end product would not be recognisable as 'whisky' today. Distilleries were not built with extensive maturing warehouses, and the product was tampered with – or flavoured – as each recipient or public house saw fit.

"In these early days, however, the public taste had not yet

become so refined as it is now, and whisky was used much newer than it is at present day. Consequently warehouses were smaller and fewer than in these latter days."[3]

Legislative changes in the excise laws meant that from 1797 until 1817, no legal distilling took place in Campbeltown. Duty had been increased to £9 per gallon of the Still volume, and the legal distillers went underground, refusing to pay up. Another running sore was the matter of the Highland Line, which acted as a legislative boundary between two areas of Scotland – the Highlands and the Lowlands – creating a two-tier system of Excise regulation. It was devised and implemented to be of help but was actually a hindrance with the distillers on either side of the line complaining that the grass was always greener on the other's patch. The problem lay in that Highland distillers made malt whisky in small pot stills, while Lowland distillers were flash-distilling amounts of execrable cereal-based spirit in larger shallow pot stills.

Neither side saw eye to eye. Campbeltown, for reasons best known to the Excise, was part of the Highland region. Consequently, a lengthy Memorial was drawn up by the local distillers on the 24th of August 1797 and presented to the Commissioners of Excise for Scotland:

"If they are confined as the last Act directs, they certainly can never take out Licenses and I humbly presume to say that if the Duty is above half more of what is presently paid, they cannot live. Even upon the present Duty, and though the line should not be circumscribed, he has enough to do to compete with the smuggler and Low Country Distiller: and if the Duty is augmented above what is here stated, private distillation will be introduced in Defiance of the Officers, and the Revenue will be entirely lost, particularly as the Highland private distiller will have nothing to lose, but everything to gain. The exorbitant tenant will have it in his power to sell his Bear [grain] to these smugglers at a rate that must put it entirely out of the power of the poor to purchase it for Bread: an instance of which happened the beginning of

this season, before the Licensed Distillers commenced, when the Bear was bought up at from Thirty to Thirty-five shillings."

For the next twenty years, not a solitary Still was licensed in the burgh. The first modern - and legal - distillery in Campbeltown was built in 1817, with, no doubt, competition from a readily available supply of illicit spirit still being made. The Town Council minutes from the 30th of January 1800 provide a glimpse into the constant battle the authorities were experiencing:

"The Council is informed that smuggling is carried on in Town and Country to a degree that is prejudicial to the object in view as well as to the poor in general. The Magistrates and Council are of the opinion that the Excise Officer or Constables, assisted by parties of Volunteers, ought to scour the country in order to seize and secure stills, thereby to prevent the abuse or consumption of grain by distillation, and to induce the tenants to bring their grain to market, and the Magistrates are requested to apply to Major McNeal, the Commanding Officer in the Volunteers, for their assistance accordingly. The Magistrates and Council earnestly recommend to the Country Gentlemen to take the subject into their serious consideration."

During 1815, on just one farm near Campbeltown, there were no fewer than 195 transactions in copper stills carried out on behalf of individuals in Kintyre and Arran. These stills, which were around eighteen gallons in volume, were sold complete with head and condensing worm for £3 to £5. They were often the joint property of several men and women through informal companies, sometimes with as many as six partners to one still. The women of Campbeltown appear to have been particularly skilled as brewers and distillers, as their names appear frequently in the few records that still exist.

Cuthbert Bede[4] wrote that prior to the year 1821, the smuggling trade was very lucrative, and a majority of cottagers and day labourers in Kintyre supported large families by the profits of smuggled whisky. At that time, a professional smuggler could clear ten shillings a week after all his expenses were paid. In his book, 'Highlands and Western Islands of Scotland' (1824), Dr John McCulloch described the illicit distillation in Argyllshire:

"The Highland process of distillation is very simple: the smallness of the capital engaged, with the risk of seizure limiting the apparatus to that which is absolutely necessary. The malting is generally carried on by a distinct class, by the dealers in grain themselves, and the wash is manufactured in a rude hut in some retired or concealed spot, poorly provided with a few casks and tubs. The remainder of the apparatus consists of two or three casks to receive the spirit, and of a still, generally of eighteen gallons in capacity with a very short worm and tub: the great command of water rendering a long one unnecessary. Sometimes a hut is erected to protect the still from the weather, but it is frequently set up in the open air, under some bank or rock which permits a stream of water to be easily introduced into the tub. On the seacoast the shore is generally chosen for this purpose, as it enables the operators to keep watch of their commodity with greater ease: but in inland situations a wood or some secluded mountain glen is the common seat of operation. These stills are generally discovered by the smoke, though expert Excisemen also trace them by examining the water of the mountain streams impregnated by the waste."

Stills for distillation within Campbeltown were most frequently obtained due to the expertise of Robert Armour, the town's plumber. He built up a considerable sideline in still-making and, given that his (known) records range from May 1811 to September 1817 and that distilling on a legal basis was virtually non-existent between 1797 and 1817, his traffic must have been the mainstay of illicit distilling in Kintyre during these years.

Robert Armour's business took in over £2,000 for the period covered in his records, so he must have lived in some degree of comfort. Curiously, in 1885, when structural alterations were being done to Armour's shop at the corner of Main Street and

Shore Street, workmen found a Still Vat buried pretty deep in the ground and a secret vent leading up into the main chimney in the gable. *"It is supposed,"* remarked the Campbeltown Courier, *"That at one time, the ground beneath the flooring of the shop has been a vault, where secret distilling operations were carried on."* It seems that Robert Armour had practised what he had preached – or, at the very least, had a working shop model for potential customers.

The Campbeltown Distillery broke the distilling deadlock - the first legal distillery, built in 1817, and the first to challenge all the 'sma' stills' in the burgh.[5] Founded by John Mactaggart, maltster, and John Beith, banker, the distillery can be viewed as Campbeltown's first modern or industrial distillery. Situated in the middle of Glebe Street, its construction could not have foreseen how the area would become the epicentre of Campbeltown's distilling industry, although it would take another seven years for the next distillery to be built. John Beith may be the same person as listed in the still books of Robert Armour, having bought illicit stills prior to the legal Campbeltown Distillery (as his name appears several times - see Appendix G). Despite having the highly reputable job of 'banker', was the first businessman in Campbeltown to own a legal distillery, a rogue-turned-legitimate?

Across Scotland, the Excise Act (or Wash Act) passed on 18th of July 1823, finally sought to give parity and fairness across the entire industry. Gone were the favourable conditions to certain distillers (as outlined by Duncan Colville in Appendix B) and, for the set fee of £10, distillers could now license a still without fear of regional differences in excise later crushing their business.

No less than 216 distilleries across Scotland were licenced from 1823 to 1830 as entrepreneurs saw the potential benefits of this new legislation. Printed in the 'Inverness Courier' on the 14th of March 1827 were 281 firms of malt distillers. Argyll South[6] could boast 26 distilleries, whilst the Elgin region (incorporating much of what we now consider Speyside) had 37, with Perthshire having a table-topping 43.

Despite these numbers, there is little doubt that the addition of 14 new distilleries before 1830 in such a small town and population went a long way to forming Campbeltown's moniker of 'Whiskyopolis'.

Much of the early success of the Kintyre distillers had been developed during the rebellious illicit years. The neighbouring towns, harbours, and in particular, Glasgow, all played a large part in distributing the spirit made within the burgh. In 1814, it was reported that less than six weeks after the barley harvest, 'public houses were selling whisky distilled from it'.[7]

The Scotch whisky trade flourished with the urbanisation of cities such as Glasgow and the development of the English market. From a national output in 1823 of 3,000,000 gallons, distillation increased to over 8,000,000 just two years later (hitting 10,000,000 proof gallons in 1828).[8]

For the first half of the century, exports (beyond the UK) were not a considerable part of the business. Indeed, for the Campbeltown distillers, there was little interest beyond the merchants of Glasgow.

However, success for these new distillers was not guaranteed. Within Kintyre, proximity to the town and harbour appears to have been a key determiner in those concerns that persevered - a fact that is eminently apparent to anyone visiting the area. A guidebook entitled 'Views of Campbeltown' written by William Smith Jr and published in 1835 goes some way to explaining this:

"...the greatest advantage derived from this mode of conveyance [referring to the introduction of steamboat communication with Glasgow] has accrued to the Distillers in Campbeltown, for they are thus enabled to send their whisky to the Glasgow market at a very moderate expense, besides avoiding the delay, which causes a considerable decrease in the quantity and strength of the spirits, and the risk which the former mode of conveyance had.

"These advantages have tended considerably to the erection of new distilleries so that, although it was only in 1817 that the first distillery was erected, under the new laws, by Messrs John Beith & Co., there are now upwards of twenty-three in full operation. The draff, or refuse of the grain, is sold at almost a

nominal price, for although the distilleries are generally on a limited scale, the produce is great compared with the consumpt. There being but little of it made use of in the dairy, it is generally sold to poor people, who feed their swine with it, and this tends greatly to keep up this filthy infliction.

"The whisky, which is of an excellent quality, is sold wholesale, principally by means of agents in Glasgow. There is a good part of it also sent into the Ayrshire markets, and a small portion of it sometimes find its way into England, although, from the extra duty per gallon, this must always be a very limited quantity.

"The contrast between the extensiveness of the present and former distilleries, has been often remarked by every person connected in the slightest degree with the trade. At one time, if 300 gallons were in bond, the whole work stopped until a market had been found for this amazing quantity. Whereas now some of the distillers may sometimes have on hand, when prices are low, nearly 3,000 gallons, and still continue working, feeling confident of a sure market for their produce, which has acquired a considerable reputation throughout the whole West of Scotland, and, in fact, wherever it has been found in its genuine purity.

"Each of the present distilleries now produces on an average 20,000 gallons. The 'Duke of Lancaster' Steam-Packet carried to Glasgow, in the year ending 1834, nearly 300,000 gallons of whisky from Campbeltown.

"Steam Navigation has been of immense advantage to the community – the voyage to Glasgow, the chief mart where the whisky made in Campbeltown is sold, being in 1835 performed in nine to twelve houses, when, previous to its introduction, the voyage often consumed as many days. In fact, at no very distant date, the voyage to Glasgow was considered of such momentous importance that wills were regularly drawn out by parties hazarding the expedition. Although about twelve days might then be considered rather a tedious passage, yet often did the packets take much longer. In some instances goods [had] been ordered from Glasgow and regularly shipped and bills at three months drawn from the day the vessel sailed, and those bills have become due before the goods have arrived in Campbeltown!"[9]

With the invention of the 'Stein', or 'Continuous Still', the perception of Scotch whisky changed as markedly as the product. Whereas grain whisky had previously been manufactured in a similar way to malt whisky – just in much larger stills – the continuous still allowed a purer and plainer spirit for blending with the more fiery Highland spirits. The invention of this method for continuous distillation, although at first slow to take off, would have a lasting impact on the industry and Campbeltown whisky.

Despite the continued growth in demand for Scottish spirits from the English – especially Lowland grain – the whisky industry suffered along with most other industries in the 1840s. The Campbeltown distillers, despite losing a few of the smaller and more remote distilleries, continued unabated and, in 1848, were able to set up the Campbeltown Distillers' Association. Sadly, no records remain from this organisation, but – according to correspondence and media coverage – the association acted on behalf of all of the distillers within the district. At times, motions regarding pricing and best practices would be brought in front of the association. And whilst as a group they were able to help the burgh find solutions with regards to effluent and waste (including draff and potale), it is clear that the individuality of each business was maintained.

Much of the mid-part of the 19th century was a steady progression – at least for those distilleries that persevered. Between 1824 and the first full account of the district (provided by Alfred Barnard in 1885), no less than eleven distilleries were started and then closed.

When John Walker of Kilmarnock died in 1857, his personal estate was valued at £4,256 (around £400,000 ATTOW), with whisky *"accounting for over half the value of the entire [shop] stock, some £750 (of which £370 was under bond). The holdings were dominated by Campbeltown whiskies, now mostly forgotten names like Kinloch, Lochhead, Lochruan, Rieclachan, Springside (and the still very well-known) Springbank... Geography, or rather proximity, apparently dictated what John used in his blends, possibly along with a local preference for the stronger flavours of the West Coast and island distilleries, relatively available through the ports of Troon and Ayr."*[10]

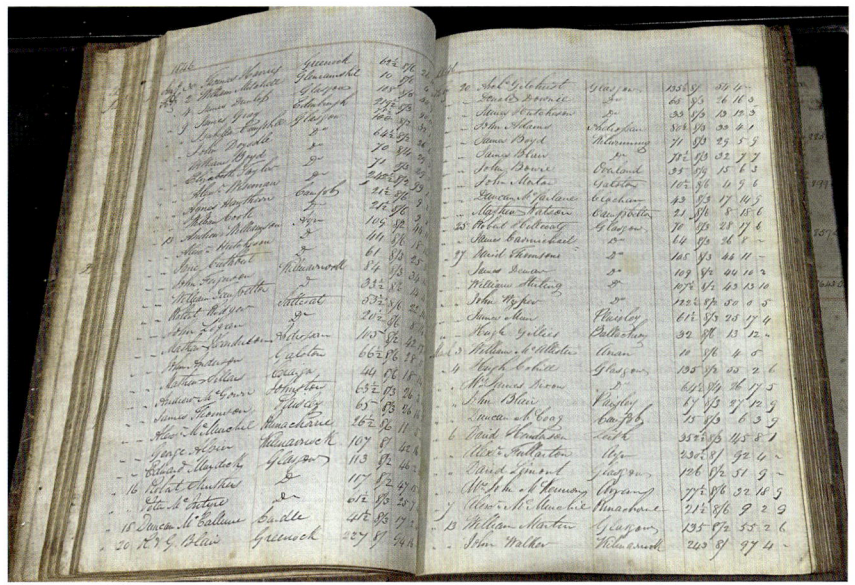

Springbank's sales ledger from 1846 showing John Walker.

A decade later, John Walker & Son – as the shop became known – had increased their whisky stocks by a third, much of which was still dominated by 'West Coast' whiskies such as Springbank and Rieclachan.[11] John Walker appears in the ledgers of J. & A. Mitchell in 1846 along with numerous other accounts, many of which were publicans and shop owners, but also private individuals and buyers for large estates. The addresses are dominated by Glasgow, Paisley, Leith, and the surrounding areas, including Campbeltown. John Walker would continue to be a customer of J. & A. Mitchell up until the crash of the 1980s.

Kintyre was not the most fertile farmland and had never made an abundant amount of grain. Prior to Campbeltown receiving regular visits by the large steamers, there were several years where bad harvests led to a scarcity of distilling activity.

Due to its hardiness, Bere, a six-row barley strain, had been grown as a priority for the distilling industry – at least in the parts of Scotland that were conducive to its growth. In 1811, one-half of the Hebridean crop was given to this grain due to its early harvest and ability to thrive in the western climate. In coastal areas, seaweed was abundant and could be used as a manure, allowing Bere to be grown in poor topsoil. As the industry thrived, 'Bere' gave way to barley, although it was still farmed until the 20th century.[12]

Joseph Pacy noted that *"The supply of Bere and Bigg[13] was not sufficient for the demand, therefore the distillers and maltster imported barley from the north of Ireland, which is of easy access to Campbeltown at a cost, freight included, not much over that for the lighter grain… The difference of the tax on the two kinds of malt was a temptation to attempt to pass barley on the Excise for Bere and Bigg, which considering the regulations I have alluded to, was not easy to resist."* (See Appendix C)

Maps from 1801 – and more clearly in 1820 – show how the area known as Dalintober was separated in a way that is hard to fathom now, with the Esplanade Road linking the Old Quay on the Campbeltown side to the Dalintober Quay opposite. The 'Loch Head' reached as far as Longrow and Lochend Street (hence the name). The harbour was ideally sheltered for the steamers and cargo ships, and much of the stonework that went in to building the distilleries was brought in as ballast from the great boats coming and going.

In 1774, the Town Council built a wall from the north side of the old quay to the bottom of Main Street and: *"Ordered boats to deposit their ballast hitherto 'thrown out in different parts of the harbour' as infill behind it."*[14]

A much grander proposal was put forward in 1823 by Archibald McNair, a timber merchant on Bolgam Street, who proposed to improve the road behind the wall and to build a row of sea-front properties. The council liked this idea, and plans were approved to build up a suitable embankment, allowing the buildings to be built on top. By 1828, the deed had been received from London and was ready for signing. However, in the interim five-year period, whilst only the Campbeltown Distillery had existed when the project was first envisioned, there were now around fifteen additional distilleries bordering the Mussel Ebb.

The town was already synonymous with whisky and its production, but now, due to its industrial output, the nickname 'Whiskyopolis' was coined – most likely sometime in the 1870s. Barnard omitted to use the phrase, preferring Whisky Metropolis, in his writings - it is possible he whiffed an air of dislike for the term whilst he was visiting. An advertisement in the 'Ardrossan and Saltcoats Herald' in 1878 offered excursions to Campbeltown with *"ample time to see 'Whiskyopolis'."* Evidently, the moniker had been in use long enough to allow its use in marketing. The earliest reference in the 'British News Archive' was from the 'Glasgow Herald' in February 1877:

"The inhabitants of Campbeltown, or properly Whiskyopolis, the capital of Kintyre, are just now threatened with a visitation that is expected to inflict more damage than a plague of locusts. It is well known by all travellers in the Peninsula of Kintyre that the people of Campbeltown are in many ways a superior race. They are simple in their habits – cleanly, moral, God-fearing, and untainted even by the faintest dream of that audacious spirit of scepticism which has so long been 'tirling the Kirks'[15] in the great centres of the so-called civilisation."[16]

The article – a great lament against the evils of the 'Argyll and Bute Militia' descending upon Campbeltown – called out a certain Mr John Ross as the potential saviour from this egregious and conspicuous intrusion. Ross was the owner of Longrow Distillery, which sat perpendicular to the street of the same name and adjacent to Springbank Distillery. The article goes on, and leaves the reader wondering if John Ross was in some way responsible for the prose:

"But who is John Ross? ...surely no one who has sipt [sic] his tumbler of Campbeltonian nectar can be ignorant of the

identity of John Ross. Why, John Ross is, in fact, the greatest Whiskypolitan living. Good, shrewd man, he has retired from business with as much money as would fill a mash tub. But if he no longer distils the beautiful 'peat-reek', he is by no means an idle man; and he does not hide his siller either in a 'hedge' or a 'hugger'. He is generous, and spends much of what he made by selling unadulterated whisky in the propagation of an undiluted gospel."

Other terms such as 'Whiskyville' and 'Whisky Capital of the World' (and perhaps least used was 'Whiskeytown')[17] were all coined but only for a few decades until the prefix 'once' was necessary – a signal for the decline of the sobriquets. Possibly the best use of 'Whiskyopolis' came from the 'Oban Times' in February 1879. Whilst discussing the 'obnoxious practice' of *"engaging their neighbours' servant[s] in an underhand way… as a breach of the fourth commandment, which says 'Thou shalt not covet thy neighbour's man-servant nor his maid-servant', the decalogue has evidently got into a muddied condition in Whiskyopolis. The clergy should see to the matter at once, and get it rectified, or serious consequences may follow."*

Evidently, there were those who believed the product of Campbeltown was a detrimental element to society, causing decent men to stray against the many commandments.

Circa 1900. The new warehouses for Glen Nevis Distillery are clearly visible on Glebe Street, next to Ardlussa Distillery on the right.

CHAPTER 2

THE LAST DISTILLERY

"We have all heard of Campbeltown whisky, and many excellent men among us have tasted it. The racy qualities of this species of strong waters have been widely appreciated by Churchmen and Dissenters. The Campbeltown tap is known throughout the civilised world. It has a flavour of its own, and though, as compared with 'North Port', it is decidedly underproof, it is largely sold by evangelical victuallers and is pronounced a 'Scriptural' drink by ardent volunteers."

'The Campbeltown Apostle On Disestablishment'
Montrose Standard, October 1885

"Scotch whisky achieved its world fame and acceptance through the skill and acumen of the blenders. The distillers certainly did their share; they produced superlative spirits. There lay part of the disadvantage: none of the hundred or more of them was able to produce year after year a consistently uniform beverage in sufficient quantity to make a world-wide appeal for itself alone. That was where the blenders stepped in: they blended, or mixed, the spirits of many distilleries to market in increasing amounts a beverage of consistent and uniform quality, a quality adjusted to appeal to the palates of their customers."

'Scotch – The Formative Years'
Ross Wilson, 1970

John Syme noticed too late as the scaffolding he was working on began to sway. Two storeys up and looking onto Glebe Street, at the north end of the new malting barns, Syme and his five co-workers had just moved some of the larger stones. Now, as Syme was ready to position the stones on what would make the top tier of the wall, the momentum of shifting this extra weight stressed the scaffolding beyond its limit. As the structure collapsed, several fellow workers were able to land safely, but Syme and John Michie, who had also been at the top, came off the worst.[18]

"It was a relief no one perished." Stated Dr Gibson as he tended to the wounded.

Just six months earlier, in September 1876, Dr Gibson had attended one of the worst and most distressing accidents of his career. Whilst trying to avoid cockroaches crawling about,[19] William Court, an officer of the Inland Revenue attached to the Kintyre Distillery, fell into a large heater of boiling water. Court, who had only just been assigned to the distillery and was likely unacquainted with the layout, managed to free himself and crawl to the nearby house of David Ralston, an employee of the distillery. Ralston, along with another distillery worker, Daniel Bowie, conveyed Court to his lodgings on Glebe Street whilst Dr Gibson was summoned. Dr Gibson did all he could to alleviate Court's great suffering, and despite being in and out of consciousness for the next day, he eventually passed away the following night.

Dr William Gibson moved to Campbeltown in 1854 and lived there until his death in 1922, aged 98. Born in 1824 in Haddington, East Lothian, Gibson moved to Campbeltown after graduating from Edinburgh University and, within a year, was appointed Parochial Medical Officer. At the time of his death, he was Scotland's longest-serving medical practitioner, having served the Campbeltown and Kintyre communities for over 60 years. During his time, he witnessed numerous accidents and deaths of distillery workers and tradesmen.

The lack of permanent injury or fatality greatly relieved the owners of James Ferguson & Sons, the business behind the new distillery. Not being locals, James Ferguson and his business partner and brother, George Ferguson, were keen not to have the spotlight shone on their new enterprise. Certainly not in a negative way. Glebe Street was already the hub of distilling activity within Campbeltown. With the addition of Glen Nevis in 1873 and Ardlussa in 1879, the street was one long parade of distilleries from Albyn Distillery at its northern tip (situated on The Roading) and, heading south, the Glengyle, Rieclachan, Campbeltown, Springbank and Longrow distilleries all on the east side.

Perhaps Dr Gibson's decision to live at 'Kirkland' on Dell Road, adjacent to Glebe Street, ensured he was never that far from the next accident.

For any other town, the construction of a new distillery would be something novel and newsworthy, but Campbeltown was not like any other town. Ardlussa began operating in September 1879 and received the following brief news coverage buried deep within the long columns of the local 'Courier':

"The New distillery erected in Glebe Street by the Ardlussa Distillery Company, and which is to be called the Ardlussa Distillery, has now been so far completed as to admit of operations being commenced, and we understand that on Thursday the first grain was wet. The erection is in the form of an oblong square, having a frontage of three storeys, and extends 256 feet along Glebe Street. The following are the dimensions of the different parts of the work: - Two malt barns, with granary overhead, 165 feet by 48 feet; drying kiln, 48 feet by 42 feet. There will be no sacks required for ground or unground malt, all being done by machinery and hoppers. The malt store is 42 feet by 48 feet, and the mash room underneath is of the same dimensions. The still house with tun room is 130 feet by 40 feet. Bonded warehouse along Dell Road, 210 ft by 60ft.

"There is only one pump in the distillery, which is used for pumping the worts up to the refrigerator. Everything else, which in many other distilleries in town requires to be worked

by means of pumping, is here carried on by gravitation. This is unquestionably a vast improvement on the old system, and will be a great saving of labour and expense. The wash still is capable of charging about 3,200 gallons, and the spirit still 1,800 gallons. The engine in the works is 20 horsepower (nominal), and the boiler, which is perhaps the largest in town, is 22 feet by 7 feet 6 inches. The smoke from the distillery is discharged from a chimney stalk reaching a height of 85 feet, a sufficient guarantee that the smoke emitted will not become a nuisance to the neighbourhood.

"The Excise and other offices required are commodious and suitable, while an excellent house for the manager and another for a workman have likewise been added. All the internal arrangements and fittings have been constructed on the newest and most approved principles, and everything about the work reflects credit alike on the architect and contractors. This new distillery makes the twenty-second work of the kind in town; and it is estimated that, when the whole are in full operation, something like 50,000 gallons[20] will be turned out per week. The contractors were as follows: - Messrs Neil Ferguson & Son, mason work; Mr C. Martin, joiner; Mr Andrew Griffen, engine and machinery; and Messrs Robert Armour & Sons, copper work."[21]

James Ferguson & Sons were based at 7 Cadogan Street, Glasgow. The firm were spirit merchants and distributors of their own brands and had already acquired the Jura Distillery in 1875. It is more than likely that Fergusons were already trading in Campbeltown whisky (often referred to as 'Highland' rather than 'Campbeltown') and building the distillery was a natural diversification to ensure future supply.

Forty-seven years before the Fergusons broke ground on Glebe Street for what would be Ardlussa Distillery, David Colville was planning a new distillery with a business associate, Peter Reid, in Glasgow. Their correspondence, at least what survives, allows us some insight into the planning and thinking behind a new distillery during this era. Colville was already a partner in the Dalaruan Distillery, built in 1825, and by the first letter we have, had already located buildings, previously maltings, in the area

Circa 1880. A closer view from Gallowhill. The 'oast' style pagodas were uniformly adopted until Benmore changed theirs to a Doig style.

known as Dalintober.

Peter Reid wrote on the 15th of February, 1832: *"Your letter is not so definite as I could have wished - the greater part of it being describing the property - of the capabilities of the place you should be a good judge - on that we can speak afterwards. To your most important inquiry of will it pay, I say I believe it would and handsomely – you should know, last year was no criterion. A great deal of good has been done with these works in Campbeltown – Glasgow is extending daily and becoming more and more the great mart of Scotland."*[22]

During the 1800s, Glasgow was one of Britain's fastest-growing cities. Between 1801 and 1901, the population increased tenfold. From what was considered a large town in the 18th century emerged Britain's third largest city and one of growing importance to the trade with the rest of the Kingdom.

This growth mirrored that of the Campbeltown whisky industry, which relied on the city's ports as the first destination for their whisky. After the Campbeltown Distillery was completed in 1817, the town witnessed a further 16 distilleries erected by 1832. Albyn, Argyll, Burnside, Caledonian, Dalaruan, Glenramskill, Hazelburn, Highland, Kinloch, Kintyre, Lochhead, Lochside, Longrow, Meadowburn, Rieclachan and Springbank had all been completed, with Scotia being built directly adjacent to the planned Dalintober.

Reid was an established merchant in Glasgow, and his role within the new firm, to be named Colville & Reid, was as its agent on a commission of two pennies and a farthing in the pound. Being based in Glasgow, Reid relied on the letters from Colville but was better placed to judge the success of the venture from a sales perspective.

"In a word, if you managed at Campbeltown and I'm here, I am sure (that is with the surety of all terrestrial things) that it should do well.

"Now as to 'could such an additional quantity be got easily quit of without more than ordinary risk': as to easily, I say no, but that I could see some more than I have been doing for you, of late, I think might be accomplished by increased expenditure which I am ready to undertake. I think that I could command a somewhat steady consumpt[ion] of produce, and you and I cannot and must not hide from ourselves the fact that we are both at the time of life for such exertions and when they will most likely be successful."

Reid was also concerned about word getting out about the town as plans like this can often spread like wildfire in small communities.

"I suppose you will not yet have divulged your project to any. I hate when these things make a 'sough' [rumour or gossip] through the town. I say let it be done now, fit it up properly with every possible new improvement of your experience, but with economy over cutting every procedure. The outlay expense would be (proportionately) small, I think. What sum would be required to set it in working order, and how much money? Are you correct in saying five hundred gallons weekly? Of course, the largest quantity in shortest time is the proper way."

Five hundred gallons a week was the output of Colville's Dalaruan Distillery and matched many of the other newly built distilleries. Reid wrote another letter the same day, reiterating much of what he had already posted but adding that *"the last five years, as an average, that most of the works at Campbeltown [distillers] have done well. Glasgow is yearly extending and becoming more and more the great mart of Scottish merchandise.*

"The communication with Campbeltown is good, and my present acquaintance, and to be supposed increasing acquaintance, in the trade should be of some avail with regard to the 'easily' getting quit of the extra quantity, of course — no, not easily — but increased exertions could be made. And we are at the best time of life for these; neither too young to be overlooked

nor too old to take it as a serious evil. However, I think that I could get through a considerable quantity more than what of late D.C. & Co. [Dalaruan Distillery] have sent me."

Only one letter survives from David Colville to Peter Reid. Sent two days after Reid's letters on the 13th, Colville confirms that, to prevent any rumours, he *"spoke to none except my father today. He thinks about 600 pounds should set it going except stock for carrying it on, and I think four percent or more should do this. I would incline that he and I should be the only partners or perhaps if John Hart learned to be mashman that he could also do all the writing that might be necessary here and take his [illegible] under my superintendence. My father is to be silent in the meantime and thinks that although we may be consulting about it, I think it will be advisable to be at no expense until the land is positively fixed, which will likely be very soon. We both think the place will do five hundred gallons weekly by doing a period every week. What ground should a four or five horsepower engine necessary apparatus cover? What is the expense of keeping it moving? Is there much risk of it going wrong, or is it easily managed more fully by post etc, will the engine do the work of four or five horse, what will it cost?"*

The steam engine revolution removed the need for horse or water-driven wheels and was a driving force in the increased output of distilleries – allowing them to run for longer. Although the steam-driven boats had vastly decreased the time it took for mail to come and go between Campbeltown and Glasgow, it did not prevent the overlapping of mail. Subsequently, Reid was able to send out another letter on the 18th of February before he had received the full reply from Colville.

"Economy must rule all the proceedings. However, I must say that one thousand, to one thousand two hundred pounds, as you state, is but a small sum to start us. As to partners, I dare say thirds are as good as any. I am not a sanguine fellow and don't wish to take large risks. What will either make or unmake me

suddenly a larger share than one-third I don't wish to hold, it would keep me too anxious. To more than three partners I would object however. ... As to an engine, 'twill cost about £40-50 low power.

"I am going to see a very fine new one about four or five horsepower on Monday. The room required will be very little. I'll measure exactly and also ascertain cost; I will do more. The horses drink incessantly. Keep in mind the continued supply of water it will require. It will pump itself, all that it wants is plenty. The expense of keeping it moving will be small I think and no risk of its going wrong. A person who understands it will be proper to have. 'Tis easy to make it work but if not attended to rightly it may spoil itself; want of cleanliness or oil in proper time or place will make it go done quickly, otherwise 'twill last fifty years and more."

On the 28th, Reid wrote again:

"You say you may perhaps come here to see an engine working and stills etc. Would it not be best to do so now or that we might speak and arrange more decidedly on every matter before concluding all the terms? If you did so it strikes me our calculations could be made more close and carefully because taking an engine by the hand and afterwards it costing too much or perhaps not found to suit at all would be rather serious. I would return to Campbeltown with you if you thought it necessary so as to arrange all the preliminary of our procedure."

Sadly, no letters survive that allow an insight into the actual costs of building the distillery – nor the apparatus and its installation. Despite further letters expressing concerns over the increase in the barley duty that was delivered on the 6th of April and some panic selling in the 'Ayrshire' trade, the company partnership was signed within a week of commencing the distillery.

The 1823 Excise Act was the great catalyst for the conversion of the many of the smaller distillery setups, mostly illegal, to a more industrial setup. The majority of the modern Campbeltown distilleries were built between 1823 and 1834 – part of the great boom in Scotland. Success, however, was not guaranteed and many, especially those still considered 'small' did not survive beyond the 1850s. Several of the distilleries were advertised for sale within a decade or two of being established - often being stripped of any useful plant by neighbouring distilleries. Of those that are traceable, Caledonian, Drumore, Glenramskill, Highland, Lochside, Union and West Highland distilleries all closed sometime within the late 1840s and early 1850s. Through the partnership of Reid & Colville, Dalintober survived the purge of the mid-part of the 19th century.

The distilling season of Autumn to Spring avoided the summer months when the heat hampered the malting process. This was naturally dependent on suitable barley being harvested and available. Steamers loaded with barley were setting off from the east coast of Scotland bound for Campbeltown. From the border counties of Roxburgh and Berwick to Moray and Caithness in the furthest north, barley was not just grown in abundance but generally accepted as where the best quality barley was harvested. Within Campbeltown, however, the distillers never showed any sign of favouritism regarding who or where the barley came from other than to the local farmers - assuming the quality was up to standard. Regular updates of barley shipments would grace the pages of the newspapers, such as:

"Lord Reidhaven of Banff, Runcie, from Konigsberg, 238 tons barley, consigned to Lamb, Colville & Co.; Vestuta of Banff, Fowler, from Konigsberg, 206 tons, consigned to Reid & Colville; Lady Bute of Rothesay, Service from Wick, 140 tons, consignees Glenside Distillery Company; Lizzie from Padstow, 80 tons, consignees Greenlees & Colvill."[23]

As the distilling industry grew, so did the list of potential barley suppliers. Barley was shipped from all over Scotland, supplemented by ships loaded from England, Ireland, Denmark, Moldova and the Danube. By the latter part of the 19th century, steamers of 3,000 tons were familiar sights on the quays of Campbeltown Loch. OMIC in Campbeltown commented in June 1897:

"In Campbeltown, we are blessed by the daily visit of the barley agent. He brings the gossip of the day, local and national, and conveys information as to the state of the markets throughout the countries of the world. His functions are thus twofold, and it is hard to say which side is most appreciated. The barley market, it is true, is of great importance, but at times we dearly love a chat, and tit-bits of general information are not infrequent, the barley merchant and the distiller both profiting thereby. When one is in the genial frame of mind induced by intelligent conversation, it is more easy to order 500 tons of barley than it is to buy 50 tons when one is confined to the purely commercial aspect of the case."

Barley was the continued topic of conversation amongst the distillers. With low prices for labour, coal and peat, it was barley, above all other supplies, that dictated the profit margin for the owners. It was continually referred to during all of the journals and articles of the period:

"A large proportion of Scotch and Irish barley is being used by the Campbeltown distillers this season. The colour rendered this barley unsuitable for the brewers, and consequently the bulk of the Scotch and Irish barleys have found their way into the hands of the whisky producer. The quality is excellent and the price reasonable, while the fermentation and produce are all that can be desired." * April 1897

"The absorbing topic amongst the distillers here is the abnormal rise in the price of barley. Matters were bad enough in the early part of the season, when 24s to 26s was being paid for Scotch [barley]. Now that the price has risen to 32s the outlook is indeed serious. Did the selling price of whisky advance in a

like ratio, distillers would not complain, but dealers apparently expect the old prices to hold, which is simply absurd. So far as I can gather, the opinion seems to be general that the best way out of an impossible position it to make the working season a very short one. Foreign barley has not maintained the position it held last year, the quality being much inferior, hence the importation is much less." * February 1898

"A considerable quantity of the barley used by many of the Scotch distillers for the last two or three years came from the Black Sea. This year there will be little or no barley to export from these districts in consequence of deficient crops. This is to be regretted, as the quality of the barley was invariably such as to make it well suited for distilling purposes, especially with a mixture of home barley wrought along with it." * October 1899

From the brief accounts available from Dalintober Distillery, a typical month in 1832 saw £500, 15s, 6d spent on barley with 'Wages and Coals etc' costing only £35, 4s, 11d.[24] Despite these early accounts showing a loss, it soon became a profitable enterprise, and barring those distilleries that closed soon after starting, most flourished. So much so that in 1841, the Town Council revised their rateable values for the distilleries:

"The meeting having revised the amended list of assessment for the Distilleries prepared by the Clerk from the last information we could obtain care of opinion that the sums attached to their names respectively should for the charge against them viz:"

Dalintober Distillery to be assessed on	£240
Lochruan Distillery to be assessed on	£200
Scotia Distillery to be assessed on	£200
Highland Distillery to be assessed on	£400
Kintyre Distillery to be assessed on	£200
Glenside Distillery to be assessed on	£200
Dalaruan Distillery to be assessed on	£200

Lochhead Distillery to be assessed on	£200
Kinloch Distillery to be assessed on	£160
Union & Campbeltown Distillery to be assessed on	£160
Rieclachan Distillery to be assessed on	£200
Tober an Righ Distillery to be assessed on	£80
Longrow Distillery to be assessed on	£200
Lochside Distillery to be assessed on	£160
Mountain Dew Distillery to be assessed on	£40
Caledonian Distillery to be assessed on	£200
Meadow Burn Distillery to be assessed on	£240
Burnside Distillery to be assessed on	£240
West Highland Distillery to be assessed on	£100
Hazel Burn Distillery to be assessed on	£200
Glenramskill Distillery to be assessed on	£200
Spring Bank Distillery to be assessed on	£200
Albyn Distillery to be assessed on	£200
Springside Distillery to be assessed on	£200

In March 1841, the Town Council Minutes explained the rationale for the new rates; *"The meeting resolved that in place of the mode in which the Trade of the Distilleries has been hitherto conducted, that they be adapted according to the quantity made at each on a graduating scale."* Thus, it is possible to determine, to a degree, the size of each distillery from how much tax they were expected to pay.

In these days of trading, before distillate had to remain in bond for some time prior to its removal, the distilleries, through their agents mainly in Glasgow, could sell and ship their wares immediately.

In such a small community, the appeal against the rates must have appeared odd, juxtaposed as it was with the apparent wealth of the distillers. Within decades of the mad rush to erect distilleries, a similar 'peacock' event began with the building of grand houses, especially those on either side of the Loch. From the Georgian houses that sit juxtaposed to the tenement blocks of the town - those that give Campbeltown the look and feel of Glasgow (as designed by Glasgow architects and hence the commonly used nickname 'Wee Toon') – to the mid-19th century.

"The continued prosperity of the spirit trade is reflected in Campbeltown. The general prosperity of the old town is dependent on it, and, judging from the numerous new villas springing up on the slopes of either side of the loch, evidence is not wanting that we participate in good times. After all, we rather pity the producer in the far north when we read of Arctic weather, blocked railways and frozen streams."* April 1897

Many of those villas, such as Auchinlee, Craigard, Hazelbank and East Cliff remain. Craigard, an 'Italianate Villa', was built for William McKersie, owner of Albyn Distillery. The house was designed by Henry Clifford, a prominent architect in the village. Clifford was also responsible for designing Auchinlee (Built for John McKersie[25]), Redcliffe (built for William Greenlees), Redholme (built for Arthur Gardiner) and 'The Club' on Main Street. Hazelbank, now the Ardshiel Hotel, was built by John Burnet for Duncan Colville. Burnet also designed the Longrow United Presbyterian Church in 1869 (now known as the Lorne and Lowland Parish Church).[26]

Whilst barley was a common topic of conversation amongst the distillers, the townsfolk were often more concerned with their water supplies. In the early part of the 19th century, several small lochs and wells were the primary water source for the inhabitants of the burgh, but no one could have envisioned the explosion of industrial-sized distilleries and the drain this would have on the resources.

Wells had been dug at several distilleries, including Scotia, Argyll, Benmore and Dalintober. Those distilleries near Lochend could utilise water coming through the Town Burn. To satisfy the growing distilling industry and to update the town's water

Crosshill Reservoir looking out towards Davaar. Picture courtesy of John Mcfadyen.

supply, the Crosshill Reservoir was commissioned in 1848 and completed in 1852. As the land belonged to George Campbell, 8th Duke of Argyll, a fee of 2d per 1,000 gallons was levied to the distillers. This returned an estimated £600 per year although the water was often accused of being poor quality and infested.[27] The water from the reservoir fed into Campbeltown via a single pipe until the issue was brought up as part of the Campbeltown Burgh and Harbour Bill in 1876.

Dr Gibson, Campbeltown's Parochial Medical Officer, stated to the Select Committee at the House of Commons (meeting to consider the Harbour Bill) that *"the water was dirty. Some tenements had not taps and the people in these tenements had to carry it from the public taps."*[28]

Complaints had been made about the want of water for the hospital. *"In the winter of 1874 there was no water for six weeks,"* Dr Gibson continued, *"Nor was there any for about two months later that summer. The water in addition to being very brown, was in the summer full of small crustacea, and sometimes human hair and worms were seen."*

The local agent for the Duke, Duncan Ferguson, retorted that in 1861, a pipe had been laid to Dalintober without any communication to the Duke's agent. However, a later agreement of £5 per annum, to be paid annually, was put in place. It was noted that the 2d rate per 1,000 gallons had been fixed in 1871, and in that year, *"the distillers amounted to 70,320,000 gallons, in 1872 it was 59,653,000, in 1873 there was a slight increase and in 1875 it was 73,040,000 gallons."* Ferguson added that the estate had collected water rates from the distillers for the last twenty years, and *"if there was cause of complaint, he should certainly have heard it."*

Duncan Colville, Managing Partner of Reid & Colville (Dalintober Distillery), replied tersely:

"The reason we never formally complained to the Duke's chamberlain was because we found from experience that our best interests were secured by simply taking whatever supply was allowed us, and being thankful."[29]

When Charles Greenlees of Dalaruan Distillery was then asked why the firm had not complained directly regarding the water problems, his answer was met with laughter by those within the room:

"*Well, the supply might be cut off altogether!*"

The Bill would see the creation of two pipes from the Crosshill Loch, one servicing the distilleries and one the townsfolk. In 1884, a water filter was installed, but problems remained, and in October 1887, the Campbeltown Courier reported that:

"We understand that both Crosshill and Lochruan water supplies are very low, and that measures are being taken to conserve them as much as possible… intimation has been given to the various distilleries that, in the event of matters not improving within ten days, the supply to these works from Crosshill loch will be shut off."

The water problem persisted until the middle of the 20th century when the town purchased the Crosshill Reservoir from the Duke's estate in 1945, and a new reservoir at Auchalochy began alleviating the supply issues in 1950. Crosshill Loch (as it is more commonly referred to) remains the source of water for the town's distilleries as the water is free from chemical treatment.

Whilst most of the more common distillery jobs drew in workers from the immediate area, those positions commanding experience or further education were advertised far and wide. Distillery managers would often serve time all over the country. On average, each Campbeltown distillery employed around twelve men, and whilst jobs would be interchanged, the head brewer was often second only to the distillery manager. The carting of barley and then the maltings were the most labour-intensive, and shiels (barley shovels) would be held proudly in the rare moments a photo of the staff was taken.

Peat had long been the preferred choice for keeping the fires lit in the kilns. Local peat cutters working the Laggan of Kintyre, the land between Machrihanish and Campbeltown, supplied much of the early requirements. In the mid-1800s, Irish peat was being imported from County Donegal, and by the 1880s, the import was causing much concern to the local harvesters due to it being nearly half the price. Angus Martin writes in his encyclopaedia:

"In December 1899, a Campbeltown smack (sail boat), on passage to Lough Swilly in County Donegal for peat, was wrecked, a mishap which elicited from a writer in a Glasgow evening newspaper the quip that 'Campbeltown whisky derives something of its reeky flavour from Ireland, and is thus a kind of international spirit'. 'Kintyre peat', he added, had 'pretty well given out', and 'Irish turf' was now being 'regularly brought to the distilling town'."[30]

The life of a peat farmer was tough and weather-dependent. A local cutter, John MacKay, along with a fellow worker, would drive three 'recks' (loads), starting at four in the morning, in order to be at the distillery by six, before moving on to the next distillery. Mackay was dismissive of the Irish peat being just 'turf' (more or less calling it mud) and not the big, black and heavy stuff that he harvested from Aros Moss. MacKay and his colleague would cut about 200 tons (400 cartloads) in an average season and he continued supplying the distilleries until the collapse in the 1920s.

"An uncommon sight was witnessed at the harbour this week in the export of two cargoes of Kintyre peat. The shipments were for despatch to the distillery at Ardrishaig. Hitherto the local distilleries have entirely absorbed all the peat cut in the district, but this winter, owing to the short working season caused by the abnormally high price of barley, the distilleries did not lay in an average stock of peat and the peat-cutters had a prospect of having considerable quantities left on their hands. This has now been avoided by a market for the fuel being found elsewhere. The circumstance of Kintyre peat being exported for industrial purposes is probably unprecedented."[31]

Circa 1900. The chimney of Springbank and Ardlussa distilleries are clearly visible.

CHAPTER 3

BARNARD'S TOUR

"We got a little amusement out of our fellow travellers – one of them a gentleman in clerical attire, catching some fragments of our conversation on spirits, evidently mistook us for important officers of the Salvation Army. Seeing this we puzzled him, and in answer to his enquiries, informed him that we had just started on a long and tedious pilgrimage to the spirit land, and that ours was a mission of investigation into the creation, development and perfection of crude spirits into 'spirits made perfect'.

"One of our party here produced his flask and explained to our reverend friend what kind of missionaries we were, when, to our surprise after taking a 'wee drappie', and like Oliver Twist, asking for more, the pious-looking brother offered to join us in our excursions, that he might do the tasting, and we the writing. This generous offer was declined."
'The Whisky Distilleries of the United Kingdom'
Alfred Barnard, 1887

Alfred Barnard

Barnard tipped his hat against the sun. His decision to forego the usual steamer 'Davaar', which sailed from Glasgow to Campbeltown, had paid dividends. Whilst the smaller steamer 'Columba' - leaving from Princes Pier, Greenock - was busier than usual, it was considerably quieter than the Davaar laden with the 'Glasgow Fair' tourists. Late July was proving to be an inspired time to sail to Campbeltown, and Barnard revelled in the freedom to move about the boat, having spent so many hours sitting on trains.

Glasgow Fair was, for many Campbeltonians, the highlight of the year. Most of the numerous distilleries were either finished for the season or were in the final throes of cleansing and repairing the plant for the months of idleness, before the next maltings began. The town spent much of the beginning of July preparing for the influx of visitors, which could feel at times like the local population had doubled. On the Saturday of the Fair weekend, it was not uncommon for around 2,000 visitors to step off the steamers and onto the quay. Every visitor looked forward to the parades, regatta and the many activities laid on by the townsfolk.

Guest houses, hotels and spare rooms would fill to the point where tents were erected on any spare patch of ground to ensure everyone had somewhere to stay. When the weather permitted, it was not a surprise for the morning dog walker to find numerous souls asleep on the grass or wherever had been deemed suitable the night before. This year, despite a depression in the Glasgow trade, the number of visitors did not appear to be affected. As the Columba puffed its way past Gourock, Barnard did not realise that he had missed a rather 'Bacchanalian' Glasgow Fair the year before his visit. Drunken revelry around midnight became the bane of all wishing to retire from the day's activities.

There was no such revelry on the Columba, and Barnard noted with pleasure when a few loose children, caught up in some sort of game, raced past him. Leaving the small bay, crowded with small yachts and then passing Dunoon, whose beach was thronged with summer visitors, it was not long before the scenery became more rugged. Upon reaching Rothesay, and true to form for the weather that particular year, the heavens opened. Heavy rain then harassed their journey until the boat left the Kyles of Bute. As they steamed past Ardlamont Point, the Isle of Arran came into full view, and Barnard could easily make out the highest mountain, 'Goatfell', rising three thousand feet above sea level. To the starboard side was Skipness Castle, with its two rectangular towers rising from opposite corners of the ruins.

Having reached Tarbert, Barnard made little time in disembarking the boat to locate the coach, thus allowing him to secure the box seat (much to the annoyance of slower passengers hoping to ride alongside the driver). The six-hour journey, covering 40 miles, was spent enjoying the scenery as the weather remained moderately fair. The route kept to the west of the Kintyre peninsula,[32] and Barnard marvelled at the odd lane darting off from the main road, often overshadowed by trees and leading to impressive houses. The 'smiling cornfields' spread out as a testament to the cultivation carried on to the highest perfection.

As the coach bobbed merrily along, Barnard noted several villages not large enough to be called hamlets. The occasional shower did not dampen the traveller's spirits. Rather, it was welcomed due to the rain's dampening effect on the otherwise dusty roads. This ultimately led to a more comfortable ride, if a slightly wetter one. Shortly after six in the evening, the coach passed the Drumore Nursery and entered Campbeltown.

Barnard noted several chimney stacks puffing grey smoke into the sky – buildings that would take up much of his time over the next fortnight. Eventually, the coach stopped outside the White Hart Hotel on Main Street, and after much negotiation, Barnard (not realising how busy the town would still be from the Glasgow Fair tourists) secured a room. Suitably settled in, and after a restorative meal, Barnard ventured into the town, noting in his leather-bound notebook:

"Campbeltown is certainly a most attractive place and we were charmed with its appearance. It is situated at the head of a beautiful bay, which is almost landlocked and engirt by heath-covered hills. The foremost of these is Bengullion – Hill of the Wind – 1,224 feet high, which is on the southern shore, and Knock Scalbert of nearly the same altitude on the northern shore. At the entrance to the bay like a sentinel stands the bold and rocky island of Davaar on which there is a Beacon Tower. The harbour, which is two miles long and one broad, is admitted to be the best roadstead in Scotland; at the time of our visit its waters were teeming with life and hundreds of sail were riding safely at anchor on its ample bosom. Campbeltown is a royal burgh and one of the most interesting towns of Scotland."

Finding the locals extremely convivial, Barnard gleaned some regional history of the illicit distilling trade carried on before industrialisation. One story of an aged woman who resided near Hazelburn warranted retelling. She was of a rather doubtful character and was charged before the Sheriff with smuggling. The charge being held proven, it fell to His Lordship to pronounce the sentence. When about to do so he thus addressed the culprit, *"I daresay my poor woman it is not often you have been guilty of this fault." "Deed no Sheriff,"* she readily replied, *"I haena made a drap since youn wee keg I sent to yersel."*

On the morning of the first full day of Barnard's tour, he retraced the coach's journey that brought him into the town. Crossing Main Street at the crossroads of Castlehill, Argyll and Lorne Street, Barnard turned left onto Longrow and, within a five minutes' walk, was presented with the street-fronted offices of Hazelburn Distillery. The total distillery, being one of the largest producers within Campbeltown, covered over three acres of ground - and was believed to have been built on the site of the Parliament House, where James IV held a parliament when he emancipated the vassals of the McDonalds. Upon entering through the archway,[33] Barnard was greeted by the Distillery Manager, Mr Samuel Greenlees, who provided all information and a personal tour of the works.

"The water we use," Greenlees informed Barnard, *"is taken from various sources, that for mashing is brought from the Crosshill Loch, for other purposes, there are two excellent wells on the premises forty feet deep, containing spring water of the finest quality."*

Greenlees led the party through the three granary floors, each averaging 110 feet in length and 31 feet in width, capable of storing ten thousand quarters of barley and, on the ground floor, malt barns with tiled floors of the same dimensions to the granaries. Each malt barn was fitted with elevators that moved the grain to the malt floors. A single mill used steel grinders to prepare the dried malt for the next stage. Capable of grinding 2,500 bushels every ten hours – the entire process being powered by steam. In an adjacent building to the rear, two heating tanks, each holding 2,500 gallons, supplied hot water to the mash tun. Next to this room was the mash and still house – 64 feet long, 32 feet broad, and 42 feet high.

Onwards, they marched through the impressive set-up. Samuel Greenlees, despite being 71, continued the tour in a sprightly and energetic manner. Upon reaching the mash tun, Barnard once again brought out his length of measuring tape; 14 feet in diameter and 6 feet deep. The underback and worts receiver was placed high in the same building to allow the worts to pass through a Morton's Refrigerator before filling the fermenting tuns.

The tour passed through a doorway into the next room, revealing nine washbacks, each holding 6,000 gallons. Heading upstairs, Barnard was shown to a gallery in the still house where the wash charger had been installed next to the low-wines and feints charger capable of receiving 2,800 gallons. Down different stairs, the group returned to the ground level next to the three pot stills. Hazelburn, Barnard was informed, contained the largest wash still in Campbeltown at 7,000 gallons. The two low-wines and feints stills could each hold 1,800 gallons. All three stills were fired by kilns, so arranged, that the flues carry the heat all round.

"There is a peculiarity in the form of the heads which we have not seen at any other distillery. The tops, instead of being of the ordinary pear-shaped heads, are composed of 32 chambers or tubes in each still, terminating in a dome just before passing into the worm. These tubes are enclosed in a copper case which serves as a condenser, a stream of cold water being kept flowing around the pipes whilst the stills are 'at work'. By this means a large proportion of the fusel oil which otherwise would pass off in the form of vapour along with the spirits is thrown back into the still, and the pure spirit is allowed to pass through the columns into the worm free from impurity."

Outside of the still house, and within the inner court, the worm tubs were inspected before being guided to what was referred to as the 'Ball Room' where the spirit safe was distributing the day's clear spirit output.

Samuel Greenlees watched his visitor intently as the group moved to the racking store. Even from the furthest south of the country, Englishmen were not strangers to Campbeltonians, but Samuel had never seen anyone take the dimensions of parts of his distillery before. He completely understood the studious note-taking with regard to capacities and output – this was, after all, a common occurrence for any distiller when being visited by a customs officer. But, as he watched Barnard once more unroll his tape measure, muttering to himself, '23 feet' as he measured the steam boiler, Greenlees could not, for the life of him, explain the interest in these measurements.

Moving onto the warehouses, Greenlees informed Barnard that currently, there were 302,200 gallons of maturing whisky on site, but if the warehouses were full, that number would be closer to half a million gallons. Much of the stock was immediately taken to the Osborne Street, Glasgow, warehouses of Greenlees Brothers.

"We employ twenty-two men," Greenlees informed Barnard, watching him scribble that number into his leather-bound writing pad. *"In addition, we have three Inland Revenue Officers. We only make Campbeltown malt, and last year we produced 192,000 gallons. However, we can make 250,000 gallons."*

Barnard thanked Greenlees for his time, and by chance, he and his entourage accepted the offer of a drive from one of the neighbouring distillers. The July sun was bright, and the coach set off towards the coast. The drive allowed the trio to inhale the bracing sea air and shake off some fatigue from their exhausting travels.

That evening, the group were entertained in the Drill Hall by Nelly Howitt and the 'two-voiced' vocalist Clarence Hallet. Howitt gave a singular performance as Carlyle from 'East Lynne', whilst the group felt the abilities of Hallet, as a falsetto, were unique if not something they would subject themselves too again - if given the choice.

The following day, a similar route was taken to arrive at Springbank Distillery. The walk took the group by the splendid-looking United Presbyterian church, with its tower at the front reaching up to God in the heavens. Its trio of black doors made the front of the church appear like a giant fork or shiel. Taking the next turn on their left, Well Close, the group found themselves betwixt two busy works. Springbank was identified to the right as the much larger of the two - covering around ten acres.

In a rare demonstration of extravagance, within such a crowded burgh, the firm of J. & A. Mitchell & Co., boasted a small park. The grass was somewhere that the owners, renowned farmers, could bring their prized tups or sheep needing attention during the lambing season.

Upon entry into the small courtyard, Springbank's Head Brewer met the travelling companions and directed them to the two granaries. From his side pocket, Barnard produced his tape and measured the interior, *"100 feet long by 44 feet wide,"* Barnard stated to the Brewer. *"If you say so, sir,"* he replied with bewilderment before adding, *"I've never thought to measure it before."*

The granaries were currently empty, as the distillery would not require more barley until around September. Passing through the four floor maltings, the brewer kindly demonstrated how the steam lift and hand elevators would raise the germinated malt to the kiln floors ready for drying. The two kilns were contiguous to the malting floors; each was floored with English perforated tiles, allowing the hot smoke from the peat fires to permeate the wet malt.

From the kiln, the tour passed the malt deposit and the mill, which, although idle, was powered by steam. More elevators brought the ground malt, now known as grist, to the loft. Entering into the mash house Barnard remarked how crisply-white the stone walls were. Further measuring led Barnard to scribble down the cast-iron mash tun dimensions, 14 feet in diameter and 5 feet deep. Further notes were taken of the underback, a large hot water heating tank and a Morton's refrigerator – a recent acquisition.

The tun-room was next, housing seven washbacks, each capable of holding 6,000 gallons, with a wash charger of 7,000 gallons capacity. Heading back on themselves, the Brewer brought them to the base of the three stills: 3,000, 1,700 and 1,500 gallons capacity, respectively. In close proximity was a capital 16 horse-power Steam Engine, complete with boiler.

Beyond the still-house was a small cooperage and cask shed with offices for the distillers and Excise clerks adjacent. Barnard enquired about the water and was informed it came from the Crosshill Loch, and the number of employees was 15. Output was confirmed as 145,000 gallons, which, the brewer stated, was predominantly sold in London and Glasgow.

As that appeared to be the end of the tour, Barnard thanked the nameless brewer for his time,[34] who watched in some bemusement as the tape measure came out one final time. Barnard paced the frontage of the distillery and noted that it was 600 feet.

With the business of the day attended to, the small troop made their way back towards Main Street. Another fine July morning had seen the arrival of a large crowd of holidaymakers, and the town was still abuzz with the festivities of the Glasgow Fair. The Steam Packet Co., were doing a roaring trade – Barnard noted in the local paper that praise was heaped upon them for their foresight in laying on extra sailings 'shipped such a long distance without hurt or accident'.[35]

Having spent a few days as residents, Barnard and his entourage began to feel at home in the town. By chance or design, Barnard had already met several of the curious distillers, and day three of the tour started with a most propitious invitation to join Duncan MacCallum, proprietor of the Glen Nevis Distillery, for a sail. The morning was ideally suited to the activity; a brisk breeze was blowing off the land, and white crests were gleaming in the sunshine. Before long, the group were scudding[36] through the water, making straight for the Isle of Davaar. Behind was a view of Campbeltown and its harbour that had been forsaken by the group, having taken the coach from Tarbert.

MacCallum guided the boat to Dalintober Quay, as Barnard's appointment was the distillery of the same name. Dalintober, occupying over two acres, fronted onto Kinloch Park ('500 feet' of frontage Barnard noted in his jotter) and commanded the finest views of any distillery in the district. Entering under a stone archway, the group found themselves in an oblong courtyard with offices, stores, and warehouses on the right and the maltings, grain lofts, and main brewing and distilling houses on the left.

DALINTOBER DISTILLERY.

Distillery Manager, Mr Archibald Pursell, warmly greeted the visitors and spent several hours explaining the entire process. Pursell explained that the three granary floors could hold 3,500 quarters of barley. Having been soaked for 48 to 50 hours (to begin the germination process), the moistened barley is then laid out by hand on the four malt floors, all concreted and capable of working 2,500 bushels per week. Once it is green malt, it is sent to the kilns, some fifteen feet above the peat fires, where it is dried.

Pursell continued the tour, watching Barnard in particular as the journalist nodded and jotted down notes at every pause. Arriving at the mash tun, Pursell watched as Barnard produced a tape measure, noting the diameter and depth: 14 feet by five feet deep. Bemused, the distillery manager kept up his guided tour: *"The mash tun possesses double action revolving stirring gear driven by steam. As the crushed malt falls into this vessel, water of a sufficiently high temperature is added."*

The tour moved on to the six washbacks, each holding 8,000 gallons, and placed against the walls of a lofty and well-lighted hall. The still house was a separate room containing three pot stills. The wash still was 3,293 gallons capacity, and as was usual for the time, the low wines would pass through a worm condenser and via the spirit safe into a timber low wines receiver - Barnard's tape measure re-appeared: 10½ feet in diameter and 3½ feet wide. The low wines are then split into the two smaller spirit stills, 1,073 and 1,066 gallons, respectively.

The spirit is then filled into casks before being weighed and marked by the Excise Officers. They then either head to one of the five bonded warehouses at the distillery or straight out to a customer. Pursell pointed out that warehouse number four was being re-built. *"And when finished,"* he added, *"It will be one of the largest in Campbeltown."*

The entire site is run from an 18-horsepower engine and a steam boiler, 20 feet long by 6 feet in diameter. In addition, there are cask sheds and offices for clerks and the Excise Officers. *"Our water comes from the nearby hills and a deep well on the premises. The latter,"* Pursell reassured his visitors, *"is of fine quality and highly suitable for mashing purposes. This last season, we made 120,000 gallons."*

When David Colville, owner of Dalintober, enquired with his distillery manager how the tour had gone, Pursell replied, *"They were an attendant and engaged party. Although,"* Pursell paused, *"I have to admit, I had never expected anyone to measure our Low Wines Receiver."*

"A walk of a quarter of an hour, past the quay and across the Kinloch Park, brought us to Benmore Distillery. We could never quite understand why this piece of land reclaimed from the sea and without a shrub or flower thereon should be called a Park; at present it is a nursery ground for children, and sacred to the repairs of fishing nets and domestic washing. What might have been made of a smiling paradise of flowers and greenery down to the very borders of the sea, is left a wilderness by a parsimonious local board. It may be that the Campbeltown magnates are satisfied with making fine whisky, and let things remain as they are rather than as they might be. A thousand times during our stay in the Whisky Metropolis did we wish for the shade of trees, or some quiet sheltered seat whereon to rest and gaze at the beautiful sea, and distant hills which guard the entrance to the bay, and are the redeeming features of the scene."[37]

Benmore Distillery, situated on Saddell Street, faced the Loch and Park, albeit without the prominence of Dalintober, allowing such splendid views. Barnard's first impressions reminded him more of a municipal building than a manufactory of 'Barley Bree'. The buildings consisted of one square block erected around a handsome paved courtyard. The entire site was around two acres entirely enclosed. One feature that stood out was the brick chimney stack – recently rebuilt after a storm blew the last one down.

William Ferguson, the Distillery Manager, was waiting for the travelling journalist and his colleagues. The tour followed in a similar vein to the three already undertaken: Granaries that could take 4,000 quarters of barley;[38] the malt barn – the largest in Campbeltown – measured pedantically by Barnard, was 156 feet by 48 feet broad; a single kiln, 48 feet square and floored with wirecloth. The furnace was of a newer construction than that seen so far in Campbeltown – bricks had replaced the sheet iron, saving on fuel and causing an advantageous draught when fired up. An adjoining malt store was measured at 42 feet by 30 feet, and the mill was noted to be similar to most others.

Ferguson, who had never witnessed anyone measure his malt store, took the trio across a short passage into the mash house. Continuing his guided tour, he described the mashing process and how the liquid, now known as worts, was pumped into the 1,600-gallon underback before being pumped again to the 'coolers' through a patented refrigerator and then into the washbacks – six in total with a capacity of 5,400 gallons each.

The tour crossed a short platform to a step ladder, allowing a shortcut to the still house. Ferguson was relieved to see there was no return of the tape measure as he explained that they were able to use just two pot stills that had patent air valves and both heated by furnaces. The wash still had 2,500 gallon capacity, whilst the low wines was half that.

"Wherever possible," Ferguson informed the group, gesturing to pipes above him, *"We have used gravity to feed each stage of the process. This allows us to have just one pump on the entire premises. To guard against fire, every floor is provided with extincteurs [extinguishers] and hand grenades, besides a complete arrangement of fire-plugs and sets of hose and reels."*

Barnard jotted down the final few details; the water was taken from springs inside the works (Ferguson insisted it was superior to the Loch waters), and the output was 125,000 gallons a year.

The following day, the summer weather that had been enjoyed thus far vanished as rain clouds moved in and let loose their load. Thankfully, the day's visit was to Ardlussa Distillery, Campbeltown's newest works, and one close to the White Hart Hotel. Having donned waterproofs, the trio set out to see a distillery not yet in its tenth year of production.

Upon arrival, Barnard busied himself once again with his tape measure whilst James Murdoch, Distillery Manager, watched on with a befuddled look. The maltings, Barnard noted, were 180 feet long, 48 feet wide and nearly 40 feet high. Underneath were two malt barns with concrete floors and the usual elevators to the kiln. Next door was the mash house with a cast-iron mash tun, 15 feet in diameter and 6 feet deep.

"*We have used gravitation to our advantage throughout,*" claimed Murdoch. "*This has saved us much in labour. But we do need a pump to get the worts to a second tun above.*" Murdoch finished by indicating the second iron tank up above the party. This second tank allowed the six washbacks, 8,200 gallons capacity each, to be filled using gravity.

From here, Murdoch led the party to the still house, which gleamed but was silent. "*The Wash Still can hold 3,200 gallons,*" he continued, pointing at the larger of the two stills, "*and the Spirit Still 1,800 gallons.*" Barnard distracted wondering what dimensions the still house might be, noted down in his jotter "*18,000 Wash and 3,560 Spirit*" – quite where he got those numbers from would bemuse Murdoch and the owners of the distillery after publication.

Murdoch led the group back to the courtyard and into one of the two bonded warehouses. Barnard was impressed with the arched roofs that required neither central supports nor pillars.

"*We currently house 18,000 casks,*" Murdoch informed the group, standing in front of the row upon row of stowed casks. "*And during this season, we produced 118,000 gallons, almost entirely bound for the Glasgow market.*" Barnard thanked Murdoch for his time and patience.

"*Did you get to measure everything you wanted?*" Murdoch asked Barnard, glancing down at the pocket that contained the tape measure.

"*Oh, yes, thank you, Mr Murdoch.*" Barnard hastily replied before bustling his group back out the way they had come in.

As the rain dissipated, the afternoon's visit took Barnard and his companions to Dalaruan Distillery, passing the Argyll and Lochhead distilleries. Charles Colvill Greenlees, Managing

Partner of David Colvill & Co., and the grandson of Charles Colvill, who built the distillery in 1824, greeted the tourists. The distillery had only recently completed extensive additions and now covered three acres.

From the distillery's courtyard, Greenlees conveyed the group up a staircase to the offices where Barnard outlined the intentions of his book.[39] Understanding that this was a production tour, Greenlees took his visitors to the barley lofts, three in total, and the four stone malt barns. The lofts could contain 5,000 quarters of barley, and Barnard took his time measuring each of the four malt barns, which were nearly identical.

"I have the distillery plans, if that would be more convenient for you?" Greenlees directed at Barnard who, having finished his measurements, was rolling back up his tape. *"Oh, no, that won't be necessary. But thank you."* Barnard replied, hastily jotting the final figures down.[40] Connected to the malting floors were two 'capital' kilns, floored with Bridgwater tiles where only peat is used in the drying process.

Greenlees described the mill, noting that Barnard omitted notes for this section. The pen returned to the pad, however, when Greenlees informed the group that the mash tun could mash 2,000 bushels at one time. *"The iron coolers,"* Greenlees continued, *"are larger than normal and are placed outside so that the worts can be cooled rapidly. And once cooled, we can fill the seven washbacks we have."*

Barnard scribbled this down. He had quite forgotten his tape measure for much of this tour. Next, the group were taken to the three stills. The wash still was 2,750 gallons capacity and the spirit stills 1,886, and 850 gallons respectively. Uniquely, Dalaruan had sunk their three receivers into the floor.[41] Having been guided through the spirit store and nearby 7-horse power steam engine, Barnard remembered his tape and measured the boiler at 20 feet long and 7 feet in diameter.

Having completed the production cycle, Greenlees directed the group to the five bonded warehouses, which sat in a triangle behind the distillery plant, fronting onto Mansfield Street. In total, the distillery could warehouse 3,000 casks. The 'reducing' water came from two wells situated within the distillery grounds. Sixteen men were employed, producing 112,000 gallons.

With the return of summer weather, Barnard noted how much a 'pleasant place' the burgh was with its *"boundless sea, plenty of boating, fishing and golfing."* With time before his next visit, to Lochhead Distillery, Barnard and his companions took a trap out to the Salt Pans situated at Machrihanish. From this location, the famous Machrihanish golf course could be viewed and was said to be the best and most extensive in Scotland.

"At the time of our visit a party of Oxford students were playing a match with the Club, among whom we descried many of our friends the Distillers who are noted Champions of the game. We returned home very unwillingly, being loath to leave the animating scene…"

On returning from Machrihanish, the trio found their lunch waiting for them at the White Hart Hotel. Barnard, in a rare moment of acknowledgement, noted, *"We were comfortably entertained at the White Hart during our stay, and both the landlord and his good wife did everything in their power to render our visit both comfortable and agreeable. Their horses and traps were the best we had used during our tour and would be a credit to any city hiring establishment."*

Suitably refreshed, the trio strolled the few minutes' walk around Kinloch Park before arriving at Lochhead Distillery. The distillery's old-fashioned appearance reminded Barnard of the burgh's 'romantic smuggling days'. Built on the banks of the Lochhead Burn, which ran adjacent to the distillery, a stream had been diverted through the works, which rejoined the burn that ran into the sea.

"What was once a cluster of old houses and an ancient mill, with doubtless several illicit stills, is now a licensed Distillery, and time has indeed dealt leniently with its old stone walls and fences."

A shortened tour ensued – so short that Barnard omitted to jot down the name of his guide nor to unleash his measuring tape. From four antiquated barley lofts, leading to four malt floors and two kilns – each fitted with German tile flooring. Only peat was used in the kilns for drying. Lochhead possessed the largest mash tun, but Barnard could not measure, having forgotten his tape. Eight washbacks, each holding 8,000 gallons, fed two stills. The wash still held 3,300 gallons, and the spirit still 1,800. The coolers, as was the case at Dalintober, are left in the open and stretched right across the burn. Five small warehouses hold a capacity of 3,000 casks, and the distillery produced 111,000 gallons in the past year.

The next morning, Barnard continued his habit of taking a stroll down to the quay. The early promenade caught the spectacle of the boats heading off in search of fish or shipping precious cargo. *"Steam navigation,"* Barnard reasoned, *"is of incalculable benefit to Campbeltown, there being no railway within 80 miles."*

At the Quay, he watched as barrels of either whisky or gutted herring were rolled onto awaiting boats. Occasionally, the cargo was fattened cattle being sent to Glasgow for either sale or slaughter. The constant stream of cargo in and out demonstrated how crucial Glasgow's primary market was to the town. The steamboat had revolutionised this rural life.

"The farmer of Laggan or the Highlander who spends his life on the Kintyre Hills can descend in the morning from his lovely home, and setting his foot on board a steamboat at some neighbouring pier or jetty, suddenly finds himself in company with tourists from all parts of the world, and he who slept last night in the blue mists of the mountains, the next, is traversing the gas lighted streets of Glasgow, or Edinburgh."

The town's clock striking ten jolted Barnard from his musings. From the bustle of the quay, Barnard headed back up Main Street before turning onto Glebe Street to arrive at Glen Nevis Distillery. Despite Glebe Street being the most populated street in Scotland for distilleries, Glen Nevis commanded fine views of the bay and hillsides.[42]

Glen Nevis, being so new, was of a modern appearance and contained all of the 'new improvements'. The warehouses, barley stores, and kilns all run parallel to the road. The kilns, with their distinctive round, leaning vents, could process ninety-quarters of barley every four days. A modern mash tun, complete with improved patent revolving machinery, fed six washbacks. The modernity was evident throughout with a new eight-horsepower steam-driven engine, a centrifugal pump driving the grains and sparge, and a large Morton's refrigerator for cooling. The washbacks could hold 6,000 gallons, and the two stills held 3,200 and 2,200 gallons, respectively.

Two adjoining warehouses, one of them two-storey high, could hold 5,000 casks and an on-site cooperage allowed for repairs and storage of empty casks. The water was taken from the Crosshill Loch, and twelve distillery employees were employed. The past season saw 100,000 gallons produced and sent almost exclusively to Glasgow.

GLEN NEVIS DISTILLERY, CAMPBELTOWN.

By now, the novelty of Barnard's presence, for the distillers at least, had worn off – as had the novelty for Barnard of being in Campbeltown. The small town had become a home away from home, and Barnard found the distillers a courteous, kind and hospitable group. As the tour of the new day was Kinloch Distillery, the trio passed by the New Quay, where they witnessed large cargoes of barley being transferred from the steamers to the distillers' carts. The park adjacent to the distillery was 'so thickly covered with fishing nets, laid out to dry' that the group had to carefully pick their route around each so as not to disturb any.

The distillery, Barnard discovered, had previously been a Malt House *"for the purpose of supplying malt to the numerous smugglers who carried on their business... and from whose products arose the far-famed Campbeltown Whisky - now so well known in the market."* The building was a fine old work, and, as Barnard had remembered his measuring tape, he took great pleasure in noting that the frontage to Kinloch Park was over 400 feet with a depth to Longrow of 240 feet.

Being close to the harbour, with its bustle and traffic on the wharf, gave the distillery a 'life and animation' more than some of the others. The distillery had been greatly enlarged over the past few years and now covered two acres of ground. James Dunlop, the Managing Partner (and son of the founder of the same name), was on hand to personally take the tour. The group started with the three barley stores, each containing a metal steep. In conjunction, there were three malting floors, which each had their own kiln fired by peat. Down a flight of stairs, Dunlop brought the group to the mash tun, which he stated was 14 feet in diameter and 5 feet deep. Barnard's tape measure remained redundant in his coat pocket.

From the mash tun, the group were led to the tun room, where eight washbacks stood, each capable of holding 7,400 gallons and with switchers driven by steam. By retracing their steps, the group, via the courtyard, entered the still house – a quite neat and spacious room, Barnard thought, where three pot stills sat. Two were heated by furnaces, and one by steam. The wash still held 2,900 gallons, whilst the spirit stills were 1,800 and 1,700, respectively.

Dunlop then directed the group to the four warehouses occupying one side of the complex. Alas, at this point, Dunlop paused too long, and Barnard seized the moment, unfurling his tape measure. It had not occurred to Dunlop that anyone would want to know the dimensions of his warehouses. As Dunlop watched Barnard measure each one, he informed the group of what he felt was the more important number in that the warehouses could contain 3,000 casks.

"The water is from the Crosshill Loch," Dunlop continued, watching Barnard measure across the warehouse where they were situated. *"Although we also have excellent water obtainable from a deep well on the premises."* Barnard, despite jotting this information down, was unmoved as he took his final, measurement. *"And last year we produced 97,000 gallons, but we have acquired neighbouring land to expand,"* Dunlop stated, effectively finishing the tour. Goodbyes were said, and Dunlop wondered just how his tour would read on the printed page.

With the morning free before heading to Burnside Distillery, Barnard joined a coaching party headed to Glen Lussa - five miles north of Campbeltown, along the peninsula's east coast. Legend had made the area famous for 'the strength, beauty, and intelligence of its inhabitants'. With distillery names running through his mind, Barnard misheard the river's name and jotted down 'Ardlussa River' instead of 'Glen Lussa River'. Ardlussa Distillery had been named after a hamlet on the Isle of Jura - and had nothing to do with the burgh of Campbeltown.

Passing through ripe barley fields, the coach dropped the small party off at Burnside Distillery, southwest of Campbeltown. Situated on the banks of the Bengullion Hill, after a short climb, allowed a splendid view of the town and harbour. The fine malt barns were once used as a banqueting hall when the 9th Duke of Argyll, John Campbell, came of age.

A short tour, hosted by Managing Partner James Greenlees, moved on to the kilns, one each for the three malting floors, which are fired using peat and 'blind coal'.[43] Barnard took the time to measure the mash tun, 14 feet in diameter and 5 feet deep, before Greenlees headed them into the tun room with its six washbacks (each with 5,500 gallons capacity). Two pot stills distilled the wash and low wines, 3,000 and 1,250 gallons, respectively, and a large 15-horsepower steam engine powered the plant. Barnard's tape was once again put to use, measuring the boiler at 20 feet in length by 7 feet in diameter. At the time of the visit, seventeen men were employed, and the distillery produced 96,000 gallons in the previous season. The Campbeltown malt was sold almost exclusively to customers in London and Glasgow.

LOCHRUAN DISTILLERY

Another day meant another distillery for the intrepid trio. Having breakfasted, the familiar route to Glebe Street was made, this time bound for Glengyle Distillery. Before travelling far, John Ross of Longrow Distillery invited Barnard to meet Provost Colville, of Dalintober Distillery, and several other distillers who had not yet made his acquaintance. Barnard took the opportunity to make an official appointment to visit Longrow Distillery in a few days. The group then continued on a few hundred yards to their intended destination - further along Glebe Street.

Upon arrival, and much to the chagrin of Barnard, it was

discovered that William Mitchell, Glengyle's Managing Partner, was absent and had not left provisions for a tour. Thankfully, the Head Brewer rose to the occasion and performed a perfunctory and expedited tour of the 'neat and compact' works. Barnard was able to note that there were two malt barns; a single kiln with wire cloth flooring (peat fired); a mash tun, 12 feet by 5; a 10 horse-power steam engine and boiler (30 feet long and 9 in diameter); two pot stills (3,100 and 1,860 gallons respectively) and three warehouses holding 2,000 casks. The water was taken from the Crosshill Loch, and fourteen men were employed, producing 90,000 gallons of spirit. In the haste of the tour, however, Barnard omitted to record the brewer's name.

Lochruan Distillery, situated on the corner of High Street and Princes Street, formed part of the block of distilleries along with Scotia and Dalintober. Covering two acres, the distillery was acquired by the present owners two decades prior. Granted a tour by John McKersie, the Managing Partner, Barnard was afforded more time to unravel his measuring tape. The four malt barns, each 86 feet by 27 feet, fed two good-sized kilns (each 36 feet by 27 feet) with tiled floors, where only peat is used in the drying process.

The mash tun measured 16 feet in diameter and 4½ feet deep. In an adjoining room was a large 16-horsepower engine with a boiler 20 feet long by 6½ feet in diameter. The tun-room, 58 feet long, 30 wide and 34 high, housed seven washbacks, each with 6,708 gallons capacity. The still and mash house, 70 feet by 28 feet, contained three pot stills holding 3,245, 1,835 and 1,785 gallons, respectively. Distributed about the premises, five large warehouses contained, at the time of the visit, 2,000 casks.

Twelve men produced 85,000 gallons in the previous season, and McKersie stressed that the Lochruan Whisky owed its fine reputation to the 'peculiar excellence of the water, and the care exercised in the manufacture'. As Barnard and his fellow tourists thanked McKersie for his valuable time and walked out of the courtyard, the owner could not help but chuckle that he was lucky not to have been measured himself. *"Most peculiar"*, he would mutter later to his brother when asked.

William McKersie, John's brother, did not have long to wait before Barnard visited his Albyn Distillery. Situated the furthest north of the burgh distilleries, Barnard was impressed with the 'delightful view of Bengullion and the woods of the Lime Craigs, the property of the Duke of Argyll'. As McKersie speedily took his guests through the distillery, he allowed Barnard little time to measure much more than the 14 feet in diameter mash tun. No measurements were taken of the four malt barns, two kilns (fired only by peat) or any of the stores or rooms. Passing the six washbacks (each with a 5,000-gallon capacity), Barnard had to act quickly in order to measure the 24-foot-long boiler (8 feet in diameter) sitting next to the 14-horsepower steam engine.

Barnard jotted down that Albyn Distillery used three pot stills, 2,500, 1,650 and the third, just 580 gallons, respectively. Once again, his thoughts were distracted as the third still was 1,580 gallons. Five warehouses held 2,000 casks and an on-site cooperage. The water is from the Crosshill Loch, with eleven employees producing 85,000 gallons. The whisky was sold as Highland Malt, predominantly to Glasgow, Ayrshire and London.

Midway through their stay in the town, Barnard and his companions awoke to glorious sunshine. As the trio made their way around Kinloch Park towards Scotia Distillery, they encountered many sunburnt 'hardy fish women'. Scotia Distillery appeared to be hidden away out of sight, 'as if the art of making whisky, at that time, was bound to be kept a dark secret'. The buildings gave a straggling and old-fashioned appearance whilst the additions have been implemented with ease and convenience in mind.

The tour began at the three malt barns, one of which Barnard measured at 300 feet, each with a kiln floored with perforated tiles. The kilns were fired with mostly peat and a little blind coal. Next was the mash tun, 12 feet in diameter and 5 feet deep. In the tun room were six washbacks, each with a capacity of 4,306 gallons, feeding three pot stills, 1,640, 850 and 520 gallons, respectively. Scotia, like others nearby, kept the coolers outside but had fans fitted and driven by the 8-horsepower steam engine (the boiler being 20 feet by 7 feet in diameter). Seven small warehouses keep 1,700 casks stowed, and the water used is from the Crosshill Loch. Additionally, two wells are bored down to the rock, 80 feet deep, and yield a never-ending supply. Last year's production was 85,000 gallons.

Basking in the sunshine, the small group left Scotia and headed back across Lochend to Longrow, the principal street in Campbeltown. Their next destination was Rieclachan Distillery. The group made their way down a short lane, entering through an old-fashioned pair of gates *("evidently made to shut in the secrets of the distillery from the outside world")*. Barnard considered the distillery *"a fine old place... distinctly one of the old 'Sma' Still' works; but from time to time additions have been made... so that it is gradually losing its old romantic touch of age."*

Managing Partner Hugh Mitchell afforded the gentlemen a brief tour, starting with the two large barley stores adjacent to two malt barns (170 feet by 42 feet wide), a mash tun 10 feet in diameter (4 feet deep), seven washbacks each with a 5,000 gallon capacity and two pot stills; 2,139 and 1,600 gallons. The obligatory boiler measurements were taken (22 feet by 7 feet in diameter) situated near the 14-horsepower steam engine. Like so many of the local distilleries, the water was sourced from the Crosshill Loch, and ten employees produced 70,000 gallons.

The next morning, again being a glorious summer's day, Barnard and his companions hitched a ride to Saddell Castle with Andrew Douglas, landlord of the White Hart Inn. The castle, situated ten miles north on the eastern side of the peninsula, was the residence of a McDonald known as 'Righ Fiongal' – a despot who 'for sport, and to keep himself in practice, would shoot people with his long gun'. On returning to Campbeltown, the trio headed straight for Glenside Distillery on Dalaruan Street.

The guide for their tour was Managing Partner John Orr, who immediately drew the group's attention to a conduit that brought the distillery's water directly from the Auchalochy Loch[44] with additional water coming from a well within the two-acre enclosure.

Orr then directed the group to the three barley lofts capable of holding 2,000-quarters of grain. These supplied four malt barns, which in turn fed three kilns, each fitted with tiles and heated by peat. The mash house contained a heating copper and a mash tun[45] incorporating the patented stirring gear and a metal underback. Barnard remembered his tape measure and was able to jot down the boiler dimensions being 24 feet by 6 feet in diameter – all next to a 12 horse power engine. Orr then directed the group to the tun room, which led to the still house. Four washbacks, each holding 8,000 gallons created the worts that were first distilled in the wash still, 2,483 gallons and then by the spirit still with a capacity of 1,372 gallons. The five warehouses contained 1,600 casks, and the twelve employees produced 70,000 gallons, which was principally sold in London, Liverpool and Glasgow.

GLENSIDE DISTILLERY.

"Sunday, in Campbeltown, is carried to its Jewish length, and is quite a day of gloom and penance. The churches and chapels, which are scattered all over the town are crowded with well-dressed and staid looking people, and everybody carries a pious look on that day. Neither music nor whistling is allowed in either the houses or streets, and the landlady of the hotel was quite shocked at our proposing to play some sacred music on the piano. We might have expected this, as it is said that there are as many places of worship as distilleries in the town."

Suitably, after Barnard's brooding over the Sunday practices, the group's next visit was to meet with John Ross at his Longrow Distillery. Ross, who, at 83, would proclaim to be the oldest living distiller to anyone in earshot, was in fine form as Barnard and his companions greeted him. Longrow Distillery was situated on the street from where the name was derived and opposite Springbank Distillery. The tour was filled with wit and racy anecdotes from the 'hale and hearty' Ross, all within the presence of the United Presbyterian Church tower - built mostly at the expense of Ross himself. The distillery was *"so built in by the houses and shops in Longrow that it would be difficult for a stranger to find it."*

Ross directed the tour through the two barley lofts and three malt barns built with low-pitched roofs. These in turn fed two kilns, each floored with tiles where the smoke from peat and coal could filter through, drying the barley. Ross' natural charm and storytelling caused Barnard to forget he was carrying his measuring tape and, in a rare lapse, the old-fashioned mash tun was not measured, nor were any of the rooms. Barnard even forgot to record the capacity of the six washbacks, the two pot stills (of the 'Smuggler's Pattern', heated by furnace), the receivers and chargers or even the boiler attached to the steam engine (not even a mention of the horsepower).

At long last, the group reached the three warehouses, and finally, Barnard recalled he was in attendance to record the distillery apparatus. Seeing the appearance of the tape measure, Ross launched into another tall tale about local smuggling. Barnard could only run his measure along one wall, recording a single warehouse to be 130 feet long. The water was taken from the Crosshill Loch, supplemented by a spring rising from a deep well on the premises. Longrow, being one of the smallest distilleries in the burgh, produced just 40,000 gallons in the previous season.

Having finished at Longrow and with an afternoon to spare, the trio made their way to the Kintyre Distillery. Situated on Broad Street behind the Benmore Distillery and opposite Dalaruan, Kintyre had been erected a few years after Longrow and appeared more modern and less 'scattered'. Barnard's group were afforded the briefest of tours starting at the two Barley Lofts, three malt barns feeding two kilns (fired by peat and coal). A fine mash tun fed six washbacks, and the entire plant was run by an 8-horsepower steam engine with a boiler (20 feet long and 6½ feet in diameter). The still house contained three stills fired by furnaces and five small warehouses containing 500 casks.

The water for condensing purposes was taken from a well, and an unidentified Loch supplied the rest – the distillery production was 67,000 gallons last season. In a rare moment of relaxed formality, Barnard was given the chance to try a sample of eight-year-old Kintyre malt and gave it no higher praise than stating it to be of the same quality as Longrow.

Reeling from the extravagant whisky tasting the day earlier at Kintyre Distillery, Barnard was restored to his professional best as the troop headed to Campbeltown Distillery – the final distillery to be visited on Glebe Street.

"This distillery was erected in the year 1815 by John Mactaggart, great-grandfather of Mr Daniel Mactaggart, the Procurator Fiscal of Campbeltown, and is an old-fashioned work according to the present ideas of distilling, but when it was first built it was a great advance on the 'Smuggler's Kettle'. On passing through a pair of ancient gates and turning to the left, the visitor comes upon a veritable 'smuggler's work', so ancient is its appearance and tumble-down look."

The distillery, despite having undergone several alterations since it was first built, retained its 'old-world look'. There were two barley stores, two malt barns and a single medium-sized kiln floored with old English perforated tiles. An ancient mill ground the finished barley, and a more modern mash tun (complete with revolving machinery) with a capacity of 4,000 gallons was measured at 13 feet in diameter and 4½ deep. A large 14-horsepower steam engine powered the distillery, and the steam boiler measured 17½ feet long by 4½ feet in diameter. Five washbacks held 3,000 gallons each, feeding two 'Sma' pot stills', holding 1,400 and 960 gallons, respectively. The coolers are in the open, in addition to a Morton's refrigerator. Four small warehouses contained 1,300 casks (some of them 'very aged'). The water is from Crosshill Loch and only peat is used in drying the malt. The previous season's production was 60,000 gallons, sold principally in Glasgow and Ayrshire.

As Barnard's fortnight approached its finale, just two distilleries remained. The town had left an indelible impression on the travellers. Nowhere else on their two-year-long odyssey would they come close to being in an area with such a heavy concentration of distilleries. Campbeltown had its own unique way, and what would have seemed a distinct peculiarity to all those visiting was commonplace to the locals. The penultimate distillery for Barnard to tour was Argyll Distillery, which bordered the much larger Hazelburn Distillery on Longrow. Despite being over forty years of age, the distillery was 'a clean and compact little work'.

A single barley store and malt barn (120 feet long by 28 feet wide) fed into a kiln - heated solely by peat. The mash tun, 12 feet by 5 feet, supplies five washbacks, each containing 3,900 gallons. Two pot stills, 1,070 and 686 gallons, produce 40,000 gallons of spirit a year. There are five small warehouses on site holding 600 casks. The water is taken from the Crosshill Loch, supplemented by a deep well on the premises.

The afternoon of their last day presented the intrepid distillery hunters with their final distillery and the one closest to the White Hart Hotel. As if by design, the tour had begun at the largest distillery in Campbeltown, Hazelburn, and finished with the smallest, Springside.

"The works consisted of three small granaries and Maltings, two kilns floored with tiles and heated with peat, a Mill House and Stores. A Mashing and Distilling House, which contains a Mash Tun, 10 feet in diameter and 3½ feet deep, Underback and heating Copper. In the Tun Room, we observed six Washbacks and a Wash Charger; and in the Still House two Pot Stills holding 1,205 and 394 gallons respectively, also the Receivers, Chargers and Safe. There are four bonded Warehouses which contained 600 casks, and a small Spirit Store. The water used for all purposes comes from the Crosshill Loch. The make is called Campbeltown Malt and the annual output is 30,000 gallons."

Thus ended the first formal, authorised tour and categorisation of Campbeltown's distilling industry. Barnard, complete with tape measure and notebook, headed off to Islay the next day as he and his colleagues were still very much at the beginning of this quite epic undertaking.

Barnard's Tour Guides:

Hazelburn: Samuel Greenlees died two years after Barnard's visit at his home, Hazelbank House (now the Ardshiel Hotel). His son, also Samuel, moved back from London to carry on Hazelburn Distillery.

Dalintober: Andrew Pursell died in Dalintober at the tragically young age of 52 in 1893. His wife, Jean, died two years after him. Their life had been blighted by tragedy, having lost four infant children.

Benmore: William Ferguson died aged 83, passing away at his home of Dunalaister, Kilkerran Road. His son, George, was awarded the Military Cross in 1918 before disappearing in 1948.

Ardlussa: James Murdoch is not mentioned in Barnard's book, but was likely the Manager of Ardlussa Distillery at the time of his visit. Murdoch was still Manager when 'The Wine and Spirit Trade Record' returned in 1905.

Dalaruan: Charles Colvill Greenlees died in 1908, aged 77. 'The Wine and Spirit Trade Record' described him as 'one of the most interesting personalities in the town', and he is a likely candidate for Our Man In Campbeltown.

Lochhead: It is possible that Barnard's guide was Robert Colville. Colville - much to the delight of the 'Campbeltown Courier' that covered the story in January 1900 - went on to secure a place within Customs & Excise.

Glen Nevis: Samuel Thomson is the likeliest candidate to have shown Barnard around the distillery. Thomson began as a clerk in 1897 and remained with owner Duncan MacCallum throughout his life, ultimately as a Director, until 1953.

Kinloch: James Dunlop represented the Campbeltown region as part of the 1891 Select Committee hearing. He died in 1901, aged 66, and was well respected within the community.

Burnside: James Greenlees died at his home of Seafield, aged just 44 in 1888, three years after Barnard's visit. Along with being Managing Partner of Burnside Distillery, Greenlees was also a Director of Highland Distillers Co.

Lochruan: John McKersie was an influential distiller and respected member of the community, becoming Provost in 1875. A position he held for six years. He died in 1904, aged 62.

Albyn: William McKersie was John's younger brother and, although less conspicuous in public life, was generous in spirit. William took on Lochruan after his brother's death and died twelve years later in his home of Craigard.

Rieclachan: Hugh Mitchell was one of the most respected distillers and townsfolk being elected Provost in 1896. Hugh died at Seafield in 1935, aged 82.

Glenside: Little is known of John Orr, the son of another John, who was a partner in Glenside from around 1850. He left little impression on Barnard. But then we are given very little impression of most of his guides.

Longrow: John Ross is arguably Campbeltown's most interesting character within the distilling fraternity – certainly from this period. A pious yet feisty character, he was as likely to give to a church as he was to publicly air grievances. He once took out an indictment against the 'Campbeltown Courier' to prevent an unflattering letter from being published. Ross died in March 1886, aged 84 (Barnard got his age wrong). Longrow Distillery closed shortly after Ross' passing.

A note on this chapter:

Please allow plenty of writer's discretion with the above account. Barnard's work is sometimes difficult to comprehend - not due to technical jargon or convoluted prose but due to the randomness of the information provided and, perhaps more pertinently, what is not. A chronicle of life and times, it is not. Nor is it a travel guide, a manual, or a diary. Puzzling measurements follow important omissions and head-scratching inclusions. Now and again, we are given glimpses into the writer's humour and the occasional local person, custom or tradition.

Considering the intended reader - those who would never see most of these locations, never mind the inside of these factories - we are rarely invited to behold the scene or walk in the author's footsteps. I have attempted to add something to the narrative and correct some of the errors. That being said, this is our only guide from the era, making it invaluable. Priceless, in fact.

There was very little critical response to Barnard's book - much of it being a cut-and-paste job from whatever was sent by the publisher to the media. Some of the Irish newspapers dived slightly deeper, and from the 'Campbeltown Courier', the following was published:

> *The Whisky Distilleries of the United Kingdom.*
> *"A volume under the above title has been issued by the proprietors of 'Harper's Weekly Gazette' from the pen of Alfred Barnard. As might be expected, in dealing with such a subject, the writer has a lot to say about Campbeltown and its neighbourhood, and we are very glad to say it is, generally speaking, of a very favourable character.*
> *"General critical remarks are interspersed throughout the notices of the various distilleries, by which we are able to come to the conclusion that the writer much enjoyed his visit to our shores. He is somewhat sarcastic on our 'Kinloch Park', and confesses inability to understand why it should be dignified with the title. He was pained to see 'what might have been made a smiling paradise of flowers and greenery down to the very borders of the sea left a wilderness by a parsimonious local board'.*
> *"This is how it strikes a stranger, and the 'parsimonious local board' referred to might take some degree, the idea of a 'smiling paradise of flowers and greenery', at a spot that at present is only a little removed from a quagmire. The writer's descriptions of the various distilleries are extremely interesting, and are distinguished by clearness and conciseness. To those interested in the distillery industry the volume must prove of considerable value, and to Campbeltonian readers generally its remarks, critical and otherwise, regarding the town and its staple trade will be regarded as unusually interesting and pointed."*[46]

View from behind Gallowhill Farm (bottom right).

CHAPTER 4

TRADITIONS

"Kintyre is truly a land flowing in its outlying districts with milk, and in its inland quarters with whisky. After all, there is no better blessing than milk and whisky. Does it even excel that favourite mixture of Prince Bismarck, champagne and beer?"
The Marquis of Lorne addressing a Kintyre Club reunion
'Campbeltown Courier' 5th November, 1898

"The distillers at Campbeltown were respectable, intelligent, clever men of business, and were disposed, I believe, to render to Caesar the things belonging to Caesar. The town itself, although isolated, I considered pleasant, and the splendid deep bay at its entrance is magnificent. It was a remarkably cheap place for a family to live in, and had I been a private individual instead of a Gauger, I could very well have settled down there."
'Reminiscences of a Gauger'
Joseph Pacy 1873

*"The topic of the day here is the visit of a company promoter from London who desires to buy up the Campbeltown distilleries on what he considers favourable terms to the holders. Unfortunately for the officer, the distillers don't 'bite'. They are mainly gentlemen who have been in the trade from boyhood, whose fathers before them made the business, and who don't see their way to give up their independence for any present or future gain however fair the promise may be."** May 1897.

By the mid-late 1800s, the Campbeltown distillers were experiencing the golden era for their whisky. Although signs pointed to a change in consumer habit, demand for Campbeltown whisky remained strong. Glasgow remained the destination for almost all of the whisky removed from bond, and blends were still keen to highlight their 'Highland' pedigree.

The visit by the 'London promoter' is a glimpse into how the rest of the market viewed those within Whiskyopolis. There was, in reality, little chance of the proposal being successful, as OMIC pointed out later in the article:

"I know Campbeltown and its staple trade exceedingly well. To me the idea of a syndicate organising and working, as reported, the twenty-two distilleries of Whiskyopolis is irresistibly comic. To persuade all the firms engaged in the profitable manufacture of aqua so famous to merge themselves into the happy family of a gigantic limited company is a project too ridiculous."

The anomaly of a supposedly high-quality product, combined with a low price, was enough temptation for someone loaded with an offer of 'favourable terms' to approach the mass of Campbeltown distillers. That the financier who entertained the idea wasted so much time and effort in what was a long and expensive journey was, as noted, irresistibly comic.

But was the idea of a conglomerate so absurd? The industry (which would, as we will see, crash from its own weight of tangled dealings) would dictate otherwise - but not until the turn of the century. By then, the distillers would have long forgotten the Londoner and his proposition. The low price issue, was a thorn in the Campbeltown distiller's side. This was not a new concern, and also not one that was solved easily.

Almost from the beginning of the industrialised era, Campbeltown's whisky had been sold at a price below that of all other districts. An 1826 article in the 'Bath Chronicle'[47] listed Campbeltown whisky at the same price as grain whisky (15s per eleven-over-proof gallon), whilst Glenlivet was 19s to 21s for the same quantity. As was noted by Pacy in 1873, the burgh was an incredibly inexpensive place to live; there were plenty of jobs and more than enough means to make ends meet during the summer months when the distilleries were idle. At least that was the case when times were good – which they were through much of the 19th century. This cheapness caused a fixation on the prices of raw materials, especially barley.

"The price of barley is causing some anxiety in Campbeltown. Dealers expect to purchase whisky at last year's prices but it is evident, in the unsettled state of the barley market, that it would be unwise for Campbeltown distillers to fix a price for the whisky. The Campbeltown price is bound to be higher than last year. The north country distillers with their long prices and consequent large profits can afford to drop a bit in their quotations without serious loss, but in Campbeltown during recent years prices have been so low that the enhanced cost of materials is bound to cause an upward tendency. Any other policy would be suicidal."*
October 1897

The Campbeltown Distillers' Association, formed in 1848, allowed the distillery owners to come together in the closest they would get to a conglomeration. From the few letters and articles that exist, it appears that much of the discourse was around price and practices. In November of 1897, OMIC allowed a rare glimpse into how cooperative the members were - at least in voice. In response to the high barley prices, the Association made a decision:

"The Distiller's Association, which includes all the Campbeltown distillers, held a meeting in their offices on the 1st October, under the presidency of Provost Mitchell. After full consideration of the subject, it was unanimously decided to make an advance of two pence per gallon on last season's price. The 'trade' don't quite take the same view of this subject as do the Campbeltown Distillers' Association, and a vigorous attempt is being made to get orders booked at the old price. So far as I can hear, these efforts have not been attended with any degree of success. Distillers having so recently been engaged in balancing books and ascertaining profits, are in a position to realise exactly what would be the result of selling new whisky at the same price as last season's with barley at its present figure.

"One cannot blame dealers for trying to buy on the best terms possible for themselves; one can hope that so far as Campbeltown is concerned they may not succeed. ...at the best the price of Campbeltown whisky is cut down to the water's edge and the smallest margin left for profit, so perhaps buyers will see the reasonableness of conceding the small advance asked for in consideration of the enhanced cost of materials."

The effectiveness of this cooperation, certainly with regard to forcing the market to accept any price increase, was less than limited. Campbeltown whisky had always traded at a marked discount to the other 'centres', at times on a par with what the industry labelled 'plain malts' – those from the Lowlands. When OMIC wrote of the Distillers' Association's intention to increase prices, nearly all of the Campbeltown distilleries were offering bulk newly made spirit for 2s 6d per bulk gallon - compared to most of Scotland's whisky trading at around 1s higher.

Despite the threatened small increase of 2d extra for Campbeltown spirit, the opening prices remained the same until at least 1904 with almost no variation. As prices of raw materials and other costs (including wages) increased, the price of a gallon of bulk spirit from Campbeltown did not alter.

Thus, every fluctuation in the price of barley, coal, peat and transport markedly affected the profitability of distilling each season. This is clearly evident with how much emphasis is given in the letters of OMIC continually bemoaning the cost, in particular of barley. When rumour got to Campbeltown that the distillers of the North were going to combine in an attempt to agree on a barley price, it was hoped it could operate in a similar vein to the Campbeltown Distillers' Association. Encouragement, in the hope of resulting in lower prices, was given freely:

"...no difficulty is experienced here in fixing a uniform price every year for Kintyre-grown barley mutually satisfactory to the distiller and the farmer. The custom is for the Distillers' Association to fix the price early in the season according to prices ruling outside, but, of course, should barley prices in the outside markets materially change as the season advances, either up or down, the association alters the prices here in sympathy with those ruling outside.

*"It has been found that the system works well, and has stood the test of many years, the Distillers' Association being one of the oldest institutions in Campbeltown. At one time the price of whisky was fixed in the same way, but for years back the agreement annually come to in this respect was more honoured in the breach than in the observance, and came to be regarded by the trade as a sort of farce. In these days of keen competition, it has been found better to allow each distiller to fix his own price and endeavour to dispose of his brand to the best advantage, without being hampered by the risk of either breaking a price which he was a party to fixing, or else losing an order which would be jumped at by some less scrupulous neighbour and competitor."** November 1898

For much of the 19th century, sales were sought through 'travellers' (salesmen), or agents. A few of the distillers acted on behalf of themselves, visiting customers and obtaining orders, whilst most relied on new business their travellers or repeat orders. As each firm acted in its own best interests, and with a history of low-price working against them, price hikes, even when universally agreed, were often sabotaged.

exclusively from Europe.

Early on, and possibly due to the combination of supposed health benefits and how well the product travelled, ex-Sherry casks were the popular choice for distillers. As is the case today, the Sherry industry was not able to keep up with the whisky

Burnside Distillery is on the right. The road past the side of the distillery leads to the old burial ground at Whitehill.

industry's demand of what were considered 'genuine fresh sherries'. Despite many believing that 'seasoned casks' (those that have had Sherry resting in them before being transported, often wet with 'some' liquid for transport) are a modern phenomenon, it became a necessity over a century ago as the whisky industry began to demand longer maturation and greater cask influence.

> *"[There is] an excellent substitute for fresh sherries, for which we are indebted to Messrs. W. P. Lowrie & Co., coopers, Glasgow. Their 'Wine-seasoned casks', prepared by their patent process, have evidently turned out a success. The other day my attention was drawn to several samples of whisky of various ages matured in these casks, which were being compared with samples of whisky of similar age from 'fresh sherry' and 'plain wood'.*
>
> *"It was gratifying to observe that the 'wine-seasoned' casks of Messrs. Lowrie & Co., had imparted the true sherry flavour, while the spirit had developed a soft, palatable quality which was absent in that taken from 'plain wood' and could not be surpassed by the best samples of the 'sherry'. The colour from a blender's point of view was simply perfect. If the general results equal these, a great future may safely be predicted for these casks, and the patentees are to be congratulated on supplying an article which is likely to have an influence for good on the whisky trade. Matured spirits of good colour, excellent flavour, and soft palate, are especially necessary at a time when the public taste at home and abroad demands Scotch blended spirits at the highest class."*

As this was a repeat of a paragraph included in the magazine's first issue, one can only assume the author had a vested interest in the success of this process. The patented process was to blast the interior of the cask with pressurised steam, opening the pores and allowing the impregnation of Sherry or other wines. This substitution for casks that had traditionally matured fortified wines became very popular, although it was noted that the authentic casks remained *"indispensable to the blenders… to do for whisky what no substitute of added wine or colour can effect."*[54]

W. P. Lowrie's success would eventually see them own

Lochruan Distillery and the site of the neighbouring Dalintober Distillery. Seasoned casks are still widely used today.

Whilst Campbeltown's distilling industry had grown out of the antiquated and basic 'sma stills' activity in and around the burgh, the distillers were often keen to update and modernise their distilleries with the latest improvements and inventions. During Barnard's visit, he noted that many had visible additions, including the latest in refrigeration and other patents improving yields, consistency and labour. In 1898, the famous distillery architect and inventor Charles Doig visited Benmore Distillery, and likely others, before heading to Islay.

Doig is today remembered as the inventor of the Doig Ventilator (better known as a Pagoda) for the kilns – an invention that allowed a greater draw of smoke from the kiln fire through the barley. Benmore was likely the first Campbeltown distillery to replace the more common Cowl or 'Cardinal's Hat' adapted from the English Oast House (for the drying of hops). It does not appear, from the black and white photos that exist, that this invention caught on, and in 1920, Hazelburn, despite being thoroughly modernised, was still using the cowl.

In 1890, the Campbeltown Bonding Company, as part of Greenlees & Colvill Co, was established. Having identified a site at Lochend, a contract was awarded to Robert Weir & Sons for a building *"three storeys in height and raised high enough to have four floors, each floor easily holding up to 700 puncheons. When completed, the building will prove an acceptable addition to the neighbourhood, being built in uniformity with its surroundings."*[55]

James Greenlees, at the Select Committee on British and Foreign Spirits of 1891, bemoaned the difficulties in obtaining permission to erect new distilleries in the burgh:

"In Campbeltown, where we [Greenlees Brothers] have three distilleries, two of the warehouses were very full; in fact, the Inland Revenue were complaining, and when their inspector came down from Somerset House, they complained of the state that those warehouses were in on account of the number of casks. We bought a piece of ground a little bit away from the three distilleries, and proposed to build a general warehouse there, so that whichever distillery wanted room to warehouse, if the warehouses were too full, we could take the whisky and put it into the warehouses."

The Committee asked what reasons the Excise had given for not approving the application for new warehouses. In reply, James stated that the only excuse provided *"was that if that were granted to us other distilleries might want the same, and they would have to grant it to them."*

The Commission, in part, was to decide upon a minimum period of bonding of spirits and a general curiosity about how the experiences differed for distillers around the UK. James Greenlees was most obliging with his information,[56] and when asked if compulsory bonding for a period of time would come as an inconvenience. James replied:

"Yes. I do not know if we could do it at all. In our present warehouses we have 922,000 gallons, while the actual quantity which should be in those warehouses is only 780,000 gallons… which means passages filled up, so that you cannot get casks out or in."

The platform for airing these grievances evidently had the desired results. The new bonding warehouses on Glebe Street were finally given approval, alleviating the burden on the strained existing space. A year later, Glen Scotia also added a new warehouse, and over the next seven years, new warehouses were built at Glenside, Albyn, Campbeltown, Glen Nevis, Lochhead and Springside distilleries.

The main thrust of the Select Committee was to determine whether *"on grounds of public health, it is desirable that certain classes of Spirits… should be kept in bond for a definite period before they are allowed to pass into consumption."* Despite the Select Committee not introducing a minimum bonding period, the erection of these warehouses demonstrates a change in how business was being conducted. The Campbeltown Bonding Company was a success, as by the end of 1891, 103,543 gallons had been imported from Islay and Jura distilleries for warehousing.

Greenlees, as a witness, was called for his expertise and knowledge with regard to blending. Asked if he found the taste for milder whisky had increased, he answered: *"enormously; people want a much more silent and much older whisky than they did 10 or 15 years ago."*

Representing the Campbeltown distillers was James Dunlop of the Kinloch Distillery, accompanied by William McEwing, the long-time manager of Hazelburn Distillery (employed by James Greenlees' brother Samuel, and their father Samuel before his death in 1887).

Having established that Dunlop was representing the Campbeltown Highland Malt Distillers and that all of the distilleries only used malted barley for their whisky, the question over current designation of malt whisky was brought up. Dunlop was not impressed with the new description. Lyon Playfair, chairing the group, asked: *"It formerly was described as 'malt whisky', was it not, under the old law?"*

"It was so," Dunlop replied, *"and the phrase was withdrawn, and afterwards renewed. It was then withdrawn a second time."*

Dunlop's concern, and on behalf of his fellow Campbeltown distillers, was that malt whisky was sent out with the designation 'plain British spirit' – a labelling that Dunlop felt would cheapen the product in the eyes of the consumer. Another member of the panel asked what the *"advantage in reviving the old permit on which was stated 'From malt only', seeing that most spirits go into the hands of blenders who may mix them in any way they please?"*

Tellingly, and in a way campaigning for something that would have repercussions long after Kinloch Distillery had closed, Dunlop replied: *"It would be a protection, to a certain extent; that is to say, you send it to the blender and he is satisfied it is malt whisky; then, if a dealer buys from him, he can see whether he is getting malt whisky or blended whisky."*

When the panel discussed the core of the Committee's purpose, the mandatory ageing of spirits, Dunlop was not sure there was any benefit to be had from changing the regulations.

Playfair: *"What is your opinion about the desirableness of keeping whisky in bond?"*

Dunlop: *"We think it unnecessary to legislate for compulsory retention."*

Playfair: *"What is the average age of whisky cleared from Campbeltown distilleries?"*

Dunlop: *"A few months ago the excise officials collected statistics hearing on that point, and they found that the average of whisky cleared from Campbeltown was two years and four months. A considerable portion of that was removed to other warehouses, where it would be still further matured. We, therefore, think it unnecessary to legislate for the compulsory retention of spirits in bond, when traders retain it for maturing of their own accord."*

Playfair: *"Does your whisky go into the trade as your own malt whisky, or is much of it used in blending?"*

Dunlop: *"It goes both ways. Personally, ours goes nearly half and half. We pay duty on about half of our own make; barely half now."*

Playfair: *"Is the blending with other kinds of malt whisky, or is a great deal of the blending with grain whiskies?"*

Dunlop: *"I cannot state that for certain, but our understanding is that it is principally with the grain whiskies."*

Playfair: *"And that gives a better tone and quality to the grain whiskies?"*

Dunlop: *"Yes, and cheapens it; makes a medium price."*

Greenlees was equally nonplussed by the idea of a minimum age in bond: *"I do not see that there is the slightest necessity for compulsory bonding, because the test of competition will get whiskies old enough for the people."* When asked whether the consumer was asking for older whisky he replied: *"You will [now] get very old whiskies anywhere; there are public houses in London where they are serving whisky from six-and-a-half up to twelve years old."*

1891 was the start of Scotland's second great race to build distilleries (the first being the period after 1823), particularly in the area now known as Speyside. The Select Committee were keen to understand this sudden burst of activity and investment. Greenlees, in stark contrast to the figure that would be called as a witness in 1908, was forthright with his information and views:

"There is a very large amount of money invested by the public; men who have money saved, instead of investing it in railways and other things, invest it in whisky – it is a very good and safe investment."

"How much would it increase in value?" Playfair asked.

"It should always net the investor from 10 to 15 per cent if he buys well and has a market for selling it again. Of course there are some whiskies which do not pay, sometimes you lose." Greenlees candidly replied.

His words, although unlikely to have haunted him, were

prescient, and whilst the suggested returns were conservative for almost a decade, lots of people did indeed lose. But before the sharp drop in the industry, the rise of the Greenlees Brothers is a story worth considering.

Hugh and William Mitchell sitting in front of a 'dogcart' outside Glengyle Distillery. Their nephew sits at the rear and maltman Hugh Muir stands at the office door next to the resident exciseman smoking a pipe. The horse was called Billy.

CHAPTER 5

THE GREENLEES BROTHERS

Dr Adeney: *"You made a remark… as to the fall in the Irish trade and the rise in the Scotch blending trade, and you referred to educating the taste of the English. What did you mean by that?"*
James Greenlees: *"By educating the public up to a blended whiskey of a pleasant description."*
Dr Adeney: *"Is it not fair to say 'Down to a blended whiskey'?"*
James Greenlees: *"No, educating it up, most decidedly."*
'Royal Commission on Whiskey and Other Potable Spirits' 1908

"To Messrs Greenlees Brothers belongs the credit of having made the trade in Scotch whisky, and of having introduced that beverage to the British public in a wholesome and agreeable form, blended with the utmost nicety and judgement, so that delicacy of flavour and absolute purity are, as far as possible, combined."
'Wyman's Commercial Encyclopaedia' 1890

James and Samuel Greenlees

At the height of Campbeltown's whisky popularity, it may have come as an odd suggestion when James and Samuel Jr Greenlees stated their intention to head to London and set up a new whisky business. The two men, aged 22 and 20 respectively, were not greatly experienced in either the distilling trade or in running a business. Both had been educated at the United Presbyterian Academy in Campbeltown, and upon leaving school, James had gone to Glasgow as an apprentice in the firm of Bairds & Co, iron merchants, whilst Samuel Jr had joined his father at Hazelburn Distillery.

Samuel Sr had joined his cousins and the original Hazelburn partners Mathew and Daniel Greenlees in 1845. This coincided with his marriage to Agnes Greenlees, Mathew and Daniel's sister, and also with the retirement of Archibald Colvill (the other original founder of Hazelburn Distillery). The couple had four children together, but Agnes passed away whilst all their children were infants. Despite Samuel remarrying in 1861 and having four more children, James and Samuel Jr remained the only boys from his first marriage.

The firm of Greenlees Brothers was registered in 1870 and initially partnered along with their father and Charles Colville Greenlees (Managing Director, Dalaruan Distillery).[57] In early

1871, the two brothers took up official residence at the Gresham Building in the centre of London. Using warehouses and bottling facilities of an existing firm in Glasgow, they lost no time in getting started and it was clear that they intended to use clever marketing to get ahead.

England at this time was still in its infancy when it came to appreciating Scotch whisky. Weaning itself from a diet of brandy[58] and other foreign and domestic spirits, the English drinker was more likely to receive (and expect) a glass of Irish whiskey than to know to ask for Scotch. In the early days of their business, the Greenlees Brothers 'sold about three vats of Irish to one of Scotch'.[59]

Clearly, the brothers were astute enough to ease their way into the English market by pandering to the crowd and had great success marketing the brand, 'Royal Connaught Irish Whiskey'.

But these were boys from Kintyre, and it did not take them long to bring Scotland's finest to London. From the distinct lack of advertising for the Royal Connaught Irish whiskey, one can see the direction in which they wanted to take the business.

Coinciding with the Greenlees Brothers setting up in London, there was much coverage of the pending marriage of Princess Louise, Queen Victoria and Prince Albert's sixth child, to John Campbell, Marquess of Lorne. Due to the geographical relevance (John Campbell being the heir to the Dukedom of Argyll) and no doubt playing heavily on the media coverage, the Greenlees Brothers released their first branded whisky, Lorne Highland Whisky.

On the day of the wedding, James and Samuel announced themselves to the trade and media by holding a large and 'representative banquet'.[60] Steadily, the brothers began to advertise in local newspapers and by April, they had appointed Marshall and Elvy as their sole agents for London. In contrast to the unfortunate marriage (which drifted apart after several childless years), the Lorne Highland Whisky took off and, through an aggressive marketing campaign, quickly put Greenlees Brothers firmly on the lips of London drinkers. James and Samuel were never shy about proclaiming the quality of their whisky – often by quoting reviews from newspapers:

"This whisky has that pure mellow flavour which results from age and judicious blending of whiskies distilled from malt of the finest quality, prepared under the personal supervision of the Proprietors. Not only may it be safely asserted that there is not a 'headache in a hogshead of it', but it also possesses all those qualities which the best medical authorities value so highly, and which render it one of the best agents in their pharmacopoeia. So long, then, as alcohol has to be prescribed for constitutional ailments, it cannot be taken in a more agreeable, safer, or beneficial form than the Lorne Highland Whisky, which is worthily named after the most popular of Scotchmen, the Marquis of Lorne."

An advertising mirror produced to promote Lorne Whisky. The firm produced a host of brands with three obscure ones included here.

"To those who, like the great national poet, Burns, think Scotch Whisky the pearl of all drinks, the Lorne Highland Whisky will recommend itself as a boon long sought after. Its delightful mellow

flavour may be attributed to the selection of the very finest malt, to purity in distillation, and that tone which age alone can impart. Distilled by the proprietors, Messrs. Greenlees, on the Argyll Estates, the name and title given to it are doubly appropriate. It may be safely pronounced, after a trial and comparison with other whiskies, to be superior to any in the market."

"This whisky is a pure, unadulterated spirit, very mellow, in quality excellent, and, in our opinion, perfectly wholesome. Where a stimulant is required, it is to be preferred to Brandy."[61]

Commercial Street, London circa 1900.

With the success of Lorne Highland Whisky, the brothers developed a plethora of further brands, including 'Davaar' – named after the small island at the head of Campbeltown Loch, 'Dew of Bengullion' – named after the highest hill in southern Kintyre, 'Glenlussa' named after a part of Campbeltown, another called 'Claymore', and again playing on the popularity of the monarchy at the time, 'King Edward VII'. From the outset, James and Samuel were the agents for their father's Hazelburn distillery and, although to a lesser extent than the blends, began to market Hazelburn pure malt, adding the Dalaruan and Lagavulin distilleries shortly thereafter.

The firm had notable success when landing the contract with the Admiralty to supply them with whisky in 1878.[62] Within a dozen years of leaving Campbeltown, the brothers had achieved a dominant place in England as a premium and trustworthy supplier of Scotch whiskies. The original London offices within the Gresham Building quickly proved wholly inadequate, and the business was moved to 29-31 Commercial Street, near the busy Spitalfields area of London.

Their success also allowed the brothers to open a large warehousing, blending, and bottling facility on Osborne Street in the heart of Glasgow.[63] The magazine, 'Leading Firms in British Commerce', provided a detailed description of how meticulously they had planned their Glasgow enterprise:

"Messrs. Greenlees Brothers bonding stores were located right in the heart of the city proper, and could scarcely be more conveniently situated to rail or river, the former running direct overhead, while the latter lies within stone-throw. It is not the convenience of situation alone that has been made the name of the firm a 'household word' at home and abroad. The scrupulous attention given to the smallest detail, the high class and quality of the liquor, the method and punctuality in executing commissions, have placed this House among the foremost of the kind in the world.

"With a frontage of 300 feet, occupying 14 of the large arches

GREENLEES BROTHERS,

Highland Pure Malt Pot Still Whisky Distillers, and Blenders of Fine Old and Thoroughly Matured Whiskies.

Prices ranging from 2/- to 16/- per gallon (in Bulk), F.o.b.; or from 8/- to 35/- per dozen (in Cases), F.o.b.

Sole Proprietors of KING EDWARD VII. Yg SCOTCH WHISKY, "LORNE" Highland Whisky, and "CLAYMORE" Rare Old Scotch.

BEING WHISKY EXPERTS WE SUPPLY

The Best Obtainable Value in Whisky.

Special Labels and Brands reserved for Buyers' use.

Bonded and Export Stores—GLASGOW.   Distilleries—ARGYLESHIRE.

SAMPLES AND PRICES ON APPLICATION TO
Head Offices and Stores:—
29B & 31B, COMMERCIAL STREET, LONDON, E.

Telegraphic Address—" GREENLEES, LONDON."
Codes—A.B.C. 4th and 5th Editions, A.1, Liebers, and Hamiltons' Numerical Code Condenser.

---

under the Glasgow and South-Western Railway, and covering an acre of ground, this vast warehouse was capable of storing 500,000 gallons. So methodically are the casks stacked that any given one can be turned out at a few minutes notice without disturbing its neighbours. The flooring was composed of solid concrete to a depth of 14 inches, and consequently always level and dry.

"Overhead, the arches are lined with galvanized iron. The casks were stowed three high on wooden blocks to protect them from any possible dampness, the lower consisting of puncheons and butts, hogs-heads come second and quarters and octaves make up the top tier. In the long narrow arches which branch off and where the cased goods were stored, the same precautions of block raising was taken to perfect dryness secured, insuring protection to expensive capsules and labels.

"Two features of special value to which was directed were first, in the interest of the owner of the goods, the cool, equable temperature, aided by sufficient ventilation, which reduces the lowest point the falling off in bulk or strength of the spirits stored and second, in the interest of the warehouse keepers themselves, *in having as already stated, a smooth floor, well-drilled assistants, ample passage room and even kept stacks, all tending to reduce labour to a minimum.*

"The blending carried on in these stores was of exceptional magnitude, three-quarters of a million gallons passed through the vats within a year. For filling these from the casks a large double suction pump was used which throw 5,000 gallons per hour. There were six blending vats in this warehouse of various contents from 7,000 gallons. Both the pumps and mixing apparatus was driven by a powerful gas engine from the firm of Messrs. L. Sterne & Co. of the Crown Iron Works. Messrs. Greenlees had made the proper blending of different spirits a subject of special attention, and on which they have spent much time and money in perfecting.

"In the bottling department again machinery was used to minimize labour. The bottles used were all new, with a view to remove effectually what goes under the term of Bloom, the bottles were steeped in an acid solution. After having been subjected for a sufficient length of time to the action of the acid bath they were removed and placed upon rotary brushes driven by the gas engine, and were scoured out first with lukewarm water, succeeded by cold water.

"The spirits passing by gravitation from the vats were received in the filter, whence it was filled into bottles by means of a bottling machine, which was one of McGlashan's patents. After it leaves the corker's hands the bottle was examined to see that the contents were perfectly bright and the quantity contained was rigidly verified by H. M. Inland Revenue Officer, appointed specially for the purpose. The capsules and labels were then affixed. The enveloping of it first in a paper wrapper then in a straw one, prepared the bottle for the hands of the packer. When the case received a dozen bottles the lid was nailed down ready to have the affixed address and permit. Judicious division of labour enabled the two fold operation of bottling and packing to be carried out quickly and economically.[64]

The English – and predominantly London – whisky trade was dominated by a small number of large firms, and the Greenlees

ADVERTISEMENTS—(WHISKY BLENDERS).

GREENLEES BROTHERS,

BONDED VATTING
AND
BOTTLING WAREHOUSE PROPRIETORS.

Vattings & Bottlings made in Customer's own name.

DIMENSIONS.		OPERATIONS 1886.	
Frontage -	384 Feet.	Received	1,302,060 Gallons.
Superficial Area	56,502 Sq. Feet.	Vatted	1,470,726 ,,
Cubic Area -	739,158 Feet.	Delivered	1,378,998 ,,

Bonded and Bottling Warehouses:

37 TO 53, AND 59, OSBORNE STREET,

Offices:

38, STOCKWELL STREET, GLASGOW.

Brothers' dominance did not go unnoticed. James Buchanan once remarked, *"the wants of the licensed Trade in London were pretty well met by Messrs Greenlees, whose Lorne whisky practically held a monopoly of supply."*[65] In October 1886, Alexander Walker, son of the famous John Walker, discovered in the Midland Grand Hotel[66] that the Greenlees Brother's whisky *"was being 'pushed' by the bar staff at a lower price to Walker's."*

The Midland Grand was not only Alexander Walker's favourite place to stay in London but also a significant account offering high visibility to his brand. In addition, the Midland Railway was one of his principal carriers. In an angry letter, Walker wrote, *"If it suits you to get a commission of a few hundred pounds a year from Greenlees Brothers, it might well suit Walker's to withdraw their business from the railway, seeing that they, through you, refuse to do business with one of their best, and largest customers."*[67]

The firm continued to see notable growth as new agencies were gained in Canada, Australia, Japan and several British colonies. The magnitude of the business made the papers when one of the largest shipments of whisky Scotland had ever seen was moved by a special train from the Highlands to Glasgow. *"About 50 lorries were required to convey it from Buchanan Street Station to the bonded stores in Osborne Street."* It was noted by the 'Glasgow Mail' in April 1885 that *"Some of our readers on seeing the huge procession of carts passing through our streets this morning, must have reflected that the total abstainers do not appear to be having it all their own way."*

The success and resulting demand for Lorne whisky and the trend of forgery, or 'passing off', caused numerous incursions on the Greenlees brand. In 1888, the brothers were forced to take legal action against a firm called Ramsay & Co., of Liverpool, in order to:

"Restrain the defendants from selling or offering for sale, invoicing, or otherwise passing off, or attempting to pass off on the trade or public, under the name or description of 'Lorne Blend Whisky' or 'Lorne Whisky', any whisky not sold by or obtained from the plaintiffs, and from using any labels or marks, or branding or affixing on any case, box, or other receptacle, any label, mark, or design with the words 'Lorne Whisky', 'Lorne Blend Whisky', or any colourable imitation of the words 'Lorne Whisky', and from using any mark, label, or design to induce flee trade or public to believe that whisky not sold by or obtained from the plaintiffs is Lorne Whisky, and from selling, or offering for sale, or endeavouring to pass off on the trade or public, whisky not sold by or obtained from the plaintiffs as and for plaintiffs' whisky."[68]

From the outset, and no doubt having learned about the issue from their early days with Hazelburn, adverts would often have a warning message included: *"Please observe that each bottle has Lorne Highland Whisky on Label, Cork, and Capsule, without which none is genuine."*

In May 1886, Samuel Greenlees Sr passed away at his home in Campbeltown. He was described in his obituary as *"possessed of great natural energy, unwearying perseverance. His punctuality and promptitude, his perfect straight-forwardness and honesty, his clearly conceived and tersely expressed plans, his thorough trust-worthiness, made him an excellent businessman, and one with whom business could be transacted with perfect confidence and satisfaction."* He had travelled for many years, and was highly respected throughout the trade and had been working the day before his death.

The death of their father irrevocably changed the setup of the Greenlees Brothers' business. Almost immediately, Samuel Jr returned to Campbeltown to continue running the Hazelburn Distillery. Having bought Glendale House in Kilkerran Road, he then purchased Argyll Distillery in 1887 and Burnside Distillery in 1888. All three distilleries, under his management and ownership, continued to remain separate from the Greenlees Brothers firm which James now took to managing predominantly on his own.

Despite the loss of their father and the now geographical split of the brothers, the business continued to flourish, and in 1889, secured the contract as the sole supplier of Scotch whisky to the Olympia, as it hosted the world-famous Barnum circus show. In June 1891, the Reading Standard commented:

"Advertising is no longer a business, but has become an art; an idol at the feet of which so many sit proclaiming their goods to the world. Every day one sees or hears of some novel form of advertising that has been adopted by some pushing business house. The latest form of bringing the wares of the manufacturer before the public is that which has been adopted by Messrs Greenlees Bros., the well-known distillers; and from what I know of human nature I think this is likely to secure them the extended popularity which they desire.

"This firm arranged with Messrs. Chas. Green Spencer and Sons, the aeronauts, to have a large quantity of advertising circulars distributed by them from their balloons during their several trips from the Naval Exhibitions at Chelsea. Among the

circulars distributed there are a number bearing a coupon on the back, which entitles the finder to a bottle of Messrs. Greenlees celebrated Lorne whisky. Last week the balloon passed over Mortimer and Silchester, at which places no less than six coupons were found, and the finders were each supplied with one bottle of Lorne whisky by Messrs. Butler and Sons, of Chatham Street, Reading, who are agents for the above firm."

In 1894, the Greenlees Brothers released a small booklet, free of charge, titled 'A Tourist's Visit to Argyllshire and West Highlands'. Whilst all copies of this booklet appear to have been lost, the 'Lincolnshire Echo' allows this glimpse into the contents.

"In addition to the touring information a full description of Messrs. Greenlees business is given, and a great number of 'Facts about Scotch whisky', a beverage that Messrs. Greenlees Brothers may be considered to know something about when it is stated that they have now on hand over 2,000,000 gallons of the popular spirit, 'a quantity that would suffice to give half-a-pint of whisky to every inhabitant of Great Britain, France and Germany." Alfred Barnard had been invited to write about Hazelburn Distillery (he had first visited in 1885[69] when Samuel Greenlees Sr was Managing Director), and he remarked that *"the whole contents of all the warehouses comprised a stock of 7,626 casks, representing 437,170 gallons."*

James and Samuel, never shy of giving the Temperance movement something to consider, concluded the pamphlet with:

Truth Versus Fiction.
"The British Medical Association appointed a Committee to make enquiries in order to ascertain the average age of the different categories of drinkers – that is to say, those who completely refrain from alcoholic drink, those who indulge more or less in moderation, and those who drink to excess. The Committee has handed in its report, Its conclusions are drawn from 4,234 deaths, which are divided into categories of individuals, with the average age attained by each:

Total abstainers	*51 years 22 days*
Habitually temperate drinkers	*63 years 13 days*
Careless drinkers	*59 years 67 days*
Free drinkers	*57 years 59 days*
Decidedly intemperate drinkers	*53 years 3 days*

The figures show, singularly enough, that those who reach the shortest age are those who drink no alcohol whatever; after them come the drunkards, who only exceed them by a trifle. The greatest average age is reached by those who drink moderately."
'Revue Scientifique' and 'London Daily Telegraph'

Now on his own in London, James Greenlees began a steady program of investing in a wide range of industries. Between 1895 and 1897, James was listed as a Director of the Captain Cook Brewery in Auckland, Walker & Meimarachi Ltd (The Egyptian Supply Store) and the firm of India-Mexico Ltd. Despite this divestment, there was sufficient funding and requirement to back the building of the Speyside Distillery,[70] Kingussie, in 1895. The late 1890s witnessed a boom in production and demand, and it was becoming clear at this stage that the English palate was more suited to the softer, sweeter style of the Highlands, in particular, the Glenlivet area – what we now refer to as Speyside. Greenlees Brothers were by this point agents for several Campbeltown and Islay makes but were looking for a steady supply from a Speyside distillery.

The new distillery was in co-operation with the Macpherson Grant family of Ballindalloch (an area that had seen a recent explosion of distilleries around this time). Quite how the firm was established is unknown and the absence of either James or Samuel Greenlees at the opening ceremony points to their involvement as being simply financial. The distillery was spared little expense becoming one of the largest in Strathspey, covering several acres which included houses for the manager and much of the workforce. A siding was built by the Highland Railway to facilitate the arrival and dispatch of casks and materials.

The building of the distillery was poorly timed as shortly after completion the industry witnessed a large slump in demand. In 1904, 210 casks, comprising 13,434.6 proof gallons of whisky, were shipped to the Osborne Street warehouses. It was recorded at the time as being *"an exceptionally large consignment for a comparatively new distillery, especially considering the prevailing depression in the trade."*[71]

Things were not right at the distillery, and Charles Doig, the great distillery architect and inventor, was brought in to troubleshoot the problem.[72] Whether due to the great depression, the product or a combination of both, the large withdrawal of stock by the Greenlees Brothers marked the end of the Speyside Distillery. Just nine years after commencing distilling, it was closed, and the sad process of finding a buyer began:

"Owing presumably to the present unsettled state of affairs in the trade, it seems very difficult to dispose of such a thing as a distillery. Offered for sale for the sixth time in Dowell's room, Edinburgh, last week, the Speyside Distillery, Kingussie, failed to find a purchaser. At the first exposure some time ago, £5,000 was asked; at the second time ago, £4,000; at the third, £3,000; at the fourth, £2,500; at the fifth, £2,000; and on Wednesday at £1,500. The distillery was built in 1896, and is situated close to the Highland Railway Company's Station at Kingussie, and the main line to the south, with which it is connected by a line of rails.

"The buildings stand upon a site of about 10½ acres, and include manager's house, Excise officer's house, and four workmen's cottages, in addition to ample warehousing accommodation. It may be mentioned that the Speyside Distillery, which went into voluntary liquidation in July 1909, was incorporated in May 1895, with a capital of £20,000. In the 1908 balance sheet the property account and distillery plant represented a figure of £20,536 8s 9d."[73]

The new owners, Highland Industries Company, converted the distillery to manufacture petrol gas machines and to extract malt. This business also floundered, and today, all that can be seen of a once sprawling distillery complex are the homes that were built. Quite how exposed the Greenlees Brothers were to the collapse from this venture is unknown, but their business appears to have carried on without the slightest hint of financial loss from the press.

Despite their continued advertising campaign for their brands, James and Samuel did not seek personal coverage in the way that contemporaries within the whisky industry, such as James Buchanan and Tommy Dewar, were known to do.

In 1910, Samuel Greenlees was interviewed by 'The Globe' regarding the growth of New York. Samuel had visited the city thirty years prior to this trip and remarked *"What struck me most were the huge commercial buildings which sprung up and the immense growth of the city northwards."* Samuel was a member of the Old Players Club, a group of well-to-do businessmen and would have been acquainted with the Public Relations skills of Tommy Dewar, who was President of the club.

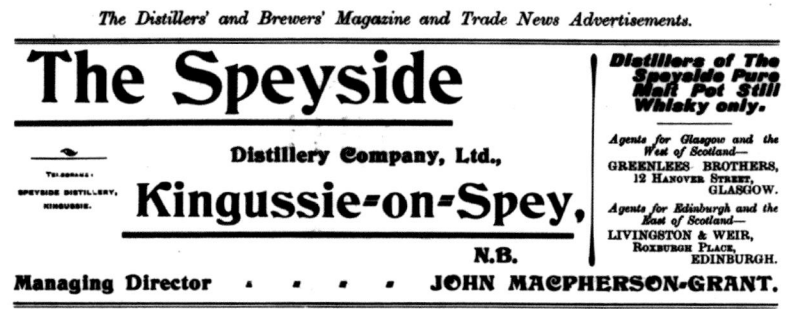

Neither brother courted much publicity and each shunned notoriety, but we are provided two glimpses into James' character from his appearance as an expert witness firstly in 1891, at the Select Committee report on British and Foreign Spirits and then in 1908 for the Royal Commission on Whiskey and other Potable Spirits.

The 1891 Committee had been appointed 'to consider whether,

on grounds of public health, it is desirable that certain classes of Spirits, British and Foreign, should be kept in bond for a definite period before they are allowed to pass into consumption'. The James Greenlees we see in this report now has two decades of experience running Greenlees Brothers and his answers are full and detailed. Sir Lyon Playfair, the Chairman of the Committee, enquired why James thought 'blending is such an important part of the whisky trade':

"I would say that in Scotland particularly," James replied, *"Each district makes a different whisky, a whisky of a different flavour and having its own peculiarities. The taste for whiskies nowadays is such that you cannot get people to drink these*

MR. JAMES GREENLEES.

distinct flavours by themselves; it is an acquired taste for a man to drink Islay pure, or Campbeltown pure, or Glenlivet pure; but by mixing those whiskies in certain proportions, you make them much more palatable and pleasant, and produce a better article."

Chair: *"Did you say that you considered that the public taste requires more of an admixture of silent spirit?"*

James: *"No, I said they like an older whisky, more silent, with less flavour."*

Chair: *"To attain that new process of blending are the grain spirits used for blending... made in the patent still?"*

James: *"Yes, a grain spirit made in the patent still; that is the advantage you have in blending. If you use patent still spirit you make your blend more perfect by using a little grain. If you unite different characters of whisky, if you make a blend of, say, five fine malt whiskies, without grain, unless they have been blended for a very long time together, you can almost detect the different distilleries they have come from."*

Chair: *"If you have expert taste?"*

James: *"Yes, if you are accustomed to seeing whiskies and mixing them; then if you put in a very small quantity of grain spirit into your blend you at once marry them, and you cannot detect the difference in the slightest."*

In 1908, almost two decades on, and having experienced the Pattison crash and subsequent recession in the industry, we see a very much more circumspect James Greenlees - this time called as an expert witness to the Royal Commission on Whiskey and Other Potable Spirits.[74] This Commission had arisen due to a court case that began in the Islington Borough against local spirit merchants accused of passing off a liquor that was not 'whisky'. Much of the discussion revolved around the differences between English, Irish and Scotch whisk(e)y and what defined them. In the interview, we get a clear indication of the manner and intelligence of James Greenlees from his continual use of single-word answers and political astuteness to avoid certain questions, traps, and revelations.

The board of commissioners was chaired by The Right Hon.

Lord James of Hereford, who tried his best to glean blend recipe information from his witness:

>Chair: *"How did you regulate your blending?"*
>James: *"By what we considered was the blend of whiskey to suit the palate of the public at the time. The Irish whiskey having less flavour than the Scotch, we reduced the flavour and made it more palatable than an individual whiskey."*
>Chair: *"I presume you had to follow the public demand, which meant the public taste?"*
>James: *"Certainly, and we tried to educate the public."*
>Chair: *"In what direction did that public taste go?"*
>James: *"In the direction of a more silent whisky."*
>Chair: *"And silent means not so pungent?"*
>James: *"Not so heavy, not such a heavy flavour; rather less flavour than the malt whiskies."*
>Chair: *"Practically, giving me a rough average, what percentage of malt would there be?"*
>James: *"It would a great deal depend on the price of the whisky and the age. If it was a cheap whisky you would have to put in a greater percentage of patent still whisky. If it was a high class whisky, a dear whisky, you have less patent still in it."*
>Chair: *"Would you be disposed to make public the exact proportions of the blend you make?"*
>James: *"No, I do not think that would be fair."*
>Chair: *"You treat it, I will not say as a trade secret, but a trade possession?"*
>James: *"Certainly, it is one's business pure and simple. If everybody had to put on their label the exact proportions of grain and malt each one would know exactly the other man's business, which I do not think would be fair."*[75]

During both interviews, James gives clues from someone outside of the Campbeltown bubble as to the changes in consumer behaviour. James offers his sorrow that *"the Commission could not go and visit Campbeltown, because it would have been very interested. There are 20 distilleries within half a mile of one another. The whiskies of all those distilleries differ to a certain extent although they are made exactly the same way. Two distilleries next door to one another will make a whiskey of a different flavour."* Despite this, and as quoted at the start of this chapter, his insistence never waivers that blended whisky is the present and future for Scotch whisky.

The economic downturn began to take its toll, and perhaps due to this slump or a longing to be closer to his children, Samuel Greenlees moved back to London in 1908. By the time the First World War settled into its bloody quagmire, the Greenlees Brothers were reaching the latter years of their business together.

Due to James' poor health, the 1914 edition of 'Who's Who In Business' listed just Samuel Greenlees as the 'Present Principle'. James' health deteriorated further, and on the 1st of September 1916, he passed away in a London nursing home. Such was the continual devastating news from the war front that James' death barely registered in the newspapers. One of the most influential whisky barons of the 19th & 20th centuries passed away with barely a flicker of acknowledgement.

As the industry tried to recover from the devastation of the First World War, the ensuing economic depression, and the closures within the whisky industry, Samuel struggled on running the business. Without his brother James and a lack of interest from any potential heirs, moves were made to change the structure and nature of the company. In 1919 the firm of Alexander and Macdonald Co. Ltd., of Leith, was absorbed, and the two firms became 'Macdonald Greenlees'. As a result the head office then moved to Leith. The merger brought with it the brand of 'Sandy Macdonald', which had a more impressive pedigree (or at least a longer history) than the Greenlees brands, having been marketed since 1840.

In 1918, the Greenlees family association with Hazelburn Distillery ended when it was sold to Mackie & Co. (later becoming White Horse Distillers), and the Burnside Distillery was also sold off to United Creameries. Samuel's ties to the Campbeltown distilling trade were completely severed when Colvill, Greenlees & Co., and with it the Argyll Distillery, was sold in 1921 to the recently merged firms of James Ainslie & Co., and David Heilbron Ltd (forming Ainslie & Heilbron Distillers Ltd).

In December 1925, Macdonald Greenlees was acquired by William Williams & Co. Ltd., of Aberdeen and became Macdonald, Greenlees & Williams. It was the end of the London connection for the Greenlees Brothers and coincided with the retirement of Samuel Greenlees' involvement within the whisky industry. Just a year later, the all-encompassing Distiller's Company Limited absorbed the firm of Macdonald, Greenlees & Williams.

"Inquiries made in Aberdeen yesterday with reference to the announcement that it is proposed to wind up the company of Messrs Macdonald, Greenlees and Williams (Distillers) Ltd., elicited the fact that Messrs Macdonald, Greenlees and Williams have merged their interests with those of that great concern, the Distillers Company, Ltd., which within recent times has absorbed several distilling companies. This combining of interests has been anticipated for some time, and was no surprise to the trade.

"In preparation for the new arrangement, Messrs Macdonald, Greenlees and Williams transferred some months ago from their former branch at 36, 37 and 38 Regent Quay, Aberdeen, to smaller premises at 27 and 29 Virginia Street, upon which extensive structural alterations were made in order to equip the premises as suitable offices… The export warehouses at Leith, Aberdeen and Glasgow are likely to be maintained. These contain large stocks of matured whisky."[76]

On the 24th of January 1939, Samuel Greenlees passed away at his residence, 8 Wilton Place, London. He was 89, and his passing was felt most keenly in Campbeltown. The 'Campbeltown Courier' published a fitting tribute:

"Messrs James and Samuel Greenlees proceeded together to

London, where, as a result of their investigations, they became convinced that a big market could be developed for Scotch Whisky, provided a whisky could be produced suitable to English tastes.

"As a result of their investigations, they decided that the single malt whisky, then practically the only Scottish product, was not popular in England, but that a blended whisky found a ready sale.

"They had the courage of their convictions and decided to establish the firm of Greenlees Brothers, Whisky Blenders and Bottlers. Greenlees Brothers may, therefore, be regarded as the pioneers of whisky blending and as the pioneers in popularising Scotch Whisky throughout the world."

Samuel had remained a loyal stalwart to Campbeltown throughout his years and was known for his continual telegrams and news reports to family and colleagues whilst living in London or travelling.[77] His wife, Jessie Eliza Weir Greenlees, had died in 1908 and they left behind two sons, Weir Loudon and James Walter. Captain Weir Loudon (born 26th December 1882, the year after his father married Jessie) was a first-class cricketer and a graduate of Magdalene College, Cambridge.

Weir died in Marylebone, London, on 10th January 1975, aged 92. Weir Loudon received his names via his mother's maiden name and Weir's grandfather, Reverend Walter Weir. The Reverend had tragically lost four of his five children to diphtheria in 1863 before dying himself a year later. His widow (Jessie's mother) then married again to Captain James Loudon, and the surname of Loudon Greenlees was adopted. Weir's younger brother, James Walter, was named after both of his grandfathers and made a Captain during the First World War. James, who was eight years Weir's junior, died in 1972 in Ballantrae, South Ayrshire.

There is little trace now of the Greenlees Brothers and their impact on the Scotch whisky industry. As two quintessential Victorian and quite stoic men, they were not obsessed with any legacy nor with the business being passed down through generations. Perhaps, as can be seen by their business acumen, the young distillers realised that the time had passed for their town's old way of doing business. Their position within the blending fraternity and fashions of the day will have allowed them to foresee the dark clouds gathering around Campbeltown whisky. However, they remained committed to the burgh throughout their lives.

All that remains from the once great Greenlees Brothers is the brand 'Grand Old Parr'. First introduced as 'Old Parr' in 1909, the blended whisky was named after the legendary Thomas 'Old Tom' Parr, who reputedly lived from 1482 to 1635. Quite how, or why, the Greenlees Brothers decided on this story for a brand is lost to us, but given their proclivity for stating the health benefits of pure Scotch whisky, it must be assumed there was an emphasis on longevity through consumption. The prefix 'Grand' was added long after any Greenlees' association with the brand, but the whisky remains defiant and, to this day, is exported around the world. A reminder of two young Campbeltonians who took on the centre of the world and shone.

Circa 1902 - Gauging two casks at Glengyle's Duty Free Warehouse No 1. Hugh Muir, now with a white beard.

CHAPTER 6

SHOCKWAVES

"The company boom and its effect on the trade is also deserving of serious attention. So long as times are good things go on swimmingly, but let a general depression of trade occur – and the present labour troubles indicated that the country may at any time be plunged into the throes of an industrial war – what is to be the result? Distilleries are increasing largely in number; in other cases the output is being doubled!
"The consumption is not increasing at the same rate, consequently stocks in bond go up by leaps and bounds. A time must therefore come when the market will be flooded with Scotch whisky, prices will fall, the investing public will be startled, and – but we prefer not to dwell on the probable result; a word to the wise man is sufficient."
OMIC
August 1897

"The Jury, by a majority, find Robert Paterson Pattison guilty as libelled of charges one, two, three and four. The jury find Walter Gilchrist Gray Pattison guilty of charges two and four and find the first and third charges as against him not proven. Robert Paterson Pattison the sentence is that you be imprisoned for eighteen calendar months."
Robert Pattison: "My brother is entirely innocent of charges one and three."
'Opening the Case – The Affairs of the Pattisons' Whisky'
Justine Hazelhurst, 2024

The Pattison Crash, as it would come to be known, affected the entire whisky industry.

Whilst there had been the odd blip, closure, or collapse of a firm, warehouse or trader, the Scotch whisky industry - certainly the legal part of it - had enjoyed a sustained period of growth for much of the latter part of the 19th century. It was a mostly prosperous period when the growing consumer base kept pace with the building of new distilleries and increased output.

However, if there is one trait we can ascribe to the Campbeltown distillers of this period, other than a steadfast belief in their practices and quality of spirit, it is a level of conservatism concerning growth outside of their control. From the outside, there is a certain irony in a corner of Scotland possessing more distilleries per square yard (and per capita) than any other part of the country, casting a critical eye over what was going on elsewhere. Whilst OMIC In Campbeltown was just one voice, it is unlikely that support had not been garnered from his fellow Kintyre distillers before sending his 'In Campbeltown' letters for publication – especially when they were critical.

"Where is Scotland to find a market for her whisky? The question is coming to be a serious one for the distillery companies; for it is evident that the supply present and possible in the near future has not only gone far beyond the demand but far beyond the point which it is desirable for the good of the world that it should ever touch. According to the statistics given by Mr Thomas R. Dewar, who can speak on this point with the special information of an expert, Scotland is now producing double the quantity of whisky that it did ten years ago. Neglecting fractions, it produced a little over 18 million gallons in 1888, and in 1898, the production of whisky had reached a little more than 33 and one third million gallons. But the world has not taken, and is not yet prepared to take, that amount of whisky off the hands of the producers. Therefore, it is going into bond, and at present, there are 89 million gallons of whisky in Scotland maturing and waiting for a market... [if] the world does not increase in its demand

for whisky, then to what extent are the Scotch distillers to go on storing up and maturing it? There is evidently a difficult question maturing about the disposal of the surplus Scotch whisky if the world is to keep its head clear."* November 1898

It is unlikely that this article was written without credible insight and knowledge of the mood and whisperings within the Scotch whisky trade. Based in London, James Greenlees was a constant messenger of all tidings within the whisky world and kept the Campbeltown distillers in the loop. Despite the industry's size, it remained a small network of companies and individuals.[78] The warning signs, especially from those in and around the Pattison Brothers of Leith, were there for most to see.

Robert and Walter Pattison joined their father's firm, originally a dairy wholesaler, establishing the firm Pattison, Elder & Co., and diversifying into blended Scotch in the mid-1880s. This coincided with an explosion in the building of distilleries and new ancillary firms. Brokers, in particular, grew in numbers, sensing the chance of profits through the speculation of buying and selling casks. The Pattison Brothers, as the firm was renamed when it went public in 1896, quickly established themselves as, if not the largest, then certainly one of the most impressive brokers, blenders and bottlers of spirits. Although, predominantly, they were known as owners of bonded Scotch whisky.

From the outside, and indeed for those witnessing the growth in Leith, where the Pattison Brothers were based, everything just appeared like an incredible success story. Whisky flooded in as newer, more extensive and impressive warehouses were built. Billboards and signs sprang up; plush offices were decked out with the finest livery, and company owners, particularly Robert and Walter, lived the millionaire life.

The barbed concerns and premonitions printed in the 'Distillers Magazine' were fairly steady, leading up to the inevitable crash of the Pattison Brothers. Initially, the response from Campbeltown was stoic - a standalone defiance, albeit, perhaps without the hindsight, knowing the size of the fraud and debt.

Advert in the 'Illustrated London News' June 1897.

"Recent events in the East of Scotland do not directly affect distillers here, as I am informed that Pattisons did little or no business in Campbeltown, but at the same time, the collapse of a firm doing business on such an extensive scale would be bound to make its effect felt here as elsewhere."* January 1899

There was a continued backlash to the 'speculative trade', a blight, as far as the Campbeltown distiller was concerned, that did not enter into their order books. *"Distillers here,"* OMIC reassured readers a month later, *"have never encouraged the speculative buyer, the bulk of the whisky manufactured going into the hands of those who were going to use it. The wisdom of this course cannot be disputed, and had distillers in other centres confined the sale of their whiskies to those engaged in the trade, stocks in bond over the country would not have increased at the rate they have done during the last two years or so."*

The failure to realise, or admit, to the symbiosis of all distilling centres and aspects of the whisky industry is further evidence of a slightly pious, or at least 'us and them' mentality that prevailed. The Campbeltown distiller, out on a limb and for so long heavily reliant on just Glasgow and surrounding merchants, was not interested in the speculator, accumulator or the demonstrable success of 'Leith Merchants'. The fact that whisky from all regions, including Ireland and England, was part of this continual trade seems to have been overlooked, ignored, or not considered.

Whilst most Campbeltown whisky was sent to Glasgow for blending, either to be used immediately or in the near future, the

The Distillers' and Brewers' Magazine and Trade News Advertisements.

ESTABLISHED 1846.

GLENALBYN DISTILLERY CO., LTD.

DISTILLERS OF

Finest Highland Malt Whisky,

INVERNESS.

Agents: **F. W. & O. BRICKMANN, 46 Constitution Street, Leith.**

The Licenses Insurance Corporation and Guarantee Fund, Limited.

No other business than that of License Insurance is transacted by this Company.

AUTHORISED CAPITAL, £1,000,000.   SUBSCRIBED CAPITAL, £140,870.

THE OBJECTS OF THE CORPORATION are to compensate persons interested in Licensed Property for loss sustained through forfeiture of Certificate of License. At each annual Licensing Court the opportunity occurs to destroy the Licenseholder's means of livelihood and ruin a prosperous business. Insurance protects him from such disasters, maintains his security, and relieves him of the harassing anxieties which other traders are free from. The following are prominent dangers covered by Insurance :—
1 Untrustworthiness of Servants.
2 Severity of the Police and Magistrates.
3 Unruly Customers.
4 Adverse Local Feeling.
5 Applications for Transfer, owing to death or otherwise.

Proprietors, Bondholders, Brewers, Distillers, Wine Merchants, and others, are also protected against the risk of the forfeiture of Certificates of License in which they are interested.

Chief Office for Scotland, - - - 63 GEORGE STREET, EDINBURGH—J. M'CANKIE, Manager.
Head Office, - - - - - 24 MOORGATE STREET, LONDON, E.C.

change in the business-to-business model of the whisky industry had altered drastically from the 1880s onwards. As blenders adapted to changing tastes, new markets and changing prices, whisky was required in a variety of makes and ages in a way that had simply not been the case in the early to mid-part of the 19th century.

Stock was being laid down in the warehouses of the Campbeltown distillers, some already acquired by customers looking to mature in situ, some laid down by the distillers themselves. As can be seen by the proliferation of new warehouses being built by the distillers in the late 1880s onwards, speculation, in one form or another, was now part and parcel of the Campbeltown whisky business.

The expansion of the Speyside region as a distilling powerhouse was often the cause of the frustration for the Campbeltown distillers, who felt that these were short-term profit businesses.

"The quotations of distillery spirit trade shares have been rather on the downgrade lately, and it looks as if the public is becoming rather shaky about some of their investments. This will likely have the effect of putting an end to further flotations for some time to come, which may not be altogether a matter of regret on the part of the trade in general. There was always the temptation to go on building and floating distilleries so long as the public were eager to obtain this class of investment."

The banks, seeing the success of the share take-up of these new distilling firms, as Pattisons would do so in 1896, happily leveraged the companies against valuations and stock. The web of investment, debt, credits, and who owned what became so entangled that eventually the British Linen Company Bank[79] refused the Pattisons a further extension on their overdraft in December 1898. Rumours were already circulating throughout the industry that trouble was brewing, but the scale of the web of credits and bills was beyond anyone's expectations.

All previous thoughts that the Campbeltown distiller was in any way shielded, or outside, of the sphere of influence from this

OPENING PRICES FOR NEW WHISKY—SEASON 1899.

The following opening prices have been announced:—

HIGHLAND.	Per bulk gallon.
Aberlour-Glenlivet	3/11
Aberfeldy	3/6
Ardmore	3/8
Auchinblae	3/3
Auchintoshan	3/3
Balblair	3/7
Balmenach	3/8
Balvenie	3/7
Banff	3/3
Ben Morven	3/7
Ben Nevis	3/8
Blair Athol	3/4
Brackla	3/7
Cardow	3/10
Clynelish	4/8
Coleburn-Glenlivet	3/8
Craigellachie-Glenlivet	3/7
Dalmore	3/8
Devanha	3/6
Dufftown-Glenlivet	3/6
Dallasdhu	3/9
Ferintosh	3/6
Glenalbyn	3/6
Glenburgie	3/7
Glendullan-Glenlivet	3/9
Glenfarclas-Glenlivet	3/7
Glenmoray-Glenlivet	3/8
Glenlivet	4/6
Glen Mhor	3/4
Linkwood-Glenlivet	3/6
Longmorn	3/6
Macallan-Glenlivet	3/11
Miltonduff	3/6
Milton (Keith)	3/6
Glenfiddich	3/8
Glentauchers	3/7
Millburn	3/3
Glengrant	4/1
Glenmorangie	3/6
Glenturret	3/2
Highland Esk	3/4
Highland Park	4/1
Inchgower	3/8
Parkmore	3/8
Pollo	3/6
Pulteney	3/2
Scapa (Orkney)	3/10
Speyburn	3/8
Speyside	3/8
Strathisla	3/6
Stronachie	4/
Teaninich	3/8
Tobermory	3/9
Towiemore	3/8
Tullymet	3/6

CAMPBELTOWN.	Per bulk gallon.
Benmore	2/7
Campbeltown	2/6
Glen Nevis	2/5
Kiuloch	2/8
Lochhead	2/7
Scotia	2/7

ISLAY.	
Bowmore	3/10
Caol Ila	3/11
Lagavulin	3/9
Laphroaig	3/11
Lochindaal	3/9
Glencadam	3/6
Glencoull	3/0
Glendronach	4/2
Glenfyne	3/6
Glengarioch	3/6
Isla	3/
Knockdhu	3/8
Lochnagar	4/9
Port Ellen	3/6

CLYDE DISTRICT.	
Greenock Distillery	2/11

LOWLAND.	Per proof gallon.
Annandale	2/4
Auchtertool	2/4
Auchtertool Peat	2/6
Bankier	2/5
Clydesdale	2/6
Drumcaldie	2/8
Edinburgh	2/7
Glenforth	2/6
Glengoyne	2/6
Grange	2/9
Linlithgow	2/8
Littlemill	2/6
Lochnagar Royal	2/9
Loch Katrine (Camlachie)	2/4
Rosebank	3/4
Saucel (Paisley)	2/3
St. Magdalene	2/8

GRAIN WHISKY.	
Adelphi	1/4
Ardgowan	1/3
Bo'ness	1/3
Cambus	1/4
Cameronbridge	1/4
North British	1/3

fallout quickly evaporated as trade ground to a halt. Writing in February 1899, OMIC noted:

"Bonding orders since the New Year have been rather scarce, while the enquiry for whiskies with age has also been comparatively flat. The reason of this is not far to seek. Indeed, the wonder would be if, under existing circumstances, it was otherwise. Dealers have with one consent been going in for reducing stocks, and in the meantime, seem to have resolutely set their faces against giving fresh orders. Until something definite is known regarding the ultimate fate of Pattisons' concerns and whether their stocks are to be thrown on the market, distillers need look for nothing more than a hand-to-mouth business being done."

Like a house of cards, the fallout of the Pattison crash brought down merchants and dealers all over Scotland (many of whom were completely innocent casualties of the over-extending of credit lines). This did not affect consumption, which slightly increased over the period. This was an industry reeling from a loss of confidence in the profitability of buying, holding and selling stocks of bulk whisky. For the consumer, however, a glass of whisky was still a glass of whisky.

The numbers, when finally revealed, were quite staggering. F. W. & O. Brickmann, an established and respected agent also based in Leith, had been deeply invested in the Pattison Brother's business. The collapse of Brickmann in October 1899 sent further shock waves through an already jittery industry. Reporting on the 18th of October, the Glasgow Herald stated, *"The gross liabilities, actual and contingent, were not far short of three-quarters of a million. The contingent liabilities and bills discounted amounted to no less than £400,000, while the other liabilities exceeded £300,000. Creditors held security to the amount of about £200,000."*[80]

The 'Distillers' Magazine', on behalf of many of its subscribers, lamented the loss of such a popular firm:

"The announcement made of the financial difficulties in which the firm of F. W. & O. Brickmann, whisky brokers, Leith, find themselves, created a considerable sensation in commercial circles. It was known in the beginning of the year that the firm had been heavily hit with the Pattison failure, and it came out that the two firms had had several 'joint' transactions which were not of a profitable nature. There were doubts at that time as to whether the Brickmanns would weather the storm; but they pulled through, and it was hoped that the worst was passed. But since the Pattison collapse whisky broking, on which the firm largely depended, has been at a complete standstill, and payment has now had to be suspended.

"Much sympathy was expressed with the firm at the position in which they were placed, which has been entirely brought about by losses by bad debts in Pattisons Limited, and other, and the utter stagnation of the whisky broking trade in Leith. It was decided that the speediest mode of winding-up the estate would be by sequestration, and instructions were given to apply for this."[81]

This second shockwave, once again, pulled with it several smaller firms that barely received a shilling in the pound for their loss. By January 1900, halfway through the regular distilling season, the full impact of the downturn had hit the burgh.

"The year which has recently come to a close was none too bright for distillers. Orders for new whisky were difficult to get unless at prices which could scarcely be regarded as remunerative. The various failures which took place during the year in the trade, to a certain extent, paralysed the bonding business more especially. In consequence of this, distillers closed down earlier than usual last summer and were later of resuming again in the winter."

Whilst the Campbeltown distilleries were producing a great deal less than they had in the last two decades of the 19th century, the warehouses continued to send healthy amounts from their warehouses. The previous year had seen 1,199,376 gallons of whisky shipped - 'the largest quantity cleared from bond in twelve months for the last fourteen or fifteen years'. It is likely that a large majority of this stock had been sold previously and was being transferred by its owner - and much of it had been imported from Islay and Jura. 1899 saw 84,324 gallons moved into Campbeltown's warehouses.

This exodus of bulk spirits, and reduced production, gave OMIC extra fuel to his fulminations against the distillers in the 'North'. *"In Campbeltown there has been no increase in stocks for the last few years, in fact last year the quantity cleared from bond was substantially more than was manufactured. Distillers in other centres might, with advantage to themselves, and the trade generally, have copied the policy of our friends here, who regulated their production with the output from bond, and gave speculative buyers pretty much the go-by."*

These accusations went by, at least in the printed media, without reply – possibly as it was the expansion in the Highlands, specifically the Speyside region, that experienced the greatest fallout from the crash a year earlier. From this depression, the Distillers Company Ltd, incorporated in 1877, began to use its might, buying up many of the now troubled distilleries and whisky firms, to restrict the production and as much as possible, speculation. Many of these 'absorbed' distilleries were closed; very few were ever revived. The growth and expansion of the Distillers Company Ltd would have a large impact on Campbeltown two decades later.

The exposure of the Pattison Brothers' crash brought a new level of interest from the general public – many who had never considered whisky 'investable'. Articles from supposed experts sprang up with suggested yields or returns on maturing whisky. Some proposals were wildly inaccurate, often accusing those around the crash of profiteering, whilst others attempted to show healthy returns when the product was matured for a period of time.

In 1901 an attempt by one London publication to demonstrate how age increases the value stated that *"Roughly speaking, in from eight to nine years Highland malt whisky is doubled in value. Campbeltown make, which when placed in bond early in 1891, was worth 2s 6d, is now being sold at 5s."*[82] Islay malt of the same age was 7s 10d. Whether they liked it or not, the Campbeltown distiller was part of the larger buying public, and by default, part of the speculation.

The end of the 19th century, rather than marking a period of industrialisation and invention that revolutionised the whisky industry, instead marked a sustained period of depression and difficult trading. Barley prices rose to levels never seen before and for the Campbeltown distiller, still the cheapest 'make' on the market, the price squeezed profit margins beyond feasibility.

An already strained industry bemoaned the cost of raw ingredients and was often loathe to make much whisky with so little interest. In the immediate aftermath of the crash, the Campbeltown distillers or their representatives, visited customers to gauge the mood of the industry. Reports back were 'conflicting', as consumption remained good, whilst it was still the policy of dealers and blenders to reduce stock due to the uncertainty around the industry.

*"The wisdom of this course is undoubted, and the effect will no doubt be to cause a marked reduction in the quantity of whisky manufactured in Scotland during the season which has just commenced."** Dec 1899.

At the turn of the century, the distilling business carried on, albeit at a reduced capacity. There were still what was considered 'regular customers' – whether that meant consistent or in keeping with how their business behaviour was perceived - but distilling seasons began late and finished early. The lack of business, and prolonged depression, was by no means exclusive to the whisky trade. The start of the new century had seen many industries in a depressed state.

"It is to be regretted that general business in Campbeltown is

slacker this winter than it has been for some years back, and it is a matter of importance to many workmen that the distilleries are now started, as there are more idle men to be seen about the streets just now than is usually the case. The local shipbuilding yard, which, as a rule, gives employment to several hundred men, is very slack, and this, combined with a comparative failure in the herring fishing, makes money rather scarce in the meantime. It is to be hoped that the distilleries, on which so many people here depend, will have a good long working season." * December 1901

The talk of the wider whisky industry was of a great 'whisky loch' drowning out the supply, or demand, of new production. William Greenlees, Chairman of the Campbeltown Distillers' Association, wrote to the press to correct some erroneously printed stock figures as OMIC noted in November 1900:

"With reference to the recently published returns of whisky in bond... of the 10,236,529 proof gallons whisky shown in Campbeltown collection there was only 6,500,607 gallons, while the quantity exported for last year was 1,523,731 proof gallons, showing an excess of clearances over production of 379,978 proof gallons. The satisfactory feature regarding this output is that the great bulk of the whisky sent out was intended for immediate use and not merely removed for storage in other bonds. If every distilling centre in Scotland was in this position, we should be hearing less in these days than we have been doing regarding the 'enormous accumulation' of whisky in bond."

The opportunity to point a wagging finger at the root of the trouble was never missed (again, without rebuttal from the 'other centres'). Distillery output, in the new century, was down one-third from the highs of the late 1890s. Although production would climb steadily until 1904, it would never reach anywhere near its height, and in reality, the lull from the Pattison fallout marked the initial slow decay of the Campbeltown industry.

By 1901 the mood was especially dispirited, with OMIC noting, *"The past year has been a more than usually interesting one, in as much as it brought to a close a century which has been marked by an amount of business enterprise and push such as perhaps none of its predecessors could show. The distilling trade has shared to a certain extent in the prosperous times, but unfortunately the closing years of the century were anything but bright ones for malt distillers."*

The downturn in production and surplus of aged whisky caused a shift in what blenders could offer and what the public expected. Whilst the Campbeltown distillers were finding less interest in their new fillings, stocks of older, matured whisky were still being drawn on in good numbers. Bulk shipments were, on average, spirit two years older than had been the case before 1900. There was a brief hope that this new trade marked an increase of malt whisky in blends against what had been a growth in the proportion of grain whisky used. By the end of the year, the mood was slightly more sanguine.

"There is no doubt that the general trade of the country is rather less buoyant than it has been, more especially for the last two years, but these were years of exceptional briskness, and we can hardly look for a continuance of the same volume of trade to last for ever. There is no doubt, however, that a good steady all round business is yet being done and likely to continue for some months to come at least." * Dec 1901

The case against the Pattison Brothers had dragged on into 1901. Any lingering or lasting notion that Campbeltown distillers were not part of the tangled web was dashed when James Ferguson & Sons, owners of Ardlussa Distillery, were named as a supplier.

In March of 1901, The 'Distillers' Magazine' ran an in-depth article considering the whisky industry during the 19th century. Titled 'Progress of Scotch Distilling in the Last Century' by a Campbeltown Distiller (due to the prose and diction, unlikely to be the same author as the In Campbeltown letters), the piece covered much of the taxation and consumer trends before getting to the latter part of the century as the author makes it clear where the blame must be placed for the crash:

"Like all businesses, the distilling trade in Scotland has had

its vicissitudes, prosperous times and times of depression. For many years back the public taste, especially in England, has been gradually drawing towards Scotch whisky, and thanks to the enterprise of several well-known firms, who spared no expense in the way of cultivation and extending this trade, the demand for high class Scotch blends has become very great. Unfortunately, this extra demand led to a speculative trade being begun and to the manufacture of whisky far in excess of the requirements of the trade. Businesses were converted into Limited liability companies, and the public, who seemed to think that to put money into distilling was going into an undoubted investment, rushed at every chance of subscribing for the shares of these new companies as they came out."

The article highlighted the incredible production growth; between 1886 and 1899. In one year alone, the stock (in bond) increased by 13.5 million gallons - almost the entire production of 1885/86. Stock in bond, during the same period (1886 & 1899) more than doubled from 40.5 million gallons to 109.9 million gallons.

Consumption, whilst also increasing, was never going to keep up with the supply. As was noted in The Distillers' Magazine (1901): *"This consideration is of serious import, and though it by no means betokens a 'syncope', suggests 'a solemn pause', or, at least, a careful look ahead.... 'Booms', as they are called, followed by over-production and succeeded by periods of restriction and depression, following each other in succession, until something like a normal equilibrium is attained."*

By 1902, with some confidence returning to speculative buyers, distilling saw a return to growth; however, high material costs tempered this. Campbeltown distillers, who hadn't seen a price increase for over a decade, began to seriously feel their margins were becoming unworkable. Whilst dozens of distilleries had either been shut down or gone to the wall, there was still incredible competition from distilleries in the north – all able to command a shilling or more for their make than the Campbeltown distiller.

"One effect of the low prices is that a superior quality of whisky has been finding its way into the leading blends, and so raising the standard of quality, to the advantage of the public. To distillers of fine malts this is a matter of the utmost importance, and is bound to lead to good results in time to come. Looking at the rate at which parcels of old 'Campbeltowns' have been moving off the market for the last twelve months, the surplus stocks are bound to be getting pretty well used up, and this, in the ordinary course of business, is certain to lead to brisker demand and better prices before long."* Jan 1902

The stock of Campbeltown whisky in bond, at least that which remained in the burgh, hit a peak of 6.5 million gallons in 1899. As production fell, clearances from the bond remained fairly steady at around 1.4 million gallons each year. The continued import of bulk spirit kept the appearance of a busy whisky centre and provided several jobs. This could not disguise the fact that Campbeltown whisky production was heading in the wrong direction.

"Parcels of Campbeltown with any age are now becoming so scarce, the enormous quantities which have gone into consumption during the last few years having very materially reduced stocks of anything but the more recent years' bondings. As the quantities of new whisky manufactured here during the last three years more especially were very much curtailed, blenders will shortly be finding some difficulty in supplying their wants with old 'Campbeltowns'."* Jan 1903

1903 had not begun in auspicious circumstances as January brought some of the worst flooding Campbeltown had ever seen. Two distilleries had entire malt floors ruined, and parts of the town had become inaccessible. Little glee was taken when the part of the street where the Inland Revenue office was situated turned into a lake, causing *"various means to be devised in order that parties having official business to transact at the office might gain admission. The town authorities are endeavouring to take steps to prevent a recurrence of this sort of thing again."*[83] The weather had already seen to a poor harvest before the distilling season, forcing many of the distillers to purchase all of their malt from beyond the burgh.

By late 1903, the greater part of the whisky being cleared from the bond was now between six and twelve years of age. This was a seismic change in the whisky landscape. Ages that had previously been a novelty or at least rarely seen were now being traded as near commonplace. There were growing fears that aged stocks were becoming nearly exhausted *"and better paying prices ought soon to be looked for by holders of old whiskies than they have been getting for some time back."**April 1903.

This was reiterated at the end-of-year Campbeltown Distillers' Association meeting. In the four years since 1899, the total decrease in bond stood at 788,663 gallons (although this did not take into account the amount of Islay and Jura whisky maturing within the burgh). It was noted that *"Comparatively little whisky is now sent out from distillers' warehouses under from two to four years old and upwards. Within the last ten to fifteen years the trade has undergone a complete change."** Jan 1904

OMIC lamented how business was now conducted. Gone were the days of clearing spirit six months to two years old, nearly all duty paid, for delivery to a middleman whose business it was to sell to the retailer and order as required. The new blending house, often capable of much larger offerings, now traded directly to the retailer or publican. *"Whether this is to the advantage of the consumer is a matter of optimism regarding which a good deal could be said pro and con."*

What wasn't up for debate was whether this new system would be fleeting. The large blending firms, the likes of which Samuel and James Greenlees had established, were now the new norm, and customers looked to large centres such as Glasgow, London or Leith, and the large firms within, for the product. It was now the period of big brands and brash marketing and a period where the distillery or region name became less of a draw.

Towards the end of the first decade of the 20th century, the gloom had well and truly set in. Campbeltown whisky production was down to half of what it had been during the heyday, and clearances from bonds were also down around 40%. Despite the occasional positive outlook, writing at the end of 1907, the 'Campbeltown Courier' summed up the mood of the industry.

"The depression from which the Scotch whisky trade has suffered for several years made its influence felt here, and with stiff markets and decreasing sales there has been a decided tendency in late years to restrict and reduce each season's output, with the view of preventing stocks in bond from increasing, if not of bringing about a considerable reduction. But this year a new element has brought about quite an unprecedented situation in the history of the industry here.

"When the period usually recognised for the opening of the distilling came round, manufacturers found the price of raw material a substantial barrier to the possibility of their producing whisky at a profit. There was a big increase in barley prices, and even the lowest quotations failed to meet their needs. The price of fuel, also, demanded serious consideration. No attempt was made to start manufacture at the ordinary time, and so far, only one or two works have commissioned operations.

"Early in the new year it is expected that there will be a general start, but at least two distilleries will not work at all this season. For some years too, distillers have complained frequently about the unsatisfactory nature of the prices ruling for Campbeltown whiskies but no concerted effort was made to raise them. In the autumn, however, in keeping with a movement by distillers in other parts of the country, and in view of the increased cost of production, it was resolved, at a meeting of the Campbeltown Distillers' Association, to raise the price of whisky 2d per gallon. There was a disposition among dealers at first to oppose the rise, but latest reports point to the change being generally accepted."[84]

Whilst no minutes from the Association's meetings remain, it was reported that 'a unanimous determination to stand out for an increase in the price of the new season's make'. This increase would still leave Campbeltown whisky a full shilling less than most other malt distilling regions. As the article stated, *"The proposed increase in the price of Campbeltowns does not approach the prices of the dearer makes in a way that will bring them into competition in the market."*[85]

The stubbornness, or singularity, of the Campbeltown distillers - 'no suggestion of combination in the matter' – was noted as the 'especially weak point' of the Campbeltown Association. As had been evidenced in the latter part of the last century, it was one thing for the distillers to agree around the table, but when market forces applied pressure, cracks in decisions appeared.

Many of the distillers, unable to find enough business for new fillings, curtailed their season or did not begin. 'Silence reigns supreme', was how the journal put it, adding that *"by this time of the year [late September 1907], under ordinary circumstances, even the most backward [distiller] would have been at least in the initial stages of manufacture."* Many of the works were waiting until the end of the year to commence due to a usual late rush of customers wanting that year's vintage on the cask, as it was customary at this time to sell whisky on its vintage.

The 1907/1908 season witnessed the first time the burgh's production had dipped under one million gallons since the early 1840s and a full million gallons less than the peak reached in 1897. What had hoped to be an early harvest was ruined by a wet summer. *"Stocks [barley] stood for weeks in flooded fields under pouring skies with the straw blackening and rotting, and the grain sadly deteriorating."* The result was a poor harvest across Scotland and high prices from beyond. Coal was being used more regularly from the local Argyll Colliery mine at Machrihanish, although it was noted that its *"quality is somewhat inferior, but its accessibility and price are important considerations."*

Whilst there had been an acceptance of the price increase a year ago, the orders for new fillings were not returning to previously seen levels. Instead, it was felt that a 'hand to mouth' practice prevailed. Buyers were more circumspect in regard to growth or demand and thus reluctant to lay down great stocks. This left the Campbeltown distiller with a choice to either fill in the hope of future orders or to decrease production.

More favourable barley prices the following season saw

the Campbeltown distillers' output return to above one million gallons. Much of this extra production was aided by a *"remarkably good harvest reaped in [the Kintyre] district, probably the best for twenty years."*[86] The positivity was short-lived. Demand fell, and barley prices once again rose due to yet another bad harvest. What the industry, and one still heavily reliant on UK ('home') consumption, desperately needed was a friend in high places.

On the 29th of April 1909, as David Lloyd George, Chancellor of the Exchequer, exclaimed, *"This is a war budget!"* it is doubtful anyone within the Scotch whisky industry was hoping for either help or a positive message. As Ross Wilson described in his book 'Scotch – The Formative Years' this was *"a war budget conscribing the spirit industry of the country and, with pathological savagery, attempting to wreck it."*

Lloyd George was an ardent Temperance advocate and believed that alcohol lay at the root cause for much of the social decay and current economic slump. Believing spirits to be a 'somewhat different' case to beer (arguing that a large increase in the duty of beer would lead people to drink more spirits – but at no point reasoning the reverse), Lloyd George increased the duty by a third. Ross Wilson summed it up perfectly:

"A diabolically clever presentation of a devilish scheme of taxation. [Lloyd George] hoped to drive a wedge between different sections of the trade: License duties were up, so that licensees would concentrate on their own troubles; wine was not touched at all; beer only indirectly; spirits were savaged."

The last two decades of the 19th century saw the greatest expansion and the worst collapse of a century-old industry. The Pattison Brothers' crash, and they were not the only guilty party, sparked a downturn in the Scotch whisky industry that continued well into the first decade of the 20th century. Demand had not drastically waned, but production had.

Despite the hopes of the Campbeltown distillers for a return to the days of selling whisky and clearing it in its infancy, the demand for aged whisky, of eight to ten years maturation, remained high, and the price remained low. Lloyd George's crusade heaped misery on an industry fighting high production costs and fairly stagnant demand. Exports had yet to hit the giddy heights they would one day attain, and Campbeltown, which had once boasted 21 working distilleries, saw the decade close with just seven in production.

All of these concerns and tribulations would soon pale into insignificance as the world plunged into the greatest crisis it had ever known.

A funeral cortege returning from Whitehill cemetery passes the Burnside Distillery circa 1905.

CHAPTER 7

THE GREAT WAR

"Kintyre's contribution to the war services of the country in the present times must be proportionately large according to population. The two companies of the 8th Argyll & Sutherland Highlanders will be 235 strong; the Campbeltown section of the Mountain Battery will have about 10 men; there will be some 20 Scottish Horse; while 25 Naval reservists have gone away. That is roughly 370 men."
'Campbeltown Courier'
8th August, 1914

"Drink is doing more damage in the war than all of the German submarines put together… We have got great powers to deal with drink, and we mean to use them."
Lloyd George
February, 1915

"In the early days of the war, Mr Lloyd George had the idea that the whole distilling trade should be stopped."
William Ross
Ex-Chairman of the Distillers Company Ltd, speaking in 1932

The remaining few years of peacetime saw the whisky industry in a sombre, wound-licking mood. In January of 1911, 'The Wine and Spirit Trade Record' reflected with the grim appraisal that *"It would be difficult to find a more trying or unsatisfactory period than that just closed."* A large portion of the blame was laid squarely on Lloyd George's shoulders: *"Prior to the introduction of the Budget of 1909, the industry has shown unmistakable signs of emerging from the heavy cloud of depression which had overshadowed it since the collapse of Pattisons Ltd... The immediate effect was to cut down the consumption of home-made spirits by one-third."*

As so many of the Campbeltown distilleries were either silent or reducing output, combined production from the region steadily dropped – as did removals from the bond. With a depressed market, the annual distilling report stated, *"distillers are showing now disposition to risk capital in the industry, and the manufacture of new whisky is quite clearly confined to what is wanted for an apparent market."* Demand remained for older whiskies, now ten years and older, and it was felt that *"the industry is passing through a serious crisis, and the position of the smaller firms is critical."*[87]

The following season did not bring any relief. The summer mood had promised a revival, and word spread around that Campbeltown whisky was in favour. However, a particularly poor harvest from a drought experienced all over Western Europe had led to high barley prices (jumping from 24s the previous year to 34s a bushel). Whereas it had been hoped most, if not all, of the workable distilleries would be back online, production dipped once again by nearly a quarter. *"From the point of view of employment, especially,"* noted the 'Campbeltown Courier' in October of 1911, *"the rise in the price of the raw material is thus most unfortunate and regrettable."*

1912 did not fare much better, with the Courier's end-of-year résumé referring to the distilling industry as *"a black spot on the local industrial survey."* The paper expressed that the depression in the industry was becoming a familiar story, although the blame was not always levelled at the same concern:

THE GREAT WAR

"First, it was the imposition of the new spirit duties; now, it was the abnormal prices of fuel and raw materials." The distilleries had ever so slightly increased production, but it was still the case that the narrow profit margin, with weak market prices prevailing, kept the furnaces from being lit. Whilst barley had been the big riser in cost for 1911, the cost of coal was now causing issues. In conclusion, and with a dark foreboding, the paper summed up the mood: *"As long as the present prices for barley continue, the outlook for Campbeltown is rather hopeless."*[88]

The lowest point came in 1913 when several distilleries added to the number already silent in Campbeltown. Production for the year barely nudged past 500,000 gallons as continued high barley and coal prices were now complicated by high freight costs. However, as 16 distilleries had begun the Autumn season, the mood was one of having weathered the worst. That was despite *"an all-round increase of wages, amounting from 2s to 3s a head, granted to workmen at the beginning of the season [as] a new item to be reckoned with in the calculations of the distillers."*[89] The troubles of the pre-war years experienced by the Campbeltown distillers were in stark contrast to the northern distilling centres, which posted record production in 1913/1914.

What the Campbeltown distillers needed was a period of sustained growth and a return to stardom within whisky circles. What they didn't need was a crisis the likes of which the world had never previously experienced.

'WAR IN EUROPE', declared the 'Campbeltown Courier' on the 8th of August, 1914. Due to publication dates, the announcement arrived four days after King George's official declaration. *"War,"* the article began, *"loaded with issues probably more fateful than any which this country has had to face at any previous period in our history, has begun in Europe."*

Although many more men would be called up, than the original 370 mobilised at the start of the war, it is no less a sombre thought that at least 348 of those who left, did not return to the burgh. Their family names, now immortalised on the Kintyre War Memorial, have a familiar look to many that still inhabit the area: Armour,

Black, Campbell, Colville, Galbraith and on the list goes.

In the early stages of the Great War, life carried on with a certain level of normality for the town and distillers. Soldiers sent from the burgh began arriving in Canada to start training. Private Alex McIntyre, son of Albyn Distillery's mashman of the same name, landed on the 28th of October along with 33,000 other soldiers. Even the Provost's son, James McMurchy, joined the Seaforth Highlanders in Vancouver. Distillery vacancies were still advertised, and in November, the sad news was published that James Morrison, 'employed at a distillery in Campbeltown', had drowned when the steam trawler he was taking a berth on sank off the coast of Wigtownshire.

Early skirmishes and war information were reported in great detail, and the odd letter demonstrates the spirit and humour of the young men who left Campbeltown, many who had never travelled as far as England, let alone Europe and beyond. Private James McCrank wrote to Mr A. Ollar of Kilkerran:

"I take the pleasure of writing to you to let you and all the old friends about the Quay Head know that I am still in the land of the living. Although our marches and trials have been many I have kept in the best of health. Well, you would like to know some of the fighting I have seen with my regiment, the good old 93rd Argyll and Sutherland Highlanders. ...one was to defend a village at all costs. We went out early on the morning of the 21st of October, and soon we got stuck into it hot style... Then we got the word to retire, and during the retirement, we lost one of our brave men. Among them was Private J. McVey, belonging to the town."

In November, the 'Campbeltown Courier' reported that *"Several of the distilleries have laid in cargoes of barley, and it is hoped that a number of works may commence operations before the New Year. The season, however, is expected to be a short one."*

By December, the full horrors of the war were laid bare. The atrocious and attritional Battle of Ypres, claiming over 250,000 lives, had touched all of the warring nations. For Campbeltonians, who watched as their young men were drafted and waited anxiously for letters to arrive, everyday life became a truncated and war-directional affair. The town was rarely idle as troops from all over the Commonwealth continually landed in the harbour to train.

For the distillers, the pre-war season had looked like a reversal of the downward trends since the beginning of the century.

"In our résumé of the distilling industry at this time last year, our estimate as to the prospects for the past season was in some measure realised. Out of twenty distilleries, fourteen were in active operation for the greater part of the season, making 736,685 proof gallons, as compared with 523,240 gallons produced in the previous season. The barley used was said to be the finest in quality and productive value for many years. We are pleased to hope that notwithstanding increased costs, chiefly in respect of fuel and wages, the balance sheets of the various firms, whole not by any means 'rosy', were on the right side."[90]

But that was where the good news ended. *"We anticipate that through a variety of causes the present season will probably show a greater decrease. The crisis in which we find ourselves has seriously affected every commercial enterprise... and it was to be expected that the distilling industry would be severely hit."*

Just three Campbeltown distilleries had begun the 1914/1915 distilling season, and *"should the beginning of the year see a revival in distilling, an added difficulty will be the question of labour, so many skilled workmen having joined the various units of His Majesty's forces."*

'The Wine and Spirit Trade Record' summed up the 1914/1915 distilling season: *"Distillers have experienced boom years and lean years, but never before have they seen a single year cut in two – one half calm and fairly prosperous, the other fraught with tumultuous dealings and the terrors of war."*[91] Despite the war footing, a delivery of between 400 and 500 tons of barley was expected to arrive in Campbeltown in January 1915.

The outbreak of war caused a period of panic buying in anticipation of rationing and price increases. Reporting on a piece from the 'Glasgow Herald', the 'Campbeltown Courier' noted that: *"Everybody who uses alcohol seems bent on having a reserve supply in his cellar or cupboard. The manager of a big West End store informs me that the rush of orders for whisky is unprecedented, with great quantities being sold every day."*[92] This rush on distillate did not equate to an increase in the production of Campbeltown malts. At the beginning of 1915, 'The Wine and Spirit Trade Record' noted, *"Campbeltowns and Lowland Malts were very seldom asked for, although a few parcels of 1908 and 1909 changed hands… Campbeltown distillers are also curtailing their output."*[93]

Many of the patent still (grain) distilleries had already been directed to provide yeast, acetone and fusel oil for the war effort. This caused the first and only occasion where grain whisky achieved higher prices than malt whisky. This led to a brief increase in the bottling of 'all-malts'.

One of Lloyd George's last acts as Chancellor was in passing the Immature Spirits (Restriction) Act of May 1915. This resulted in the compulsory bonding of spirits for a minimum of three years.[94] Any lingering hopes the Campbeltown distillers had for a return to spirits being shipped and bottled between six months and two years of bonding were now extinguished.

In late May of 1915, Lloyd George was appointed Minister of Munitions and then in 1916, Secretary of State for War. Believing that Britain was 'fighting Germans, Austrians and drink', Lloyd George established the Central Control Board, whose lasting legacy to the whisky industry was a reduction in bottled strength.

Aged Campbeltown whisky continued to be sought after, with little interest in new fillings. Prices of the older malts appeared attractive until compared to what the northern distilleries could command. The inflation had done nothing to close the gap. Those distillers that had sustained production during the depressed first decade of the century were now reaping the reward from the change in demand:

"For a considerable time back old makes had been languishing. Now they are taking their fair share in the clearances, and at prices which are affording distillers a very satisfactory amount of

*remuneration."*⁹⁵ A brisk trade was being achieved with whisky now from 1897 onwards and saw a renewed interest in brokering and speculation. The sharp rise in price for older whisky, in turn, led to a run on younger two to three-year-old whisky. This caused the dilemma of when to sell, for the Campbeltown industry that had greatly reduced production over the last few years. The older whiskies were commanding great prices, but *"the makes of two and three-year-old 'Campbeltowns' were very restricted, and the few firms who [held] these bondings could easily realise a handsome profit if they chose to sell."*⁹⁶

With the Campbeltown distillers realising good prices on their old parcels of whisky and a renewed interest for younger spirit, the distilling season of 1915/1916 should have signalled a return for many of the distilleries to return to production. Unfortunately, another particularly bad harvest, a scarcity of wood, shipping and men curtailed any such ambition. On top of all of this, Campbeltown was experiencing a water shortage due to the decaying nature of the Crosshill Reservoir and the pipes feeding the town. The issue became so hazardous that emergency powers were *"given to the Convener and the Master of Works to turn off the water supply from Crosshill Loch and Lochruan at times to be decided by them for the conversation of the water supply."*⁹⁷

In May of 1916, the Ministry of Munitions instructed all distilleries to stop production, except those making products required by the government. It was felt that the wider industry had enough stock to survive several years' hiatus. That was little comfort to the Campbeltown industry, which was now running dangerously low on stock. For most of 1916, very little Campbeltown whisky had been on the market, and those who owned it were either moving it or leaving it in bond until it was required. The Highland or Northern distillers had been producing good numbers prior to the war. Campbeltown's sustained drop in production, however, was now leaving them out of the pages of the trade news and, more importantly, with little means for revenue.

In March of 1916, Duncan Colville, Senior Partner of Dalintober

Distillery, died. Four months later, on the 7th of July, Duncan's brother David died suddenly. David, described in his obituary as having a 'genial and amiable disposition, and highly respected in the town', was the main force behind the distillery. Duncan, despite being the senior of the two, had taken more interest in local affairs, being at one time the Dean of Guild and Provost from 1881 to 1890, and upon retiring from that post, was elected Chairman of the Campbeltown Distillers' Association.

Despite David leaving four sons (David, William, Augustus and Duncan), and the distillery having been re-built in 1900, the firm was wound up by trustee Peter Dewar. The economic downturn and forced war closures likely led the family to see no interest or future in the firm.

Many of the letters from Peter Dewar to all those associated with the distillery survive in the Argyll Archives. One of Dewar's first letters sums up the dire situation the distilleries were facing, despite calls for their products.

"With reference to your enquiry for Dalintober Whisky, we regret that the Trustees are not selling at all at present, and in any case, we have no whisky in stock suitable for your requirements." 9th September, 1916

Customers, including Thomas Eaglesome (which still exists), were requested to return emptied wood, which was scarce during the war. Cheques had to be re-routed and addressed to Messrs F. J. Mackenzie & Colville, 55 West Regent Street, Glasgow, as the firm Peter Dewar was working for. Within the same month as David's death, Charles Doig,[98] the renowned architect, was employed to 'finish the valuation'. As accounts were settled, one company, who had been a staunch supporter of Campbeltown whisky, wrote to complain about an unexpected loss:

"I enclose a letter from Messrs John Walker & Sons, claiming credit note for an excessive deficiency on cask no 193 of 1905, sent out on July 10th last. I find there is a special 4 gallons on above. I leave the matter in your hands to deal with." 7th August,

1916

In August, the Paisley firm of Wm Foulds & Co., wrote asking to buy the option of distilling for the ensuing year. Distilling in 1916 was heavily regulated and it was noted that, supplies and regulations permitting, there had already been interest locally to buy the option to distil.

"I had a call today from Mr Duncan MacCallum [Glen Nevis Distillery] and he asked me to write you and see if you were selling the option to get working at Dalintober, if so, you might reserve the purchase in his favour. He is prepared to give the highest price that is agreed upon by the Distillers. I think you would get over one shilling per gallon." 5th September, 1916.

Dewar's letters also express the dilemma over seeking the best prices for the dwindling older stock. Dewar wrote to the trustees:

"Excuse me taking the liberty but I think you ought to hold on to the whisky we have for sale as in conversation with Mr John Colville and again with Mr Smith, Hazelburn I learnt that whisky has not nearly reached its highest peak yet.

"Mr Sam Greenlees said when he was here a fortnight ago that it would reach £1 per gallon yet. Without divulging the price we were getting, Mr Colville told me he was getting 14/- per gallon some time ago. As mentioned in your letter, there is only one Hogshead left unsold of 1906." 15th October, 1916.

This was again reiterated in December:

"I had a conversation with Mr John Colville about prices. He says apart from himself he has heard of no sales lately, but he sold a small parcel of 1905 a week ago and got 16/6 for it quite easily. He advises not to sell below that figure.

"The demand is for 3 & 4 years old and more can be got for it than the older whiskies as both bulk and strength is higher, age & quality not being considered nowadays. I have not yet heard what is going for new make." 4th December, 1916

1917 proved to be an excellent year for the barley harvest. A glorious summer did little to raise the spirits of all those whose lives had been touched by the war. Although the Battle of Verdun was not over, the death of one million soldiers and Germany's return to unrestricted submarine warfare hung over the land. America's declaration of war in April 1917 added much to the spirit of the Allies, and by the summer, the first of the US soldiers had arrived in France.

For the whisky industry, it was a period of marked frustration, as the prohibition on production prevailed, but for the Campbeltown distillers, it was a period of complete stagnation. For the first time in the burgh's proud history, it was no longer a contributing centre or region of the Scotch whisky scene. Unable to produce and with nothing to sell, the only activity (other than the occasional use of buildings for the war effort) was the dispatch of casks to Glasgow when called upon by owners – although even this was heavily restricted by government-imposed conditions.

Prices continued to rise, leading Dewar to inform the trustees of recent activity:

"I saw Mr John Colvill today and he told me he sold some 1915/14 whisky at 22/- per gallon, and is inclined to think the prices are still going up, in fact he is in the belief that it will ultimately reach 30/-. In the meantime he is not selling any. I have received your letter of 31st. I note that you made no mention about selling empty casks in your letter to Mr Colvill. In the course of our conversation the question of prices for empty casks cropped up. I regret I mentioned we had sold some casks and the prices that I thought were current just now i.e. 33/35/- and 17/6. Mr Gardiner called about the feints and regrets in the meantime he cannot make an offer. They have barley to fulfil their quantity allowed to be made, and application to the Ministry of Munitions to make another 100 gallons they were flatly refused."

In addition to the regulations over how much spirit could be made, the War Office, in an attempt to prolong stocks and control what was released onto the market, regulated the amount of bulk spirit that could be released from bond.

"I enclose a letter received tonight from Messrs Forsyth Ltd mentioning that they are getting their average clearances for last year at Springbank Distillery added on to their average here with the intention of clearing equal to 4 puncheons by 31st March. They are under a misapprehension as to the working of the restrictions, in the first place the average is not the yearly average, but the daily average, and traders are not allowed to anticipate the quantity to be duty paid. This applies to Distillers as well, and we are advised to see that our customers besides them they will require to take their turn in being served, strictly they are only entitled to 25.2 gallons from date of issuing restrictions up to today." 9th February, 1917

In May of the same year, the Ministry of Food asked the Campbeltown Distillers' Association if the unused mills could grind maize. Peter Dewar informed the trustees, adding, *"I have seen some of the other Distillers, and they are agreeable to place their machinery at the disposal of the Ministry. As maize has never been ground in Campbeltown we cannot say if the rollers as they stand, would be suitable for the purpose."* 8th May, 1917.

Argyll Distillery ran some experiments, putting some maize through their mills *"for the horses, and found them unsuitable for the purpose."*[99] In the same letter, John Colville, owner of Argyll Distillery, brought up the issue of 'insurance against war risks' during transit. *"Owing to the presence of mines in the Firth of Clyde there is a certain risk that did not exist before and the Distillers want to make it clear that the responsibility for loss rests with the customer, therefore he advises me when I receive an order to write the customer and ask the customer if they wish their whisky insured or are willing to take the risk."*

From Dewar's letters, it is clear that the intention was to preserve Dalintober Distillery until such time as it could be sold as a going concern. Attention was drawn to crumbling brickwork, the condition of the chimney after heavy rain, and the work required to 'putting the washbacks in order'. As Burnside Distillery had recently been stripped of all 'utensils' by Mr Mackenzie, it was felt that the wood from their washbacks would be available for repairing the bottoms and staves requiring replacement. However, it was discovered that as the washbacks had already been rebuilt, they were beyond repair. Indeed, the previous manager, Mr Howe, noted that the wood, bought from W. P. Lowrie & Co., had not been seasoned correctly and *"the last season the distillery worked was hopeless."* October, 1917

On the 20th of November, Dewar wrote to the Commissioners of Excise to inform them of the sale of the remaining feints to Melrose Drover Ltd, Links Distillery, Leith. The feints, Dewar stated, were suffering great evaporation due to the unusually wide Feints Receiver. The letter also revealed that Dalintober had been silent since the end of the 1913/14 season, a period of almost three years.

1918 proved to be a particularly cruel year for the distillers in Campbeltown. Private David McKerral, who had left his job with Lochhead Distillery to fight for the cause, was killed in France aged 33. Peter Mackie, who would later play a part in the Campbeltown whisky story, lost his only son, James Mackie, a Lieutenant in the Yeomanry. Hugh Mitchell of William Mitchell & Co, Glengyle and Rieclachan Distilleries, lost his only son, Willie. Second Lieutenant Mitchell, serving with the RAF, was shot down in 1918 and died, aged 19, of pneumonia as a prisoner-of-war in Leuze, Belgium.

The weather just added to the misery of the burgh. In November, a 'terrific rain storm' flooded much of the town. Dewar wrote to the trustees, informing them of the damage:

"On entering the Distillery this morning empty casks were scattered all over the yard, all the ground floors were flooded; in some parts to a height of three feet. In the warehouses the loose

skids were all heaped about and the wedges swept away from the casks. No damage was done to the contents of the casks and I have been over them replacing the wedges. Nothing more can be done in the warehouse until the water drains away." 5th November, 1918

An update on the flooding situation was provided on the 9th of January, 1919:

"There has been no action taken by the public so far with regard to the flooding, but as far as one can make out it was the outlet that was too small to carry away the heavy volume of water running into the town, and some make out that it is choked at the outlet. I was talking to Mr Dan MacTaggart today and he says the 'poor' Town Council are getting all the blame, how are they to know that the drains and sewers are choked. I shall let you know if anything transpires and if any action is going to be taken by the sufferers of the flood."

By October of 1918, it was clear that the end of the war was near. 'The Wine and Spirit Trade Record' wrote *"Consequent on the general belief that the war is rapidly drawing to a close, distillers are considering with keen interest how their industry will be affected. The renewal of operations and the consequent supplementing of supplies would, in their estimation, be the only sensible and adequate way of bringing business back to its normal condition."*[100]

Fears were growing that without a speedy return to production the industry was in danger of depleting stocks to such a level that would cause the cessation of exportation and/or further UK rationing. The trouble facing the distillers wasn't simply one of waiting on the government to say 'go' either. The barley harvests during the war had been of mixed results, and prior to the war breaking out, around ninety per cent of barley was sourced from various ports – many of which remained closed and with little chance of reopening for some time. There was a continued shortage of wood for maturation, and Campbeltown was still suffering from a lack of shipping to and from Glasgow.

One returning soldier remarked, *"Everybody has been wishing us a merry Christmas and a Happy New Year, and they are all very good to us, but we can't get liquor for love or money, and so it's a sober time."*[101] Clearance was eventually given to distillers in January 1919 to recommence works, and whilst this was felt as 'the tide turning in the affairs of the distillers', there were still significant concerns. Barley had to be secured and that was proving difficult with limited supply and large requirements from business' in the South.

More pressing was the need for a workforce. Britain's casualties during the war were around 660,000 dead and a further 2 million wounded. A gap had formed between experienced distillers and new workers. Advertisements began appearing in all of the periodicals looking for maltsters, mashmen and general workers. Campbeltown and Kintyre would not be the first part of Scotland these skilled, scant and in demand workers would consider.

As the second decade of the 20th century came to a close, most of the Campbeltown distilleries filled their malt barns, fuelled their steam engines and fired up their kilns. This was despite the knowledge that the distilling landscape had irrevocably shifted. The first decade of the century had been the hardest trading conditions any of the distillery owners had ever faced. All were still recovering from the worst collapse the industry had ever known, barley harvests were unpredictable, barley prices remained high, and market prices for Campbeltown whisky were not keeping up with inflation. And just when there was a glimmer of hope, the world plunged into the bloodiest war it had ever seen.

Predominantly, in Campbeltown, the distilleries were owned and run as family affairs. Second, third or even fourth-generation owners who had enjoyed the lifestyle and income that owning a distillery brought, bereft of the hard start-up costs. Now, in the face of rising material and employment costs, low product prices, and the loss of life & lineage, the unthinkable was becoming a reality; the distilleries began to change hands.

Duncan MacCallum, unlike many of his peers, had not been born into a distilling dynasty - nor even from farming stock. His father, Peter, had built up a large fishing fleet, so large he was known as 'The Admiral'. Duncan, who was born in Campbeltown in 1847, was brought up with the work ethic of his father and, having seen how the whisky industry was flourishing, acquired land on Glebe Street, where he constructed - with the financial assistance of his father - Glen Nevis Distillery in 1877. Ably assisted by his manager, Samuel Thomson, MacCallum made Glen Nevis a success. In 1891, MacCallum, heading a consortium, purchased the Scotia Distillery, which was then radically improved and modernised. MacCallum had also bought substantial shares in the Glenside and Kinloch distilleries, making him the most prominent (or powerful) distiller in Campbeltown.[102]

The shift away from selling directly to numerous smaller merchants created an emphasis on ties with larger blending houses. These companies offered greater security for orders, allowing distillers to lay down stock in anticipation of purchases once the stock had reached a suitable age.

The Distillers Company Limited, whose strategy after the Pattison Crash was one of purchasing many of the smaller firms, or partnering with the larger blending and brokering firms, had begun to dictate the direction of the industry. Whilst there had been talks previously, during the more profitable years, it was now a time of great depression and action was required to bring Campbeltown whisky back as a respected and sought-after style of whisky.

West Highland Malt Distilleries, a new consortium headed by MacCallum, with the backing of several other notable distillers, including the large blending firm of Robertson & Baxter, was created to 'acquire the undertakings of Scotia, Glen Nevis, Glengyle, Kinloch, Dalintober and Ardlussa Distilleries'.[103] How this deal was struck and what state the finances of these distilleries were in is unknown. MacCallum's business acumen and notable success may have been the only chance these distillery owners saw of clawing back to a profitable enterprise.

In October 1919, Dewar wrote his last letter to the trustees informing them *"that two of Robertson & Baxter's Directors were here on Saturday looking over the new distilleries. Dalaruan is not working yet but I hear they intend to work this season."*

Having secured new owners for Dalintober Distillery, Dewar's next role was to oversee the final years of the Campbeltown Distillery. Campbeltown Distillery had stopped production in 1917 before being permanently closed around 1921. Peter Dewar, having wound up the businesses of both Dalintober and Campbeltown distilleries, died on 25th March 1935.

Additional changes of ownership also occurred in 1919. Argyll Distillery, as part of the Greenlees Brothers' exit from the industry, moved to the newly formed Macdonald, Greenlees & Williams (Distillers) Ltd. Hazelburn Distillery - remaining under the banner of Greenlees & Colville, Ltd - was sold to Peter Mackie & Co. Burnside Distillery, one of the earliest works built, situated just outside of the town on Witchburn Road, was sold to United Creameries. Having had its plant stripped prior to the breakout of war, the distillery had lain dormant for years.

The continual decline of the Campbeltown distilling industry from 1899 onwards was now given a lifeline. MacCallum's new West Highland Malt Distillers consortium would lead by example, bringing the malts of Campbeltown to the new blending powerhouses - adding Campbeltown's weighty whiskies to the blends that were now reaching across the globe. Several other Campbeltown distilleries were now in new hands, some undergoing modernisation, others continuing as they were, making the best spirit they could. In a new market where so much product was laid down in the expectation of customers after the mandatory three-year maturation, the remaining Campbeltown distillers began refilling their warehouses. With the knowledge that Campbeltown whisky was once highly sought after, the distillers looked forward to the new world, the one re-building from the carnage of WWI, getting a taste for their whisky.

Surely, the very worst was now behind the distillers of Campbeltown whisky?

CHAPTER 8

UNWANTED GOUT IN THE TEEN YEARS

"Campbeltown whisky was somewhat celebrated, and was in great request both in the home and in the foreign markets. Distilled in stills of small size, and made from peat-dried malt, there was a flavour about it peculiar to itself, and which was much relished by consumers of that kind of spirit."
'Reminiscences of a Gauger'
Joseph Pacy, 1873

"Stocks of anything over from three to four years old are now becoming scarce in Campbeltown, and holders of old whiskies are beginning to feel the effect of this scarcity in a general all round hardening of prices. It is of course universally admitted that the prices of old Campbeltowns have been abnormally low, and gave a very poor return for their money to holders, more especially for the last two years back. Considering the value of this whisky for blending purposes, it is only fair that those who had to make sacrifices when the market was fully supplied should get the benefit now that there is a comparative scarcity in the popular blending ages."
The last instalment of the 'In Campbeltown' letters
'The Distillers' Magazine and Spirit Trade News' May, 1904

'When does a point of difference become a singular issue?'

This question must have been what was going through the minds of the Campbeltown distillers as the economic downturn post-WWI turned into a drought. As we read, when James Greenlees was asked in 1891 by the Select Committee on British and Foreign Spirits why he thought that blending was such an important part of the whisky trade, his answer must not have come as much comfort to the Campbeltown distillers:

"The taste for whiskies nowadays is such that you cannot get people to drink these distinct flavours by themselves; it is an acquired taste for a man to drink Islay pure, or Campbeltown pure, or Glenlivet pure; but by mixing those whiskies in certain proportions, you make them much more palatable and pleasant, and produce a better article."

The era of the bottled-in-bond 'self-whisky' or 'pure malt' and district-driven marketing (such as referring to the Highland, Glenlivet, Islay or Campeltown regions) was losing ground to the blended brands being marketed by the Greenlees Brothers and others such as John Walker & Sons or James Buchanan & Co. In truth, it was the very singularity of Campbeltown whisky – the reason for its rise throughout the 19th century – that was partly the cause for its undoing. Every account of Campbeltown whisky, as a collective, noted its difference, its uniqueness and the demand for it:

1825
"There are some places more famed for the goodness of their whisky than others, such as Glenlivet, Ferintosh, Campbeltown, Crieff, etc. of which intimation is given in the houses where it is sold upon tickets almost in every spirit dealer's window in Glasgow, Edinburgh and other places."[104]

1835
"The whisky, which is of an excellent quality, is sold wholesale, principally by means of agents in Glasgow."[105]

"At an election meeting held last week at Campbeltown, Sir William Cunninghame said that the whisky of Campbeltown was the best in the world."[106]

1884
"Campbeltown is perhaps most widely known for its whisky, which is sent to all parts of the world."[107]

1905
"The Whisky occupies a place of its own because of its distinctive character."[108]

As markets developed a taste for a milder product, Campbeltown's famous richly flavoured malt went out of fashion. James and Samuel Greenlees, acknowledging London as the burgeoning market for this new type of Scotch, threw a certain level of caution (and stability) to the wind. The tried and tested method of business for the Campbeltown distiller, selling direct to merchants and agents throughout Scotland – bottling around half of the output in bond as pure malt, the other half shipped in bulk – must have appeared an ancient business to the two young men. England, and primarily London, was the new customer base. But this meant a new product, something more 'silent'.

The first shots across the Campbeltown distiller's bows was an article printed anonymously in September of 1898.[109] An extraordinary piece, titled 'Campbeltown Whisky Redivivus' [reborn], bemoaned the changing in drinking habits:

"Indications are not wanting that 'self' whiskies may again resume their old place in markets for the product of Scottish distilleries and in the estimation of former patrons. Till this recently arrived age and rage for blends, Campbeltown whisky, Islays and Glenlivets, then in limited supply, held the field almost unassailed, and if there was sometimes an admixture of these famed makes, it was compared within the bounds of the private cellar. Now, blends multifarious and multiplied, are being turned

out on all hands, and a public, not always wise, are by reiterated advertisement educated into the belief that to affect a whisky which has not been variously and curiously compounded, is to be ignorant of the supreme virtues of Scotch drink."

The lament at the loss of pure malt whiskies, with their fuller flavour and uniqueness, is quite evident. This wasn't just occurring in the 'Home' market, but was also driving exports. The new 'softer' version of Scotch, a more constant and interchangeable style of drink, was becoming the norm. The author's prophecy for Campbeltown's style of whisky was prophetic:

"...if a taste for an individual or self-whisky is again to prevail, it surely behoves Campbeltown to apprehend the signs of the time, and bestir itself to reap benefit by a change so distinctly to its advantage. Blends have doubtless become the fashion: the Highland 'fine malt spirit' solus, it would be idle to deny, has ceased to be in its former appreciation.

"There is temptation in a now keenly competitive trade, to use a large proportion of the newer, and in a sense stronger forms of alcohol, as the mainstay of the blend, and to add in lesser volume the high flavoured matured malt that gives a 'gout' to the mixture. If this were not to some degree an existent evil, why the recent outcry?"

The term 'gout' was taken from the French word 'goût', meaning taste or flavour. Its use in the article is to describe a uniqueness of flavour emanating from some malt whiskies and, in particular, those from Campbeltown. The 'newer' and 'stronger forms of alcohol' are in reference to the grain whisky made at the patent stills - mostly from Scotland's central belt. The author is highlighting a trend that would continue, and never stop being a concern to some quarters, of using a greater proportion of this cheaper and more neutral spirit as the bulk of blended Scotch whisky. This, in turn, decreased the demand for flavourful malts - a watering down of the flavour profile of what was Scotch whisky into something, at least to this drinker, causing ignorance 'of the supreme virtues of Scotch drink'.

Was this an issue with blender's finding the malts too strong? Was it burgeoning markets, having tried pure malts, determining that the heavier single malt Scotch was not to their taste? Or was it a style of whisky forced upon the consumer through marketing and propaganda? The cheapness and ease of production of grain whisky has to be taken into consideration. Blender's could adjust styles and ratios to suit price and consumer.

"Till human nature has reached immaculateness, there is possibility of a whisky being sold, which not being 'self' and reputable on its own character, may be a something, if not fearfully, at least wonderfully made. It is to the catching on of this idea of doubt that is pointing to a possible return to the 'single' spirit as a refreshment or tonic stimulant, and many things less likely have happened than a recurrence to old ideals. How then is Campbeltown to benefit by return of the favouring tide! Although an outsider, I would say if the biggest outlet for its manufacture is not mainly with the wholesale blending trade (which is not likely), take a leaf out of their book. Improve, it may be possible, the quality, by somewhat 'silencing', where needful, the product."

This last statement, reinforced by James Greenlees' testimony to the Select Committee in 1891, was not what the Campbeltown distillers wanted to hear. They were of a mind that it was just a fad or phase, and no doubt the English drinker would progress – and the distillers hoped quickly – to appreciate the fuller flavour and robustness of the Campbeltown malt Scotch whisky.

The timing of the article in 1898 also coincided with the best year the Campbeltown distillers and the wider whisky industry had ever experienced. Demand was high, the Pattison credit crisis was yet to break, and feelings were bullish about the future. Despite this, the author, evidently well-versed on the subject, suggested, again prophetically, some options to the distillers:

"Keep it in the warehouse for a proper but not an extravagant period, and to publish its merits send out able, energetic

travellers, who need not be of the barmaid-bribing stamp; also not to be forgotten, advertise Campbeltown whisky (every trade now advertises) as what it really is, a fine malt spirit, unmixed, untouched, and absolutely under excise custody from the time it runs from the still until it leaves the warehouse for the retailer's premises. The question of quality will then be one entirely between the purchaser and the retailing merchant, in whom, as the last hand, the buyer ought to have full confidence. Further, should there be any difficulty, now that the burgh is to have general duty-free warehouses, in the way of distillers themselves, if they so elect, bottling under bond and sending out in handy cases pure and old Campbeltown, more especially to the ever-expanding foreign markets. The subject deserves further discussion."

As it turns out, the author was decades ahead of the curve. The suggestion of embracing the individuality of the region, and marketing it as such, was very much against the business model and practices of the times. Whilst the 'bottled-in-bond' element did hark back to a previous era, the distillers were not at the time presenting their wares on an individual basis.

There was little to no marketing of the whisky as a 'single distillery' output. Being distinctive, not just to other Scottish regions, but amongst the Campbeltown distilleries was not the unique selling point it is today. Perhaps there was a camaraderie that prevented any one distillery from promoting their distillery over and above the region. Perhaps it was just not the done thing - bad manners, if you will. More likely, is that the industry had yet to engage consumers on a 'single malt - single distillery' basis - something that is taken for granted today with the single malts of nearly every distillery bottled and marketed for retail.

Signed 'W. McD.' the author provides an interesting postscript:

"Just a concluding word about 'self' whiskies. The taste for these is a growing one here, but it is seldom attempted to be met. It may be prejudice or want of education on my part – I don't think it either – but I am fond of a drop of, say, pure Glenlivet (Smith's),

Glen Grant, Highland Park, Talisker, Long John, Lochnagar and others, the particular flavours of which have been familiar to me in the past.

"Why cannot certain establishments keep a supply of these – or some of them at any rate – in cask and bottle, and provide their customers as desired? It would pay them quite as well to do so as does their hundred-and-one blends. A cask of, say, ten year's old grain, in sherry wood, too, would not be a bad thing to have at hand'; depend upon it, there would be a run on the article, not a few preferring such to the more highly flavoured malts. But I have said enough for the present."

Whilst the prose may be quite different, the sentiments will be repeated almost a century later. For decades, there will be calls for greater availability of single malt expressions. This letter suggests that even in the 1890s, single malts, were available, just not in large quantities or available in enough establishments (interesting to note that not a single Campbeltown malt is mentioned). Even into the 1980s, there was a fear from the large blending houses, now controlling the industry, that the fiery malts may turn drinkers against Scotch - or, and this may be more telling, against blends. The pure malt could not compete on price, nor in quantity, to the grain distillers. Surely the rapid growth of the sector was through the promotion of blended whisky - not from single malts?

The only retort to this article, again from someone outside Campbeltown, was from one publican wondering why 'W. McD.' was struggling to find what he wanted:

"…a letter from Mr John Stewart, the proprietor of the three 'Clachans' in London, in which he says that if our correspondent cares to call at either of these places, he will be supplied with almost any self-whisky he cares to name."

With sales of Highland malt still strong, it is probable that the 'gout' references were not interpreted by the Campbeltown distillers as anything other than a compliment. Little attention was likely paid to the calls to change their spirit or practices.

Why, after all, would you change a product you have made for nearly a century when that same product built up a reputation for 'purity' and 'excellence'? Surely, it is the new customer, uneducated and only at the start of their whisky journey, who must be in the wrong. Given time and education, won't these blended drinkers move on to the more flavourful malts?

Having survived the storm of the Pattison and Brickmann crash, bringing in the new century and seeing whisky now shipped to all parts of the empire, the Campbeltown whisky industry remained circumspect but hopeful:

"The past year has been a more than usually interesting one, in as much as it brought to a close a century which has been marked by an amount of business enterprise and push such as perhaps none of its predecessors could show. The distilling trade has shared to a certain extent in the prosperous times, but unfortunately the closing years of the century were anything but bright ones for malt distillers.

"The circumstances were somewhat peculiar, as while on the one hand the consumption of whisky never was better, on the other hand the curtailed production, combined with heavier working expenses, left the very smallest margin for profit.

"In Campbeltown the distilling business was carried on during the year very much on the principle of 'marking time'. Distillers kept their works going for the sake of keeping their regular customers together, but with the certainty that there would be little or no profit left at the end of the year's work. Such being the case, the last working season was made a short one, and the quantity of whisky manufactured very much under an average year. The works were really all late of starting again this winter, and the prospect is that the present working season will be longer than its predecessor."*- February 1901

Just two years later, in 1903, the usually broad and neutral Distiller's Magazine printed the following article that contained warnings in addition to the hopes of the 1901 article:

"Campbeltown makes do not occupy the position they once did. They are, in common parlance, slow to move, and their low price is out of all proportion to their value, yet we see a brighter future for them, for from statistics the removals from bond are becoming regularly greater than the make. If this continues it will show that blenders are beginning to know the value of Campbeltown, and more judicious selling and handling their makes by the distillers will make them valuable, and they will pay to hold, as they formerly did.

"Campbeltown five years old can be bought for 3s bulk gallon – very little more than the price of grain spirits – and in proportion to the price of 'new', very much cheaper. There is, however, really no ruling price for new Campbeltown, which is a pity, as it shows a decided want of combination, resulting at the present day in little or no profit to some, and frequently loss.

"There are good stocks in bond of the years 1892, 1893 & 1894, but overall we should say that there is only some five years' supply in bond of Campbeltowns. The majority of distillers are curtailing the 'new' make, which will make their position the healthier."

As can be seen in the sales ledgers for Springbank Distillery, large blenders were buying Campbeltown spirit, but either Springbank was bucking the trend or sales were considerably down on what had been moving previously. It is clear that the change in demand was dropping production - despite their being good orders for aged spirits.

"As to the late unpopularity of Campbeltown it is difficult to speak, as the publicans have used as much as before. It is the larger blenders who have been using less. Much of the make is filled into hard oak wood, unseasoned, which never mellows properly, and gives the whisky with age a decidedly 'new look'. Indeed blenders have often rejected samples – good enough, but not all of the maturity the age should make them. This may be obviated by filling better casks, and Campbeltown distillers, as they value their industry, should take warning."

The use of 'hard oak wood' was not a unique tendency amongst Campbeltown distillers who were buying their casks from the same brokers and cooperages as the rest of Scotland. This is a ruse or excuse - perhaps even a prod - for the Campbeltown distillers to ensure they all used the very best casks available so that all of the distilleries were shown in the best light.

"And, again, there is a tendency in Campbeltown 'new' [spirit] to emit a stunning odour which has baffled many to avert, and which has prejudiced many a buyer. The sting wears off with age and open bungs, but the whisky never shows the same quality. We hardly think that the water is to blame, nor yet the barley. It may be rather dirty dishes, with bad fermentation, and this again causes the whisky to marry badly and come out 'top' in a blend, killing other good ingredients."

Remembering that this article is printed in 1903 is perhaps the best evidence we have that Campbeltown whisky did not suddenly fall out of favour with the blenders. The 'stunning odour' that 'prejudiced many a buyer' suggests that this problem had been around for a while. Exactly what it was, science had yet been able to explain. But perhaps today's Springbank, which makes arguably one of the least pleasant new-makes, and yet one of the best matured malt whiskies, may go some way to explain this; Without explaining how Campbeltown whisky was once so sought after prior to the mandatory maturing period or when spirit was drunk less than two years old.

"It is not such a far cry from Campbeltown to Islay, yet the makes of the latter are presently in the first rank as to demand, price, and use, and deservedly so, for no blend can be complete without some 'softening', and this characterises the Islay makes. Islays after six years old are very scarce, and their value is greater than any gilded security, though it has to be admitted that some of the makes are of greater intrinsic value than others. It would be invidious to name any, but undoubtedly the prices gauge the values, as we can trace more distinctiveness in these

than between the various Campbeltowns.

"The popularity of the Islay make has not built new distillers, though it has enlarged the output of some existing, which is good for it, as although few, there are enough. They have had their bad day, too – they were not always popular – but we believe that they will always continue so now. There is a full five and a half years' supply in bond at Islay and Glasgow, which is by no means too much – just healthy.

"'Plain malts' or 'Lowlands' are almost in the same position as Campbeltowns – slow to move, though they, too, are come away. Some are very popular, and aged are readily picked up, but in general they are low priced and worth more money. 'New' is often difficult to sell, but the distillers know that it will be needed someday, and being in most cases able to afford it, lay aside a good stock against blenders' requirements."[110]

Blenders, according to the article, were being turned away due to Campbeltown whiskies' inability to mix well with others. Like a disruptive child, it was being excluded. Lowland malts, the article continues, *"are not unpopular. It is not that which keeps them low in price, but blenders have always used them as so much padding, doing no harm to a blend, nor much good, but balancing rather the other malts and the grain spirits without affecting price."* Another reminder that it was Campbeltown whisky's distinctness that was now causing the problems.

The Campbeltown distillers were not oblivious, or blinkered, to the noise coming from blenders, and, one assumes, via the general public not appreciating any blends that may omit a 'stunning odour'. In 1905, the editor of 'The Wine and Spirit Trade Record' dedicated seven pages of the April issue to 'Campbeltown and its Whisky'. Again, despite the magazine tending to take a neutral position, being more a vessel for scientific, factual and advertising means, the author presents what he sees as the current situation:

"Campbeltown Whisky occupies a unique position because of its cheapness as a pure Malt, and it is quite safe to say that

it is more largely used in blends than many people imagine. The all-Malt crusade has undoubtedly benefited the town of Campbeltown."[111]

The author wonders why, having taken stock of the drop in demand after the Pattison crash of 1898, the Campbeltown distillers were not heeding warnings on current stock levels:

"...figures also show that the Campbeltown distillers were wise enough to learn a valuable lesson from the collapse of the 'boom', their production dropping from 1,810,226 gallons in 1897 to 1,141,753 gallons in 1900, the result being that their stocks were in 1903 only equal to a four years' supply. This would have been a good proportion to maintain, but since 1900 there has been a steady increase in the output, while the clearances from bond have stood still, the consequence being that the stock at the end of last September showed an excess of 120,000 gallons over the total at the corresponding date in 1903. The net result is that the distillers now find themselves in the possession of stocks equivalent to 4½ years' consumption at last year's rate. Here again combination might be of great utility in bringing about a restricted output."

Time would negate the writer's concerns as the growth in production was stunted and by 1905 there was an almost unabated decline. The article continues and for the third time in as many pages, the author reiterates that 'Campbeltown Whisky is of a pronounced character'. The tendency now, it claims, is all the time towards making it, as one of the distillers put it, more 'soft, sweet and silent'. The author goes on to suggest that *"Londoners, in particular, are all the time asking for a lighter tobacco, milder cheese, and more neutral whisky.*

"The desire for 'all-malt' has to be met, but at the same time the growing taste of the public for a more neutral spirit has to be catered for. Hence peat is gradually being supplanted by coke or anthracite coal. In fact, under some kilns, peat finds no place except for the initial kindling.

"Furthermore, a large and increasing quantity of Whisky is wanted for export to hot countries which are ill-adapted for the consumption of heavy, indigestible Whiskies."

Entirely what the average drinker north of the border, accustomed to their 'peat-reek' and less 'silent' whiskies, must have made of these comments are not recorded. Or at least was unrecordable. Perhaps that is where we now get the 'Hard Northerner' and 'Southern Softy' monikers that continue to this day.

More damning evidence was highlighted when Dr Phillip Schidrowitz was called as a witness to the highly publicised Royal Commission in 1908. Having researched the whiskies of Scotland, Dr Schidrowitz was asked to describe the regions and districts that made Scotch whisky:

"Then finally the Campbeltowns, which are perhaps not quite so fine in quality as similar whiskies made elsewhere, but I do not wish to be understood that there are no fine Campbeltown whiskies."

(II.) "Impurities" in Five different Classes of Scotch Whiskey.
Using the Allen-Marquardt Method.
(Based on the Tables of Schidrowitz and Kaye.)

Number of Samples.	Class of Whiskey.	Average "Impurity" per 100,000 of AA.	Max.	Min.
16	Campbeltowns	335	510	201
5	Islays	294	337	260
39	Highlands	292	431	223
16	Lowlands	255	350	165
16	Grains	120.	191	63

The scientific findings of Dr Schidrowitz did not make for pleasant reading for the Campbeltown distillers.

His hastily added defensive statement would not have assuaged the masses, especially when it was omitted from his summary statement. In an industry that prided itself on purity and the medicinal qualities of its product, the findings from analysing the output of Scotland's distilling regions would not have made comfortable reading – reinforcing what blenders believed they knew: Campbeltown whisky was not fit for their blends.

There was time for a further boot into the Campbeltown distillers when Mr Robert Bowes, Wine & Spirit Merchant on Frederick Street in Glasgow, took to the stand. Being interviewed by Dr W E Adeney, Bowes was asked:

"I see from your précis that when you commenced the business in 1872, you blended Islay and Campbeltown?
"Yes," Bowes replied.
Adeney: *"Has your experience shown that you had to make a change?*
Bowes: *"Yes, a lot of customers were complaining of the nauseous flavour and the higher taste, the peat, and so on. I suppose you would term them ethers."*
Adeney: *"You had to alter your blend to meet the change in taste, do you mean?"*
Bowes: *"Yes."*
Adeney: *"It was not to meet a reduction in the price?"*
Bowes: *"No."*
Adeney: *"It was really to meet a change in taste?"*
Bowes: *"Yes."*

In December of the same year as the Royal Commission findings, it would have come as no surprise that the Campbeltown Distiller's Association announced a reduced output for the year.[112] Whilst this was blamed on higher production costs and 'super-abundant' stocks, the lack of demand was hitting the prospects of selling new offerings.

Although coming nearly sixty years later, the book 'The Whiskies of Scotland' (1967) by R. J. S. McDowall gave an uncredited quote to Campbeltown's supposedly poor quality whisky.

"There was a time when the Campbeltown malts were known as the Hector of the West, the deepest voice of the choir – a

compliment indeed. When the financial slump came in the late 1920s the public and the blenders became more choosy and turned up their noses at the Campbeltown 'stinking fish' especially when plenty of good whisky from the Highlands was available. The poor distilleries destroyed the reputation of the others, a warning indeed to the many blenders today who are harming if not destroying the reputation of Scotch whisky abroad."

Taking into consideration how wrong McDowell's timeline is and the lack of any supporting evidence to his statement, the quote barely warrants attention. But since it allowed a constant cut and paste for writer's afterwards and a long association with herring casks, or 'fishy' whisky, it is worth inclusion just to dismiss.

It is unlikely that the 'Restless' Sir Peter Mackie would have been oblivious to the concerns surrounding Campbeltown whisky when his firm purchased Hazelburn Distillery in 1918. His commitment to the distillery, if not to saving Campbeltown's reputation within the wider Scotch whisky fraternity, was made evident with the immediate modernisation of the distilling plant and implementing more scientific methods to produce a better (read 'different') spirit.

When 'The Wine and Spirit Trade Record' visited (publishing their piece on 14th December 1922), they found:

"The change of ownership… has taken the local trade out of an old-fashioned rut that was slowly paralysing initiative and diverting the eyes of the distillers from the up-to-date methods that modern science has placed at their disposal… Hazelburn Distillery has undergone changes which may be legitimately described as revolutionary."

The new owners of Hazelburn were keen to distance themselves from the reputation of Campbeltown whisky that had permeated the blending industry:

"The actual process of distilling differs slightly from the method by most of the firms in the town, and owing to scientific control, special treatment of the water supply [whether this is the

spring or Crosshill Loch is not specified], *and close co-operation between the theoretical and practical staffs, Hazelburn can produce a Whisky which will bear comparison with any made in the district."*

Mackie wasted no time in offering his new distillate alongside his existing malts. A customer circular was sent in October 1919:

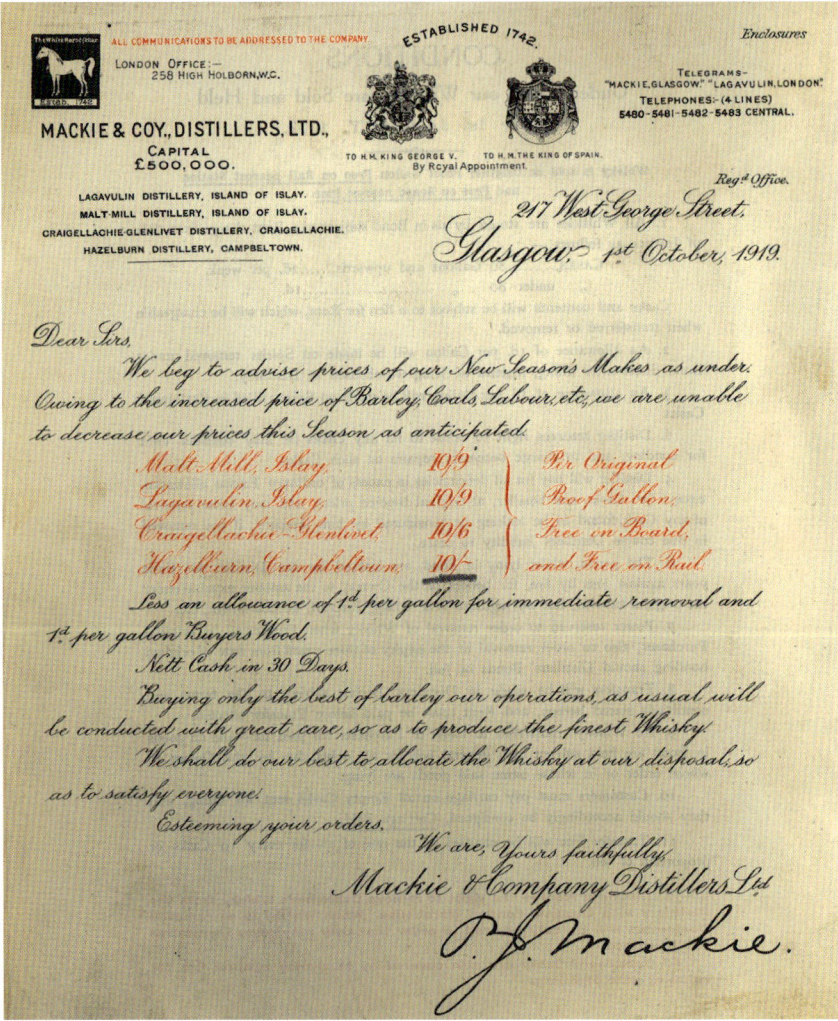

Within the same month, probably from lack of sales within the blending and brokering community, an amended price list was sent out.

"Referring to our former opening Price List, we have decided to reduce the price of our new 'Hazelburn Campbeltown' Whisky to 9/- per proof gallon."

All assurances were provided to anyone having already purchased at the old price, but more worryingly was the statement that accompanied the reduction:

"'Lagavulin' and 'Malt-Mill', Islay, and 'Craigellachie-Glenlivet' Distilleries are all fully booked up for this season."

Despite the assured changes to the distillery, the resulting new spirit, and the drop in prices, Mackie & Co., were still struggling to convince blenders and brokers to order stock of Hazelburn whisky. In January of 2020, another letter was sent to customers once again, full of assurances that the new spirit was a high-quality malt.

> Dear Sirs,
>
> We are sending you, under separate cover, a small sample of this Season's New " Hazelburn-Campbeltown " Whisky, of which we think you will approve.
>
> Extensive alterations have been made at Hazelburn Distillery with a view to eliminating that objectionable "gout" which has always been characteristic of Campbeltown Whiskies, thereby preventing them being so extensively used as the North Countries.
>
> We think we can claim to have eliminated this and to have given the Whisky a full Malty Flavour, which we are certain you will find equal to the finest quality of the Highland Whiskies.
>
> We may mention we are fully booked up for this Season's Make, but, as Bonders, we should like you to see what you are getting.
>
> We are,
>
> Yours faithfully,

The above letter was sent to all Hazelburn customers during the 1919/20 season and is the clearest evidence that 'Campbeltown' whisky had completely fallen out of favour. Something 'objectionable' was coming out of the region, whether from all of the distilleries or just a few, is arguable. Hedley Wright, the late owner of J. & A. Mitchell & Co Ltd, suggested that some Campbeltown distillers *"confident of their Glasgow monopoly, became careless and produced an inferior spirit, which they filled into poor-quality casks. These distilleries were the first to fail but... they dragged almost the whole Campbeltown trade with them."*[113]

This, sadly, is just hearsay or a theory and is perpetuated in books of the mid to late 20th century. It must be argued that the proud Greenlees family, linked to the Hazelburn distillery until just before its bitter end, could never have been accused of making inferior whisky. There was no Glasgow monopoly for the Campbeltown distillers from the turn of the century onwards - indeed, the reverse was true. And when one considers the decades of work done by Samuel and James Greenlees in establishing themselves within the English markets - promoting Campbeltown whisky as best they could - the notion is hard to fathom.

Mackie, who was no fool, would not have taken on the Hazelburn Distillery had its reputation been so poor within the industry as to make sales unfeasible. Yet, despite the new laboratory, new equipment, and new distilling techniques, by 1921, the firm had completely distanced itself from any association with 'Campbeltown':

"Hazelburn is no longer Campbeltown Whisky. We have therefore, dropped the word 'Campbeltown', and call it Hazelburn-Kintyre. We have made extensive alterations in water, stills, and general manufacture, as a result of experiments in our Laboratory, and we are now making a very fine whisky equal to the best North Country Makes and possessing all their body and character."

Determined to convince his customers, Mackie had organised a blind tasting for *"two of the best judges*[114] *in the Whisky Trade in Scotland,"* where *"Hazelburn was placed alongside the three best North Country Glenlivets."*[115]

ALL MALT POT STILLS.		
LAGAVULIN, ISLAY,	5/6	Per original proof gallon Free on Rail and Free on Board.
MALT - MILL, ISLAY,	5/7	
CRAIGELLACHIE - GLENLIVET,	5/-	
HAZELBURN - KINTYRE,	4/3	

Price list sent out 19th November 1921. Despite the reduced prices, Hazelburn remains the cheapest.

In true Campbeltown fashion, the price of Hazelburn spirit was a good shilling to a shilling and a half cheaper than all other malts. A year later there had been no change in the industry's attitude towards Campbeltown whisky. Mackie's re-branding as 'Kintyre' whisky, expert analysis and conviction that the spirit Hazelburn was making was the best it had ever made had done little to result in new orders.

Perhaps most galling of all to the old brigade of Campbeltown distiller, watching the disintegration of their once-proud industry unfold, was the promise from Mackie that Hazelburn was now *"made by a Glenlivet Distiller according to the latest methods of that district."*

A century of being the capital of the whisky world, and being renowned as a centre of whisky excellence was burst with the realisation that blenders wanted Speyside whisky first and foremost. Mackie pushed the piercing barb in a little further by concluding the letter:

"It is yet too early to definitely determine the exact quality of this whisky when fully matured, but bondings (casks of spirit) since we effect the alterations show every prospect of maturing into a first-class North Country style with a clean malty flavour and the necessary body."[116]

MacDowall's earlier quote about 'stinking fish' and Hedley Wright's passed-down anecdote relating to either poor quality wood or badly made whisky goes against the fact that the Campbeltown industry experienced sales into the 20th century. The majority also re-opened after WWI once barley supplies had been reallocated. Campbeltown whiskies were renowned for being distinct and unique. Could a couple of rogue distilleries tarnish an entire region due to simply cost-cutting or bad practices? Or was the demise and sharp decline due to changing drinking habits - the rise of more 'silent' blends to the detriment of flavourful single malts?

In September 1924, the 'Campbeltown Courier' published (adjacent to the obituary of Sir Peter Mackie), an appeal by White Horse Distilleries (as Peter Mackie Co Ltd were now known) against a rates valuation for Hazelburn Distillery. Within the report, Mr Theodore Scott, Secretary of White Horse Distillers, gave evidence that stated:

"Campbeltown whisky, he stated, was in very great disfavour with blenders, few of whom would buy it. The result was that while the industry was experiencing a boom in the North of Scotland and in Islay, it was very seriously depressed in Campbeltown. His company had a highly trained sales organisation, yet they could not sell Campeltown whisky, and if they could not sell it, he considered it would be difficult for anyone else to sell it. Blenders simply wouldn't have Campbeltown whisky."

Also in attendance was Archibald Stewart, a solicitor acting on behalf of White Horse Distillers, who looked to back up Scott's statement: *"Campbeltown whisky refuses to blend: it preserves its individuality in any company."* Perhaps feeling the discomfort these statements were causing for those in attendance (the local audience including the Campbeltown Town Council), Stewart diplomatically added, *"Like the Campbeltown people, it always comes to the top."*

Mr Scott submitted tables showing the current prices for Campbeltown whisky at various ages versus that of *"North Country and Islay makes. For 1922 whisky, Hazelburn was quoted at 8s; Craigellachie, 16s; and Ardbeg (Islay) 18s 3d. At Hazelburn last season they only worked 10 mashing periods, while a full working season was reckoned at 50 mashing periods. His firm had attempted to sell Hazelburn [Distillery] repeatedly but had received no offers."*[117]

One can only deduce, from a lack of accounts, comments and replies, that the Campbeltown distillers took this shunning from the blenders in silence. Attempts were no doubt made all over the burgh, like at Hazelburn, to use less peat in their malting process. But to no avail. Their once proud industry had, in part, been undone by a change in direction - a move towards a more easily promoted product. That is not to outright blame either the blenders or the consumers. Tastes change and the Campbeltown distiller was simply caught in the crosshairs.

Low prices and availability were no longer enough of a draw to keep the Campbeltown whisky trade flowing, and as orders dried up, so did all of the distilleries.

Well, almost all of them.

CHAPTER 9

RATES, RANTS & RUPTURES

Ho! Campbeltown, by steep Davaar,
So famed for Kings and deeds of war,
Thy beauties like a fadeless star,
Are every bright;
But one dread art thy fair shores mar-
A nation's blight!

There's grandeur in thy rugged hills,
And music in thy flowing rills,
But oh! Your curse is whisky stills,
Dread mischief brewing;
That oe'r old Scotland spreads such ills-
Outrage and ruin!

Your drink destroys the peaceful cot,
Your drink makes virtue's path forgot,
And loving fathers turn a sot-
Makes home a hell!
The early grave, the drunkard's lot,
Proclaims the spell.
'Ode to Campbeltown' 1881[118]

Alleyways, wells, walls, and warehouses were constant places to explore and play for the youth of Campbeltown during the distilling heyday. Mirth and mischief were possibilities at every turn for anyone so inclined. Sadly, accidents were an ever-present possibility and not exclusive to those working within the distilleries.

On a fine Friday afternoon in June 1876, a young boy named David Muir was playing near the edge of the Mussel Ebb. This area was a common playground for the local children but also where the boiling hot potale was discharged from some of the numerous distilleries surrounding Lochend. Muir, who had no doubt played in the area before, took one gamble too many and *"before he could get out of the way the liquid got about his feet and scalded the poor little fellow in a fearful manner. He lingered in great pain until late on Saturday night when death mercifully put an end to his sufferings."*[119]

A death that would have likely made national news today received scant coverage. Whilst deaths like this were extremely uncommon, especially to those not working within the distilleries, the nuisance and hazard that was the great expanse between Campbeltown and Dalintober was an issue raised constantly by the public. Mussel Ebb was reachable by the tide, and whilst the banks on either side of the loch were man-made, *"they had become coated with stinking ooze from the decades of discharges from the distilleries and rendered useless for fishing. After all, Campbeltown Loch was practically land-locked and such wastes were not flushed out effectively."*[120]

In 1871, the Duke of Argyll, through his agent James Leslie, raised the issue of the following *"principle nuisances affecting the Mussel Ebb*:-
1. *The discharge of all the sewers at high water mark.*
2. *The placing of privies directly over the burns or sewers or otherwise over the water.*
3. *The want of public privies, so that the whole line of beach wherever at all sheltered, and often even when quite exposed, is used as a universal privy.*

4. The communication between butchers' slaughtering places (there being no public slaughter house) and the burns or sewers, in consequence of which great quantities of entrails and other offal are washed down upon the beach.
5. The throwing of fish garbage upon the beach.
6. The non-removal of sea-weed from the beach;
7. The discharge of the dreg or potale from the distilleries upon the beach at high-water."

It was pointed out that during the cold months, the potale was not very objectionable but 'extremely offensive in hot weather or low water; when it deposits and putrefies on the beach'. The Duke wondered why other distilleries could not apply the potale to the 'manuring and irrigating of some neighbourhood lands' as had been successfully applied by James Stewart of Glen Scotia Distillery, along with the output of two other distilleries (possibly Dalintober and Lochruan). Stewart, it was argued, through pumping the potale, *"applies with considerable profit to 182 acres of land mostly situated as high as 300 feet above the sea."*

In response, Charles MacTaggart, the Town Clerk, acknowledged that the offensive state of the Mussel Ebb is 'undoubtedly the dreg or potale thrown upon it by the various Distillers in or near the town'. MacTaggart reminded the Town Council that the Public Health Act (Scotland) 1867 stated:

"The owners or occupiers of Distilleries, Manufactories, or other works, shall be compelled, where possible, to dig, make, and construct pools or reservoirs within their own ground, or as near their works as possible, for receiving and depositing the refuse of such works, so far as offensive or injurious to the health of those living in the vicinity thereof, or to use the best practical means for rendering the same inoffensive or innocuous before discharging it into any river, stream, ditch, sewer, or other channel."

MacTaggart agreed that the nuisance caused by the distillery's discharges had 'become so serious that the requisite steps ought no longer be delayed'.

A year prior to David Muir's tragic death, during the usual

Town Council Meeting, an extract of a letter was added to the minutes[121] 'from some of the inhabitants… and a report from Mr Storry, C.E., on the Mussel Ebb'. Whilst the letter was not printed, the response to the 'nuisance' was slightly awkward considering the Councillors in attendance included Samuel Greenlees, Duncan Colville, Charles Greenlees, Alexander Greenlees, and John Ralston (all distillery owners or connected directly to distilleries). Despite the conflict, they responded:

"The Distillers, while they consider that the complainers exceed the fact in stating that it is injurious to health, are willing to do everything in their power to remove any cause of complaint."

There was also a consensus that the Distillers were *"prepared to bear a fair proportion of the outlay in addition to their proportion by assessment."* All of which came too late for David Muir, who sadly, and in the worst way possible, nullified their premise that the current mode of discharge was not 'injurious to health'.[122] Over a year before Muir's death, locals had already begun to refer to the 'Lake of Death' in reference to Campbeltown Loch and the surrounding area. A breakout of typhoid blamed on the poor sewage works, often clogged by the potale, did not help the distiller's argument.

The second meeting determined that *"any plan intended to remove the nuisance by carrying the potale to low water mark will not effectually remove the evil."* Later in the same month, the new breast wall and road that had been constructed from the Old Quay to Dalintober were inspected by Alexander Campbell from the Board of Supervision, Edinburgh. Whilst the Local Authority believed that this new partition, when complete, would leave 'little if no cause for to complain of the Mussel Ebb being offensive', Campbell was not convinced:

"I am of the opinion that the nuisance of the Mussel Ebb is modified by lessening the area of it, and that the removal of the foul sludge from within the harbour will also contribute to lessen the stench of which the inhabitants of Campbeltown generally complain.

"I consider, however, that the Local Authority is far too sanguine in believing that there will then be little or no cause to

complain... So long as the distilleries continue to pour out their dreg or potale on the Mussel Ebb, the nuisance must exist."[123]

The Duke of Argyll, whose agent was inundated with complaints of the nuisance, offered to *"erect machinery for utilising this refuse matter, provided the distillers' become bound to give it to him in perpetuity."* The distillers, most of whom were still annually paying for their water from the Duke's reservoir, were wary of this potential bind.

"The Distillers object to give it in perpetuity, in the case at any future time the means are found to make this refuse matter valuable to them." An offer of a guaranteed ten years of rates was tabled along with the cost of the machinery at any future valuation (or even original outlay) should they wish to send their potale elsewhere.

The issue, as it affected the burgh works, caused an amendment to the existing 'Campbeltown Harbour and burgh Act 1846', which caused the dragging of the Bill through Westminster. This unnecessarily pro-longing and expensive adjudication did not sit well with those wishing for works to commence. One anonymous Campbeltonian's letter of complaint was published in the 'North British Daily Mail':

"By far the most interesting question involved in the Campbeltown Bill – a question which affects all Scotland, and indeed the whole United Kingdom – is, Why, 'in the name of all that is wonderful', the parties interested should have required to proceed to London to fight their battles?

"Why should any poor little Scottish burgh be compelled, when it wants an additional supply of water or gas, to go to London in order to obtain the necessary authority?

"We don't object to as much argument as may seem good to either side, nor would we even feel sore when twitted a good deal about our whisky-drinking proclivities; nay, we would suffer with much equanimity all the jokes that might be thrust at us regarding either the water flea or the terrible 'pot ale' nuisance, if we could only free ourselves from that long journey to London, the dread array of 'Counsel', and the accumulating items of lawyers' bills. As we have indicated this 'Parliamentary bill nuisance', is not

simply a Campbeltown question, it is a question for all Scotland and for all England likewise."[124]

The new Harbour and Burgh Bill was passed in 1876 and work commenced immediately to dredge parts of the harbour. Unfortunately, the Bill did not address one of the main scourges of the town: the discharge of potale into the sewage system. In 1890, Mr McWilliam campaigned against the *"great nuisance existing in our midst which is deterrent to the health and prosperity of the place, and we know also that the distilleries are the principal cause of that nuisance."*[125] McWilliam spelt out the issue and compared it to a similar issue that faced Kelvingrove, Glasgow:

"If they [the inhabitants of Kelvingrove] had reason to complain of the nuisance from one or two distilleries, I think we have much more reason to complain when we have over 20, and not only that, but at Kelvingrove they have a constant current flowing past, which tends to a great extent to carry away any refuse; whereas, here, we have not current, and whatever finds its way into the public sewers goes direct into the harbour, where by the action of the tide, it is spread over a small area and there settles down and putrefies, so that we have a constant stench and continual nuisance."

The Potale Tank, situated near Rieclachan Distillery, Longrow.

A tank had been erected at the head of Longrow and adjacent to the Rieclachan Distillery around the middle of the 19th century, and whilst this had allowed some of the distilleries to discharge their potale, it continued to be a nuisance to the burgh. By the latter part of the century, the problem persisted, forcing the Campbeltown distillers to authorise a report by Dr Gibson, Medical Officer, and Dr McKecnhie, Sanitary Inspector. Their findings were that:-

- *The 'Potale Tank' is more than fifty yards from any dwelling house.*
- *It is presently filled with water and is free from effluvia.*
- *The smell of fresh potale is not offensive, and if occasional offensive effluvia emanates from the tank, it must be owing to the potale being kept until it decomposes.*
- *In the walls of the tank there were crevices that required filling.*
- *To cover the tank would, in our opinion, make entering to clean it dangerous to life.*
- *Captain Stewart should not only be encouraged to continue their operations in the feeding and fertilising properties but even to increase them.*

The Campbeltown Distillers' Association, led by Chairman, Charles Greenlees (Managing Partner of Dalaruan Distillery), replied that *"The Distillers' again repeat that they do not acknowledge that the refuse of their works is the chief cause of the alleged nuisance."* Greenlees went on to state that with the exception of one distillery, Ardlussa, all were built prior to the Public Health Act.

This was disingenuous, and erroneous as several distilleries had been erected since the act, and, in any case, as was pointed out by, Captain Stewart, the 83rd section of the Act allowed the householders to present a petition to the Sheriff for an order on the Local Authority. Stewart clarified the situation: *"the distilleries [are] the chief cause of the offensive state of the Mussel Ebb and shores of the Loch."*[126]

Also not agreeing with some of the findings within the report were the many inhabitants of Longrow who complained of the 'disagreeable smell' caused by the tank. The solution, it seemed, was to blend the potale with the local sewage and 'the whole conveyed by means of large pipes in the loch beyond low water mark'.[127] Six months later the pipes had been laid. Writing in October 1897, OMIC stressed:

"...we are all anxiously awaiting the result of the experiment. So far as one can judge at this stage, there is every reason to expect that we have heard the last of the 'Mussel Ebb' nuisance. We shudder to think what is to become of our municipal rulers when they address their constituents on public matters now that this hitherto fertile topic of discussion has been removed. Let us hope that the much-maligned distiller will have a period of rest vouchsafed him now that the word 'potale' is divested of its terrors." *November 1897

Reading this with today's health, safety and environmental laws, conditions and concerns, the state of mind of the distillers seems cavalier and at times dismissive. Living in apparent splendour and out of the central areas - clogged with distilleries, tenements and other businesses, the distillery owners were accused of 'failing [to provide] a satisfactory answer'.

Eighteen months later the experiment appeared to be a success. *"I am glad to notice that the troubles which have for so long worried distillers in the North in connection with the vexed question of pollution are on the fair way to being grappled with. Here we have quite got over this difficulty, which at one time provided a fertile topic of debate at Town Council and municipal meetings. The experiment which was tried upwards of a year ago of carrying the whole town sewage by means of large metal pipes into deep water has been sufficiently long in existence to enable a fair idea of its effectiveness to be ascertained, and it is generally admitted that the success of the undertaking is no longer a matter of doubt."* * February 1899

Despite the optimism, this turned out to not quite be the all-conquering solution the distillers had hoped for. The 'Courier' continually raised the question of the 'disagreeable odour' and, in 1921, ran a front-page piece titled 'The Mussel Ebb. Causes of Offensive Smell'. The article gave a history of the issue but now demonstrated a better understanding of what was causing the issue:

"The offensive odours are caused by sulphuretted hydrogen, sulphide of ammonium, and other gases derived from the decomposition and putrefaction of accumulated sewage deposits. The action of certain germs is to break up or analyse the organic matter which forms part of sewage into such consistent gases."[128]

In simple terms, although the discharge had been moved far out towards the centre of the loch, the level at which some of the pipes had been laid was not sufficient for the discharges to 'fall' when the tide was full. It was claimed that due to the 15 distilleries working in the previous season, around 50,000 gallons of potale, along with 10,000 gallons of steep water, were sent into the sewage system. That was, each day, they were operating those processes. It was also claimed that potale was 40 times as strong as ordinary sewage.

"The offensive odours rising from this putrefying sewage will be most noticeable:-
- *In warm weather, as heat favours the growth of the micro-organisms which are associated with putrefaction.*
- *For the same reason, after hot pot-ale and waste waters have recently been added to the sewers.*
- *When the tide is low, and the deposit exposed to air.*
- *When the wind is from the East, or, even more so, when there is no wind to disperse the offensive gases.*
- *After the distilleries have been at work for some time.*
- *As the accumulation of deposit increases year after year."*

The radical solution, and one not put forward by the 'Courier' in its long list of conclusions, was already presenting itself as the third decade of the 20th century began for the Campbeltown distillers. Of the twenty-one distilleries that Barnard had visited in 1885, Longrow had already closed, Burnside had been stripped of its plant and the buildings sold, and around five others had not been distilling since the 1912/13 season.

It was not all bad news. Occasionally, some serendipity would occur; a clerical anomaly resulted in one of the rarest whiskies to have ever been bottled:

"A queer story comes from Rothesay about a forgotten barrel of Campbeltown whisky. At the final accounting of the books of a prominent Glasgow firm of distillers and bonded warehouse proprietors, it has just been proved that through a clerk's error, a cask of whisky warehoused at Campbeltown in the year 1892 had been forgotten. The cask was the property of the father of ex-Bailie John Lyle, Lorne Hotel, Rothesay, and has now been cleared from bond and delivered in Rothesay.

"The favoured few who have so far been permitted to taste this aged nectar pronounce it a fit drink for heroes, and experts say that by some fortunate chance the liquor has escaped the 'woody' flavour naturally associated with such prolonged bonding. Not only has the storage rent accumulated, but the quantity of spirit has come down by natural process from 33½ gallons to 14 gallons. The proprietor, of course, finds that it would be impossible to obtain locally a price for the liquor commensurate with its cost, and among the suggestions were that it should go to an American millionaire or be distributed in tiny phials in dry areas for the 'conversion' of teetotallers."[129]

Sadly, what became of this unicorn whisky is unknown.

A continual thorn in the side of the distillers, especially during economic downturns, was the issue of business rates. In 1876, a good year for the distillers, a slew of appeals were made by the Campbeltown distillers, and not just on their businesses (for comparison, see the Rates Table in Chapter 2):-

1. *Appeal by Colville, Greenlees & Co., against the valuation of £130 on Argyll Distillery.*

2. Appeal of Robert Colvill & Co., against valuation of £167 on Meadowburn Distillery.
3. Appeal of Greenlees & Colvill, against valuation of £345 on Hazelburn Distillery.
4. Appeal of Lamb, Colville & Co., against valuation of £226 on Kinloch Distillery (appeal withdrawn).
5. Appeal of Lochruan Distillery Co., against valuation of £285 on Lochruan Distillery.
6. Appeal of Wm. McKersie & Co., against valuation of £208 on Albyn Distillery.
7. Appeal of Wm. Mitchell & Co., against valuation of £223 on Glengyle Distillery.
8. Appeal of Reid & Colville, against valuation of £275 on Dalintober Distillery.

And the following appeals against distillers' homes (numbered as per Town Council Minutes):

9. Appeal of Mrs David Colville, against valuation of £66 on East Cliff House.
10. Appeal of Mr Samuel Greenlees, against valuation of £84 on House, Kilkerran Road.
11. Appeal by Mr William Mitchell, Drumore, against valuation of £105 on Drumore House.
12. Appeal by Mr Robert Colville, against valuation of £70 on Rock Bank House.
13. Appeal by Mr John Galbraith, against valuation of £63 on North Park House.

The Board for the meeting included Provost - Charles Greenlees, Treasurer - John Greenlees, Dean of Guild – Duncan Colville and Councillors including Alexander Greenlees and Samuel Greenlees. It must have appeared, at least to anyone outside of the burgh, a strange case requiring recusal. At times, even those within the area accused the Councillors of being lopsided. Whilst the Provost, Charles Colville, had (for sake of scrutiny perhaps) not appealed the valuation of his Dalaruan Distillery, one wonders how Duncan Colville argued for and against his own appeal against the valuation of Dalintober.

Despite a clear conflict of interest, the appeals were mostly futile:

"The Magistrates and Council, having considered the above appeals, remit to Mr Campbell, Assessor for Glasgow, to inspect the machinery and buildings in Nos 5 & 8, being Lochruan and Dalintober Distillery, and adjourn consideration of these cases till the following day at 12 o'clock noon. Dismiss the appeals Nos 1, 2, 3, 4, 6, 7, 9, 10 and 11; reduce 12 from £70 to £60 and dismiss 13."[130] (The appeals by Lochruan and Dalintober were later dismissed.)

In 1910, with 'Depression in the Trade' as the 'Courier's' article described the times, the Town Council met once again as the Valuation Appeal Court.[131] In 1909, the Assessor had granted the distilleries a reduction of 20 per cent. Whilst the original valuations had been prepared 30 years ago, the Assessor (Mr Hart) stressed that *"...their Honours would remember that at that time the distilling industry in Campbeltown and Scotland was in a very different position from what it is present. It was a matter of general knowledge that during the past ten years the distilling industry has been passing through a period of great financial depression and his clients, the Campbeltown distillers, had shared in that depression."*

Mr Hart went on to demonstrate how much production had fallen. *"In one distillery, in the year 1897, the output was 37,000 gallons, last year it was reduced to 13,000 gallons; in another distillery in one year 1905-1906 the output was 96,000 gallons, and this was reduced to 39,000 gallons last year."* In all of the cases, it was noted that there had not been large jumps from one year to the next. Instead the decline had been gradual over the last 15 or 20 years. This was an exaggerated claim due to peak production being in 1897, just 12 years before the current assessment - Hart was, after all, working on behalf of the distillers.

There was no debate from anyone present over the downward trend in the industry. With regards to the 'capital value' of each distillery, Mr Mackelvie (Glen Scotia Distillery) referred to the case of Kingussie Distillery, that had been built ten years ago just as the depression began. *"The owners, were unable to work it at a profit, and so it was put up for sale. It was advertised to go at*

£15,000 without an offer, and then at a reduced price of £8,000 without an offer. About three months ago that distillery was sold at the ridiculous figure of £700."

When the distillers had accepted the 20 per cent reduction at the previous year's valuation, it was 'hoped that things would get better, but instead, they went from bad to worse, and the outlook is indeed black for the season'. A new relief of 50 per cent was requested. After consideration, the Court granted a reduction of 10 per cent.

Peter Mackie & Company Ltd., having acquired the firm of Greenlees & Colvill, which included Hazelburn Distillery, contested the Campbeltown Burgh Valuation throughout their brief ownership. In 1922, the firm appealed Hazelburn Distillery's valuation of £1,020, wanting it reduced to £800 – the previous year's valuation. Mr Archibald Stewart, on behalf of Peter Mackie & Co., argued that *"It was notorious that there was at present no market for Campbeltown whisky. Blenders were showing a pronounced antipathy to the local make, which had in consequence become very difficult to sell."*[132]

Stewart added that parts of the world were experiencing prohibition, *"particularly on the American continent, reducing the world market for Scotch whisky, conditions which affected Campbeltown very decidedly."* In truth, this was just an added extra for effect. Prohibition in the US, whilst affecting the entire Scotch whisky trade, had little additional impact on the downturn in the trade for Campbeltown whisky. By this time, the large blending houses dictated what whisky was bought and blended.

The Assessor, Mr J. B. McClement, wondered why only Hazelburn was appealing the rates increase. *"Mr Stewart's address,"* McClement replied, *"had consisted of some doleful statements and prophecies which might or might not come true. All Messrs Mackie's swans were geese when it suited them. Last distilling season might not have been very successful in the matter of sales, but who could say that the portion of the make unsold would remain unsold after it had matured."*

McClement went on to quote a recent piece in the Glasgow Herald, suggesting that the industry was in a better place now than it was before the War. As he began with: *"I have some Islay whisky cases,"* a chorus of voices in attendance shouted, *"Where?"*

Stewart irritated with the waiving away of his concerns, did not ingratiate himself with the Assessor by replying that 'he had no knowledge of whisky'. The appeal was dismissed. The plight of the distillers, however, was exactly as Stewart described. Around 1920, the Kintyre Distillery ceased production, and in 1921, Stewart Galbraith & Co., entered into voluntary liquidation.

The attempt by Duncan MacCallum, with backing across the industry including Robertson & Baxter, failed. In 1923, West Highland Malt Distilleries entered into Voluntary Liquidation. Duncan MacCallum bought back Scotia Distillery for £2,500, whilst Glengyle was sold for its buildings at just £350.

W. P. Lowrie, who owned the neighbouring Lochruan Distillery, bought the warehouses of Dalintober Distillery. From the West Highland Malt Distilleries stable that left the Glen Nevis, Kinloch and Ardlussa Distilleries, all of which were put up for sale in late 1923. The Kinloch and Ardlussa Distilleries each fetched £1,500, whilst Glen Nevis was bought for only £500. From the six distilleries that began within the West Highland Malt Distilleries Limited, only Scotia would ever distil again.[133]

By the time of the 1924 Rates Valuation, the full realisation of the dire state of the Campbeltown distilling industry was no longer in doubt. Again, only White Horse Distillers Ltd appealed their valuation. The assessment of £928 was, in the opinion of Archibald Stewart, who was on better behaviour this time, £428 too high. Mr Theodore Scott, Secretary of White Horse Distillers Ltd., stated that *"Campbeltown whisky was in very great disfavour with blenders."* This time, the appeal was partly successful as the rates were dropped to £750.

The appeals in business rates proved to be a lesson in futility. White Horse Distillers, unable to sell the whisky nor the distillery, closed Hazelburn in 1925. Despite the best efforts of the Distillery

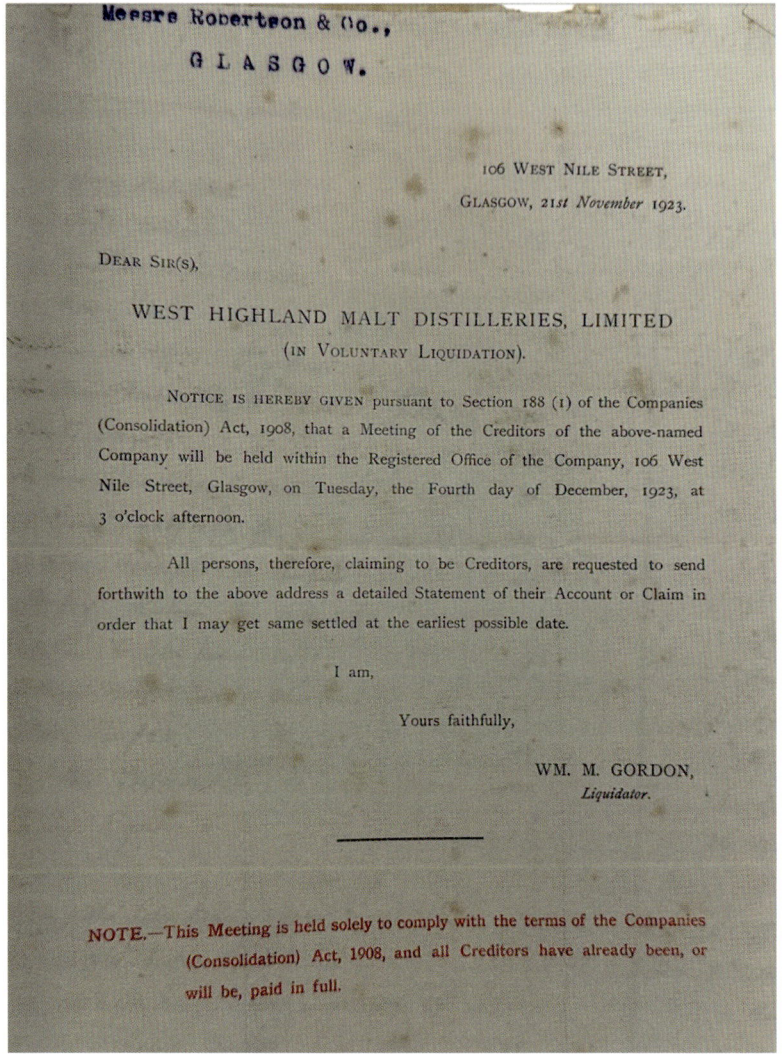

Held within the Robertson & Baxter Archives is the liquidation letter of West Highland Malt Distilleries, Limited.

Manager Peter Innes, who had been specially brought in by Peter Mackie, having worked at the Tamdhu and Yoker Distilleries, the overbearing reputation that Campbeltown whisky now had with blenders could not be altered.

Mackie's brief ownership did allow for one unusual visitor on the streets of Campbeltown. Masataka Taketsuru had travelled to Scotland from Japan to learn just how Scotch whisky was made.

His employers in Japan, Settsu Shuzo, wanted to discover what made Scotch whisky superior to other matured spirits, and in July 1918, Masataka set off for Glasgow. Having studied Chemistry at Glasgow University, he travelled to Elgin and spent time at Longmorn Distillery.

Back in Glasgow, he rented accommodation from a family named Cowan and fell in love with Rita, the eldest daughter. With additional time spent at the Bo'ness and Gartloch grain distilleries, the pair eventually managed, via Professor Forsyth Wilson, to spend several months in early 1920 at the Hazelburn Distillery. Sadly, there are no accounts of his stay and Masataka kept the majority of his notes primarily on the production of whisky. Of Campbeltown, he wrote:-

"Campbeltown lies on the west side of the Kintyre Peninsula, roughly five hours journey by steamship from Glasgow down the River Clyde. Apart from being one of the country's foremost centres of whisky distilling and fishing, all year round, and especially in summer when visitors are at their most numerous, the town boasts the most wonderful scenery and a good harbour. In the past there were more than twenty distilleries but seven became amalgamated so that now only fourteen remain, lined up across the western side of the town, in competition with one another for survival both day and night."

Masataka and Rita married, and the pair settled in Japan where no doubt Rita experienced the reverse of the culture clash that had faced Masataka during his time in Glasgow. His time and work experience were not wasted and through the financing of Shinjiro Torii, a Japanese entrepreneur, Masataka was responsible for the construction and running of Yamazaki, which opened in 1924. This is considered the first Japanese whisky distillery, and Masataka Taketsuru the instigator, or spiritual father, of the Japanese whisky industry.

Had Taketsuru been more interested in the decline of the Campbeltown whisky industry, he may have offered more clues as to what the mood of the distillers had been. As his time at

Hazelburn coincided with the shift towards making a more 'silent' style of whisky – something adopted by the Japanese distillers – a chance of some clues as to why Campbeltown whisky was so different, was also missed.

The largest customer of the Campbeltown distilleries, certainly after the First World War, was Robertson & Baxter of Glasgow. The firm began in 1860 and, by 1881, had built the Bunnahabhain Distillery on the Isle of Islay and the Clyde Cooperage in 1884. R & B, as they became known, were part of the group that founded Highland Distillers in 1887, which merged Bunnahabhain (operating under the Islay Distilling Co) and Glenrothes Distillery in the village of the same name. Further acquisitions brought Glenglassaugh Distillery in 1892 - later added to the Highland Distillers stable - and a part share in Tamdhu Distillery.

In 1919, and no doubt because of the amount of Campbeltown whisky being purchased, R & B backed the West Highland Malt Distilleries, bringing the six distilleries that were incorporated even closer to the firm. Differences within the family led to the release of Haig & Haig subsidiary (purchased in 1907) and R & B later entered into voluntary liquidation. Whilst the purchasing of Campbeltown whisky continued in the interim period, the new firm of Robertson & Co., headed by James and Alex Robertson, was not buying anywhere near the quantity of fillings as the previous version of the firm had. This was partly due to prohibition, partly due to the decline in demand for Campbeltown whisky, and partly due to the decline across the industry in the early 1920s.

From the log books and blending ledgers of R & B, it is clear just how much Campbeltown malt was used. Much of the very last distillate was bonded by R & B, and it is a wonder that blends were sent out with a spirit make that would never be seen again. The loss of one of the largest accounts, as well as the liquidation of West Highland Malt Distilleries, sent a destructive wave through the burgh. Dalaruan, having lost its enigmatic and highly-esteemed owner, David Colville, limped on but went silent in 1924 and was put up for sale in 1925. There were no buyers.

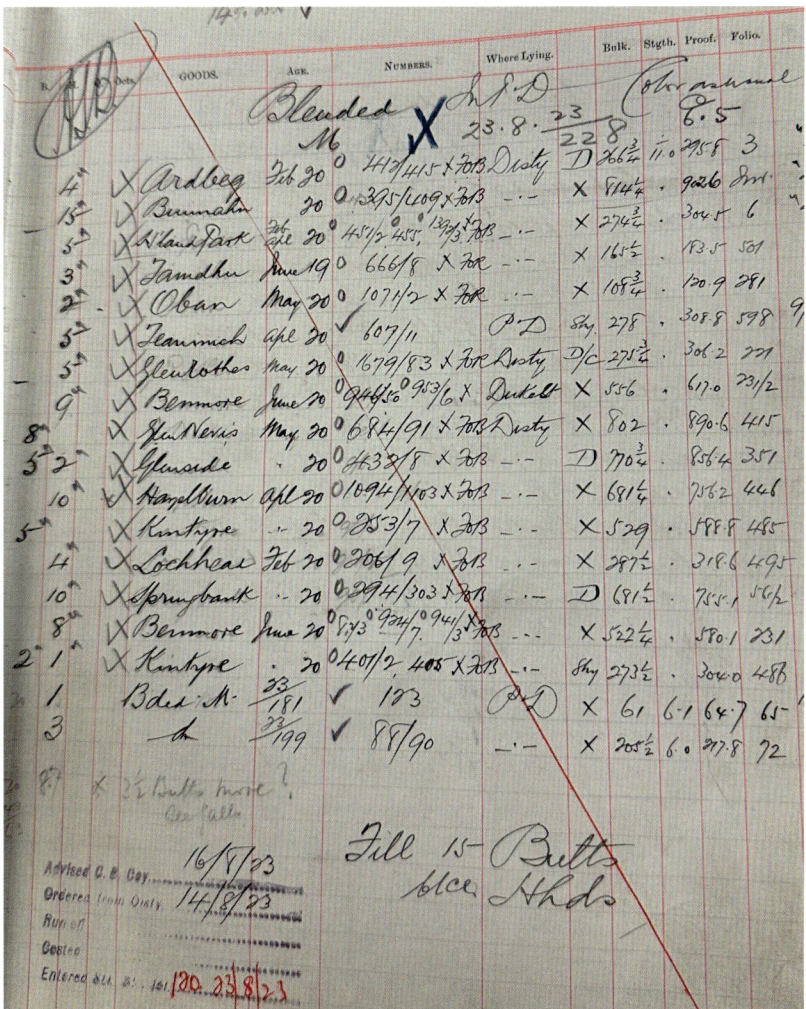

The blending ledgers of Robertson & Baxter 1923. Many of the blends used large quantities of Campbeltown whisky. This blend included Benmore, Glen Nevis, Glenside, Hazelburn, Kintyre, Lochhead, Springbank and Kintyre.

W. P. Lowrie & Co. Ltd., being a subsidiary of Buchanan & Co., was part of the conglomeration with the Distillers Company Limited and Lochruan Distillery, being surplus to requirements, was closed in 1925. It had likely been silent for quite a while prior to this. Little is known about Springside Distillery but it too went silent sometime before 1926. Albyn, Benmore and Lochhead had a stay of execution, but by 1928, only three distilleries were left in Campbeltown. William McKersie & Company Limited, owners of Albyn Distillery, went into liquidation in April 1927. An attempt was made when the new firm of Benmore Distilleries Ltd was formed to keep two of the Campbeltown distilleries in operation (Lochhead Distillery being the other). This too in 1928, was bought by the Distillers Company Limited, and whilst it is not known if the distilleries had already been silent for some time, the acquisition was the final nail in their coffins.

It is a distinct point of speculation and wonder that so little attention was paid to the near-total wiping out of a once-thriving industry. Possibly, the hangover from the war, with recent memories of rationing, Ministerial orders to cease production, and the economic depression that had hung over the industry since 1900, all contributed to a feeling of inevitability - a numbing of the loss. In the trade journals Campbeltown simply ceased being considered a centre of distilling. In the local media, hope was pinned on the smallest of chances that a revival may occur.

Whilst distilleries lay idle, dormant and often empty all over the burgh, warehouses remained full, and the sight of whisky casks being loaded on and off boats kept up the pretence that there was still a thriving whisky industry.

Campbeltown, once known as Whiskyopolis, now traded this moniker for a lesson to be learned. The Campbeltown whisky industry was now renowned as a 'once' something or other. A great cloud had gathered, and as if due to a contagious plague running rampant, the distilleries had, one by one, gone silent.

Where twenty-one distilleries had once thrived in Campbeltown, only three now remained.

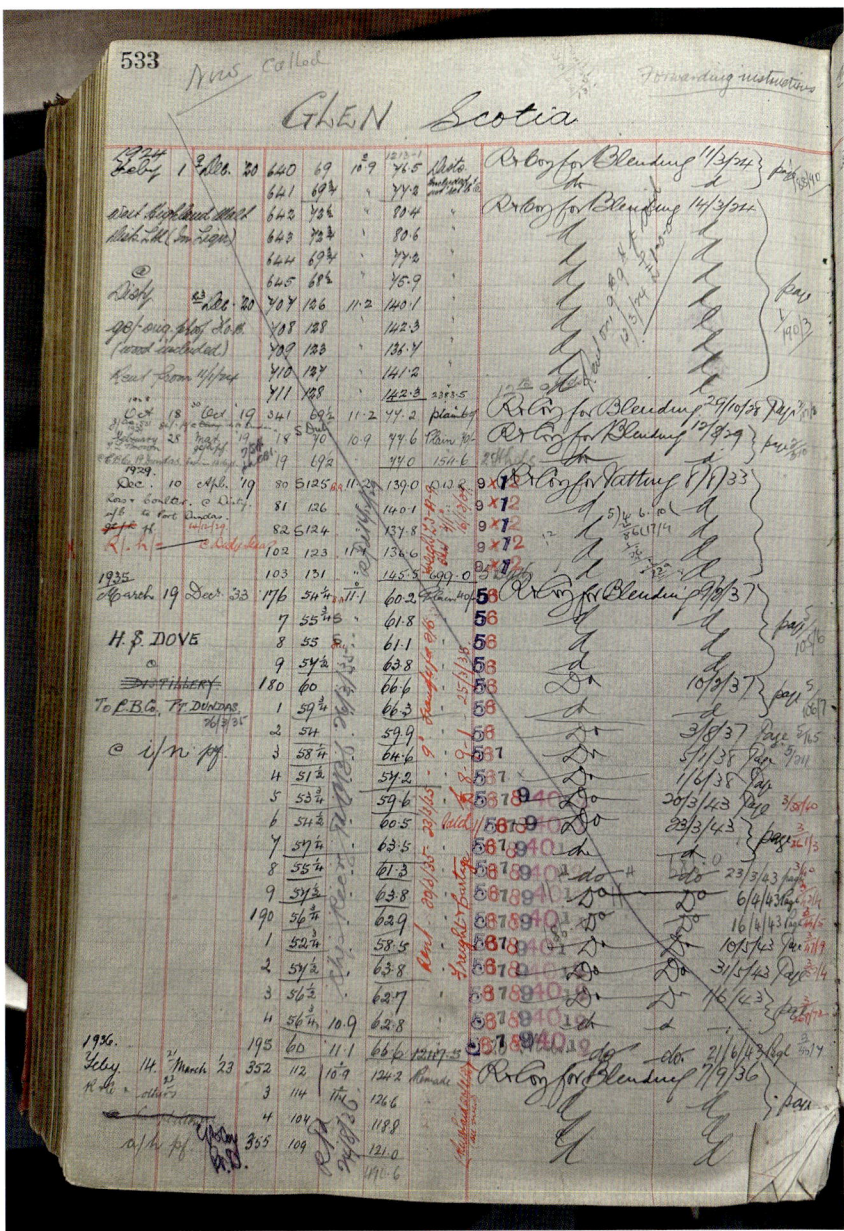

The stock ledgers of Robertson & Baxter contained some of the last spirit made at several of the Campbeltown distilleries. Attention is drawn to the addition of GLEN to Scotia's title. The stock of Campbeltown whisky was extensive, but by the mid 1930s only Springbank was being used in Robertson blends.

CHAPTER 10

TEETERING

"[On] my first visit to the distillery town, and in my three hours stroll, I was not favourably impressed... The only object of interest was an ancient sculptured Cross, with Celtic carvings, in Main Street. A gallows, I reflected, would have been more appropriate. ...if the distillers had not done much for the architecture of the town, they had built stately mansions for themselves on its fringes along the shores of the loch."

Campbeltown as seen by William Power, Parliament candidate for Argyll
'Campbeltown Courier', 27th July, 1940

"Distilling is by no means dead in Campbeltown."
'Campbeltown Courier'
2nd December, 1939

Hedley Wright, previous Chairman, David Stirk, author, Neil Clapperton, Chairman and Lillian Campbell, previous Company Secretary at the opening of Glengyle Distillery.

On a slightly overcast day in March 2004, Thursday the 25th to be exact, Frank McHardy, a few of the distillery workers, and I watched as the first distillate was produced at Glengyle Distillery. Admittedly, my youth and naivety prevented me from giving the occasion the attention and admiration it deserved. Watching the birth of a new whisky was, if more in hindsight than at the time, a rather momentous occasion.

What I had failed to realise was that Glengyle signified the first malt whisky distillery ever built in Scotland to be self-sufficient – in other words, built to bottle its entire output as single malt Scotch whisky. It was also the first distillery built in Campbeltown for 125 years. Perhaps, more significantly than either of those two facts, was that it brought the burgh up to three distilleries – matching that of the Lowlands – ensuring that Campbeltown, as a known and respected centre of Scotch whisky, was kept firmly on Scotland's regional whisky map.

The completion of Glengyle Distillery signified the first time

Campbeltown had three operational distilleries since the early 1930s. Rieclachan, once considered the most esteemed whisky from the burgh, had been owned and run by Hugh Mitchell, son of William Mitchell, who had built the original Glengyle Distillery in 1873. Hugh was a hugely popular figure within the burgh, having been elected Provost in 1896 but had sold Glengyle Distillery in 1919 to West Highland Malt Distilleries only to watch it subsequently close in 1925. This, perhaps, was one reason for Rieclachan's longevity.

In 1933, Hugh's health forced a step back from the running of Rieclachan Distillery, and having lost his only son, William, during WWI, he called upon his daughter, Helen ('Ellie'), to run the distillery. This was a highly unusual move - for the period - but as a graduate of Glasgow University and a chemistry tutor, Helen proved to be a more than capable manager.

Commenting in 1934, Hugh stated: *"Helen took her B.Sc. at Glasgow University and for some years was a lecturer at a London agricultural college. Last winter, she came home for a holiday, and during that time, my manager fell ill. She gave up her London job and did his work. He died, and now I am only too glad to have her as manager. As my son was killed in the war, I am pleased that she is able to carry on the family tradition."*[134]

Hugh Mitchell died two years later, signalling the end of Rieclachan Distillery. It is not known whether he had expressed a wish that the distillery be wound up to allow Helen to pursue her own career, but with her new distillery management skills, Helen became the Company Secretary for J. & A. Mitchell. The move reunited her side of the Mitchell family with those of Springbank (having split acrimoniously over 60 years prior). Miss Mitchell was considered *"rigorous in her control of the company's finances. Helen was also very firm with staffing and with the length of time in the year that they could justify distilling. It was widely held that it was her strict and careful local management that largely saved the company during what was a very difficult time."*[135]

The loss of the distilleries during the early 1920s was as if a giant loader had pushed them, one by one, over a cliff edge. Within the decade, most of the distillery's futures were decided.

Duncan MacCallum, who had become the local magnate of distilleries towards the end of the distilling era, ensured many of the sites would never again be a distillery. Writing to the 'Courier' in December of 1928, MacCallum disclosed his intentions for the Kinloch Distillery:

> *"I am naturally anxious for the development and amenity of the town, and if my proposition is agreeable to the Town Council, I would be prepared to hand over the property (retaining only the utensils etc therein), free from any encumbrances and without consideration of any kind.*
>
> *"It is perhaps well to point out that the stones of the buildings would form material of excellent quality for the new erections to be determined upon."*

There was little uproar, outrage or even resistance to what, on the face of it, appeared a very benevolent act. Provost Smith stated, in accepting the offer, that *"He only wished he could express his thoughts and [those of the Town Council] in better language than he could command. He knew they all appreciated very highly the spirit in which this offer was made by their fellow townsman, Mr MacCallum. The only regret in the matter was that it made them realise that a man of Mr MacCallum's undoubted ability in his own walk of life had come to the conclusion that he had no further use for the distillery, and his action meant a further and definite reduction in what was once an important local industry."*[136]

Not everyone saw the great demise in the same vein as the Provost. A month later, a letter from A. S. Miller was published that, whilst hinting at behind-the-scenes disagreements, suggests some of the locals were keen to see industry be revived, not reduced to rubble:

> *"Sir, in your issue of 15th December, I note that the owner of the Kinloch Distillery intends demolishing, or otherwise making a gift of that work to the town.*
>
> *"With no desire to detract from the munificence of the gift, as a ratepayer and one who during recent years has spent much time*

and a good deal of money in an endeavour to bring industries to the town, I would take exception to the further destruction of about the only work now available for industrial purposes, a building and plant which would be a valuable asset to any company who may yet desire to start an industry in Campbeltown. The dried grain work is one example, and there have been many others lately in Leven, Stirling, Jedburgh etc. Why not instead gift one of the already demolished works or even the old Highland Distillery if it is to improve the amenities.

"It is a scandal to see the town in its present state, and the parties responsible are not without cause for censure. Several of the works already demolished have been twice bought and sold at a good profit to the owners, and if they grudged the taxes they fitted the burden themselves. I know for a fact that two of them would be working today but for the astuteness of these individuals. Public opinion is freely expressed against any further demolition. Certainly a man can do as he likes with his own, but as an unemployed Ratepayer I object to pay taxes which should be paid by others. Had the distillery trade been good (it need not have been lost to Campbeltown) I feel sure this offer would have never been made. In November I was given an option of purchase in the Kinloch to run for six months if I wished. On desiring written confirmation, I was informed that it had been offered to the town.

"I always understood a man's word was his bond, but I presume a resumption of distilling there would be antagonistic to that gentleman's other interests in town. The recent acquisition of Albyn Distillery has blocked one scheme which was under way, and one which would have been of great importance to the town and district and also the colliery.

"Some time ago it was remarked in our Town Council that Heaven and Earth were being moved for help. There is plenty of evidence in the Press of attempts to move the earth, but like in the case of the Baalites of old, the fire is not yet. Much preparation has been made in the town for recreation and the grave, a waste of National money. Then we seek to lick the hands of the alien for sustenance while British brains are allowed to starve.

"The status and well-being of our town is at stake, and this is *no time to make capital of its extremity. I challenge the donor of the Kinloch Distillery to give the support he promised, and any others who really have the good of their town at heart, to join me in the endeavour to build up an industry in our valley of Achor."*[137]

This outcry, certainly the only one published in the 'Courier', was to no avail, and Kinloch was demolished a year later. A similar fate faced the Dalintober, Lochruan, Dalaruan, Kintyre and Glenside distilleries, with housing schemes replacing all of them. Albyn was also given to the Town Council and demolished, as would the Lochhead Distillery, albeit much later. Argyll Distillery, owned by the Distillers Company Limited (which also owned the neighbouring Hazelburn Distillery), was sold in 1929 to the Craig Brothers, who converted the buildings into a workshop. The Craig Brothers also acquired the remaining buildings of the Rieclachan Distillery in 1935. These were converted into a car showroom but have since been demolished and are now the site of the Co-operative Supermarket.

Perhaps the most poignant demise was that of the Campbeltown Distillers' Association, which entered into liquidation in 1927. The group, which had been a unilateral collective of the burgh's distillers, had met continuously during the heyday and into the 20th century. Collectively, they used their voice to challenge duty rises, law changes and misinformation. Now, with barely a fraction of the distilleries still in production, the meetings stopped, the draff plant went quiet, and the body disintegrated. The Campbeltown Textile Company acquired all of the remaining buildings, and the association ceased to exist.

It would be wrong to suggest that Springbank was completely immune or shielded to all the closures and loss in demand of the period. The surviving ledgers tell a tale that paints a slightly rosier picture of the troubles within the district, particularly the singular issues that Peter Mackie was having in selling Hazelburn.

John Mitchell, the original partner of the distillery, died in 1892, and Archibald (the 'A' in J. & A. Mitchell), continued as

Chairman until he tragically fell off a haystack in 1903. His death at age 58 almost mirrors his grandfather Archibald's, who fell off a chair and died at age 59. Archibald, the grandson, had preferred farming to distilling and left his younger brother Alexander to run the business from Glasgow.

When Alexander died with no heirs in 1912, the business's running passed to the youngest of the Mitchell siblings, Martha, who had married John Bennet Wright, a merchant in Glasgow. John Bennet Wright had been made a Director of the firm in 1897 when J. & A. Mitchell had been incorporated as a Limited Company.

During the latter stages of Alexander Mitchell's management, in the 1900s, Springbank had been experiencing fluctuating production, averaging around 74,000 gallons a year from 1906 to 1912. This was well below the distillery's capacity of over 100,000 gallons a season but was in keeping with the depressed times. In 1912, with the passing of the reigns to John Bennet Wright, Springbank, along with the other Campbeltown distilleries, struggled to produce spirit due to the cost of barley. With John Bennet Wright's appointment as Managing Partner, the 'Mitchell' period for the firm ended, and the era of the 'Wright' family's stewardship began. John Bennet Wright's tenure as chairman was a brief spell as he died in 1916, four years after Alexander. The position of Chairman was then passed to his son, Gordon Mitchell Wright. Like his father and grandfather, Gordon ran the business from his homes in Edinburgh and Bridge of Allan.

Hedley Gordon Wright, the last of the Wrights to be Chairman, possessed a quiet stubbornness borne perhaps from his remarkable upbringing. Hedley Gordon Wright was born in Cambridge in 1931 and spent his early life in Bridge of Allan, just north of Stirling. After school, Hedley returned to Cambridge to study Geology at St. John's College.

As a tall, athletic man, Hedley joined the rowing team and was awarded a 'Blue' in riflery (the highest honour a sportsperson can achieve at Cambridge University). Further education was gained at St Andrews University before the university appointed Hedley as a Reader. Hedley's older brother, John Bennet Wright, who died in 1974, had been the intended inheritor of J. & A. Mitchell, but having expressed no desire to manage or be involved in the distillery, Hedley altered his life's trajectory and took control.

According to Hedley, his father had instructed him to sell Springbank Distillery and end the family's connection with the albatross. Despite not being born in Campbeltown nor a resident, Hedley had no such intention and ploughed his mind and financial capabilities into giving Springbank a fighting chance.

The sales ledgers of J. & A. Mitchell in 1912 - the customers had become dominated by larger blending firms.

In 1960, after his father's death, Hedley became Chairman – and would continue for over sixty years before his death in 2023 aged 92. During Hedley's early reign as Chairman, the Scotch whisky industry was experiencing a turbulent time of ups and downs. Indeed, the Wright family's tenure of J. & A. Mitchell is a story of battling against the odds to keep the business going.

The marriage of Hedley's father, Gordon Mitchell, to Georgina Briggs Constable allowed the family a certain level of financial stability. Georgina's family were wealthy landowners in Fife, and it is believed the Wrights lived a comfortable existence from external investments and incomes. Hedley Wright's term as chairman was undoubtedly one of benevolence rather than a profit-making exercise.

After the First World War, and once distilling restrictions had been lifted, Gordon Mitchell Wright oversaw a more productive period between 1920 and 1925. The sales ledgers, instead of being filled with countless small merchants and traders, as had been the case during most of the 19th century - were now filled with the large blending and brokering firms of the times:- Wm Teacher & Sons, James Harvey & Co, W. P. Lowrie & Co., John Walker & Sons, Macdonald & Muir Ltd, Bloch Brothers, Arthur Bell & Sons and even several consignments to the Drambuie Liqueur Company. The company was also now exporting to Italy and Norway among other international markets.

Whatever trouble Mackie was having with selling his Hazelburn whisky, having re-designed the distillery, making the whisky more 'silent' and replacing 'Campbeltown' with 'Kintyre', does not appear to have held back Springbank's sales during the same period. At least on paper, it appeared that way.

Likewise, the often repeated notion that the Campbeltown distillers were overproducing during the downturn does not hold up against the figures produced or the fact that Springbank's warehouses entered 1905 with 417,715 gallons of spirit and, when the ledgers available end in 1937, had halved to 206,344.9 gallons.

In 1922, a large cargo was shipped from Speyside to Campbeltown by Peter Mackie – a shipment that would not have been possible had the company's Campbeltown warehouses been overflowing with maturing Hazelburn spirit.

"The consignment which totalled no fewer than 2,240 barrels of about 56 gallons each — or over 124,000 gallons — was the property of Messrs Mackie & Co., proprietors of 'White Horse' whisky, and to make room for the coming season's spirit it was transported from the firm's Craigellachie Distillery to their bonded warehouses in Campbeltown.

"It is stated that the consignment was the largest single one that has ever left Speyside, the biggest on record previously being 500 barrels. Including the Excise Duty the value represented by this large quantity of spirit approaches £1,000,000.[138] To convey it from Craigellachie to Lossiemouth where it was shipped on the steamers Avington and Royal Firth, required eight special trains. No mishap of any kind, it is understood, befell a single barrel at either end of the journey."[139]

The movement speaks volumes in how the different distilling centres were faring during these times. Craigellachie, being in the heart of the most desirable region for malt whisky, close to the river Spey and Livet Valley, was being run at a level no Campbeltown distillery could match - not with demand for Campbeltown whisky in such a depressed state.

Gordon Mitchell Wright witnessed Springbank's most depressed era. Between the distilling seasons of 1926 and 1936, the stills ran for just a couple of months, making only 103,540 gallons (and were completely silent for four of the seasons). Campbeltown witnessed the first unenforced period without any distillation since the modern industry began in 1817. Rieclachan was closed permanently in 1934, and Scotia had been silent since the beginning of the decade. Campbeltown was no longer making whisky; The Whiskyopolis tap had been turned off.

For the Scotia distillery, plans were afoot to recommence distilling. Duncan MacCallum, who had died in mysterious circumstances in 1930, had retained ownership, and his trustees sold the distillery to the Bloch Brothers in 1933. Distilling recommenced, and in December of 1933, 2,000 gallons were recorded.

Why Gordon Mitchell Wright decided, in 1936, to recommence distillation is lost to us – as are most of the ledgers of production from this date onwards. By early 1939, with trouble brewing again in Europe, the Scotch whisky industry, having learned lessons from the First World War, set about laying down as much stock as possible. September 1939 signified the German Nazi invasion of Poland, forcing Chamberlain to declare on the 3rd of September 'a state of war exists between us'. The pre-emptive production in 1939 was now looking propitious.

War efforts meant rationing and a depressed trade. A gloom quickly spread over an industry - just as signs had indicated a return to better days. Despite the outbreak, the 'Campbeltown Courier' noted, *"The war has made little difference to the work of Messrs J. & A. Mitchell and Co. Ltd., Springbank Distillery... finding the demand as great as ever for good Campbeltown whisky."*[140]

Springbank's whisky, sold entirely for blending, was finding customers as soon as it was made. Had there not been a looming threat of rationed production hanging over the industry one may have concluded business was on the up. In truth, this heightened demand was from lessons learned after the First World War.

The 'Courier', ignoring the obvious repeat of history, concluded optimistically, *"It is hoped there will never be any slackening off for as long as Springbank is still working a full pressure 'Old Campbeltown' is still alive."*

The 20th Century, so far, had proved to be a crushing period for the Campbeltown distillers. Yet, despite this, and the ongoing war, the Bloch Brothers, owners of the newly renamed Glen Scotia Distillery (no doubt named to distance itself from Campbeltown and appear more like the in favour Glens of the North), acquired Glengyle Distillery in January 1940.[141]

Sir Maurice Bloch, along with his brother Joseph, made no commitment to the recommencing of distilling, but the change of ownership did signal the immediate cessation of the Rifle Club from using the premises. Glen Scotia, like Springbank, had been working at 'full pressure' with the war so far having 'no effect on the business'. The 'Courier' remained optimistic that *"the distilling business may be extended to Glengyle when the reconstruction work has been completed."*

Campbeltown Corporation Compulsory Purchase Order No. 1 1935

NOTICE IS HEREBY GIVEN that the Department of Health for Scotland have in pursuance of their powers under the Housing (Scotland) Acts 1925 to 1935 confirmed with a modification the above mentioned Compulsory Purchase Order submitted to them by the Provost, Magistrates and Councillors of the Burgh of Campbeltown the Local Authority under the Housing (Scotland) Acts 1925 to 1935 authorising the Local Authority to purchase compulsorily for the purposes of Part III of the Housing (Scotland) Act 1925 the lands including any houses or other buildings thereon described in the Schedule hereto.

Copies of the Order as confirmed and of the Map referred to therein have been deposited at my Office, Union Street, Campbeltown, and may be seen at all reasonable hours.

The Order will become operative at the expiration of thirty days from the date of publication of this notice but if proceedings in the Court of Session are instituted within that period by an aggrieved person desirous of questioning the validity of the Order the Court may, if satisfied that the Order is not within the powers of the Act or that the interests of the applicant have been substantially prejudiced by any requirement of the Act not having been complied with set aside the Order either generally or in so far as it affects any property of the applicant or do otherwise as shall appear to the Court to be just.

SCHEDULE

Numbers on Map Deposited at Office of the Local Authority.	Quantity, Description and Situation of the Lands	Owners or Reputed Owners.	Lessees or Reputed Lessees	Occupiers (except tenants for a month or less than a month)
1.	Piece of Ground in Saddell Street, Campbeltown, bounded on the West by Saddell Street, on the South and East by Kinloch Park and on the North by property believed to belong to Miss McArthur and others	Scottish Malt Distillers Ltd. 15 Coates Crescent, Edinburgh	None	Proprietors
2.	Ground in Dalintober, Campbeltown, on which the Buildings known as Dalintober Distillery stand with the exception of the Warehouses of said Distillery at present actually being used for storing whisky therein	Do.	None	Proprietors
3.	Ground in Princes Street, Campbeltown, on which the buildings known as Loch Ruan Distillery stand with the exception of the Warehouses of said Distillery at present actually being used for storing whisky therein	Do,	None	Proprietors

Dated this 27th day of February, 1935.
THOS. MACKELVIE, Town Clerk, Campbeltown

A Public Notice printed in the Campbeltown Courier in 1935.

By March 1940, the 'Courier's' optimism had all but evaporated. Reporting on the near three-month premature cessation of operations by Springbank, the blame was placed squarely on the government's restriction of barley for distilling purposes. *"Only the skeleton staffs necessary to keep the plant in order have been retained."* It was questioned whether distilling may recommence at the beginning of 1941.

The effect of the Second World War, whilst having a much more significant impact on the world, was less arresting to Campbeltown. Four times as many soldiers from the burgh perished in the Great War than in the Second World War. The Campbeltown industries had already suffered catastrophic depressions prior to the war; Shipbuilding had all but disappeared; the fishing industry was a fraction of what it had been, and only two distilleries had survived beyond the early 1930s. The war effort and restrictions, this time around, were more limiting to the public than to industry.

That in no way diminished the continual losses on the beaches, seas and deserts, adding to the gloom that prevailed in the town and nation. A former resident, referring to themselves as 'Dalintober', wrote to the 'Courier':

"If the present state of affairs is allowed to continue then Campbeltown, I am afraid, is doomed to become nothing but a third-rate holiday resort. It is pleasing to find the fisherman still so energetic and their calling is not likely to disappear like the mining, ship-building and distilling (partly) and woollen manufacture."[142]

With distillation on hold during much of the war, J. & A. Mitchell continued to retain staff on their books – mostly dealing with dispatching casks from their warehouses.

Post WWII, the distillers were allocated barley to distil restricted quantities. Customers for J. & A. Mitchell, from the late 1940s onwards, continued to be the big players in the blending industry. Wm Teacher's remained the most significant customer, along with continual orders from the likes of Chivas Bros, Hiram Walker, Lang Brothers, Whyte & Mackay, John Walker & Sons and Arthur Bell (among many others).

In 1954, Glen Scotia, along with the bonded warehouses on Glebe Street, was sold to Hiram Walker & Sons (Scotland) Ltd before being sold a month later to A. Gillies & Co – a company founded by Sir Maurice Bloch - thereby buying the distillery back.

Springbank returned to full distillation, producing 88,826 gallons in 1954, 115,570 gallons in 1955, and 129,129 gallons in 1956. The customers continued in the same vein: Wm Grant, Barton Brands, Hiram Walker, Arthur Bell, and with larger brokers such as Stanley P Morrison, Hay & Macleod and Mackinlay McPherson (a division of Scottish and Newcastle Breweries Ltd). The war years had seen a shrinking of the brokering activity, but in the subsequent decades, a scramble for stock saw a return of the established broker and speculator.

In 1965, 'The Scotsman' ran a report on Campbeltown stressing that the transport links were holding the region back. *"The bus,"* stated John Clark, *"makes the trip in about six hours [from Glasgow], compared with the 20 minute B.E.A. flight while a motorist can reach Glasgow in about four and a half hours."* But despite the remoteness, J. & A. Mitchell were in rude health and had 'started construction work on a new £30,000 bonded whisky store on the site of the old Longrow Distillery'.[143]

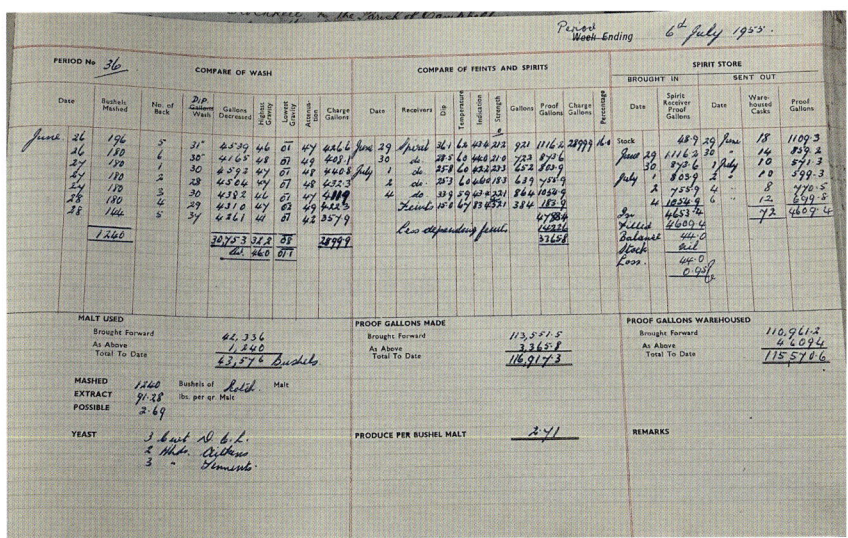

Production records from Springbank Distillery, 6th July 1955. The 1950s were a sustained period of growth for the whisky industry.

At some point during the late 1960s, the malting floors were abandoned, as Springbank began using malted barley supplied by malting companies. By the 1970s, the decrepit malting floors had become an entangled mess of storage for casks and bits of machinery.

In 1972 Hedley Wright, purchased the firm of Wm Cadenhead - supposedly in search of the considerable stock of glass that was part of the sale. What was instead purchased was Scotland's oldest independent bottler and considerable stocks of incredible whisky (at the time, considered the largest stock ever sold at auction containing no less than 650 hogsheads of malt whisky). J. & A. Mitchell now possessed a second string to its bow and Wm Cadenhead proved to be a boon to the business during the years that Springbank was either out of production or low in stock.

Meanwhile, Glen Scotia Distillery had been sold again in 1970 to Amalgamated Distilled Products (ADP) which was formed to take over A. Gillies & Co., (Distillers) Ltd. This signalled an extended period of renovation and in 1977 the distillery was reopened.

The 1970s was a return to former glory for much of the industry as it witnessed total production blast its way past 400 million litres of pure alcohol in a year. Whilst that figure would dip in the middle of the decade, mainly because of the overproduction in 1972 & 1973, the decade was seen out as being one of satisfying output.

The early 1980s, however, marked a significant change in the habits of drinkers around the world. Glen Scotia and Springbank, both almost entirely reliant on the blended Scotch whisky trade, felt the change as markedly as any other distillery. In 1983, Glen Scotia closed, and in September of that year, eleven of the twelve employees were made redundant. Springbank only recorded two full seasons of production during the entire decade.

John McDougall, who had been appointed Springbank Distillery Manager in 1986, used the downtime in 1987 to reinstate the floor maltings. A decision that not just created work for the remaining skeleton staff, but would hold Springbank in good stead for the future's change in drinking habits.

By the late 1980s the industry had cleared enough of its 'Whisky Loch', and, with sales picking up, distilleries began to bubble back into life. Glen Scotia began distilling again in 1989. By the early 1990s, the future was looking very much brighter with the 'Courier' in January 1991 declaring 'Round the clock whisky: a future for Glen Scotia'.

In the late 1980s and early '90s, there was a remarkable change in the public perception of Springbank whisky. Spearheaded by Hedley Wright's nephew, Gordon Wright, Springbank single malt Scotch whisky began to get recognition and a following from the new breed of engaged whisky drinkers. Although there were large and frustrating production gaps over the last decade, the warehouses had a not inconsiderable amount of aged, and quite glorious Springbank whisky.

Whilst these incredible bottlings had cleared much of Springbank's warehouses, the quality of the product had garnered the whisky much-needed and warranted international attention. The UK and export markets began to look beyond the bulk-driven blends, and single malts were now produced in ever-increasing numbers. Springbank was at the forefront of this movement, albeit with limited offerings.

Frank McHardy, who had first managed Springbank in 1977, returned in 1996 and this period saw the fires truly lit under the stills. Under Frank's stewardship, the distillery began to make three different types of distillate. Longrow, which had first been distilled in 1973, was brought back into production. This was a traditional double-distilled, heavily peated malt whisky - a hark back to an earlier style of Campbeltown whisky; and a triple distilled make called Hazelburn that omitted peat from the kiln, thereby containing little, if any, of the smoky esters that some drinkers were not so keen on.

Springbank and Glen Scotia remained as a time capsule to the distilling of a bygone era. To tour either, which was not the easiest before the millennium, was to travel back in time. No computers, sensors or technology to guide the distiller. This was old-fashioned whisky, and, as if by a miracle, was exactly what the new breed of whisky drinker was looking for.

In 2008 Iain McAlister was appointed Distillery Manager of Glen Scotia Distillery. The distillery had been acquired by the Loch Lomond Distillery Company in 1994 and had received little attention prior to McAlister's appointment. In his first year as Manager, just 80,000 litres of alcohol were produced. Much modernisation was required to get the old works up to modern standards, and in 2014, the distillery was part of a management buy-out by the firm Loch Lomond Group. This was the start of a major overhaul of the business, moving away from bulk-driven, blended sales to a greater concentration of single malt Scotch whisky. Further investment in Glen Scotia Distillery ensued before Loch Lomond Group was itself bought out by another leveraged buyout, which continued with the name of Loch Lomond Group. From a distillery that barely distilled a few months a year, by 2024, the stills sent 750,000 litres of alcohol to casks - all destined to be bottled as a single malt whisky.

Before the millennium, Hedley Wright was thinking of how to truly bring Campbeltown back as a destination for the whisky drinker - and with a watchful eye on the regional map of Scotch. When the old Glengyle buildings went to public auction in 2000, the initial reason for purchasing them was simply that they bordered Springbank Distillery.

Once acquired, it took little time for the germ of an idea to form, leading to Frank McHardy planning a new distillery. With frugality at the heart of the plan, Frank was able to acquire used plant from the mothballed Ben Wyvis Distillery, once part of the Invergordon complex.[144]

Initially, the focus of the distillery was to produce a lightly peated, double-distilled whisky using the malted barley from Springbank's floor maltings. In recent years Glengyle has maintained an output of around 95,000 litres per year made up of roughly 60% lightly peated, 25% heavily peated, 10% unpeated and 5% triple distilled. Springbank's output is 260,000 litres of alcohol, 10% of which is the triple-distilled Hazelburn and 10% is the heavily peated, double-distilled Longrow.

The remains of what was Glengyle Distillery - and what J. & A. Mitchell were faced with, having purchased the buildings in 2000.

Glengyle, whose whisky is called Kilkerran due to Loch Lomond Group owning the trademark for 'Glengyle', has proved that a distillery just a few hundred yards away, using the same barley and water, makes a different whisky. Similarly, J. & A. Mitchell and Glen Scotia have proven that when a whisky is made with passion, its product can find a market as a single malt.

The two companies, by the thinnest of chances, have kept a sliver of Scotland as an important part of the Scotch whisky story. Who knows, perhaps the Scotch whisky region loved and respected as 'Campbeltown' may have slipped off the map - lumped in with the mass of others known simply as 'Highland'.

Instead, the region is now on the map in permanent ink, as relevant and respected as any other region.

This was achieved with the purchase, re-build and recommissioning of Glengyle Distillery in March 2004. Thursday the 25th, to be exact.

Glengyle completed March 2004.

CHAPTER 11

EPILOGUE

"Campbeltown cannot be described as being in the middle of nowhere; it is the end of nowhere.
A destination where one simply has to turn around and head back the way they came.
Its location and the journey to get there are not much of a deterrent when one considers the reward is a dram of Campbeltown whisky. To drink Campbeltown whisky is to share a moment with our ancestors.
No whisky comes closer to evoking a historical context than that made at the end of the Kintyre Peninsula."
The Author

"Ask for a whisky which is not available. A good malt to start with is Longrow, which is made at the Springbank Distillery when the distillers can be bothered to make it."
'How to be a malt whisky snob'
'The Scotsman' 21st December, 1995

I began this book by recounting the first impressions from my inaugural visit to Campbeltown over two decades ago. The town then suffered a malignant and brooding cloud from a lack of enterprise that had no intentions of shifting. There was a melancholic atmosphere. It seemed that whatever business hadn't already closed was soon to be shut. Jobs were sparse and often poorly paid. Those who had done well at the excellent Grammar School often left Kintyre, taking their joie de vivre and energies elsewhere. The migrations were nothing to contend with those that left in their droves to the New Worlds during the 19th and early 20th centuries, but the exodus of talent, often never to return, gave the town a sinking feeling.

One thing that never altered, despite the factory closures, empty shops, crumbling housing schemes and diminishing public amenities, was the spirit of the locals. It is hard to stress just how much of an 'island mentality' exists in these extreme towns and villages – and whilst the local population, at times, felt helpless to prevent the decay – there was never any indication of a waivering pride of where they lived, or where they hailed from.

That survival mentality, bonhomie, and sense of community were all evident when I lived there. The fact that I worked for one of the two whisky companies helped my integration. I was never made to feel like I had taken a job from a local, but rather that I was there to help rejuvenate a once thriving industry. Glen Scotia Distillery, at the time, was more or less being held together by duct tape and ancient mortar, whilst Springbank was slowly building up stock from having its warehouses nearly emptied (during lean years of production). My then colleague, Euan Mitchell, Sales Director for Springbank, would often joke that his job title should have been 'Sales Prevention Manager', such was the dire state of the company's stock holdings.

From 2004 onwards, the town began to see real change. Whilst jobs were few and far between, J. & A. Mitchell slowly began increasing staff, Glengyle was in production, Glen Scotia was being revived, and work started on the new swimming pool and gymnasium built on Kinloch Park. Perhaps more importantly, certainly for the whisky industry, was the emergence of an entirely new demographic of whisky drinker. Gone were the brand-loyal, tumbler with soda, blended Scotch drinker. Gone too, was the fuzzy, 'old-man' image of the drink.

   A new, engaged, and flavour-hunting drinker began arriving at distillery doors; at first, a trickle, but soon a torrent in their numbers. Eager to seek out single malt Scotch that offered powerful, flavourful and different whiskies, it did not take long before 'Campbeltown' was once again the talk of the whisky-drinking community. Recalling Mr Archibald Stewart's words one hundred years prior, when asked why blenders were no longer buying Campbeltown whisky, he replied:

"Campbeltown whisky refuses to blend: it preserves its individuality in any company. Like the Campbeltown people, it always comes to the top."

Stewart's attempts at ingratiation aside, a better compliment to Campbeltown whisky has perhaps never been uttered. Whilst there are more reasons than simply being out of favour with blenders (granted, that is a big reason) for the demise of the Campbeltown distilling industry, the 'individuality' of the spirit is now its saving grace. In a saturated marketplace for single malts, where many Speyside whiskies struggle to find pre-eminence with such similar rivals, the three distilleries of Campbeltown have quietly sold everything they release, continually gaining new fans and demand. Their uniqueness is now their strength.

   When I first toured Springbank Distillery in 2004, with Frank McHardy as my guide, had you told me that there would once be a guided tour every day, I would have found that inconceivable. Had you then gone on to inform me there would be three tours a day – frankly, I would have laughed. During my time in Campbeltown I lived in the now-condemned flats built on the site of what was the Dalintober Distillery, directly adjacent to the crumbling and sorry-looking Glen Scotia Distillery. My partner worked at the offices within the Benmore Distillery – we really lived in and amongst the ghosts of the industry.

Occasionally, the whiff of mash would waft its way into my flat, or the tell-tale sign of steam from the boiler would inform me that Hector Gatt, on loan from Springbank, was operating the distillery for a short run. For anyone passing on a day without signs of distilling, the building had an air of 'the past' about it, a lost and forgotten distillery. There were no tours or access to Glen Scotia (unless you were lucky enough to know Hector or Frank, of course), and now there are two every day.

Glen Scotia Distillery looking tired and forgotten in 2005.

The transformation over the last twenty years in Campbeltown is remarkable, and this time, it isn't a sticking plaster like a call centre doomed to fail once the grants run out. When I was part of the team at J. & A. Mitchell,[145] I was one of approximately 48 employees. Today, that number is around 114. Glen Scotia had one full-time employee and now has 14. Iain McAlister is likely now overseeing the best whisky the distillery has made this century - possibly ever.

From a period with almost no likelihood of finding Glen Scotia single malt whisky anywhere other than a few specialist shops, the whisky is now exported to all of the major whisky-drinking countries – and continuing to find new fans.

But what is it about Campbeltown whisky that makes it so

special? Why, two hundred years ago and more, was it so sought out, infamous or famous, whichever you prefer, by those finding its style to be a such agreeable flavour profile? And can it be that the very same trait that made it so popular was the one factor that turned blenders away and collapsed an industry?

Frank McHardy, who served two stints as Springbank's Distillery Manager over forty years, firmly believes that the location contributes greatly to the whisky's flavour; something commonly referred to - and with great reverence - as 'Campbeltown funk'. To a greater or lesser degree, all three current Campbeltown distilleries (and their incarnations) have a singular quality – a regionality.

"If you take the Campbeltown malts," Frank reasoned, *"most of them display what can be described as 'funky' notes coming from the Campbeltown area. These can be reminiscent of salt, from the maritime location, coal dust, oiliness but also displaying both sweet and fruity notes."*

Glen Scotia Distillery in 2024 - now looking resplendent and reinvigorated. Photo courtesy of John Mcfadyen.

One theory, put forward in the late 1920s, and science has since given evidence towards it, is the notion that yeast played a large part in the regional aspect of Scotch whisky. For much of the 19th century, yeast had been provided by the brewing industry, in particular, the yeast created from the production of dark beers such as Porter. This then had to be shipped, either in casks (known as 'Skimmings') or pressed yeast in sacks. A lengthy and in-depth article was written for 'The Wine and Spirit Trade Record' sometime in the 1920s:

"The pot-still distiller is often at a serious disadvantage in regard to yeast supply, owing to the remoteness of his distillery, and in isolated instances his knowledge of yeast may be limited to acquaintance with the article in poor condition."

By the time of the article, the Campbeltown distilling trade was already reduced to a fraction of what it had been, but from the journals of Masataka Taketsuru, we learn that Hazelburn was still using bagged yeast:

"As for the yeast, some of the wort is drawn off and yeast is dissolved in it... The compressed yeast is obtained from companies producing beer or stout. The sediment from the beer or stout-making process is compressed and put into sacks."

There was not sufficient beer production in Campbeltown to provide the distillers with yeast. Therefore the theory of yeast deterioration due to time shipping from the central belt to Campbeltown goes some way to explain the uniqueness of the region's whisky. As 'The Wine and Spirit Trade Record' article mentions:

"This yeast theory is supported by the geographical division of Scotch Whiskies. Lightly-flavoured 'malt' is produced in Lowland distilleries that are favourably situated for receiving supplies of fresh and healthy yeasts. Highland distilleries, particularly those of the far north, seldom receive yeast in the same condition as it is despatched from the brewery: Highland whiskies develop medium malt flavours. Yeast delivered to Islay and other remote distilleries may be indifferent (from laboratory standards) by the time it is pitched, and sometimes it is a fortnight old: the distillates are characterised by very heavy flavours, heavy by comparison even with Campbeltowns."

EPILOGUE

This does not explain why there remains such a geographical difference - Springbank has been using distiller's yeast for over fifty years. Certainly for J. & A. Mitchell, the traditional methods of floor maltings, distinct distillation processes and ensuring every single cask is matured on-site must play a part in it being such a unique whisky. As Serge states in his Foreword, 'the best soups are made in old pots' and it could be argued that as Springbank and Glengyle are whiskies made to maximise flavour, and not to fit a blender's palette (or palate), attention is not fixated on yield and consistency. At least not in the same manner.

Ronan Currie, Melanie Stanger, Cara Clements, David Allen, Nathan Currie, Ian Rich, Mitch Graham & Grant Macpherson, Campbeltown Malts Festival. Photo courtesy of John Mcfadyen.

On what the whisky was like before even the 1950s, we will really never know, and for those lucky enough, there are only a few bottles of whisky from Campbeltown with any great history. I must mention that the oldest expression of Springbank is a 1919 vintage, bottled in 1970 as a 50-year-old whisky. I have had the pleasure to taste this, and I can relay that it was much softer than I had expected. Very little peat smoke, but then it had 50 years to mellow in wood – and it was made during the great call for more 'silent' Campbeltown whiskies. There was certainly no 'objectionable gout' to report.

Regarding why the blenders shunned it, we can only take the feelings expressed at the time. On why the whisky now tastes as it does is part science, part location and a large, and healthy part mystery. As much a mystery as to how such great whisky region ever fell from favour.

The nearest regional neighbour and an island that escaped with just a light bruising from the early 20th century troubles is the Isle of Islay. All contemporary accounts, certainly from the 1800s onwards, talk about how unique Islay malts were, whilst being recognisably 'Islay' in style, and likewise how unique the Campbeltown malts were, but, again, collectively similar. Both distilling centres were buying barley from whichever source it could be obtained, assuming it was of the highest quality. So, any difference cannot be ascribed to an issue - or policy - of local agronomy.

Is the uniqueness a question of local peat used in the kilns? The Islay distilleries all relied on peat from the island and often from their own specific bogs. While Kintyre peat was harvested and used by the distilleries, from the evidence, it is clear that predominantly Irish peat was preferred. Could this explain the uniqueness of Campbeltown whisky? Quite possibly. But it doesn't explain why Campbeltown whisky today is still considered such a special Scotch whisky region, as Irish peat hasn't been used for decades. Not being technically minded or concerned, I prefer the alchemy side of this industry rather than the cutting open of the 'Golden Goose'. Campbeltown whisky is unique because it is, and let's leave it that way.

EPILOGUE

So, 'whodunnit'? Who shot down the Campbeltown distilling industry? Was it the Pattison Crash? Overproduction? Inferior spirit? Uncompetitive practices? Changes in drinking habits? The wars, the depression, etc and so on? Try as I may, I have found no evidence to corroborate the tale that some of the Campbeltown distillers began cutting corners, making an inferior product, and thereby tarnishing the great name of the burgh's spirit.

With the evidence presented, Hedley Wright's tale suggesting in-fighting resulting in a poor quality spirit, has more of a passed-down anecdote about it. That is not to say it can simply be dismissed. On the contrary, the very fact that Glen Scotia and Springbank survived suggests that within Campbeltown, certain whiskies were of a style that had, at the very least, a broader appeal and were the best that the town could offer. Their existence, in other words, is evidence of a Darwinist 'survival of the fittest'. But even that explanation needs quantifying, as possibly not relevant when considering today's preference for single malt Scotch.

Arguably, the demise, or contraction, of Campbeltown as a whisky powerhouse was always on the cards. The moment those first distillers, using the new patent or column still, confidently brought their aged grain whisky to market, and coupled with validation from the 1908 commission, the abundance of fiery whisky from Campbeltown was always likely to be thinned. And though the finger has been pointed, ad verbum, by writers down the years, at depression, blenders, prohibition (which in truth played a very minor part), war and competition, the simple truth is there were always too many distilleries - and many of them too small. Where the tragedy lies is that rolling on one hundred years, the malt whisky enthusiast's question is not 'Why now so few?' but, rather, 'What did we miss?'

Campbeltown was not just famous for possessing a certain regional style, but for all of the distilleries being markedly different from one another. Using the Isle of Islay again as an example, a half dozen or so distilleries survived past World War II, and in the last twenty or so years, as malt whisky drinkers have exploded in numbers, the greatest strength of Islay whisky, along with their pungency, is their uniqueness to each other.

The longing for all those fans of existing Campbeltown whisky is to taste what we lost. If Glen Scotia and Springbank were the few that the large whisky houses could 'blend' with, what were the others like? With today's penchant for fiery, smoky and flavourful single malts, are some of those lost distilleries now the ones that would be highly sought after? After all, Rieclachan was often considered the best whisky in the region, whilst Hazelburn was the poster child of Campbeltown's distilleries. Imagine what gems we lost when the blenders turned their back on an entire region due to its weight of flavour.

We'll never know, of course.

To visit Campbeltown now is to enter an adults' playground for all things single malt Scotch whisky. Gone are the days of hoping a tour might be your best bet to get close to the local spirit. To quote a recently printed book on touring some of Scotland's distilleries:

"Across from Springbank's distillery shop is the Washback Bar in what used to be the joiner's workshop. Here, you will find all of the available Springbank and Glengyle whiskies [and many unavailable]. Beyond that is a small museum dedicated to Hedley Wright, the previous chairman, and beyond that is the Springbank blending room where you can take part in the 'Barley to Bottle Tour'. This culminates in being able to blend your perfect Springbank dram from several aged whiskies.

"As if that wasn't enough, you can also join a Cadenhead Warehouse Tasting, tour Springbank and/or Glengyle, and stay for three nights as part of the 'Eat, Sleep, Dram, Repeat' package (including a guided historical tour of Campbeltown). And for those who want a truly immersive experience, you can even wait several years to join the 'Whisky School' and learn how to make whisky the Springbank way, from malting to bottling. I feel like I've just written a promotional piece for the company, which I have, but in reality, J. & A. Mitchell has created a 'Whisky

EPILOGUE

Disneyland' for enthusiasts.

"And if that hasn't exhausted you, just a few minutes' walk from Springbank is Glen Scotia Distillery – here you can choose from a 'Distillery Tour', a 'Dunnage Warehouse Experience', a 'Distillery Manager Tour', a 'Whisky Heritage Walking Tour' and 'The Warehouse Journey'. It's a far cry from the occasional and never more than once-a-day tour (only of Springbank) that existed when I lived there."[146]

I returned to Springbank twenty years or so after my first visit, this time with tour guide Finlay Wylie. A local, propitiously finding employment during a round of golf, who delivered one of the best tours I've ever had. Nothing had really changed at the distillery in the two decades separating my tours. It still felt like stepping back in history. Had the distillery staff been toiling in heavy woollen suits and large caps with soot and peat stains, little else would need altering to achieve the sense of time travel.

And yet, everything had changed. There was life and activity around each corner, and not just the mice and birds in the malt barns. This is not to suggest that there has been a return of pride. That was always there. The rejuvenation has brought a feeling, or sense, of 'I told you so – you just needed to be patient'.

The whisky was always good; it just needed the world's tastes to develop, stocks to return to healthy levels, and owners and managers (especially in the case of Glen Scotia) who knew how best to present the product to the world.

I spent time with the owners of the planned Witchburn and Machrihanish distilleries. Each very different in their approach, modus operandi and intended customer – but both very much adding to the region. In a few weeks, I and many other mad malt whisky aficionados will participate in the seventeenth Campbeltown Malts Festival. The gathering will be a cross-section of the wider whisky-drinking public that enjoys Campbeltown whisky.

It would be an illuminating experience to witness the reactions of the Mitchells, McKersies, Colvilles, and Greenlees (et al.) to a festival celebrating Campbeltown whisky. Perhaps they would first question, 'Why so few?' when confronted with just three working distilleries. Or maybe they would simply admire a product being received and appreciated as they had intended. Whatever ghosts there were or spirits left in purgatory, the renaissance of Campbeltown has allowed them all to rest in peace. The doom and gloom has been exorcised.

The robustness and uniqueness of Campbeltown whisky is not in dispute - the region will never again be questioned as being worthy of retention on the Scotch Whisky Regional map. The lessons from history have been learnt, and the future is very much golden, full-flavoured and singular.

Campbeltown whisky, once spurned by the great blending houses as being 'too much at the top', has had the last laugh.

It is now considered very much at the 'top'.

APPENDIX A:

DISTILLERY HISTORIES

This list entails all of the known Campbeltown distilleries that were built in the 19th century. I have omitted much of what Alfred Barnard concluded from his visit in 1885 due to it being the bulk of Chapter 3. For a more comprehensive list of all of the distilleries that have come and gone, at least those we know of, I can recommend Angus Martin's 'Campbeltown Whisky – An Encyclopaedia' which has been extremely helpful with the compiling of these histories. As Martin mentions in his book, some of the years are dubious and possibly do not correlate to the actual records of when the distillery commenced distilling. Likewise, the closure of many of the distilleries is down to part detective work and part guesswork. Many were mothballed (a period where they were silent) before finally closing – and some of the 'mothball' periods were several years.

ALBYN DISTILLERY 1837 - 1927

Having secured a lease for the land from the Duke of Argyll, William McKersie erected the Albyn Distillery in 1837. McKersie had already established the Lochside Distillery in 1830, built behind the firm of Robert Armour & Sons on Longrow. Soon after, William's younger brother Alex joined the firm but left in 1852 (when Lochside Distillery closed), emigrating to Australia. When visited in June of 1923, 'The Wine and Spirit Trade Record' noted that Albyn Distillery was, *"a pleasant little group of buildings on the outskirts of the town, overlooking the bay."*

William McKersie, having retired, passed the distillery onto his two sons in 1876, and in turn, they paid him an annuity of £1,150 each year in lieu of purchasing the going concern. Despite this hefty annual payment (over £100,000 today), the sons, William and John, were not spared the succession duties (introduced in 1853, this has since evolved into inheritance tax).

The business was valued at £28,000 (£2.5 million ATTOW),[147] but the annuities and taxes did not prevent the two McKersie brothers from prospering.

In 1893, the distillery fared the worst after a large storm, having its stalk (chimney) blown into the roof of the still house, causing considerable damage. Despite this setback, a new warehouse was built in 1895. When John McKersie passed away in 1904, William took control of both Albyn and Lochruan distilleries. Albyn distillery eventually left the McKersie family when in 1920 the lease was taken on by the new firm, Wm McKersie & Co, Ltd., with the Glasgow based subscribers: A. N. Murdoch and James Cradford. This firm was a wine and spirit broker based on Wellington Street, and no doubt, due to the good will of the business, kept the McKersie association.

Alfred Barnard noted in 1885 that the distillery had three small stills with capacities of 2,500, 1,650 and 580 gallons each. However, in 1905, 'The Wine and Spirit Trade Record' reported that the distillery had *"three stills with a capacity of 3,000, 1,600 and 1,500 gallons."* Considering the errors that Barnard was culpable of, it would appear that the later numbers are more accurate. By the time 'The Wine and Spirit Trade Record' returned in 1923, the set-up had changed:

"In the still-house are two pot-stills with the usual air valves and other fixtures. For many years three stills were employed, but the installation of the indicator on the Spirit receiver has enabled the management to dispense with the third still, and incidentally to save four working hours per week."

The article, published in June, described the distillery:

"Rusty fastenings, used by the Excise officers in the days when the heavy duty on malt made it necessary to keep the entire distillery under close surveillance, still hang limply on the doors of the malting-house, and high up on the fermenting floors lies

a dingy cooling tank; now replaced by a polished refrigerator."

The firm was renowned for its long-serving staff. Archibald Keith had, over 40 years' service, worked his way up to Distillery Manager, before his sudden death in 1914. In the article published in 1923, the brewer was the son of a Mr McIntyre, who had held the same position for 50 years, and one of the maltmen was Donald McCallum, who had been serving the firm for 48 years. It was noted in the article that *"Campbeltown distilleries contain a number of old employees, who seem unconsciously to have blended their personalities with the aged buildings in which they have worked all their days… A sturdy old Scot, and a well-known local character, Donald McCallum remembers clearly the days when the whole of the distilling machinery was worked by horses."*

With the downturn in the industry and falling foul of blender's preferences, the new firm did not last long before entering into voluntary liquidation:

"William McKersie & Company, Limited (In Liquidation) At an extraordinary General Meeting of the above Company held within the Registered Office of the Company on Thursday, the 21st day of April, 1927, the following Resolution was duly passed, and at a subsequent Extraordinary General Meeting, also duly convened and held within the same place on Monday, the 9th day of May, 1927, the said Resolution was duly confirmed as a Special Resolution, viz:- 'That the Company be wound up voluntarily'."[148]

By 1928, it was quite clear that the distillery as a going concern was of little value, and the liquidators *"offered to the Town Council to acquire as it adjoins the Corporation Gasworks. The committee after fully considering the matter, were of the opinion, in view of the high fue duty (£71 11s 6d) that they could not make any recommendation to the Council to acquire the ground and premises."* The Council rejected this offer, and in 1928, Albyn was leased by the Franco-British Oil Trust as a laboratory for a

Dr Aicher to conduct experiments into the extraction of oil from coal. In 1929, the work ended due to an inability to raise sufficient capital, and the process was relocated to the River Medway.[149] In 1942, part of the building was used as a mortuary, and in 1955, part of the works were converted to a clothing factory operated by Andrew Douglas Ltd. This was later taken over by Jaegar Tailoring in 1977 but closed in 2000.

John and William McKersie were highly respected and valued members of Campbeltown and Kintyre. John's obituary struggled to list his many offices and contributions to the burgh:

"In the life and work of his native town he took a keen and active interest. His public services were practically wholly confined to the Town Council, in which he served for twenty-one years, retiring after holding for six years the highest honour which that body can confer upon one of its members. He was elected to the Council in November, 1875, and was in continuous service til 1896.

"In 1879 he was appointed convener of the Gas Committee, and a year later was elected to the office of Dean of Guild. After holding the latter office for ten years, he was in 1890 elected to the Provost's chair, a position which he filled with the highest credit to himself and to the community.

"When his term expired in 1893 his health was beginning to trouble him, and he expressed a desire to retire from public service. However, it so happened that the burgh was in much need of him still, there being a hitch in connection with the election, and at the earnest and unanimous request of the Council he returned to office, being again appointed Provost. He finally retired in 1896, when his brother-in-law, Provost Mitchell, was appointed to the important position for which he vacated."[150]

On the day of his funeral, as a mark of respect, *"the local steamers have carried their flags at half-mast, and today on all the vessels at the harbour and on public buildings the flags are flying half-mast high. The town bell was tolled during the funeral hour."* John McKersie's estate was valued at £82,768 (£8.5 million ATTOW). His health had deteriorated after the loss of his first daughter, Jane, who died in 1903, and on his passing was survived by his widow Helen, two sons, William and Archibald and a daughter Edith who was just 15 years old. John's brother, William, was a much less prominent member of the community, but his 'business aptitude and ability were beyond question'.[151] William died in 1916, aged 72 at his home, Craigard House.

ARDLUSSA DISTILLERY 1879 - 1927

Undoubtedly, it would have come as a massive shock to the proprietors of James Ferguson & Sons, the commissioners of the building of Ardlussa Distillery in 1878, that their distillery would be the last one built in Campbeltown until Glengyle was rebuilt in 2004.

James Ferguson and son James Jr were Glasgow wine and spirits merchants based at 9 Cadogan Street. As their business, and the demand for whisky expanded the Fergusons purchased the Jura Distillery;

"Distillery For Sale, by Private Bargain. The JURA DISTILLERY, Island of Jura, with the whole machinery, fitting, utensils, and others, belonging to the tenants, with the right to the unexpired term of a least for nineteen years, from Whitsunday, 1863. The distillery is presently at work, and may be seen in all its operations. Entry can be given to suit the views of intending purchasers. For further particulars apply to J. K. and D. Orr, 29, Waterloo Street; or to Macleod and Ralston, Writers, 205, St. Vincent Street, Glasgow."[152]

It is from Jura that the name Ardlussa was taken for their new Campbeltown project. James Sr was then joined by his brother George not long after the purchase to assist with running the new endeavour.

Rumours abounded that *"another large distillery was about to be erected in the neighbourhood of the Gallowhill for a Glasgow firm."*[153] In April of 1878 it was confirmed *"that James Ferguson & Sons, Cadogan Street, Glasgow – owners of Craighouse Distillery, Jura – had feued a piece of ground next to Glen Nevis Distillery."*[154] In 1879 the distillery was commissioned and received the following coverage in the 'Campbeltown Courier':

"The New distillery erected in Glebe Street by the Ardlussa Distillery Company, and which is to be called the Ardlussa Distillery, has now been so far completed as to admit of operations being commenced, and we understand that on Thursday the first grain was wet. The erection is in the form of an oblong square, having a frontage of three storeys, and extends 256 feet along Glebe Street. The following are the dimensions of the different parts of the work: - Two malt barns, with granary overhead, 165 feet by 48 feet; drying kiln, 48 feet by 42 feet.[155]

"There will be no sacks required for ground or unground malt, all being done by machinery and hoppers. The malt store is 42 feet by 48 feet, and the mash room underneath is of the same dimensions. The still house with tun room is 130 feet by 40 feet. Bonded warehouse along Dell Road, 210 ft by 60ft. There is only one pump in the distillery, which is used for pumping the worts up to the refrigerator. Everything else, which in many other distilleries in town requires to be worked by means of pumping, is here carried on by gravitation.

"This is unquestionably a vast improvement on the old system, and will be a great saving of labour and expense. The wash still is capable of charging about 3,200 gallons, and the spirit still 1,800 gallons. The engine in the works is 20 horse-power (nominal); and the boiler, which is perhaps the largest in town is 22 feet by 7 feet 6 inches. The smoke from the distillery is discharged from a chimney stalk reaching a height of 85 feet, a sufficient guarantee that the smoke emitted will not become a nuisance to the neighbourhood.

"The Excise and other offices required are commodious and suitable, while an excellent house for the manager and another

for a workman have likewise been added. All the internal arrangements and fittings have been constructed on the newest and most approved principles, and everything about the work reflects credit alike on the architect and contractors. This new distillery makes the twenty-second work of the kind in town; and it is estimated that, when the whole is in full operation, something like 50,000 gallons will be turned out per week. The contractors were as follows: - Messrs Neil Ferguson & Son, mason work; Mr C. Martin, joiner; Mr Andrew Griffen, engine and machinery; and Messrs Robert Armour & Sons, copper work."[156]

There is little trail for the firm of James Ferguson & Sons nor how they were able to afford both Jura Distillery (which required re-equipping post-purchase to the tune of £25,000)[157] and then the building of Ardlussa in fairly quick succession. Nor are there many details as to how the business grew and distributed the spirit from the two distilleries. We know that an Alex Ferrier of Port Bannatyne, Isle of Bute, worked as a 'traveller' or salesman for part of the period of the Fergusons ownership but how this arrangement was organised remains a mystery.

Along with Benmore Distillery, Ardlussa was the only other distillery to be built by outsiders to Campbeltown but it appears this was not of any concern to the Campbeltonian distillers. Ardlussa Distillery Co. are mentioned as part of the Campbeltown Distillers' Association throughout their period of operation and, as well as Ferguson being a common name in the burgh, it appears that James Ferguson & Sons were fairly benevolent to local concerns. James Ferguson was an early supporter of the Machrihanish Light Railway and was listed as one of the Directors when it launched in 1905.[158] The first Distillery Manager was James Murdoch, who in 1894, along with his wife, was presented with a marble clock, a set of studs and a gold brooch by 'Captain John Reid' (the oldest employee of Messrs James Ferguson & Sons) to mark their Silver Wedding Anniversary.[159] Graciously Captain Reid *"expressed the hope that Mr and Mrs Murdoch would be spared to celebrate their golden wedding."*[160]

Ardlussa was the final distillery to be built on what must have been the most congested distilling street in the world. Sandwiched in between Glen Nevis Distillery and Witchburn Road, the Ardlussa Distillery had little room to grow. Despite this, a new warehouse was erected in 1893 and it is evident the distillery was a successful enterprise. So much so, that in 1900 the company was able to employ Springbank's Manager, Alex Greenlees, as their agent. There appears to have been no ill feeling towards this appointment as J. & A. Mitchell presented Alex with a 'handsome gentleman's travelling case' in addition to a 'handsome present from the workmen at Springbank Distillery'.[161]

'The Wine and Spirit Trade Record' published the following account in 1905:

"Ardlussa, which dates from 1879, and owned by Messrs. James Ferguson & Son, of Glasgow, has two stills, holding 4,300 and 2,400 gallons respectively. Owing to the various altitudes at which the vessels are located, practically the whole of the operations are performed by gravitation, pumping being thus reduced to a minimum. The five wash-backs are large vessels, holding 12,500 gallons each, the malting floor has an area of 290 feet by 48 feet, and the kiln measures 48 feet by 48 feet. The manager here (Mr. James Murdoch) has been more than a quarter of a century with the firm."[162]

In 1910, the company changed the name of the business to James Ferguson & Sons Ltd., perhaps to align all of the assets of the business. Jura Distillery, which had hit hard times in 1901, eventually closed in 1911, never to re-open under the ownership of James Ferguson & Sons.

"In consequence to the long continued dry weather the water supply of the [Jura] distillery has failed, and the distillery season has been abruptly brought to a close several weeks earlier than anticipated."[163] Jura would not distil again until being rebuilt in 1960.

Bombardier David G. Lorimer succeeded James Murdoch

as Distillery Manager, before leaving to manage Glentauchers Distillery in Speyside. Lorimer, who was well-liked within the communities he had worked, was killed in Heuvelland, Belgium in 1917.

Ardlussa Distillery, in addition to many others, hit hard times during WWI and, in 1919, was sold to the West Highland Malt Distilleries Ltd, who also acquired the Scotia, Glen Nevis, Glengyle, Kinloch and Dalintober distilleries. James Ferguson Sr died on 1st November 1921; his short obituary was titled 'Distiller's Fortune':

"James Ferguson of the Knowes, Bearsden, and of Glasgow, distiller of Messrs James Ferguson and Sons, a director of the North British Distillery Company (Limited) and of the Campbeltown and Machrihanish Light Railway Company (Limited), who died on November 1 last, left, in addition to real estate, personal estate of the total value of £233,884 of which the personal estate in the United Kingdom amounts to £217,487."[164]

The West Highland Malt Distilleries experiment, despite having a good number of backers and being proactive within the market, was a short-lived affair, going into voluntary liquidation in 1923. Soon after, the process of off-loading all assets and liabilities commenced, with advertising for sale of the distilleries, including Ardlussa. Ardlussa escaped the ignominy of a forced sale at 'Public Roup'[165] as it was bought sometime in 1924 for £1,500 (despite having been valued at £4,205).[166] By this time, the distillery was silent, and the only value was in the warehouses for storing whisky under bond.

"For sale by Private Bargain, the following Distilleries situated at Campbeltown, Kintyre.
Glen Nevis Distillery
This is a substantial building fully equipped as a distillery. Area 1 acre, 3 roods or thereby. Ground Burdens, including redemption price of duplication of Feu-duty. £39 3s 6d per annum.
Glengyle Distillery

This is a substantial building fully equipped as a distillery. Area 2 acres, 1 rood, or thereby. Ground Burdens, including redemption price of duplication of Feu-duty, £62 16s 3d per annum.

Ardlussa Distillery

Substantial building partially equipped as a distillery but principally used as a bonded store and malting. Area, 1 acre 2 roods, or thereby. Ground Burdens, including redemption price of duplications of Feu-duty, £53 8s 4d per annum. Each property includes a dwelling house."[167]

A brief promise of activity was sparked with an article that appeared in the Campbeltown Courier in March 1936:

"New Company Formed to carry on Business of Bonded Warehouse Proprietors.

"A development which may be of great interest to Campbeltown has occurred with the formation of a private company, The Glen Nevis and Ardlussa Warehouse Limited.

"The subscribers to the company are Mr Samuel Thomson, Glen Nevis Campbeltown, Distillery Manager, and Mr Alexander Wright Gow, 200 Glencroft Road, Cathcart, Glasgow.

"The chief object for which the company is formed is to carry on the business of bonded warehouse keepers, blenders and bottlers. The Share Capital of the company is £5,000 issued in £1 shares. A considerable quantity of whisky has already been brought in, and further supplies are to arrive both from Islay and the North. It is hoped that when the new development gets underway, much employment will be provided for Campbeltown men in the way of blending and perhaps bottling."

This enterprise was also short-lived, and the last tenant was A. Gillies & Co., who purchased the remaining warehouses in 1955, along with neighbouring Glen Nevis Distillery (Glen Scotia Distillery had been acquired earlier in the same year). These warehouses remained in use up until the early 1970s when McFadyen's Contractors bought them and the site was levelled.

DISTILLERY HISTORIES

ARGYLL DISTILLERY 1844 – 1924

Little is known about the original Argyll Distillery, nor when the name changed from MacKinnon's Distillery. It is possible that the distillery was never named MacKinnon's but rather referred to as MacKinnon's distillery. Angus Martin, in his encyclopaedia, has almost certainly exhausted all available material as to the origins of the partners, and it is likely that the original partner can be identified from Angus's research: *"In Kilkerran graveyard, a Duncan MacKinnon died in 1835, aged 58. He is described as 'Distiller' on the headstone."*

This distillery, known locally as 'Wee Argyll' was built in 1825 at the Big Kiln on Lorne Street (although its malt barns were on Longrow). Wee Argyll was defunct by 1844 when the new Argyll Distillery was built on Millknowe, adjacent to Hazelburn Distillery. The original partners were Robert Colvill,

The washbacks of Argyll Distillery - as featured in 'The Wine & Spirit Trade Record' article in 1923.

Hugh Greenlees and Robert Greenlees Jr. When Robert Colvill and Hugh Greenlees retired the distillery was carried on by the junior partners, including Robert Greenlees who ultimately ran it on his own.[168]

After Robert retired, the distillery was sold to the firm of Greenlees Brothers who, after their father, Samuel's, retirement, had taken on the neighbouring Hazelburn Distillery. Although keeping the distillery on the smaller side, the new owners, operating as the firm Greenlees, Colvill & Co., embarked upon a series of steps to modernise the plant. 'The Wine and Spirit Trade Record' visited Argyll Distillery in 1905, describing it as *"a miniature model of Hazelburn, but with only one drying malt kiln and half the number of wash-backs,"* and again in 1923:

Argyll's spirit receiver - as featured in 'The Wine & Spirit Trade Record' article in 1923.

"Argyll is entered through the narrow old-fashioned yard that is so typical of the local distilleries, but one requires to walk only a few paces before discovering proofs of progress. Three years ago, men carried the ground malt from the mill-room and deposited it by hand in a mash-tun. Instead of that clumsy process a system of conveyors now does the same work. Similarly, the

draff used to be thrown out of the mash-tun by hand, but the installation of a large drainer (or No.2 mash-tun) enables the hot refuse to be pumped out, drained and passed through a chute to carts for removal to the drying plant. A special feature… is the upright Cochrane boiler, 16 feet high and 8 feet in diameter. This is the only boiler of its kind in Campbeltown, and it is fitted with a supply pump of the latest pattern, which feeds it with water at a temperature of 200°F."

This new boiler must have appeared like something out of a science fiction novel when it was installed (sadly, no photograph of this or much else inside the distillery was provided). The reporter also noted that the distillery had recently been fitted with electric light and storage batteries. Being one of the smaller concerns, Argyll had a capacity of 50,000 gallons and warehousing, 200 yards from the distillery, offered a capacity of 4,000 casks.

After the retirement of Samuel Greenlees Jr, the firm was reshuffled, and in 1919, Argyll Distillery briefly operated under the firm of Macdonald, Greenlees & Williams (Distillers) Ltd before being sold to Ainslie and Heilbron (Distillers) Ltd of Glasgow. It is unknown just how long the distillery continued to run after 'The Wine and Spirit Trade Record' article was published in March 1923, or if it was still in operation. Ainslie & Heilbron were swallowed up by the great purchasing strategy of the Distillers Company Ltd., and by 1929 the distillery had been emptied of its plant and machinery.

In 1930, the premises were bought from the Distillers Company Ltd by the Craig Brothers, who *"converted the property into a spacious and well-equipped garage and workshop."*[169]

BENMORE DISTILLERY 1868 - 1928

Benmore Distillery in 2005. The only distillery known to have adopted the Doig Pagoda above the kiln.

Perhaps as remarkable as the scramble for distilleries within Campbeltown was also that it took until 1868 for 'outside' investment to fully realise a distillery within the burgh. Originally called Bulloch & Co., the firm of Bulloch, Lade & Co., began in the spirits business having built the Dunochter Distillery in Dunbartonshire (now named Auchentoshan Distillery), in 1817. Several generations later, and having lost the influential William Robertson in 1855, who left to start the firm of Robertson & Baxter, Archibald Bulloch merged with D. Lade & Co., in which Archibald was already a partner (they also had adjoining offices in Glasgow)

Having purchased the land for the new distillery from a local merchant named Thomas Brown, the original partners of Archibald Bulloch (Archibald is listed as 'London' so may have been the agent for the business), William Carswell Lade, Matthew Bulloch and Robert Sutherland set about building what would be Benmore Distillery on the corners of Saddell and High Street. Once completed, Benmore joined the firm's other distilleries: Caol Ila Distillery, purchased in 1863; Camlachie Distillery, purchased in 1852 (renamed Loch Katrine in 1867); and the warehouses of the silent Islay distillery, Lossit, which were purchased in 1867.

John Carrick of Islay, was the original manager of Benmore who likely had to deal with the much-publicised exit of Dugald Mathieson, Clerk and Mashman:

"We hereby give notice, that Dugald Mathieson, for some time employed as Clerk and Mashman at Benmore Distillery, Campbeltown, is no longer in our Employment, and has no power or authority to represent us in any way. Bulloch, Lade & Co."[170]

"Public Sale of Superior House Furniture and Plenishing also, a 14-ft Pleasure boat with mast, sails and moorings (Belonging to the Trust Estate of Dugald Mathieson and sold by order of Thomson McLintock, Accountant, Trustee, 87 St Vincent Street, Glasgow). Robert McTear & Co are instructed to sell the above by public auction at Benmore Distillery, Saddell Street, Campbeltown, on Thursday 11th September, at Twelve o'clock prompt."[171]

[Three years later a 'Dugald Mathieson, fisherman' was fined for punching a fellow fisherman, Charles Durnan in a crowd on Longrow.]

In December 1881, a new warehouse was approved, which was likely built adjoining the neighbouring Highland Distillery. Tragically a local builder, John Morran, collapsed whilst building the warehouse. A sudden fit dropped Moran into a puddle and before help could arrive, he had drowned. Aged just 28, his widow 'came down on Tuesday and… a small sum of money was collected from a few benevolent friends in town.'[172]

Additional warehousing was built nine years later after the purchase of the estate of David Campbell, a publican and landlord on Saddell Street – 'at the upset price of £95'.[173]

It is curious that around this time a Benmore Whisky was

heavily promoted within India (Murray & Co., Meerut and Kara Distributors) that had nothing to do with Bulloch, Lade & Co. Given that they had almost certainly ruffled feathers with the Adelphi company who owned the Loch Katrine Distillery (before Bulloch, Lade & Co., renamed Camlachie Distillery, Loch Katrine) it is possible the infringement was ignored - a lesson learned in litigation.

Benmore's mash tun and under back - as featured in 'The Wine & Spirit Trade Record' article in 1923.

When James died in 1888 the distillery went to public sale. However, the distillery failed three times to make its reserve, having first been brought to sale at the Faculty Hall in Glasgow in October, with a reserve price of £6,500. As there were no bidders, a second attempt was made in November this time with a reserve price of £5,000. Again, there were no bids and the distillery went to auction for a third time:

"Burnside Distillery with a portion of the effects and fittings, and the goodwill of the firm, was exposed for sale at the Faculty Hall, Glasgow, on Wednesday last, at the upset price of £4,000 but failed to find a purchaser. The distillery was sold by private treaty the same evening to the firm of Greenlees Brothers, Hazelburn Distillery, of 'Lorne Whisky' fame for £3,500."[177]

In 1905, the distillery was visited by 'The Wine and Spirit Trade Record' which described Burnside as *"the most remote distillery from the town, being fully half-a-mile out on the road to Machrihanish – the famous golfing course on the shores of the Atlantic. This 'work' has a unique appearance from the road, being painted on a grassy slope, with its white-washed range of buildings and peaked warehouses forming a bright contrast to the sombre hues of the heather-clad mountain called Bengullion, immediately behind."*

Burnside suffered a slightly earlier fate than its peers when, after Samuel Greenlees withdrew from the industry, the distillery was closed and sold to United Creameries in 1919 for £4,000. This enterprise, which also purchased the site of the Meadowburn Distillery, ran under several names until 2019 when it was closed, and McFadyen Contractors purchased the site. The site was demolished in early 2025.

CAMPBELTOWN DISTILLERY 1817 – c.1921

Campbeltown Distillery is yet another distillery that leaves little trace of its existence – all research is hindered by having a distillery with the name 'Campbeltown'. John Mactaggart and his financial partner, John Beith, were the first enterprising pair to take on the illicit distillers, thereby breaking the two-decade absence of a licensed distillery in the burgh. That they came in for criticism is undoubted but they were certainly ahead of the game with regards to the Excise Act that would revolutionise the industry six years later. Mactaggart, listed as 'maltster', would have been an experienced distiller and Beith, noted as a 'banker' with the Renfrewshire Bank, was prepared to use his financial clout to bring to fruition a more modern attempt at distilling in Campbeltown.

It is a testament to their enterprise, that despite numerous distilleries being built after 1823, Campbeltown Distillery outlived so many and was still in operation in the 20th century. The 'Inverness Courier' listed the distillery in 1822 as making '4,905 gallons from 10th November 1820 to 10th November 1821'. Sadly, the 'Campbeltown Courier' was not in existence until 1875 and very little local news made any of the earlier newspapers thus the agreement between Beith and Mactaggart is lost but it is clear that John Mactaggart's son Charles was owner of both the Campbeltown and Union distilleries in 1835 - this is also the year that the tenant Hector Henderson, trading as H. & F. Henderson, went into sequestration.

After briefly trading as Charles Kelly & Co., having been acquired by Captain George Melville and Duncan McMillan, the firm then traded as the Campbeltown Distillery Co. Neil McNish began his career as a clerk and worked his way up through the company before being appointed a Director of the firm Messrs Stewart, Galbraith & Co., a position which he retained up until his death."[178]

When Barnard visited in 1885, he stated that the distillery was erected in 1815 although this is likely when building work began. Barnard also states that *"The distillery has undergone some changes since it was first erected, and some additions and machinery have since been added, nevertheless, nothing can take from the place its 'old-world look' and ancient appearance."* 'The Wine and Spirit Trade Record' visited in 1905 but afforded the distillery just two sentences:

"Campbeltown Distillery is one of the smaller works, dating from 1815. It has a mash tun 15 feet in diameter, five wash-backs holding 3,000 gallons each, and two small pot stills containing 1,400 and 960 gallons each."

The similarity and sparseness of this information makes one wonder if it was simply lifted from Barnard's report – certainly, the reiteration of the starting year of 1815 corroborates this. In 1888 the firm of Robert Hillcoat & Sons endeavoured to create *"the largest blend of whisky ever made in Scotland."*[179]

Included in the blend were a number of distilleries, including 'Campbeltown' but the likelihood is that this is not specifically from Campbeltown Distillery as malt from the region was referred to as Campbeltown spirit or malt. The article also lists whisky from Glenlivet and Tullymet - there was no distillery of that name at the time - demonstrating how ambiguous the research into individual distillery names was for the period.

Even so, it is worth noting that the blend required a vat that could contain 12,000 bulk gallons. Alas, it never occurred to anyone reporting on the giant production to record even a single brand name the blend was intended for.

Campbeltown Distillery was omitted from 'The Wine and Spirit Trade Record' review of all United Kingdom distilleries visited between 1922 and 1929. Therefore, we must date its closure prior to 1923.

It must have been quite a sight for Campbeltown Distillery to watch as distilleries were erected on all sides of its grounds. Its own expansion took it from Longrow to Glebe Street, wedged in by the Springbank and Rieclachan distilleries on either side of Longrow (Millknowe Road).

Anyone now taking the tour of Glengyle Distillery, which starts in the yard of Springbank Distillery, will pass the one remaining warehouse – a stone testament to the instigation of the industrial period of Campbeltown's distilling industry.

DALARUAN DISTILLERY 1825 – c.1924

Dalaruan Distillery was built on Broad Street, on the site of an earlier brewery established in 1770 by Orr Ballantine & Co. The distillery was named after the village it was built in, Dalaruan - meaning 'Field of the Red Place'. Built within touching distance of the larger Hazelburn Distillery but separated by the 'Town Burn' that used to run in parallel to Lady Mary Row.

Specifications for the distillery were drafted on 20th January 1824 for the roofing and joisting of the distillery building by architect Nathaniel McNair. While the distillery was originally intended to be established by Colvill Langlands, it was ultimately founded under the name David Colville & Co., named after one of its principal partners, David Colville, a lawyer and banker. Colville was also a key figure behind the Dalintober Distillery, and the partners included his father John Colville (a maltster), Charles Colville (a cartwright), Ralph Langlands (merchant), and Daniel Greenlees, who was also involved with the Hazelburn Distillery. The company's full list of founding partners thus reflected a combination of local business expertise and distillery experience.

In 1838, following the death of Ralph Langlands, John McMurchy purchased the share held by Langlands' estate, securing a significant role in the distillery's future. Under the Colville family's direction, Dalaruan Distillery expanded its operations, increasing its output and refining its processes. By 1877, the distillery had grown significantly, prompting the construction of a new two-story granary to accommodate the increasing demands of malt production. This was followed in 1893 by the addition of a new bonded warehouse, a crucial development to store the growing stock of whisky.

On 6th July 1896, a devastating fire broke out at Dalaruan Distillery, causing extensive damage to several of its key buildings. The fire engulfed the distillery's granaries, kilns, stores, and lofts, and for a time, 200 casks of whisky were at risk. The swift action of workers and the local fire brigade, including 50

'Bluejackets' from HMS Northampton, helped avert a total loss. Fortunately, the whisky casks were saved, though 900 bushels of grain were destroyed. The fire's destruction was significant but the damages were covered by insurance, allowing the distillery to recover and rebuild.

At its peak, the distillery had a distilling capacity of 3,400 proof gallons per week, with a malting capacity of 175 quarters of barley per week. Its bonding capacity was estimated at 500,000 proof gallons. A 1905 article in 'The Wine and Spirit Trade Record' highlighted Greenlees *"as a deeply knowledgeable figure in the local whisky scene, proud of Dalaruan's connection to the ancient Dalriads, the original inhabitants of Kintyre who had migrated from Ireland."*

In November 1905, the distillery saw a major technological upgrade when a new 10-ton boiler and its mountings were delivered for installation at the distillery. The equipment came aboard the S.S. Pirate and was built by Messrs Wilson of the Ladybank Boiler Works, Glasgow.

Unfortunately, in 1908, tragedy struck when Charles Colville Greenlees, the Managing Director and grandson of the original founder, passed away. After Charles' death, the distillery continued operations under new management but faced mounting challenges.

In 1925, it was announced that the distillery's assets, including its substantial stock of whisky, would be sold:

"The property of David Colville & Co Ltd, with frontages to Broad Street and Mill Street, and extending to three acres or thereby. The buildings, which are stone built, include two kilns with maltings, a mash tun of about 14 feet in diameter, a still-house with a wash still with a capacity of 4,027 gallons (including the head), and two other stills. There are also capital duty-free warehouses and the appropriate office stores and other appliances of a distillery and malting.

"There will be included in the sale the loose tools and utensils,

and the following empty casks: - 39 puncheons, 218 hogsheads, 114 quarters, and 7 octaves.

"Distilling capacity, 3,400 proof gallons per week. Malting capacity, 175 quarters barley per week. Bonding capacity, 500,000 proof gallons or thereby.

"The water is derived from public sources at a cost of 3d per 1,000 gallons and from an adjoining burn. Assessed rental temporarily fixed at £450. Ground Burdens, £6 per annum. Casualties redeemed.

"It will be open to the purchaser to arrange to take over Customers' stocks at the distillery amounting to 46,000 proof gallons or thereby.

Upset Price £15,000."[180]

There were no buyers and by 1931, the distillery was demolished. Tragically, during the demolition, a wall collapsed, killing 20-year-old Charles Stalker from Millknowe. The site is now entirely given to housing, whilst a kite-shaped park is situated in the heart of what would have been the old distillery.

DALINTOBER DISTILLERY 1832 – c.1923

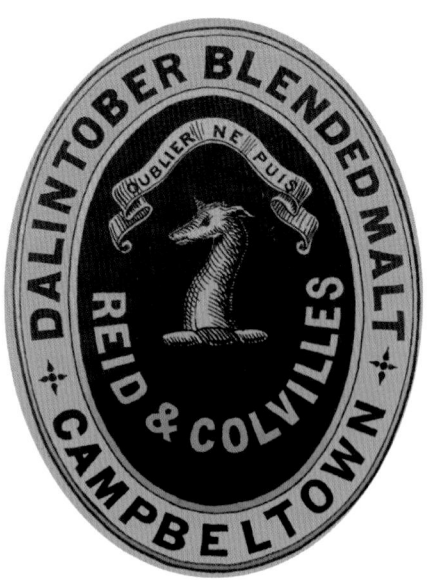

DISTILLERY HISTORIES

The distillery was founded by the partnership of Reid & Colville, which included Peter Reid, a Glasgow merchant and the son of Hugh Reid, a cooper by trade, David Colville, a writer, and Archibald McCorkindale, the son of Bailie Duncan McCorkindale. Dalintober Distillery was built on John Street in Campbeltown and named after the village of the same name. The name means 'Field of the Well' - a reference to the natural spring that contributed to the distillery's water supply.

The 'Glasgow Herald' published an advertisement on 7 January 1867, noting that Dalintober Distillery, along with the goodwill of the established Reid & Colville business, was for sale. The distillery, situated on roughly three-quarters of an acre, was capable of producing 1,300 gallons of spirit per week, with potential to expand production to 3,000 to 4,000 gallons. The kilns were described as 'commodious and in perfect working order', enabling immediate production. The Colville's continued running the business.

This period marked the peak of Dalintober's early success, and the distillery's operations were known for their quality and efficiency. The firm had built strong connections, via Reid, within the whisky trade, establishing itself as a trusted name.

In the years that followed, ownership of the distillery passed to the sons of David Colville—Duncan and David Jr. The business was rebranded as 'Reid & Colvilles'. In December of 1899 the distillery suffered a catastrophic fire with the damage estimated at £4,000.

"A rather serious fire took place early on Sunday morning, 17th December, at Dalintober Distillery, Campbeltown, belonging to Messrs Reid & Colville. The alarm was given soon after four o'clock. By the time the Corporation hose, in charge of Firemaster McCallum, was on the ground, the fire had got a good hold, and it was quite evident that the distillery buildings, comprising millroom, maltstore, mashhouse, stillhouse, and tunroom, were doomed. The wind, which was blowing strongly

from the south-east, made the works of destruction very rapid, and fears were entertained that nothing could save the adjacent distilleries, Lochruan and Scotia, as well as the many duty-free warehouses in the immediate neighbourhood. Fortunately, the efforts of the firemen were successful in preventing the fire spreading, and thus, although the damage done is serious enough, an appalling catastrophe such as might have happened had those duty-free warehouses caught fire was averted.

"Coming at this season of the year, the inconvenience caused by the fire will be very great. The premises were covered by insurance. Much activity was shown by those engaged in extinguishing operations, and to their exertions, assisted by an excellent supply of water, the localising of the fire is due. The Campbeltown distiller have reason to congratulate themselves on the immunity they have had from any very serious fire for many years past." * January 1900

A visit to the distillery in 1905 by 'The Wine and Spirit Trade Record' noted the picturesque view of the distillery from the park and described the distillery's three stills: of 3,300, 1,080, and 1,070 gallons' capacity, as well as six washbacks, each holding nearly 8,000 gallons.

Following the death of David Colville in 1916 (leaving an estate of £39,618), his surviving partner, Duncan Colville, continued to manage the business. After Duncan's passing in the same year, his estate valued at £15,247, the trustees of David Colville appointed Peter Dewar to manage the affairs of the business. Dewar oversaw the distillery until November 1919, when it was sold to West Highland Malt Distilleries.

By 1923, Dalintober Distillery had been taken over by W. P. Lowrie & Co., owners of the neighbouring Lochruan Distillery. However, Lowrie's use of Dalintober was limited to the malting floors and warehousing rather than to continue whisky production. By 1926, it was reported that some 600,000 gallons of whisky were stored at the site.

In 1936, land formerly occupied by Dalintober Distillery and now owned by Scottish Malt Distillers (a subsidiary of the Distillers Company Ltd) was compulsorily purchased through the Housing (Scotland) Acts of 1925 to 1935. A housing scheme was approved in 1938, covering the site of both Dalintober and the nearby Lochruan Distillery, with an estimated cost of £24,000 for the development. Those houses offered splendid views over Kinloch Park and Campbeltown's harbour. I should know, having bought and lived in one of the flats. Now, the buildings stand derelict and condemned – a sad chapter on what was such an industrious part of the town.

GLENGYLE DISTILLERY 1873 – 1924
RE-OPENED 2004

A violent argument about sheep led William Mitchell to fall out with his brother John and ended William's time at Springbank Distillery. This broke a near 35-year partnership and caused William to build Glengyle Distillery just 500 yards along from his brother's distillery. The brothers had bought Springbank Distillery in 1837 from William Reid, Jr & Co. In 1873, it was noted by the 'North British Daily Mail':

"Operations are shortly to be commenced at the west end of the Roading for erecting a new distillery premises for William Mitchell, Esq, for a long time one of the partners in the firm of J. & W. Mitchell in the Springbank Distillery, Longrow. The work is to be on a pretty large scale. Mr Neil Ferguson, builder, has obtained the contract for the mason work."

Glengyle was noted in 1905 as having two stills holding 4,000 and 2,000 gallons, respectively. The six washbacks had a capacity of 6,600 gallons each. At the time of the visit, Hugh Mitchell, the son of the founder, was Provost (Mayor) of Campbeltown. Mr Mitchell, we are informed in the article, *"holds strongly by the conviction that blended whiskies should be sold as such and not passed off as fine Highland malt. At the same time, he readily admits that grain whisky improves with age."*[181]

William's two sons joined the firm; William Jr having left school and Hugh having spent a number of years working for James Watson & Co, iron merchants, in Edinburgh. When William Sr died in 1887, aged 68, the sons took control and tragically when William Jr's poor health took him at the age of 43, Hugh ran the business on his own.

In 1897 new warehouses were erected adjacent to the Roading (part of the walls of one of these remain). Hugh Mitchell lost his only son Willie during WWI, having been shot down and contracting pneumonia as a prisoner of war, aged just 19. Hugh was a tireless campaigner for the region and was noted in his obituary by the author as having *"never met anyone keener to do and sacrifice in the interests of Campbeltown's prosperity or more ready stoutly to defend its honour than ex-Provost Mitchell. He was a perfervid patriot as far as Campbeltown was concerned all his life, and nothing grieved him more than the depression which has touched his native place so sorely."*

When the West Highland Malt Distilleries Co., was launched, Glengyle's future was for the first time taken out of the family control with its purchase in 1919. This new venture did not last long and when, in 1923, the company went into voluntary liquidation, Glengyle, along with Glen Nevis and Ardlussa distilleries were put up for sale. Incredibly, Glengyle changed hands for just £350.

Over the next 80 years there were three more attempts to revive the distillery. Firstly, in 1940, the Bloch Brothers acquired the buildings and promised a full renovation. Their timing could not have been worse as the Ministry for Food curtailed almost all distilling activities during the war. The second attempt, in 1957, seemed more plausible as the firm Campbell Henderson, wholesale wine and spirit merchants, submitted plans to Campbeltown Town Council to revive the distillery – costing £250,000 'as a modern distillery, which would be a model of its kind'. Despite the Town Council using their powers of compulsory purchase, it was reported that 'The District Valuer has failed to reach an agreement with the proprietors of Glengyle Distillery for the acquisition of the property'.

In 1960 the buildings were bought by Kintyre Farmers who were a local co-operative. The buildings, then fell into disrepair being a preferred spot for pigeons to congress and discharge. That was until Hedley Wright, the great-great-nephew of William Mitchell acquired the buildings. Under the careful management of Frank McHardy, J. & A. Mitchell's Distilleries Manager, the buildings were restored and new plant was fitted (albeit some of it second hand). Hedley Wright returned Glengyle Distillery into the family firm and also shone a much-needed spotlight on the Campbeltown region – which now, importantly, had three distilleries to boast about.

GLEN NEVIS DISTILLERY 1877 – c.1923

Being part of the last great flurry of distilleries built in the 1870s, Glen Nevis was afforded greater exposure than either Glengyle that came a few years before, or Ardlussa that was built two years later. In a rare moment of disclosure, the 'Campbeltown Courier' (20th October, 1877) allowed us a glimpse into the new works:

"This new distillery, erected by Messrs D. McCallum & Co in Glebe Street, is now all but complete, very little requiring to be done to put it into fair working order. The first stone of the new work was laid on the 15th of March last, and it is certainly creditable to the contractors that the various portions of the structure were pushed on so rapidly and yet so substantially, as that by Tuesday last the first wetting of the barley took place. The whole building has been only about seven months in construction. The Glen Nevis is the twenty-first distillery in town, and as will be seen from the following description its dimensions are not much behind any of the other large works in town, and we understand

when in full working order it will be capable of producing 4,000 gallons weekly

"The erection is in the form of an oblong square having a frontage of 3 storeys in height, extending 260 feet along Glebe Street. The following are the dimensions of the different parts of the work: - two malt barns with granary overhead, 130 feet by 36; drying kiln, 36 feet square, fitted with a malt measure, which is so arranged that no bushel is required for measuring the dried malt. The malt store is 36 feet by 30, with grist room and mash-house underneath. The still-house with tun room extends at right angles to the last-named building 120 feet, and at the corner is situated the spirit store, office, and mashman's house. The wash-still is capable of charging about 3,000 gallons, and the spirit still 2,000 gallons, being the largest in town. All the internal arrangements and fittings have been constructed on the newest and most improved principles, with a view to give as little labour as possible to the workmen, as well as to insure good work.

"The engine is 18 horse-power (nominal), and the boiler is a very large one, being 20 feet by 7. The chimney stalk reaches an altitude of 80 feet, so that the smoke from it will not be likely to become a nuisance. The whole erection is covered with a substantial slate roof, and certainly gives a fine appearance to this part of the town. The first malting, as already stated, took place on the 16th instant, and Messrs McCallum expect to have their produce in the market in a short time. The contractors were as follows: - mason work, Mr Neil Ferguson; joiner work, Mr Charles Martin; copper work, Messrs R. Armour & Sons; engine and machinery, Messrs R. McNair & Sons; smith work, Mr Andrew Griffin."

Built by Duncan MacCallum, who also appears to have been the sole director, Glen Nevis had additional warehousing erected the year following its construction. This was not uncommon as new distilleries built up maturing stocks. More unusual, however, was the sale of the distillery to The Scotch Whisky Distillers Limited in 1887. The directors of the new firm included several distillers, although not Duncan MacCallum. Of the five well-known distilleries, *"The present proprietors of four of the Distilleries are advanced in years, and one of them has very bad health; they are therefore desirous of retiring from the sole active management of the respective Distilleries."*

Although the Scotch Whisky Distillers Limited was a short-lived affair, it did allow us this humorous interaction that was printed in the 'Scottish Wine, Spirits and Beer Trades Review' shortly after the new firm had been announced. Mr D. P. Macdonald, of Long John's Ben Nevis Distillery stated in a letter date 2nd May, 1887:

"I find a great deal of confusion has arisen about my business and this new company, 'The Scotch Whisky Distillers (Limited)', with which I have no connection at all, and it is only fair that this should be known to the public. Glen Nevis, one of the five distilleries concerned, is a Campbeltown work, the name a fancy one, as the glen itself is about 100 miles from that place, and close to the mountain of Ben Nevis from which my pure Highland malt whisky, Long John's Ben Nevis, takes its name. The similarity of names is, to say the least, misleading."

As the directors of the new company were mostly industry veterans, there was evidence of some history, or 'niggle', within the reply that was published on 14th July:

"In your last issue our good friend, 'Long John', gives a cheering account of his season's business. The merry way he blows his own trumpet is amusing. He never misses any chance of keeping his 'brew' before the public. One time it is a letter to the 'Scotsman' on the growing evil of blending grain with fine spirit; at another, when a 'Glen Nevis Distillery, Campbeltown' is included in a Distillery Company, he writes in order that shareholders may not be 'deceived' by supposing this whisky to be his 'Mountain Dew'. According to Inland Revenue rules, every distillery must have a name, and Mr McCallum when he erected his distillery at Campbeltown in 1877 selected the name

'Glen Nevis', there being no other distillery of that name. Mr McDonald erected his new distillery in 1878, and called by the name of the river passing the work 'The Nevis', in contradiction to his other work 'The Ben Nevis'.

"The joke is that he infers that Campbeltown is not in the Highlands, and that its whisky has no claim to be classed as a Highland whisky, and that really the only two Highland distilleries are his own. The fact is that Highland whisky was made in Campbeltown, and celebrated, too, many years before 'Ben Nevis' was thought of.

"The popularity of Campbeltown whisky accounts for the number of distilleries now there, but the competition has reduced the price, and 'Long John's' would be no higher if 'Ben Nevis' were surrounded by half the number of distilleries at Campbeltown. Many whiskies are puffed till they are over-rated, while others of equal quality are under-rated. I may say, in passing, that the 'Scotch Distillers Co.' is fortunate in having a variety of whiskies: - The Dean and Gleniffer, two excellent malt, the Glen Nevis, a good Campbeltown, the Ben Wyvis, which can be made the finest 'self' whisky in Scotland and the Glendarroch, a whisky similar to the best of the 'Islay' which, notwithstanding Mr McDonald's remarks, will always stand the first rank of stylish whiskies.

Yours, etc
Little John"

The new company, in spite of, or perhaps due to, the backing of The Royal Bank of Scotland, did not last long and two years later was advertising their liquidation - no doubt allowing an element of schadenfreude for Mr Macdonald at Long John.

"The Scotch Whisky Distillers Limited, in liquidation.
Sale of four well-known Scotch whisky distilleries by tender, by order of the Chancery Division of the High Court of Justice: -
Lot 1. Ben Wyvis Distillery, situated in Dingwall, near Inverness. One of the finest distilleries in Scotland. Held permanently upon payment of a Feu-Duty of £40 13s 10d per annum.
Lot 2. Glen Nevis Distillery, situated at Campbeltown, to the

County of Argyle. One of the most modern and complete of the celebrated distilleries at Campbeltown. Held permanently at a Feu-Duty of £37 11s 7d per annum.

Lot 3. The Dean Distillery situated at the Water of Leith, Edinburgh, Held permanently at a Feu-Duty of £60 per annum.

Lot 4. Gleniffer Distillery, situated at Paisley. Held under a Lease, of which, about fifteen years are unexpired, and a rent of £79 per annum, as to which it is believed that shortly a Feu will be granted."[182]

The Glen Nevis filling store circa 1922. The casks state West Highland Malt Distilleries.

By 1891 MacCallum was operating under the name of Stewart, Galbraith & Co Ltd having acquired the Scotia Distillery in 1891 (the original firm for Scotia being Stewart, Galbraith & Co) from the liquidators. MacCallum also had a controlling influence in the Benromach, Glen Albyn and Glendronach distilleries.[183]

Glen Nevis then went through considerable alteration and modernisation. In May of 1905 The 'Wine and Spirit Trade Record' noted that *"here was an apparatus for regulating the draught of the kiln furnace. It is worked automatically by means of two brass rods which expand and contract according to the heat, and so open or close a swing-door in front of the fire. The result is an equable temperature produced without any attention on the part of the stoker.*

"There are two kilns at Glen Nevis, one measuring 40 feet by 400 feet, and the other 36 feet by 36 feet. The water comes from below and above the grain – mainly from below, so as to rouse and aerate it. Two waters are always used, and sometimes three, if the barley be unusually dirty. The time the barley remains in the steep depends on the quality of the grain and the time of year – generally from 50 to 60 hours.

"English and Scotch barley require more time in the steep and on the growing floor than foreign grain. In the mash tun no less than four different waters are used; the first two going as wort to the receiver, the third going back to the heater to be used as the first water for the next mashing, and the fourth being used to enable the draff or grains to be pumped to the draff drainer, this fourth water being used as the second water for the next mashing. There are two stills at Glen Nevis, the larger one having a capacity of 3,200 gallons, and the smaller one, 2,350 gallons."

Stewart, Galbraith & Co., went into voluntary liquidation in December 1921 and Glen Nevis Distillery then formed part of the firm West Highland Malt Distilleries Ltd. This firm also entered into voluntary liquidation two years later and in 1924 Glen Nevis was sold for £500. Much of the machinery went to Ian Hunter at Laphroaig whilst, along with the Ardlussa warehouses, were combined in a new venture, Glen Nevis and Ardlussa Warehouses Ltd in 1936. Subscribers of this new firm were Samuel Thomson, previous Glen Nevis Distillery Manager, and current Manager of Scotia, along with Alexander Wright Gow of Glasgow.

Gillies & Co., bought the warehouses in 1955 and they remained in use as bonded warehouses until the 1970s when McFadyen's Contractors bought them, levelling the site shortly afterwards. Duncan MacCallum died, having drowned at Crosshill Loch, on the 23rd December 1930. He left an indelible mark on the Campbeltown community, as was shown by the incredible turnout to his wake. He also died a wealthy man, leaving an estate of £284,000 (£15 million ATTOW). His lengthy obituaries included the following:

"The death of Mr Duncan MacCallum, distiller, East Cliff, Campbeltown, which occurred on Tuesday, 23rd December, cast a gloom over the Christmas season in our community such as it has seldom known. He was a notable townsman, known and esteemed by Campbeltown people wherever they may be, and in the business world a personality to all with whom he came in contact.

"During the war years Mr MacCallum left instructions with the stewards of the Campbeltown Steamers to provide with dinner on board at his expense, every serviceman travelling home or returning on leave from overseas."

GLEN SCOTIA DISTILLERY 1832

It would be unfair to refer to Glen Scotia Distillery as the 'other' Campbeltown malt to survive the mass closures of the 1920s. The truth is that both Springbank and Glen Scotia clung on, at times by their fingernails, and for several years both were completely silent. Scotia Distillery was built around 1832 but it would appear the true date of commencing distillation was in 1835. There is some contention as to whether Scotia is older than Springbank.

The original firm of Stewart, Galbraith & Company, consisted of James Stewart, John Galbraith, James Napier, William Galbraith and John Colville (the latter two holding one-eighth shares each, whilst the others were equal partners with 25 per cent each). By 1864 Alexander MacKelvie had been made a partner.

In 1841, land was acquired to expand the distillery, which was said to resemble a 'maze of old buildings' as late as 1891 when the distillery was bought by Duncan MacCallum (owner of Glen Nevis Distillery). The firm of Stewart Galbraith was changed into a limited company, the additional directors being Colonel

Thomas Brown and Neil McNish.

The new owners set about to completely modernise Scotia and in June 1897 it was reported *"Last year the 'Scotia' was practically reconstructed, and we hear that further additions are to be made to the same distillery this season."*[184] In 1898, the 'Campbeltown Courier' stated that neighbouring houses had to make way to construct the four-storeyed premises that stand to this day. *"The ground and second floors will be used as duty-free warehouses, while the upper floors will serve as commodious maltings and granary loft."*[185]

When visited by 'The Wine and Spirit Trade Record' in 1905, it was reported that, *"At Scotia, there are three stills. In 1897 this distillery was practically reconstructed, but so anxious were the proprietors not to interfere with the character of the spirits that they retained the principal vessels and the stills."*

In 1919 Duncan MacCallum sold his distilling interests to the new firm of West Highland Malt Distilleries Ltd, which he headed. A few years later, 'The Wine and Spirit Trade Record' returned as part of their tour of the entire United Kingdom.

"Not many yards from the site of the original Parliament House built by Fergus is Scotia Distillery, in recent years acquired by the West Highland Malt Distilleries, Ltd., and although erected as far back as 1832, it can compete successfully with most of its neighbours. The introduction of modern improvements, however, has not stolen from Scotia its air of tranquillity, and about the solid old buildings, almost hidden from the eyes of curious strangers on the roadway, there is an indefinable atmosphere that takes one's mind back to the days when smuggling was the staple industry of Kintyre."

The manager at the time of the visit was Mr Hardie, who had 40 years' experience having moved from the north-east to Campbeltown. The visit also coincided with the commissioning of *"six new wash-backs, each vessel having a capacity of about 6,000 gallons, as compared with the old backs which held only 4,000 gallons. Other additions to the distilling plant include a new pump and engine drives, and a draff-drainer. The machinery is worked by a vertical steam engine of 12 h.p. There are two pot-stills, the wash still of 2,600 capacity, and a spirit still containing 1,900 gallons. Both are heated by a furnace. The fuel is peat, followed by coke... with a staff of twelve men the output would normally be 3,600 gallons."*

The new firm lasted just two years before the distilleries were put up for sale. Scotia, probably due to its renovations and higher esteem for the quality of whisky, fetched the highest price of £2,500 – this was still a long way from either what had been spent on it, or its market value (in 1924 it was valued at £7,733 for rate purposes).[186]

The new owner was almost certainly Mr Duncan MacCallum, although it appears he may have leased the distillery, or at least contracted the spirit production, to a John and James Buchanan of Glasgow and London who eventually traded as Scotia Distillers Ltd before going into liquidation in 1936.[187]

In November of 1930 it was noted that despite there having been *"good prospects that at least one Campbeltown Distillery – Mr Duncan MacCallum's 'Scotia' – would work this winter... we regret to learn that owing to the state of the market the project has been abandoned, and it is certain that all our effective distilleries will remain 'silent'.*"[188] It could be suggested that MacCallum, someone who had thrived and hugely benefited from the Campbeltown distilling heyday, felt acutely the total desolation of the industry as every distillery went silent. His unexpected death a month later, was a total shock to all, and there were a great many who knew and admired him,

In late 1933, Scotia Distillery was sold by MacCallum's trustees to Bloch Brothers, a blending firm based in Glasgow. This signalled the end of a prolonged silent period as 92 tons of Australian barley was delivered to the distillery late in the year. Perhaps believing that all blenders preferred those makes prefixed with 'Glen' (or perhaps, like Mackie at Hazelburn, in an attempt to distance the spirit from 'Campbeltown'), the Bloch Brothers renamed the distillery Glen Scotia in 1935.

Under their stewardship the distillery was given a second (or third or even fourth) lease of life. In 1958 Hiram Walker (Scotland) Ltd., the Scottish division of the large Canadian distilling firm that had moved into the UK market after the Second World War, bought Bloch Brothers. This brought Glen Scotia distillery into the company's portfolio, which included the large grain distillery Dumbarton and the Glencadam Distillery.[189]

However, the very next month a new consortium called A. Gillies & Co, founded by Sir Maurice Bloch, bought Glen Scotia and the Glen Nevis and Ardlussa warehouses.[190] In 1970 the distillery changed hands once again, this time being taken over by the Amalgamated Distilled Products (ADP). The distillery had fallen into serious decline and was rebuilt, albeit sporadically, over four years, and costing £500,000 until it re-opened in 1977.

The new developments included a pre-heating system which could help cut the length of part of the process to half an hour instead of a week, a new mash-house and the most up-to-date distilling plant and equipment installed throughout. All of the existing warehouses had been extensively refurbished and new warehousing facilities developed.[191]

Despite ADP's Chairman, James Gulliver, stating in an ad

taken out in 'The Scotsman' (7th July) 1983 that *"We are well positioned to continue our development,"* eleven of the twelve staff at Glen Scotia were made redundant in September of the same year. In 1987, the Argyll Group, part of the ADP, sold Glen Scotia to Barton International Ltd (later Gibson International Ltd). The new owners had no immediate plans to re-open the distillery but in 1989, having been silent for five years, the distillery recommenced distilling.

In 1994, the distillery once again changed hands, having been bought by *"The Loch Lomond Distillery Company from the receiver who were called in after Gibson International disposed of their interest in the Campbeltown distillery."*[192] Like an unloved and abandoned pet, Glen Scotia moved from owner to owner until finally, and really only in the last decade or so, it has been given the spotlight to shine. The quality of its distillate – it makes great whisky – is perhaps why this often-forgotten gem survived when so many failed, and its scarred and bruised history is in every single bottle. I once lived next door to it and could smell the moment it started operating. At the time, it was just ticking over, like a rare car in a garage, as one of the Hector's, on loan from Springbank, would rev up the engine and kick out some dust.

GLENSIDE DISTILLERY 1835 – 1926

The first glimpse any traveller by road would have had of Campbeltown's distilling industry, prior to its demolition in the 1930s, was Glenside Distillery. Situated almost at the corner of Millknowe Road and Dalaruan Street, Glenside was described as being *"one of the most picturesque buildings in Campbeltown. The curious old-fashioned offices… have a quaint charm of their own, and they contain a fascinating little fireplace of which has been copied by visitors from all parts of the country."*[193]

The original firm of David Anderson & Co, was partnered by David Anderson, merchant; James Armour, maltster and Manager of the Campbeltown Gas Company and Miss Jessie Miller. In

1836, Joseph Hancock joined the firm and in 1844 Mr T. Wilkie also gained an interest in the firm.

By 1845 the distillery was up for sale:

"The Glenside Distillery, Situated near Campbeltown, with Malt Barn, Mill, and other buildings, and all utensils connected with the works. The distillery is in complete working order, has an ample supply of good water, and is capable of distilling, in each period of 10 days, from 900 to 1,000 gallons of excellent whisky. The working utensils consist of two copper stills, copper boiler, mash tun, ten fermenting backs, two spirit vats, and a number of casks. The malt barn is commodious, and the ground will admit of the premises being greatly enlarged if necessary."[194]

On 10th October, 1849, the new owners then dissolved their co-partnery and the business was *"carried on by the subscribers, Hugh Ferguson & James Armour under the same firm."*[195] James Armour died on 10th January 1865, and as Hugh Ferguson agreed to retire, the company was dissolved.

On 24th September 1866, J. K. Orr, described as 'distiller in Campbeltown and Jura and merchant in Glasgow', signed a contract of co-partnery with his brother Daniel, to carry on the Glenside Distillery Co.

Ten days later J. K. Orr died and in 1870 the contract became the subject of a Scottish Court of Session action, Orrs Trustees v Orrs. In this action Dugald Campbell Macintyre was identified as the Manager of Glenside, on an annual salary of £100, and from 1867, a partner in the Glenside and Jura firms. In 1878, a feu contract was signed by John MacIntosh Orr, Margaret Kerr Orr, William Jarvie Orr and Robert Louis Orr.[196]

In 1876 a journalist writing for the 'Renfrewshire Independent' having been 'kindly shown the entire process of distillation minutely explained', was given a sample to try.

"We were kindly invited to taste a sample of the fine 'Glenside',

and though we do not pretend to be a great judge, yet we have seldom or ever tasted finer, and a fellow could easily partake of a few halves of Glenside without having occasion for B & S [Brandy and Soda] in the morning."

The distillery staff of Glenside Distillery in 1921 with resident cat.

New warehouses were erected in 1878 and 1894 – likely the ones that sat adjacent to Dalaruan Road. In 1908 a new firm, Glenside Distillery Co Ltd., was formed; subscribers were Duncan MacCallum and J. Duff, distiller, Glasgow along with J. Robertson and Thomas W. Dewar.

By 1921 Robertson & Baxter, the large blending firm, had a controlling interest but the distillery remained trading as the Glenside Distillery Co Ltd. Despite the association with MacCallum, Duff, Dewar and the firm of Robertson & Baxter, all who backed the West Highland Malt Distilleries Ltd, the distillery was not made part of the group.

In February 1924, 'The Wine and Spirit Trade Record' published an article on the distillery but omitted any current directors or partners in the firm:

"The premises, covering two acres, are entered under a

narrow stone archway, and reaching the main building one notices many modern improvements that have been introduced since the distillery changed hands in 1908."

The author noted a new drainer for receiving the draff, pumped up from the mash-tun, and the abolition of the old 'fanners', which formerly did the work now more efficiently accomplished by refrigerators. A 'Neil's' patent rocking bar kept the fuel in the furnace from 'caking'.

"A striking feature of some of the older Campbeltown distilleries is the manner in which additional plant and accommodation have been cunningly built into the original structure without overcrowding the premises. In Glenside, for instance, a new storey was recently added to the tun-room to provide space for depositing the malt above the mash-tun, yet there is no sign of congestion, although the distillery is literally crammed to the roof with necessary apparatus... weekly output is roughly 2,800 gallons.

"The distillery is fortunate in having a splendid water supply, coming from a neighbouring loch known by the tongue-twisting name of 'Aucholochie', which might be recommended to police surgeons as a good test of sobriety."

Robertson & Baxter went into voluntary liquidation in January of 1923, and whilst the firm of Glenside Distillery Co Ltd., remained, it too entered into voluntary liquidation in 1930. A year later, in September, the liquidators of the distillery *"offered the site occupied by the Glenside and the Highland Distilleries, now dismantled, with the material, standing thereon, except such part of as had been disposed of, to the Town Council as a gift to the town. The feu duty on the whole ground is 3 guineas per annum."*

Today, the entire two-acre site is occupied by housing, part of which is suitably called 'Glenside'. Just a small part of an original warehouse wall remains that signalled the apex of the side of a warehouse that neighboured Dalaruan.

HAZELBURN DISTILLERY 1825 - 1925

    The original site of Hazelburn Distillery, built in 1825, was on Longrow, but due to increased production, the distillery moved to Millknowe in 1845 (in essence, a move further up the road). The original partners were brothers Mathew & Daniel Greenlees and Archibald Colvill, the son of Charles Colvill, founder of the Dalaruan Distillery, built in the same year as Hazelburn.

    Around 1845, Archibald Colvill left the firm and Samuel Greenlees, Mathew and Daniel's cousin, joined the business. Samuel, a local farmer, had married his first cousin Agnes (the sister of Mathew and Daniel) in 1840. The original name of the firm, Greenlees & Colvill remained until being sold out of the Greenlees family in 1919.

    The business prospered and in 1858, Daniel and Samuel purchased the 300-acre estate of Moy. When Daniel retired in 1881, Samuel was able to take full control of the distillery and the estate:

"The fine estate of Moy, in the neighbourhood of Campbeltown, was on Friday offered for sale amongst the joint proprietors, and became the property of Captain S. Greenlees of Hazelbank. The distillery business of Greenlees & Colville, Hazelburn Distillery, Campbeltown, was also disposed of privately at the same time, and was likewise purchased by Captain Greenlees."[197]

Hazelburn was 'considerably enlarged' in the summer of 1863, making its capacity the largest in Campbeltown.[198] In 1878 a *"petition, with relative plans, for the erection of a duty-free warehouse on the grounds of Hazelburn Distillery, belonging to Messrs Greenlees & Colville, was produced, and, after being examined, permission was given to proceed with the erection."*[199]

Hazelburn was considered the showpiece of the Campbeltown distilleries. Not only was it the largest, but it also received the most coverage in the trade journal and books. When Barnard visited, the distillery received pride of place, as was the case in the two visits by 'The Wine and Spirit Trade Record' in 1905 & 1922. Barnard noted the distillery was capable of producing 250,000 gallons a year, although the season of his visit (1884-1885, the distillery had produced 192,000.

Samuel Greenlees' two sons, James and Samuel Jr left the family firm in 1871, heading to London having started the firm of Greenlees Brothers the year before. Samuel Sr was an original Director of this new firm, and his sons found early success with the launch of 'The Connaught Irish Whiskey', and the 'Lorne Highland Whisky'.

When Samuel Sr passed away in 1886, Samuel Jr returned to Campbeltown to continue running the distillery. Samuel Jr acquired the Argyll Distillery, shortly after his return in 1887, before adding the Burnside Distillery to the company fold in 1888.

In his May 1897 letter, OMIC informed the readers that *"Last year the Scotia was practically reconstructed, and we hear that further additions are to be made to the same distillery this season. The Hazelburn [Distillery] (Greenlees & Colville, Ltd) was also added to last year, and the electric light introduced. A large general warehouse is this summer to be erected by the same firm having a frontage to Long Row and extending back to Kinloch Road. The site is presently occupied by shops and dwelling-houses, which have to give way to the requirements of the trade. It is an expensive process, however, and rather hard on distilleries who charge no warehouse rent."*

During much of its operation, the day-to-day running was controlled by William McEwing. Having joined the company as a young man, McEwing, who stayed loyal to the firm for more than 40 years, was appointed as Company Secretary and 'looked after the whole of the organisation and supervised the rebuilding of the distillery'. In 1905 a new boiler and fittings were delivered by S.S. Pirate for the distillery. At 18 tons it was the largest, and heaviest boiler ever landed at the quay.

In 1902 McEwing was made a Director and was given £1,000 'in consideration of my long and faithful services at Hazelburn Distillery'. This gift would have been sufficient to have bought one of the larger two-storey houses within the town. McEwing accompanied James Dunlop, Kinloch Distillery Manager, when he was called to the Select Committee in 1891, such was his esteem within the Campbeltown distilling community.

McEwing died unexpectedly aged 59 in 1907.[200] He was remembered as possessing *"a thorough knowledge of every branch of the industry, and was acknowledged to be one of the ablest and most practical managers in broad Scotland, in addition to being a man of rare business acumen."*

In 1919, just a few years after the death of James Greenlees, Greenlees & Colvill Co Ltd, which included Hazelburn Distillery, was sold to Mackie & Co Ltd (who shortly afterwards, renamed the firm White Horse Distillers Ltd. Led by the enigmatic and quite brilliant Sir Peter Mackie, White Horse Distillers embarked on a complete renovation of the distillery and revolution of the distilling practices. Mackie, who had already achieved success bringing Lagavulin to a wider audience, struggled to convince the blenders of Hazelburn's new and improved quality and the distillery was put up for sale in 1921:

"Greenlees & Colvill, Limited (In Voluntary Liquidation). For sale, Hazelburn Distillery, Campbeltown. This distillery, together with General Warehouses, feu-duties etc, in full working order as a going concern is offered for sale by private tender in one lot, including all sales and contracts: date of entry will be 31st December 1921. Sealed offers to be lodged on or before 11th November 1921."[201]

Hazelburn Distillery and neighbouring Argyll Distillery circa 1900.

The distillery failed to sell and Mackie was left pushing the whisky, with ever reducing prices, right up until his death in 1924. The distillery went silent sometime in either 1925 or 1926. In 1927, White Horse Distillers was taken over by the Distillers Company Ltd, and as part of their program to reduce production, Hazelburn's plant was removed and the distillery closed for good.

The once state-of-the-art laboratory, installed during Mackie's tenure, was utilised until the 1970s by the Scottish Malt Distillers, and the warehouses remained in use for maturing Islay whisky by United Distillers (part of the Distiller's Company Ltd), until 1988. In 1990, United Distillers PLC gifted the distillery to the Campbeltown & Kintyre Enterprise Trust. Although only the original offices, dwelling house and malt barns exist, all having been converted to offices, the building remains as one of the best-preserved distilleries within Campbeltown.

KINLOCH DISTILLERY 1824 – c.1923

What began as maltings, established as far back as 1792 (and almost certainly aiding the not-so-legal local distillers), was converted into Kinloch Distillery in 1824. Situated at the corner of where Longrow and Lochend Street meet, the distillery bordered the Mussel Ebb. In November 1823, Alexander Dunlop applied to the Duke of Argyll's chamberlain for an extension of his father James's lease of ground near Longrow in order to build a distillery.

The original firm of Lamb, Colvill & Co., consisted of partners James Dunlop, Robert Lamb, writer, and John Colville Jr, banker with the Clydesdale Bank. After the death of Robert Lamb in 1826, Robert Ralston, of Glenramskill Distillery, joined the firm. Ralston died in 1840 and his one-third share passed to his relatives. When John Colville passed away in 1851, Robert's son, David Ralston, offered Colville's trustees £700 for his interest in Kinloch Distillery.

James Dunlop was said to be sole partner of Lamb, Colvill & Co., when he died in 1901. He became a partner after the death of his father in 1871, and was described as Managing Partner by Alfred Barnard when he visited in 1885. Dunlop died in 1901 and received the following obituary in the December issue of 'The Distillers' Magazine'.

"The death of Mr James Dunlop, Managing Partner of Messrs Lamb, Colville & Co., Kinloch Distillery, which took place here on 5th November, removes one of the shrewdest and one of the best known of the Campbeltown Distillers. Succeeding his

father, with whom he had been for many years previous to the death of the latter associated in the management of the business, Mr Dunlop had a thorough practical knowledge of distilling, and under his supervision many alterations were made and improvements introduced at the distillery with which he was connected. Although never a very robust man, Mr Dunlop took a deep interest in all pertaining to his native place, and held many public positions of trust and responsibility which he ably filled. He had been laid aside from business for about six months, and although his many friends had hoped for his recovery, his death was not altogether unexpected. Mr Dunlop, who was unmarried, was 66 years of age at his death."

Tragically less than two years later, James' brother Robert was discovered in the Campbeltown Harbour. *"The night was wet and stormy, and [Robert] is supposed to have stumbled over the pier in the darkness."*[202]

After James Dunlop's death, the trustees of the firm appointed David Colville as manager having been a distiller at Cameron Bridge Distillery in Fife. When 'The Wine and Spirit Trade Record' visited in May 1905, they clearly had used up too much copy on Hazelburn (and telling tall tales about Kintyre in general), giving the distillery just a few sentences:

"The buildings occupy a site of two acres, extending from the (Kinloch) Park to Long Row. There are three stills, containing 2,000, 1,400 and 1,000 gallons respectively."

In 1919, the firm of Lamb, Colville & Co., was bought by Thomas L Brown, acting for West Highland Malt Distilleries Ltd. Perhaps the final official visit, as a going concern, came in 1923 as 'The Wine and Spirit Trade Record' continued their tour around the United Kingdom. At the time, it was noted that Kinloch Distillery was acting as the *"headquarters of the West Highland Malt Distilleries Ltd; Kinloch, Scotia, Glen Nevis, Dalintober, Glengyle and Ardlussa. The group is under the direction of Mr Duncan MacCallum, formerly of Messrs Stewart, Galbraith and*

Co Ltd., who has been associated with the trade in Campbeltown for some 45 years.

"Like most of the Campbeltown distilleries, Kinloch has an old-world air, although the appliances in use are up to date and in splendid condition. The grain germinates on three concrete malting floors, and there is one kiln floored with tiles.

"Peat is the principal fuel, and fifteen hundred bushels of malt are mashed each week. The tun room is a model of efficient arrangement. Three large receivers with gauges and indicator stand side by side; above them is the wash-charger, holding 5,224 gallons, and at the further end of the room are six washbacks, each with a capacity of 7,400 gallons. A picturesque detail is the old-fashioned windowed recess in the whitewashed walls containing the spirit safe."

Kinloch's Spirit Safe - as featured in 'The Wine & Spirit Trade Record' article in 1923.

After the voluntary liquidation of The West Highland Malt Distilleries Ltd in 1923, Kinloch became the property of Duncan MacCallum and it is unlikely that the distillery continued distilling much afterwards, if it was producing at all. In 1928, MacCallum gifted the land and buildings to the Town Council. Writing a letter, that was printed in the 'Campbeltown Courier', MacCallum stated:

"I am naturally anxious for the development and amenity of the town, and if my proposition is agreeable to the Town Council I would be prepared to hand over the property (retaining only the utensils etc therein), free from any encumbrances and without consideration of any kind."

Today stands the second incarnation of the houses that were built on the land that once occupied Kinloch Distillery. New flats replaced the old brick and stone tenements that were erected in the 1930s - what stands now is a modern and desirable development that looks over Kinloch Park and Campbeltown Harbour.

KINTYRE DISTILLERY 1830 – c.1920

Kintyre Distillery is yet another of the works that very little is known about. Constructed in 1830 on Broad Street (now known as New Parliament) the original owner was John Beith, banker, having helped finance Campbeltown Distillery and was at the time a partner in the Longrow Distillery. Kintyre was noted as the first distillery to have gas pipes fitted in 1831, from the newly built gas works.

When John Beith died in 1840 a new co-partnery was commenced in the name of Beith, Ross & Co., partners being John Beith Jr, merchant, John Colville Jr, Clydesdale Bank and John Ross, distiller.

A fire broke out in the distillery in March of 1875, and despite alarmist headlines such as 'Destruction of Kintyre Distillery by Fire'[203] in truth only the malt barn and kiln were destroyed. The damage, although covered by insurance was £225, including 190 bushels of barley that were lost.

In 1876, the company changed to John Ross & Co., which also incorporated the Longrow Distillery. Although, supposedly visited by 'The Wine and Spirit Trade Record' in 1905, the distillery was only afforded one sentence: *"Kintyre (John Ross and Co.) is another of the smaller distilleries, with three stills, however, and a compact set of buildings."*

Little more is known about the distillery other than it being offered in 1926 by a Mr R. W. Greenlees, on behalf of Messrs John Ross & Co (John Ross had died in 1886 – the business had been carried on by William and James Greenlees) to the Campbeltown Town Council. The asking price requested was for £100 *"which sum is to be handed in its entirety to the Campbeltown and District Cottage Hospital."*[204]

LOCHHEAD DISTILLERY 1824 – 1928

What was once arguably the most striking distillery in Campbeltown, was also built in one of the most commanding positions. When first erected in 1824, Lochhead Distillery was a ramshackle of old buildings. The original firm was A. & R. McMurchy with the founding partners being Archibald, a lawyer, and Robert who died in 1831, less than a decade after the distillery's completion. After Robert's death the new partners with Archibald were Donald Andrew, coppersmith and James Taylor, mason.

In 1833, ownership changed to William Taylor & Co, comprising father and son James and William Taylor. James died in 1847 and William in 1851, leaving his brother, Archibald, in charge of the business. By 1854 the distillery was advertised for sale by private auction. The package included: The distillery 'in full operation', comprising still-house, two malt-barns, two bonding warehouses, malt-mill house, counting house, stable and an extensive stock of casks. The distilling capacity was estimated at from 1,300 to 1,400 gallons a week. There was a copious stream with the premises which supplied water for the distillery, as well as water-pipes which had been recently fitted up and could be continued or not as the owner may incline. The sale also included a dwelling-house of two stories, with attics and a piece of vacant ground, with a frontage of 86 feet extending for 160 feet to the sea. The site contained a 'commodious bonded warehouse, a garden, and a stock of empty casks, but would be a very eligible stance for building purposes'.[205]

In 1857 a public notice anonymously announced the distillery was under new ownership but traded under the same name until 1895 when it was sold to J. B. Sheriff & Co Ltd. Campbeltown's proliferation of distilleries meant there was little end to the attempted thefts of whisky and in 1876 ten feet of gas pipe were stolen from the Lochhead Distillery and used as a syphon to steal whisky from Glenside Distillery.[206] One can only assume the gas pipe was not cut from the line that fed the distillery from the gas works.

In 1896, Mr Moir, a merchant in Belfast was advertising a 'Special Blend' of Campbeltown and Islay Pure Malt Whisky:

The Blend of Thirty Years Ago.
"Mr Moir having visited these districts lately, purchased from J. B. Sheriff & Co. 6 Hogsheads Lochhead Distillery Malt and 2 Hogsheads Lochindaal Distillery Malt, bonded in 1890, and now transferred to H.M. Customs, 'Stack C' Belfast.
"These whiskies are made from home-grown barley only, thereby ensuring that aroma and flavour so well known to connoisseurs of Scotch Whisky.
"I guarantee that there is nothing but these two whiskies in the blend."[207]

J. B. Sheriff began an extensive program of modernising and expansion: *"owing to the congested state of the old work, business facilities have been considerably hampered, and the alterations have become a necessity."*

The entire frontage of the works, from Lady Mary Row to Parliament Lane, were demolished, and in its place was easily one of the most impressive buildings that the distilling trade had added to the burgh.

"The buildings facing Lochend Street will be four storeys in height, and built probably of Kilkivian and Ballochmyle red stone, with turreted corners, and finished in accordance with the requirements of such an important thoroughfare. Altogether,

judging from plans just passed by Dean of Guild Court, the structure will be artistic and prove a handsome addition to the architectural features of the town. The kilns will be in the courtyard of the distiller, disconnected from the main block of buildings, and are to be of the most approved type. The Inland Revenue and general offices of the company are to be close to entrance gates and in keeping with the rest of the work. The architect is Mr Clifford from plans supplied by the firm."[208]

When 'The Wine and Spirit Trade Record' published their 1905 article, they noted that Lochhead was *"now one of the best equipped distilleries in the town, its maltings being imposing and quite modern; in fact, they are not yet finished, but will in the course of another year be considerably extended. Unfortunately, the firm are hampered for room here, so that they have to go off the ground for warehouse room. Their largest warehouse is in Saddell Street, and holds over 4,000 casks – say 380,000 proof gallons. The distillery is now one of the largest in the town, its mashing capacity being 2,000 bushels per week. Several years ago, the mash tun and stills were increased to twice their original size. The latter now have a capacity of 5,000 gallons for the wash one, and 2,500 gallons for the low wines one. Throughout the 'work' the utmost care is taken to ensure cleanliness and the production of a superior article, the object being to procure a soft, sweet but full-flavoured spirit. Preferably a large proportion of peat is used to Welsh anthracite coal."*

J. B. Sheriff sold out to J. & P. O'Brien sometime in 1920 who soon after entered into liquidation and were themselves bought out by the Benmore Distilleries Co., owners of the Benmore (Campbeltown), Lochindaal (Islay) and Dallas Dhu (Forres) distilleries. When 'The Wine and Spirit Trade Record' returned to highlight Campbeltown distilleries again in 1923, they afforded Lochhead quite a few column inches. The writer was certainly impressed by the finished works:

"In 1870 pressure of business doubled its size, and again in

1898 the maltings were remodelled, and a large warehouse added. Today the distillery is one of the largest and finest buildings in Campbeltown, overlooking the bay, and flanked by handsome red-brick turrets that give an artistic finish to the old-fashioned premises. Purchased in 1920 by the Benmore Distilleries Company, who have spared no effort to introduce modern methods and machinery, the distillery has an output during the average season of over 100,000 proof gallons of Campbeltown Malt Whisky. The water supply comes from the Crosshill Loch."

The distillery went silent sometime in the late 1920s, and very little is known of what purpose, if any, the impressive buildings were used for. In the late 1980s, the entire area, including the Lochend Church, was demolished, and the once magnificent, architecturally-inspired, and prominent buildings were replaced with a Tesco's complete with a car park. I very much hope, that, say in one hundred years, no historian is compiling a list of the supermarkets of Campbeltown. Or of any town.

The four-storey front of Lochhead Distillery. What was the grandest facade of any distillery in Campbeltown. Circa 1900.

LOCHRUAN DISTILLERY 1833 – 1925

An artist's impression of Lochruan Distillery. It is fanciful as ignores most of the buildings to its right side.

It must have appeared, at least to anyone from outside the burgh, that there were specific locations within Campbeltown that offered a supreme advantage to distillers of whisky. Perhaps a sort of 'Ley line' or supernatural advantage given to one location over another – even if just yards apart. Glebe Street would have been one such area of wonder to any traveller passing the numerous distilleries on either side of the street, and certainly, the almost four-acre, rectangular site in the village of Dalintober would have been another.

Lochruan was built on the corner of Princes Street, with its main entrance on the High Street. Dalintober Distillery sat behind it with the views over the harbour, and Scotia was the next-door neighbour. The original firm of Johnstons & Co., were partnered by two brothers, Robert and Charles Johnston with James Johnston joining in 1847.

In the same year, the firm signed an agreement with Buchanan,

Wilson & Co., Glasgow whisky agents who had acquired Ardbeg Distillery in 1838. This agreement granted the firm exclusive rights to all whisky produced at Lochruan. By 1st November 1848, Lochruan had been converted over in security to the Glasgow agents.[209]

Robert Hunter later took over the distillery in 1856 when it was claimed to be the largest in town. Despite the new owner, the firm still traded as Messrs Johnston & Co. In 1870, the company entered into litigation against a Dundee trader named James Blackwood Anderson. Allan Anderson, one assumes a member of the family, had been the acting agent, working on behalf of Johnston & Co., and was accused of 'absconding' with funds:

"The nature of the agency was that Allan Anderson should take orders for whisky, collect accounts as they fell due, and remit the amounts thereof when paid to the pursuers... At the time of his absconding, he was owing to the pursuers the sum of £345 1s 6d..."[210]

The firm of James Blackwood Anderson went bankrupt in 1871, with their books showing assets to be £732 15s and the liabilities £4,108 13s 7d.[211] It is unknown if Johnston & Co., received anything from the failed firm.

Lochruan Distillery appeared to be a prime target for whisky thefts and one of the most daring occurred in June 1871 when, John McFadyen, a distillery workman *"was charged with the crime of theft, by taking from a pipe leading from the still to the spirit safe in the Lochruan Distillery to which he got access by boring a hole in the pipe, about half a gallon of whisky."*[212] Crime did not pay back in the late 19th century and for this petty offence McFadyen was sentenced to three months' imprisonment.

In 1865 the distillery was bought by William McKersie and immediately went through a period of renovation – circumstances that led to the jail sentences, with hard labour, served by Daniel Mitchell (six months) and Daniel Robertson (four months) for the theft of '127lbs weight of copper or other metal, 30lbs solder and two copper-padlock covers' from the site.[213]

In 1879, new warehouse plans were also approved. Further

alterations were made, including, in 1909, the proposal of a revolutionary new still that was either never installed, or did not last long at the distillery.

RULES & REGULATIONS

TO BE OBSERVED BY

THE WORKMEN

AT

Lochruan Distillery.

I.—No Person shall be entitled to leave his service until after the expiry of fourteen free Days after he has given Notice to that effect, nor shall the Employers be entitled to Dismiss any one without a similar Notice, unless in the case of Misconduct, as aftermentioned.

II.—Absent from the Work during Working Hours (except in the case of sickness), without leave obtained, shall be visited with a Fine of Two Shillings, or instant Dismissal, in the option of the Employers.

III.—If any Person is found, without permission, taking Liquor out of any Cask, Utensil, or Vessel, or concealing or away-putting of Liquor with a theftuous purpose, he shall forfeit One Week's Wages.

IV.—If any Person shall be found to be the worse of Liquor, he shall be fined Two Shillings and Sixpence.

V.—If any Person is found in the Cellars, Warehouses, or any other part of the Premises where Liquor is kept, except in the course of his duty, and with the Knowledge of his Employers, he shall be liable to a Fine of One Shilling.

VI.—Smoking in any part of the Premises is most strictly prohibited. Any one failing to keep this Rule shall be fined One Shilling.

VII.—All Quarrelling or Fighting shall subject the Offender to a Fine of Two Shillings and Sixpence.

VIII.—No Stranger shall, on any account, be admitted into the Distillery without the consent of the Employer.

IX.—Every necessary Assistance to be given and utmost Civility shown to the Inland Revenue Officers; and the Orders of the Manager and those in charge of the several Departments must be rigidly obeyed.

X.— In event of any violation of the above Rules, it shall be in the power of the Employers instantly to dismiss and discharge the offender, without warning or payment of Wages due at the time, which, in that case, shall be held as forfeited,—any law or practice to the contrary notwithstanding.

XI.—Any Fines which may be enforced under these Regulations shall be paid over once a year to some Charitable Institution in the Town as may be named by the Employers.

PRINTED BY R. WILSON, JR.

'The Wine and Spirit Trade Record' noted that W. McKersie & Co., were still owners in 1905, and that the Lochruan spirit still was 4,500 gallons capacity and the two spirit stills were 'about 1,850 gallons each'. In 1920, W. P. Lowrie & Co. Ltd., acquired the business (this was a subsidiary of Buchanan & Co.) and were owners in 1923 when the 'Wine and Spirit Trade Record' returned to cover the Campbeltown Distilleries once again (see Appendix E).

Despite installing several modern alterations, Buchanan's, along with its subsidiary W. P. Lowrie, were acquired by the Distillers Company Ltd., in 1925, and the distillery was closed immediately. The entire site, along with that of Dalintober Distillery, was converted into housing that now sits derelict, awaiting demolition.

LONGROW DISTILLERY 1824 – c.1888

Built between the Lorne and Lowland Parish Church (Longrow Church), Longrow Distillery was a small group of buildings built close to the main commercial and residential parts of Campbeltown.

The original firm of Colville, Beith and Co., with partners John Colville Jr, banker, Clydesdale Bank, John Beith, banker and John Ross, distiller. In 1852 after the death of Colville, the firm became Beith, Ross & Co., partners being John Beith Jr, John Ross and John Galbraith who replaced Colville. This partnership was dissolved in 1876, and the two distilleries within the firm, Kintyre and Longrow, were sold by private auction.

Beith and Galbraith were bidding against Ross, who secured the distilleries for £8,010 and, probably, due to needing the financial commitment incurred by the purchase, brought another partner William Greenlees into the new firm of John Ross & Co.

The resulting split caused a great deal of acrimony and litigation at the end of the year. The affair became highly publicised as John Galbraith v John Ross. Ross, who was a noted character and story teller (and known for his piety) took much displeasure in the 'Campbeltown Courier's' coverage. The dispute, which centred over how the capital worth had been derived and monies divvied, cause Ross to write:

"I believe that both Mr Beith and Mr Galbraith are plentier of money just now than ever they were. The money that they have among their hands at present they got very easily, and it appears they do not grudge to lay out some of it in advertising the case, but whether they are laying it out judiciously or not time will tell. What their object is in giving it to the public is not easy to see. To give such rubbish to the public at a time when their minds ought to be occupied with something of infinitely more importance, to say the least of it, is greatly absurd."[214]

In such a small community, Ross's words would have been sensational and no doubt added to the bitter affair being the talk of the town. Ross died on the 3rd March, 1886, aged 84, his estate was valued at £12,394 (around £1.3m ATTOW), his obituarist in the courier noted diplomatically:

"Mr Ross was born and brought up, lived and died in Campbeltown. When a lad he learned the trade of mason, but, when quite a young man, he commenced malting and distilling, and, for more than half-a-century, he has been one of the most active and successive distillers in town. Mr Ross had a great amount of individuality of character, frequently indulged in versifying and in other modes of writing, and took an interest in movements for the benefit of the community."

After Ross's passing, the distillery passed to his surviving partners, James and William Greenlees although it is unlikely that the distillery was producing much, if at all, from his death onwards. In 1930, most of the buildings were purchased by Archibald Watson, noted as a painter, and in 1971, J. & A. Mitchell, whose Springbank Distillery was situated not more than 50 yards opposite, acquired the remaining buildings. These were converted into a warehouse and bottling facility. The yard is now the Springbank Distillery visitor's car park.

RIECLACHAN DISTILLERY 1825 - 1934

Rieclachan (often spelt Rie-clachan) was built at the start of Millknowe Road (the 'Head of Longrow') and part of the large expanse of distilleries with Glengyle and Campbeltown as neighbours - the latter's warehouses situated behind Rieclachan, on Glebe Street. The original firm of Wylie, Mitchell & Co., with original partners Archibald Mitchell, distiller, James Ferguson, cooper and maltster, John Harvey and Alex Wylie (of Toberanrigh Distillery).

Following James Ferguson's death in 1860, his share of the business was sold to Archibald Mitchell. By 1869, James Harvey, son of John, was Managing Partner. James died aged just 51, and in 1881, after his death, the distillery was bought by Archibald Mitchell's son William, of Glengyle Distillery.

William Mitchell died on 22nd December 1899. His obituarist wrote of him fondly as being, *"Highly esteemed in the trade and honoured and respected by the workmen. His loss will be keenly felt by these, while the members of the community will also regret his demise, as he was of a kindly genial nature. A personal favourite with all ranks, his popularity was unsought."*[215]

When 'The Wine and Spirit Trade Record' published their 1905 series of articles on the Campbeltown distilleries, Rieclachan was described as a *"smaller 'work', its two pots still have a capacity respectively of 2,139 and 1,600 gallons."*

When the 'Record' returned in 1923, they afforded the distillery more than a solitary sentence noting that *"a narrow path leading to Rieclachan Distillery, [was] a picturesque old building erected in 1825."*

It was stated that with all of the changes of companies and conglomerations, it was *"One of the two privately-owned distilleries in Campbeltown, Rieclachan has retained its primitive appearance, although certain additions have been made at intervals in order to cope with increased business. The buildings are so well protected from the prying eye of the outside world, and, as a visitor remarked thirty-five years ago, the seclusion of the premises was evidently designed to guard the secrets of making good Malt Whisky… Home-grown or Danish barley is used, and the fuel is Welsh anthracite coal (brought from Cardiff) and peat. Eleven hundred bushels are dealt with at each mashing and fermentation is carried out in six wash-backs. Two pot-stills of 2,434 and 1,800 gallons' respective capacity produce a normal weekly supply of 2,200 proof gallons."*

The 'other' privately owned distillery was Springbank Distillery, also in the hands of Mitchells, and the 'visitor' mentioned was Alfred Barnard, who included Rieclachan in his 1887 book. Being privately owned by Hugh Mitchell stayed the closure of Rieclachan. Mitchell continuously kept open, or re-opened the distillery, after forced closures, and through the depressed times of the early part of the 20th century. Whenever the distillery was operational during each season of the 1930s, the announcement was deemed newsworthy. In 1932, the 'Campbeltown Courier' stated:

"It is reported that ex-Provost Mitchell intends to begin full-time work at the Rieclachan after the New Year. Such an eventuality depends of course, upon whether sufficient supplies of barley will be available.

"The Rieclachan Distillery, at the head of the Longrow, is one of the oldest in the town, having been opened over eighty years ago. It has been referred to more than once as 'Campbeltown's Leading Distillery'.

"On many occasions, ex-Provost Mitchell has earned the gratitude of many workers in the town by his efforts to keep this distillery active."[216]

An illustration of how well the Mitchell owners treated their staff appeared in the reporting of the death of James Sillars:

"A native of the burgh, Mr Sillars commenced his working life as a draper, but after a year or two, he changed his occupation to that of clerk in the Rieclachan Distillery, being three years with the original firm before the distillery was acquired by the late Mr William Mitchell, the father of the present proprietor, ex-Provost Hugh Mitchell. It is a notable fact that Mr Sillars' father

was mashman in Rieclachan up to the time of his retirement as an old man, so that the service of father and son with the same employers is a notable and outstanding record.

"Altogether, the late Mr James Sillars was 56 years in the Rieclachan Distillery. It was not only a remarkably long record, but it was characterised by faithfulness, efficiency and conscientious attention to business such as was not uncommon with many of his generation."[217]

Hugh's only son, Willie, had died from pneumonia as a prisoner of war in 1916, so when Hugh, due to ill-health, retired around late 1933, he appointed his daughter, Helen, as distillery manager. This was relatively novel and possibly unique in the industrial era of distilling in Campbeltown. It is worth noting that women were heavily involved in the distilling of small, privately, or co-operatively owned stills before the industrialisation in the early part of the 19th century.

Speaking in 1934, Hugh Mitchell said *"Helen took her B.Sc. at Glasgow University and for some years was a lecturer at a London agricultural college. Last winter she came home for a holiday, and during that time my manager fell ill. She gave up her London job and did his work. He died, and now I am only too glad to have her as manager. As my son was killed in the war, I am pleased that she is able to carry on the family tradition."*[218]

Hugh Mitchell died on 10th February 1935. Rieclachan Distillery closed shortly afterwards, and by May 1936, the buildings were in the ownership of the Craig Brothers, who converted much of the site to suit their West Coast Motors business. All of the buildings have since been demolished and, like the once magnificent Lochhead Distillery, the town benefits from a supermarket on the site. Helen Mitchell stayed in Campbeltown and continued her father's efforts in aiding the local community by joining the Town Council and later, as Bailie Mitchell, becoming the first woman to sit on the bench in a burgh court.[219]

SPRINGBANK DISTILLERY 1828

Springbank's wash still - as featured in 'The Wine & Spirit Trade Record' article in 1923.

Springbank Distillery was built in 1828, although it is likely distillation likely did not begin until 1830. Whilst the premises stretch along Glebe Street, access is more commonly from Well Close, off Longrow. The original firm of William Reid, Jr & Co., with partners William Reid Sr, maltster, William Reid Jr, grocer, and John Reid, distiller.

The Reid's tenure did not last long as they immediately entered into financial difficulties. Included in the fifty-one creditors were the builders of the distillery and plant, McNair and Armour, and £285 to the commercial bank (allowing us an insight into how these distilleries were funded). The business was then sold by public auction and bought by J. & W. Mitchell, of whom the partners were brothers John and William Mitchell.

The Mitchell brothers fell out over a disagreement about sheep, and William left in 1871. This forced the sale of the business.

"Springbank Distillery, Campbeltown, has been sold to Mr John Mitchell, one of the former partners, for £5,055, the upset price being £3,500."[220]

John Mitchell, now sole owner of the distillery, brought his son Archibald into the business, changing J. & W. Mitchell, to J. & A. Mitchell - as the firm remains to this day.

The distillery was hit by several storms over the years. The worst, in 1884, levelled Springbank's smoke stack. Another storm, in 1904, ripped the roof off of the mash tun house. In 1890, Archibald's brother, Alexander, who was Managing Partner of Springbank, was sequestered but this appears to have been a minor issue as was able to pay off all debts and continued as partner.[221] In 1897, J. & A. Mitchell was incorporated into a Limited company.

"The capital of the company is £24,000, divided into 2,400 shares of £10 each, of which 1,200 are preference and 1,200 ordinary shares. The first directors will be Archibald Mitchell, Alexander Mitchell, Robert Dickie, John Bennett Wright, and Timothy Warren, Glasgow. The qualification of a director shall be the holding of preferences or ordinary shares of the nominal value of £100 in all."[222]

John Mitchell died in 1892 with an estate valued at almost £40,000 (over £4 million ATTOW), and the business passed to his sons, Archibald and Alexander. Archibald died in July of 1903 after tragically falling from a hay stack aged 58.

When 'The Wine and Spirit Record' reported on Campbeltown in 1905 it noted Springbank *"is one of the older works in the town,* dating from 1828. It has three stills – one of 4,000 gallons and two of 1,700 and 1,300 gallons respectively." The final Mitchell to run Springbank, Alexander Mitchell, died in December 1912 at his house in Glasgow.

When the 'The Wine and Spirit Trade Record' returned to cover Campbeltown again in May 1923, slightly more coverage was given to describe the distillery and its activities:

"Entering the premises, which cover ten acres of ground in the heart of Campbeltown, one looks in vain for the signs of age that might be expected in such an old distillery. The premises, with the exception of the warehouses, are lighted by electricity, the cobblestones that used to pave the yard in former days have been replaced by smooth concrete, and the dazzling cleanliness of the whole distilling apparatus and machinery makes it look as though it had been newly installed. Across the yard from the comfortable offices is the still-house, with three pot stills of 4,000, 1,700 and 1,000 gallons' capacity.

"Early this year these stills were fitted with 'wheeling flue', which distribute the heat evenly around the circumference of the vessels, thereby effecting a considerable saving in fuel. Another modern touch in the still-house is the arrangement by which the spirit, worts, wash and feints' pumps are worked by one horizontal engine of 16 h.p., so that there is no longer any need for subsidiary machinery. The compactness and efficiency of the electric generating plant are also notable features, and there is a second powerful steam engine for driving the revolving gear in the mash-tun. Seven large wash-backs, a wash charger of 5,000 gallons capacity, a refrigerator, and the usual receivers, complete the equipment of the still-house and tun-room.

"The distilling process at Springbank is similar to that of the other local distilleries. There are two barley lofts and four malt floors, each a hundred feet long by forty-four wide. The two kilns are floored with English perforated tiles, and the enclosed furnaces are fed mainly with peat from the vast moorlands in the neighbourhood of the town. In the mill-room is a mill, old in pattern, but extremely modern in regard to grinding capacity.

Although it has been in use for over sixty years, this mill can grind 1,600 bushels in five hours. Stretching fifty yards behind the distillery are eight warehouses, whose capacity would be conservatively estimated at seven thousand casks. Slate roofing is being added to these buildings.

"In a good season the average production of malt whisky is roughly 100,000 gallons, and most of the spirit is shipped to Glasgow. The water supply comes from the Crosshill Loch, which feeds most of the Campbeltown distilleries."

When Rieclachan closed in 1934, Springbank and Glen Scotia were the only remaining distilleries in Campbeltown. Scotia's survival, whilst no less remarkable than Springbank's, has a lot less to do with commitment to previous generations and the burgh itself. Gordon Wright, the grandson of John Mitchell and nephew of Archibald and Alexander Mitchell, continued the family link to the distillery. His father was a Glasgow merchant, and his mother was Martha Mitchell, youngest daughter of John Mitchell.

When Gordon passed away in 1960, the firm passed to Hedley Wright, John Mitchell's great-grandson. When Hedley Wright passed away in 2023, the firm of J. & A. Mitchell was run without a direct relative to the founders for the first time in its nearly two-hundred-year existence. The firm has been left in three trusts to continue operating and endeavouring to benefit the Campbeltown community.

SPRINGSIDE DISTILLERY 1830 – 1926

Springside Distillery was founded in 1830 by John Colvill. Colvill, often referred to as 'The Saddler' due to his origins as a saddle-maker and leather cutter in Burnside Street, established Springside Distillery after years of involvement in the whisky trade. Colvill was a man of diverse interests and talents, having previously been listed as a director of Burnside Distillery, which had been founded in 1825.

Springside's warehouse in May 2005.

In 1858, Colvill made a significant acquisition, purchasing the Machrihanish Estate for £12,300 (equivalent to approximately £1.3 million today). Just two years later, in 1860, he acquired the Muasadale Estate for £20,150 (roughly £2 million today) from Captain Fleming, a former naval officer who had served under Admiral Horatio Nelson.

Colvill expanded the distillery's facilities and infrastructure, including the construction of a three-storey warehouse in 1899 to meet growing demand and the increasing need for duty-free bonding space. This expansion marked a significant shift in distillery practices, as it became standard to build larger, multi-storey warehouses in response to the industry's rapid growth, and limited room nearby.

John Colvill's personal life was not without hardship. His wife died in 1847 at the age of 41, a devastating loss for the family. Despite this, Colvill continued to build his business empire, overseeing Springside Distillery until his death. His son, Robert Colvill, succeeded him as the head of the distillery, carrying on his father's legacy of expansion and innovation in the whisky business.

Springside bonded warehouse, May 2005.

The Colvill family was also astute in promoting their whisky. Mr J. Rae, an agent for Springside whisky alongside other famous names such as 'Auchintoshin [sic], Kirkleston, Lagavulin, and Ben Nevis' in the mid-19th century, secured the brand's. In September 1893, John Colvill & Co. advertised for a Mashman, and a few years later, in 1896, they placed another ad for the same position.

In addition to recruiting staff for the distillery, Colvill also engaged with the wider whisky industry. In 1905, he was involved in advertising for the Campbeltown Distillers' Association, offering a salary of £80 for the position of secretary.

On 21 December 1905, John Colvill & Co. was embroiled in a legal case regarding the death of a horse. The horse, which had been lent to the distillery by a local postmaster and horse hirer, was injured while in the care of the company and had to be put down. The case, widely reported in the press, involved a dispute over whether the horse had been used for a purpose outside of what it was originally lent for. The case was settled in favour of the plaintiff, with Colvill's company being ordered to pay £50 and expenses.

Tragedy struck in March 1896 when John Taylor, an employee at Springside Distillery, tragically died in an accident at the coal depot on Argyll Street.

The closure of Springside Distillery is believed to have occurred around 1926 (although likely much earlier). As the closest distillery to the busiest part of town, Springside's closure may have come as a blessed relief to those living and working nearby. There is no coverage of its closure.

OTHER DISTILLERIES

CALEDONIAN DISTILLERY 1832 – c.1850

Founded in 1832, Caledonian Distillery was erected by the firm of Peter Stewart & Co., formed by brothers William, Edward and Peter Stewart. The distillery was situated opposite Big Kiln corner with its entry through 'Warm Water Close'. By 1845, the partners were Boyle, John Keys and James Johnston.

The partnership was dissolved in 1851 and the distillery, which still had 34 years left on the lease, was placed for sale. It was stated that the distillery had not been working for some time and was advertised at the upset price of £600. There were no bids, and the price dropped to £400, at which point it was bought by Stewart, Galbraith & Co, owners of Scotia Distillery (the 'Stewart' was James Stewart, the brother of the original three Stewarts).

DRUMORE DISTILLERY 1834 – c.1847

Built in 1834 by Templeton, Fulton & Co, Drumore Distillery was situated at the Drumore Farm steading. The original partners were Robert Templeton, farmer, West Drumore; William Templeton, distiller (Robert's brother); John McMillan, saddler, Campbeltown and Mrs Mary Mitchell or Fulton, widow of Robert Fulton, merchant in Campbeltown. Mary was the sister of distillers Archibald, William, John and Hugh. The firm was sequestrated in 1847, and its assets put up for sale.

GLENRAMSKILL DISTILLERY 1828 – c.1854

It is thought that Glenramskill Distillery, or at least some of the buildings, situated near the present Glenramskill House south of Campbeltown, were built before 1828 as it was sold in 1828 to McMurchy, Ralston & Co, who were also proprietors of Burnside Distillery. In 1829 a contract of co-partnery was then arranged in the names of McMurchy and Ralston. In Smith's 'Views of Campbeltown' 1835, he noted that the distillery was 'the largest work of the kind in or near Campbelton'. Despite this, the 'Argyllshire Herald' classed it as a distillery of 'Wee Stills'. In 1855 the distillery and business were advertised for sale in 'Kay's Argyllshire Magazine' and then was advertised 'To Let' but there are no records suggesting it continued:

"Distillery to Let. The Glenramskill Distillery, situated in the Bay of Campbeltown, in good working order, capable of consuming about 70 to 80 qrs. Malt, or producing about 10 Puncheons weekly; attached to which is a supply of Water capable of working all the Machinery. The distance from Campbeltown is only 1½ miles, where Malt Barns may be had at moderate rents. Has been given up of late in consequence of the decease of the proprietor."[223]

HIGHLAND DISTILLERY 1827 – c.1852

Built in 1827 by Daniel Mactaggart & Co, Highland Distillery was situated on Broad Street. By 1833, John Grant was the proprietor, and shortly afterwards, the firm became McLennan & Grant, with George McLennan being the new partner. The distillery was put up for sale in 1859 'with or without utensils'. In 1861 the business rates were appealed against and the distillery was described by John Kerr Orr, of Glenside Distillery, as an 'old work… in a state of great dilapidation. At some point, if the below article is to be believed, the distillery was run by Messrs Duncan & Baird, but it is likely that the distillery had closed long before the article in 1874.

Disappearance of Scotch Distilleries.
"Strange as it may seem, and notwithstanding the large production of whiskey in Scotland, both for home consumption and for exportation, fully a score of distilleries have either disappeared entirely during the last twenty years or have ceased to continue in an active state. Campbeltown has been a great sufferer, having added four to the list, including Messrs Duncan & Baird's well-known Highland Distillery."[224]

LOCHSIDE DISTILLERY 1830 – c.1852

Built in 1830 by Gilkison, McKersie & Co (original partners were Peter Gilkison, William Hunter and William McKersie), Lochside Distillery was situated behind Robert Armour & Sons, plumbers, on Longrow (Kinloch Road). McKersie retired from the business, having built Albyn Distillery in 1830, and the firm became Wilkinson & Hunter, with Peter Hunter, William Hunter's son, becoming a partner. Lochside Distillery was one of the shortest-lived distilleries in Campbeltown and shut down around 1852. In 1856 the Argyllshire Herald advertised the private sale of 'Distillery Utensils' at Lochside Distillery.

MEADOWNBURN DISTILLERY 1824 – c.1885

Thought to have been built in 1824 by William Armour, Alex Kirkwood, James Taylor (who acted as the master mason) and Matthew Greenlees, later of Hazelburn Distillery, Meadowburn Distillery was situated just out of town off the Witchburn Road. The partnership changed in 1840 and in 1852 the distillery was advertised for sale:

"All, and whole, the Meadowburn Distillery, at Campbeltown, the property of Messrs. Kirkwood Taylor and Company, together with the whole buildings, utensils, and apparatus thereto belonging. The Premises consist of Still House, Two large Malt Barns, with Kiln Head, Spirit Cellar, Two Bonding Warehouses, and other buildings, all of which underwent alterations and a

thorough costly repair within the last Eighteen Months. The apparatus and utensils comprise a Ten-horse-power Steam Engine and Gearing, Water Cisterns, Copper Boilers, Mash Tun and Underback, large Cast Metal Cooler, Seven Wash Backs, Low Wine and Wash Still, Feint, Low Wine and Spirits Receivers, Wash, Low Wine and Feint Chargers, and are equal to the manufacturing of Two Thousand Gallons of Spirit per week. Grinding, Mashing, Pumping, and Fanning the Cooler are all performed by Steam, and the Works are now in complete order, and in full operation. Water is obtained partly from a Well on the Premises, and partly from a stream led into the premises by pipes. There is a large stock of casks, and other articles on hand, which a purchaser of the premises may have at valuation."[225]

In 1854 the distillery was sold to Robert Colvill. The distillery appears to have closed around 1882 or perhaps later and was not open when Barnard visited in 1885. The 1924 OS map clearly shows it as 'Distillery (disused)'.

MOSSFIELD DISTILLERY 1834 – c.1837

Thought to have been built in 1834, Mossfield Distillery is the joint shortest-lived of all the distilleries in Campbeltown. It was situated through Kirk Close on Longrow and possibly linked by William Hervey to Mountain Dew Distillery. It probably closed in 1837, as in 1838, the distillery was sold at public auction for £1,950 to John Colville (bidding on behalf of the Burnside Distillery partners). The site today is used for flats.

MOUNTAIN DEW/THISTLE DISTILLERY 1834 - c.1837

Sharing in Mossfield Distillery's fate, Mountain Dew Distillery carried on for around four years from 1834, when it had been built and run by Hervey & McMillan (William Hervey and Malcolm McMillan), until 1837 when Peter Watson & Co ran the distillery. The distillery was situated next to Springside Distillery on Burnside Street.

TOBERANRIGH DISTILLERY 1834 – c.1860

Built in 1834 by Alexander Wylie, the Toberanrigh (or Tober An Righ) Distillery was situated at No. 48 Longrow. John Wylie joined Alexander as a partner. In 1851, the distillery was acquired by John Mitchell, Hugh Ferguson and Daniel McMurchy, although it possibly only operated for another nine years, closing before 1860. The site is now shops and houses.

UNION DISTILLERY 1826 – c.1850

Built in 1826 by Mactaggart and Henderson, Union Distillery was built next to the Campbeltown Distillery on Longrow. The distillery's original partners were Charles Rowatt Mactaggart and Hector Henderson. In 1835 the distillery was sold to John Grant & Co with the new partners being Charles Kelly and John Grant. The distillery is believed to have been silent from about 1850. There are no remains.

WEST HIGHLAND DISTILLERY 1830 – c.1852

Built in 1830 by Andrew Montgomery and Archibald Andrew, the town's treasurer, West Highland Distillery was situated on Argyll Street. Little is known about the distillery, but it is believed that it stopped production before 1856. It is now a garage.

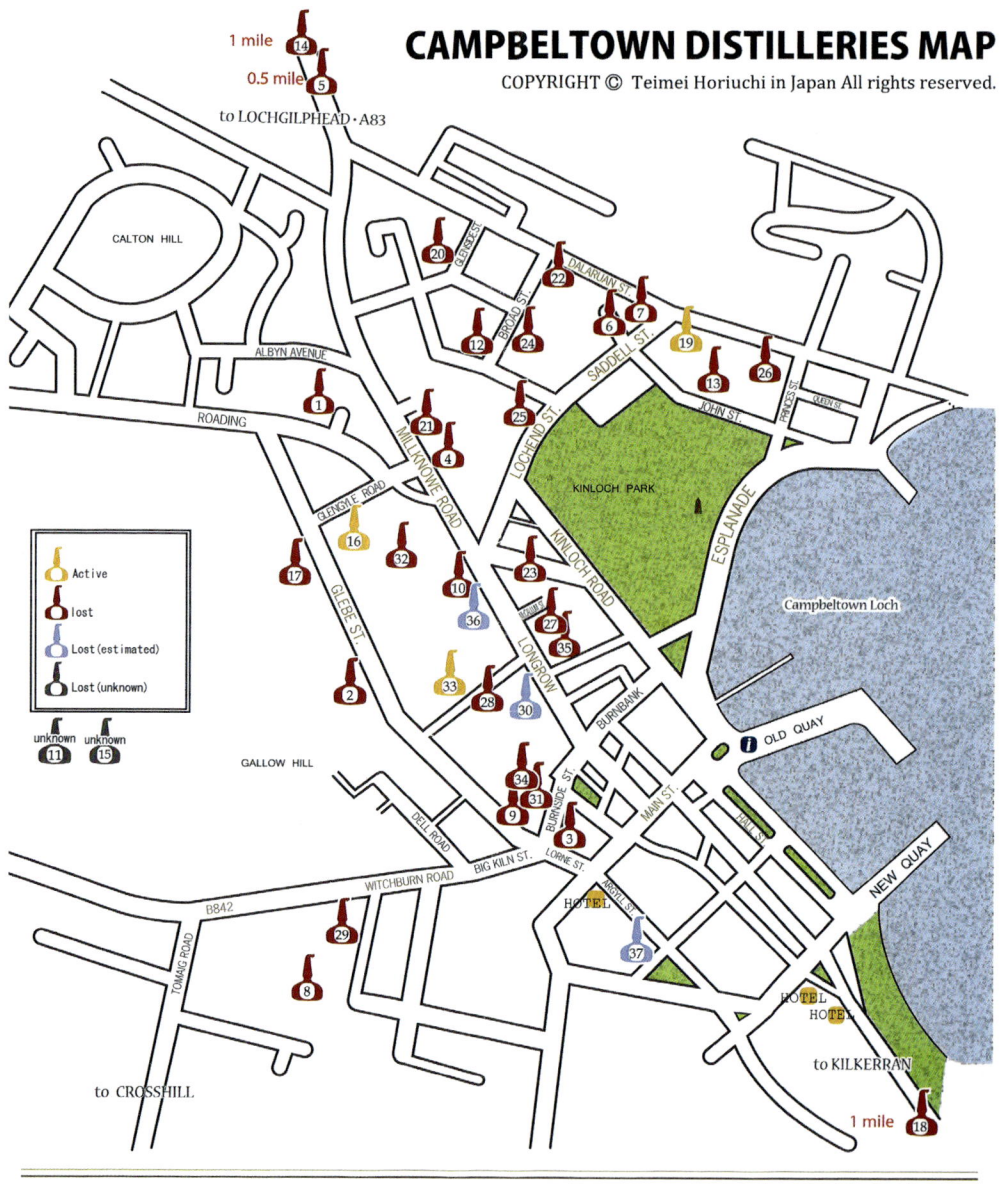

APPENDIX B:

'Origin & Romance of the Distilling Industry in Campbeltown' - Duncan Colville

"Being a Paper read to Kintyre Antiquarian Society, 10th January, 1923, by Mr Duncan Colville. Published in the Campbeltown Courier between January and March, 1923."

I have begun at the third instalment as the first three covers early Kintyre and settlements. I have also omitted instalments seven through nine as these deal with illicit distilling. Although copied directly, I have removed the large lists of names from certain sections and other parts I have felt were not relevant to this book. The entire nine instalments are available from the online British News Archive.

Town Council Records

From the beginning of the eighteenth century, it is possible to follow the course of events in Campbeltown much more closely, as fortunately the Records of the Town Council have been well preserved, and the references in them to affairs concerning distillers and maltsters are quite numerous.

First, we may note that in the list of articles imported or exported on which original dues were levied by the Town Council, was included malt, but no mention of whisky or aquavitae.

Then in the year 1703 we read of the election of a 'visitor' for the maltmen: and I may here explain that these 'visitors', who were regularly elected by the Council from amongst themselves for nearly a century and a half after this, were really inspectors who at that time would appear to have performed the work done by Public Health and Factory Inspectors at the present time.

The same year a complaint was raised by William Kelso, maltman, against John Wyly and James Mitchell, both maltmen, anent closing of the water runs.

In 1709 Donald Campbell of the Clachan, Provost of Campbeltown, by virtue of a privilege of making of two burgesses of the burgh as Provost each year, appointed William Mitchell, lawful son of William Mitchell, maltman, to be one of these two burgesses.

One of these individuals would appear to be the same William Mitchell who died abroad in 1712, and whose Will was recorded in the Commissariat of Edinburgh by his sister Helen Mitchell. The estate amounted to £179 3s 4d.

On 15th May, 1710, an Act was passed by the Magistrates prohibiting washing the Town Water (which is described as "the burn of Campbeltown on the north side of the town"), *"because said water is used by the inhabitants of the burgh for their Meal [sic], brewing, and other such uses and ought to be kept clear and not to be abused."* A penalty of One Shilling sterling was to be inflicted for each offence, and among the offensive objects specified were such varied articles as *"flesh, herring guts and heads, washing cloas [sic], yearn, bleaching and whitening of linen cloas."* A maltman named William Dunbar, had some influence in promoting this Act.

In 1712 the Council agreed to contribute £100 sterling for the *"leading of the stones ye several quarries about ye loch' for the erection by John Chiderson, mase on 'Air', of a Key and harbour at that part of the Campbeltown Loch opposite to Gortnachoquer, to be payed by the whole feuars, tacksmen, merchants, craftsmen of all kinds, brewers, maltmen, burghers, and inhabitants of this burgh."* This, I may explain, refers to the construction of what we now know as the Old Quay. (Since reading this paper, my attention has been drawn to the fact that this project was apparently not proceed with, as the 'Old Quay' was not built until some years later. In this connection see extract from Minutes of 26th July, 1735).

But the first actual mention of distillers, in the minutes at least, that I could discover, was under date 16th March, 1713, when an Act was passed by the magistrates *"anent the sufficiency of waters."* This Act, I am afraid, scarcely redounds to the credit of the distillers of that period, but nevertheless it is a link in our chain of evidence, and as such I give the following particulars of it.

"*Act Anent the Sufficiency of Waters*"
16th March, ESEA.
"The Council, considering the great abuse done by Distillers of Spirits in the Burgh, their venting and selling of insufficient stuff, whereby the greatest part of Distillers not only do cheat the people, but likewise do prejudice their neighbours that brew sufficient waters by underselling same to foreigners. They therefore appoint Walter Forrester and Alex. Cooper, and Donald Stewart, 'Taylor,' to be visitors of the sufficiency of said spirits, with power where they find any insufficient waters within the liberties of the Burgh, to seize the same and secure it till the magistrates be informed. Who are hereby empowered to fine each person guilty, according to its insufficiency... not exceeding Two Pounds Scots each gallon, and if the waters be found insufficient, the is to be distilled of new again..."

It would be interesting to know what strength of whisky was considered "sufficient" by the "visitors" – nowadays it is considered a serious offence to retail strong whisky?

Beyond the names of various maltsters connected with the Council, no further reference to our subject is made in the Council Minutes until 1732, but in the Burgh Court Records, which are bound up at the reverse end of the volumes containing the Town Council Minutes, we find an important Enactment which I will now read: -

"We, Maltsters, Brewers, Innkeepers, Victuallers, and Retailers of Beer and Spirits within the Burgh of Campbeltown subscribing, in consideration the great loss and damage sustained by us and others concerned in respect to the low rates and bad consumpt of the Spirits made of the barley of the produce of this country by ourselves, on account of the frequent importation and retail of foreign made spirits in this town and country, do therefore heartily and unanimously enact and bind and oblige each of us in the Burrow Court Books of the said Brugh, that we shall not on any account consider any inducement, motive, or respect whatsoever, either by ourselves or any other person or persons in our hames, or for or upon any of our accounts *import, or cause to be imported, sell or order of case to be sold with the bounds and liberty of the said Burgh, or reset, hide, keep, or conceal in any house, cellar, storehouse or other part or repository whatsoever, unto or in the possession of any of us, any Brandy or Spirits of whatever kind or denomination made without the Kingdom of Great Britain, and that for the term of three full and complete years which shall commence after and immediately upon lapsing of three months from and after the third day of this current month of March, which term of three months is allowed for the consumption of what of the said foreign made spirits is on hand within the said Burgh, and... we shall give information unto the proper officers of this Maties Customs of Excise... of any importation and running into this place of any of the foreign made spirits without lawful entry, that importation be effectually discourage, and the importers punished conform to law. And the premises, and every part thereof, fairly to observe under the penalty of Twenty Pounds Scots to be payed by the none-observers and each of us contravening the same, to the Pro. Fiscal of said Burgh for the use of the Common Good thereof. In testimony whereof we have subscribed this present Enaction. At Campbeltown aforesaid, the fifth day of March seventeen hundred and nineteen years."*

The Enactment is signed by fifty individuals, or in numerous instances instead of the individual's signature, "his mark" is substituted – showing that the art of writing was unknown to many in those days.

When we remember that the population of Campbeltown at that period was very much smaller than at the present time, we may infer from this Enactment that there must have been a considerable demand for alcoholic liquor in the burgh.

The next entry in the Town Council Minutes, which has some bearing on our subject, occurs on 18th March, 1732, when the Magistrates enacted that owing to bad malt having been brought to town by country maltsters, all malt from the country had to be first deposited at the Laigh Tolbooth on Wednesday, the weekly market day, to be inspected by the "Visitors of liquors and Mercates." It was ordained that this should be published by 'Tuck of Drum' – the ancient substitute for the Bellman's Bell of which I have no doubt most of us have a vivid recollection: if not the Bellman may still be seen – portrayed in his uniform, in McKinnon's Picture at our local museum!

William Mitchell, Town Officer, was appointed to keep the key of the Laigh Tolbooth till the ensuing election of Magistrates, and was authorised to charge one shilling Scots for each boll of malt sent in to the Tollbooth from the country, whereof one third was to become the property of the 'Visitors', and the other two-thirds to be retained by the said William Mitchell. Each person discovered carrying malt to the town or private houses clandestinely and upon other days of the week, was to be find in two pounds Scots money for each boll so carried, one sixpence thereof to be paid to the informer, and the balance to the Treasurer for the use of the Common Good of the burgh. The Enactment also applied to all malt brought to the town by sea,

In 1734 the tacksmen of the Town Mills appear to have had a grievance against some of the inhabitants of the town, who in time of drought and consequent scarcity of water, had made use of their own 'steel milns' to grind malt for the supply of the Burgh. The Council, however, requested the Magistrates not to come to any final sentence in the action then pending against one of the bailies *"till such times as the Tacksmen of the Milns within the Burgh shall keep sufficient water or steel milns within the Burgh for serving the inhabitants in grinded malt – so that it will not lie more than eight days at either of the said tacksmen's milns, and thereafter the proprietors of the malt to be entitled to get it ground elsewhere, and to be free of all multures and dues."* If, however, the malt was crushed elsewhere before lying eight days, or without compounding with the Tacksmen, the proprietors were to be liable to pay the abstracted multures.

The next entry in the Minutes of the Council at this period, which is of relative interest to our subject concerns the transport of coal, when on 31st May, 1735, it was enacted that *"Carriers and cadgers pay 2d for each Ticket of coals from Drumlemmill to*

Campbeltown in summer and 2½d in winter." The term 'ticket' I am told, signified a certain quantity, possible the load which a certain type of horse or pony could carry on its back.

On 26th July, 1735, we find that the Magistrates and Council decided to apply to the Duke of Argyll for a lease of the town milns which had previously been leased to individual tacksmen. And. Which had not for some time past been kept in such order as they ought, whereby the Burgh, which was thirled [sic] thereto, had been put to great charge and inconvenience in carrying their malt, etc., to other milns in time of drought: *"whereas were the miln dams and water courses of the said milns kept clean the said charges would in a great measure, if not wholly, be prevented."* At the same time the Council offered to devote any profit which they might derive from the milns, to the carrying on of the pier and the building of a new one to the southward thereof. Their application was granted by the Duke, and accordingly we find that on 2nd November, 1736, it was decided to build *"a new quay opposite to the Coal Fold or place commonly called the Kirk Roof."*

Having succeeded in obtaining a lease of the milns, the Magistrates and Council on 20th March, 1738, enacted *"that all grinded malt, brought from the country within the town's privileges, shall pay the Town Treasurer as Tacksman of the Town Milns, sixpence per Boll in lieu of the multure and groat in use to be paid for the malt made in the town, and ordain the purchasers or receivers of the said malt to pay the same."*

The same year no less than nine 'Visitors of Liquors and Mercates' were elected, including three to act as 'Judges of the Sufficiency, or Insufficiency of Malt Liquors', and at the same time the Clerk was instructed to send for a spirit proof of ivory.

The question of the water supply next crops up. On 25th June, 1742, the Council granted liberty to the inhabitants to make use of the Town River for washing therewith, and revoked all former Acts preventing the same, *"in regard there is now a good well at the Cross which may server the Town for their Victuals Drink, Brewing and Malting. And they prohibit and discharge the said inhabitants to wash anything nearer the Cross well than* the Strand, under the penalty of sixpence sterling for each Act of Contravention." This well, I may here remark, was originally thirty feet deep, but in the year 1845 its depth was increased to ninety feet by further boring (Minutes 18th July, 1845).

The following year the Council, on 16th October, 1743, received a Petition from the Campbeltown Maltsters, narrating that they had been accustomed to send men to the neighbouring farms to receive, clean, and measure the barley purchased by them: that these men not being skilful, made the maltsters suffer a great loss in bad cleaning and bad measure: and requesting that the Council enact that the farmers must deliver the cleaned barley at their kilns or other stonehouses. The Council agreed to enact accordingly.

Town Council Minutes, 1750-1800
Relief Church

And now we find a reference to peats which had long been used locally as fuel, and which by this time would doubtless be used also by the maltsters. On 18th July, 1753, the Council prescribed the size of the bags to be used by 'carriers' bringing peats to town, as complaints had been received of the smallness of bags, and that these were not sufficiently filled by the 'carriers'. At the same time rates were fixed for the cartage of these peats. I might mention an interesting entry in the Council's minutes of 12th April, 1722, where there appears in detail a list, apparently compiled in 1674, of fifty-five persons *"to whom the several moss rooms does belong, beginning at the miln damn, and coming round about to the Gallow Hill."*

A serious state of affairs apparently required the consideration of the Magistrates in January, 1757, when the minutes read, *"Considering the present distress of the inhabitants of this burrow for want of provisions, the Magistrates and Council enact that from this date no barley or other grain shall be malted within this burrow by any maltster or other person without liberty previously obtained for that effect."*

The following year we read (18th August 1758), that the

Magistrates and Council decided to let the Malt Miln and Meal Mill of the Burgh by public roup [sic] to a good tenant, as it was considered that this would tend more to the advantage of the Burgh. From this it is evident that there were two mills in operation during the period with which we have been dealing, and in this connection we find a reference to the 'two mill knows' in the year 1738 (10th October). Where the second of these two 'knows' was perhaps someone can enlighten us, but we are all familiar with what was presumable one of them – the Millknow of our own time. (Since reading this paper I have been told that the second Town Mill was situated in Burnside Street, at a spot near where the Salvation Army Hall, recently burned, is built).

Before proceeding further with the Council's minutes, I would like to refer to the building by Lowlanders of the Campbeltown Relief Church in 1767, this, as most of you are aware, being the predecessor of the present Longrow United Free Church. Amongst the original subscribers we find 14 maltsters, 14 coopers, and 2 coppersmiths, but so far as distilling at that period was concerned, we must bear in mind that most of the work performed by these coopers was in connection with barrels used in the herring fishing industry, which in the course of the previous thirty years had assumed large proportions.

Reverting to the Town Council Minutes, we find that on 1st April, 1775, *"the Magistrates and Council being informed that the Brewary Company at Dalaruan are in the practice of grinding the malt they make use of by a steel miln for which they pay no multure, tho' within the Thirl of the Milns of Campbeltown, and being determined to assert the right of the Burrow to all such abstracted multures as Tacksman of the said milns, they therefore appoint the Magistrates, with Mr Ronald Campbell, Collector of Customs, and Dugald Campbell, Sheriff Substitute, to meet with the proprietors of the Brewary, and confer with them anent the quantity of multures abstracted and what settlement they propose for the future, and make report thereanent."*

This, I may observe, refers to one of the only two brewaries I have found mentioned in Campbeltown (the other being a small one in Bolgam Street), and its name still lives, as to this day Dalaruan Distillery, which was built on the same site fifty years later, is locally known as the 'Brewaree'. I have been able to ascertain from Chartulary Deeds that the firm which owned this brewery was Orr. Ballantine & Co., of which the individual partners were Robert Orr, John Orr, Daniel Ballantine, James Ballantine, John Campbell, Sr, all merchants in Campbeltown, and Archibald Fleming, merchant in London. From the same source it would appear that the brewary was erected about the year 1770, and eventually it was purchased in 1825 by the firm who erected Dalaruan Distillery on the same site. In this connection the Rev. Dr Smith mentions that in the year 1791 the quantity of grain made into ale in Campbeltown was 400 bolls, and as the same author tells us that the Kintyre boll was equivalent to 442lbs., it follows that this brewery, being the only, so far as I am aware, in Campbeltown at that time, would use about 90 tons of grain per annum. This may enable anyone to estimate the capacity of the brewary.

Up to this we have heard much concerning the maltsters, but little to indicated the experiences of the distillers in regard to their branch of the industry. There is not much doubt, however that the stills in use here up to this stage must have been very diminutive, and this is borne out in the Minutes of 6th March, 1783, when owing to the scarcity of grain and meal, and the distress amongst the poorer inhabitants of the Burgh, with a view to affording temporary relief, the Council recommended the Magistrates to call in all the stills in the Burgh, and to keep them temporarily in some proper place of safety. With respect to such distillers as did not deliver up their stills, it was recommended to the Magistrates to take such steps as they might deem necessary for compelling them, and particularly that they deliver a List of these distillers to the Collector of Excise. At the same time the maltsters agreed to stop steeping bere for malt…

Commenting on this state of affairs, a correspondent to the 'Glasgow Herald' (17th Nov. 1821), recently remarked that Shire of Argyll was voted bone-dry in 1782 by a general meeting of the

Commissioners of Supply. In that year the harvest had proved a failure, and as the scarcity of provisions would be accentuated by the conversion of barley into pot still whisky, the Commissioners took the bold step of prohibiting its manufacture by ordering the seizure of all private stills in the county. Agents were appointed for every parish, and these were empowered *"by themselves, their factors, or others, to be employed, to take up the stills within their respective parishes and to retain the same in their natural possession from and after the 16th day of Dec."* Refusal to surrender a still on the request of the Commissioners' agent was punishable by the complete destruction of the apparatus at the hands of the Excise.

An import step towards the development of the town's industries was about to take place at this time, namely the construction of a canal from the Coal Pit, and accordingly we find that on 3rd June, 1783, the Council decided to apply for interdict against Charles McDowall, *"the tacksman of the Coal works at Drumlemman, who had begun to cut a canal at the High Miln Dam."* Further difficulties are also mentioned in the Council Minutes before the construction of the canal was finally completed.

I might here remark that in 1799 Shore Dues appear to have been first levied on whisky in Campbeltown, as we find in the Schedule of Rates then drawn up: - *"Every pun. of whiskey or aquavita... 1/-."* In the Shore Dues Tables drawn up in 1741 and 1757 Wine is included, but not whisky.

Again, in the Table of 'Customs of the Trone and other Pettie Customs of this Burgh' in 1801, we find these clauses – *"Each gallon of aquavitae going out of town for retailing, 1/-,"* and *"Each gallon ditto in time of Fair, 2/-."* Also, under the heading of 'Ladles out of Victual coming to Mercate' we find 'A ladle out of each boll malt'. These facts may perhaps be taken as an indication that by this time a considerable trade in whisky had been developed, and that its export in considerable bulk to other parts of Scotland, had commenced.

In the Table of Ladles, Causey Customs, Tronage, and Petty Customs in 1799, the following note occurs:- *"And in order that the country and town distillers may, as nearly as possible, be put upon the same footing, it is a statute and ordained that in all time coming, all sort of whisky or spirits distilled in the country and brought within the liberties of the Burgh, or shipped off from any part of the Harbour by freemen or unfreemen, shall pay a causey-custom, of one-fourth part of a Scotch pint for every sixteen pints said measure."*

Legal Stills for Private Use

Before entering into the subject of the whisky duties and their effect in promoting or encouraging illicit distillation, I would like to refer to what I suggest had much to do with the moral aspect of the matter. We have already seen that from ancient times the brewing of ale in private houses for the use of the household was permitted, and if I mistake not, the privilege was continued in regard to houses of small annual value, up to quite recently. Again, the Statutes of Icolmkill… permitted an individual to distil as much aquavitae as his own family might require: that was in 1609.

Subsequently we find that up to the year 1774, a ten gallon still was permitted to be so used in private households. In 1779 the privilege was modified by a reduction in the size of still so used, to two gallons content, but two years later in 1781 the privilege was entirely withdrawn.

It is not difficult to image the views of the people at that time, when deprived of a privilege which probably they had come to regard for generations as a right. And in view of the enormous extent to which they subsequently indulged in illicit distillation, it is scarcely to be wondered at if, at first they did not consider that in so doing they were committing a serious offence against the laws of the country. I was informed within the last fortnight, by a man whose father had suffered six months' imprisonment for this offence, that it was not regarded as such by those who indulged in it!

Still Licenses

Up to the year 1785 the duty on whisky in Scotland was charged on a presumptive number of gallons distilled, that is the quantity of wash before distillation was first ascertained, and duty was charge on the whisky which it was assumed this quantity of wash would yield. Thus, a capable distiller would benefit by getting a relatively larger yield from his wash than his less skilled neighbour, and in point of fact we find it stated in the report of the Scottish Commissioners of Excise in 1783 that many distiller could then obtain from a given quantity of malt, double the quantity of whisky which could be produced in 1705, in consequence of great improvements in the arts of fermentation and distillation.

The duty had gradually been raised since the Union of the Crowns in 1707, until now in 1787 it had reached 2/1 per gallon, a rate no doubt considered high at the time.

The revenue arising from spirits in Scotland, however, fell very far short of what ought to have been produced from the quantity known to be manufactured there, and this led to the adoption of a new principle in the imposition and collection of the duty.

Thus in 1766 the art of distillation was supposed to be so fully known that persons skilled in it could compute with sufficient exactness the quantity of spirits which a still could produce in a year, in proportion to the number of gallons of liquid it was capable of containing. This computation being made, and the amount of the duty meant to be charged on each gallon of spirits settled, the whole sum a still ought to yield in a year was easily calculated at so much for every gallon of its capacity. This annual amount was to be imposed, and collected, under an annual licence granted to the distiller, who was to declare the number of gallons to be contained in the still he intended to use through the year, and the duty was to be paid by anticipation in quarterly instalments.

This plan of licence was first proposed to be tried in the Highlands in 1785, but a year later it was extended in a modified form to the Lowlands. For this purpose Scotland was divided into two sections, Campbeltown being with that described as the Highlands. The duty on the cubic gallon of the still was first fixed at 30/- in the Lowlands and 20/- in the Highlands, and the duty on malt used in distillation was to some extent remitted. The reasons for these distinctions were that the grain in general in the Highlands was of an inferior quality, and the harvests more precarious: and that in skill and capital, the manufacturers there were also much inferior to those in the Lowlands: but to prevent the Highland distiller who might possess sufficient skill and capital, from deriving an undue advantage over the Lowland distiller in consequence of the lower duty on his still he was by law confined to a still not exceeding 20 gallons cubic capacity, a limit that a year later was to not less than thirty and not exceeding forty gallons: to the use of a limited quantity of malt: and to the production of a given number of gallons of spirits per annum: if he exceeded those he was to pay the malt duty for the excess of malt, and a duty per gallon for the excess of spirits. He was prohibited from buying grain or selling spirits in the Lowlands.

In 1788, as it was found that the distillers, particularly in the Lowlands, soon outwitted the Excise authorities by making improvements in the construction of their stills, so that, instead of taking several days to complete one distillation, a charge could be worked off in a very short time: and eventually still of 40 gallons content, the maximum size permitted in Campbeltown, were so designed – wide and shallow – that the whole operation could be actually completed in less than three minutes. To meet these ingenious devices, the duty in the Lowlands was first raised to £3 per gallon of still capacity in 1788: again in 1793 to £9, while on this occasion the Highland duty was also increased to 30s. Then in 1795 a further increase took place, making the Lowland duty £18, and the Highland 50s per gallon content of the still.

On account of the scarcity of food which then prevailed, Parliament suspended the manufacture of spirits throughout the Kingdom from that period up to 1797, when the Lowland duty was once more raised to £54 per gallon of still content. At the same time the Highlands were sub-divided into two districts: in that next to the Lowlands (which included Campbeltown) the duty was fixed at £9, and in the new Highland district, £6

10s per gallon of still capacity. This arrangement caused a great controversy throughout Scotland: resulted in the appointment of a Parliamentary Committee to consider the whole question of the Distilleries in Scotland: and so far as Campbeltown was concerned, was the last straw which broke the camel's back.

It is sufficiently significant that, so far as I have been able to ascertain, legal distilleries ceased to exist in Campbeltown for a period of twenty years from 1797 to 1817, when the first modern distillery, such as we have here today was erected.

Licensed Distilleries Established

What was the position in Campbeltown during the last quarter of the eighteenth century? To begin with, we may observe that in twenty-one years, according to a letter written to the treasury by the Scottish Commissioners of Excise (31st March, 1781), there was less than £500 whisky duty raised in the whole of the Highlands from 1760 when a substantial increase in the rate of duty was imposed, up to 1781, as the whisky had generally, if not always, been distilled in stills below the size allowed by law to 'entered' distillers, and on pretence of being for private use, by which means they were not chargeable with duty. Here also it is mentioned that the greatest part of distillation in the Highlands at that period was done by women.

When the licence was transferred to the still instead of the whisky, however, a number of such licenses appear to have been taken out by Campbeltown distillers, and accordingly about this time, we find the question of the erection of such distilleries raised in connection with Dalintober Quay, in a Memorial and Queries for the Magistrates and Council of Campbeltown, 1785, as follows: -

"The houses at Dalintober, and a brewery in the neighbourhood, but likewise without the limits of the royalty, contain convenient accommodation for erecting such distilleries as are lately authorised for the Highland Counties of Scotland, and the memorialists are informed that two or three of these are actually to be set up there by the inhabitants of Campbeltown,

which will occasion the storing of considerable additional quantities of grain without the royalty that were formerly in use to be malted within the Burgh where the Town Dues were paid. It is not improbable that the same please may be used by these distillers which is already held out by the storers of grain at Dalintober, and an attempt made to withhold from the Burgh the Ladles and Petty Customs due for the grain and malt they malt and distil, and as the chief consumption of their spirits will be on board of the herring busses while on the fishery, the memorialists are apprehensive that the distillers may also endeavour to put their spirits on board of the busses from the Quay of Dalintober, so as to evade any dues the Town might have a right to exact, if they were brought into the Burgh and shipped at the Quay."

In regard to this Memorial, the following Opinion was obtained from Mr Ilay Campbell, Advocate, Edinburgh, on 22nd November, 1788: - *"I see no way by which any person can be prohibited from establishing a brewary or distillery at Dalintober, or having granaries and dealing in grain there. IF that grain, or the ale or spirits made from it, are brought into the town of Campbeltown for sale or consumpt there, the usual dues exigible in such cases within the Burgh may be taken: or if any of those commodities are importer into, or exported from the Loch of Campbeltown, there may be room for taking anchorage and harbour dues from the vessels engaged in such trade, but I do not observe that there can be any further claim."*

In the Town Council Minutes of 13th January, 1787, we find an allegation that for some time past considerable quantities of malt had been abstracted from the Town Mills by licenced distillers within the Burgh to the prejudice of the revenue of the Burgh: this, however, was not admitted by the distillers. At the same time we ready (5th April, 1787), that a practice prevailed for some time of filling water casks and brewing vessels at the public wells, to the great inconvenience of the inhabitants. The Magistrate and Council accordingly *"discharged this practice in all time coming, under the penalty of five shillings sterling every cask of brewing vessel filled."*

At this time, also, the multure malt at the Town Mill had

accumulated to a considerable extent, and there was apparently some difficulty in finding purchasers for it. It was accordingly agreed to accept the offer from the 'licenced distillers' to receive back each his own portion of such multure malt and to pay eightpence sterling per half pack for same, and also in future to accept a composition of one shilling sterling for grinding each boll of malt in full of the price of the half-peck of malt and the groat of money multure which up to then had been payable for each boll of malt 'grinded at the Town Mill'. It was accordingly agreed to request Mr Laur. Mackenzie, Collector of Excise, to collect these sums quarterly from the distillers, along with the King's duties. A year later this agreement was renewed, and at the same time it was acknowledged that Collector Mackenzie had been of great assistance.

A short reference to the distilleries of this period is made in the local Custom House Records under date 9th March, 1789 (it may be explained that a number of typed extracts from these Records are available for the use of the public, at the Free Library here). This extract proceeds as follows: - *"Some of the bondholders here, particularly Colonel Campbell of Barbreck, signified the material injury sustained by the distillers of British spirits poured in upon us of late from the Island of Sanda."* This appears to refer to smuggled rum and brandy and suggests a state of affairs similar to that already mentioned in 1719.

Forty Gallon Stills

Writing in the year 1791 in the Statistical Account of Campbeltown, Dr Smith stated that there were then 22 whisky stills in the Town and 10 more in the Parish, making in all 32 licenced stills of the forty-gallon type. These 32 stills, he tells us, together produced 26,150 gals. of whisky in that year – a quantity which the smallest distillery now in operation here is probably capable of producing in one season. In the same Statistical Account we also find a note of the following license stills throughout Kintyre, namely, Kilcolmonell and Kilberry, 5: Killean and Kilchenzie, 3: Gigha, 1: Saddell and Skipness, 0.

The subject is not referred to in the Account of Southend, but Dr Smith, in his "Agricultural Survey of Argyllshire, published 1798, mentions that 400 bolls malt were distilled in that Parish. If we assume that this represented 2 licenced stills, we have a total of 43 stills of the forty-gallon type in Kintyre at that time.

I will now give a few particulars which are available relative to a forty gallon still operated in Campbeltown at this period, several original licences for which have been preserved. A facsimile of one of these dated 1791 was reproduced in the 'Wine and Spirit Trade Record' of 14th December 1922, in the name of James Armour, Jr, while another for a thirty-seven gallon still in the same name, dated 1796, is now preserved at Hazelburn Distillery, appropriately enough, perhaps as I am told it was on part of the present Hazelburn site that this original still was located. A third license of the same nature was some time ago presented, as I understand, by our townsman Mr Archd. D. Armour, to the Customs and Excise Museum in London. In 1789 the quantity of whisky produced by this still was 4,138 pints 'mixed' which sold at 1s 6d per pint, and 119 pints "unmixed" – a more costly commodity – selling at 2s 4d per pint. The partners in the business were originally James Armour, cooper, and John Armour, merchant: the, after the death of the latter, Hugh Ferguson and James Galbreath joined James Armour in the partnership. The profits for the three years ending 1789 averaged £70 per annum. In addition to local customers, whisky was supplied by the firm to residents in Arran, while regular supplies were purchased for use on board sloops and brigantines trading from Campbeltown. There was very little evidence of any trade being done beyond that which I have stated, but one entry showed a consignment of six casks to the Highlands.

Campbeltown Cooper Society

I happen to have in my possession the original Cash Book of this Society which was formed on 1st April 1777, when 34 Coopers each subscribed the sum of 10s to form the nucleus of a fund for the benefit of the *"reduced or ailing members of the*

Society or the widows of the members of the Society." At the same time each member agreed to contribute sixpence to the funds of the Society every three months. The following year there were 61 journeymen members in addition to a number of apprentices, and when the names are carefully examined, it is fairly evident that many of these coopers also carried on the business of maltsters – a very frequent combination at that time. It is easy to understand one reason for this – that in a poor fishing season these men were able to fall back upon their other resources.

In this connection we find in the 'Beauties of Strathclyde' (1839) that while in 1744 Campbeltown possessed only two or three small vessels, yet in 1772 there were 78 sail of from 20 to 80 tons burden belonging to the port, all build for and employed in the herring fishing, and employing about 800 men. Dr Smith in the Statistical Account says that in the seven years ending 1791 there were on an average 50 fishing busses operating from Campbeltown, and it was the custom to carry a cooper in each vessel, and probably also his apprentice in addition. I have seen several apprenticeship indentures relating to the coopers of this period, generally for a term of four year, binding the apprentice cooper, amongst other things, to serve 'on sea and ashore at the herring fishing during the seasons thereof'.

When the system of fishing then in operation, entailing absence from home for considerable periods, was gradually abandoned owing to the withdrawal of the herring bounty, these coopers and maltsters in many instances appear to have then devoted their attention and capital to a new combination, namely malting and distilling, and indeed many of their descendants were engaged in the distilling industry here up to recent years.

The Cash Book to which I have referred contains entries up to the year 1817, when the accumulated funds of the Society amounted to £164, but subsequent to that date I have no information regarding its career.

Modern Distilleries

We have seen that for a period of twenty years up to 1817 there were apparently no licenced distilleries in Campbeltown. During these years the Excise duties on stills and also latterly on whisky had been further increased and at the same time the practice of illicit distillation had grown enormously, so that in sheer desperation the Government in 1814 prohibited the use of stills of less capacity than 500 gallons in the Highlands: this, however, only resulted in further increasing the use of small illicit stills. At length in the following year the distinction between Highland and Lowland districts was abolished and the still licence duty was discontinued, but the high duty of 9s 4½d per gallon of whisky produced, was imposed.

Under these new conditions we find that the first of the modern type of distilleries in Campbeltown was erected, but in view of the enormous quantity of illicit whisky at that time being produced here, it is probably that for some years the existence of this distillery was seriously threatened. I have been shown by Col. Mactaggart a George III Crown Piece stamped 'J. McT. 1822', traditionally said to be part of the first dividend paid by this distillery, which I understand was erected by his great-grandfather, and this circumstantial evidence rather goes to support my suggestion. At all events, smuggling continued rampant until the year 1823, when, in the hope that legitimate distillers could compete against and extinguish these smugglers, the Government drastically reduced the duty on whisky to 2s 4d per gallon.

This change, so far as Campbeltown was concerned, resulted in the immediate establishment of numerous large and well-equipped distilleries, many of which have continued in operation up to the present time, and as a contrast to the notorious forty-gallon stills, there may now be seen, I believe, in Glen Nevis Distillery here, a wash still capable of containing nearly 7,000 gallons.

APPENDIX C:

'REMINISCENCES OF A GAUGER'

Excerpts on life in Campbeltown by Excise Officer Joseph Pacy
Published in 1873

I left England for Scotland in 1834, on promotion to a division at Campbelton, a town in Argyllshire, noted for its many distilleries. When I went there first the number would be about thirty. A very large revenue was derived from them, which necessitated a considerable staff of Gaugers to look after it. Each Gauger had a distillery and a certain number of malt-houses placed under his immediate charge and inspection.

Campbelton whisky was somewhat celebrated, and was in great request both in the home and in the foreign markets. Distilled in stills of small size, and made from peat-dried malt, there was a flavour about it peculiar to itself, and which was much relished by consumers of that kind of spirit.

The peat-dried malt from which this whisky was produced was made from grain designated in Scotland 'Bere' or 'Bigg', a small kind of barley grown on the light sandy soil of that country. The tax on that description of malt was something like one-fifth than that of malt made from barley, a kind of boon or protection to the grower of this lighter kind of grain. To guard against any abuse of this privilege, and to prevent imposition on the revenue, stringent and vigorous laws were in force relating to malt, subject to these different rates of duty, or tax, similar to the laws applying to every other indirect tax, which were found very difficult strictly to adhere to at all times; especially when there happened to be a limited supply of home grown grain, which would sometimes be the case in bad harvests. An illustration or two will be sufficient to show how these laws affected the makers of malt.

For instance, to give the maltster a right to the lesser tax on the malt made from bere and bigg, he was required to produce to the Excise a certificate from the grower of such grain, that it was really what it was represented to be.

Then again, the maltster was not allowed to malt barley and bere and bigg at the same time, on the same set of premises. They were required to be kept entirely apart, which was found to be a great hindrance to business, and led to infraction of the law, as I will presently explain.

The supply of bere and bigg was not sufficient for the demand, therefore the distillers and maltster imported barley from the north of Ireland, which is of easy access to Campbelton, at a cost, freight included, not much over that for the lighter grain, bere and bigg. The difference of the tax on the two kinds of malt was a temptation to attempt to pass barley on the Excise for bere and bigg, which considering the regulations I have alluded to, was not easy to resist.

A smart young Irishman whom I was friendly with, and who understood more about the importation of barley than I did, suggested to me that the revenue was imposed on by that system. We acted in concert, and by watching carefully the stocks of grain, bere and bigg, at the maltster under our survey, we found them increase much beyond what the growers' certificates would cover. There was sufficient evidence to satisfy us that barley was being introduced into stock to be malted under the regulations applicable to the lighter grain, with a view of evading the higher rate of duty.

In every case where we considered barley had been introduced into stock surreptitiously, we laid the whole under seizure, much to the consternation and dismay of the parties implicated in these transactions, and to the distillers in general.

The whole trade of Campbelton was up in arms against us on the account of our large seizure. Landowners and proprietors were in our favour, and in the prosecutions that ensued the magistrates who adjudicated were landowners, and therefore were not entirely disinterested. The onus was on the parties implicated, to prove that the impounded grain was bere and bigg. This they failed to do. They were fined heavily, and in addition forfeited the seizure.

My colleague and myself were commended by the whole bench of magistrates for our vigilance and zeal, praise that I look upon now as rather equivocal, when I think of the feeling that dictated it. Could the free trade policy of Sir Robert Peel, which has proved so successful, have been foreshadowed to my mind, I should have strongly recommended its application to Campbelton at the period I am writing about. I would have advocated an equalization of the malt duty, a free import of barley for malting or otherwise, without restriction, leaving the landlords and tenants to settle the matter of rent between themselves. Blinded somewhat by official zeal I did not view the matter in the same light then as now, or I might possibly have been a little more forbearing.

The distillers at Campbelton were respectable, intelligent, clever men of business, and were disposed, I believe, to render to Caesar the things belonging to Caesar. The town itself, although isolated, I considered pleasant, and the splendid deep bay at its entrance is magnificent. It was a remarkably cheap place for a family to live in, and had I been a private individual instead of a Gauger I could very well have settled down there.

I had previously offended the trade in the part I took in the great seizure of barley, and had to endure a good deal of petty persecution by reason of it. This I expected. I had no right to suppose that men smarting under severe penalties, inflicted on them partly by my agency, would be likely to offer me the right hand of fellowship, or even common civility. I could not help this; my duty was clearly defined, I did it, and braved the consequences.

There was an absence of all litigiousness connected with what I may call an unpleasant duty. I had no personal desire of a conflict with what I knew to be a powerful interest; but when I was convinced the law was being evaded and the revenue defrauded, I could not rest satisfied without joining, in all the vigour I could command, to break down the system. The more powerful the interest I had to combat, the more gratifying to my nature. I was delighted in meeting a formidable foe, for in such a case defeat is not ignoble, whilst victory is glorious.

APPENDIX D:

CONTRACT OF REID & COLVILLE
DALINTOBER DISTILLERY
16th OCTOBER, 1832

The parties hereto, viz Peter Reid, Merchant in Glasgow, David Colville, writer in Campbeltown and Archibald McCorkindale residing there agree to become partners in carrying on the trade of Distillers under the firm of Reid & Colville on that property in Dalintober, on which a Distillery is in the course of being erected, and that under the following conditions, —

First, the partners are to take the property at the price of Four Hundred and Fifty Pounds Sterling, as formerly agreed on, and to contribute on equal proportions of the whole expense of erecting the works thereon and for this purpose and for carrying on the works, they agree that the Capital worth of the firm be One Thousand Four Hundred and Fifty Pounds Sterling to be paid in cash, but if a greater sum be required the partners shall contribute the same equally, or instead to be paid by any partner who advances more than another,–

Second, the said Archibald McCorkindale shall forthwith at his own expense qualify himself to become Manager of the said concern, by learning mashing, fermenting and Distilling in all its branches and shall take the active superintendence of the same, and also act as clerk and bookkeeper to the company, for all which he shall receive a salary of Fifty Pounds Sterling per annum.

Third, the said David Colville shall in the meantime act as Cash Keeper and alone subscribe the firm of the Co-partnership, and the said Peter Reid shall act as agent and sell at two and one half farthing commission on his sales and other agents who may be appointed.

Fourth, regular books shall be kept and balanced every year on the 10th October, when a full state of the Company affairs shall be shown, and a dividend ordered, if considered advisable, but the Books shall at all times be open for the inspection of the partners.

Fifth, the endurance of the company shall be at least Five years, and as long thereafter as the parties may consider beneficial with a breach at the end of every five years, and any partner intending to retire at any breach, shall give six months previous written notice of such intention to the others, and at the breach the whole property and effects shall be duly ascertained and the Partner intending to retire shall be bound within one month of the date of such valuation to make offer of his share to the others, who shall within three weeks be bound to decide on said offer and the retiring Partner shall not be at liberty to sell at a lower price than the other partners are willing to give.

Sixth, In case any of the partners shall die during the currency of this contract, his interest shall cease as on the day of his death and with all convenient speed the whole property and effects shall be truly valued and the books of the company balanced as of that date, and the surviving partners shall have it in their power to take the deceased's share of the property and utensils at the then valuation and be bound to pay the heirs or other representatives of the deceased, the price by equal instalments, at six and twelve months from the date of the balance and if the surviving partners agree to take the said share, the heirs or other representatives of the deceased partner shall before receiving any part of the price be bound to make up the necessary title, and to execute and deliver a proper conveyance of the share of the deceased to the others.

But if the heirs of the deceased be dissatisfied with the valuation they shall be bound within one month of the death of the deceased partner, or within fourteen days after the valuation, to make offer of his share to the others, who shall within three weeks be bound to decide on said offer and the representative of the deceased shall not be at liberty to sell at a lower price than any of the other partners are willing to give, and they shall have the first offer and a preference to all others,— In either case the outstanding debts of the company shall be collected by the surviving partners and after payment of the debts due the balance shall be equally divided every three months as collected.

APPENDIX E:

'SCOTCH WHISKY'

'The Distillers Magazine and Spirit Trade News' 1st July 1903

A great deal has been written and said of the position of various years of the Scotch whisky trade from the distiller's, the blender's, the retailer's, and other points of view, but we do not remember any article in recent years which dealt of the position in regard to each other of the various 'makes'.

The 20th century was prophesied to usher in prosperous times for all concerned in the make and sale of 'Scotch', and certainly it has to some, yet every section of the trade is complaining of quiet times. Speculation in parcels is now unknown, and the broker sells but little on the street; his commission is small, and as a rule he only now handles the makes which he knows can be very shortly disposed of to some blending house.

Nor does he (the broker) job much with his fellows, which inflates values, but buys direct from the original holder, and has a certain market. Then, too, he buys for cash and sells for cash, rather refusing an order than grant a bill.

Now, the broker is a very necessary party to the trade, and unless he fails to deliver, that is, has sold a parcel which he cannot get or is off the market when he goes to purchase it for his client, he is not grudged his commission. Many brokers with large capital lay in stocks against their client's requirements, in which case they can quote firm, and such houses have numerous enquiries, are kept busy, and make money.

There is no branch of the trade more encroached on than the broking, for the dealer's license permits of broking, and consequently distillers, blenders, and publicans do a little on their own, but the brokers live and let be.

Many distillers are also blenders, having a license which permits of them sending out two gallons, and as most of them were blenders before acquiring distilleries, the wholesale merchants can have no strong objection.

At the same time a little more combination on the part of the distributing houses might create a 'taboo', which would tend to a neat distinction, as in many other trades. It is undoubted, too, that the distillers tread on the family wine merchants, as at many distilleries quite a large trade is done in small casks, sent out to private people, duty paid. The distillers may say that this has been caused by complaints from private people that their brand has been tampered with by the merchant, and they must either get it direct from distillery or have another whisky.

If so, then the family merchant can only blame himself, just as the wholesale houses have caused the distillers to deal directly with retailers, by reason of their putting off buying makes until they have a full book, leaving the distillers with surplus stock which must get a market.

But to the actual present position of the distiller. A good many find ready enough sales for their make, but they must canvas for their orders, and what is sold is mostly to firms likely to use it. There is very little sold for pure investment, though we find that when the distillers go round they are quite willing to buy 'old' of their make against 'new', which makes the transaction look like investment or speculation. This is obvious, as no sane man would sell his old 'Per contra' unless he foresaw a good return or got a guarantee that the 'new' would ultimately be bought back. Some distillers formerly gave a written (often 7½ per cent per annum) guarantee, which is bad business, and, continued in, is sure to be fatal to one or other of the contracting parties, while others content themselves by promising to repurchase at ruling rates.

'Grains', mostly controlled by one company, have come more into line as to price with malts, and are being used in greater proportion than ever before in blends, though some of the large advertising houses will tell you that less gain is being used and more malt. Granted that some of the grain distilleries find it convenient to close down longer than formerly for their annual cleaning, but may that not be because of less speculation? And it is well, too, for some years ago very old grain could easily be got, say ten years old, at 3s 6d per gallon, now it is hardly procurable, and any odd lots fetch 5s 6d, per gallon quite easily, whereas before five years old grain cost about 2s 6d and can now be bought for 2s per gallon. This latter is more in line with the price of malts, and increases the proportion of grain used in blending.

We seldom see any blend advertised or puffed but its qualities as to maltiness are mentioned, yet some grain is very necessary in a good blend, and not one of the blends most sold but has a good proportion of grain in it. We do not think that there is more than three and a half to four years' supply of grain spirit in the country, while we consider that there is at least an overhead full seven years' stock of all malts.

Taken in all, one would say that this is as it should be, for grain spirits mature much quicker, and is always used younger in blends than malts. Quite so; but the real inference is that the grain distilleries may go on making, and that malts should curtail, or blenders be advised and use more malts, which might certainly be for the health of the consumer.

Campbeltown makes do not occupy the position they once did. They are, in common parlance, slow to move, and their low price is out of all proportion to their value, yet we see a brighter future for them, for from statistics the removals from bond are becoming regularly greater than the make. If this continues it will show that blenders are beginning to know the value of Campbeltown, and more judicious selling and handling their makes by the distillers will make them valuable, and they will pay to hold, as they formerly did.

Campbeltown five years old can be bought for 3s bulk gallon – very little more than the price of grain spirits – and in proportion to the price of 'new', very much cheaper. There is, however, really no ruling price for new Campbeltown, which is a pity, as it shows a decided want of combination, resulting at the present day in little or no profit to some, and frequently loss.

There are good stocks in bond of the years 1892, '93, '94, but overall we should say that there is only some five years' supply in bond of Campbeltowns. The majority of distillers are curtailing the 'new' make, which will make their position the healthier.

As to the late unpopularity of Campbeltown it is difficult to speak, as the publicans have used as much as before. It is the larger blenders who have been using less. Much of the make is filled into hard oak wood, unseasoned, which never mellows properly, and gives the whisky with age a decidedly 'new look.' Indeed blenders have often rejected samples – good enough, but not all of the maturity the age should make them. This may be obviated by filling better casks, and Campbeltown distillers, as they value their industry, should take warning.

And, again, there is a tendency in Campbeltown 'new' [spirit] to emit a stunning odour which has baffled many to avert, and which has prejudiced many a buyer. The sting wears off with age and open bungs, but the whisky never shows the same quality. We hardly think that the water is to blame, nor yet the barley. It may be rather dirty dishes, with bad fermentation, and this again causes the whisky to marry badly and come out 'top' in a blend, killing other good ingredients.

It is not such a far cry from Campbeltown to Islay, yet the makes of the latter and presently in the first rank as to demand, price, and use, and deservedly so, for no blend can be complete without some 'softening', and this characterises the Islay makes. Islays after six years old are very scarce, and their value is greater than any gilded security, though it has to be admitted that some of the makes are of greater intrinsic value than others. It would be invidious to name any, but undoubtedly the prices gauge the values, as we can trace more distinctiveness in these than between the various Campbeltowns.

The popularity of the Islay make has not built new distillers, though it has enlarged the output of some existing, which is good for it, as although few, there are enough. They have had their bad day, too – they were not always popular – but we believe that they will always continue so now. There is a full five and a half years' supply in bond at Islay and Glasgow, which is by no means too much – just healthy.

'Plain malts' or 'Lowlands' are almost in the same position as Campbeltowns – slow to move, though they, too, are come away. Some are very popular, and aged are readily picked up, but in general they are low priced and worth more money. 'New' is often difficult to sell, but the distillers know that it will be needed someday, and being in most cases able to afford it, lay aside a good stock against blenders' requirements.

Lowlands are not unpopular. It is not that which keeps them low in price, but blenders have always used them as so much padding, doing no harm to a blend, nor much good, but balancing rather the other malts and the grain spirits without affecting price. A really good sample of ten years' old plain malt is always in demand for those very old curio blends, and we think deservedly so, as by that age it has acquired a liqueur style which makes it very useful, and a 'sine qua non' to the blender, besides its cheapness. It is not easy to reckon the years' stock in bond of Lowlands, because often Campbeltowns are used instead, but we consider that there is six years available at the moment.

'Highlands' – Under this title we group the Spey makes – the many so-called Glenlivet makes and others north of that district. They are the hardest to speak of, being the most numerous. They are all good, but some of them, we fear, will be short-lived. There are too many of them. Those with big blending houses behind them have an assured sale, but some have great difficulty in finding markets, and must go to the wall.

Taking them in all, we consider that there is a nine years' stock in bond. We don't find fault with that, but when we consider that the average age of blends sold in the country is not more than two years, it is a big supply. We grant that of some Highland distilleries there is no more than a few years' requirements in bond, but as blenders are using more Lowlands, Campbeltowns, and cheaper Highlands, along with Islays and grains, it will be apparent that over-production amongst Highlands generally may assume alarming proportions. Of course there are houses with their pet blend, who use 10 Highland to 3 other malts in such, but few houses have only pet blends, and indeed for every hogshead or 30 cases sold of such, they sell 10 hogsheads or 300 cases of cheaper blends where the average proportions are 3 Highland to 10 or 12 other and much cheaper malts, and at least 70 per cent of grain spirits.

Highland distilleries have made a show of reducing stocks, but they accumulate, which is apparent from prices ranging. One can buy three to four years old of many makes at the price paid for the whisky new. As we already said, there are a few exceptions, but we believe that these exceptions, besides their reputation, are because many smaller blenders use them, not that the larger houses use such makes in greater proportions.

The only healthy feature of the Scotch whisky distilling trade at the moment is the sparse use of Highlands in blends. Undoubtedly, they give tone and flavour which are pleasing to the connoisseur, and they are used in blends which the connoisseurs can afford to pay for, but they are sparingly indeed used in blends which the consuming public drink.

Distillers who are blenders sell blends to the wine merchant, who again sells to the publicans, and in the first case the profit averages 30 per cent, in the second 50 per cent, while again the consumer pays another 50 per cent, so that a blend originally costing 2s 6d per gallon is sold at 3s 3d to 3s 6d to the wine merchant, by him at round 5s to the publican, and the consumer at that only gets about two-years-old whisky, which is absurd. Many publicans do their own blending, and then the consumer gets a better article; but publicans are getting lazy, and can't be bothered blending, so the public get a poor quality. Blends are fragrantly called ten years old which are no more than three, often less; indeed, 'tuppenny' is oftener new spirit than not, and yet the public are no wiser.

Legislation is much needed to improve the blended Scotch whisky trade, but the most effective legislation would come from the consumer if he would only demand a brand he knows rather than simply place his 2d and ask for a 'half'.

APPENDIX F:

LOCHRUAN & LOCHHEAD DISTILLERY PRODUCTION
'THE WINE AND SPIRIT TRADE RECORD' 1923

As so few distilleries were afforded an in-depth description of their production process and none of their actual spirit, here is the latter half of the article published in the above-mentioned trade magazine. What is remarkable, and difficult to comprehend, is the impressive, modern, functional and expansive description of Lochhead Distillery in 1923 - and yet, how, just a few years later, it produced its last spirit.

It is also a puzzle as to why such an elegant and well-made building (the 1899 four-storied warehouse situated on Lochend Street) was ever approved for demolition. Again, a search was made in the hope of discovering letters and articles demonstrating suitable outrage; pointing out the futility of destroying such an elegant building… to be replaced with a Tesco supermarket! The demolition of neighbouring Lochend Church to make way for the supermarket car park is also a striking loss to the town. Interesting to note that the 80-year-old stained glass windows from within the church went to Wellington, New Zealand, due to the family that donated them, having emigrated, wanting their return. They remain in place at the Church of St John in the City.

LOCHRUAN DISTILLERY
Published 14th July 1923

The distillery occupies two acres of ground within convenient distance of the quay. An elevator carries the grain, home-grown or the best foreign, to a system of up-to-date conveyors that pass it on to the steeps, each with a capacity of forty quarters. The steeping process takes about 70 hours, and the barley is then dropped to the four malting floors below. Installation of the conveyors has reduced the number of men required to handle the grain as it passes to the granary lofts from six to two, and since there is now no need to use sacks after the barley has been emptied into the hopper from the lorry, much labour is saved in connection with the malting operations. The conveyors, the elevator, and electric lighting plant are all worked by a new 8 h.p. Marshall steam engine.

The two kilns have tiled floors, and sixty hours is the usual period for drying the malt, which afterwards passes to the malt deposit. The mill-room machinery is exceptionally compact, and a novel feature is the system of screw conveyors and elevators that take the grist from the mill into a hopper above the mash-tun, which is sixteen feet in diameter and five deep. From the mash-tun the wort is drained into the underback, whence it is conveyed to the wort receiver by a powerful Tangye steam pump. This pump also removes the wash from the wash-backs to the wash-charger. A Morton's refrigerator is used for cooling the wart to the required temperature before it is run to the wash-backs for fermentation. Switchers in the wash-backs are worked by another newly-installed Marshall engine. Three stills are in use, all heated by furnace, and the present proprietors have replaced the old low-wines receiver by a new one of 1,600 gallons capacity.

Lochruan distillery is well provided with storage accommodation, and the premises include six large warehouses with space for 5,000 casks.

The output in a busy season is over 120,000 proof gallons of Malt Whisky, and the quality of the Spirit is no doubt partly due to the excellence of the water supply, which comes from a private tank in a neighbouring estate.

This distillery is one of two in the town that employ draff-drying machines. Spent grain from the mash-tun can thus be drained in a large tank, and then dried in the draff-drying plant. The machine in use was made by Messrs. Blair, Campbell and McLean, of Glasgow, and when driven at full speed it can dry 4 cwts. in an hour. Wet draff is sold to local farmers as cattle food, and dry draff is shipped to various parts of Scotland.

Most of the other distilleries in Campbeltown send their draff to a store belonging to the Campbeltown Distillery Association, where it is dried. The best methods of dealing with draff are being closely studied in the West of Scotland distilleries, and scientific research is revealing new ways of increasing its agricultural value.

Among other modern devices in Lochruan distillery is a Green's economiser – the only apparatus of its kind in Campbeltown. By providing a constant supply of hot water for the multifarious cleansing activities that are carried out in the distillery, the economiser saves much time (and several tons of coal) each week. The boiler is fed by a Weir's pump, and the water comes out of the economiser at a temperature of from 200 to 300 degrees.

LOCHHEAD DISTILLERY
Published 14th September, 1923

Only the finest distilling barley is used, being shipped to the wharf within half-a-mile of the distillery, and removed to the premises by lorry. Entering the four-storied malting house, one finds two large upper lofts for barley storage. On the third door are two steeps some 50 feet apart, which might well be mistaken for swimming baths. The grain is hoisted from the ground floor to the barley lofts, and then passed by pulley conveyors to the steeps, Each steep deals with 75 quarters of barley per week, and the water is changed twice during the steeping process. The actual malting is carried on in the two lower floors, whence the dried malt is raised by elevator to two kins, each about 40 feet square, and fitted with King's patent regulators, and Herman's wire flooring.

Following the drying process, the malt is removed by conveyor to the malt deposit, and ultimately passes to the upper mill-room for conversion to grist. In this room the 'boot' is fitted with paper shutters to prevent danger of explosion that existed in the old days when the 'boots' were occasionally blown through roofs of distilleries. Below in the mill-room one sees evidence of the new owners in the form of a 'two-high' Boby malt mill of the latest pattern, capable of grinding from 18 to 22 quarters per hour. For the removal of obstructions this mill is supplied with internal magnets, and so powerful are these that when a workman accidentally dropped his hammer into the machine, the tool was safely isolated.

In the tun rooms 1,450 bushels are mashed weekly, and the worts pass via the underback and the worts receiver to a Morton's refrigerator. There are eight wash-backs with a total capacity of 60,000 gallons. During fermentation revolving switchers are employed to release carbonic acid gas, and break up the surface froth. After some 30 hours in the wash-backs the wash is ready for distillation, and is run to the wash-charger and thence to the wash-still, said to be the largest in Campbeltown, with capacity for 9,000 gallons.

The worm-tubs, or condensers, are situated in the open air on the north side of the building, and in the spirit store is a vat of 2,000 gallons' capacity. The yard is enclosed by five warehouses with accommodation for 3,000 casks.

Draff is removed by chute to the ground level, and carted to the common store-room (which is the joint property of a number of distilleries), and ultimately dried and sold as cattle food. Some distillers in Campbeltown fail to realise their good fortune in having premises adjacent to the sea, into which the spent liquor from the wash-still is discharged by means of pipes. In the case of inland distilleries, as is well known, the problem of disposing of waste products is often a source of continuous worry and annoyance.

APPENDIX G:

EARLY 19TH CENTURY DISTILLERS IN KINTYRE

The following names have been culled largely from information contained in the still books of Robert Armour of Campbeltown, 1813-1817 and the accounts book of maltster John Colville, also of Campbeltown, 1817-19 & 1823-26. The location is given first, followed by the OS Landranger map reference and names of the distillers if known. I am grateful to Neil Wilson, who first published this list in 'The Island Whisky Trail'.

AMAD (NR707382) John McNish.
ARNICLE (NR708381) Charles McMillan.
ARUS (NR682212) Dugald McTaggart.
AUCHADADUIE (NR690368) John Taylor.
AUCHNASAVIL (NR790396) Mary Blair.
ACHAGLASS (NR789559) Alexander McDugald.
BACK STREET (NR718204) Mrs Clerk, Mrs David Broun, Mary Wright, Mary Armour.
BOLGAM STREET (NR719204) Missy McKinlay, Mary McMillan, Duncan McLean, Gavin Greenlees, Baby McEacheran, Widow McKivan, Jean Ferguson, Mary McKiney, More McEacheran.
BREWERIE (NR718209) Florence Galbraith, Blew, Mrs Tarbert
CORBETT'S CLOSE (NR719205) Isobel Sharp, Isobel Dunlop, Jeny Jeremy & Co
DALINROWAN (NR7410499) John Beith, John Smith, John Sillars, Archibald Sillars, James McLean, Nancy Allan, Peggy Taylor, Nancy Loinachan.
DALINTOBER (NR721209) Andrew Smith's wife, Cursty McCarmig, David Smith & Co
LOCHEND (NR718208) David Addam, More McCost, Duncan McTaggart, Bell Campbell, Big Kill, Jenet Eddum, Mary McKilup, Jeny McKinlay, Keat McKinvin, Keat McKeog, Keat Stewart, Peggy Clark, Jean McMillan, Mary Blew, Jeny Blew, Nany Shaw, John McColack, Keat McKinvin, Keat Campbell, Agness Shaw, Mary Kelly, Jenet Taylor, Barbra McTagart, Jenet Rowe, Mary McDonald, Gilbert Currie's wife & sister, Betty Currie, Betty McLean, Jean Graham, Missy McKinvin, Peggy Cast, Peggy Langswill, Mrs Quin, Mary McKillup, Jenet Adam,

Peter McKoag, Peggy King, Ket Kenzie, Ket McNaught, Donald Tyre.
LONGROW (NR717206) Archibald McKendrick & wife, Peggy McKillup, Widow Harvie, Widow Johnston, Mrs McCalester, Mrs Thomson, Nancy Armour, Florence Armour, Isabell Sheadan, Mrs Kilpatrick, Jean McKinvin, Bell McLean, Keat McIsaac, Jean McMillan, Bell McMillan, David Mitchell, More McEacheran, Agnes McFatter, Mrs McGlachan, Mrs McSporran, Keat Bride, Mrs Ross, Jenet Mitchell, Bell Dunlop, Florence Armour.
MILNOW (MILL KNOWE) (NR715209) John McTaggart, Jenet Metland, Duncan McTaggart, Mary McLean, Mary McMillan, Mary Conlie.
BALLOCHANTUY (NR666322) Malkom Currie, Duncan Morison, Niel Currie, Edward Currie, Peter McSporran, John McKeith.
BALLOCHROY (NR728522) Johnnie Blue.
BARR (NR683368) John McAlister, Mary McCallum, Wm McFater, Angus McMillan, Flory McTaggart, William Armour, Donald McLean.
BLARY (NR695371) Duncan McCallum, Archibald McFarland, John McFarland, Rodger McDonald, Neill McNeill
CALLIBURN (NR720255) James McKinlay & Co
CLACHAN (NR765561) James Brodie, Duncan Gilchrist, Donald McCoig (also at Loch Ciaran) Charles Mertin.
CLOINAGART (NR670342) Archibald McEachen, Donald McLeod (also at Margmonagach).
COALHILL (NR661193) Frank McKinvin, John O'May, John Campbell, Margaret McGaichy, Flory McCalister, Archibald Williamson, Nany NcArthur, Mary McKinven, John (Mc)Murphy, Bell McSporran.
CRUBASDALE (NR690406) Archibald Blair
DALBUIE (NR691139) James McGill
DARLOCHAN (NR672231)
DRUMLEMBLE (NR661193) John McInnis.
DRUMORE (NR706221) Andrew McKinvin, Archibald Downie.
DRUMORE-NA-BODACH (NR674329) Malkom Currie, Neil, Currie, Edward Currie, Duncan Morison.
HIGH FIELD, GIGHA (NR656511) Angus Smith, Donal Smith.
HIGH PARK (NR695257) Sandy Heman (Hyndman).
HOMESTON (NR673156)
KERRAFUAR (NR678149) Robert McGill, Robert Watson.
KILDAVIE, SOUTHEND (NR724106) John McGlachan, Donald McMillan.

EARLY 19TH CENTURY DISTILLERS

KILKIVAN (NR656204) Angus McMath, Alexander McNeil, J Taggart, John McNeil, Andrew McNeil, James Hue.
KILLAROW (NR662280) James McMillan, John Blair, Peggy McKay.
KILLBLAUN, SOUTHEND (NR702098) Hugh Breckenridge, Hugh McEacheran,
KILLEGRUAR (NR667359) Neill McDonald, John McAlister (also at Barr).
KILLOWCRAW (NR661306)
KILMALUAG (NR693376)
KNOCKHANTY (NR641201) Flory McTaggart
KNOCKNAHA (NR688180) Alexander Campbell, John Kelly, Keat Bralachan, Archibald Boid, Alexander Craig, Mrs Craw, James Craw, Alexander McKeith, Archibald McKeith, Malcolm Kelly.
KNOCKRIOCH (NR700195) Donald Kelly.
LAGALGARVE (NR660297)
LOCH CIARAN, CLACHAN (NR766549) John McLean, Archibald Milloy, Alexander McKoag, John McKeargan.
LOSSIT (NR634193) Sandy Cameron, ? Gardener, ? Gardener's widow
MACHRIEMORE (NR694091) Michael McKilop, William Brown
MIDDLE BARR (NR677367) James Kelly, Angus Downey.
PUTECHAN (NR668313) John McMillan.
RANACHAN (NR696245) John Maloy.
SADDELL (NR787322) Alexander McMillan & Co.
SALTPANS (NR632208) Donald Cameron, Dugald McClaverin, Hector Reid (also at Lossit), John Smith.
STOCKADALE (NR678368) Archibald Gilchrist.
TEANCHOISIN (NR745405)
TANGY (NR674277) Robert Clerk.
TIRFERGUS (NR662182) Hector McEacheran, Sandy Munro, Neil McEacheran, Donald McCallum, Alexander Martin.
TORCHOILLAN (NR661190) Nancy Watson.
TRODIGAL (NR649207) William Armour, John Hendry, John McKendrick, Donald McTaggart.

APPENDIX H:
TABLE OF CAMPBELTOWN PRODUCTION, STOCK DISPATCHED AND STOCK IN BOND

Year-end Sept 30th	Produced	Cleared bond	Stock in Bond
1855	1,014,800		
1865	1,140,946		
1875	1,636,484		
1889		1,159,567	
1890		1,153,352	
1891	1,575,810	1,288,287	4,200,202
1892	1,573,765	1,273,808	4,500,000
1893	1,617,133	1,416,151	4,700,882
1894	1,628,468	1,167,682	5,161,668
1895	1,653,352	1,288,732	5,526,288
1896	1,754,373	1,414,612	5,866,051
1897	1,810,226	1,431,414	6,246,863
1898	1,620,478	1,413,229	6,454,112
1899	1,447,652	1,391,878	6,509,886
1900	1,141,753	1,408,078	6,243,561
1901	1,162,393	1,405,338	6,000,616
1902	1,228,600	1,402,946	5,286,270
1903	1,314,255	1,419,219	5,721,223
1904	1,435,065	1,314,098	5,842,190
1905	1,360,525	1,266,212	5,936,504
1906	1,240,199	1,296,252	5,974,279
1907	1,275,490	1,181,388	5,974,297
1908	865,995	1,123,385	5,716,889
1909	1,161,063	883,587	5,994,335
1910*	917,576	679,028	6,232,903
1911*	717,059	859,481	6,090,481
1912*	755,368	860,838	5,985,011
1913	523,240	825,926	5,682,405
1914	736,685	775,685	5,642,405
1915	<200,000		

* end of October (Proof gallons)

APPENDIX I:

SPRINGBANK PRODUCTION TABLE 1905-1937
(Proof gallons)

1905	
JAN	9,162.5
FEB	12,692.6
MAR	14,140.9
APR	12,257.1
MAY	13,257.0
JUN	1,446.7
NOV	2,777.3
DEC	15,987.5
TOTAL	81,721.6

1906	
JAN	10,245.5
FEB	13,254.6
MAR	13,108.6
APR	12,703.9
MAY	14,929.2
NOV	6,904.8
DEC	13,310.4
TOTAL	84,457.0

1907	
JAN	9,211.6
FEB	12,494.5
MAR	13,677.2
APR	13,654.4
MAY	13,957.1
JUN	850.2
TOTAL	63,845.0

1908	
JAN	1,252.8
FEB	12,237.1
MAR	14,185.7
APR	12,542.0
MAY	14,516.6
JUN	9,643.9
NOV	6,427.8
DEC	14,012.3
TOTAL	84,818.2

1909	
JAN	10,332.9
FEB	12,195.5
MAR	13,817.7
APR	13,918.3
MAY	8,396.0
DEC	6,655.4
TOTAL	65,315.8

1910	
JAN	9,154.1
FEB	10,013.0
MAR	10,200.3
APR	12,257.1
MAY	13,257.0
JUN	1,446.7
NOV	2,777.3
DEC	15,987.5
TOTAL	75,093.0

1911	
JAN	9,496.7
FEB	11,752.2
MAR	13,701.1
APR	12,184.9
MAY	7,362.7
TOTAL	54,497.6

1912	
FEB	11,398.0
MAR	13,319.3
APR	12,763.6
TOTAL	37,480.9

1913	
JAN	4,452.6
FEB	12,488.5
MAR	11,761.5
APR	9,621.0
JUN	1,446.7
NOV	1,289.4
DEC	13,792.7
TOTAL	54,852.4

1914	
JAN	11,272.9
FEB	12,779.5
MAR	14,707.5
APR	6,115.6
TOTAL	44,875.5

1916	
FEB	4,508.8
MAR	12,771.7
APR	11,371.3
MAY	11,840.4
JUN	10,403.5
DEC	7,380.9
TOTAL	58,276.6

1917	
JAN	9,405.4
FEB	9,996.1
TOTAL	19,401.5

1919	
FEB	168.9
MAR	8,739.2
APR	13,288.8
MAY	9,351.8
NOV	10,847.2
DEC	12,726.9
TOTAL	55,122.8

1920	
JAN	1,133.0
FEB	12,109.9
MAR	15,216.7
APR	14,371.6
MAY	12,353.3
JUN	13,410.8
NOV	7,572.0
DEC	11,685.7
TOTAL	87,853.0

1921	
JAN	12,354.3
FEB	12,369.6
MAR	13,862.3
APR	8,725.1
NOV	11,995.1
DEC	15,158.9
TOTAL	74,465.3

SPRINGBANK PRODUCTION

1922	
JAN	10,463.3
FEB	13,760.8
MAR	14,150.6
APR	12,827.4
MAY	10,335.4
OCT	5,964.5
NOV	13,266.3
DEC	14,843.4
TOTAL	95,611.7

1923	
JAN	8,899.3
FEB	12,937.9
MAR	14,074.4
APR	14,079.8
MAY	6,975.2
NOV	12,938.1
DEC	14,741.1
TOTAL	84,645.8

1924	
JAN	10,676.3
FEB	9,504.9
MAR	13,789.0
APR	12,060.4
MAY	5,126.6
NOV	10,596.4
DEC	14,765.0
TOTAL	76,518.6

1925	
JAN	10,548.5
FEB	12,373.6
MAR	8,199.1
APR	13,846.4
DEC	6,160.8
TOTAL	51,128.4

1926	
JAN	10,645.0
FEB	13,709.0
MAR	4,229.0
TOTAL	28,583.0

1930	
FEB	3,525.3
MAR	12,041.0
TOTAL	15,566.3

1936	
MAR	10,396.2
APR	10,748.6
MAY	8,179.8
NOV	5,425.4
DEC	13,922.4
TOTAL	48,672.4

1937	
JAN	12,447.0
FEB	14,052.8
MAR	12,515.6
APR	15,349.1
MAY	13,357.5
OCT	4,777.0
NOV	13,059.6
DEC	13,760.4
TOTAL	99,319.0

SPRINGBANK PRODUCTION BY SEASON 1906-1937
(Proof gallons)

Year	Gallons	Year	Gallons
1906	83,006.6	1922	88,691.5
1907	84,060.2	1923	85,076.3
1908	64,378.1	1924	78,836.4
1909	79,100.5	1925	70,329.0
1910	62,983.6	1926	34,743.8
1911	73,262.4	1927	Silent
1912	37,480.9	1928	Silent
1913	39,770.3	1929	15,566.3
1914	59,957.6	1930	29,324.6
1915	Silent	1931	Silent
1916	50,895.7	1932	Silent
1917	26,782.4	1933	Silent
1918	Silent	1934	Silent
1919	31,548.7	1935	29,324.6
1920	92,169.4	1936	29,324.6
1921	66,569.0	1937	87,069.8

APPENDIX J:

SPRINGBANK DISTILLERY, CAMPBELTOWN

By Hedley G. Wright, M.A.

Springbank Distillery is situated in the heart of Campbeltown and the premises to-day, comprise not only the original buildings of 1828, but also parts of the extinct distilleries of Longrow, Rieclachan, Union, Springside and Argyll. It was originally the fourteenth distillery to be built in the golden days of the early 19th century but is now the senior and larger of the two remaining distilleries. It is in the nearly unique position of being the only distillery left in Scotland which is exclusively owned and controlled by the original family of distillers.

The story of the Mitchell family is in a way a history of recent Campbeltown distilling and it is impossible to give an account of Springbank Distillery without mentioning the several of the other distilleries of old Campbeltown.

Local records suggest that the Mitchell family came to Argyll with the second wave of Lowland settlement about 1660. Many of the family were maltsters and, in those pre-Jacobite days, it must be assumed that they were also distillers. Some Mitchells were a little more colourful, for instance James Mitchell, a weaver in Campbeltown, was a rebel in the Marquis of Argyle's rising in support of Monmouth in 1685, but his error was counterbalanced by other members of the family, James and Archibald Mitchell, who, in 1692, are recorded as being Fencible Men of Argyle: in other words they were members of the Home Guard of those times.

The history of Springbank Distillery can be conveniently begun with Archibald Mitchell (1734-1818), a farmer near Campbeltown and great-great-great-grandfather of the distillery's present managing director. Archibald's sister married Hugh Ferguson, a maltster in Campbeltown and his son, Archibald (II), married this sister's daughter: so it is not surprising that Archibald (II) traded as a maltster, the business of his uncle/father-in-law. Archibald

(II)'s malt barns were on the site of the future Springbank Distillery and were indeed to become the original maltings of the distillery. Although it is known from the private ledger of a local coppersmith that Archibald operated a still for Whisky, he never troubled to put himself on the right side of the law by taking out a licence: it was left to his sons, Hugh, Archibald (III), John and William and one of his daughters, Mary, to bring themselves within the law. Archibald (III) was one of the original partners of Rieclachan Distillery where he was later joined by his brother Hugh. Springbank Distillery was built on the site of Archibald (II)'s illegal distillery in 1828, by the Reid family who were in-laws of the Mitchells but, as the Reids soon found themselves in financial trouble, John and William Mitchell bought the property in 1837 and thereby restored their father's distillery to the direct line of descent. The new and legal firm of J. and W. Mitchell made their first sale on 14th November 1837, to one, Isabella Brown of Campbeltown, who 24 gallons at 8s. 2d. per gallon. This price included the government duty; the present price of a proof gallon of new Springbank whisky is £12 7s. 5d. inclusive of duty!

Not all of the new firm's early customers were to disappear into obscurity like Isabella Brown: during the first year's trading, on 8th October, 1838, John Walker of Kilmarnock, bought 112 gallons at 8s. 8d. per gallon and all the world knows that this John Walker is 'still going strong'. Samuel Dow of Glasgow, who made an earlier purchase on 12th March, 1838, is another well-known name in the trade that has survived through the years.

However, trouble lay ahead, for John and William, who were farmers as well as distillers, quarrelled violently, not about whisky but about sheep. William left Springbank to join his brothers at Rieclachan Distillery, so John took his own son into partnership and thus changed the firm's name to J. and A. Mitchell which it still remains. It should be noticed that William was not content to rest in partnership with his Rieclachan brothers for, in 1872, he started Glengyle Distillery as sole proprietor. Neither, for that matter, did John remain satisfied with Springbank and, in 1851, he was one of three partners that bought out Toberanrigh Distillery which, had been built by his cousin, Alexander Wylie, in 1834.

Mary Mitchell, daughter of Archibald (II) and now a widow, was one of the four partners of Templeton, Fulton and Co., who built Drumore Distillery in 1834. In this way did the Mitchells establish their position among the other distilling magnates of Campbeltown: the Colvilles, the Fergusons and the Mactaggarts, to name a few.

Springbank Distillery prospered and in 1897, when the firm became a limited company, it was one of the largest in Campbeltown. Springbank, although affected adversely by the depression of the 1920s and '30s, fortunately managed to avoid the wave of prejudice that built up against Campbeltown Whiskies at about the same time and it is probably due to this alone that the company managed to survive that difficult period. It is interesting to note that in September, 1924, when White Horse Distillers applied for a rates reduction on their evidence was given to the court that the market price for Ardbeg whisky was 18s. 3d., for Craigellachie 16s. and for Hazelburn 8s.; furthermore, Hazelburn had only worked ten periods during the previous year in place of the normal 50. Springbank was fortunate in having a full year's production at that time: but what of the other Mitchell distilleries? Both Drumore and Toberanrigh were already closed and Glengyle had just been sold for £300! It was only a matter of time before Ricclachan was caught up by economic conditions and, although it produced probably the finest of the Campbeltown Whiskies, the business was wound up. An interesting souvenir from the period of growing Campbeltown disfavour remains in the warehouses of Springbank in the form of a hogshead of 1919 Whisky: it is a fine clean tasting Spirit without any trace of woodiness which might have been gained by the use of a poor cask; it will be kept for another seven years before bottling.

Springbank Distillery to-day has changed in several features from older times. The company has been one of the pioneers in mechanisation within the distilling industry and the movement of barley and malt is now performed entirely by belts, screws and elevators. The barley intake of the distillery was adapted several years ago for the receipt of bulk supplies and anticipated considerably the method of transport and delivery that is now becoming popular. The actual maltings have been rationalised so that there is only set of floors and one kiln where formerly there had been two independent maltings. Modern techniques of box or drum maltings were rejected in favour of the traditional system as they did not affect an adequate economy to compensate for the poorer quality of malt produced by these methods. The green malt is dried on a pressure kiln of modern design and this item of equipment has been found to give a superior quality of malt and also effect considerable economy of time and fuel.

The peat used to dry the malt is cut within a few miles of the distillery by the company itself. Springbank can manufacture all its malt requirements and is one of the few distilleries in Scotland that can do this. The dried malt is stored in metal bins before being ground to a coarse flour or 'grist'. The grist is mashed with hot water in a large iron and copper tun of conventional type and the resulting sweet solution, the 'wort', is strained away from the undissolved malt husks, the 'draff', and is cooled by passing through a Paraflow heat exchanger and run into the fermenting vessels, the 'wash-backs'. The unwanted draff is a high-quality cattle food and is sold entirely to local farmers. The actual wash-backs are made of Scottish 'boat skin' larch wood, for it is the belief of the proprietors that a steel wash-back, although less expensive to install and maintain, gives a distinct taint to the final Whisky, in an analogous manner to the distinctive tone given to a violin by the use of steel strings. In the wash-back yeast is added to the worts which then ferment to become a sour Beer-like liquid called Wash.

From this stage onwards operations are acutely watched by officers of H. M. Customs and Excise to ensure that no alcohol goes into consumption without payment of duty. The wash is pumped into a large copper still which is heated by a coal fire underneath and also, simultaneously, by an internal coil through which super-heated steam is passed. This method of heating a wash-still is the traditional Campbeltown technique and has been used at Springbank for as long as memory and records indicate; it is thought that no distilleries outside Campbeltown use this method. The hot vapours that are driven off the wash are condensed again by passing them through a long coiled 'worm' of copper tube which is cooled with running water. When all the alcohol has been driven off the wash, distillation is stopped and the alcohol free 'pot ale' remaining in the still is run to waste. The collected distillate, known as the low-wines, is carefully divided into two portions, one of which is distilled again in a small 'doubling still' to give 'feints' which are mixed with the remaining low-wines and run into a third still where the final distillation takes place. A large portion of the Spirit condensed in the final distillation is rejected and it is only an accurately controlled 'middle cut' that is run into the Spirit store for filling the customer's casks.

A noteworthy feature of the plant at Springbank is the recently installed coal-burning boiler which produces the large quantities of steam required for heating purposes. This is fully automatic in action and regulates its own draught and coal supply to suit the varying amounts of steam being used. Coal was selected as the fuel because oil, the only competitive alternative, was considered too risky a substance to have anywhere near Whisky either in manufacture or maturing warehouses. The ability of Whisky to pick up any stray odours is proverbial.

In spite of the mechanisation that has taken place in recent years all the vital processes in the manufacture of Springbank Whisky have remained unaltered so the actual quantity of Whisky produced to-day is only slightly greater than at the beginning of the century. The water used for the malting, mashing and cooling all comes from the Crosshill Loch which lies on the outskirts of the 'Whisky City' about one mile from the distillery.

This article first appeared in 'The Wine and Spirit Trade Record' on 17th April 1963.

ENDNOTES:
1 By car or bike at least.
2 It is likely many of these were associated with either existing distilleries or breweries.
3 TDBASMM 1st March, 1901. Article titled *'Progress of Scotch Distilling in the Last Century'*, by a Campbeltown Distillery.
4 The pseudonym of English author, Edward Bradley, who visited Kintyre in 1859, and published *Glenreggan*, two years later.
5 I can't help wonder at the genius of the naming of this distillery. However, it has made research difficult…
6 The list was predominantly that of Campbeltown distilleries but also included eight Islay distilleries – with two distilleries situated at Bowmore and Lagavulin.
7 Moss & Hume, *The Making of Scotch Whisky*, p. 62.
8 Moss & Hume, *The Making of Scotch Whisky, p. 216.*
9 CC – 16th January 1886.
10 'A Long Stride' Nicholas Morgan p.26.
11 Ibid p. 37
12 The Campbeltown Book, p. 125 & 126
13 Bere and Bigg are both types of barley.
14 'Campbeltown Conservation Area Appraisal', Gray, Marshall & Associates, 2009.
15 Spinning, or causing concern, for the churches.
16 Glasgow Herald 16th February, 1877.
17 CC – 30th October, 1886 quoting from a "London contemporary, 'Land and Water'".
18 CC - Accident took place on 20th February 1879. Reported in Campbeltown Courier 1st March 1879.
19 Argyllshire Herald 16th September 1876
20 This is clearly a typo and likely closer to 500 gallons per week.
21 CC – 6th September, 1879.
22 All letters from Lochgilphead Archives.
23 CC – 22nd May, 1875.
24 Lochgilphead Archives, Duncan Colville papers.
25 John McKersie was supposed to have said to Clifford "Make it like my brother's [William] only better."
26 The Campbeltown Book p.283.
27 Campbeltown Whisky Encyclopaedia, Angus Martin, p. 254.
28 Oban Times and Argyllshire Advertiser, 20th May, 1876.
29 Argyllshire Herald, 13th May, 1876.
30 P. 202.
31 CC – 22nd February, 1913.
32 As the A83 does today.

ENDNOTES

33 Still visible today.
34 Barnard was not a great chronicler of names. Far too preoccupied with measuring frontages and diameters.
35 CC – 26th July, 1884.
36 This is the English use of the word Scudding, 'to move fast in a straight line' and not the Scottish definition, 'to slap, beat or spank.'
37 One hundred and ten years before Barnard visited Campbeltown, a slightly more famous English writer had also vexed lyrical due to parts of Scotland being sans trees. Samuel Johnson, albeit on the other side of the country, in Fife, had bemoaned St Andrews' lack of any large trees.
38 It is worth pointing out, perhaps a touch late in the book, that a quarter of barley is 448 lbs, and a bushel is roughly one-tenth of a quarter.
39 And what would have been far more interesting to us reading a century later was never recorded. It is slightly surprising that the office wasn't measured.
40 It would appear that none of the distillery plans or drawings remain. Each distillery, including alterations and warehouses, would have been submitted to the Dean of Guild – alas, their records have either been lost or destroyed.
41 Although not named, it is possible these were the Low Wines, Intermediate and Spirit receivers.
42 I have to take Barnard at his word here. Looking at contemporary maps it is hard to conceive of how the distillery had a view of anything but the Campbeltown and Glengyle Distilleries opposite. The hills behind yes. The bay, hard to imagine.
43 Another term for Anthracite.
44 Angus Martin thinks this quite unlikely but as errant as Barnard was, it is unlikely he invented this reservoir.
45 Not sure how Barnard forgot to measure that.
46 CC – 16th April, 1887.
47 The ad noted that "It is now beyond a doubt that whisky will supersede the common gin in this country, and at present whisky, although sold high, is generally called for." Bath Chronicle and Weekly Gazette, 23rd February 1826.
48 Duncan Colville files.
49 Grain whisky had previously meant a mixture of malt and other grains in large pot stills. This form of distillation is still carried on in parts of Ireland.
50 Grain whisky production would continue to be the dominant force until 2017.
51 CC – 8th April, 1893.
52 OMIC January 1898
53 Although at this time, there was no stipulation to use oak. This would become part of the Scotch Whisky Act of 1988 that came into law in 1990.
54 'Scotch and Sherry', Iain Russell, Unfiltered.
55 CC – 21st June, 1890.
56 A more circumspect James Greenlees would be interviewed in 1908 by a Select Committee.

57 Under the terms of the partnership, Samuel Greenlees Sr, and Charles Colville Greenlees retired from the company in 1880.
58 The phylloxera aphid destroyed much of the French vineyards in the mid-late 1800s.
59 Royal Commission 1908
60 The National Guardian 1895.
61 The ad, taken out in the Surrey Advertiser, 7th December, 1878, quoted the Morning Post, the Standard, and the Medical Review respectively.
62 London Morning Advertiser.
63 Although no date is provided for the date of entry to the Osborne Street premises, we know that Greenlees were operational by 16th August, 1884 due to Messrs James McGuire and Andrew Paton, who *"pleaded guilty to housebreaking with intent to steal… [as] they feloniously entered the bonded warehouses of Messrs Greenlees Brother, Osborne Street, by kicking in one of the panels of the door. They were each sent to prison for six months."* Glasgow Herald.
64 The frontage still exists (the arches are now bricked up), while much of the warehousing is now gone.
65 Scotch Whisky Review, Richard Joynson – no original source reference provided.
66 Now the St Pancras Hotel.
67 A Long Stride, Nicholas Morgan. Pages 72 & 73.
68 Launceston Examiner 9th March, 1888.
69 It is not known if he returned to write his chapter in the Greenlees Brother's booklet.
70 Banffshire Journal 28th May, 1895: *"Messrs Greenlees Brothers, distillers have just completed contract for the erection of a large distillery at Kingussie, to be called Speyside Distillery, and capable of distilling about 2,500 bushels of barley weekly."*
71 Inverness Courier 27th May, 1904.
72 Scotch Missed, Brian Townsend p.73.
73 Stonehaven Journal - 24th March 1910
74 James is asked if he is a director of three different companies: Greenlees and Colvill, Limited of the Hazelburn Distillery; Colvill, Greenlees and Co., Limited, Argyll Distillery and Burnside Distillery; and the Speyside Distillery Company, Limited, Kingussie-on-Spey. He confirms he is. It has already been established he is a partner in the firm of Greenlees Brothers.
75 See Appendix D.
76 Aberdeen Press and Journal 1st January, 1926.
77 See Appendix F for Samuel Greenlees obituary in the Campbeltown Courier.
78 This is still often the case today.
79 This became part of Bank of Scotland in 1969.
80 £700,000 is £76 million ATTOW.

ENDNOTES

81 November, 1899.
82 Aberdeen Press and Journal 28th August, 1901.
83 OMIC February 1903.
84 CC – 28th December, 1907.
85 TWASTR 8th October, 1907.
86 TWASTR 8th November, 1908.
87 CC – 31st December, 1910.
88 CC – 28th December, 1912.
89 CC – 27th December, 1913.
90 CC – 26th December, 1914.
91 TWASTR 8th January, 1915.
92 CC – 24th April, 1915.
93 TWASTR – January 8th, 1915.
94 And still the law today.
95 TWASTR 8th June, 1915.
96 TWASTR 8th July, 1915.
97 CC – 25th September, 1915.
98 This is a guess. It could have been Charles Doig Sr who remained active during WW1 or one of his two sons Charles Jr or William.
99 Peter Dewar letters 14th May, 1917.
100 TWASTR 12th November, 1918.
101 TWASTR 10th January, 1919.
102 MacCallum was also a director and investor of several other firms including Benromach Distillery near Elgin.
103 The Scotsman, 22nd November, 1919. Capital was £150,000 which is £6.5 million ATTOW.
104 'The Hotel Inn Keeper Vintner and Spirit's Dealer's Assistant' Alexander Peddie, (Glasgow, 1825), p. 276. Sourced from A Long Stride, Nicholas Morgan 2020.
105 'Views of Campbeltown' William Smith, 1835.
106 Edinburgh Evening News, 8th April, 1880.
107 Kintyre and the Kintyre Club, Sinclair, Alex, 1884.
108 WASTR – 8th April, 1905.
109 CC – 17th September, 1898.
110 Distiller's Magazine and Trade News, 1st July, 1903.
111 TWASTR – 8th April, 1905.
112 Aberdeen Press and Journal 26th December, 1908.
113 Angus Martin, Campbeltown Town Whisky – an Encyclopaedia, P. 281.
114 I assumed one of these had to have been Charles Maclean, but he assures me there was no request.
115 Letter dated December 1921 from Mackie & C., Distillers Ltd sent to customers from the Diageo Archives.
116 Letter dated October 1922 from Mackie & C., Distillers Ltd sent to customers from the Diageo Archives.

117 See Hazelburn Distillery History in Appendix 1.
118 CC – 20th August 1881. Anonymously submitted by 'A Glasgow Visitor'. The final verse reads, *"Tho' Burns has said that drink inspires, And fills the herd with war, desires, It makes us sit by cheerless fires, In want and woe; And makes us slaved for petty hires, And mean and low."*
119 CC – 3rd June, 1876.
120 Campbeltown, Ann Glenn p. 140.
121 CC – 29th May, 1875
122 CC – 10th July, 1875.
123 CC – 31st July, 1875.
124 19th May, 1876.
125 CC – 28th June, 1890.
126 CC - 10th July, 1875.
127 OMIC May 1897
128 CC – 16th July, 1921.
129 CC - 9th December, 1922.
130 CC – 30th September, 1876.
131 CC – 24th September, 1910.
132 CC – 16th September 1922.
133 Until Glengyle was rebuilt in 2004.
134 The Recorder 10th March, 1934.
135 A Sense of Place: Kintyre's Remarkable Diaspora, Ronald J Roberts, 2013.
136 CC – 15th December, 1928.
137 CC – 19th January, 1929.
138 £48 million ATTOW
139 CC – 23rd September, 1922.
140 CC – 2nd December, 1939.
141 CC – 6th January, 1940.
142 CC 2nd November 1940 "Is Campbeltown Done?"
143 The Scotsman, 25th May, 1965.
144 Frank McHardy had previously worked at Invergordon Distillery.
145 As Sales Manager for Wm Cadenhead in case anyone was interested.
146 'Pioneering Spirits' David Stirk, 2024.
147 CC - 24th December, 1881.
148 CC – 14th May, 1927.
149 CC – 5th January 1929.
150 CC – 12th November, 1904.
151 CC – 5th August, 1916.
152 The Hour, 15th January, 1875.
153 'Campbeltown Whisky – An Encyclopaedia' Angus Martin p. 7
154 Ibid – no source provided.
155 As this article is so close in style to Barnard's book, an apology must be made for my earlier comments. Although I maintiain that the Courier's article

is more engaging.
156 CC 6th September 1879
157 The Scottish Whisky Distilleries Misako Udo p.287
158 The Campbeltown & Machrihanish Light Railway Nigel S. C. MacMilan
159 CC - 17th March 1894.
160 You will be pleased to hear they were indeed spared and celebrated their Golden Wedding Anniversary in 1919.
161 TDABMATN – 1st April 1900. This custom of giving employees gifts was still in practice when I left J. & A. Mitchell & Co. Ltd., in August 2004. I received a rare bottle of whisky, sadly now gone, and a handsome hip flask inscribed with Springbank which I still possess.
162 The Wine and Spirit Trade Record 8th May, 1905.
163 Oban Times 8th June,1901.
164 Around £8 million today. Aberdeen Press and Journal 19th February, 1921.
165 A 'Public Roup' is another way of saying auction.
166 CC 27th September 1924.
167 CC 5th January, 1924.
168 Whisky Encyclopaedia Angus Martin p. 8 & 9.
169 CC – 5th July, 1947.
170 CC – 19th April, 1879.
171 CC – 6th September 1879.
172 CC – 24th December 1881.
173 CC – 11th February 1888.
174 CC – 17th January, 1920.
175 The Yorkshire Post - 4th February, 1920.
176 Edinburgh Evening Courant 23rd June 1828.
177 CC – 8th December, 1888.
178 CC – 18th February, 1905.
179 The Dunfermline Saturday Press, 24th March, 1888.
180 The Scotsman 17th March, 1925.
181 The Wine and Spirit Trade Record 8th April, 1905.
182 Dundee Advertiser 5th October, 1889.
183 The Wine and Spirit Trade Record, May 1905.
184 TDMASTM – June 1897.
185 CC – 15th October 1898.
186 CC – 27th September 1924.
187 The Scotsman 23rd September 1936.
188 CC – 22nd November 1930.
189 The Scotsman 16th October 1954.
190 Glen Scotia Distillery: A History, Angus Martin p.38.
191 Glen Scotia Distillery: A History, Angus Martin p.41.
192 CC – 9th December 1994.
193 The Wine and Spirit Trade Record 14th February, 1924.
194 Glasgow Herald 24th January, 1845.

195 Glasgow Chronicle 24th January, 1849.
196 The Star, 17th February, 1870.
197 Oban Times and Argyllshire Advertiser 9th July, 1881
198 Argyllshire Herald 25th September, 1863
199 CC - 13th July, 1878
200 Whisky Encyclopaedia Angus Martin p.150 -151.
201 The Scotsman 25th October, 1921.
202 Edinburgh Evening News 10th August 1903.
203 North Briton 3rd April, 1875.
204 Oban Times and Argyllshire Advertiser 24th April, 1926.
205 Whisky Encyclopaedia Angus Martin p.130 – quote taken from Argyllshire Herald 4th February, 1854.
206 Renfrewshire Independent 15th July 1876
207 Ulster Football and Cycling News 1896.
208 CC 29th April 1899
209 Whisky Encyclopaedia' Angus Martin p.134.
210 Dundee Courier 16th November, 1870.
211 Dundee Advertiser 24th January, 1871.
212 Oban Times and Argyllshire Advertiser 17th June, 1871.
213 North British Daily Mail 15th May, 1865.
214 CC - 9th December, 1876.
215 CC - 23rd December, 1899.
216 CC - 10th December, 1932.
217 CC - 4th November, 1933.
218 The Recorder 10th March, 1934.
219 Whisky Encyclopaedia Angus Martin p.187.
220 Dundee Courier 28th November ,1872.
221 Dundee Courier 9th July, 1890.
222 TDBASMM 1st October, 1897.
223 Glasgow Herald 21st July, 1856.
224 Weekly Examiner (Belfast) 4th April, 1874.
225 Glasgow Herald 2nd July, 1852.

BIBLIOGRAPHY:

BOOKS:

Barnard, Alfred, 'The Whisky Distilleries of The United Kingdom', Harper's Weekly Gazette, 1887.

Gillies, Freddy, 'In Campbeltown Once More', Northern Books, 2000.

Glenn, Ann, 'The Campbeltown Book', Kintyre Civic Society 2003

Hazlehurst, Justine, 'Opening The Case – The Affairs of Pattisons' Whisky', 2024

Martin, Angus, 'Campbeltown Whisky – An Encyclopaedia', The Grimsay Press, 2020.

McDougall, John, 'Wort, Worms & Washbacks, Memoirs From the Stillhouse' 1999, Neil Wilson Publishing.

Morgan, Nicholas, 'A Long Stride – The Story of the World's No. 1 Scotch Whisky', Canongate, 2020.

Morrice, Philip, 'The Schweppes Guide to Scotch', Alphabooks, 1983.

Moss, Michael S and Hume, John R, 'The Making of Scotch Whisky', Canongate Books 2000.

Stirk, David, 'The Distilleries of Campbeltown – The Rise and Fall of the Whisky Capital of the World', Angel's Share, 2005.

Stirk, David, 'Independent Scotch – The History of Independent Bottlers', 2023, SC Publishing.

Taketsuru, Masataka, 'On the Production Methods of Pot Still Whisky', Humming Earth, 2021.

Townsend, Brian, 'Scotch Missed - Scotland's Lost Distilleries', The Angel's Share, 2004.

Udo, Misako, 'The Scottish Whisky Distilleries', Distillery Cat Publishing, 2005.

Wilson, Ross, 'Scotch – The Formative Years', Constable & Company Ltd, 1970

'The Wine & Spirit Trade Record, The Distilleries of Great Britain & Ireland 1922-1929', Printed by James Eadie Ltd, 2022.

'The Distillation of Whisky' Notes and Observations on its Historical and Practical Aspects 1927-1931, Printed by James Eadie Ltd, 2023

BOOKLETS:

Martin, Angus, 'Glen Scotia Distillery: A History 2019'
'Kintyre and The Kintyre Club – Historical Sketch of the Peninsula 1825 to 1883', published by The Kintyre Club 1884.
'Campbeltown – The Official Historical Guide to Southern Kintyre' (1930s) published by the Campbeltown Advertising Committee.

GOVERNMENT REPORTS:
Interim Report of the Royal Commission on Whiskey and Other Potable Spirits, 1908.
Report from the Select Committee on British and Foreign Spirits, 1891

JOURNALS, NEWSPAPERS & ARCHIVES:
The Distillers Magazine and Spirit Trade News 1897-1905
The Wine and Spirits Trade Magazine 1898-1930
Campbeltown Courier
Scotchwhisky.com

Diageo Archives
Lochgilphead Archives
Glasgow University Archives
Glasgow City Archives
J. & A. Mitchell's Accounts and Ledgers

IMAGE SOURCES:

Page 7 - National Library of Scotland.
Page 9 - Argyll & Bute District Archives.
Page 31 - J. & A. Mitchell Records.
Page 35 - Argyll & Bute District Archives.
Page 40 - Argyll & Bute District Archives.
Page 50 - John Mcfadyen.
Page 54 - Argyll & Bute District Archives.
Page 87 - Argyll & Bute District Archives.
Page 97 - Argyll & Bute District Archives.
Page 104 - Argyll & Bute District Archives.
Page 128 - Argyll & Bute District Archives.
Page 148 - Argyll & Bute District Archives.
Page 180 - Diageo Archives.
Page 183 - Diageo Archives.
Page 200 - Glasgow Archives.
Page 203 - Glasgow Archives.
Page 205 - Glasgow Archives.
Page 207 – Frank McHardy.
Page 213 - J. & A. Mitchell Records.
Page 219 - J. & A. Mitchell Records.
Page 223 - Frank McHardy.
Page 224 - Frank McHardy.
Page 228 - Neil Wilson.
Page 229 - John Mcfadyen.
Page 231 - John Mcfadyen.
Page 247 - Argyll & Bute District Archives.
Page 248 - Argyll & Bute District Archives.
Page 249 - Argyll & Bute District Archives.
Page 250 - Neil Wilson.
Page 252 - Argyll & Bute District Archives.
Page 271 - Argyll & Bute District Archives.
Page 279 - Argyll & Bute District Archives.
Page 281 - Diageo Archives.
Page 284 - Argyll & Bute District Archives.
Page 287 - Argyll & Bute District Archives.
Page 292 - Argyll & Bute District Archives.
Page 295 - Argyll & Bute District Archives.
Page 301 - Argyll & Bute District Archives.
Page 305 - Neil Wilson.
Page 306 - Neil Wilson.

ACKNOWLEDGEMENTS:

Thanks to my ever-patient wife for indulging me, once again, in another time-consuming, passion project.

A huge thanks to Leon Kuebler at James Eadie & Co. Ltd., for his painstakingly methodical research going through 'The Wine & Spirit Trade Record' at the British Library. Thanks also to Iain Russell for his continual editorial help, fact-checking, and contributions, and to my mother, Carol Taylor, for her editing and encouragement.

Thanks to Mark & Kate Watt, Graham Fraser, Nicholas Morgan, Mark Davidson, and Alia Campbell at the Diageo Archives. Thanks to everyone at J. & A. Mitchell - particularly David Allen, Grant Macpherson and Fiona Brown. Also to Iain McAlister, at Loch Lomond Distillers.

A special thanks to those who work in the shops and bars in Campbeltown for keeping me entertained whilst I spent a small fortune (Cadenhead's still do the best coffee in the 'toon').

Thanks for additional help from Serge Valentin, Frank McHardy, Alan Winchester, Mark Davidson, David Tjeder, Simon Thompson and Stuart Robertson. Thanks to John Mcfadyen and Frank McHardy for the use of their photos.

An important thank you to the current Chairman of J. & A. Mitchell, who once took a chance on a mercurial, whisky-mad graduate. One of those life-altering, sliding-door moments. Ask me about it one day.

David Stirk has spent his adult life making, bottling, branding, selling, writing and talking about Scotch whisky. His other books include 'Independent Scotch – The History of Independent Bottlers', 2023 and 'Pioneering Spirits – A Tour of Scotland's 21st Century Whisky Distilleries', 2024. If not busy visiting a distillery or whisky festival, David can be found either on the golf course or reading non-fiction – primarily historical. Despite this book being on the academic side, it is the people and the product, first and foremost, that keeps David interested in Scotch whisky.

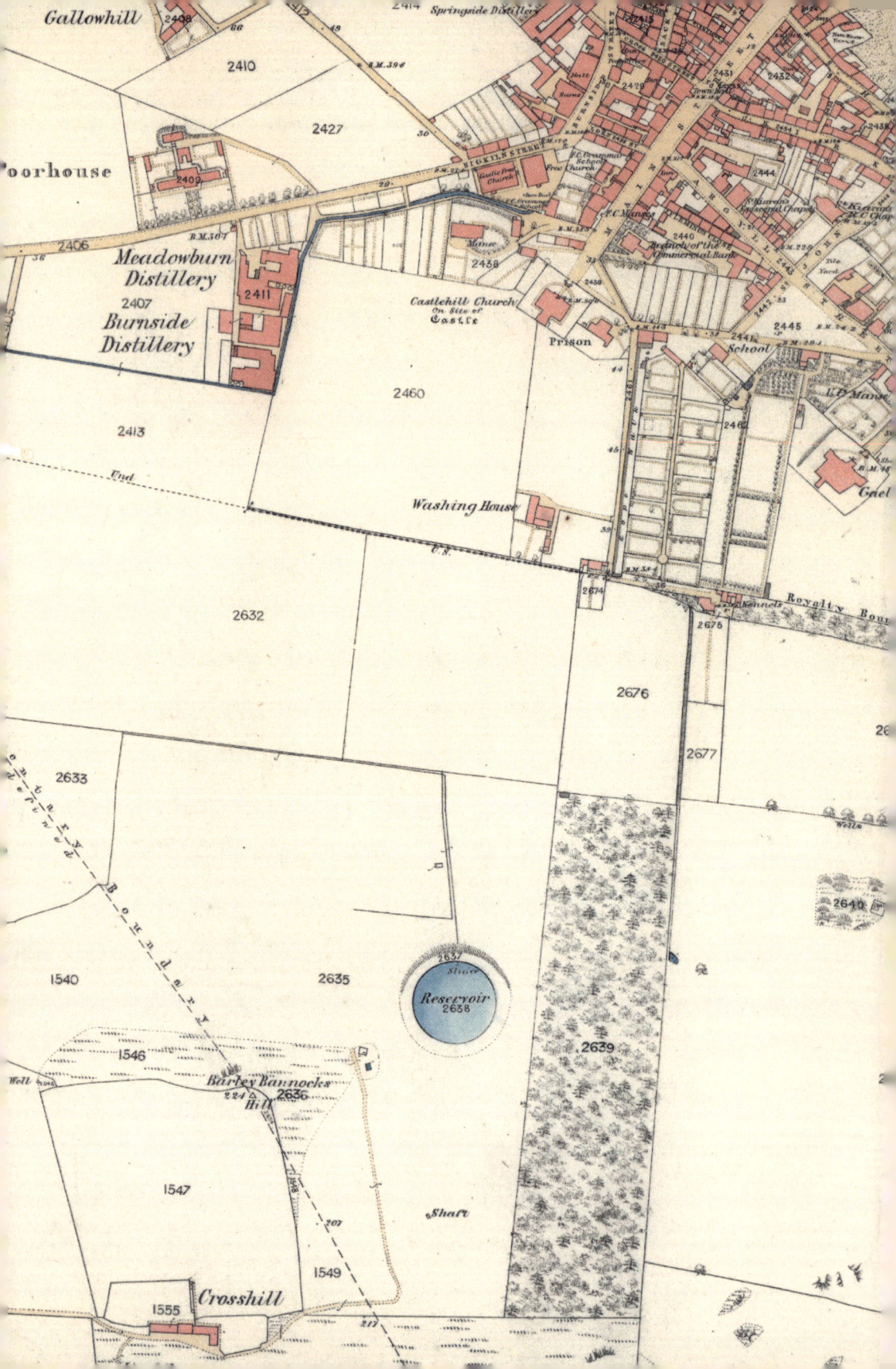